MEXICAN HISTORY

MEXICAN HISTORY

A Primary Source Reader

Edited by

NORA E. JAFFARY
Concordia University

EDWARD W. OSOWSKI
John Abbott College

SUSIE S. PORTER
University of Utah

A Member of the Perseus Books Group

Published by Westview Press,
A Member of the Perseus Books Group

Library of Congress Cataloging-in-Publication Data

Mexican history : a primary source reader / edited by Nora E. Jaffary, Edward W. Osowski, Susie S. Porter.
p. cm.
Includes bibliographical references and index.
ISBN 978-0-8133-4334-1 (alk. paper)
1. Mexico—History—Sources. I. Jaffary, Nora E., 1968– II. Osowski, Edward W. III. Porter, Susie S., 1965–

F1203.M49 2010
972—dc22

2009014008

10 9 8 7 6 5 4 3 2 1

For

Luc, Simon,

Charlie, and Cecilia

And our students and readers, past and future

Contents

Part 6. Liberalism, Conservatism, and the Porfiriato (1856–1911) 241

Part 7. The Mexican Revolution (1910–1940) 293

Part 8. The Institutionalization of the Revolution (1940–1965) 351

Part 9. Neoliberalism and Its Discontents (1968–2006) 385

Preface

As teachers of Mexican history, this is the book we had long wished was available for our use. We wanted a book of sources that told the fascinating story of Mexico's past through the words and images of those who experienced it firsthand. We wanted to engage students and provoke discussion. We wanted a compilation that paid significant attention to Mexico's Pre-Columbian and colonial eras as well as to its postindependence period. In addition, we wanted a collection that included "essential readings" on major events and themes from Mexico's past, but that also introduced readers to lesser-known material, exposing them to different vistas of the past. The book we sought would reproduce such canonical sources as Bernal Díaz's description of the first encounter between Hernán Cortés and Moteucçoma, and the Mexican Revolutionaries' 1911 Plan de Ayala, but it would also feature such documents as the petition of an eighteenth-century Afro-Mexican maroon community and the biting satire of a 1970s comic book. Finally, we wanted a reader whose length, contextual introductions, analytic questions, and other features facilitated classroom use. Since that book did not exist, we assembled it.

This reader depicts Mexico's history from 200 CE to 2006 through the examination of nine themes central to Mexico's development: indigenous people, state formation, land and labor, urban life, religion, the northern frontier, race and ethnicity, gender, and popular culture. At least one document in each of the reader's chronological sections addresses each of these themes. Readers will discover here how indigenous people made Mexican history through their actions and words from the Pre-Columbian era to the turn of the twenty-first century. They will learn how Mexico's rulers, from the emperors of the fifteenth century to the leaders of the Party of the Institutionalized Revolution (PRI) in the twentieth, wielded power and extracted wealth from the Mexican populace, and they will witness how and why the population responded: with acquiescence, with satire, and in 1692, 1810, 1910, and again in 1968, with rebellion.

The range of sources will appeal to those interested in different types of history—political, economic, legal, social, and cultural. Indeed, primary sources often allow the reader to understand how historical actors may have construed certain issues without separating them into such distinct categories. Thus, an excerpt from work by the economist José I. Iturriaga will allow the student to see how some Mexicans associated economic modernization with the disintegration of dearly held institutions such as the family. Readers will also discover Mexican social and cultural formations as they changed over time by tracing, for example, the topic of urban markets from the era of European Contact through the colonial era and as depicted in Salvador Novo's musings from the 1930s. Sources that allow for discussion of how life on the northern frontier differed from experiences in the urban south for both sixteenth-century missionaries and twentieth-century farm laborers will lead students to expand their notions of diversity in Mexico.

We have made an effort to represent a range of different Mexican voices in this collection. Students can assess, for example, the gender idealism of different ages by examining a sixteenth-century codex, a nineteenth-century didactic letter, and a twentieth-century interview. The written sources collected here include journals, petitions, laws, newspaper articles, manifestos, plays, essays, and devotional literature; maps, paintings, codices, and cartoons comprise the visual sources. Many of these documents appear in English translation for the first time in this reader. For the aid of non-Spanish-speaking readers, Spanish words are always translated upon first use within each source, and a glossary of frequently used Spanish terms appears at the end of the collection.

We envision that the sources will work most effectively when read in conjunction with other material. The sources complement and bring to life the detailed analysis and theoretical contributions of academic essays and monographs, the insights of literature and media, and the important work of synthesis found in textbooks. While a textbook might briefly describe, for example, the nineteenth-century Disentailment Law written by Benito Juárez, when students read the letter of the law provided here, they can make their own discoveries about it; for instance, they can think about how the law construed the rights of non-Church entities or how the implementation of the law led to unintended consequences. The documents collected here also help to overcome the perhaps inevitable impression of the seamless movement of history often provided in textbooks; these primary sources reveal difference, conflict, and complexity. Such is the case, for example, with the documents that celebrate and criticize the Mexican Revolution from both the left and the right. In these and other sources, the reader will gain a sense of the language of distinct historical moments.

The collection will be useful for instructors who teach Mexican history from Pre-Conquest to contemporary times, as well as for those who emphasize modern Mexican history. For those who teach the broad sweep of Mexican history, the sources will allow students to delve quickly into the subtleties of each historical period. Those who emphasize modern Mexican history will find ample material on this era and can selectively use documents from Pre-Conquest and colonial Mexico to present a richer portrait of contemporary Mexico. For example, when discussing nationalism in postrevolutionary Mexico, instructors might point to seventeenth-century Sor Juana Inés de la Cruz's use of Nahuatl in her poetry as an example of the roots of uniquely "Mexican" cultural expressions. The book's sections are divided into standard temporal divisions that will facilitate adaptation to course organization.

The volume's general introduction presents an overview of the nine historical themes portrayed in these sources and includes a discussion of how readers should approach the analysis of primary source materials. Each section also opens with a brief introductory essay that describes the era in general terms and locates each source within the central themes of the period. More detailed source introductions set the context for analysis by locating each document in a specific historical moment, often in relationship to Mexico's past or future developments. These introductions also provide the reader with information on how document genres shape the potential analysis of primary sources. How, for example, should we read a petition? What do we need to know about the tradition of political manifestos in order to be able to evaluate their place in Mexican history? What are the possibilities and limits of what we can learn from the observations of Spanish friars about indigenous cultures? Finally, each document introduction provides discussion questions or guidance. More extensive introductions are provided with the visual sources, especially those from the Pre-Conquest period. The document introductions do not do the work of analysis for the student, which would leave him or her, in the face of expert opinion, without much to contribute to in-class discussion or written work; rather, the introductions frame and position readers to do the work of analysis themselves—the work of the historian.

Each source is also appended with a list of central themes, suggested readings, and related sources found in the volume. The theme list is intended to provide instructors—and students—with a quick index of the issues addressed in each document, which could serve as the basis for tracing continuity and change in Mexican history. For example, students are guided to read Mexico's 1917 Constitution in conjunction with Andrés Molina Enríquez, an intellectual precursor and contributor to Article 27; revolutionary ballads (*corridos*) written about the Constitutional Convention; and documentation generated when the federal government applied articles of the Constitution twenty years later to its nationalization of the petroleum industry. The theme list might also facilitate the design of the course syllabus and assignments. The lists of suggested readings—which, given our anticipated audience, we have restricted to English-language material—provide instructors and students with a reliable starting place for pursuing further research on individual topics.

Our own students have responded enthusiastically to the sources in the collection and to the way we have presented them here. We hope that other readers are similarly engaged, provoked, and entertained as they use the material collected in this volume to develop their sense of Mexico's history.

Acknowledgments

We wish to acknowledge the following individuals and institutions for their material, practical, and intellectual contributions to this book: Karl Yambert, Kelsey Mitchell, Brooke Kush, Meredith Smith, and Cynthia Buck of Westview Press for their editorial expertise; Jason Smith and Sarah Comrie for their administrative assistance; Concordia University's Inter-Library Loan Office and the university's Professional Development Fund; the University of Utah Office of the Associate Vice President for Diversity and the University of Utah Gender Studies Program. For their input regarding particular documents, we thank: Frances Berdan, Merle Greene Robertson, Joel Hancock, Claudio Holzner, Rebecca Horn, James Lockhart, Robert J. Sharer, Sergio de la Torre, Eric Van Young, Nicole Von Germeten, and Fernando Winfield Capitaine. We would also like to acknowledge Tanya Huntington for her excellent translation work. Thank you to Jerry Root for his constant support. For material aid and lively Friday seminars, we are grateful to the HHFF group. Finally, we thank all our family members, particularly our children, Charlie, Cecilia, Luc, and Simon, who endured the competition for their attention this book represented as generously as it is possible for small children to do.

Central Themes

The sources excerpted in this anthology portray nine central themes in Mexican history.

Indigenous People

Sources 1–18, 20–22, 24, 27, 28, 30, 32, 37, 40, 42, 46, 47, 49, 50, 53–55, 57, 65, 67, 72

State Formation

Sources 6–10, 13, 14, 16–20, 27, 29, 32, 33, 35, 36, 39–45, 47, 49, 51–58, 61, 62, 65, 68–74, 76

Urban Life

Sources 1, 3, 6, 8, 10, 15, 19, 20, 27, 30, 34, 46, 49–51, 59, 60, 64, 68, 71, 74

The Northern Frontier

Sources 14, 18, 19, 28, 37, 39, 41, 48, 63, 66, 75

Popular Culture

Sources 15, 20–22, 24–26, 30, 31, 34, 51, 55, 60, 65, 68, 70, 74

Land and Labor

Sources 5–8, 14, 17, 19, 22, 23, 27, 29, 30, 32, 33, 41, 42, 45–50, 52–55, 57, 59, 61–64, 66, 67, 69, 71–73, 75

Religion

Sources 2–4, 10, 11, 14–16, 18, 20, 21, 23–26, 28–30, 32–35, 37, 38, 42, 43, 46, 47, 49, 50, 54, 56, 62, 63, 66, 74

Gender

Sources 2, 3, 5, 7, 10, 12, 20, 26, 30, 31, 37, 38, 41, 46, 49, 51, 54, 57, 59, 64, 71, 74, 75

Race and Ethnicity

Sources 1, 2, 9, 13, 21, 23–29, 31, 32, 40, 41, 62, 65, 66, 72

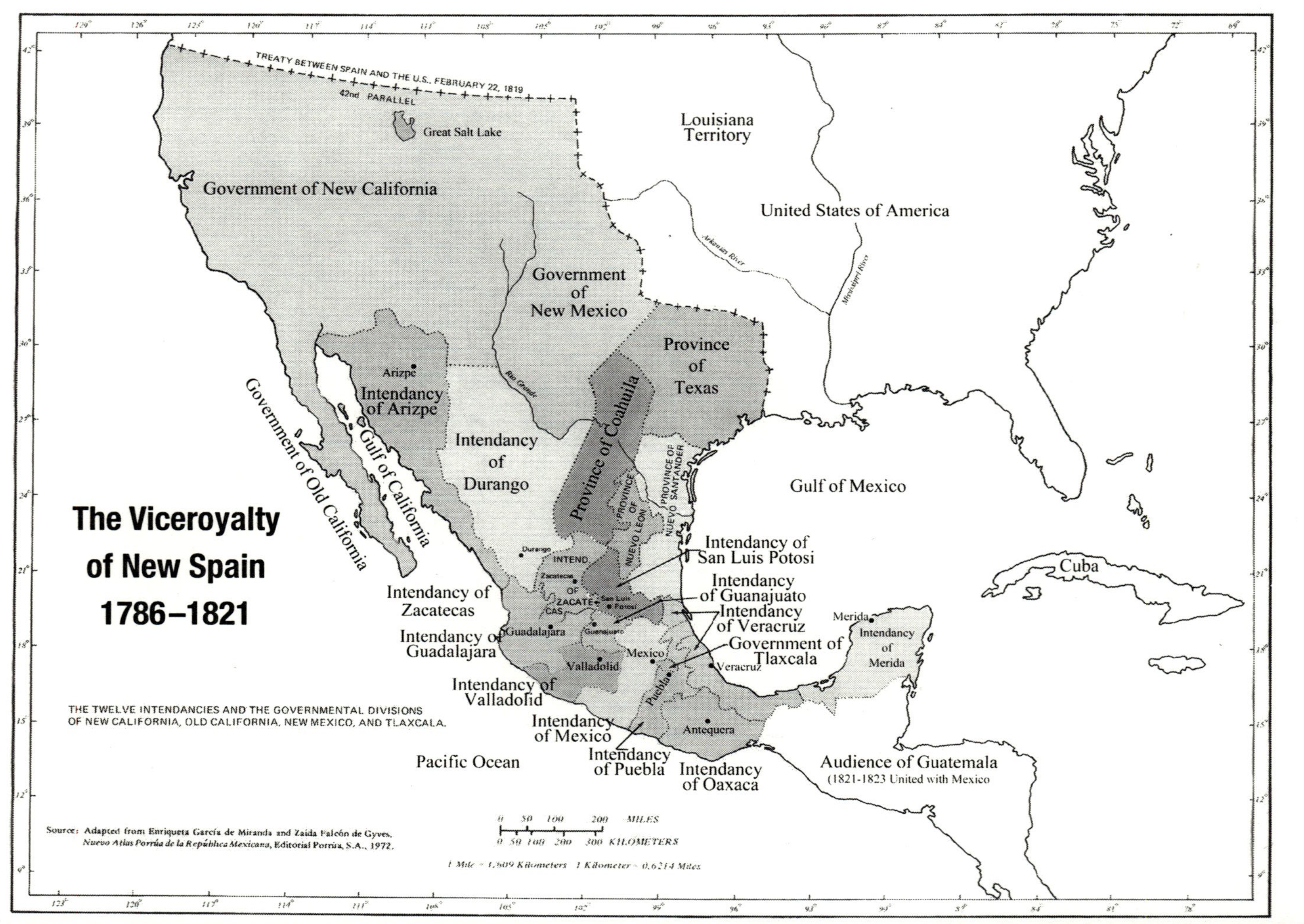
The Viceroyalty
of New Spain
1786–1821
THE TWELVE INTENDANCIES AND THE GOVERNMENTAL DIVISIONS
OF NEW CALIFORNIA, OLD CALIFORNIA, NEW MEXICO, AND TLAXCALA.
TREATY BETWEEN SPAIN AND THE U.S., FEBRUARY 22, 1819
42nd PARALLEL
Great Salt Lake
Government of New California
Louisiana Territory
United States of America
Arkansas River
Mississippi River
Government of New Mexico
Rio Grande
Province of Texas
Intendancy of Arizpe
Arizpe
Gulf of California
Government of Old California
Intendancy of Durango
Durango
Province of Coahuila
PROVINCE OF NUEVO LEON
PROVINCE OF NUEVO SANTANDER
Gulf of Mexico
INTEND. OF ZACATECAS
Zacatecas
San Luis Potosi
Guanajuato
Guadalajara
Valladolid
Mexico
Puebla
Veracruz
Antequera
Merida
Intendancy of San Luis Potosi
Intendancy of Guanajuato
Intendancy of Veracruz
Government of Tlaxcala
Intendancy of Merida
Cuba
Intendancy of Zacatecas
Intendancy of Guadalajara
Intendancy of Valladolid
Intendancy of Mexico
Intendancy of Puebla
Intendancy of Oaxaca
Audience of Guatemala
(1821-1823 United with Mexico)
Pacific Ocean
0 50 100 200 MILES
0 50 100 200 300 KILOMETERS
1 Mile = 1.609 Kilometers 1 Kilometer = 0.6214 Miles
Source: Adapted from Enriqueta García de Miranda and Zaida Falcón de Gyves,
Nuevo Atlas Porrúa de la República Mexicana, Editorial Porrúa, S.A., 1972.

States of Modern Mexico
The Mexican states commonly known as Coahuila, Michoacán, Quetéraro, and Veracruz are officially named Coahuila de Zaragoza, Michoacán de Ocampo, Quetéraro de Arteaga, and Veracruz-Llave.
BAJA CALIFORNIA
BAJA CALIFORNIA SUR
SONORA
CHIHUAHUA
COAHUILA
SINALOA
DURANGO
NUEVO
LEÓN
TAMAULIPAS
ZACATECAS
SAN LUIS
POTOSI
NAYARIT
JALISCO
GUANAJUATO
QUERÉTARO
HIDALGO
MEXICO
CITY
D.F.
COLIMA
MICHOACÁN
PUEBLA
VERA CRÚZ
GUERRERO
OAXACA
TABASCO
CAMPECHE
YUCATÁN
QUINTANA ROO
CHIAPAS
FEDERAL BOUNDARY
STATE BOUNDARIES
NATIONAL CAPITAL
0 50 100 200 MILES
0 50 100 200 300 KILOMETERS
1 Mile = 1.609 Kilometers 1 Kilometer = 0.6214 Miles

Introduction

The sources in this collection portray nine important topics in Mexican history: indigenous people, state formation, urban life, the northern frontier, popular culture, land and labor, religion, gender, and race and ethnicity. Readers new to the subject of Mexican history may benefit from the narrative of the major political, economic, military, and institutional events that these sources can be used to tell. Those who would like to examine history in terms of social structures and cultural processes and from the point of view of the non-elite will discover ample material here as well. This introduction provides an overview of the significance and historical development of these subjects and a discussion of how the sources included in this reader can best be used for their analysis.

Indigenous people were the first authors of the history of Mexico, and native people have remained key historical agents up until the present. Using phonetic alphabets, the Mayas and other indigenous peoples had written their own history since before the arrival of Europeans. We include many examples of indigenous writing, starting with the inscriptions on Maya King Hanab-Pakal's tomb more than 1,300 years ago (Source 3) and ending with Zapatista communiqués disseminated on the Internet (Source 72). One of the aims of this volume is to dispel the view—particularly widespread outside of Mexico—that Europeans obliterated indigenous civilizations. The sources included here recount the fascinating story of how and why indigenous people survived and maintained important aspects of their civilizations. Indigenous history has played a more central role in the development of Mexican national identity since the Independence Wars (1810–1821) than in any other part of North America. Today Mexico has one of the largest indigenous populations in Latin America. According to a Mexican census of 2000, the indigenous population of Mexico numbered 10 million, including 2.5 million speakers of Nahuatl, the language of the Nahuas, sometimes called the Aztecs.

This volume includes a substantial section on Pre-Columbian history because we believe that Mexico's ancient peoples established historical patterns that were carried forward into subsequent periods long after the arrival of the sixteenth-century Spanish *conquistadores* (conquerors). The most fundamental of these trends was a settlement pattern that concentrated human populations in the central and southern portions of Mexico. The Pre-Columbian Mesoamerican cultural zone included the areas of greatest indigenous population concentration on the North American continent, stretching from central Mexico through the Yucatán Peninsula into present-day Guatemala, western Honduras, and El Salvador. The dense population, productive soil, and complex societies of this region virtually determined that upon their arrival in the sixteenth century the Spanish would concentrate their colonization efforts here. Although silver strikes in the 1540s pulled more settlers north of Mesoamerica, the majority of the population of colonial Mexico remained in the south-central region, as ancient populations had also done (Source 19).

Many of the primary sources collected here treat the topic of state formation, broadly defined as the centralization of political power in a single government that controls a territory from a capital city. From ancient to modern times, Mexican states have exerted powerful control over the shape of urban life, frontiers, labor, and religion in the territories they control. When Europeans first arrived on the mainland in 1519, the powerful Mexica (Aztec) state had developed an advanced urban culture in its capital city of Mexico-Tenochtitlan in the central highlands of Mexico (sources 5 and 6). Called simply "Mexico" soon after the Conquest, the city became the capital of the colonial Viceroyalty of New Spain and the post-1810 independent Mexican republics.

State governments centralized in Mexico City have always had to contend with challenges on their frontiers, and sometimes the outcome has been a loss of influence over territory or the shrinking of borders. Almost fifty years into the nineteenth century, Mexico's weak federal government scarcely exercised dominion over its national territory owing to endemic civil wars, an anemic economy, and foreign intervention. When the Yucatec Mayas rose up in rebellion in 1847, they established an independent Maya government, and Mexico City almost lost the entire state, which the army did not completely secure until 1901 (Source 40). The Mexican-American border in the north presented an even greater challenge. In the aftermath of independence from Spain in 1821, Mexico's proximity to the United States of America shaped its subsequent history to a much greater degree than would be the case with more distant Latin American countries. In 1848, as the loser of the Mexican-American War (or as it is called in Mexico, *la guerra de la invasión Yanqui*), Mexico relinquished half of its national territory to its northern neighbor (sources 39 and 41). Modern Mexico's uneasy relationship with the United States has been central to the formation of its modern identity.

The study of state formation also examines how Mexicans challenged or consented to the power of their governments from within the country's borders. The form that the Mexican state has assumed is the result of the interplay between different actors over the distribution of political, economic, and social resources. Thus, state formation is often founded in labor relations, control over land, and negotiation over religious practices. State power has undergone major reconfigurations repeatedly in Mexican history, most notably during the Pre-Columbian Classic (200–900 CE) and Post-Classic periods (900–1519), at the time of the Spanish Conquest (1519–1610), with independence from Spain (1810–1822), and during the Mexican Revolution (1910–1920). Each time an invasion, revolution, or coup d'état transformed the state, new governors tried to win some voluntary support from the people so as not to perish in continual rebellion or revolution.

After 1521, when the Spaniards removed the indigenous hereditary ruling classes from state power, the Europeans in charge still required indigenous labor, tribute payments, and souls for conversion. If the political elites wanted to secure the basic material necessities of life and prosper in the colony, they depended on the labor of the non-elite indigenous, black, and mixed-race people, who vastly outnumbered the wealthy Europeans (sources, 19, 23, and 24). The political elite's dependency on common people gave the latter some bargaining power (sources 20 and 29). The colonial state could not simply force subjects to comply with governmental authority but had to convince them that they had some stake in this government. In exchange for consent, the state at times offered its subjects humane treatment on the basis of a shared Catholic religion. It also sometimes relinquished political authority by granting local autonomy to communities of indigenous people or escaped African slaves (sources 13, 20, and 25). The formation of states has never been a purely top-down process. Indigenous people and the mixed-race poor frequently disturbed the peace of the colonial period with protests when the government reneged on its side of the bargain, as illustrated by the Mexico City Riot of 1692 (Source 27). One century later, while the Spanish monarchy barely held on to the colony, independence fighters like José María Morelos demanded government by the people (Source 33).

After the Mexican republic won its sovereignty from its colonial masters in 1822, expectations for popular participation in state power rose because, at least formally, Mexican democracy had expanded. Conflicts over church-state relations and federalist-centralist political models hampered the Mexican government's development in the nineteenth century. These conflicting positions crystallized into violent clashes between the Liberal and Conservative Parties at mid-century. Modern Mexicans reenacted the traditions of participation in state-making initiated in the colonial period when they rose in revolt against the oppressive government of Porfirio Díaz (1876–1911) and when they helped shape significant clauses of the Revolutionary Constitution of 1917 (Source 54). Similarly, the governing party brought to power with the close of Mexico's 1910 Revolution, adopting the name Partido Revolucionario Institucional (PRI) in 1939, reenacted the colonial state's strategy of incorporating the populace into the rhetoric and practice of its rule through bureaucratic institutions that addressed the demands of many sectors of society, particularly in the arenas of health care, education, and housing. The student movement of 1968 and the Ejército Zapatista de Liberación Nacional (EZLN, or the Zapatistas) insurgent movement, which declared war on the federal government in 1994, are latter-day heirs to the tradition of popular challenges to state authority (sources 68 and 72).

One of the Zapatistas' major grievances with the Mexican government was the privatization of communally owned land. Land and labor are central themes in Mexican history that take on different meanings in changing historical contexts. In Mexican history, control over land and labor has also been linked to conceptions of race and ethnicity. During the colonial period, for example, access to indigenous communal lands was in part defined by ethnicity; non-indigenous peoples were prohibited from purchasing communally held indigenous lands. In the mid-nineteenth century, the liberalizing Laws of Reform reversed this prohibition, with varying effects on indigenous peoples according to their differing economic positions and possession of written or oral records of land ownership (Source 42). The Mexican Revolution of 1910 threw into question the basis for the ownership of private property, and conflicts over the land, some that dated back to the early colonial period, erupted again in the language of revolution (Source 54). The argument of revolutionaries like Rubén Jaramillo for the rights of Mexicans to land and labor effectively limited the federal government's control of workers, production, and political participation (Source 67).

Throughout the time period treated here, as availability permits, we have included examples from Mexican popular culture (widely distributed culture produced outside of the state) because they reveal how broad sectors of the population viewed the political actions of the elite, as well as how they understood a variety of other topics, from sex to art to the economy. These sources include newspaper articles, sardonic comics, passionate ballads (*corridos*), and transcriptions of performance art (sources 47, 51, 55, 68, 70, and 74). They present readers with an entertaining means to access the viewpoints of members of society not represented in more traditional documentary forms. Frequently political, these popular culture sources allow readers to research the question of whether the non-elite consented to or resisted political regimes, mainstream moralities, and established economic orders.

As well as supplying the populace with a measure of power, Mexican states from the Pre-Columbian era up until the onset of the postrevolutionary secularist PRI state used religion as a means of legitimizing rule. Conversion was an integral aspect of Spain's conquest of Mexico's indigenous population. Catholicism became the predominant ideology in colonial Mexico, shaping how people conceived of such diverse issues as gender, justice, and race. However, throughout Mexico's history, religion has served purposes beyond that of legitimizing the state, and across time spirituality has sprung from sources beyond its reach. Through their creation myths, for example, Pre-Columbian peoples meditated on such issues as the ephemeral quality of human life and the dangers of excess. In their spirituality, they recognized that human beings are part of the order of the natural world. Although they sought to eradicate Pre-Columbian religions, sixteenth-century Christian friars also brought the first kernels of humanism and the first notions of human rights to Mexico.

Under the influence of the European Enlightenment, the eighteenth-century Bourbon state introduced secularizing reforms to its colonies. Postindependence governments, unlike Pre-Columbian and colonial states, constructed their authority without theological underpinnings. And despite the presence of powerful dissent from such figures as conservative Lucás Alamán, by the end of the nineteenth century liberal democratic citizenship had replaced shared Catholicism as the ideological justification for social harmony (Source 41). Objections to this secularist position were manifest, however, in such events as the 1928 Cristero Rebellion and the growth of the political party that grew from it, the Partido de Acción Nacional (PAN) (Source 62), the party that broke the PRI's monopoly on state power in 2000. Today, despite two centuries of anticlerical state policy, an overwhelming majority of Mexicans continue to identify themselves as Christian, and a majority of those Christians remain Catholic.

From the time of the Spaniards' arrival onward, another important legacy of Catholicism was its influence on the development of powerful gender ideologies in Mexico. The new religion increased paternalism and encouraged a stronger separation of women and men in the private and public spheres. Although Pre-Columbian women were not warriors and generally not rulers, they did act as religious leaders, educators, and medical professionals, as in the case of Mexica society (Source 5). Mesoamerican motherhood was political because dynastic marriages built empires and increased state power (Source 7). Catholicism pushed a paternal vision of the cosmos and replaced Pre-Columbian deities, which possessed both masculine and feminine guises, with God the father and his son Jesus. During the colonial era, Spanish Catholicism reinforced the notion of distinctive public/masculine and private/feminine spheres and emphasized the centrality of honor and sexual purity in the lives of women. Even so, it was the nun Sor Juana Inés de la Cruz who questioned accepted female norms (Source 26). With early industrialization and the separation of home and work, gender ideology privileged men's realms over women's in new ways. In the late twentieth century, significant sectors of Mexican women challenged the country's gender ideologies, often doing so most powerfully from within the very occupation that gender ideology had dictated would be women's work: motherhood (sources 71 and 75).

As well as exerting a formidable influence on the development of gender ideology, Catholicism played an important role in shaping notions of race and ethnicity in Mexico. The ability to trace genealogical lines back to old, Spanish Christian families determined one's degree of racial purity, not pseudo-Darwinian ideas about race, as found later in the nineteenth century. The Spanish, however, did not introduce the notion of distinctive ethnicities into Mexico, nor did their arrival initiate the notion of racial and cultural mixing. Pre-Columbian Mesoamerica was a multilingual, multinational culture zone. Indigenous people like the Mexica and the Mixtecs had strong ethnic identities, not because they were isolated from each other, but because they were aware of each other (sources 1, 5, and 7). One of the significant features of the Mesoamerican zone was that different indigenous linguistic groups changed when they came into contact with each other. Cultural mixing happened prior to the arrival of Europeans.

After the Conquest, the ongoing process of *mestizaje* (race mixing) mixed people from three major continents: the indigenous people of North America; Europeans, mostly from the Iberian Peninsula; and West Africans. For the first three centuries after Contact, the indigenous population far outnumbered the small number of Hispanic immigrants, who were disproportionately male. This fact, combined with an early influx of a substantial number of African slaves, virtually guaranteed that a large mixed-race population would be created in the Viceroyalty of New Spain (sources 25 and 31). Try though they did, colonial authorities could do little to prevent it from happening, and in spite of the widespread social privileging of racial "purity," by the nineteenth century at least half of Mexico's population was mixed. After independence, race became more difficult to trace since the laws of the republic abolished the colony's legal classification of the population by race. But Mexicans were ambivalent about their mixed-race heritage throughout the nineteenth century and beyond, even while intellectuals and artists in the postrevolutionary period in the early twentieth century began to celebrate this background as the source of nationalist unity and liberation.

This volume provides students and teachers with a wide range of primary sources from which to examine Mexican history. These firsthand accounts are the raw materials that historians use to write history. Readers, whether professional historians or students enrolled in introductory survey courses, are likely to approach them initially in the same way: they will use evidence from these sources to challenge and question preconceived notions and received wisdom. Doing history is like having a conversation. Each interpretation of a primary source is made in response to what other readers, whether in classrooms or in printed materials, have said about the past. In this sense, every generation's way of doing history is revisionist. People who are new to reading primary sources are sometimes unsure about exactly what it is they are supposed to do with them. The art of reading primary sources is the art of asking questions that are appropriate to the sources. But how do you know which questions are appropriate, especially if you are not a professional historian? First, readers must consider the historical period from which the source emerged, the type of source it is, and how both of these factors affect the way in which it presents information. The introductions to each section and to each source will equip readers to analyze the influences of each source's context and its genre.

Readers should consider how the intended purpose of each genre influences a source's content. This anthology contains a wide variety of types of sources ranging from the lofty political statements of Mexican constitutions to the comical parodies of cartoon skeletons. Some writings are personal narratives in which authors seek to explain their lives or justify their actions to their contemporary audiences. Readers should consider whether the author intended to report, legislate, satirize, argue for change, or convert people to a religion or political ideology. Readers should also recognize that many sources have more purposes than those their authors might explicitly articulate. What authors call a "history" (*historia*) or a "report" (*relación*) or a "map" (*mapa*) may also be a demand for a change, an appeal to higher authorities for favors, or a very local and culturally specific view of the world.

In considering primary sources, readers should also think about their intended audiences. Who was the audience? How much of the population did it represent? Answering these questions will prevent readers from exaggerating the importance of the source for the author's contemporaries. Until the modern period, none of these sources were written or drawn for popular consumption because only a minority of the population was literate. How might political inequalities have influenced the creation of a source? What might contemporary readers have wanted to hear? Knowing the audience and purpose allows readers to formulate questions that they will reasonably be able to answer. For example, one of the sources in this reader is an excerpt from a comic book called *Los Supermachos,* produced in the late 1960s and 1970s; as an inexpensive publication, *Los Supermachos* could reach a large audience of Mexicans who were literate. It was also a satire whose jokes were funny only if audiences could relate to what it was saying. *Los Supermachos,* then, would probably be an appropriate source from which to gauge with some accuracy what educated but non-elite Mexicans of the period thought about their society.

Source analysis also considers authorship in terms of the influences of class, political position, or membership in an interest group. Did the writer compose the piece under negative circumstances? For example, was he or she acting as an agent or victim of coercion, expressing animosity for others, or responding to threats to his or her class or position in the world? Many of the people in this anthology wrote when something vital to their lives was at stake. If their society was on the verge of a revolution, witnessing the dissolution of an older order, or trailing in the wake of an invasion, that position would inform their writing.

Additionally, *when* the source was written must be taken into account. Knowing "when" means having some information about the historical moment during which the source was produced as well as knowing how events in the past might have influenced the source's outcome. Readers should recognize that a historical subject in the middle of an event does not know its outcome. Does the author write during the time the event transpired or forty years in retrospect? Immediately experiencing something does not necessarily guarantee that the author was correct about what was happening. In fact, when people are caught up in big events or changes, they often have only a vague notion, or no notion at all, of its meaning. What is called a "revolution" in retrospect may simply have seemed like a disaster or a civil war to the people living through it.

Think also about where the document was composed. Did the author write about events that were happening far away? Was the author living in Mexico City but commenting on the frontier? Once again, sometimes immediacy is better, but not always. A local person writing about his own city or town might exaggerate its importance, defend it, or, conversely, unduly deride it.

In a different vein, readers should also consider their own positions and attitudes with respect to the sources studied. How do you, the reader, plan to use each primary source? Will you compare it with others in order to track changes and find patterns over time? Or are you more focused on immersing yourself in a snapshot of one moment of a long-past world? Good readers become aware of their own set of cultural, educational, and experiential assumptions because historical interpretation is a dialogue with the self. This becomes apparent when two people have opposing interpretations of a single source whose evidence may support either viewpoint.

Overarching narratives that explain why the past is important and what "really" happened have shifted over time too. The meta-narratives that people tell about the past are subject to changes in politics, fictions, and academic trends.

Finally, readers should recognize that, like the written sources, the visual sources included in this volume must also be placed in the historical contexts of time, place, purpose, and audience. Sometimes the immediacy of a picture compels viewers to believe that they inherently understand what they are seeing regardless of context. People often assume that pictures cannot lie. Like written primary sources, however, visual sources are embedded in history. Readers will get the most out of the visual sources reproduced here by thinking about them in relation to the written primary sources from the same time period in order to flesh out the larger context. The ways in which illustrators visually arrange information in two-dimensional space are culturally determined. Without knowing something about the creators' worlds, viewers will miss what they were trying to communicate to their audiences.

PART 1

Pre-Columbian Mexico (200–1519 CE)

Knowledge of Mexico's Pre-Columbian period, the time prior to 1519, when the Spaniards arrived on the mainland, is essential for understanding modern Mexican culture. Mexicans' knowledge about ancient indigenous civilizations continues to influence national identity, architecture, the arts, and official state policy toward indigenous people, among other things. The primary sources in this section document the histories of the Mayas, the Nahuas (Aztecs), and the Mixtecs, the three major ethnic groups who formed Mesoamerica and are still represented in significant numbers in Mexico's population today. A fourth group, the people of central Mexico who built the city of Teotihuacan, is identified here by the city name because the historical record does not tell us what they called themselves. Despite the fact that each group spoke a separate language, they shared a set of common attributes, identifiable in the primary sources here: intensive agriculture that produced surpluses, sedentary populations, urbanized social life, hierarchies, writing systems, religious justifications for politics, and a vision of a nondualist universe governed by creation/destruction cycles. A fifth indigenous group whose history is also included here, the Seris (Comcáac), was one of many nonsedentary and semi-sedentary tribes that lived beyond the frontiers of the Mesoamerican zone (Source 9). As is illustrated here, in many ways the Seris were as different from the sedentary indigenous people as they were from the Spaniards.

Historians and archaeologists have created the historical periods of Pre-Columbian history to track the fluctuations of state formation. Historians used to speak of the rise and fall of entire civilizations. Now scholars understand that during the Pre-Columbian period was the rise of Maya, Nahua, and Mixtec state governments in particular cities. Cities like the Maya city of Chichén Itzá consolidated their power by allying with or conquering independently governed city-states belonging to other Mayas on the Yucatán Peninsula. With the falling of central governments that had incorporated other city-states, the ethnic groups did not disappear. Instead, they practiced their lifeways on a smaller scale back in their city-states.

This section covers the Classic (200–900 CE) and Post-Classic (850–1519 CE) periods, when the growth of powerful states fostered cultural achievements that left their marks on posterity with monolithic ruins and hieroglyphs. During the Classic age, the dynastic ruling families of Maya city-states such as Tikal in Petén (modern-day Guatemala) and Palenque (modern-day Chiapas State) allied with neighbors and expanded their power. To the north, on the outskirts of contemporary Mexico City, Teotihuacan built massive pyramids and palaces along straight avenues (sources 1 and 3). The Post-Classic period began with the collapse of Maya Tikal and the central Mexican Teotihuacan states. The contemporaneous Toltecs of Tula in central Mexico and Mayas of Chichén Itzá rose in their places (Source 8). In the last century of the Post-Classic period, Nahuatl-speaking people rose to prominence, and one nation, the Mexica, created what was later known to history as the Aztec Empire. By 1470 CE, Mexica state power encompassed the territories of the Valley of Mexico and much of central Mexico from the eastern Gulf Coast to the western Pacific Ocean. The Mexica built their empire outward from their city of Tenochtitlan, the remains of which are buried beneath modern-day Mexico City (sources 5 and 6). In all these instances, Mesoamerican rulers used not only warfare but also the expansion of kinship through marriage alliances to expand their kingdoms (sources 5, 7, and 8).

Like all of the earlier centralizing governments, the Mexica's state-level society concentrated its most important political, economic, and religious institutions in its capital city. The earliest settlements were constructed around a central cluster of high ceremonial and administrative buildings, and every subsequent culture copied this plan. The cities were designed as models of the cosmos. Most Mesoamerican cities had square or rectangular ceremonial centers that represented the four cardinal directions of the universe: north, south, east, and west. A major god was associated with each of the directions. Often found in the middle of these city squares were pyramids that represented the center of the world, imagined by the Nahuas as the hearth-fire in the center of a house or the hole where the Maya world-tree grew (Source 3). City plans were also grids that zoned people according to social inequalities and political hierarchies (sources 5, 6, and 8).

Many of the sources in this section illustrate the deeply political nature of indigenous cultural achievements. Rulers justified their power over territories through writing, maps, and art that traced their lineages back to mythic origin places, the first people or gods in creation stories, and fabled golden age cities (Source 7). Ruling elites also used religion to justify the class systems of their authoritarian states (Source 3). Pre-Columbian land tenure is not fully understood, but it was most likely a combination of private and public ownership. All land technically belonged to the lord because of his divine origins, but residents possessed it when they cultivated it (sources 7 and 8). When imperial states like the Mexica expanded, they harnessed the labor of subject peoples by demanding raw materials and manufactured goods as tribute tax and did not conquer land per se (Source 5).

Mesoamericans were able to produce the agricultural surpluses needed to support cities because of civil engineering and human planning, which needed the coordination of leaders. At the same time, these agriculturally based societies operated under environmental constraints. Some of the forces of nature necessary for agriculture were predictable and came in cycles, like the sun, but others, like water, could be unpredictable. People turned to the gods, who were personifications of these fickle natural forces, to secure fertility. Readers can explore how a people's desire to secure fertility might lead them to consent to the rule of hereditary elites (sources 2 and 3).

The Nahuas, Mayas, Mixtecs, and Teotihuacans all had rain, maize, and sun deities, whom they called by different names depending on their language (Source 1). Distant divinities who ruled the heavens were almost abstract principles. The heroic friend of humankind, the Feathered Serpent, was found in all of these mythologies (sources 2 and 4). No Mesoamerican god, however, was purely good or evil. Like the forces of nature they personified, divinities could be both helpful and harmful to people. Most Pre-Columbian gods and goddess had multiple forms and guises. Pairs of divinities were often shown as opposites (Source 4). These agricultural peoples also saw that fertility was helped by decay and that life came from death. In both the Nahua (Source 4) and the Maya (Source 2) stories about the creation of humanity, gods struggle with the lords of the underworld to rescue or animate humans and bring them to the land of the living.

Anyone who studies archaeological and written sources for Pre-Conquest religion will be bewildered by the different versions of the same stories, often with different gods and goddesses involved. Much of the confusion stems from the fact that each written source presents, not a standard "Aztec" or "Maya" mythology, but a local version of the myths. They are "official" myths in the sense that they belonged to the most politically powerful of the indigenous city-states at the time they were written down. The authors of the histories often made their tribal divinities play starring roles. When the Mexica of the island of Tenochtitlan consolidated their power in 1428, they declared that their tribal war-god Huitzilpochtli was now also the sun-god. As in Europe, even in Pre-Conquest times, the winners wrote history, not the weak. The term "Aztec" was not coined until the early nineteenth century and is a historical anachronism. We use the general "Nahuas" to refer to all communities speaking the Nahuatl language and "Mexica" to refer to the Nahuas who created the empire based in Tenochtitlan. Much confusion has resulted from the use of this term because the written and archaeological sources on these people are all local sources, not documents of one unified Aztec nation.

Many of the primary sources in this section and the following one on the Spanish Conquest can be used for a dual purpose: to understand the Mesoamerican cultures in Pre-Columbian times and to understand how indigenous people deployed their culture to make sense of European contact. Standing in the waters of Post-Contact written primary sources, archaeologists often methodologically go "upstream" to corroborate archaeological evidence about Pre-Columbian cultures. They use written sources that indigenous people produced in the Post-Conquest period, almost always with some help or influence from Spanish churchmen, in order to draw conclusions about indigenous society in the time before Contact. All of the written sources in this Pre-Columbian section, except for artifacts in the photographs, fall into this category. Are these sources too tainted by contact to use? Perhaps this is the wrong question. The fact that indigenous people had a history means that their culture was always evolving, never static. Before Contact, they too shaped their own history as times changed. Things changed rapidly with the arrival of the Spaniards in 1519. How might the upheaval of the early sixteenth-century conflict and contact have been the impetus for indigenous people to make more powerful statements of indigenous history and identity than during the times when they knew nothing of the Europeans?

1. Copán and Teotihuacan: Shared Culture Across a Great Distance (200–900 CE)

The two images with which this reader begins show objects with shared iconography found in two geographically distant ancient cities: Teotihuacan and Copán. During the Classic period of Mesoamerican civilization (200–900 CE), the Maya city-states of Copán (Honduras), Kaminaljuyu, and Tikal (both in Petén, Guatemala) flourished, with Tikal acting as the dominating power. Over 600 miles northwest, Teotihuacan (30 miles north of modern Mexico City) was a city with a population of around 150,000 and an equally impressive culture. It is not known what the people of Teotihuacan called themselves, or even what language they spoke, although it was not Maya. During the 700s CE, both Teotihuacan and Tikal went into decline. Although it is not clear what happened to Teotihuacan, the strains of increased war may have brought the city down in 750, when the temples and palaces were burned. As a hegemonic state, Tikal most likely collapsed at the end of the 700s because of environmental degradation caused by the lethal combination of overfarming, famine, and endemic warfare.

In 1936, archaeologists uncovered a quadratic architectural feature called *talud-tablero,* distinctive of contemporaneous Teotihuacan, from the ruins of Kaminaljuyu and Tikal. This arrangement of platforms and slopes can be found in the image (on page 14) depicting the Temple of Quetzalcoatl, Teotihuacan. The next image (page 15) is of a ceramic tripod vessel from the Margarita tomb of Copán, which was executed with major Teotihuacan features, including the *talud-tablero.* Atomic analysis has revealed that the materials came from somewhere in central Mexico, but the artistic style of the Copán vessel is a blend of Teotihuacan and Kaminaljuyu.

Painted on the Copán tripod vessel (page 15) are two eyes peeping out of the doorway of a temple or palace. They are the goggle eyes of the ubiquitous rain god, called Tlaloc in Nahuatl and Chac in Maya. The Teotihuacan temple image features the goggle-eyed deity, who continued to be central to Mexican religion even into the Post-Conquest period. The direction of cultural exchange may not, however, have been one-way. Archaeologists also discovered that an entire quarter of Teotihuacan was decorated with Maya artistic styles.

The Copán vessel painting also includes the name K'inich Yaax K'uk'Mo, the Maya king who founded the ruling dynasty of Copán in 426 CE. A frieze on Copán Altar Q depicts K'inich Yaax K'uk'Mo being inaugurated wearing a warrior costume from Teotihuacan that included goggle eyes and a serpent shield. He is called Lord of the West, and evidence suggests that he arrived in Copán after a 152-day journey from an unspecified "lineage house." Scholars still ask: Did he come from Teotihuacan? Was he a Maya ruler "crowned" there? Or does the vessel simply reflect the movement of culture rather than the relocation of an actual person?

Clearly the people of Teotihuacan and those of the Maya city-states within the political orbit of Tikal shared culture during this period of time, but what was the nature of their encounter? For many years, the prevailing view among archaeologists was that the central Mexican people from Teotihuacan had been the primary agents of change, perhaps even invading or colonizing Maya lands to the south. Teotihuacan was envisioned as a belligerent northern nation menacing the more peaceful Maya cities. Since then, the Mayas have been shown to have been much more militaristic—even practicing human sacrifice—than previously believed. More important for our understanding of these two visual sources, archaeologists have recently questioned a one-sided Mexican-centric model of cultural interaction. Mayan merchants who traveled north to Teotihuacan and other central Mexican towns may have been responsible. Perhaps the Mayas back in Petén had encouraged the introduction of foreign culture for their local reasons? What social, political, or economic value might exotic foreign goods have had in Tikal or Teotihuacan?

All controversies aside, these artifacts demonstrate that prior to the arrival of Europeans, indigenous Mexico was international and multi-ethnic while being united by the shared cultural elements of Mesoamerica. Mexico had a long tradition of cultural contact and assimilation of foreign culture into local city-states, whether through warfare or trade. If we consider this long-term context, the arrival of Spaniards in 1519 looks less unusual and may not have been as shocking to indigenous Mexico as we might think.

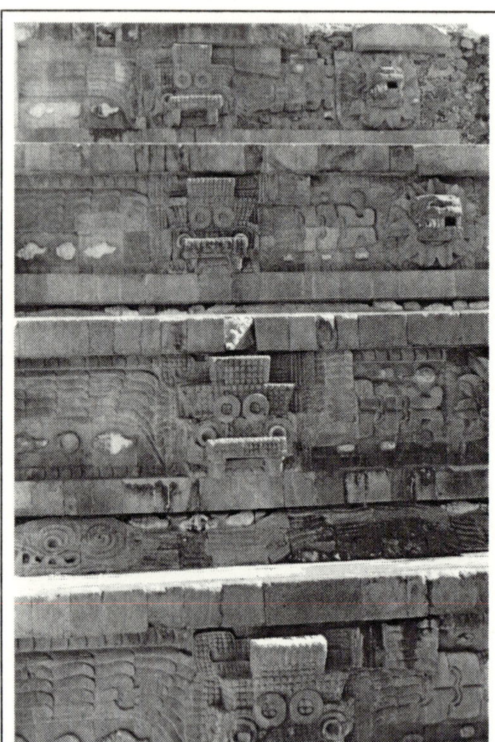

Temple of Quetzalcoatl, Teotihuacan, detail showing talud-tablero *and the rain god*

Photograph by Edward W. Osowski.

Painted vessel from the Margarita tomb, Copán, painted in the Teotihuacan style

Photograph by Robert J. Sharer. Used courtesy of the Early Copán Acropolis Program, University of Pennsylvania Museum and the Instituto Hondureño de Antropología e Historia.

Central Themes

Indigenous people, urban life, race and ethnicity

Suggested Reading

Braswell, Geoffrey, ed. *The Maya and Teotihuacan: Reinterpreting Early Classic Interaction.* Austin: University of Texas Press, 2003.

Carmack, Robert M., Janine Gasco, and Gary H. Gossen. *The Legacy of Mesoamerica: History and Culture of a Native American Civilization.* Upper Saddle River, NJ: Prentice-Hall, 1996.

Carrasco, David, Lindsay Jones, and Scott Sessions, eds. *Mesoamerica's Classic Heritage: From Teotihuacan to the Aztecs.* Boulder: University Press of Colorado, 2000.

Related Sources

2. The *Popol Vuh* ("the Community Book"): The Mythic Origins of the Quiché Mayas (1554–1558)
3. Maya Royalty and Writing (c. 667 CE)
8. The Urban Zoning of Maya Social Class in the Yucatán (1566)
16. The Spiritual Conquest: The Trial of Don Carlos Chichimecatecotl of Texcoco (1539)

2. The *Popol Vuh* ("the Community Book"): The Mythic Origins of the Quiché Mayas (1554–1558)*

From 1554 to 1558, unknown Quiché Maya lords wrote down the *Popol Vuh* using glyphic texts and oral renditions. They penned this work in the European Latinate alphabetic script, which they had learned from the Christian friars, but hid the book from the Catholic clergy. While working as the priest of the highland town of Santo Tomás de Chichicastenango, Guatemala Dominican friar Francisco Ximénez copied the manuscript sometime between 1701 and 1703. As Munro Edmonson's literal translation of the Quiché Mayas shows, the verse was crafted according to a poetic style common in Mesoamerica in which parallels are constantly made and one idea is often repeated in several ways. For example, there are two principal creator-gods in this selection. The first is called Quetzal Serpent, Shaper, Engenderer, and the second god is called Heart of Heaven, Former, Bearer Majesty, and different-colored lightning.

Prior to its recording, the mythic history was probably recited during religious rituals. Guatemala is obviously no longer administered from Mexico, as it was during the colonial period as part of the Viceroyalty of New Spain, but this passage shares common themes across time and among ethnic groups occupying the multilinguistic Mesoamerican indigenous cultural zone. We invite readers to interpret the text alongside sources 1, 3, and 4.

The first part of the *Popol Vuh* begins with the origin story of the world in which Cucumatz, the Quiché Maya name for Quetzalcoatl, who is submerged in a perfectly placid ocean, converses with the Heart of Heaven. The words of their conversation create topographical features of the natural world and the animals. The two gods then make human beings three times, but each model is a failure and they destroy them.

The second part is about the hero twins, Hunahpu and Xbalanque, who anger the death lords of Xibalba, the underworld, because of their raucous ball-playing. The lords lure them to the underworld where the twins defeat monsters, overcome treacherous obstacles, and, through their trickery, eventually gain victory over the dark lords in a ball game, which ends in the deaths of the death lords. Then they resurrect their father, Hun Hunahpu, who was buried in the underworld ball court. He rises, appearing as the maize god. Archaeological evidence shows that this story dates back to the Maya Classic period, and King Hanab-Pakal's sarcophagus lid makes reference to some of these themes (Source 3). The Mayas built I-shaped ball courts in the ceremonial centers of their cities and played games that reenacted destruction/creation stories. The Quiché Mayas called the ball court *hom,* which also means "tomb," "crack" (see "Cleft" in this selection), or "chasm." Thus, the ball

---

*Munro S. Edmonson, *The Book of Counsel: The Popul Vuh of the Quiché Maya of Guatemala* (New Orleans: Tulane University, Middle American Research Institute, 1971), pp. 145–155.

court and the tombs like that of King Hanab-Pakal represented the crack in the earth where people and gods entered the earth when they died, but also the place from which they emerged when they were created or born. Life and death, creation and destruction, are necessary opposites in the universe.

At this point, the creation story of humanity picks up again because the maize god is now alive, and he can sustain life. The following passage is about the fourth creation of humanity. Cucumatz ("Quetzal Serpent" in this translation) and Heart of Heaven succeed in engendering human beings with the help of Xmucane, an ancient soothsayer and wife of Xpiacoc. She grinds white and yellow maize flour and mixes the ingredients to make people. The four original men she makes are mostly acceptable to Cucumatz and Heart of Heaven and do not need to be destroyed. Cucumatz and Heart of Heaven animate the maize bodies but find that the four are just a little too perfect, too godlike. So they dull their intellects and senses and give them four beautiful wives to distract them and keep them happy. These four original couples then travel to Tulan Zuvia (translated as "Seven Caves and Seven Canyons"); after entering the caves, the original people emerge differentiated, speaking different languages and each possessing their own tutelary deity, including the Quiché people. The Seven Caves also appears in a Nahua creation story (Source 4).

The third part, not contained here, which is roughly one-half of the *Popol Vuh,* is a historical account of noble lineages, wars, migrations, and events up until 1550. Understood with the earlier parts in mind, the creation story culminates in the founding of the Quiché Maya territorial political unit, which they possessed when the Spaniards first arrived. The *Popol Vuh* was once viewed as "the Maya Bible." However, the third section, which is studied much less often, suggests that the rulers who wrote the *Popol Vuh* intended it to be the Quiché Mayas' own origin story, not that of all Maya cultures, let alone all of humanity's. At the same time, however, these rulers did link their local history to a narrative containing gods and themes universal to the Mesoamerican indigenous cultural zone.

How would the creation myths serve to legitimize the Quiché Mayas' sovereignty, or sense of ethnic identity, apart from other Maya groups? The *Popol Vuh* is about politics, but also about Mesoamerica morality and universal questions of human existence. What do the gods think were the first human's moral failings? What moral values does the text suggest need to be followed? What does the creation story tell us about the Maya view of gender? What is the purpose of human existence in the eyes of the gods?

The Popul Vuh, *Part 2*

And this is the beginning when man was invented, / And when that which would go into man's body was sought.
Then spoke the Bearer, / And Engenderer,
Who were Former / And Shaper, / Majesty / And Quetzal Serpent by name,
"The dawn has already appeared; / The creation has already been made,
And there is clearly a nourisher appearing, / A supporter,
Born of light, / Engendered of light.
Man has already appeared, / The population of the surface of the earth," they said.
It was all assembled and came / And went, their wisdom,
In the darkness, / In the night time,
As they originated things, / And dissolved things.
They thought; / And they meditated there
And thus came their wisdom directly, bright / And clear.
They found / And they maintained / What came to be / Man's body.
That was just a little later / There not having appeared
The sun, / Moon / And stars / Over the heads
Of Former / And Shaper.

In Cleft, / In Bitter Water by name,
There came then yellow corn ears / And white corn ears.

And there are the names of the animals; / These were the bringers of the food:
Wildcat, / Coyote, / Parakeet / And Crow.
They are the four animals / Who told the news
Of the yellow corn ears / And white corn ears to them.
There they went then to Cleft / To point out the Cleft road,
And there they found the food / Whence came the flesh
Of the formed people, / The shaped people.

And the water was their blood; / It became man's blood.
There came to Bearer / And Engenderer the corn ears.
And they rejoiced then / Over the discovery
Of the marvelous mountain, / Filled / With quantities / And quantities
Of yellow corn ears, / And white corn ears,
And also loads of cacao / And chocolate,
Numberless mameys, / Custard apples, / Anonas, / Nances, Soursops / And honey
It was full of the sweetest foods, / In the town
At Cleft, / And at Bitter Water by name.
There was food there / From the fruit of everything:
Small vegetables, / Big vegetables, / Small plants / And big plants.
The road was pointed out / By the animals.

And the yellow corn was ground / And the white corn
And nine bushels / Were made by Xmucane.
The food came / With water to create strength,
And it became man's grease / And turned into his fat
When acted upon by Bearer / And Engenderer,
Majesty / And Quetzal Serpent, as they are called.
And so then they put into words the creation, / The shaping
Of our first mother / And father.
Only yellow corn / And white corn were their bodies.
Only food at the outset / Were their bodies.

These are the names of the first men who were made, / Who were shaped:
The first was Jaguar Quiche, / And the second in turn was Jaguar Night,
And the third in turn was Nought, / And the fourth was Wind Jaguar,
And these are the names of our first mothers / And fathers.
Only formed, / Only shaped they were said to be.
They had no mother; / They had no father.
Just heroes by themselves / We have said.
No woman bore them; / Nor were they engendered
By the Former / And Shaper, / The Bearer / And Engenderer.
Just power, / Just magic
Was their forming, / Their shaping
By the Former / And Shaper,
Bearer / And Engenderer, / Majesty / And Quetzal Serpent.
And when they looked like men / They became men.
They spoke / And they talked; / They saw / And they heard;
They walked; / They grasped;
They were fine men. / They were handsome. / Manly faces / Were their features.

They had breath / And existed.
And they could see too; / Immediately their sight began.
They came to see; / They came to know
Everything under heaven / If they could see it.
Suddenly they could look around / And see around
In the sky, / In the earth.
It was scarcely an instant / Before everything could be seen.
They didn't have to walk at first / So as to gaze at what was under heaven:
They were just there and looked. / Their understanding became great.
Their gaze passed over trees, / Rocks, / Lakes, / Seas, / Mountains / And valleys.
Truly then / They were the most beloved of men,
Jaguar Quiche, / Jaguar Night, / Nought / And Wind Jaguar.

And then they were asked by the Former / And Shaper:
"How pleasant is your existence? / Do you know? / Can't you see? / Can't you hear?
Isn't your language good / And your walking?
And look now / At what you see under heaven!" / And so then they gave thanks
To Former, / And Shaper,
"Truly then twice thanks, / Thrice thanks that we are created already,
And that we mouthed / And faced.
We can speak; / We can hear; / We ponder, / We move;
We think very well; / We understand
Far / And near,
And we can see large / And small
What is heaven, / What is earth.
Thanks then to you / That we are created, / We are formed, / We are shaped,
We exist, oh our grandmother, / Oh our grandfather,"
They said / As they gave thanks
For their forming, / Their shaping.
They came to understand everything; They saw it:
The four creations, / The four destructions
The womb of heaven, / The womb of earth.
And not very happily / Did they listen to this,
The Former / And Shaper.
It is not good / What they said,
"Our forming, / Our shaping:
We know everything great / And small," they said.

And so they took back again / Their knowledge,
Did Bearer / And Engenderer.
"How shall we make them again / So that their sight reaches only nearby?
So that it will just be a little space / Of the surface of the earth that they see?
It is not good / What they say.
Aren't their names just formed / And shaped?
And quite like gods / Will they become then
Unless they begin to multiply / And begin to grow numerous
When it whitens, / When it brightens:
Unless it increases. / Then so be it!
Let's just undo them a little more. / That's what is still needed.
It isn't good what we have found out. / Won't they just equate their deeds with ours
If their understanding reaches too far / And they see everything?" they were told
By the Heart of Heaven, 1 Leg, / Dwarf Lightning, Green Lightning,
Majesty, / Quetzal Serpent, / Bearer, / And Engenderer, / Xpiacoc, / Xmucane,
Former / And Shaper, as they are called.
And then they made / Their life over
For their forming, / Their shaping.

And their eyes were chipped / By the Heart of Heaven.
They were blinded like the clouding of the surface of a mirror; /
 Their eyes were all blinded.
They could only see nearby then, / However clear things might be,
And thus they lost their understanding, / And all the wisdom of the four men
At the start, / At the beginning
And thus was the forming, / The shaping
Of our grandfathers, / Our first fathers
By the Heart of Heaven / By the Heart of Earth.
And then there were their mates; / And their wives came to exist.
Only the gods / Invented them too.
Thus it was just in their sleep / That they brought them then.
Truly they were beautiful / And they were women
For Jaguar Quiche / Jaguar Night, / Nought / And Wind Jaguar.
When their wives were there they were properly brought to life / At once their
 hearts rejoiced again over their mates.
And these are their names; / Their wives were these:
Red Sea House was the name / Of the wife of Jaguar Quiche
Beauty House was the name / Of the wife of Jaguar Night
Hummingbird House was the name / Of the wife of Nought;
Parrot House was the name / Of the wife of Wind Jaguar.
And these were the names of their wives, / Who became queens.
They were the bearers of the little tribes, / The great tribes,
And this was the root of us / Who are Quiche people.
And the worshippers became many, / And the sacrificers.
They came to be no longer four, / Though four were the mothers of us Quiche
 people.
Different were their names / For each of them.
Then they multiplied there / At the sunrise.
Many were their names. / They became the peoples:
Majesties, / Ballplayers, / Maskers, / Children of the Lords,
As they continued to be called, / The names of the people.
And there / At the sunrise they multiplied. . . .

Central Themes

Indigenous people, religion, gender, race and ethnicity

Suggested Reading

Scarborough, Vernon L., and David R. Wilcox, eds. *The Mesoamerican Ballgame.* Tucson: University of Arizona Press, 1991.

Schele, Linda, and Peter Matthews. *The Code of Kings: The Language of Seven Sacred Maya Temples and Tombs.* New York: Scribner's, 1998.

Taube, Karl. *Aztec and Maya Myths.* Austin: University of Texas Press, 1997.

Related Sources

1. Copán and Teotihuacan: Shared Culture Across a Great Distance (200–900 CE)
3. Maya Royalty and Writing (c. 667 CE)
4. The Origin of the Nahuas and the Birth of the Fifth Sun (1596)

3. Maya Royalty and Writing (c. 667 CE)

In 1952, the Mexican archaeologist Alberto Ruz opened a passage in the center room of the Temple of Inscriptions at Palenque (in Chiapas State), Mexico. Digging down through rubble that filled a staircase and past a box containing five or six sacrificial victims, he discovered one of the most significant monuments of the ancient civilizations of the world: the astounding tomb and sarcophagus of King Hanab-Pakal, who was born in 603 and reigned from 615 to 683. Thanks to Ruz and several generations of archaeologists and linguists, the world can appreciate the beauty and profundity of the ancient Maya worldview and its history. The following description and analysis is based on the scholarship of Linda Schele and Peter Mathews. In the early 1970s, Schele and other archaeologists made linguistic breakthroughs and managed to decipher ancient Maya hieroglyphs. They have proven that the Maya Classic period had a fully phonetic writing system—not just picture-writing, as formerly believed—and thus that the Mayas wrote their own history, mostly on buildings, one thousand years before the arrival of Europeans. The Temple of the Inscriptions contains the longest continuous Pre-Columbian Maya text. It recounts the history of Palenque and glorifies the roles that Hanab-Pakal and his ancestors had in it. Schele's translation of the hieroglyphs in and around Hanab-Pakal's tomb provides us with the historical information that we have about the greatest king of the Mayas.

At the age of twelve, Hanab-Pakal ascended the throne of the Kingdom of Bak to become a great patron of the arts and architecture in his city, a survivor of wars with rival Maya city-states, and a husband who would have to suffer the death of his wife. In Hanab-Pakal's time, the city, known today as Palenque, was called Lakam Ha ("Big Water") because aqueducts from the mountains fed a series of small elegant channels in the pavement of the sacred precinct in the center of the city. Hanab-Pakal ordered and directed much of the construction of the capital city as it appears to visitors today. In 675 CE, Hanab-Pakal began the construction of the Temple of the Inscriptions and his tomb underneath.

The sarcophagus lid, which is 3.8 by 2.2 meters in dimension, features a portrait of Hanab-Pakal framed by the outermost rectangular sky-band. It is oriented as modern maps are today, with north at the top. He is facing left toward the west with his chin pointing at a crescent-shaped glyph that means "moon" on the sky-band, which also says "night." Directly behind him is the east, indicated by the dotted-X figure, "sun" or "day," in the middle of the sky-band. Inscribed on the top (north) and bottom (south) sky-bands are the pictures and names of three lords who were high-ranking officials in Hanab-Pakal's government and who may have coordinated the building of the Temple of the Inscriptions and the tomb.

In the background are various emblems, such as the shields with feathers hanging down, which all represent the life force. Hanab-Pakal rests on a sacrificial plate, with an emblem of death in its center, and he is enclosed in the open jaws of a snake. A snake's open mouth represents a door to the underworld in Mesoamerican mythology. Out of the sacrificial plate resting inside the snake door sprouts a stylized, flowering ceiba tree that represents the World Tree or the Milky Way. Atop the tree is a fanciful bird depicting the animal double (*nahualli*) of the first shaman in the world, who transformed himself into this figure to travel on mystical journeys through the otherworld.

Is Hanab-Pakal falling into the underworld, or is he rising up from it? Is this a death or a resurrection scene? Or is his stance meant to be more ambiguous, possibly suggesting both? His nose ring is flying up, and his hair is flung back. Linda Schele claims that he is being flung down, while other scholars think that he looks like he is flying upward or being resurrected. Schele believes that Hanab-Pakal is pictured at the moment of his death, falling into the underworld, but elements of the carving seem to evoke the cycle of death and life. Schele observes that his bent body pose also suggests a woman giving birth.

Hanab-Pakal wears a style of netted skirt that is emblematic of the maize god and a turtle ornament on his pectoral. Written along the side of the lid (not pictured here) appears: "They closed the lid, the sarcophagus of the maize god."* The written names of ten ancestor kings and one queen in chronological order of their reigns also appear on the sides. Each ruler in this ancestral orchard is shown emerging from a hole, with a tree behind him or her. Archaeologists speculate that the stone tube connecting the Temple of the Inscriptions above with the tomb was a conduit for souls to pass from this simulated underworld to the world of the living.

In the *Popol Vuh,* the hero twins defeat the death lords and then bring their father back to life in Xibalba, the underworld. They all emerge into our world from a crack in the cosmic turtle's shell in the form of maize gods. They then build a fire in the center of the world and set up the World Tree, giving order to the cosmos. Where in this mythical narrative would Hanab-Pakal have situated himself among his ancestors? What is the implied meaning about his death for his descendants? How does Hanab-Pakal's tomb justify his rule through religion? Given the inclusion of multiple generations of rulers on the coffin and their own emergence from the underworld, what might the purpose of this tomb have been other than as a burial spot?

---

*Linda Schele and Peter Mathews, *The Code of Kings: The Language of Seven Sacred Maya Temples and Tombs* (New York: Simon & Schuster, 1998), p. 117.

Maya king Hanab-Pakal's sarcophagus lid

Central Themes

Indigenous people, urban life, religion, gender

Suggested Reading

Coe, Michael D. *Breaking the Maya Code.* New York: Thames & Hudson, 1992.
Miller, Mary, and Simon Martin. *Courtly Art of the Ancient Maya.* London: Thames & Hudson, 2004.
Scarborough, Vernon L., and David Wilcox, eds. *The Mesoamerican Ballgame.* Tucson: University of Arizona Press, 1991.
Schele, Linda, and Peter Mathews. *The Code of Kings: The Language of Seven Sacred Maya Temples and Tombs.* New York: Simon & Schuster, 1998.

Related Sources

1. Copán and Teotihuacan: Shared Culture Across a Great Distance (200–900 CE)
2. The *Popol Vuh* ("the Community Book"): The Mythic Origins of the Quiché Mayas (1554–1558)
4. The Origin of the Nahuas and the Birth of the Fifth Sun (1596)

4. The Origin of the Nahuas and the Birth of the Fifth Sun (1596)*

Fray Gerónimo de Mendieta (1525–1604) arrived in New Spain in 1554. As a speaker of Nahuatl, his lifework as a Franciscan brother was the Christian indoctrination of the Nahuas. Mendieta's *Historia,* which was not published until the nineteenth century owing to a royal ban of 1577, is a valuable source on the mythology of the Pre-Conquest Nahuas. Mendieta cites a lost writing of another Franciscan, Fray Andrés de Olmos (1491?–1571), as his source for this selection.

The following passages contain the story of the origins of humanity and the sun at the time when the world was created. Other sources, such as the Aztec Calendar Stone, tell us that the Pre-Conquest Nahuas believed that they were living during the Fifth Sun, which they called Nahui Ollin (Four Movement). According to this belief, the world and humanity had already been created and destroyed four times in cataclysmic wars in which sibling gods battled for the supremacy of each age. In Chapter 1 of Mendieta's *Historia,* the celestial creator divinities Citlalicue and Citlalatonac, goddess and god of the stars, produce a very unusual offspring: a giant flint knife that falls to the earth at Chicomoztoc, Seven Caves. Fallen gods spring

---

*Jerónimo de Mendieta, OFM, *Historia eclesiática indiana,* ed. Joaquín García Icazbalceta (Mexico, 1870), libro II, pp. 77–80. Excerpt translated by the editors.

from the Seven Caves and set out to create human beings. Chicomoztoc is mentioned in other sources (not included here), such as the *Historia Tolteca-Chichimeca* (1550), which documents the founding of many of the most powerful sixteenth-century Nahua *altepetls* (dynastic city-states). Seven nomadic bands of Chichimecas emerged from the cave—the Xochimilca, Chalca, Tepaneca, Colhua, Tlahuica, Tlaxcalteca, and Mexica—and they wandered homeless until their tutelary deities guided them to establish altepetls in central Mexico. Mendieta mentions that the people who told the origin stories to Andrés de Olmos were from some of the most important city-states, which represented these seven bands of Nahuatl-speaking people from the Seven Caves, such as Mexico (the city of Tenochtitlan), the place of the Mexica band, and Tlalmanalco, an altepetl of the Chalca people. Mendieta's mention of the caves thus implies that this should be read as the origin story, not of all Aztec peoples, but of particular Nahua city-states.

Post-Conquest sources can be used to understand the Pre-Columbian period, but with care. In this selection, Mendieta remarks on these two Nahua origin stories, indicated by parentheses, and compares the myths to the Bible. He explains the Nahua civilization's creation myths with his own civilization's creation myths. Mendieta and many other Franciscans of the time believed that the Christian conversion of the millions of indigenous people in the New World was the harbinger of the Second Coming of Christ. Anything that had happened in the past including Pre-Columbian people's understanding of how the world was created, would thus show glimmers of God's providential master plan for history. As a millenarian, Mendieta thought that God and the devil had been struggling for the upper hand throughout history and in all places, including Mexico, but that when Christ came again he would vanquish evil once and for all. In spite of the Franciscans' optimism, they were always on the lookout for the diabolic presence in indigenous religion and history.

Readers in the past have generally used this and other sixteenth- and seventeenth-century ecclesiastical writings based on indigenous sources in two ways. First, generations of anthropologists have attempted to filter out Mendieta's remarks and tried to understand the Pre-Conquest origin stories on their own terms. If we were to take this approach, there are a series of questions we might ask: What do these myths tell us about these people's views on human nature and humanity's relationship with the gods? How does this vision of humanity's place in the universe help to explain the existence of Pre-Conquest organized religion, war, and practices such as human sacrifice?

This approach does, however, have methodological problems. First, Mendieta tells us that Andrés de Olmos synthesized several versions of these stories, effectively acting as an editor. Second, we may seek to understand how a sixteenth-century Spanish Franciscan attempted to fit indigenous civilization into the general worldview of his own Christian European civilization. Readers may be more interested in interpreting indigenous civilization in the context of the Spanish Conquest or conversion, covered extensively in the second section of this volume. But what if the indigenous people themselves prompted Mendieta to supply the parenthetical remarks he includes in his writing? After all, the indigenous leaders who recounted the stories were—at least publicly—good Christian converts. During the colonial period, all of the indigenous communities named here capitalized on their avowed loyalty to the Spanish king and Catholic faith. If these leaders had assimilated some of the Christian worldview by the time Mendieta took down the stories, then this originally foreign set of assumptions may have affected which stories they remembered, how they framed them, and the order in which they told the events. There is a third way to read the myths: as snapshots of the worldview of the Nahuas who lived in two worlds—Spanish and indigenous—in the sixteenth century. Which aspects appear to be non-European, and which might have been European-influenced?

Historia Eclesiástica Indiana

Chapter 1: What They Believe About Their Gods or Demons and the Creation of the First Man

This account is from the venerable and very religious father Fray Andrés de Olmos who took it from paintings and reports that the *caciques* [local native leaders] of Mexico, Texcoco, Tlaxcala, Huexotzinco, Cholula, Tepeaca, Tlalmanalco, and the rest of the *cabeceras* [head towns] gave to him regarding the gods that they had in the different provinces and *pueblos* [towns], which served and gave adoration to the different gods.* In different ways they related various absurdities, fables and fictions, which they held as certainties because if they had not believed them as such, they would not have written them down with such diligence and efficacy as a later account of their fiestas will tell. Even though each of the provinces had different ways of relating their stories, for the most part, they came to conclude that in the heavens there was a god called Citlalatonac and a goddess named Citlalicue. The goddess gave birth to a great knife or flint (which in their language, they call *tecpcatl*) and because her children were frightened of it, they agreed to cast this knife from the sky, which they indeed did. And it fell to a particular part of the earth called Chicomoztoc, which means "Seven Caves." Out came 1,600 gods (it appears to be an attempt to explain the fall of the evil angels) and these fallen and exiled ones lacked servants. So they agreed to send a message to their mother, the goddess, saying that because they had been cast out and banished, she should give them the power to raise men who would serve them. The mother responded: if they had deserved to have them they would have always had them in their company; however, they did not deserve this. If they wanted to have servants there on earth then they would have to ask Mictlan Tecutli, who was the Lord or the Chief of hell, who might give them some

**Cabeceras*, or "head towns," had legal and administrative jurisdiction over subordinate towns. After the Conquest, the Spanish often designated the most powerful indigenous city-states as cabeceras.

bone or ash of the ancient dead. Then upon them they might sacrifice themselves and from them man and woman would come who then might multiply. (It appears here that they were trying to understand the Flood when mankind perished leaving none to remain.) Taking heed, then, of their mother's response—it is said Tlotli, "the hawk" brought them her answer—they entered into counsel and agreed that one of their number, called Xolotl, would go into the inferno for the bone and ash. He was advised that Mictlan Tecutli, chief of hell, was two-faced and deceitful and that he should make sure and not tarry after he had been given what he requested. And that is why he planned to flee without stopping to explain himself. Xolotl did it the way that he was entrusted: he went to hell and obtained from the chief, Mictlan Tecutli, the bone and ash, which his brothers hoped that he would get. He had just grasped them in his hands and was about to escape when Mictlan Tecutli, insulted that he would just run away from him, gave chase. As luck would have it, while escaping, Xolotl tripped and dropped an arm bone which shattered into pieces, great and small. This is why some men are shorter than others. Gathering up all the parts that he could, he arrived at the place where his fellow gods were. He threw all that he carried into an earthenware pot or bowl. The gods and goddesses sacrificed themselves with bloodletting from all parts of their bodies (to which accordingly the Indians were later accustomed) and it is said that four days later a baby boy emerged, and returning to do it again four more days later, out came a girl. They gave them to Xolotl to raise and he nourished them with the milk of cardoon.

Chapter 2. Of How the Sun Was Created and the Death of the Gods

Now, man had been created, and having multiplied, each one of the gods took some men to be their devoted servants. And for some years, according to what is said, there was no sun. The gods met at the pueblo called Teotihuacan, which is six leagues from Mexico [City] where they made a great fire and these gods arranged themselves in four quarters around the fire. They said to their devotees that whoever was the quickest to hurl himself into the fire would then have the honor of having created the sun because the first to leap into the fire would then spring forth as the sun. And the one who was the bravest of them pounced and threw himself into the fire, falling into the inferno. Meanwhile, standing around and waiting where the sun was supposed to rise, they bet with the quails, lobsters, butterflies, and snakes that they could not guess where the sun would rise. Some said here and some said there, but in the end none guessed correctly, and for this they were condemned to be sacrificed as later they were very accustomed to do before their idols. Finally the sun rose where it was destined to rise but it stopped and would not pass by. And seeing that the sun would not go about on its course, the gods agreed to send Tlotli as their messenger: on their behalf he might command the sun to move along his course. He replied that he would not move from his place until some of them were killed and destroyed. Some were frightened at his response. And some were angry such as the one called Citli [Hare] who took his bow and three arrows and shot at the sun to pierce him in the forehead and drive him forward. The sun went down and thus did not budge. He then shot a second time but the sun dodged the arrow. The third time he did it the sun got very angry and hurled back one of the arrows at Citli, which nailed him in the forehead and killed him. Seeing what happened, the other gods were dismayed and understood that they could not prevail against the sun. So these desperate ones agreed to kill themselves and sacrifice all. And the minister of this sacrifice was Xolotl who opened their chests with a flint knife, killed them, and then killed himself in the same way. They left each of their devotees the clothes they wore—cotton cloths—as remembrances of their devotion and friendship. In this way they appeased the sun and he went along his course. And these devotees and servants of the dead gods wrapped these cloths around poles, making notches or holes in the pole. They placed in the center some little green precious stones and the hides of tigers and snakes and this wrapping was called *tlaquimilloli.* On each one was placed the name of a demon who had given his or her garment, and each was a principal idol that they greatly revered even more so than the fantastical figures that they made from stone or wood. Father Andrés de Olmos tells of how he found these idols wrapped in many cloths in Tlalmanalco; however, at this time, half of these rotten things have been hidden.

Central Themes

Indigenous people, religion

Suggested Reading

Aguilar-Moreno, Manuel. *Handbook to Life in the Aztec World.* New York: Oxford University Press, 2007.

Burkhart, Louise M. *The Slippery Earth: Nahua-Christian Moral Dialogue in Sixteenth-Century Mexico.* Tucson: University of Arizona Press, 1989.

Clendinnen, Inga. *Aztecs: An Interpretation.* New York: Cambridge University Press, 1992.

Phelan, John Leddy. *The Millennial Kingdom of the Franciscans in the New World,* 2nd and rev. ed. Berkeley: University of California Press, 1970.

Related Sources

2. The *Popol Vuh* ("the Community Book"): The Mythic Origins of the Quiché Mayas (1554–1558)
20. Chimalpahin: Indigenous Chronicler of His Time (1611–1613)
24. The Persistence of Indigenous Idolatry (1656)

5. A Treasury of Mexica Power and Gender (c. 1541–1542)*

The *Codex Mendoza* (c. 1541–1542) is one of the most valuable Post-Conquest written sources on the Pre-Columbian Mexica of Tenochtitlan, which expanded to become what is today referred to as the Aztec Empire. The first viceroy of Mexico, Antonio de Mendoza (1535–1550), or members of his government organized the production of the *Codex* for King Charles I of Spain. The new European empire-builders required information about Mexico and its people so that they could extract resources as efficiently as possible. They already had at their disposal the meticulous records of the Aztecs. After French pirates seized the *Codex* from the Spanish flotilla en route to Europe, it ended up in the hands of the royal cosmographer of King Henri II of France in 1553.

Produced with guidance from Spanish friars, the book contains seventy-two drawings and written glyphs executed by one or several indigenous *tlacuilos* (painter-scribes). The sixty-three pages of interpretations of these pictorial elements in Spanish were probably provided by indigenous interpreters and painter-scribes. Part 1 gives the history of the founding of Tenochtitlan, including the depiction of the eagle landing on the cactus, and follows its political expansion from 1325 to 1521. Part 2 is the Aztec Empire's record of the annual tribute payments from the 371 city-states, organized into 38 provinces, that were under its control prior to the Conquest in 1521. Part 3 covers many aspects of daily life: descriptions of rituals from birth to marriage, a catalog of job occupations and the ranks of warriors, and an explanation of how the justice system functioned. The tlacuilos most likely copied the material for parts 1 and 2 from earlier native written sources that are now lost to history. They created part 3 especially for the *Codex*. Much of what we know about Pre-Columbian Nahua society—other than what has been deduced from archaeology—comes from the *Codex Mendoza* and another source produced in the sixteenth century, the *Florentine Codex* (Source 11).

The first selection is from part 2. We can see the amazing quantity of goods—such as an astounding 16,000 rubber balls made from rubber tree resin—that came from a single province located in modern north-central Oaxaca State. The Mexica tribute system reached as far south as Chiapas and northern Guatemala, the source of resources found only in the cloud forests there: liquidambar, the resin of the sweet gum tree, used for smoking and medicinal purposes; and the feathers of the *quetzalli,* the rare quetzal bird. Most likely the taxation demands of this indigenous civilization had a negative impact on the environment there.

---

*Frances Berdan and Patricia Rieff Anawalt, *The Essential Codex Mendoza* (Berkeley: University of California Press, 1997), pp. 96–97, 118–119, 126–127. Reprinted with permission.

Along the left-hand side and the bottom of the tribute record appear the Pre-Columbian place-name glyphs for each *altepetl* (city-state) that sent tribute to Tenochtitlan. For example, in the top right-hand corner is Tochtepec, written in a glyph that combines a picture of a rabbit (*tochtli* in Nahuatl) on top of a picture of a hill (*tepetl).* Then to the right of the names of the city-states are the pictures of the tribute items that the entire province owed annually. On top of the pictures are number signs, such as the little feather figure meaning 400, above each *manta* (cotton cloak). What does the diversity of the goods from just one province tell us about the specialization and coordination of labor in local city-states? What can we deduce were the methods of production? What does it tell us about how the Mexica economy was structured?

The second drawing, with accompanying text, depicts the bathing and naming rituals for newborn babies that midwives conducted, presenting male and female infants with symbols of their ideal gender roles in society. The illustration also shows the two main educational paths for boys: the temple school (the *calmecac*) or a master-apprentice relationship in which adult warriors trained young boys to fight. Given that the midwife presents a weaving distaff and spindle to all baby girls, what does this tell us about women and the tribute economy of the empire?

The third drawing shows a wedding ceremony in which a man and a woman literally "tie the knot" with their mantas. The bride and groom are symbolically arranged before a hearth with parallel lines of two old men on the groom's side of the house and two old women on the bride's side. Similar to the birth and naming rituals, a female medical professional leads the ceremony, along with a procession of women. What do these last two documents illustrate about conceptions of gender in this society? Why would the institution of marriage and the work of midwives and female physicians have been so important to an imperial state?

The Codex Mendoza

Tribute list from Tochtepec*

The number of towns of the hot and temperate lands drawn and named on the following page is twenty-two, etc. The things they gave in tribute to the lords of Mexico are the following:

First, they paid in tribute one thousand six hundred loads of rich cloaks, clothing the lords and *caciques* wore;

Also eight hundred loads of cloaks striped in red, white, and green;

Also four hundred loads of women's skirts and tunics—all of which they gave in tribute every six months;

And also they gave in tribute one warrior costume with its shield trimmed with rich feathers, with its [back] device of a bird, and in the colors drawn;

Also one gold shield;

Also one [back] device for warrior costumes, like a bird's wing, of rich yellow feathers;

Also a gold diadem of the form drawn;

Also one gold headband, one hand wide and of the thickness of parchment;

Also two strings of beads and a collar, of gold;

Also three large pieces of greenstones, rich stones;

Also three strings of round stones of greenstone beads, rich stones;

Also four strings of greenstone beads, rich stones;

Also twenty lip plugs of clear amber, decorated with gold;

Also another twenty lip plugs of crystal with their blue smalt and gold setting;

Also eighty bundles of rich green feathers called *quetzalli;*

Also four pieces, like bundles, of rich green feathers trimmed with rich yellow feathers.

Also eight thousand little bundles of rich turquoise-blue feathers;

Also eight thousand little bundles of rich red feathers;

Also eight thousand little bundles of rich green feathers;

Also one hundred pots or jars of fine liquidambar;

Also two hundred loads of cacao;

Also sixteen thousand round balls of rubber, which is the gum of trees, and when the balls are thrown on the ground they bounce very high—all of which they paid in tribute once a year.

---

*The three subheadings for the *Codex Mendoza* selections here were added by the editors of this reader.

Tochtepec / pueblo
400 loads of *mantas* of this rich design
400 loads of *mantas* of this rich design
400 loads of *mantas* of this rich design
400 loads of *mantas* of this rich design
400 loads of this *mantas* design
Xayaco, pueblo
One warrior costume of rich feathers, of this bird style
One gold shield of this fashioning
400 that is, of this *mantas*, loads, design
400 skirts and tunics loads of women's [*guipiles*]
Otlatitlan / pueblo
One shield of rich feathers
Device of rich feathers
One gold diadem of this fashioning
Coçamaloapan, pueblo
Mixtlan / pueblo
One gold headband, one hand wide and the thickness of parchment
One string of gold beads
One string of gold beads
Three pieces of *chalchihuitl*, rich stones
Three strings of *chalchihuitl*, rich stones
Michapan / pueblo
Ayotzintepec / pueblo
Four strings of *chalchihuitl*, rich stones
16,000 balls of rubber
Michtlan, pueblo
Twenty lip plugs of clear amber, with their setting of gold at the end
Twenty lip plugs of crystal, with their blue coloring and their setting of gold
Teotlilan, pueblo
Four pieces of rich feathers, made like handfuls into this form
Tlacotlalpan.
Tozlan, pueblo
Eighty handfuls of rich feathers
Xicaltepec, pueblo
Eight thousand little handfuls of rich turquoise feathers
Eight thousand little handfuls of rich red feathers
Eight thousand little handfuls of rich green feathers
One hundred pots or jars of liquid-ambar
Two hundred loads of cacao
Yaotlan / pueblo
Oxitlan / pueblo
Yxmatlatlan, pueblo
Tzinacanoztoc, pueblo
Totoltepec, pueblo
Chinantlan, pueblo
pueblo / Ayoçintepec
Cuezcomatitlan pueblo
Puctlan, pueblo
Teteutlan, pueblo

Midwife and newborn babies

[This is an] account of the manner and customs the Mexicans had in giving birth to a boy or girl, their custom and rites in giving names to the infants, and later dedicating and offering them to their temples or to the military, as shown in the drawings with their brief explanations, contained farther on, on another page, beyond the figures shown on this page.

After the mother gave birth, they placed the infant in its cradle, as drawn. And at the end of four days after the infant's birth, the midwife carried the infant, naked, and took it to the courtyard of the house of the one who had given birth. And in the courtyard they had placed a small earthen tub of water on rushes or reeds [as a mat] called *tule,* where the said midwife bathed the said infant. And after the bath three boys, who are seated next to the said rushes eating toasted maize rolled up with cooked beans, the food they called *yxicue,* purposefully put the food in the little earthen jug so they might eat it. And after the said bath, the said midwife ordered the said boys to call out loudly the new name of the infant who had been bathed. And the name they gave it was that which the midwife wished. And at the beginning, when the infant was taken to be bathed, if it was a boy, they carried him with his symbol in his hand; and the symbol was the tool used by the infant's father, whether of the military or professions like metalworker, woodcarver, or whatever other profession. And after having done this, the midwife handed the infant to his mother. And if the infant was a girl, the symbol they gave her for bathing was a distaff with its spindle and basket, and a broom, which were the things she would use when she grew up. And they offered the male infant's umbilical cord, along with the little shield and arrows used in bathing, in the place where they warred with their enemies, where they buried it in the ground. And likewise for the girl, they buried her umbilical cord under the *metate,* a stone for grinding tortillas.

And after that, at the end of twenty days, the infant's parents took the infant to the temple or *mezquita,* called *calmecac.* And, with offerings of cloaks, loincloths, and some food, they presented the infant to the priests. And after the infant had been reared and reached [a proper] age, they delivered him to the head priest of the said temple to be trained there for the priesthood.

And if the infant's parents decided that, upon coming of age, he would serve in the military, then they offered the infant to the master, promising him [to service]. The master of boys and youths was called *teachcauh* or *telpuchtlato.* They made the offering with presents of food and other things for the dedication. And when the infant was of age, they delivered him to the said master.

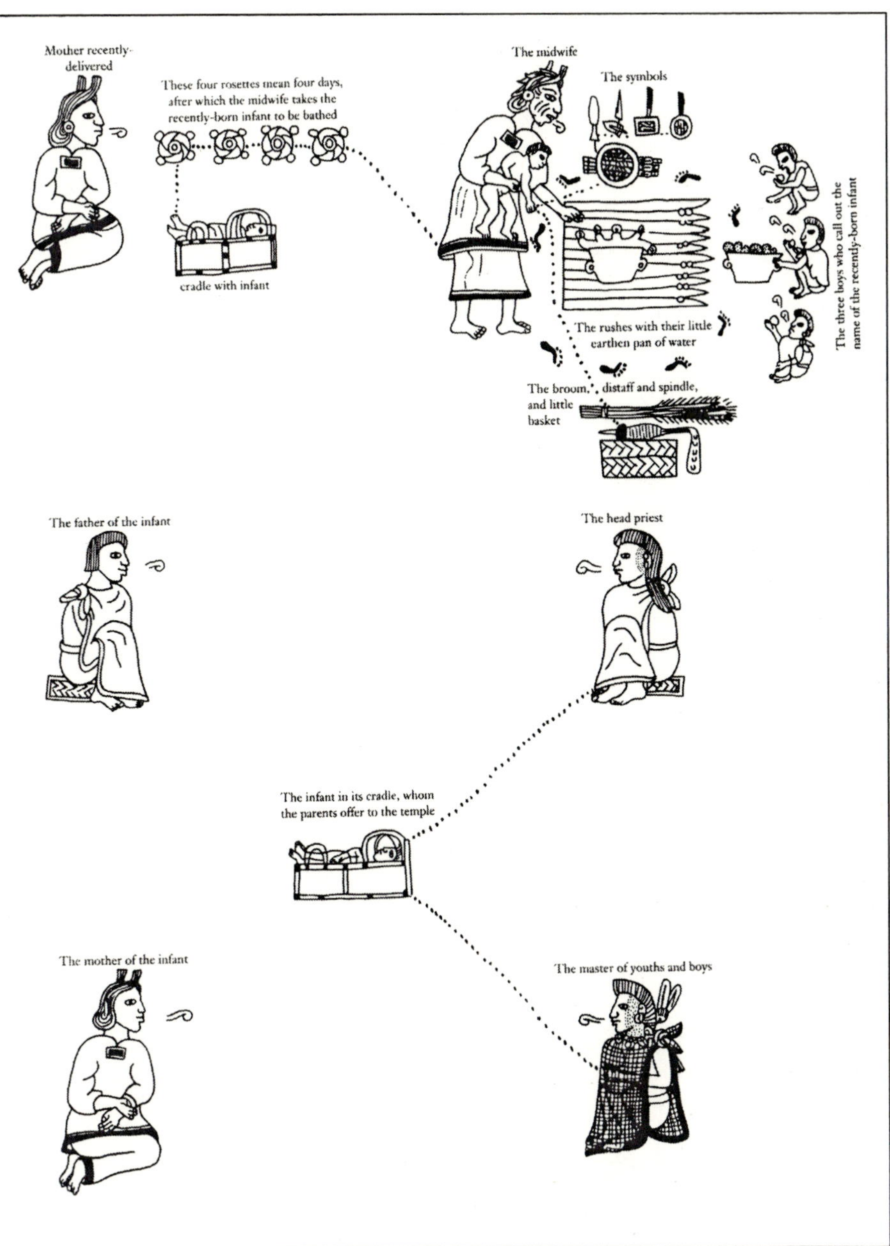
Mother recently-delivered
These four rosettes mean four days, after which the midwife takes the recently-born infant to be bathed
cradle with infant
The midwife
The symbols
The three boys who call out the name of the recently-born infant
The rushes with their little earthen pan of water
The broom, and little basket
distaff and spindle,
The father of the infant
The head priest
The infant in its cradle, whom the parents offer to the temple
The mother of the infant
The master of youths and boys

Education of children and marriage ceremony

Explanation of the drawings on the following page: In the first part, the drawing means that the father, having boys of a youthful age, took them to the two houses drawn, either to the house of the master who taught and instructed youths or to the temple, according to how the youth was inclined. And he delivered him to the chief priest or the master of the boys so the youths might be taught from the age of fifteen years.

Explanation of the drawings on the second part of the following page: The drawings depict the means and custom they had in making legitimate marriages. The ceremony began when the bride, just after dark, was carried on the back of an *amanteca,* who is a physician. They were accompanied by four other women carrying ignited pine torches, who went lighting their way. And when they arrived at the groom's house, the groom's parents led her to the patio of the house to receive her, and they put her in a room or house where the groom was waiting. And the bride and the bridegroom sat on a mat with its seats, next to a burning hearth, and they tied their clothes together, and offered copal incense to their gods. And then two old men and two old women, who were present as witnesses, gave food to the bride and bridegroom, and then the elders ate. And when the old men and old women finished eating, each one individually addressed the bride and bridegroom, offering them good advice on how they ought to behave and live, and on how they ought to perform the responsibility and position they had acquired, in order to live in peace.

Central Themes

Indigenous people, land and labor, gender

Suggested Reading

Berdan, Francis. *The Aztecs of Central Mexico: An Imperial Society,* 2nd ed. Belmont, CA: Thomson Wadsworth, 2005.

Carrasco, Pedro Pizana. *The Tenocha Empire of Ancient Mexico: The Triple Alliance of Tenochtitlan, Tetzcoco, and Tlacopan.* Norman: University of Oklahoma Press, 1999.

Dodds, Caroline Pennock. *Bonds of Blood: Gender, Lifecycle, and Sacrifice in Aztec Culture.* New York: Palgrave Macmillan, 2008.

Hassig, Ross. *Trade, Tribute, and Transportation: The Sixteenth-Century Political Economy of the Valley of Mexico.* Norman: University of Oklahoma Press, 1993.

Related Sources

4. The Origin of the Nahuas and the Birth of the Fifth Sun (1596)
6. Markets and Temples in the City of Tenochtitlan (1519)
24. The Persistence of Indigenous Idolatry (1656)
37. A Woman's Life on the Northern Frontier (1877)
46. A Positivist Interpretation of Feminism (1909)

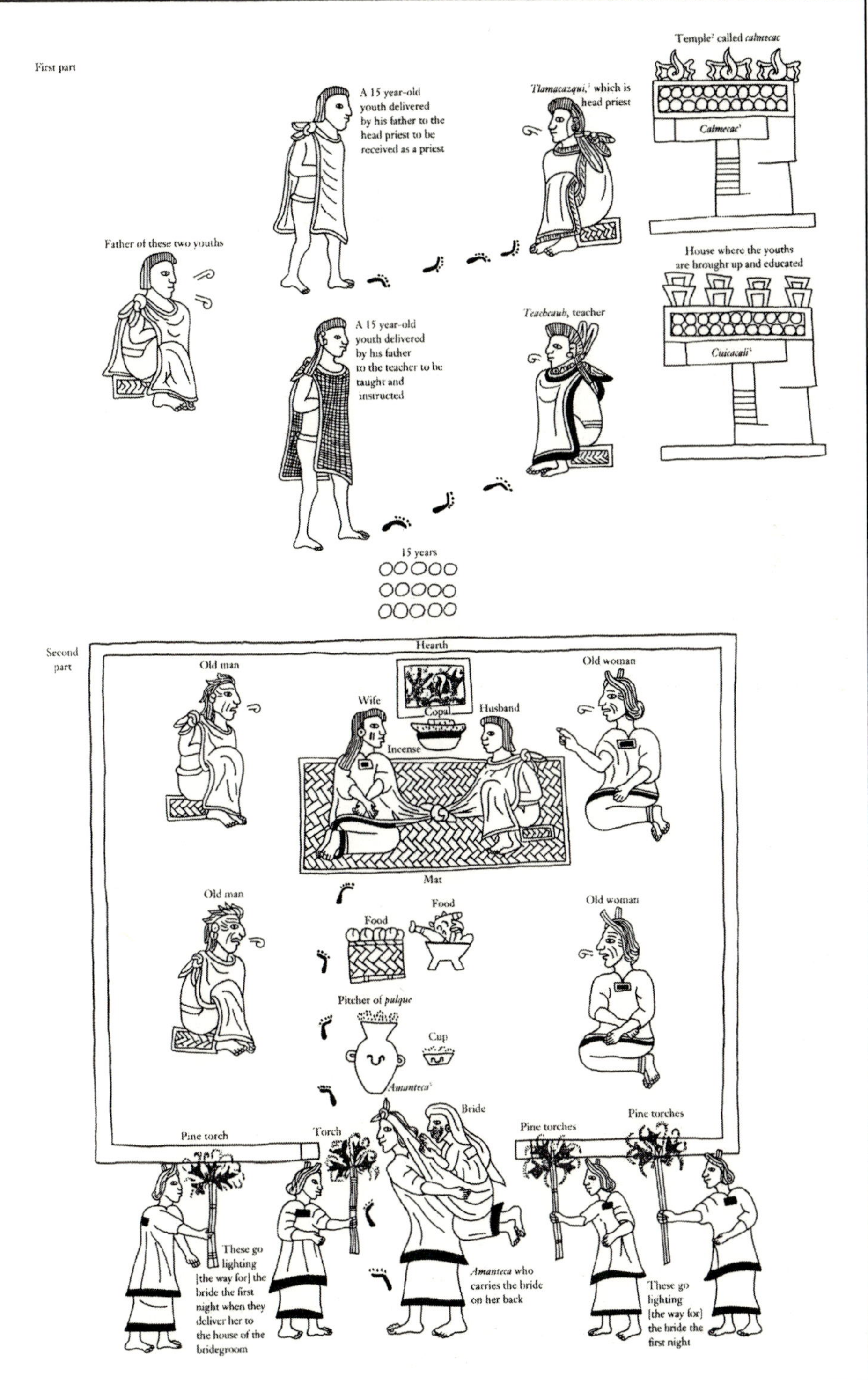
First part
A 15 year-old youth delivered by his father to the head priest to be received as a priest
Tlamacazqui,[1] which is head priest
Temple[2] called *calmecac*
Calmecac[3]
Father of these two youths
A 15 year-old youth delivered by his father to the teacher to be taught and instructed
Teachcauh, teacher
House where the youths are brought up and educated
Cuicacali[4]
15 years
Second part
Hearth
Old man
Old woman
Wife
Copal
Husband
Incense
Mat
Old man
Food
Food
Old woman
Pitcher of *pulque*
Cup
Amanteca[5]
Bride
Pine torch
Torch
Pine torches
Pine torches
These go lighting [the way for] the bride the first night when they deliver her to the house of the bridegroom
Amanteca who carries the bride on her back
These go lighting [the way for] the bride the first night

6. Markets and Temples in the City of Tenochtitlan (1519)*

Intent on conquering Mexico, Hernán Cortés (1485–1547) arrived in the Mexica city of Tenochtitlan in November 1519, which he incorrectly called "Temixtitan" in this primary source. This revealing and lively description of the city in that year comes from the conquistador's second letter to King Charles I of Spain, which was printed soon thereafter and became one of the earliest best-sellers in European history. Although readers might be wary of taking a conqueror's words as reliable information on Pre-Columbian Nahua society, Cortés's tone tends to be neutral when he is not praising. In addition, some of the information that Cortés provides is corroborated by other written primary sources, including the indigenous-authored book, the *Codex Mendoza* (Source 4).

The Mexica established the city of Tenochtitlan in the early 1300s on a small island in Lake Texcoco. They began to consolidate their political authority over the Valley of Mexico in 1428 CE with an alliance with the neighboring city-states of Texcoco and Tlacopan. Raised agricultural plots engineered from the lake mud (called *chinampas*), extensive trade networks, and tribute collected from subordinated city-states fostered an estimated population of between 150,000 and 200,000 people by 1519.

This passage describes two of the grandest locations in the city: the massive marketplace and the monumental sacred precinct. The Mexica designed the city in four administrative quarters, with the double-walled sacred precinct built where the four inner corners of the quarters met. In this religiously based urban plan, the four quarters represented the four cardinal directions of the cosmos—east, west, north, and south—and the sacred precinct represented the *axis mundi* (the center of the universe). In Mendieta's Mexica creation story, the gods arrange themselves in four quarters around this center, where they build a fire in order to create the sun (Source 4). The massive paved plaza held seventy-eight religious structures, including the *calmecac,* an educational institution run by priests (Source 5). On the east side of the ceremonial plaza was the *Templo Mayor* (Great Temple), which, at sixty meters in height, was the tallest structure in Tenochtitlan. It was crowned by two buildings dedicated to Tlaloc, the rain god, and Huitzilopochtli, the tribal war deity turned sun god. Opposite the temple, to the west, were the great ball court and the skull rack, *tzompantli,* for the heads of human sacrifices.

---

*Francis Augustus MacNutt, ed. and trans., *Fernando Cortes: His Five Letters of Relation to the Emperor Charles V,* vol. 1 (Cleveland, OH: A. H. Clark, 1908), pp. 256–260, 262–264. Some footnotes from the original translation have been omitted.

The largest marketplace in Mexico was located on the north side of the island in Tlatelolco, a city that had lost its independence to expansionist Tenochtitlan in 1474. An estimated 20,000 to 25,000 people per day shopped in Tlatelolco, and even more attended a special market held every five days. The market was organized in sections, with similar goods always sold in the same location. To this day, large outdoor street markets in Mexico City are arranged in a similar fashion, and the word *tianguis,* derived from the Nahuatl *tianquiztli,* means "market" in modern Mexican Spanish. From the multitude of goods for sale, what can we learn about the city residents' diet, appearance, and homes? Market prices were set according to a system of fluctuating values of the three forms of currency: cacao beans, cotton cloths called *quachtli,* and T-shaped copper pieces. The Mexica government did not manage this market economy, but as the passage suggests, some form of centralized commercial authority did regulate market transactions.

Assuming that grandeur was synonymous with societal importance, what do the two locations of sacred precinct and marketplace suggest were the main purposes of the city? Cortés describes a highly specialized, hierarchical, and seemingly orderly lifestyle. What types of authorities were in charge, and what aspects of society did they regulate and control? What might indigenous practices of marketing and governance have meant for the Spaniards?

Like many of the documents in this section and the next one, readers should consider this passage as both a source on Pre-Columbian Mexican society and a source for understanding the Spanish Conquest. The aspects of Mexica society that Cortés finds most remarkable reveal some of the cultural values and political goals of the conquerors from Spain. Cortés glowingly compares Tenochtitlan to Cordoba, Seville, and Granada, cities in Andalusia, Spain. What aspects of Mexica society did Cortés think were admirable, and in what ways did he believe the people were similar to his own? Which aspects did he believe warranted the label "barbarous," thereby rendering the Mexicans deserving of conquest? What might explain his divergent attitudes?

The Second Letter of Hernán Cortes

The great city of Temixtitan is built on the salt lake, and from the mainland to the city is a distance of two leagues, from any side from which you enter. It has four approaches by means of artificial causeways, two cavalry lances in width. The city is as large as Seville or Cordoba. Its streets (I speak of the principal ones) are very broad and straight, some of these, and all the others, are one half land, and the other half water on which they go about in canoes. All the streets have openings at regular intervals to let water flow from one to the other, and at all of these openings, some of which are very broad, there are bridges, very large, strong, and well constructed, so that, over many, ten horsemen can ride abreast. Perceiving that, if the inhabitants wished to practice any treachery against us, they had plenty of opportunity, because the said city being built as I have described, they might, by raising the bridges at the exits and entrances, starve us without our being able to reach land, as soon as I entered the city, I made great haste to build four brigantines, which I had completed in a short time, capable whenever we might wish, of taking three hundred men and the horses to land.

The city has many squares where markets are held, and trading is carried on. There is one square, twice as large as that of Salamanca, all surrounded by arcades, where there are daily more than sixty thousand souls, buying and selling, and where are found all the kinds of merchandise produced in these countries, including food products, jewels of gold and silver, lead, brass, copper, zinc, stone, bones, shells, and feathers. Stones are sold, hewn, and unhewn, adobe bricks, wood, both in the rough and manufactured in various ways. There is a street for game, where they sell every sort of bird, such as chickens, partridges, quails, wild ducks, fly-catchers, widgeons, turtle-doves, pigeons, reed-birds, parrots, owls, eaglets, falcons, sparrow-hawks, and kestrels, and they sell the skins of some of these birds of prey with their feathers, heads, beaks, and claws. They sell rabbits, hares, and small dogs which they castrate, and raise for the purpose of eating.

There is a street set apart for the sale of herbs, where can be found every sort of root and medical herb which grows in the country. There are houses like apothecary shops, where prepared medicines are sold, as well as liquids, ointments, and plasters. There are places like our barber's shops, where they wash and shave their heads. There are houses where they supply food and drink for payment. There are men, such as in Castile are called porters, who carry burdens. There is much wood, charcoal, braziers made of earthenware, and mats of divers kinds for beds, and others, very thin, used as cushions, and for carpeting halls, and bed-rooms. There are all sorts of vegetables, and especially onions, leeks, garlic, borage, nasturtium, watercresses, sorrel, thistles, and artichokes. There are many kinds of fruits, amongst others, cherries, and prunes, like the Spanish ones. They sell bees-honey and wax, and honey made of corn-stalks, which is as sweet and syrup-like as that of sugar, also honey of a plant called maguey, which is better than most; from these same plants they make sugar and wine, which they also sell.

They also sell skeins of different kinds of spun cotton, in all colours, so that it seems quite like one of the silk markets in Granada, although it is on a greater scale; also as many different colours for painters as can be found in Spain and of as excellent hues. They sell deer skins with all the hair tanned on them, and of different colours; much earthenware, exceedingly good, many sorts of pots, large and small, pitchers, large tiles, and infinite variety of vases, all of very singular clay, and most of them glazed and painted. They sell maize, both in grain and made into bread, which is very superior in its quality to that of the other islands and mainland; pies of birds, and fish, also much fish, fresh, salted, cooked, and raw; eggs of hens, and geese, and other birds in great quantity, and cakes made of eggs.

Finally, besides those things I have mentioned, they sell in the city markets everything else which is found in the whole country and which, on account of the profusion and number, do not occur to my memory and which also I do not tell of, because I do not know their names.

Each kind of merchandise is sold in its respective street, and they do not mix their kinds of merchandise of any species; thus they preserve perfect order. Everything is sold by a kind of measure, and, until now, we have not seen anything sold by weight.

There is in this square a very large building, like a Court of Justice, where there are always ten or twelve persons, sitting as judges, and delivering their decisions upon all cases which arise in the markets. There are other persons in the same square who go about continually among the people, observing what is sold, and the measures being used in selling, and they have been seen to break some which were false.

This great city contains many mosques, or houses for idols, very beautiful edifices situated in the different precincts of it; in the principal ones of which are the religious orders of their sect, for whom, besides the houses in which they keep their idols, there are very good habitations provided. All these priests dress in black, and never cut or comb their hair from the time they enter the religious order until they leave it; and the sons of all the principal families, both of chiefs as well as noble citizens, are in these religious orders and habits from the age of seven or eight years till they are taken away for the purpose of marriage. This happens more frequently for the first-born, who inherit the property, than with the others. They have no access to women, nor are any allowed to enter the religious houses; they abstain from eating certain dishes, and more so at certain times of the year than at others.

Amongst these mosques, there is one principal one, and no human tongue is able to describe its greatness and details, because it is so large that within its circuit, which is surrounded by a high wall, a village of five hundred houses could easily be built. Within, and all around it, are very handsome buildings, in which there are large rooms and galleries, where the religious who live there are lodged. There are as many as forty very high and well-built towers, the largest having fifty steps to reach the top; the principal one is higher than the tower of the chief church in Seville. They are so well-built, both in their masonry, and their wood-work, that they could not be better made nor well constructed anywhere; for all the masonry inside the chapels, where they keep their idols, is carved with figures, and the wood work is all wrought with designs of monsters, and other shapes. All these towers are places of burial for the chiefs, and each one of their chapels is dedicated to the idol to which they have a particular devotion. Within this great mosque, there are three halls wherein stand the principal idols of marvelous grandeur in size, and much decorated with carved figures, both of stone and wood; and within these halls there are other chapels, entered in by very small doors, and which have no light, and nobody but the religious are admitted to them. Within these are the images and figures of the idols, although, as I have said, there are many outside.

. . .

Along one of the causeways that lead to the city, there are two conduits of masonry each two paces broad, and five feet deep, through one of which a volume of very good fresh water, the bulk of a man's body, flows into the heart of the city, from which all supply themselves, and drink. The other which brings the water, when they wish to clean the first conduit, for, while one is being cleaned, the water flows through the other. Conduits as large [around] as an ox's body bring the fresh water across the bridges, thus avoiding the channels by which the salt-water flows, and in this manner the whole city is supplied, and everybody has water to drink. Canoes peddle the water through all the streets, and the way they take it from the conduits is this; the canoes stop under the bridges where the conduits cross, where men are stationed on the top who are paid to fill them. At the different entrances to the city, there are guards, in huts to collect a *certum quid* of everything that comes in. I do not know where this goes to the sovereign, or to the city, because up till now I have not been able to ascertain, but I believe it is for the sovereign, for, in other markets in other provinces, that contribution has been seen to be paid to the ruler. There are to be found daily in the markets and public places of the city many workmen, and masters of all trades, waiting to be hired.

The people of this city had better manners, and more luxury in their dressing and service, than those of other provinces and cities, for the reason that the sovereign, Montezuma, always resided there, and all the nobles, his vassals, frequented the city, so better manners, and more ceremony prevailed. But to avoid being prolix in describing the things of the city (though I would fain continue), I will not say more than that, in the service and manners of its people, their fashion of living was almost the same as in Spain, with just as much harmony and order; and considering that these people were barbarous, so cut off from the knowledge of God, and other civilized people, it is admirable to see what they attained in every respect. As far as the service surrounding Montezuma is concerned, and the admirable attributes of his greatness and state, there is so much to write that I assure your Highness I do not know where to begin, so as to finish what I would say of any part respecting it. For, as I have already said, what greater grandeur can there be, than that a barbarian monarch, like him, should have imitations in gold, silver, stones, and feather-work, of all the things existing under heaven in his dominion?—not a silversmith in the world who could do it better; and, respecting the stones, there is no imagination which can divine the instruments with which they were so perfectly executed; and respecting the feather-work, neither in wax, nor in embroidery, could nature be so marvelously imitated.

Central Themes

Indigenous people, state formation, urban life, land and labor

Suggested Reading

Broda, Johanna, David Carrasco, and Eduardo Matos Moctezuma. *The Great Temple of Tenochtitlan: Center and Periphery in the Aztec World.* Berkeley: University of California Press, 1988.

Brooks, Frances J. "Moteczoma Xocoyotl, Hernán Cortés, and Bernal Díaz del Castillo: The Construction of an Arrest." *Hispanic American Historical Review* 75, no. 2 (May 1995): 149–183.

Clendinnen, Inga. *Aztecs: An Interpretation.* New York: Cambridge University Press, 1993.

Smith, Michael. *The Aztecs.* Cambridge: Blackwell Publishers, 1996.

Related Sources

4. The Origin of the Nahuas and the Birth of the Fifth Sun (1596)
5. A Treasury of Mexica Power and Gender (c. 1541–1542)
60. Chronicles of Mexico City (1938)

7. The Mixtec Map of San Pedro Teozacoalco (1580)

The Mixtecs, who call themselves the Ñudzahui in their language, live in the highlands and the Valley of Oaxaca State. During the Post-Classic period, the most historically influential highland city-state was Tilantongo, whose ruler, 8 Deer Tiger Claw (1063–1115 CE), conquered parts of the Mixtec region. Tilantongo was legendary because the Mixtecs associated it with their mythical origin place, Apoala, where their first ancestors grew from a tree and created noble lineages. Around 1350 CE, highland Mixtec lords began to form marriage alliances with the rulers of the Zapotec ethnic group, who lived in the nearby Valley of Oaxaca. While the neighboring Mexica state became increasingly powerful, the Mixtec city-states managed only to create fragile alliances among themselves. By the time the Spaniards arrived, the Mexica had already forced the Mixtec powers to pay tribute to Tenochtitlan, and the entire region was named Guaxacac, after the Mexica garrison that enforced the tax.

The Mixtec of San Pedro Teozacoalco created the *Map of Teozacoalco* (1580) for King Philip II of Spain, whose royal cosmographer was conducting a written geographical survey of all of Spanish America later called the *Relaciones Geográficas.* We include this map here in our section on the Pre-Columbian period because, even though the Christian churches and crosses pictured on it attest to the fact that it was made after Contact, it records information about Pre-Columbian times in a mostly non-European cartographic style. The royal cosmographer's questionnaires for the survey had not included a request that local communities draw maps. Indigenous painter-scribes of Teozacoalco and other *pueblos* (towns) in New Spain created them of their own volition. The historical geographer Barbara Mundy thus believes that this and other indigenous maps of the *Relaciones Geográficas* are autonomously expressed representations of indigenous values. Without prompting, they were stating to their new colonial masters why they believed they were important. Four extremely rare Pre-Columbian Mixtec codices have allowed historians to verify that the map's information about Pre-Contact times is accurate. We can interpret this map in order to understand Mixtec attitudes toward politics, land, gender, and marriage in the Pre-Columbian period.

The most noticeable non-European convention on the map lies in the two columns of dynastic rulers to the left-hand side of the spherical representation of Teozacoalco's territory. Each generation of male ruler is paired with his wife, and both are seated on a mat. This is a Mesoamerican writing convention that indicates they were rulers. Male nobles did not assume rule until married, so political authority was symbolized by a male-female pair. Compare this inclusion of marriage to the illustration of the wedding scene from the *Codex Mendoza* (Source 5). What do these two sources say about the purposes and political subtext of Mesoamerican marriages? What does this say about how society defined gender roles for men and women? The Mixtecs considered men to be more appropriate rulers than women. Are two parallel lines of men and women an example of gender parity or "separate but equal"?

The two columns of lineages on the Teozacoalco map attest to how Mesoamerican city-states of the Pre-Columbian and early Conquest eras used marriage to form alliances with possible rival polities, which created new mixed family lines. The first column of seated figures on the left-hand side represents the ruling lines of Tilantongo, and the second column represents those of Teozacoalco. Each of the two lines springs upward from the place-name glyph for each city-state (side views of buildings with overhanging roofs), with the first generation of rulers at the bottom and the most recent ruler of Tilantongo at the very top of the tree. 8 Deer Tiger Claw, who lived during the second dynasty, is the second single figure from the bottom of the first column. Note the footprints walking to the second column. During the second Tilantongo dynasty in the twelfth century, a prince from the city-state traveled to Teozacoalco and married a noblewoman, thus beginning the second dynasty of Teozacoalco. At the top of this column are the founders of the third dynasty in 1321 CE, who are starting along a road floating in the blank space toward the circular depiction of Teozacoalco's territory. These same personages are also featured within the circle at the end of this road. The founders of the third dynasty are at the base of a third lineage column rising up from next to the Catholic Church. Six generations of ruling couples are depicted, with the top figure being the man in power during the Spanish Conquest. This lone male figure was a second Tilantongo noble son who was parachuted into power in Teozacoalco.

Mesoamerican rulers established legitimacy by documenting impressive lineages and tracing them back to divine beings or origin stories. Hanab-Pakal did this with his tomb carvings in Palenque (Source 3), and the Nahuas believed that their tribal ancestors who founded their most important city-states came from the Seven Caves (Source 4). Similarly, many Mixtec rulers of various city-states, not just those in Teozacoalco, traced their lineage to Tilantongo, the most prestigious kingdom and a player in the origin myth of the tree of Apoala. How would claims of shared ancestors from Tilantongo aid ruling families in various city-states in statecraft? Rulers of Mixtec states may have had common ancestors, but war among them was common too. What might have caused war to break out among rulers who had family relations?

In addition to creating a map of social relations, the Mixtec painters intended to represent actual topographical features and settlements, as in contemporary maps. Resting on the perimeter line of the sphere are forty-six figures that are the place-name glyphs for territorial boundary landmarks. This Pre-Columbian style of writing place-name glyphs is also found in the *Codex Mendoza* tribute lists (Source 5). The actual territorial boundaries of Teozacoalco form a shape that looks like a lumpy potato. Barbara Mundy believes that the Mixtecs depicted the territory as a perfect sphere as a rhetorical device and as a political assertion that the community was unified and significant.* If they were arguing something, what were they arguing against? Why would they have felt the need to assert themselves in this fashion during the Pre-Columbian or Post-Conquest periods?

Finally, the Mixtec mapmakers chose to convey both geographical and sociopolitical information when they drew the lineages on one side and the territorial sphere on the other. We can be certain that they wanted their audience to make a connection between lineage and territory. What does the prominent inclusion of the ruling dynasties on the map suggest about Mixtec attitudes toward ownership of land and community territory? Compare this map with the Oztoticpac Map of 1540 (Source 17) and note that the Oztoticpac map registered private property. Why might the Mixtec map not have any sign of privately owned land?

---

*Barbara Mundy, *The Mapping of New Spain: Indigenous Cartography and the Maps of the Relaciones Geográficas* (Chicago: University of Chicago Press, 1996), p. 116.

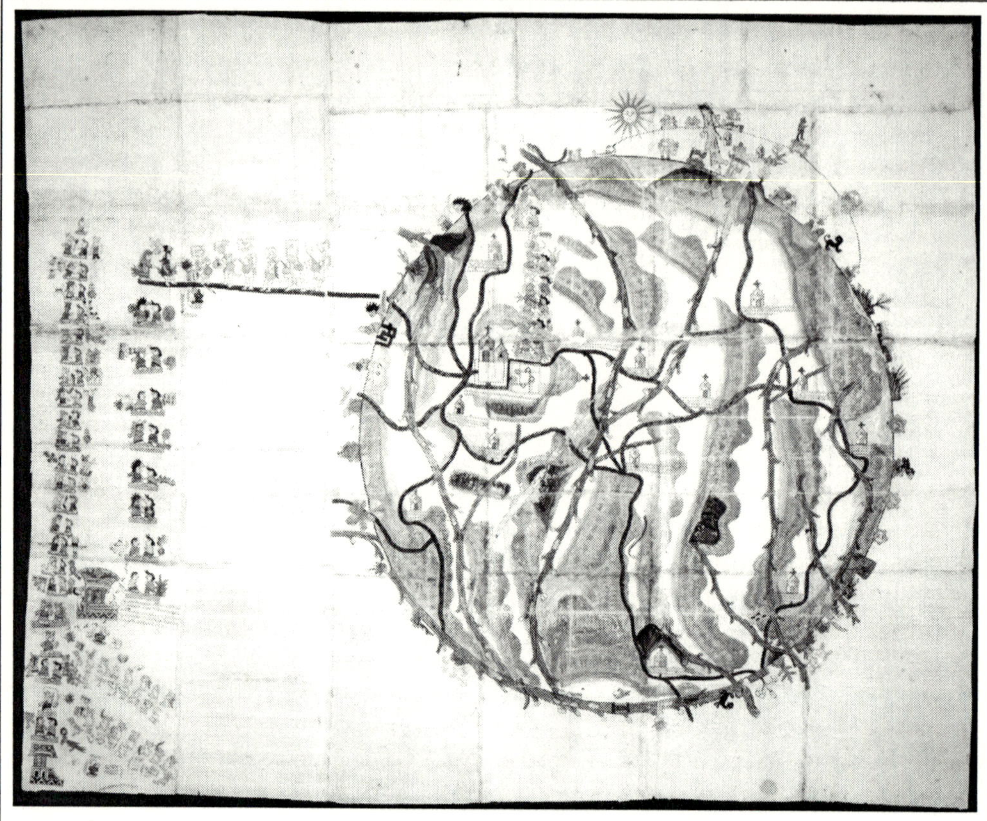

The Mixtec map of San Pedro Teozacoalco

Courtesy of the Nettie Lee Benson Latin American Collection, University of Texas at Austin.

Central Themes

Indigenous people, state formation, land and labor, gender

Suggested Reading

Mundy, Barbara. *The Mapping of New Spain: Indigenous Cartography and the Maps of the Relaciones Geográficas.* Chicago: University of Chicago Press, 1996.

Spores, Ronald. "Marital Alliance in the Political Integration of Mixtec Kingdoms." *American Anthropologist* 76 no. 2 (new series, June 1974): 297–311.

Terraciano, Kevin. *The Mixtecs of Colonial Oaxaca: Ñudzahui History, Sixteenth Through Eighteenth Centuries.* Stanford, CA: Stanford University Press, 2001.

Related Sources

5. A Treasury of Mexica Power and Gender (c. 1541–1542)
13. Acazitli of Tlalmanalco: Nahua Conqueror on the Mesoamerican Frontier (1541)
17. The Inquisition Seizes Don Carlos's Estate: The Oztoticpac Map (1540)

8. The Urban Zoning of Maya Social Class in the Yucatán (1566)*

In these excerpts from the *Relación de las cosas de Yucatán,* Bishop Diego de Landa (1524–1579) documents Yucatec Maya society as it had developed in the late Post-Classic period. The first excerpt provides evidence for the fundamental material basis that intensive agriculture provided to all of the Mesoamerican people, including the Yucatec Mayas. Their agricultural systems produced surpluses, transformed the natural environment, and made settled life in towns and cities possible. Landa mentions that they "sow[ed] in a great number of places," planting small agricultural plots while ranging over their territory. The Yucatán Peninsula has an arid climate, with little fresh surface water. *Cenotes,* the open wells formed when surface limestone collapses into aquifers, supplied the Mayas with water. Because the top soil was very thin, Maya towns needed access to large amounts of land. They practiced slash-and-burn agriculture and after a time had to abandon their plots and leave them fallow while scrub plants returned the soil to fertility.

Why would intensive agriculture encourage the kinds of social and political hierarchies associated with "civilization"? Contrast the Mayas of the Yucatán with the Comcáac of the northern Sonoran deserts. How did the sedentary life of the Mayas (and the Nahuas and Mixtecs) make them more easily governable and exploitable by centralizing states such as the Mexica and Spanish Empires?

During the Post-Classic period, with the collapse of the empire-building Yucatec Maya city-states of Chichén Itzá in the thirteenth century and Mayapán in the fifteenth century, political authority diffused into many independent dynastic city-states. Yucatec society became more localized, but each town retained, as a microcosm, many of the fundamentals that the large Mesoamerican states featured, namely agriculture and urban spaces designed to foster social and political hierarchies. The Yucatec Mayas called the local city-states the *cabob* (singular *cah*), and Bishop Diego de Landa refers to them as "republics" in this primary source. Note Landa's observation of how the most important people in society lived within the enclosure of the ceremonial religious center of the city. How did both the imperial Mexica capital of Tenochtitlan and the Yucatec Maya towns use urban planning to encourage the division of people through social and political hierarchies?

Local dynasties formed alliances with those of other towns, which centralized political authority in Chichén Itzá and Mayapán. When alliances dissolved, local ruling families were left in charge of their local city-states. Mayapán, the last Maya city-state to rule the entire Yucatán Peninsula before the Spaniards arrived, collapsed when alliances among local ruling elites broke down. In his discussion of

---

*Alfred M. Tozzer, ed., *Landa's Relacion de las Cosas de Yucatán: A Translation,* Papers of the Peabody Museum of American Archaeology and Ethnology, Harvard University, vol. 18, 1941. Reprinted courtesy of the Peabody Museum, Harvard University.

politics, Landa speaks of the house of Cocom as though they ruled all of the Yucatán, but this did not reflect the historical reality of the late Post-Classic period. The Cocom and Xiu lineages ruled Mayapán together, but when members of the Xiu family massacred some Cocoms, the resulting civil war caused the collapse of the central state in 1441. The Xiu and Cocom clans then retreated into separate parts of the peninsula, where they ruled towns independently of each other until the Spaniards consolidated their rule in 1540s. During Bishop Diego de Landa's notorious idolatry trials in 1562, he accused ruler Nachi Cocom of heresy, but Cocom, unlike many other Mayas who were burned at the stake, perished of natural causes before his conviction. Even though Landa may have gathered information on the Cocom as part of his idolatry investigation, this primary source is slanted in favor of Cocom rule. The family was supposedly the fittest to rule because all the nobles resolved that it should be this way in order to preserve the stability of the "golden age" of Kukulcan. Kukulcan is Maya for Quetzalcoatl, who, according to a controversial historical interpretation, was a mythic Toltec high priest from the northern Mexican city of Tollan (Tula) who was devoted to the Feathered Serpent and supposedly made Chichén Itzá a great power. Compare and contrast this document's use of the mythic past with that of the Mixtec *Map of San Pedro Teozacoalco* (Source 7). How is the political rhetorical spin in Landa's document similar to that of the Mixtec map?

Finally, the mention of the Cocoms cautions us that this primary source may be presenting the reader with the local perspective from the towns they ruled, not necessarily that of all Maya communities. As noted earlier in this book, the *Popul Vuh* is sometimes mistakenly characterized as a canonical "Maya bible," but in fact it is the holy book of only one Maya group, the Quiché. Is it a mistake to take Landa's description as representative of the whole "Maya world"?

Report on the Affairs of the Yucatán

The trades of the Indians were making pottery and carpentering. They earned a great deal by making idols out of clay and wood, with many fasts and observances. There were also surgeons, or, to be more accurate, sorcerers, who cured with herbs and many superstitious rites. And so it was with all the other professions. The occupation to which they had the greatest inclination was trade, carrying salt and cloths and slaves to the lands of Ulua and Tabasco, exchanging all they had for cacao and stone beads, which were their money; and with this they were accustomed to buy slaves, or other beads, because they were fine and good, which their chiefs wore as jewels in their feasts; and they had others made of certain red shells for money, and as jewels to adorn their persons; and they carried it in purses of net, which they had, and at their markets they traded everything which there was in that country. They gave credit, lent and paid courteously and without usury. And the greatest number were the cultivators and men who apply themselves to harvesting the maize and other grains, which they keep in fine underground places and granaries, so as to be able to sell (their crops) at the proper time. Their mules and oxen are the people themselves. For each married man with his wife, they are accustomed to sow a space of four hundred feet, which they call a "hun uinic," measured with a rod of twenty feet, twenty feet wide and twenty feet long.

The Indians have a good habit of helping each other in all their labors. At the time of sowing those who do not have their own people to do their work, join together in groups of twenty, or more or less, and all together they do the work of all of them (each doing) his assigned share, and they do not leave it until everyone's is done. The lands today are common property, and so he who first occupies them becomes the possessor of them. They sow in a great number of places, so that if one part fails, another may supply its place. In cultivating the land they do nothing except collect together the refuse and burn it in order to sow it afterwards. They cultivate the land from the middle of January and up to April, and they sow in the rainy season. They do this by carrying a little bag on their shoulders, and with a pointed stick they made a hole in the ground, and they drop there five or six grains, which they cover over with the same stick. It is a wonder how things grow when it rains. They also joined together for hunting in companies of fifty, more or less and they roast the flesh of deer on gridirons, so that it shall not be wasted, and when they reach the town, they make their presents to their lord and distribute the rest as among friends. And they do the same in their fishing.

After the departure of Kukulcan, the nobles agreed, in order that the government should endure, that the house of the Cocoms should have the chief power; because it was the most ancient or richest family, or because at this time he who was at the head of it was a man of the greatest work. This being done, since within the enclosure there were only temples and houses for the lords and high priest, they ordered that other houses should be constructed outside, where each one of them could keep some servants, and to which the people from their towns could repair, when they came to the city on business. Each one then established in these houses his majordomo, who bore for his badge of office a short and thick stick, and they called him caluac. He kept account with the towns and with those who ruled them; and to them sent notice of what was needed in the house of their lord, such as birds, maize, honey, salt, fish, game, cloth and other things, and the caluac always went to the house of his lord, in order to see what was wanted and provided it immediately, since his house was, as it were, the office of his lord.

It was the custom to seek in the towns for the maimed and the blind, and they supplied their needs.

The lords appointed the governors, and if they were acceptable confirmed their sons in the offices, and they charged them with the kind treatment of poor people, the peace of the town and to occupy themselves in their work of supporting themselves and their lords.

All the lords were careful to respect, visit and to entertain the Cocom, accompanying him, making feasts in his honor and repairing to him with important business, and they lived in peace with each other amusing themselves with their accustomed pastimes of dancing, feasting and hunting. . . .

Before the Spaniards had conquered that country, the natives lived together in towns in a very civilized fashion. They kept the land well cleared and free from weeds, and planted very good trees. Their dwelling place was as follows: in the middle of the town were the temples with beautiful plazas, and all around the temples stood the houses of the lords and the priests, and then (those of) the most important people. Then came the houses of the richest and of those who were held in the highest estimation nearest to these, and at the outskirts of the town were the houses of the lower class. And the Wells, if there were but few of them, were near the houses of the lords; and they had their improved lands planted with wine trees and they sowed cotton, pepper and maize, and they lived thus close together for fear of their enemies, who took them captive, and it was owing to the wars of the Spaniards that they were scattered in the woods. . . .

Beyond the house, all the town did their sowing for the nobles; they also cultivated them (the fields) and harvested what was necessary for him and his household. And when there was hunting and fishing, or when it was time to get their salt, they always gave the lord his share, since these things they always did as a community. If the lord died, although it was the oldest son who succeeded him, the other children were very much respected and assisted and regarded as lords themselves. And they aided the other *principales* inferior to the lord in all these ways, according to whom he was and the favor which he enjoyed with his lord. The priests got their living from their offices and from offerings. The lords governed the town, settling disputes, ordering and settling the affairs of their republics, all of which they did by the hands of leading men, who were very well obeyed and highly esteemed, especially the rich, whom they visited, and they held court in their houses, where they settled their affairs and business usually at night. And if the lords went out of their town, they took with them a great many people, and it was the same way when they went out of their homes.

Central Themes

Indigenous people, state formation, urban life, land and labor

Suggested Reading

Restall, Matthew, and John F. Chuchiak. "A Reevaluation of the Authenticity of Fray Diego de Landa's *Relación de las cosas de Yucatán*." *Ethnohistory* 49, no. 3 (Summer 2002): 651–669.

Sharer, Robert J., and Loa P. Traxler. *The Ancient Maya.* Stanford, CA: Stanford University Press, 2006.

Smith, Michael Ernest, and Frances Berdan. *The Postclassic Mesoamerican World.* Salt Lake City: University of Utah Press, 2003.

Related Sources

3. Maya Royalty and Writing (c. 667 CE)
5. A Treasury of Mexica Power and Gender (c. 1541–1542)
6. Markets and Temples in the City of Tenochtitlan (1519)
13. Acazitli of Tlalmanalco: Nahua Conqueror on the Mesoamerican Frontier (1541)
40. The Mayas Make Their Caste War Demands (1850)

9. The Nomadic Seris of the Northern Desert (1645)*

When the Jesuit missionary Father Andrés Pérez de Ribas came to the northern deserts of Sonora, he encountered a people who were, for him, perplexingly different from the indigenous people of the Mesoamerican core zone. The Comcáac, whom the Spaniards called the Seris, were nonsedentary hunter-gatherers who lived on the coast of the Gulf of California in Sonora and on Tiburón Island. This primary source is from Ribas's *Historia de los triunfos de nuestra santa fe entre gentes las más bárbaras y fieras del nuevo orbe* (History of the Triumphs of Our Holy Faith Among the Most Barbarous and Fierce Peoples of the New World), which he published in 1645. It does not really make sense to place the history of the Comcáac in the Pre-Columbian or Conquest periods, whose division historians tend to conceptualize in terms of before and after European victory in the heartland of Mesoamerica. When Ribas arrived in the early 1600s, it had been one hundred years

*Thomas Sheridan, ed., *Empire of Sand: The Seri Indians and the Struggle for Spanish Sonora, 1645–1803* (Tucson: University of Arizona Press, 1999), pp. 21–23. Some of the translator's footnotes have been eliminated.

since the Mexica lost the city of Tenochtitlan to the Spaniards. However, the indigenous people in Sonora had had virtually no contact with Europeans when the missionaries arrived—except for the European diseases that most likely had preceded the newcomers and had decimated the Seri population. Nor does their story fit easily into the colonial period of the more central regions of Mexico. In spite of missionary efforts through the seventeenth and early eighteenth centuries, very few Seris were converted or settled. They continued to conduct frequent raids on agricultural settlements until the mid-eighteenth century, when the Spanish finally subdued them.

In this document, we see the Jesuit Andrés Pérez de Ribas evaluating the Comáac culture by the light of his own religious and cultural traditions, as well as his experiences with indigenous peoples in central Mexico. He and other Jesuits wrote that the Comáac had no organized religion. In comparison to the Mexica and others who had great temples to their gods whom the Christians considered demonic, the Comáac, in the Jesuits' view, lived in a state of innocence. Their religious practitioners were male and female shamans who contacted animal spirits while on vision quests in nature and then returned to humanity with the animals' magical songs. Father Ribas called the unnamed Comcáac bands "excessively wild," while noting how healthy they were. Living in an extremely arid environment, the Comcáac were unable to farm, yet they still had a very diverse diet of plants and animals from the desert and from the waters of the Gulf of California.

How do we explain why the Comcáac practiced a nomadic lifestyle, and how might this have shaped their social organization? Unfortunately, small societies such as the Comcáac suffer from being defined negatively by what they supposedly lack—civilization. How does Father Ribas define civilization? How does he explain its absence among the Comcáac? Would they have had a need for "civilization"? How can the Comcáac perspective help us to understand the sedentary indigenous societies of the Mesoamerican core? How, for example, would intensive agricultural production, which the Comcáac did not practice, be at the root of many elements of the Mexica, Mixtec, and Maya cultures? Did those sedentary cultures have anything in common with the Comcáac so that we could call them part of one "Amerindian" world?

History of the Triumphs of Our Holy Faith Among the Most Barbarous and Fierce Peoples of the New World

I spoke of these nations, who ordinarily inhabit the arroyos and banks of the rivers [i.e., agricultural groups], because there are others—the most barbaric ever seen or discovered upon this earth. They neither work the soil nor sow like the others, nor do they have any manner of house or shelter, or defense against the elements. Nevertheless, their way of life deserves to be understood, even though it is the farthest removed from humanity and quite unlike that of the other peoples of the world. In this way it is possible to comprehend the misery into which man fell when through his sin he lost the delightful paradise into which God had placed him, in order that he might pass from paradise into heaven. The words of the royal prophet have been fulfilled in these people: "Thus man, for all his splendor, does not abide; he resembles the beasts that perish" [Psalms 48:13].

Because of his sin, man has fallen to the level of the beasts God created him to rule over. Of these people, some live like brute animals in bramble thickets and dense wooded hills, and others live along the shores and sand dunes of the sea. The former sustain themselves by hunting and gathering wild roots and fruit, drinking from *charcos** or small lakes of rainwater. Those who live by the sea sustain themselves by fishing in the ocean, supplementing their catch with lobsters, snakes [eels], and other such creatures. In place of bread, they eat fresh, dried, or salted fish. Nonetheless, some journey to the pueblos of their agricultural neighbors at harvest time to trade fish for maize. At another time of the year, they gather the small seed of a grass that grows beneath the waters of the sea; this also serves them for bread. The truth, though it may seem incredible to the nations of Europe, is that these people pass the greater part of the year without bread or any other grain to replace it. As I have said, they eat only fish and wild fruit.

That which grows abundantly and which they enjoy for the longest period of the year is *pitahaya*,** a tree foreign to Europe and the rest of the world. The branches of this tree look like grooved green tapers, growing straight from the short trunk in such a way that they form a beautiful crown. The pitahaya bears no leaves but its fruit grows like nipples along its branches. With its spiny skin the fruit looks something like the husk of a chestnut or the fruit of a prickly pear. Its flesh is similar to that of a fig, only blander and more delicate. In some of the fruits the flesh is very white, whereas in others it is red or yellow. They are delicious, especially when they come from dry areas such as the coast of the province of Sinaloa, where it rains very little. These pitahayas are extremely abundant, and sometimes they grow in stands of two, three, or six leagues at a stretch.

*Depressions dug in arroyos to capture runoff.

**Organ pipe cactus (*stenocereus thurberi*). The Seris used pitahayas for many purposes, eating the fruit both fresh and dried and fermenting boiled fruit pulp and juice into a wine. They also crushed the dry cactus itself and mixed it with animal fat to make pitch.

Such are the foods and sustenance of some of these migratory nations. It is worth noting that these people, especially the mountain and coastal dwellers, are the tallest and most corpulent of all the nations of Nueva Vizcaya and even Europe, despite the fact that they have so little food. They are also very swift and nimble. They live for a long time, even to the point of decrepitude, upon such sparse and scanty food devoid of largesse.

Since I have written about their strange foods, I will also write about how they protect themselves from the rain and other inclement weather. When it rains and they wish to shelter themselves, their remedy is to gather a clump or bundle of tall grass. Binding the bundle at the top, the Indian then sits down, opens it at one end, and places it over his head in such a way that it covers his body. This bundle of grass serves as his raingear, his roof, and his tent, even if it rains all night. Such is their defense against the rain.

Their protection against the extremely strong rays of the sun is no better, because their only defense is to thrust tree branches into the sand. Under this shade they sit, live, and sleep. Against the wind they have no other defense than their naked bodies. During the cold nights of December and January they avail themselves of bonfires that they light, lying down close to the flames in the cold sand. This is the type of protection they employ against the cold when they travel through unpopulated areas. Since there is never any lack of firewood in this province, of abundant thickets, they build a string of bonfires close together and stretch out to sleep between them, taking care to extinguish them when they awake. Finally, if one of these Indians wishes to travel four or six leagues on a cold night, he will carry a burning firebrand, holding it near his stomach to warm himself while leaving the rest of his body exposed. These are far fewer of these wandering people than there are farmers, yet they are happier than if they had all the wealth and palaces in the world.

There is word of another population called the Herris [Seris]. They are excessively wild, without pueblos, houses, or fields. They have no rivers or streams, and so they drink from small pools and charcos. They sustain themselves by hunting; however, when other nations are harvesting maize, the Seris come to trade deerskins and salt, which they have gathered from the sea. Those who live closest to the ocean also eat fish. It is said that others of the same nation inhabit an island in the same sea.* Their language is extremely difficult.**

---

*Tiberón Island. One group of Seris also lived part of the year on the much smaller San Esteban Island.

**Seri is close to being a linguistic isolate, although most linguists place it in the Hokan stock. It certainly bears no relationship to the Uto-Aztecan languages of the Seris' neighbors in Sonora.

Central Themes

Indigenous people, state formation, race and ethnicity

Suggested Reading

Felger, Richard Stephen, and Mary Beck Moser. *People of the Desert and Sea: Ethnobotany of the Seri Indians.* Tucson: University of Arizona Press, 1985.

Sheridan, Thomas E. *Empire of Sand: The Seri Indians and the Struggle for Spanish Sonora, 1645–1803.* Tucson: University of Arizona Press, 1999.

Weber, David J. *The Spanish Frontier in North America.* New Haven, CT: Yale University Press, 1992.

Related Sources

6. Markets and Temples in the City of Tenochtitlan (1519)
13. Acazitli of Tlalmanalco: Nahua Conqueror on the Mesoamerican Frontier (1541)
18. Father Fernández Attempts to Convert the Seris of Sonora Single-handedly (1679)

PART 2

The Spanish Conquest and Christian Conversion (1519–1610)

The Spanish military conquest, especially the stories about the war between the Mexica and the Spaniards, created iconic images, powerful myths, and strong feelings about the past, which continue to resonate today. On the heels of the conquerors came the men of the cloth who sought to convert indigenous people to Christianity. This was not simply a period of warfare. Indigenous people and Spaniards negotiated with each other while admiring and disdaining each other's cultures. The violent and peaceful interactions established contradictory patterns of social interaction that lasted throughout the subsequent colonial period.

The sources the Iberian conquerors generated have defined how the story of the Conquest has been told. In this section, we focus on many of these sources. However, we remind readers that many of the sources in the previous Pre-Columbian section were created during the Conquest era and can be analyzed to shed further light on that period (sources 4, 6, and 8). Likewise, some of the sources in this section contain information that elucidates Pre-Columbian history (sources 10, 11, 12, 13, and 16).

Readers should remember that the Spanish Conquest happened at different times in different parts of Mexico. It is certainly true that Hernán Cortés and his band of fighting men landed on the Gulf coast in 1519, and that by 1521 they had razed the once-beautiful Mexica capital of Tenochtitlan. In 1542, with the pacification of Nueva Galicia (Guadalajara), a populous but unruly frontier zone of Mesoamerican peoples, the Spaniards considered the conquest complete (Source 13). In other words, the fall of the Pre-Columbian states of the sedentary agrarian societies of central Mexico has traditionally been viewed as the end of the Conquest period. These were definitive years for central Mexico, but in other regions, like the eastern portion of the Yucatán Peninsula, the conquest of indigenous societies was not completed until the late nineteenth century (Source 40). In 1542, crown officials created the administrative unit of the Viceroyalty of New Spain, which eventually extended from California east to Texas and north of Panama. The Spanish discovery of silver deposits in the 1540s pushed the frontier of the colony farther north from those of Pre-Columbian indigenous states, but beyond the colonial silver cities and mining camps, Spanish authority was a legal fiction. Throughout the colonial period, the crown and the Catholic Church could not govern the small bands of nonsedentary and semi-sedentary people who populated the great deserts north of the modern cities of San Luis Potosí, Zacatecas, and Tampico. With continuous violence between indigenous raiders and scattered Spanish settlers and priests, the so-called colonial peace did not really exist on the peripheries of south-central Mexico. The Jesuit religious order utterly failed to convert the Seris of Sonora, and the Franciscans were so harsh that the pueblo peoples of New Mexico rose in rebellions that Spanish armies brutally suppressed in the seventeenth century (sources 14 and 18).

Readers should look out for the many ways in which indigenous peoples reacted to the arrival of the Spaniards. Mexica warriors fought to defend their empire, but other Nahuatl-speaking states, like Tlaxcala and Tlalmanalco, joined Hernán Cortés in sacking Tenochtitlan. The Spaniards might have failed had it not been for indigenous interpreters like Malintzin (Source 12). After the wars, the leaders of these communities capitalized on their early alliances with the Spaniards, and three sources in this section (12, 13, and 15) should be interpreted in this context. Because the Spaniards succeed in completing the conquest in the areas of Mexico where sedentary people lived, they were able to have more peaceful cultural exchanges with indigenous people who more quickly adapted to the newcomers. In this exchange, the Nahuas, Mixtecs, and Mayas acquired tools of cultural survival within the new Spanish order from the Christian institutions established to convert them to Christianity. Literacy was one of the most powerful means by which we see indigenous people assimilating rather than simply capitulating to Spanish culture. At the College of Santa Cruz Tlatelolco, as Nahua students taught the Franciscan friars Nahuatl, the native acolytes learned how to write Nahuatl (and Spanish and Latin) in the European Latinate script. Working with friars like Bernardino de Sahagún (Source 11) and Gerónimo de Mendieta (Source 4), the Nahuas preserved their history and myths. The Pre-Columbian tradition of writing evolved rather than disappeared. The Oztoticpac Map of 1540 (Source 17) shows old pictographic writing conventions, while imagistic language is found in the *Florentine Codex* (Source 11) and in the *relación de mérito* (report of service merit) of Don Francisco de Sandoval Acazitli (Source 13).

Although peaceable cultural interchange happened at humanistic religious institutions, the Spanish used Christianity—or rather, its absence—as a justification for conquest and enslavement. In Bernal Díaz del Castillo's account of the Conquest, when Cortés talks to Moteucçoma about religion, they are not having a polite dinner conversation. The conqueror is discharging his legal duty to attempt to convince the Mexica king to convert without force (Source 10). Those who refused to convert could be justly conquered. An epic poem written about the heroic efforts of the Spaniards to take the Acoma *pueblo* (town) in New Mexico has a jarring digression in which the coming massacre is justified on Christian religious grounds (Source 14).

For the survivors of the wars of conquest, peaceful cultural contact and violent struggle established a contradictory colonial society: harmony through a common

Christianity and domination through shear force. The lives of some of the individuals documented in this section reflect this contradiction. Acazitli, the Nahua ruler of Tlalmanalco, assists the Spaniards in vanquishing the native people of Nueva Galicia (Source 13). When he returns home as a conquering Christian, he marches under triumphal arches that are also used in a specifically Catholic religious festival in Tlaxcala (Source 15). Sahagún helped preserve indigenous culture but took a break from his labors to act as a translator at the Inquisition trial of Don Carlos Chichimecatecotl (Source 16).

During the immediate Post-Conquest period, indigenous leaders and their people had to make difficult choices that would never have completely satisfying results. Religion, politics, and personal prosperity were intertwined. If an indigenous ruler wanted to maintain some power so that he could look out for his people, he had to publicly convert to Christianity. If accused by the Inquisition of worshiping false gods, an indigenous ruler stood to lose his estates, government positions, and, in the case of Don Carlos Chichimecatecotl, his life (Source 16). As the colonial period developed, indigenous leaders maintained their political position in their local communities by being bridges between their people and Spanish priests, commercial landowners, and crown magistrates.

10. Hernán Cortés and Moteucçoma Meet, According to a Spanish Conqueror (1568)*

Bernal Díaz del Castillo (1496–1584) was a "man on foot" who accompanied Hernán Cortés on his 1519 expedition to Mexico. Nearly fifty years later, Díaz composed his *True History of the Conquest of New Spain* while languishing bitterly in the backwaters of Guatemala, where, despite his contribution to the Spanish victory, he had been rewarded with an unprofitable *encomienda* (grant of Indian tribute and labor). He wrote his account in the hopes of securing a more promising living for himself and to correct what he saw as the inaccuracies of other previously published accounts.

His dramatic and detailed narrative has long served as an essential source in the reconstruction of the Conquest's history. What does this excerpt reveal about Díaz's strengths and weaknesses as both observer and recorder of the events of the Conquest? Do you notice places where his account reveals more about Spanish preoccupations and preconceptions than it does about indigenous practices? In this selection, Díaz describes the first meeting between Cortés and Moteucçoma and elaborates on some of the details of the latter's majestic customs. "Doña Marina," mentioned in this excerpt, was the indigenous translator who was essential to the Spanish victory (Source 12), and "Aguilar" was Gerónimo de Aguilar, a Spaniard who had been shipwrecked among the Maya for eight years prior to the Spaniards' arrival. This source can also be fruitfully compared to the account of the Conquest as told in indigenous accounts (sources 11 and 12). What discrepancies do you notice and what might account for these? How does Díaz treat Moteucçoma's understanding of the Spaniards' origins?

---

*Bernal Díaz, *The True History of the Conquest of New Spain,* ed. A. P. Maudslay (London: Hakluyt Society, 1908), pp. 53–64, 66–69. Some footnotes have been eliminated.

Chapter LXXXIX [89]

How the Great Montezuma came to our quarters with many Caciques [native leaders] accompanying him, and the conversation that he had with our Captain.

When the Great Montezuma had dined and he knew that some time had passed since our Captain and all of us had done the same, he came in the greatest state to our quarters with a numerous company of chieftains, all of them his kinsmen. When Cortés was told that he was approaching he came out to the middle of the Hall to receive him, and Montezuma took him by the hand, and they brought some seats, made according to their usage and very richly decorated and embroidered with gold in many designs, and Montezuma asked our Captain to be seated, and both of them sat down each on his chair. Then Montezuma began a very good speech, saying that he was greatly rejoiced to have in his house and his kingdom such valiant gentlemen as were Cortés and all of us. That two years ago he had received news of another Captain who came to Chanpoton, and likewise last year they had brought him news of another Captain who came with four ships, and that each time he had wished to see them, and now that he had us with him he was at our service and would give us all that he possessed; that it must indeed be true that we were those of whom his ancestors in years long past had spoken, saying that men would come from where the sun rose to rule over these lands; and that we must be those men, as we had fought so valiantly in the affairs at Potonchan and Tabasco and against the Tlaxcalans; for they had brought him pictures of the battles true to life.

Cortés answered him through our interpreters who always accompanied him, especially Doña Marina, and said to him that he and all of us did not know how to repay him the great favours we received from him every day. It was true that we came from where the sun rose, and were the vassals and servants of a great Prince called the Emperor Don Carlos, who held beneath his sway many and great princes, and that the Emperor having heard of him and what a great prince he was, had sent us to these parts to see him, and to beg them to become Christians, the same as our Emperor and all of us, so that his soul and those of all his vassals might be saved. Later on he would further explain how and in what manner this should be done, and how we worship one only true God, and who He is, and many other good things which he should listen to, such as he had already told to his ambassadors Tendile, and Pitalpitoque and Quintalbor when we were on the sand dunes. When this conference was over, the Great Montezuma had already at hand some very rich golden jewels, of many patterns, which he gave to our Captain, and in the same manner to each one of our Captains he gave trifles of gold, and three loads of mantles of rich feather work, and to the soldiers also he gave to each one two loads of mantles, and he did it cheerfully and in every way he seemed to be a great Prince. When these things had been distributed, he asked Cortés if we were all brethren and vassals of our great Emperor, and Cortés replied yes, we were brothers in affection and friendship, and persons of great distinction, and servants of our great King and Prince. Further polite speeches passed between Montezuma and Cortés, and as this was the first time he had come to visit us, and so as not to be wearisome, they ceased talking. Montezuma had ordered his stewards that, according to our own use and customs in all things, we should be provided with maize and [grinding] stones, and women to make bread, and fowls and fruit, and much fodder for the horses. Then Montezuma took leave of our Captain and all of us with the greatest courtesy, and we went out with him as far as the street. Cortés ordered us not to go far from our quarters for the present, until we knew better what was expedient. I will stop here and go on to tell what happened later.

Chapter XC [90]

How on the following day our Captain Cortés went to see the Great Montezuma, and about a certain conversation that took place.

The next day Cortés decided to go to Montezuma's palace, and he first sent to find out what he intended doing and to let him know that we were coming. He took with him four Captains, namely Pedro de Alvarado, Juan Velásquez de Leon, Diego de Ordás, and Gonzalo de Sandoval, and five of us soldiers also went with him.

When Montezuma knew of our coming he advanced to the middle of the Hall to receive us, accompanied by many of his nephews, for no other chiefs were permitted to enter or hold communication with Montezuma where he then was, unless it were on important business. Cortés and he paid the greatest reverence to each other and then they took one another by the hand and Montezuma made him sit down on his couch on his right hand, and he also bade all of us to be seated on seats which he ordered to be brought.

Then Cortés began to make an explanation through our interpreters Doña Marina and Aguilar, and said that he and all of us were rested, and that in coming to see and converse with such a great Prince as he was, we had completed the journey and fulfilled the command which our great King and Prince had laid on us. But what he chiefly came to say on behalf of our Lord God had already been brought to his [Montezuma's] knowledge through his ambassadors, Tendile, Pitalpitoque, and Quintalbor, at the time when he did us the favor to send the golden sun and moon to the sand dunes; for we told them then that we were Christians and worshipped one true and only God, named Jesus Christ, who suffered death and passion to save us, and we told them that a cross (when they asked us why we worshipped it) was the sign of the other Cross on which our Lord God was crucified for our salvation, and that the death and passion which He suffered was for the salvation of the whole human race, which was lost, and that this our God rose on the third day and is now in heaven, and it is He who made the heavens and the earth, the sea and the sands, and created all the things there are in the world, and He sends the rain and the dew, and nothing happens in the world without His holy will. That we believe in Him and worship Him, but that those whom they look upon as gods are not so, but are devils, which are evil things, and if their looks are bad their deeds are worse, and they could see that they were of little worth, for where we had set up crosses such as his ambassadors had seen, they dared not appear before them, through fear of them, and that as time went on they would notice this.

The favor he [Cortés] now begged of him was his attention to the words that he now wished to tell him; then he explained to him very clearly about the creation of the world, and how we are all brothers, sons of one father and one mother who were called Adam and Eve, and how such a brother as our great Emperor, grieving for the perdition of so many souls, such as those which their idols were leading to Hell, where they burn in living flames, had sent us, so that after what he [Montezuma] had now heard he would put a stop to it and they would no longer adore these Idols or sacrifice Indian men and women to them, for we were all brethren, nor should they commit sodomy or thefts. He also told them that, in course of time, our Lord and King would send some men who among us would lead very holy lives, much better than we do, who will explain to them all about it, for at present we merely came to give them due warning, and so he prayed him to do what he was asked and carry it into effect.

As Montezuma appeared to wish to reply, Cortés broke off his argument, and to all of us who were with him he said: "With this we have done our duty considering it is the first attempt."

Montezuma replied—"Señor Malinche, I have understood your words and arguments very well before now, from what you said to my servants at the sand dunes, this about three Gods and the Cross, and all those things that you have preached in the towns through which you have come. We have not made any answer to it because here throughout all time we have worshipped our own gods, and thought they were good, as no doubt yours are, so do not trouble to speak to us anymore about them at present. Regarding the creation of the world, we have held the same belief for ages past, and for this reason we take it for certain that you are those whom our ancestors predicted would come from the direction of the sunrise. As for your great King, I feel that I am indebted to him, and I will give him of what I possess, for as I have already said, two years ago I heard of the Captain who came in ships from the direction in which you came, and they said that they were the servants of this your great King, and I wish to know if you are all one and the same."

Cortés replied, yes, that we were all brethren and servants of our Emperor, and that those men came to examine the way and the seas and the ports so as to know them well in order that we might follow as we had done. Montezuma was referring to the expeditions of Francesco Hernández de Córdova and of Grijalva, when we first came on voyages of discovery, and he said that ever since that time he had wished to capture some of these men who had come so as to keep them in his kingdoms and cities and to do them honour, and his gods had now fulfilled his desires, for now that we were in his home, which we might call our own, we should rejoice and take our rest for there we should be well treated. And if he had on other occasions sent to say that we should not enter his city, it was not of his free will, but because his vassals were afraid, for they said that we shot out flashes of lightning, and killed many Indians with our horses, and that we were angry Teules, and other childish stories, and now that he had seen our persons and knew we were of flesh and bone, and had sound sense, and that we were very valiant, for these reasons he held us in much higher regard than he did from their reports, and he would share his possessions with us. Then Cortés and all of us answered that we thanked him sincerely for such signal good will, and Montezuma said, laughing, for he was very merry in his princely way of speaking: "Malinche, I know very well that these people of Tlaxcala with whom you are such good friends have told you that I am a sort of God or Teul, and that everything in my houses is made of gold and silver and precious stones. I know well enough that you are wise and did not believe it but took it as a joke. Behold now, Señor Malinche, my body is of flesh and bone like yours, my houses and palaces of stone and wood and lime; that I am a great king and inherit all the riches of my ancestors is true, but not all the nonsense and lies that they have told you about me, although of course you treated it as a joke, as I did your thunder and lightning."

Cortés answered him, also laughing, and said that opponents and enemies always say evil things, without truth in them, of those whom they hate, and that he well knew that he could not hope to find another Prince more magnificent in these countries, and that not without reason had he been so vaunted to our Emperor.

While this conversation was going on, Montezuma secretly sent out a great Cacique, one of his nephews who was in his company, to order his stewards to bring certain pieces of gold, which it seems must have been set apart to give to Cortés, and ten loads of fine cloth, which he apportioned, the gold and mantles between Cortés and the four captains, and to each of us soldiers he gave two golden necklaces, each necklace being worth two pesos, and two loads of mantles. The gold that he then gave us was worth in all more than a thousand pesos and he gave it all cheerfully and with the air of a great and valiant prince. As it was now past midday, so as not to appear importunate, Cortés said to him, "Señor Montezuma, you always have the habit of heaping load upon load in every day conferring favours on us, and it is already your dinner time." Montezuma replied that he thanked us for coming to see him, and then we took our leave with the greatest courtesy and we went to our lodgings.

And as we went along we spoke of the good manners and breeding which he showed in everything, and that we should show him in all ways the greatest respect, doffing our quilted caps when we passed before him, and this we always did, but let us leave this subject here, and pass on.

Chapter XCI [91]

Of the manner and appearance of the Great Montezuma and what a great Prince he was.

The Great Montezuma was about forty years old, of good height and well proportioned, slender and spare of flesh, not very swarthy, but of [the] natural colour and shade of an Indian. He did not wear his hair long, but so as just to cover his ears[;] his scanty black beard was well shaped and thin. His face was somewhat long, but cheerful, and he had good eyes and showed in his appearance and manner both tenderness and, when necessary, gravity. He was very neat and clean and bathed once every day in the afternoon. He had many women as mistresses, daughters of Chieftains, and he had two great Cacicas as his legitimate wives, and when he had intercourse with them it was so secretly that no one knew anything about it, except some of his servants. He was free from unnatural offenses. The clothes that he wore one day, he did not put on again until four days later. He had over two hundred chieftains in his guard, in other rooms close to his own, not that all were meant to converse with him, but only one or another, and when they went to speak to him they were obliged to take off their rich mantles and put on others of little worth, but they had to be clean, and they had to enter barefoot with their eyes lowered to the ground, and not to look up in his face. And they made him three obeisances, and said: "Lord, my Lord, my Great Lord," before they came up to him, and then they made their report and with a few words he dismissed them, and on taking their leave they did not turn their backs, but kept their faces toward him with their eyes to the ground, and they did not turn their backs until they left the room. . . .

For each meal, thirty different dishes were prepared by his cooks according to their ways and usage, and they placed small pottery brasiers beneath the dishes so that they should not get cold. They prepared more than three hundred plates of food that Montezuma was going to eat, and more than a thousand for the guard. . . .

I have heard it said that they were wont to cook for him the flesh of young boys, but as he had such a variety of dishes, made of so many different things, we could not succeed in seeing if they were of human flesh or of other things, for they daily cooked fowls, turkeys, pheasants, native partridges, quail, tame and wild ducks, venison, wild boar, reed birds, pigeons, hares and rabbits, and many sorts of birds and other things which are bred in this country, and they are so numerous that I cannot finish naming them in a hurry; so we had no insight into it, but I know for certain that after our Captain censured the sacrifice of human beings, and the eating of their flesh, he ordered that such food should not be prepared for him thenceforth. . . .

As soon as the Great Montezuma had dined, all the men of the Guard had their meal and as many more of the other house servants, and it seems to me that they brought out over a thousand dishes of the food of which I have spoken, and then over two thousand jugs of cacao all frothed up, as they make it in Mexico, and a limitless quantity of fruit, so that with his women and female servants and bread makers and cacao makers his expenses must have been very great. . . .

Let us leave this and go on to another great house, where they keep many Idols, and they say that they are their fierce gods, and with them many kinds of carnivorous beasts of prey, tigers and two kinds of lions, and animals something like wolves which in this country they call jackals and foxes, and other smaller carnivorous animals, and all these carnivores they feed with flesh, and the greater number of them breed in the house. They give them as food deer and fowls, dogs and other things which they are used to hunt, and I have heard it said that they feed them on the bodies of the Indians who have been sacrificed. It is in this way: you have already heard me say that when they sacrifice a wretched Indian they saw open the chest with stone knives and hasten to tear out the palpitating heart and blood, and offer it to their Idols, in whose name the sacrifice is made. Then they cut off the thighs, arms and head and eat the former at feasts and banquets, and the head they hang up on some beams, and the body of the man sacrificed is not eaten but given to these fierce animals. They also have in that cursed house many vipers and poisonous snakes which carry on their tails things that sound like bells. These are the worst vipers of all, and they keep them in jars and great pottery vessels with many feathers, and there they lay their eggs and rear their young, and they give them to eat the bodies of the Indians who have been sacrificed, and the flesh of dogs which they are in the habit of breeding. We even know for certain that when they drove us out of Mexico and killed over eight hundred of our soldiers that they fed those fierce animals and snakes for many days on their bodies, as I will relate in the proper time and season. And those snakes and wild beasts were dedicated to these savage Idols, so that they might keep them company. . . .

In the house of the Great Montezuma himself, all the daughters of chieftains whom he had as mistresses always wore beautiful things, and there were many daughters of Mexican citizens who lived in retirement and wished to appear to be like nuns, who also did weaving but it was wholly of feather work. These nuns had their houses near the great Cue of Huichilobos and out of devotion to it, or to another idol, that of a woman who was said to be their mediatrix in the matter of marriage, their fathers placed them in that religious retirement until they married, and they were [only] taken out thence to be married. . . .

As I am almost tired of writing about this subject, and my interested readers will be even more so, I will stop talking about it and tell how our Cortés in company with many of our captains and soldiers went to see Tlatelolco,* which is the great marketplace of Mexico, and how we ascended the great Cue where stand the Idols Tezcatepuca and Huichilobos. That was the first time that our Captain went out to see the city and I will relate what else happened.

*"Tutelulco" in the text.

Central Themes

Indigenous people, state formation, urban life, religion, gender

Suggested Reading

Carman, Glen. *Rhetorical Conquests: Cortés, Gómara, and Renaissance Imperialism.* Purdue Studies in Romance Literatures 35. West Lafayette, IN: Purdue University Press, 2006.

Clendinnen, Inga. *Ambivalent Conquests: Maya and Spaniard in Yucatán, 1517–1570.* Cambridge: Cambridge University Press, 2003.

Restall, Matthew. *Seven Myths of the Spanish Conquest.* Oxford: Oxford University Press, 2003.

Townsend, Camilla. "Burying the White Gods: New Perspectives on the Conquest of Mexico." *American Historical Review* (June 2003). Available at: http://www.history cooperative.org/journals/ahr/108.3/townsend.html (visited February 1, 2009).

Related Sources

11. Moteucçoma and Hernán Cortés Meet, According to a Nahua Codex (c. 1555)
12. The Nahua Interpreter Malintzin Translates for Hernán Cortés and Moteucçoma (1580)
22. On Chocolate (1648)

11. Moteucçoma and Hernán Cortés Meet, According to a Nahua Codex (c. 1555)*

Fray Bernardino de Sahagún (1499–1590) was a member of the Franciscan Order who was educated at the University of Salamanca, Spain, where Renaissance humanism was in full force. He arrived in New Spain in 1529 on a mission to convince the Nahuas to embrace Christianity, and he started teaching at the College of Santa Cruz Tlatelolco in 1536. This Franciscan school prepared the sons of the Nahua aristocracy for the time when they might be permitted to be Catholic priests. Some of these young men became scribal assistants to Sahagún. The friar was extremely curious about his students' fascinating civilization, which he admired. But Sahagún wanted to know as much as he could about their culture in order to stamp out what he believed was a false religion (Source 16). The Nahua assistants went out and gathered information on their people's culture and history. Then, using the recently acquired skill of writing in the Latinate script, the Nahua assistants wrote down what they had been told in their native language, Nahuatl. Until 1580, Sahagún headed

*James Lockhart, ed. and trans., *We People Here: Nahuatl Accounts of the Conquest of Mexico* (Berkeley: University of California Press, 1994), pp. 114–118.

this project, producing several versions of the encyclopedic *General History of the Things of New Spain.* The most complete copy that survived, the *Florentine Codex,* was finished around 1578 or 1579. Sahagún's overall goal was probably linguistic. He wanted to create an authentic Nahuatl literature that would provide every possible historical use of the language and could thus be the foundation for the most authoritative dictionaries and grammars of the language.

The selection found here is from Book 12 of the *Florentine Codex;* first written down around 1555, the *Codex* tells the story of the 1519–1521 war for the city of Tenochtitlan. In this piece, we read the famous story of the meeting of Moteucçoma and Hernán Cortés when the Spaniards had arrived just outside of Tenochtitlan. The meaning of Moteucçoma's speech to Cortés was immediately controversial and the source of several of the most distorted legends of the Conquest. Hernán Cortés politically spun the speech as a capitulation, although recent scholarship has shown that such exaggerated and obsequious speeches were pro forma when people of importance arrived. Since then, generations of university professors and schoolteachers have claimed that the speech proved that the Nahuas were cowed because they believed the Spaniards were returning gods.

Clearly, a careful comparative analysis is required when such disparaging myths are involved. Although the Nahuas' narrative is authentically indigenous, it is also the product of a cultural conversation between the Nahuas and the Spaniards when they came into contact during the mid- to late 1500s. When Sahagún translated the Nahuatl into Spanish, he made annotations, most likely after asking follow-up questions of the Nahua storytellers. As a result, the Spanish version sometimes has different or conflicting information about the same events. We include here only James Lockhart's English translation of the Nahuatl, but there are intriguing differences between the Nahuatl version and Sahagún's Spanish translation of the indigenous language. For example, the Spanish version mentions Hernán Cortés by name, but in the Nahuatl version he is called simply "the war leader."

Second, readers are cautioned not to view this text as representative of a single, monolithic Indian perspective. We recommend reading this document with the *Lienzo de Tlaxcala,* which is a pictographic history of the Nahua city-state of Tlaxcala, and Bernal Díaz for comparative purposes (sources 10 and 12). Compared to Book 12 of the *Florentine Codex,* how are Díaz's views of Moteucçoma and the people of Tenochtitlan different from the opinions of the anonymous Nahuas who recounted the meeting episode? Ironically, Book 12 is one of the few primary sources on the Conquest that pushes the idea that the Nahuas believed the Spaniards were gods (*teotl*). How do we explain this? One clue may rest in the fact that the Nahuas of the *altepetl* (sovereign state) of Tlatelolco told the stories in Book 12 to Sahagún. Although Tlatelolco and Tenochtitlan shared the urbanized island in the middle of Lake Texcoco, they were separate altepetl, and Tlatelolco had been a client community of the dominant altepetl of Tenochtitlan when the Spaniards arrived in 1519. If in 1555 they still remembered or resented this, how might this have influenced their opinion of Moteucçoma?

Finally, what is the meaning of Moteucçoma's speech to the Spaniards in the *Florentine Codex?* Comparing this document to Díaz's account and the *Lienzo de Tlaxcala,* do you find evidence that the Nahuas of Tenochtitlan—or any other indigenous people—believed that they were speaking to gods?

The Florentine Codex, *Book 12*

Sixteenth chapter, where it is said how Moteucçoma went in peace and quiet to meet the Spaniards at Xoloco, where the house of Alvarado is now, or at the place they call Huitzillan.

And when they [the Spaniards] had come as far as Xoloco, when they had stopped there, Moteucçoma dressed and prepared himself for a meeting, along with other great rulers and high nobles, his rulers and nobles. Then they went to the meeting. On gourd bases they set out different precious flowers; in the midst of the shield flowers and heart flowers stood popcorn flowers, yellow tobacco flowers, cacao flowers, [made into] wreaths for the head, wreaths to be girded around. And they carried golden necklaces, necklaces with pendants, wide necklaces.

And when Moteucçoma went out to meet them at Huitzillan, thereupon he gave various things to the war leader, the commander of the warriors; he gave him flowers, he put necklaces on him, he put flower necklaces on him, he girded him with flowers, he put flower wreaths on his head. Then he laid before him the golden necklaces, all the different things for greeting people. He ended by putting some of the necklaces on him.

Then [Cortés] said in reply to Moteucçoma, "Is it not you? Is it not you then? Moteucçoma?"

Moteucçoma said, "Yes, it is me." Thereupon he stood up straight, he stood up with their faces meeting. He bowed down deeply to him. He stretched as far as he could, standing stiffly. Addressing him, he said to him,

"O our lord, be doubly welcomed on your arrival in this land; you have come to satisfy your curiosity about your altepetl of Mexico, you have come to sit on your seat of authority, which I have kept a while for you, where I have been in charge for you, for your agents the rulers—Itzcoatzin, the elder Moteucçoma, Axayacatl, Tiçocic, and Ahuitzotl—have gone, who for a very short time came to be in charge for you, to govern the altepetl of Mexico. It is after them that your poor vassal [myself] came. Will they come back to the place of their absence? If only one of them could see and behold what has now happened in my time, what I now see after our lords are gone! For I am not just dreaming, not just sleepwalking, not just seeing it in my sleep. I am not just dreaming that I have seen you, have looked upon your face. For a time I have been concerned, looking toward the mysterious place from which you have come, among clouds and mist. It is so that the rulers on departing said that you would come in order to acquaint yourself with your altepetl and sit upon your seat of authority. And now it has come true, you have come. Be doubly welcomed, enter the land, go to enjoy your palace; rest your body. May our lords be arrived in the land."

And when the speech that Moteucçoma directed to the Marqués had concluded, Marina reported it to him, interpreting it for him. And when the Marqués had heard what Moteucçoma had said, he spoke to Marina in return, babbling back to them, replying in his babbling tongue,

"Let Moteucçoma be at ease, let him not be afraid, for we greatly esteem him. Now we are truly satisfied to see him in person and hear him, for until now we have greatly desired to see him and look upon his face. Well, now we have seen him, we have come to his homeland of Mexico. Bit by bit he will hear what we have to say."

Thereupon [the Spaniards] took [Moteucçoma] by the hand. They came along with him, stroking his hair to show their good feeling. And the Spaniards looked at him, each of them giving him a close look. They would start along walking, then mount, then dismount again in order to see him.

And as to each of the rulers who went with him, they were: first, Cacamatzin, ruler of Tetzcoco; second, Tetlepanquetzatzin, ruler of Tlacopan; third, the Tlacochcalcatl Itzquauhtzin, ruler of Tlatelolco; fourth, Topantemoctzin, Moteucçoma's storekeeper in Tlatelolco. These were the ones who went. And the other Tenocha noblemen were Atlixcatzin, the Tlacateccatl; Tepehuatzin, the Tlacochcalcatl; Quetzalaztatzin, the Ticocyahuacatl; Totomotzin; Ecatenpatiltzin; and Quappiaztzin. When Moteucçoma was made prisoner, they not only hid themselves and took refuge, they abandoned him in anger.

Central Themes

Indigenous people, religion

Suggested Reading

León-Portilla, Miguel. *Bernardino de Sahagún: First Anthropologist.* Norman: University of Oklahoma Press, 2002.

Lockhart, James. *Nahuas and Spaniards: Postconquest Central Mexican History and Philology.* Los Angeles: UCLA Latin American Center Publications and University of California Press, 1991.

Osowski, Edward. "Spanish Conquest of Mexico—Two Views." Available at: World History Sources, Center for History and the New Media, http://chnm.gmu.edu/worldhistory sources/d/251/whm.html.

Schwartz, Stuart B., ed. *Victors and Vanquished: Spanish and Nahua Views of the Conquest of Mexico.* Boston: Bedford/St. Martin's Press, 2000.

Related Sources

10. Hernán Cortés and Moteucçoma Meet, According to a Spanish Conqueror (1568)
12. The Nahua Interpreter Malintzin Translates for Hernán Cortés and Moteucçoma (1580)
16. The Spiritual Conquest: The Trial of Don Carlos Chichimecatecotl of Texcoco (1539)

12. The Nahua Interpreter Malintzin Translates for Hernán Cortés and Moteucçoma (1580)

Malintzin, whom the Spanish called Doña Marina, played a key role in securing their victory over the Mexica in the conquest of Mexico. Malintzin was born into a noble family in the Nahua town of Paynala. Conflicting reports relate that either she was stolen from her family by merchants who sold her to a Maya household or that her mother and stepfather gave her away to some Maya Indians from Xicalango in order to clear the way for her younger half-brother's right to inherit his father's *cacique*-ship. After serving in Xicalango, Malintzin changed hands again and ended up working in servitude in the Chontal Maya area at the base of the Yucatán Peninsula. She was one of twenty women a Maya *cacique* (local leader) awarded to Hernán Cortés in 1519 as an act of reverence and alliance.

Malintzin's aptitude in both her mother tongue of Nahuatl and her adopted Maya tongue proved invaluable to the Spaniards' diplomatic and military campaigns against the Mexica. Beginning in the aftermath of Mexico's Revolution of Independence, however, and increasingly in the twentieth century, the figure of Malintzin began to acquire a negative connotation. Known most commonly in the modern era as "La Malinche," her chief association became that of betrayal. But sources more contemporary to the events of the Conquest, including indigenous ones, tell a different story about how her peers viewed this extraordinary woman.

The image below comes from the *Lienzo de Tlaxcala,* the most famous set of pictorial sources narrating the story of the Conquest. Copies of these images were published in Diego Muñoz Camargo's *Historia de Tlaxcala* in 1580. How did these artists represent Malintzin and the work she undertook? How does their overall depiction of the Conquest compare to those in other contemporary accounts (sources 10 and 11)? Compare the goods lying at the figures' feet to those contained in the image on page 33. What purpose might these items have served?

Central Themes

Indigenous people, gender

Suggested Reading

Boone, Elizabeth Hill. *Stories in Black and Red: Pictorial Histories of the Aztecs and Mixtecs.* Austin: University of Texas Press, 2000.

Kartunnen, Frances. "Rethinking Malinche." In *Indian Women of Early Mexico,* ed. Susan Schroeder, Stephanie Wood, and Robert Haskett. Norman: University of Oklahoma Press, 1997, pp. 291–312.

Townsend, Camilla. *Malintzin's Choices: An Indian Woman in the Conquest of Mexico.* Albuquerque: University of New Mexico Press, 2006.

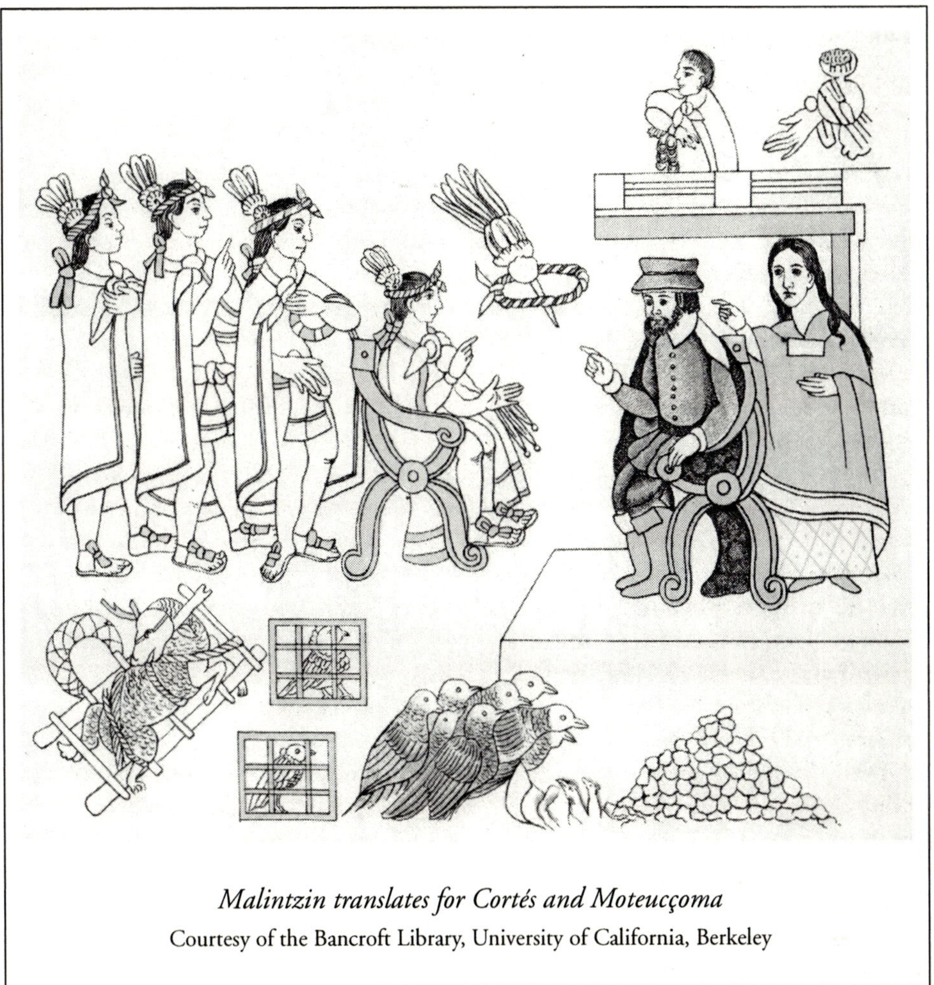

Malintzin translates for Cortés and Moteucçoma
Courtesy of the Bancroft Library, University of California, Berkeley

Related Sources

5. A Treasury of Mexica Power and Gender (c. 1541–1542)
10. Hernán Cortés and Moteucçoma Meet, According to a Spanish Conqueror (1568)
11. Moteucçoma and Hernán Cortés Meet, According to a Nahua Codex (c. 1555)

13. Acazitli of Tlalmanalco: Nahua Conqueror on the Mesoamerican Frontier (1541)*

After the fall of Tenochtitlan, many Spaniards were convinced that the Seven Golden Cities of Cíbola could be found somewhere to the north of the former Aztec Empire, which prompted military expeditions in search of them. In 1540, Governor Francisco Vázquez Coronado left his province of Nueva Galicia (Guadalajara) to lead the search, taking with him a few hundred Spaniards drawn from the tiny population of Europeans in his frontier province. Coronado made it as far north as modern-day Kansas, but his fruitless odyssey into the American Midwest pleased no one and especially angered the first viceroy of New Spain, Antonio de Mendoza (1492–1552), who ruled from 1535 to 1550. The absence of Coronado and the Spaniards of Nueva Galicia triggered the Mixtón War (1540–1541), a massive uprising of the indigenous people that Coronado was later unable to suppress. The rebellion had been gathering steam since 1530, when the Caxcan people became emboldened by a religious revival movement under the leadership of one Tenamaxtli. The Mixtón War became the biggest threat to the consolidation of Spanish power in New Spain since their arrival. Unlike the ethnic native groups that Hernán Cortés encountered, who were typically divided, the Caxcan, Zapoteca, and Nayarita peoples formed a military alliance against the Europeans.

Viceroy Antonio de Mendoza was forced to personally lead an army from Mexico City. Like Hernán Cortés, Mendoza defeated his enemies largely because he commanded a large number of indigenous warriors who outnumbered the Spanish fighters involved. In 1542, Tenamaxtli escaped northward into the lands of Nayarita, territory that the Spaniards would not control until the early 1700s. The primary source here illustrates how indigenous people, especially their leaders, made very different choices when it came to resisting or joining the new Spanish order. Don Francisco de Sandoval Acazitli, who was the Nahua *tlatoani* (lord) of Tlalmanalco, fought in Mendoza's army in 1541, an experience that he recounted in his *relación* (report). This is an example of a Conquest and colonial era genre called the *relación de mérito* (report of service merit), a kind of résumé that *conquistadores* used to petition the crown for rewards after a glorious and successful campaign. At the end of this report, when Acazitli comes home to his province of Chalco, his whole community greets him as a returning conqueror as he passes under triumphal arches that Europeans had built for their caesars since the time of the Roman Empire. Acazitli's original relación was in Nahuatl, a version no longer in existence; this translation comes from a Spanish translation from a legal case of 1641.

The Spanish called the area "la Gran Chichimeca," using a Nahuatl word that the Europeans pejoratively used to mean "barbarian." The Nahuas, in a seemingly

*"Relación de Acazitli," in Joaquín García Icazbalceta, ed., *Colección de documentos para la historia de México*, vol. 2 (Mexico: 1858), pp. 307–308, 310–314, 330–331. Excerpts translated by the editors.

culturally chauvinistic way, lumped all of the northern semi-sedentary bands of Zacatecas, Caxcan, and Nayarita under the blanket term "Chichimeca." Their attitude toward these people was more complex, however, than that of the Spaniards, who considered them total barbarians. The Nahuas believed that they were the descendants of wandering Chichimecas from the north who eventually settled in cities and towns in the Valley of Mexico. In some sixteenth-century altepetls, the top dynastic ruler was called "Chichimeca Lord." If we can assume that Acazitli and the other Nahuas who fought on Mendoza's side did not look down on the Chichimecas whom they fought, why then did they fight on the Spanish side?

Three excerpts from the much longer relación elicit many questions. The letter opens with an exact description of Acazitli's warrior costume, weapons, and clothes and evokes the pictorial representations of warrior ranks in the Nahua-illustrated *Codex Mendoza.* What other elements of Pre-Columbian Nahua warrior culture seemed to be present? How might Acazitli have used his participation to consolidate his power within the colonial system? What can we deduce about the indigenous society in rebellion from the brief description of the town of Xuchipiltepetl?

Report of the Journey That Don Francisco de Sandoval Acazitli, Cacique and Noble Native from the Pueblo of Tlalmanalco, Province of Chalco, Made with Lord Viceroy Don Antonio de Mendoza When He Went to Conquer and Pacify the Chichimeca Indians of Xochipila

When he went to war with the Chichimecas, Don Francisco Acazitli bore arms and wore the insignia of a skull of woven feathers with green plumes, a round shield inlaid with a twisted lip ring made of the same material, his sword and his *ichcahuipil.** He dressed in a red doublet, wide-legged pants, shoes and half-boots, and a white sombrero. He wore a great handkerchief wrapped around his head and a necklace of two chains of precious stones.

They left on this journey, Monday, the Feast of Saint Michael, the Archangel, on the 29th of September in the year of our Lord, 1541.

I, Don Francisco de Sandoval, *cacique* and lord of the city of San Luis Tlalmanalco, having heard news that the Lord Viceroy Don Antonio de Mendoza, who resides in the great city of Mexico and Royal Audiencia, makes war in the land of the Chichimecas of Xuchipila, went to the city to beg the Lord Viceroy to grant me the privilege that I, and those of my province of Chalco, might go and serve in this war. His lordship did benevolently grant that we might go to this war. I, then, upon returning to Tlalmanalco, forewarned all the people of this province of Chalco for war,

---

*Quilted cotton armor that originated in Pre-Conquest times.

as did Amecameca, Tenango, Xochimilco, and those here in Tlalmanalco. And all those of good will, prominent residents, and serving members of town government, soldiers and barrio officials, were allowed to go to serve in this war. I, Don Francisco, also prepared for this war with my two sons, Don Bernardino del Castillo and Don Pedro de Alvarado, who accepted my command of them. I gave them arms: ichcahuipil[i], shields, and swords. Being now the inevitable time to leave for war, we marched in review with all the people and arms prepared for war. I, Don Francisco de Sandoval, marched in the company of Don Fernando de Guzmán and all the principal officials of [indigenous] municipal government, the barrio officials and all the rest of the common people. We marched from here in Tlalmanalco on Sunday. . . .

[Following this passage is a day-by-day account of all the places marched to and camped at, and for how long. *Ed.*]

. . . We went to sleep in Yepcalco where there are hot springs and here there was a tight spot and some people were thrown over the side. We went past a great river that had a salt works on its shores. On Thursday we left there and came to sleep in Misquititlan and later they went to survey the lands to determine who were there. The following day we went there and everyone stopped on the shores and only the viceroy with all the Spaniards advanced and the natives all stayed put. Only three native lords went with the viceroy: Don Francisco of Tlalmanalco, Don Juan of Coyoacan, and Don Mateo of Cuitlahuac. They went on a reconnaissance mission of the hill where the enemies were. At the place where they halted, the whole native army began to prepare their arms and then to march. They went downhill and halted where they met the captain of Tlacotlan who brought with him the people of Tonalan who were going with Martín de Silva y Esteban of Xochimilco. They were the ones who carried the sick to Tonalan and the wounded to Tototlan, as well as those who had fallen ill when they left Acatlan. At that time there was just nothing one could do but to try to maintain order. The following Saturday, a pursuit began and there was nothing one could do, and they shot arrows and fired at some people. And we were not there for more than four days—Sunday, Monday, Tuesday, and Wednesday—and the fifth day the battle began in the morning during the time when one normally goes to mass. The combat formation was to place the artillery in the center, then bands from Tlaxcala, Huexotzinco, Cuauhquechollan, followed by the Mexicans, people from Xilotepec, and then those from Culhuacan. On the other side were men from Michoacán, Mextitlan, and Chalco. They fired the artillery towards the Chichimecas' wooden fences, then at their rock walls, which dislodged them. After that, the Spaniards began to fall upon them but then the Chichimecas turned on them at which point they struggled fiercely. Señor [Sir] Don Francisco left the people, went down below, and when he arrived, the Chichimecas were now being routed from their position, but he did not capture anyone nearby.* Then, they

*Nahuas at this time used the Spanish honorifics "señor" and "señora" as titles of nobility—"lord" and "lady"—not as just "Mr." and "Mrs.," as in modern usage.

and Señor Don Francisco with his green-plumed *quetzalpatzactli* began to charge the Chichimecas, at which time they captured the fence.* They destroyed and burned their houses and engaged in combat with the Chichimecas, who were retreating from a large part of their fences, which they had on a steep slope. They fiercely defended the last fence that was in front of their houses. The victors raised the Royal Standard above them and the *pueblo* [town] was won. They commenced to capture them. And some of ours fell with their captives, some of them dying and some of them injured. This is where everyone from the provinces gained many captives and no more than four Spaniards died in this battle. This battle lasted until we had taken Nochtlan where we stayed for four days—Thursday, Friday, Saturday, and Sunday. From then on, Chalco province took up its burden of hauling the artillery, which was double the work, and also they carried on their backs the cannon balls, the rest of the munitions, and the accessories for the artillery. They also took care of the herd of sheep. On Monday, we left for Xuchipila and we went to sleep at the edge of another forest. We left there on Wednesday and arrived in Xuchipila where the enemy was based. The next day, on Thursday morning, came Maldonado, who was called Listonco by those in attendance, and he brought with him only those of the province of Chalco. Marching very early in the morning with his retinue, which included Señor Don Francisco and all of his people, Maldonado passed by Ahuizolco. Later he commenced to climb and pass over a ridge and then a hillock. Then they climbed down to meet the Mexicans halfway. They said to him: "Señor, where are you going? The Chichimecas are coming." And the Señor could not be made to understand and he passed close by them. And when he turned to go, he encountered another person who was from Amequemecan who said the same thing: "Señor, where are you going? The Chichimecas are coming." And having gone a short distance to a river, he returned. Some of the Chichimecas beat a retreat from us while another group went up to stand their ground and attack us. No one was able to advance in the area between where they had retreated from us to the place from which the Señor held them off. The last in the line were Maldonado and Salinas who came bearing the Royal Standard and only one man died—a man from Tenantzinco who was Maldonado's vassal. The next day, on Friday morning, the two captains, Maldonado and the captain of Tlacotlan, turned to go. Just the same, they made their retreat but did not take any natives with them. The captain of Tlacotlan was wounded by arrows, one in his foot and the other in his hand. They hit three horses with arrows too. The following day, on Saturday, the viceroy and the Spaniards marched and he brought along the Mexicans only. They went to get their caudillos Tapia and Don Martín of Tlatelolco. Then the viceroy took command of the Mexicans' post so that the Spaniards were in the forward position and the Mexicans and some Spaniards flanked them. They slept in Apzolco and they now went by day as this is how they loved to advance. The viceroy was calm and the Mexicans were at their positions.

**Quetzalpatzactli* was a crest of quetzal bird feathers woven onto a frame, also worn by warriors in the Pre-Conquest times.

Having arrived at the river, they [Don Francisco's party from Chalco] began to call them and they responded: "Tomorrow, we will go to see the Señor." Later they came and took the road to the viceroy and the whole army of natives came back. The next day, on Sunday, at dawn, the enemy came down from the sierra, though they would have preferred to attack us at night. The Chichimecas came down to the foot of the sierra. The people of Chalco were the frontline men as well as those from Cuauhtitlan, Coyoacan, and Xilotepec. Only the people of Xilotepec burned settlements. The Chichimecas came by two pathways, one that went straight for Xilotepec's position and the other towards Chalco's position. The men of Chalco defended their position very well. For a little while they captured Don Francisco because he fought them unarmed with only an old buckler and without a sword. He then came back at them armed with his ichcahuipil, buckler, sword, and all the emblems of war and fiercely battled the Chichimecas, and they dared not return again. Seven of them died there and two were taken alive so that they could be seen by the viceroy. He asked them questions but they did not want to say anything. On the third day he set the dogs on them. That was Wednesday when the Spaniards were counted among the ranks that were there. And Friday they counted the men of the infantry who were musketeers and crossbowmen.

We came to the peaks of the Sierra of Xuchipiltepetl where there was a very large temple of the devil in this mountainous place. The hall was fifteen fathoms long and thirteen wide and the walls were all made of stone in an adobe style.* The building was so ancient that no one knows who the people were who built it. The hill began its structure completely from the hollows of the rocks in rugged and difficult places. Regarding the residents who were there, all their houses were very beautiful and made of stone slabs and adobe bricks with stairs made of the same. This type of stone is like the stone that is quarried in Sencoc and the exterior part was made of stone. The outline of the hill was skirted by a river which appeared to issue from the cavities of the stones, flowing very widely. There were four roads that went up to the place, rambling through the rocks through difficult and vexatious passes.

Then, on Sunday, we left marching off in search of the hill of Miztepec where we were to decamp, and [first] we went to sleep in Apzolco. On Monday, we left there and went to sleep at the foot of the hill of Miztepec. By the time that we arrived, the enemy was in our sights but they did not make war cries or a ruckus. On Tuesday we began to march and we came upon some crags below, and through a great opening, the road cut through the stone on either side. And having marched down through the great craggy rock, the Chichimecas attempted to take our army. From the summit of the great rock they pitched and shot huge rocks that rolled. Some of them were stopped and captured while others were wounded. Fighting fiercely, they were pursued to the river where they stood their ground to counterattack, and the

*One fathom equals 1.67 meters, making the hall approximately 25 meters long and 22 meters wide.

enemy defended the pass strenuously. By sheer force they were thrown into the river. They were pursued to the ledge, fighting us all the way from the top on down. There on the edge of the ravine we spent the night, and below the place of the great craggy rock slept the viceroy. This is where we were confronted by the Chichimecas.

. . . We came to sleep in Mexico [City] and we stayed there two days, Saturday and Sunday, and he still had not said farewell to the Lord Viceroy Don Antonio de Mendoza. By means of the interpreter, Antonio Ortiz, he said: "I say to His Most Illustrious Lordship that I come to kiss his hand, extending gratitude for his having returned healthy from the journey which His Lordship has made in the land of the Chichimecas with such rewarding successes and without any disasters or sickness. I pray that God blessed him with a safe return to his house and court in this city of Mexico: Rest assured, His Illustrious Lordship, that I come to beg permission to return to his pueblo of San Luis Tlalmanalco." The interpreter related all of this to the viceroy who replied through the same man: "His Illustrious Lordship says, 'I am most grateful to Don Francisco and very satisfied with the service that the people of Chalco have rendered for the marques when he came to the conquest and pacification of this kingdom, grateful that they helped him in all the wars that the marques has waged. May you go in good time to rest in your house and pueblo of Tlalmanalco. If I may offer you something, I will do what you will ask me, and I will favor you.'" And on Monday we left and we came to sleep together under a pine tree on a plain. We arrived at night. Tuesday, we left there for this pueblo of Tlalmanalco where they had been ordered to greet Señor Don Francisco. First, a party of principal men from Tochitltezacuilco came out to receive him, another group was from Ictlan. The third party was from Ostotipac and it included Don Fernando [de] Guzmán, who came to greet him in the place that is called Iztompatepec. And so did Joaquin Tlecomalhua, Cristóbal Maldonado, Bernardino Tlacochcalcatltecutli and all the rest of the principal men, the señoras, and, from all areas, the common people. All along the road there were triumphal arches and sedge on both sides, and these decorations went from the road to the inside the church. Similarly, at intervals they set up stages covered in sedge. They decorated in the same manner from the church to the palaces of Don Francisco de Sandoval, adorning all the places with flowers. This adornment began in Iztompatepec. Then, all the principal men, leaders, señoras, welcomed Don Fernando. Father Cristóbal Ruiz was the guardian of this occasion. Here ends the journey that the Señor Don Francisco made when he went to the conquest and pacification of the pueblos of the Chichimecas, which has been recounted in this report.

Central Themes

Indigenous people, state formation, race and ethnicity

Suggested Reading

Gerhard, Peter. *The North Frontier of New Spain.* Norman: University of Oklahoma Press, 1993.

Gradie, Charlotte M. "Discovering the Chichimecas." *The Americas* 51, no. 1 (July 1994): 67–88.

Matthew, Laura, and Michel R. Oudijk. *Indian Conquistadors: Indigenous Allies in the Conquest of Mesoamerica.* Norman: University of Oklahoma Press, 2007.

Restall, Matthew. *Maya Conquistador.* Boston: Beacon Press, 1998.

Warren, J. Benedict. *The Conquest of Michoacán: The Spanish Domination of the Tarascan Kingdom in Western Mexico, 1521–1530.* Norman: University of Oklahoma Press, 1985.

Related Sources

11. Moteucçoma and Hernán Cortés Meet, According to a Nahua Codex (c. 1555)
14. Poetic Attempts to Justify the Conquest of Acoma, New Mexico (1610)
18. Father Fernández Attempts to Convert the Seris of Sonora Single-handedly (1679)

14. Poetic Attempts to Justify the Conquest of Acoma, New Mexico (1610)*

In his epic poem *Historia de la Nueva México* (1610), the chronicler Gaspar Pérez de Villagrá tried to exonerate Juan de Oñate and the Spaniards who massacred the people of Acoma in 1599. Acoma was one of many indigenous towns located on hilltops in what is today the American Southwest. Pérez de Villagrá served as captain and legal notary in Juan de Oñate's expedition into the northern frontier that established the Spanish Province of New Mexico in 1598. The commanding officer of the assault on Acoma was Vicente de Zaldívar, who sought to avenge the death of his brother Juan, whom the Indians had killed in December 1598. Exploring the countryside, Juan de Zaldívar and the thirty-one Spanish fighting men under his command had camped at the foot of the rock ridge atop which Acoma rested. There are conflicting stories about why hostilities commenced. In one version, the Indians invited the Spaniards to the town with the express plan of luring them to be massacred. In another version, the Spaniards ascended uninvited, stole food, and

*Gaspar Pérez de Villagrá, *Historia de la Nueva México* [1610], Spanish/English ed., ed. Miguel Encinas, Alfred Rodríquez, and Joseph Sánchez, trans. Fayette S. Curtis Jr. (Albuquerque: University of New Mexico Press, 1992), pp. 222–224.

raped a woman. For whatever reason, the people of Acoma attacked, killing Juan de Zaldívar and twelve other men and then throwing their bodies from the cliffs.

Vicente de Zaldívar returned with a larger force and laid siege to the town on January 12, 1599. The battle raged for three days and left eight hundred Indians dead, eighty executed, and the town obliterated by fire. All male and female prisoners over twelve years old were enslaved for twenty years, and the males over twenty-five had one foot cut off. Because of the harshness of Juan de Oñate's attack on Acoma and his record of allowing his men to abuse and rape the Indians of the province, the viceroy ordered Juan de Oñate to step down from office as the governor of New Mexico in 1607, finally banishing him from the territory in 1614.

Compared to Hernán Cortés's decisive and lucrative victory over the Mexica of central Mexico, the Spaniards' spiritual and governmental colonial endeavors in New Mexico could hardly be called successful. Interestingly, two authors who participated in these respective conquests, Bernal Díaz del Castillo (Source 10) and Gaspar Pérez de Villagrá, were similar characters with similar motivations for writing. Both were underlings who tried to justify their actions and those of their respective commanders, one of whom was wildly successful, and the other a spectacular failure.

In this passage from *Historia*, the Franciscan friar who traveled with the expedition justifies waging a punitive war against the Indians on religious grounds. Compare the Franciscan priest's rhetoric in Villagrá's poem to Cortés's attempted conversion of Moteucçoma through reasonable discourse. What legal or moral purpose might these conversion attempts have served both Cortés and Oñate? Before the Acoma uprising, the Spaniards claimed legal jurisdiction over New Mexico, maintaining that the Indians had already submitted to Spanish authority. Through Franciscan interpreters, Oñate had addressed the leaders of some *pueblos* (towns) in the summer of 1598 when he asked them to accept the Christian religion and submit to the authority of God and King, to which the Indian leaders supposedly agreed. Why did the Spaniards who were about to assault Acoma think that they had a legitimate argument that their enemies were rebels rather than fighters in a just war?

Historia de la Nueva México, *Canto XXV [25]*

*How a process was drawn up against the Indians of Acoma and of the opinion the monks gave, and of the instructions given the Sergeant Major that he might go forth to the punishment of the aforesaid Indians.**

Scarce had the fresh dawn entered, defeating
The spent quarter,** when the strong General
Was, without having taken off his arms,
Conversing with the sentries, ordering
That, since the secretary now was dead,
Juan Pérez de Donís, your true subject,
One who had served well on this expedition,
Juan Gutiérrez Bocanegra should,
Being a judge and captain and well skilled,
Draw up against the folk and fort of Acoma
Beginning of a suit. And, this being done,
The cause being substantiated well,
Before giving sentence he wished
The Father Commissary and the monks
Should each give vote upon his doubts,
Whose serious writings, it seems to me,
Should be placed here unchanged in style.

The case which the Governor put, that the holy Fathers might give their opinions upon it.

Don Juan de Oñate, Governor and Captain General and Adelantado† of the provinces of New Mexico, asks what is required for the justification of war, and, supposing that the war is just, what the person who makes it may do concerning the conquered and their goods?

Reply of the Commissary and monks.

The question proposed contains two points. The first is, what is required for war to be justified? To which is replied that there is required, first, the authority of a prince who does not recognize as a superior, such as is the Roman Pontiff, the Em-

---

*Throughout this version of the poem, *religiosos* is incorrectly translated as "monks." The missionaries would have been friars, not monks.

**The reference is to the last quarter of the night. The poetic reference (fresh dawn / spent night) appears to be to the Aurora/Tithonus myth.

†The crown granted the title *adelantado* to a conqueror when he received a royal license to conquer and colonize an area. If successful, adelantados would then become the first royal governors of the conquered province.

peror, and the rulers of Castile, who enjoy the privilege of empire in or not recognizing a superior in temporal affairs, and others; they in person, or whoever may possess their power for this effect, for a private individual cannot make war, for the collection of people for it is required, which is the act of the prince alone, and he can plead to justice before his superior.

The second requires that there shall be just cause for the aforesaid war, which is in one of four manners: either to defend the innocent who suffer unjustly, to whose defense princes are obligated whenever they are able, or for the recovery of property which has been unjustly taken from them, or to punish delinquents and guilty persons under his laws if they are his subjects or under those of nature if they are not, and, finally and principally, to secure and preserve peace, for that is the principal end for which war is ordained.

Thirdly, there is required, for the entire justification of war, a just and right intention in those who fight; and it will be just fighting for any of the four causes which we have stated and not through ambition to rule nor for mortal vengeance, nor for the desire for the property of others.

The second point of the question is: what can the person who may make the aforesaid war do in regard to those conquered and their possessions? To which it is replied that the aforesaid conquered and their goods remain at the mercy of the conqueror, according to the form and manner required by the just cause which moved the war, for it was defense of the innocent, he can proceed until he leaves them free and places them in safety, and may satisfy them and satisfy himself for the damages they have suffered and for those they have incurred in this deed, like Moses in the defense of the Hebrew ill-treated by the Egyptian.

And if the cause of the war was the recovery of property, he may satisfy himself measure for measure in the same kind or in its vale in all justice, and if he wishes to use the authority of a minister of divine justice and judge human, he may, as such minister and judge, extend his hand further, penalizing and chastising his crime, without obligation or restitution, like the judge who hangs a man because he stole some maravedís or reales.*

If the cause of the war is the punishment of delinquents and those guilty, they and their goods remain at his will and mercy, according to the just laws of his kingdom and republic, if they are his subjects; and if they should not be, he may reduce them to live according to the law divine and natural by all the methods and means which in justice and reason may seem proper to him, overcoming all hindrances which may be offered to this, of whatever sort they may be, these being such that they may disturb the just result which he intends.

And, finally, if the cause is universal peace, either of his kingdom or republic, he may much more justly wage the aforesaid war and destroy all impediments that may disturb the aforesaid peace, until effectually securing it, and, having secured it, he should not make war further, because the act of war is not an act of choice and will

*_Maravedís_ and _reales_ were Spanish units of money. One _real_ equaled thirty-four _maravedí_.

be of just occasion and necessity, and so he should seek peace before he begins it if he makes war only for it. . . . Notwithstanding that it is thus true that, discounting the necessity or manifest peril of death, or victory being impossible in any other way, or by a just sentence of a competent judge, in such case, it is not the fault of the slayers, who as ministers of divine justice execute, but of the dead who, as culprits, deserved it. And this is my opinion, lacking a better one.

Fray Alonso Martínez, Apostolic Comissary.

This was agreed to and signed by all the other Fathers.

With whose opinions well-founded
On many texts, laws, and places
In holy Scripture, then the Governor,
Seeing how all these things agreed
Upon the case and doubts that he had wished
To be proposed to them, he wished
To close the case and give sentence,
Ordering war, with fire and blood,
Proclaimed against the fort of Acoma . . .

Central Themes

Indigenous people, state formation, the northern frontier, land and labor, religion

Suggested Reading

Auerbach, Jerold S. *Explorers in Eden: Pueblo Indians and the Promised Land.* Albuquerque: University of New Mexico Press, 2006.

Gutiérrez, Ramón A. *When Jesus Came, the Corn Mothers Went Away: Marriage, Sexuality, and Power in New Mexico, 1500–1846.* Stanford, CA: Stanford University Press, 1991.

Leal, Luis. "The First American Epic: Villagra's History of New Mexico." *In Paso por Aqui: Critical Essays on the New Mexican Literary Tradition, 1542–1988,* ed. Erlinda Gonzales Berry. Albuquerque: University of New Mexico Press, 1989.

Related Sources

10. Hernán Cortés and Moteucçoma Meet, According to a Spanish Conqueror (1568)
13. Acazitli of Tlalmanalco: Nahua Conqueror on the Mesoamerican Frontier (1541)
18. Father Fernández Attempts to Convert the Seris of Sonora Single-handedly (1679)
28. Indigenous Revolt in California (1737)

15. The Tlaxcaltecas Stage a Christian Pageant, "Like Heaven on Earth" (1538)*

The Franciscan brother Toribio de Benavente (c. 1490–1569) arrived in Mexico-Tenochtitlan in 1524 and participated in the first organized conversion effort of indigenous people in mainland Latin America. Soon the Franciscans had established a convent in Tlaxcala, the Nahua city-state that had allied itself with Hernán Cortés and supplied thousands of indigenous warriors and retainers to the war against Tenochtitlan. Called by the Nahuas "Motolinía" ("impoverished"), and a gifted speaker of Nahuatl, he became the guardian of the Franciscan convent at Tlaxcala from 1536 to 1542. Fray Toribio was a keen observer of indigenous cultures and a chronicler of the Franciscans' missions. Between 1536 and 1539, controversy within the Catholic Church raged over the appropriateness of the Franciscans' mass baptisms in places like Tlaxcala, and the influence of the competing Dominican Order increased in New Spain. Motolinía was a millenarian, believing that the mass conversions were the prelude to the Second Coming. Belief in Providence prompted the friar to report enthusiastically and hopefully on the Nahuas' desire to be good Christians. The Nahua leaders of Tlaxcala would certainly project this image during the sixteenth century because it helped to bolster their already elevated status due to their assistance in the conquest of Tenochtitlan.

In this primary source, Motolinía describes a massive Corpus Christi celebration of the Eucharist in which the Nahuas of Tlaxcala adorned the parade route with an amazing number of flowers and triumphal arches over the roads. Motolinía's full account of the festival of 1538 includes both the descriptive letter included here and a second description by an anonymous friar of Tlaxcala, which Motolinía quoted in its entirety. The anonymous author's account, not included here, emphasized that the nature scene was intended to depict the Garden of Eden and the snakes, the devil, and sin. Motolinía does not mention that the scene was supposed to represent the Garden in his description but instead focuses on the novelty of the wondrous ingenuity of the Indians' tableau.

Does Motolinía provide insight into the Indians' understanding or agenda for the festival, which may not be Christian- or European-influenced? Given the Tlaxcaltecas' belief that they were the descendants of hunting-gathering Chichimecas from the Seven Caves, what other purposes would this tableau have had other than to portray a scene from the Bible (Source 4)? In comparison to New Mexico, Tlaxcala was a raving success for the Franciscans. What historical factors may have facilitated the Tlaxcaltecas' relatively easy conversion to Christianity? Why would religious festivals, pageants, and processions be effective ways of converting the indigenous people of central Mexico?

---

*Fray Toribio de Benavente (Motolinía), "Historia de los Indios de Nueva España," in Joaquin García Icazbalceta, *Coleccion de documentos para la historia de México* (Mexico, 1858; reprint, Nendeln, Liechtenstein: Kraus Reprint, 1971), pp. 79–86. Excerpt translated by the editors.

On the Festivals of Corpus Christi and San Juan That They Celebrated in Tlaxcala in the Year 1538

When the Holy Day of Corpus Christi arrived in the year 1538, the Tlaxcaltecas staged a very solemn festival that merits being memorialized because I believe that if the Pope and Emperor with their courts had attended, they would have been much pleased to see it. Although there were no precious jewels and no brocades, there were other decorations that were fine to see, especially the flowers and roses that God created in the trees and in the fields—so much so that it was pleasing and worth note that a people who until now were taken for bestial, would know how to do such things.

The procession of the Most Holy Sacrament went along with many crosses and saints on portable platforms. The arms of the crosses and the adornments of the saints' platforms were made completely of gold and plumes, and so were the saints' images themselves, and they were so finely worked that people in Spain would have held them in higher esteem than those of brocade. There were many saints' banners. There were twelve Apostles, each dressed with their insignias. Many of the people who accompanied the procession carried lit candles in their hands. The whole route was covered in sedge, bulrushes, and flowers, and at one point, there were people who went about tossing roses and carnations the whole time. There were all kinds of dances that delighted the people in the procession. All along the route, one could stop at chapels with altars and beautifully adorned altarpieces from which came many singers who were singing and dancing in front of the Most Holy Sacrament. There were ten large triumphal arches that were delicately constructed. There was even more to see and to notice all along the street, such as, they had divided the street along its length in the figure of the three naves of a church. In the middle, there was a space twenty feet wide, and through this space passed the Most Holy Sacrament and ministers, and crosses, and all the pomp of the procession. All the people, who were not a small number in this city and province, walked along on the other two sides that were each fifteen feet wide. This space was created by some dividing arches that had openings of nine feet. To the amazement and admiration of three Spaniards and many others in attendance who counted them, there were a total of 1,068 of these arches. The arches were completely covered in roses and flowers of every color and style, and they estimated that each arch had a load and a half of roses—understood as the load of the Indians. They estimated a total of 2,000 loads of roses for all the chapels, for all the people to hold in their hands, and the triumphal arches, which included another 66 little arches. About one fifth of them were carnations which originated in Castile, and had multiplied in such an astounding manner, that it is incredible. The groves here are much larger than those in Spain and the flower-growing season lasts year-round. There were 1,000 round shields which were woven from flowers and distributed among the arches. And the other arches did not have shields but, instead, there were great flower designs assembled like the domes of onion skins, rounded and so finely made that they shined. There was so much more that one could not count it all.

There was another thing that was amazing to see. In each of the four corners or turns of the route, they had made a mountain—and each one a great tall rock. Down below they had created a meadow with patches of grass and flowers and everything else that is found in a wild field. The mountain and the rock [were] so natural that it was as though they had originated there. It was an amazing thing to see because there were many trees—wild, fruit, and flowering—and mushrooms, funguses, and mosses, which grow on mountain trees, in the rocks, and in old split trees. In some places it was like bushy thickets and in others it was thin. In the trees there were many birds, great and small. There were falcons, crows, and owls. In the rest of the woodlands there was the hunting of deer, hares, rabbits, jackals, and very many snakes.* These were tamed and defanged because most of them were a type of viper, which were as long as a fathom [six feet] and as thick as a man's arm at the wrist. The Indians take them in their hands, as one would do with birds, because they have an herb that tranquilizes or numbs the ferocious and poisonous ones. This substance is also medicinal for many things; it is an herb called *picietl.*** So that nothing would diminish the total naturalism, there were hunters very well-hidden in the mountains with bows and arrows. Those that normally play this role are from another language-group, and because they inhabit the mountains, they are great hunters. In order to see these hunters it was necessary to look very closely because they were so invisible behind all the branches and foliage of the trees; because they were so well-hidden, the hunted animals easily came right to their feet. They made many hand signals before they fired so that they could carefully select which of the unsuspecting animals they would hit.

This was the first day that the Tlaxcaltecas brought out their coat of arms, which the Emperor gave them when this *pueblo* [town] was designated as a city, which no other pueblo of Indians had been granted. You justifiably granted this because they were a great help to Don Hernando Cortés when he won these lands for Your Majesty. They had their coat of arms on flags, which also included the coat of arms of the Emperor, which they raised into the air on a very high pole. I was astonished, wondering where they could have found a pole that was so tall and slender. These banners were placed on the rooftops of the buildings of their municipal council because this is where they could be the highest. The procession left from the choir and organ chapel with many singers and to the music of flutes in concert with the chorus, trumpets, drums, and large and small bells. All of this was played together at the entrance and exit of the church which made it seem all the more like heaven on earth.

---

*Since jackals are not indigenous to the Americas, the animals were most likely coyotes.

***Picietl* is the Nahuatl word for tobacco.

Central Themes

Indigenous people, urban life, popular culture, religion

Suggested Reading

Curcio, Linda Ann. *The Great Festivals of Colonial Mexico City: Performing Power and Identity.* Albuquerque: University of New Mexico Press, 2004.

Diaz Balsera, Viviana. *The Pyramid Under the Cross: Franciscan Discourses of Evangelization and the Nahua Christian Subject in Sixteenth-Century Mexico.* Tucson: University of Arizona Press, 2005.

Nesvig, Martin Austin. *Local Religion in Colonial Mexico.* Albuquerque: University of New Mexico Press, 2006.

Related Sources

4. The Origin of the Nahuas and the Birth of the Fifth Sun (1596)
14. Poetic Attempts to Justify the Conquest of Acoma, New Mexico (1610)
16. The Spiritual Conquest: The Trial of Don Carlos Chichimecatecotl of Texcoco (1539)
20. Chimalpahin: Indigenous Chronicler of His Time (1611–1613)
24. The Persistence of Indigenous Idolatry (1656)
25. Afro-Mexicans, Mestizos, and Catholicism (1672)

16. The Spiritual Conquest: The Trial of Don Carlos Chichimecatecotl of Texcoco (1539)*

The Inquisition trial against Don Carlos Chichimecatecotl, the "Chichimeca Lord" of Texcoco, represents a pivotal moment in the early solidification of Spanish religious and political authority eighteen years after the fall of Tenochtitlan to Cortés. Inquisition procedures began at the church of Santiago Tlatelolco on June 2, 1539, when Francisco Maldonado from the *altepetl* (sovereign ethnic state) of Chiconautla secretly denounced Don Carlos in the Nahuatl language before Franciscan friars Juan de Zumárraga, first Bishop of Mexico, and two of the most capable Spanish translators of Nahuatl, Alonso de Molina and Bernardino de Sahagún. This selection contains Francisco's elaboration of his first testimony, which decided the fate of Don Carlos because it seemed to offer evidence of the native lord's outright rebellion against Spanish authority. Francisco was a zealous convert to the new faith of Christianity and brother of Don Alonso, the Lord of Chiconautla. The young catechist had trained at the College of Santa Cruz Tlatelolco and then returned to

---

*"*Proceso inquisitorial de cacique de Tetzcoco,*" in *Publicaciones del Archivo de Nación,* vol. 1 (Mexico: Eusebio Gómez de la Puente, 1910), pp. 22–25, 39–44. Excerpt translated by the editors.

his town to teach his people how to stage processions where they would pray to God, instead of Tlaloc, the rain god, to bring rain. Francisco provided the most damning testimony because he recounted how Don Carlos had made a long anti-Christian harangue at a meeting of indigenous nobles at Don Alonso's house. Don Carlos angrily denounced the Franciscan friars and their religion, directing his ire toward the young upstart Francisco. The Lord of Texcoco was personally offended by Francisco and his father's sympathies with the Spanish friars because Don Alonso was married to his half-sister—in the following testimony, he refers to Don Alonso as "brother."

Out of twenty-seven individuals prosecuted by Juan de Zumárraga, Don Carlos was the only one to be executed—burned at the stake for the crime of heretical dogmatism and for trying to convert people back to worshiping Tlaloc. Don Carlos defended himself by saying that he was innocent and had been denounced for political reasons because people, including some of his family members, questioned his legitimacy as Lord of Texcoco. Professor Patricia Lopes Don believes that, while other witnesses corroborated some of Don Carlos's comments, he was telling the truth when he said that the witnesses were politically motivated. Indeed, since before the Conquest, succession to the throne in Texcoco had been contentious. Kings and lords practiced polygamy and often had concubines. In Texcoco, kings always selected a son whose mother had the best social status—in this case, a mother who was a member of the Mexica royal family of Tenochtitlan. Since Nezahualcoyotl ascended the throne in 1427, the kings of Texcoco had always been sons of Mexica royal mothers. Nezahualcoyotl's son Nezahualpilli, who ruled from 1471 to 1515, had forty sons, several of whom were the children of some of Moteucçoma's sisters. But the Lord of Texcoco did not designate a successor before he died. During the Conquest, resentment over succession motivated some of Texcoco's nobility to ally with Hernán Cortés, and some with Moteucçoma—who had forced Texcoco to make his unpopular nephew Lord of Texcoco. After several rulers and dynastic struggles, Don Carlos was slated to become the next Lord of Texcoco. Don Carlos (born Ometochtli around 1505) was the son of a low-status concubine and King Nezahualpilli. Don Pedro, who was Lord of Texcoco in the 1530s, selected his half-brother, Don Carlos, to be his successor and broke with the tradition of appointing a male family member whose mother was Mexica. Therefore, most of the nobility of Texcoco viewed Don Carlos as an illegitimate heir, although Don Pedro worked hard to groom Don Carlos and make him more acceptable before he died. When Don Pedro died in the spring of 1539, Carlos took power. Almost immediately thereafter, people from Chiconautla, an altepetl subject to the jurisdiction of Texcoco, came forward to denounce Don Carlos before the Inquisition.

Don Carlos lost his life and a major piece of his family's hereditary estate, including a palace, which the Inquisition confiscated and sold to a Spaniard (Source 17). After Don Carlos's execution, Zumárraga was himself condemned. The Royal Council of the Indies in Spain stripped him of his position as an Inquisition official because of his harsh handling of this and other Inquisition cases against indigenous people. Zumárraga and other Franciscans' aggressive retribution against alleged idolaters contributed to the crown's decision to remove all indigenous people from the jurisdiction of the Regular Inquisition in 1571.

Francisco's testimony was surely political, and he and all the other witnesses made their statements in the charged and dangerous environment of the Inquisition. Suspiciously, Francisco does not testify that Don Carlos talked about Tlaloc, and the first half of the Inquisition file goes into great detail about evidence of Tlaloc worship. Whether or not Don Carlos actually said all the things that the indigenous nobles claimed he did, the words would still be subversive to the Spaniards. Why? What do Francisco's allegations and the seizure of Don Carlos's property tell us about the political choices that Post-Conquest indigenous nobility in the new Spanish order were forced to make? If Francisco was putting words in Don Carlos's mouth, he understood enough about the Spaniards to know what would alarm them. Is this a document best suited to inform us about the experience of an indigenous Christian convert who has accepted Spanish culture and authority as legitimate? Or is this best used to explain why some rebellious indigenous leaders refused to accept Spanish authority as legitimate?

Inquisition Proceedings Against a Cacique of Texcoco

10. That Which Was Declared with Regard to the Cult of the God Tlaloc

. . . *Gobernador* [indigenous governor] Don Lorenzo, Don Francisco, Don Hernando, and Don Lorenzo, *principales* [nobles] of the aforementioned *pueblo* [town] of Texcoco, said that, just as they have said in the past, when it was not raining and when there was a lack of water, they heard tell of how on a mountain called Tlalocatepetl, they made sacrifices that were offered to the god of water, known as Tlaloc; and they had heard news that in ancient times Tlaloc had been customarily on this mountain where everyone was accustomed to coming for water and to making offerings to this idol, which was one of the most ancient in all the land; in the time of the ancient wars among Guaxocingo, Mexico, Tlaxcala, and Texcoco, those from Guaxocingo would smash the Tlaloc idol on the mountain in order to anger the Mexicans; and an uncle of Montezuma who was called Auizoca, being Lord of Mexico, had ordered that the Tlaloc idol, which Guaxocingo smashed, be placed in the sierra and be fixed; and after that, they once again held it in high esteem and reverence because it was very ancient and from time immemorial it had been part of this sierra and they believed that this idol should always have been there. And with this information they put out a search and went all over the sierra looking for it until they found it buried and they pulled it out and it was fixed and returned to form with gold and copper wires and the pieces were pulled together where it appeared to be broken. And later before the most holy gentlemen they displayed a big piece of wood with wire around it that they said had been attached to the idol. And they also sent seven little round bars of gold, more or less the size of one's palm in length, which they claimed had been the gold wire with which the idol was assembled. And they said that they had melted down and made these seven little bars of gold; and then they showed three little bars of copper that they said were melted down from the same [idol]. They also presented a green jade stone with a figure in one part that they said was the sixth day-count, which they said the idol had on its forehead; and when, later, they took possession of the idol they stationed guards to see if they would come to him and make offerings and to find out who came and where they were from. And two or three times they found papers with fresh blood, copal incense, veils, small beads and other things for sacrifices. And they could not figure out who was doing it because the guards felt that they were not making the offerings where the idol usually was but instead down below at the foot of the sierra towards Guaxocingo. And there in a place towards Guaxocingo they found much fresh blood and it appeared, from the blood and the face [of the body], that some little boy had recently been sacrificed. The blood, the face, the papers, and the sacrifices that they found and took from the said sierra, are the same types of things found in Guaxocingo because, as everyone knows, each province had its own way of making sacrifices and offerings and had their distinct signs. Because of this they know that people from Guaxocingo are responsible. Thus they informed Your Lordship and surrendered the jade stone, the wire, the 3 bars of copper, and the 7 bars of gold, which are fat and are more or less one *vara* [yard] high, round and one span in length. . . .

11. The Seizure of the Goods of Don Carlos

And following the aforementioned, on this same day, His Most Reverent Lordship said that the goods of the said Don Carlos have been seized, including the houses of residence where until now he has been living, the country estate that is nearby adjoining it, and the other houses where they found the idols, all of which Don Lorenzo, *Gobernador,* has turned over for seizure.

24. The Elaboration of the Denunciation That Francisco Maldonado Made

And following the aforementioned, on the 11th of July in the year 1539, before me, the Secretary, Your Most Reverend Lordship, being in the pueblo of Chiconautla, Francisco, Indian, native to this pueblo, was made to appear, and he told all he knows and gave his testimony in the language of the Indians regarding what he knew of the matter of Don Carlos Chichimecatecotl of Texcoco. And because this is in their local language, he requested that Father Juan González, the cleric who was present, speak and translate what he knew about the case, and that he read what was written in his language, which was contained in this legal document.* Therefore, the said Francisco, having legally sworn to his testimony in this document, translated by Juan González, said the following: as he has said in other statements in Mexico before Your Lordship, Don Carlos came to the pueblo of Chiconautla at the beginning of this past June. It was the Holy Day of the Trinity during which the required fasting and spiritual exercises must be made in this pueblo the Monday prior [to the Holy Day of Trinity]. Don Carlos was annoyed and was visibly angry about this, saying that this was not a universal requirement. The following Tuesday morning, the town of Chiconautla staged a procession, and Don Carlos, being in town, did not go to the church or the procession but stayed in the inn, sulking and being angry, being dissatisfied with those who participated in the procession. And all the prominent Indians and the *macehuales* [Indian commoners] of the pueblo went to the procession singing their praises to God, begging that he would have mercy on their souls, and later that same day in the evening after the sun had set, Don Carlos said to the witness: "Francisco, come here and listen up, brother. Would you by chance, be asking, 'What is Don Carlos doing?' Tomorrow I will leave for Texcoco. Look, when my grandfather Nezahualcoyotl and my father Nezahualpilli died they did not command us, nor exhort anyone that they must attend. Understand, brother, that my grandfather and my father examined everything, front to back; as is said, they knew the past and what was to come, and they knew what must be done a long time ago; one did what parents say and prophets exhorted. Truly, I tell you that my grandfather and father were prophets and they knew what one was supposed to do, and so one did it. And so, brother, understand me, that no one should take to heart this law of God and Divinity." It was like he was saying that no one should love God or his Law. He said: "What is this Divinity, what is it like, and where did it come from? What is it that you teach and what have you exhorted?" He addressed the witness, saying that it was a sin to make old men and women and some of the noble Indians believe in God: "Brother, what have you been going around teaching and saying? There is nothing else to be said." And this is how he finished: "You all should get past this Law of God and that is that." And then he concluded: "So listen, brother, this I truly tell you. What is taught in the school is all a joke." It was as if he were saying this [teaching] would not prevail nor is it something that should be paid attention to. He then continued, saying: "Neither should you nor the others believe what is alleged to be the law. And regarding what you say and teach from your little papers and doctrine books. By chance is it true or already uncovered? There is nothing else like this. Satisfied, I believe with reason that you all accept and understand what parents say. Understand me, brother, that I have lived and traveled everywhere and have held dear the words of my parents and grandfather. So listen, brother, to what our parents and grandparents said when they died, that truly, their beloved gods were made in heaven and in the earth, as such, brother, we should only follow what our grandparents and our parents held true and said when they died. Listen, brother, Francisco, what do the parents say? What do they say to us? What do you all understand? Look how the friars and the parish priests all have their own ways of doing

*The document does not exist in the original.

penance. Look how the Franciscan friars have a type of doctrine, a way of living, styles of dress, and prayer. As everyone can see, the Augustinians, the Dominicans, and the priests each have different ways of doing things. It was the same for those who observed our gods. People from Mexico had a style of dress, prayer, and making offerings that was different from what people did in other pueblos. In each pueblo they had a way of making sacrifices and their own manner of prayer and making offerings. Just like the friars and priests, no one did the same thing as the other. We should follow this just as our ancestors followed this. In the manner that they lived, we should live. Parents teach and preach this to us so that we will understand; each one decides to follow the law, customs, and ceremonies that he wants to. Brother, all I am saying is that maybe you will all understand this but perhaps you will not accept what I say. Know that if, by chance, the words of my father, grandfather, and ancestors conformed to the word of God, then I would have also done as you do! However, it does not conform with what we understand the religious fathers preach to us. Those who carry out their duty would insist that they do not have women and scorn the things of the world and women. It is about time that those religious fathers did as they say. It is their duty, but not ours. What have you been going around saying and teaching? Relax. Calm down now that our nephews are born. The sons of Don Alonso, Tomás and Diego, will, as boys, teach this to others. What is it that you teach, brother, and what is it you go around preaching? If the Viceroy, Bishop, or Provincial orders something, then it is not a problem if you promote it very much. Listen, my nephew Lorenzo de Luna does not understand what I know is said. In another time, no one made accusations against my grandfather, my father, Moctezuma, or the Lord of Tacuba and no one scolded him"— [Don Carlos] made [Francisco] understand that he was burdening him with these things and making him feel sorry for himself for knowing them, so that no one might have been accused of stepping out of line or forcing his hand—this is how [Francisco] understood what [Don Carlos] declared. [Don Carlos] said the same things to them: "And you, what do you want to do and what do you say about this? Is it true that you say this or not? Look at what you are prohibited, what you are reprimanded for, what you are forbidden, and what you are scolded for, brother. Because you are my nephew, you do not have to do what the Viceroy, the Bishop, or the Provincial says, nor the curates who they appoint. I, also, was raised in the church and in the house of God as you were, but I do not live like you, nor should I. What more do you want? Don't the people of Chiconautla fear and obey you completely? Don't you have to eat and to drink? What more do you want? What are you going around saying these things for? Because it is not our duty to do what you do. According to what our ancestors taught and said it is not good to know the lives of others or to be like the others who are accustomed to seriousness and seclusion without authority over people of low social standing. Brother, what harm do women and wine do to men? Maybe the Christians do not have many women and so get drunk if the religious fathers do not intervene. Thus, what these fathers make us do is not our duty and this law should not impede anyone from doing what he wants to do. We should abandon and throw from our shoulders what they tell us: Oh, brother, now that you have understood me, before my brother Don Alonso, I prohibit and forbid you! Obey, I say to them, and control what you say: nephew Don Alonso, let there be no dissent among us. We should flee from the religious fathers and we should do as our ancestors did and not as those who impede us would want us to do. In the times of the ancestors, the macehuales did not sit on the mats of lords or on fancy chairs, but nowadays one does and says whatever he wants. It was not like anyone could stop us or force our hand when we would want to do something. But instead, we should eat, drink, take pleasure, and get drunk as we used to do. Take a look at yourself and your nephew Francisco, Señor. Understand and comply with my words, which are also those of the Lord of Mexico, Yoanizi and my nephew the Lord of Tacuba, Tezapilli. He should tremble before them and know that if he did something else that it would cost him dearly and it could cost him his life." This is what the witness understood him to say. And after he had made this speech, Don Carlos said with a great sigh: "Who are these people that would destroy us, they who disturb and live among us, who burden us and subjugate us? Listen there! This is what I believe here. The Lord of Mexico, Yoanizi, maintains this and so does my nephew Tezapilli, Lord of Tacuba, and there is also Tl[a]cahepantli, Lord of Tula. We are all considered equals and in agreement. We have no other equals and this is our land, our hacienda, our treasure, and our possession. This is our ancestral domain and our holding. And if anyone wants to do or say otherwise, we will laugh in his face. Oh brothers, I am very angry and emotional! Sometimes my nephews, the lords, and I talk about this, [saying,] who dares come here to seize, command, and judge us? He is not a relative or of our blood. This one who claims to be an equal thinks that this sentiment is hollow and that he could know it. This much is true: no one should mock us because our nephews and brothers are lords. Oh brothers! No one is on the same level as those liars, nor should they be. Nor should they join those who obey and follow our enemies." According to the witness, Don Carlos said all of this in his speech in the presence of the witness, Don Alonso, Lord of Chiconautla, Cristóbal, Indian commoner, resident of Chiconautla, two prominent Indians of Texcoco, called Zacanpatl and Coaunochitlli, and another Indian commoner named Poyoma from Texcoco and Acanauacatl, and a prominent Indian of Chiconautla. All of the above named were scandalized by what Don Carlos said in his speech and attest that this is true. Asked if he had hatred or rancor against Don Carlos or if he is being coerced to testify, he [the witness] said that he does not testify out of bad intentions, but only because it is the truth and he wants to unburden his conscience for the love of Our Lord God. And the witness believes that his testimony about Don Carlos will be corroborated in other testimonies and that it was God's will that he come forward to say these things so that they would be revealed. In Mexico, he states, before Our Most Reverend Lordship, that all that his testimony contains in this proceeding is true and discharged in secret according to procedure before his Lordship, the said Francisco, and abovementioned interpreter.

Signed [in rubrics], Fray Juan, Bishop of Mexico,
Juan González, Miguel López, Francisco Maldonado

Central Themes

Indigenous people, state formation, religion

Suggested Reading

Greenleaf, Richard. "The Inquisition and the Indians of New Spain: A Study in Jurisdictional Confusion." *Americas: A Quarterly Review of Latin American Cultural History* 22, no. 2 (July 1966): 181–196.

Gruzinski, Serge. *Man-Gods in the Mexican Highlands: Indian Power and Colonial Society, 1520–1800,* trans. Eileen Corrigan. Stanford, CA: Stanford University Press, 1989.

Lopes Don, Patricia. "The 1539 Inquisition Trial of Don Carlos of Texcoco in Early Mexico." *Hispanic American Historical Review* 88, no. 4 (November 2008): 573–606.

Ricard, Robert. *The Spiritual Conquest of Mexico: An Essay on the Apostolate and the Evangelization Methods of the Mendicant Orders in New Spain, 1523–1572,* trans. Lesley Byrd Simpson. Berkeley: University of California Press, 1966.

Related Sources

1. Copán and Teotihuacan: Shared Culture Across a Great Distance (200–900 CE)
4. The Origin of the Nahuas and the Birth of the Fifth Sun (1596)
17. The Inquisition Seizes Don Carlos's Estate: The Oztoticpac Map (1540)
20. Chimalpahin: Indigenous Chronicler of His Time (1611–1613)
21. The Creation of Religious Conformity (the Early Eighteenth Century)
24. The Persistence of Indigenous Idolatry (1656)

17. The Inquisition Seizes Don Carlos's Estate: The Oztoticpac Map (1540)

During the Inquisition's proceedings against Don Carlos Chichimecatecotl, Lord of Texcoco, in 1539, the court seized the accused idolater's property, including his estate of Oztoticpac. This fascinating indigenous map of the estate is believed to have been presented as legal evidence in the land dispute cases that resulted from Don Carlos's execution and were probably initiated by Don Carlos's family. Registering a total of seventy-five parcels of land, it is a rare historical source that documents Nahua property ownership during the Conquest period. It shows evidence of four different types of Nahua land tenure that were in existence during Pre-Conquest times, and it also documents changes in property ownership and the influence of new European foods and business. How were disputes over land related to the indigenous elite's loss of political power over their populations with the Spanish Conquest?

The map is organized into four quadrants. The top left is an illustration of the *tecpan,* the "lord's palace"—the seat of indigenous government and the residence of the *tlatoani,* the governor of the *altepetl* (sovereign ethnic state) of Texcoco. Don

Pedro Tetlahuehuetzquitzin had given his unpopular nephew Don Carlos the estate in order to raise Don Carlos's social status while he groomed him for power. But Don Carlos was tlatoani of Texcoco for only a few months when the Inquisition tried and convicted him. When Inquisition officials confiscated Don Carlos's estate, they sold the tecpan to a Spaniard, Alonso de Contreras. Don Carlos's family disputed the sale in court. They argued that, as was customary, ruling lords had the use of the palace and palace lands, but that they were considered patrimony to be handed down to the next lord upon assuming rule and could not be bought and sold. We see a disruption here of one of the two traditional Pre-Conquest kinds of public landownership: lands that the commoners were required to work to support the government in the palace. A second type of communal land worked by commoners, temple-land, had disappeared when the Spaniards destroyed the temples.

On the lower left are apple, peach, pear, quince, and pomegranate trees and grape vines, none of which were native to the Americas. Don Carlos had entered into a joint business venture with a Spaniard named Pedro Vásquez de Vergara to grow fruit trees and grapevines, some of which were grafted onto Carlos's preexisting native trees. These trees are pictured in the lower left-hand quadrant. Many of these trees and vines were planted on the land owned by the lord and some on the farmers' plots pictured in the right half of the map. In 1540, Pedro Vásquez de Vergara filed a lawsuit to recover his trees from the Inquisition, which was about to sell them to Alonso de Contreras.

The right side of the map features land allotments in various rectangular shapes and sizes. Boundary lines connecting four tree glyphs designate the Oztoticpac lands. The largest single section of land pictured on the top right of the quadrant is Don Carlos's privately owned estate; it appears that leaders in the Pre-Conquest times owned private property. Within the Oztoticpac boundary, however, are two other types of landholding: land allotted to independent peasant farmers (*calpollali*) and land rented to tenant farmers. Adjoining Don Carlos's large block of land are ten long, thin rectangles that designate rental properties. To the right of these strips, you can see two lines of indigenous heads running vertically to indicate the ten renters.

Further below, another line of indigenous head glyphs registers forty-five Nahuas (each little flag above a head equals twenty). These forty-five commoners (*macehuales*) are holders of calpollali (*calpolli* land). Every Nahua altepetl was divided into administrative districts called *calpolli*. In principle, the calpollali belonged to the calpolli, the corporate entity, but the land was not worked in common. Indigenous officials allotted calpollali within their territories to individuals and their families in varying sizes according to status, but individuals retained land allotments throughout their lifetimes and left them to their heirs. For all intents and purposes, the Nahuas practiced private landholding. However, such a landholder retained the right to hold the land only if he or she worked it. If left uncultivated, the lord or calpolli leader allotted the land to a landless resident or a newly married couple who would put it to good use. This practice of landownership is sometimes called "usufruct" rights to hold the land; according to the sixteenth-century Bishop of the Yucatán, Diego de Landa, this form of landownership existed among the Mayas (Source 8). The leaders distributed property to the landless not only out of a sense of communal duty to all members of the district but also because they wanted to collect a tax in agricultural produce or cotton cloth from the landholders.

In the early sixteenth century, these calpolli land allotments could not be bought and sold, but depopulation from European smallpox and measles severely disrupted the re-allotment system. Lands remained vacant as many calpolli residents died off. Indigenous leaders resorted to selling or renting these lands to Spaniards so that they could make their tribute tax payments to their new imperial overlord, the Spanish crown.

Differences in wealth come clear in the map. The holders of calpollali had land allotments that were roughly twice the size of the renters' plots, and the private land of Don Carlos's family was thirty to forty times larger than the calpollali. The entire estate within the area marked by the four trees was surrounded by the lands that commoners owned. Some of the commoners' lands within Don Carlos's estate spill across the tree-designated boundary, which has led researchers to conclude that these were properties under dispute. Why might Don Carlos's execution have encouraged his neighbors to attempt to grab land? Or was it the other way around? Did the commoners have to defend their land against the encroachments of the nobility of Texcoco? If so, why? Could it have been a loss of authority over the commoners that brought about the execution of the Lord of Texcoco and made the commoners more aggressive in expropriating the land of the nobles?

Prior to recent research on land tenure in sixteenth-century Mexico, the popular notion was that indigenous people did not have private property and held land only in common. How does this document show a much more complex and complicated system? How did the administration and distribution of land to the common people give leaders power? Was the encroachment of the commoners on the estate of Don Carlos's family a sign that the calpolli farmers of Oztoticpac gained more power after the Spanish Conquest? How might depopulation have given the surviving calpolli farmers a new advantage in negotiating with their Nahua rulers over what the farmers gave them in tax and labor?

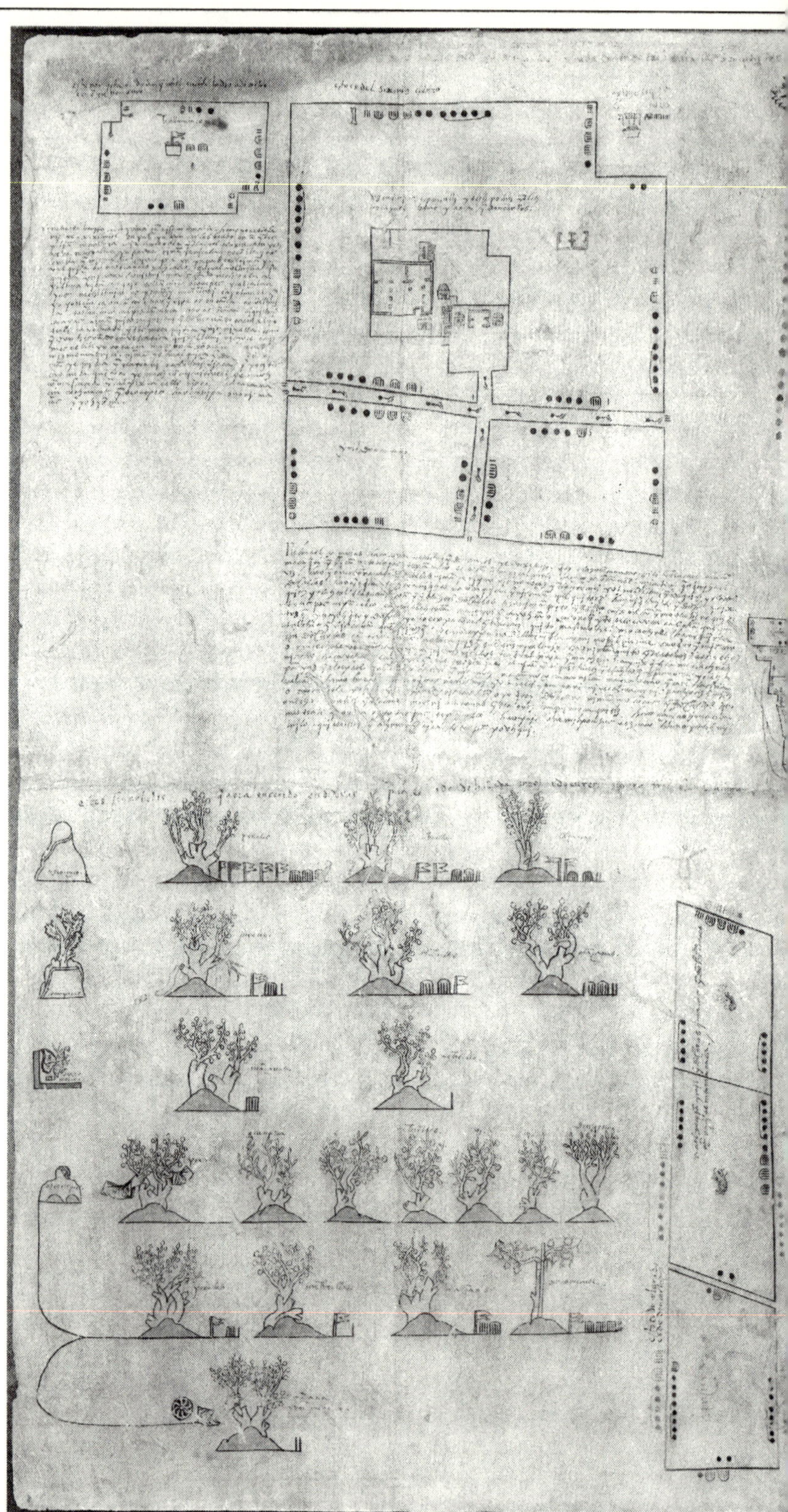

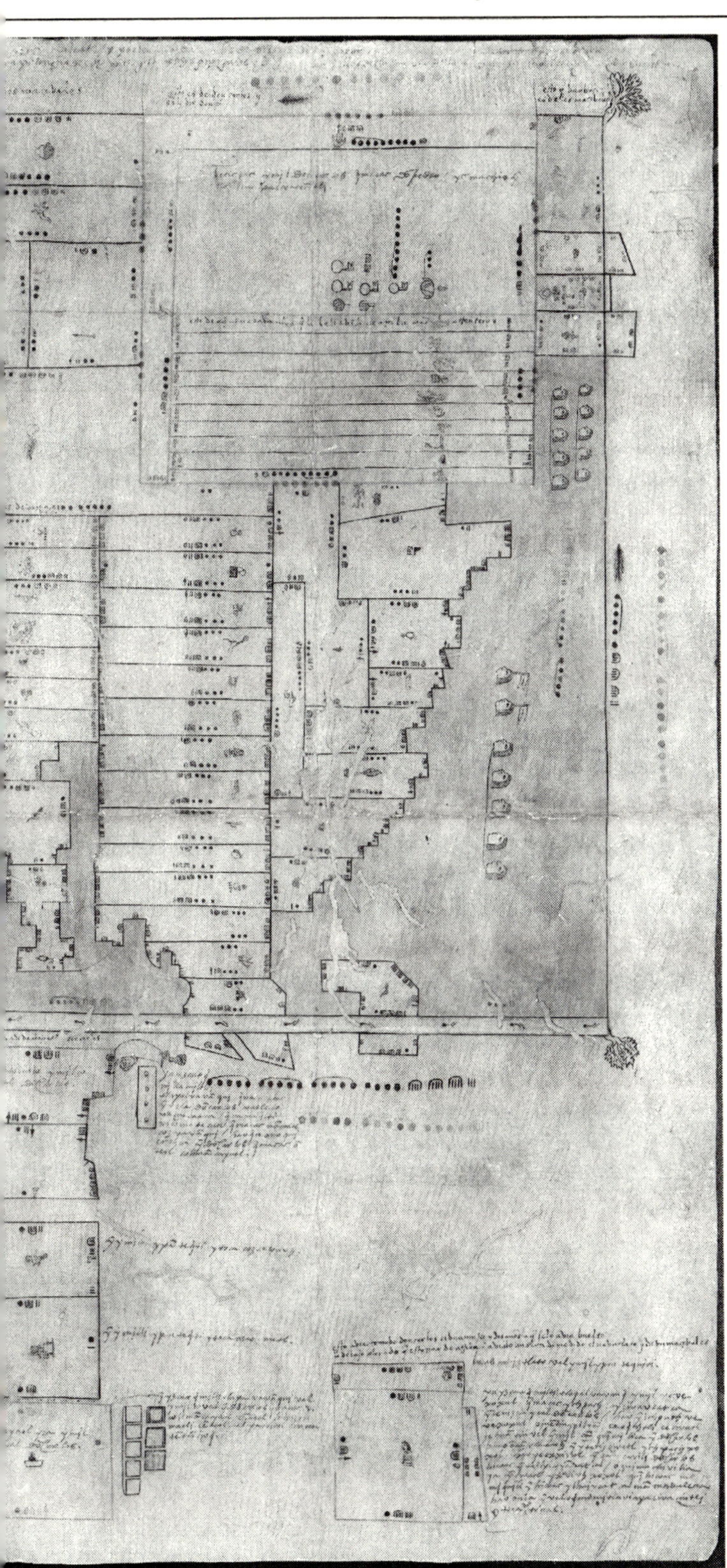

The Oztoticpac lands map of 1540
Courtesy of the Library of Congress.

Central Themes

Indigenous people, state formation, land and labor

Suggested Reading

Gibson, Charles. *The Aztecs Under Spanish Rule: A History of the Indians of the Valley of Mexico, 1519–1810.* Stanford, CA: Stanford University Press, 1964.

Harvey, H. R., ed. *Land and Politics in the Valley of Mexico: A Two-Thousand Year Perspective.* Albuquerque: University of New Mexico Press, 1991.

Lockhart, James. *The Nahuas After the Conquest: A Social and Cultural History of the Indians of Central Mexico, Sixteenth Through Eighteenth Centuries.* Stanford, CA: Stanford University Press, 1992.

Related Sources

7. The Mixtec Map of San Pedro Teozacoalco (1580)
8. The Urban Zoning of Maya Social Class in the Yucatán (1566)
16. The Spiritual Conquest: The Trial of Don Carlos Chichimecatecotl of Texcoco (1539)
40. The Mayas Make Their Caste War Demands (1850)

18. Father Fernández Attempts to Convert the Seris of Sonora Single-handedly (1679)*

Beyond the frontiers of the northern silver mining zone, the duty to spread Hispanic civilization and Christianity to the indigenous people fell mostly on the shoulders of the Franciscan and Jesuit religious orders, which ministered to the New Mexico and Río Grande region and to the northern Pacific Coast, respectively. Historians agree that the Society of Jesus, which started its conversion efforts in 1590, was completely unsuccessful in transforming the culture of the Seris (Comcáac) of the deserts of Sonora. Slowly making their way north from Sinoloa along the Gulf of California, they managed to convert the Yaquis and created a handful of viable settlements in the interior by the 1640s. When Father Fernández established the first mission to convert the Seris in Pópulo in 1679, it had already been thirty-four years since the first European, Father Andrés Pérez de Ribas, reported on these people (Source 9). Unlike the Yaquis, who lived in small, dispersed agricultural settlements and with whom the Jesuits had more success, the Seris did not farm at all. The Seris had to be settled in a *pueblo* (town), which they were forced to construct, and then encouraged to farm before any conversion would take place. The Seris

---

*Thomas Sheridan, ed., *Empire of Sand: The Seri Indians and the Struggle for Spanish Sonora, 1645–1803* (Tucson: University of Arizona Press, 1999), pp. 31–33.

thus experienced the missionary's main institution of conversion, the *reducción,* by which missionaries encouraged formerly dispersed bands to move to one dense settlement built around a mission compound where they could accept the salvation of their souls while remaining safe from indigenous enemies, Spanish settlers, and slave-hunters. In such concentrated zones, unfortunately, members of these communities ran a higher risk of catching contagious diseases and having their labor exploited by the priests who ran the missions.

Father Fernández wrote the following letter to his Provincial shortly after arriving in Pópulo in 1679. What evidence do you find here to support the assertion that the Jesuit missionaries were failing in their efforts to convert and settle the indigenous people? What challenges may have impeded Father Fernández's efforts? Analyze this document along with the previous one on the Seris (Source 9). How did the vast differences between Spanish and Seri societies make conversion difficult? Compare and contrast this source with Motolinía's description of the Corpus Christi pageant in Tlaxcala, the major Nahua town that dated back long before the Spanish Conquest (Source 15). How might some of the similarities between Spanish and core Mesoamerican societies have facilitated conversion in Nahua, Maya, and Mixtec areas?

Father Fernández's Letter

(Marginal note: the Seri language is the harshest and most difficult of all the missions, and until now no one has learned it. It has a rasping pronunciation [illegible phrase].)

My Father Provincial Tomás Altamirano:

May the Lord keep Your Reverence with the health and vitality that I wish for you. I received Your Reverence's [letter] and was overjoyed to have news of your [good] health. It is for His greater glory that Our Lord blesses Your Reverence with long life—and for [the glory] of the entire Company, with such a superior. Having given Your Reverence to us, God would not take you away but leaves you with us as our superior, to my consolation and everyone's—or so I ask of His Divine Majesty in my humble prayers and offerings. I esteem and cherish in my soul the favors and honors Your Reverence bestows upon me in your letter. Our Lord is to be the payment, for I can do nothing to repay Your Reverence for such love other than to constantly commend you to God and His mother, Mary, in my prayers and offerings.

Today I am in the district of Ures, and Father Francisco Xavier is at Bausacora [Baviácora],* assigned thus by Father Visitor Provincial Juan Ortiz Zapata. The reason for this change was the Seris' request that I minister to them, so that they might be

*Nuestra Señora de la Concepción de Baviácora was a *visita* of the mission of San Pedro de Aconchi along the Río Sonora. It was established for the Opata Indians in 1639. (A *visita* was a community that had no resident parish priest and was visited by a priest who administered Catholic rituals. *Ed.*)

baptized and establish their pueblo. I have done so. Proceeding with great joy in my soul to the valley previously called Horca, I came to Ures, and on Saturday, January 6, the day of the Holy Virgin Mary, I sang the first mass there. To ensure the success of the mission, I chose the Holy Virgin Mary as the patron saint of the Seris, and for this reason I have named the valley Nuestra Señora de Pópulo. It is through her blessed intercession that Our Lord has wished to bestow His loving kindness on such misguided souls who roamed the wilds and the pueblos, as these Seris did.

Those of the nation who are presently here are not many, but rather few in number. I have baptized more than 130, including young and old, and all the baptized and unbaptized live together in this valley. Some have already built their houses, and the rest are in the process of doing so. They have built me a small dwelling on the site. All have planted the corn I gave them, for in order to gain their goodwill, it was necessary to win them over by their mouths, and give them food. I have presented the Christian doctrine in the Seri language, teaching it to them word for word; and every day, in the morning and in the afternoon, they come together to recite it. On the days when I am with them, they come to hear mass, and little by little I am teaching them the ways of our holy faith and the things they must know for their salvation. I have instructed them in the devotion of the sacred rosary, to which end I have distributed rosaries among all the baptized, and every afternoon they gather to recite [the rosary] in their native tongue before an image of Our Lady. I recite in unison with them, the better to teach them to pray, and to move them closer to tender devotion toward the Holy Virgin. I often speak to them of the Holy Virgin, so that they will esteem her with great veneration and love.

It has been His Divine Majesty's will to take unto Himself and His Sacred kingdom seventeen of the baptized Seris: fourteen innocent children after they were baptized, two men, and one woman. One of the men died within three months of his baptism, and the other within eight days of being baptized. The woman who was in danger of death when I baptized her, died within an hour. This Seri woman sent for me and requested with great anxiety that I baptize her immediately, for she greatly desired it. I baptized her and she died within an hour. I am much consoled by Our Lord's having taken this Indian woman, who prepared herself so well for holy baptism.

This Valle de Nuestra Señora de Pópulo is ten leagues from Ures, which distance I traverse with no trouble. I travel to all the souls under my charge, attending to the children's catechism and teaching everyone the ways of our holy faith. In particular, I have instructed all those under my charge in the devotion of the sacred rosary of Holy Mary, distributing to them what rosaries I have. Every Saturday and Sunday the Pimas assemble in the church; I sing the *Salve [Regina]* for them, and then they recite the rosary to the Holy Virgin. Every night the pages and *officiales de casa* [gather] in the hall. I frequently have them make their confessions and receive communion, such as on the feast days of the Holy Virgin, together with the processions that are made on such days and on the high feast days of the year.

In this manner, I remain forever vigilant with all the souls in my charge. To do so well, I avail myself of the Holy Virgin, in whose sacred hands I place my life and all that is mine, and give thanks to the Lord, for He bestows everything—life, strength, and His grace. He has given me health, which remains at the service of Your Reverence. He has given me vitality and the strong desire to spend my life—and if I had them, all the [lives] in the world—in the conversion and salvation of souls. Thus, until my death, I can know no greater glory than to employ my life in the conversion of souls, and were it possible, as I wish for and beg of Our Lord, to shed my blood for He who shed His for the good of my soul. I have nothing further to tell Your Reverence, except that I implore you not to forget me in your sacred offerings, for I will achieve much through Your Reverence's prayers.

I am sending with the messenger this inkwell that I ordered made for Your Reverence. I had saved three bezoar stones* to send to Your Reverence, but my intention and desire was hampered by the coming of the bishop, to whom I presented them. All of Sonora is short of silver, so that there is no one purchasing provisions as before. For this reason, I am sending nothing to Your Reverence for powders. I shall be careful in the coming year and will always try to send Your Reverence some donation for the purchase of powders, and will also endeavor [to send] some bezoar stones.

May the Lord keep Your Reverence for His greater glory and that of the Company, and for my consolation. Ures, October 7, 1679.

Your Reverence's son and servant,
Juan Fernández
I would appreciate Your Reverence sending me
some rosaries with the messenger.

Central Themes

Indigenous people, state formation, the northern frontier, religion

Suggested Reading

Bowen, Thomas. *Unknown Island: Seri Indians, Europeans, and San Esteban Island in the Gulf of California.* Albuquerque: University of New Mexico Press, 2000.

Weber, David J. *Bárbaros: Spaniards and Their Savages in the Age of Enlightenment.* New Haven, CT: Yale University Press, 2005.

*Bezoars were hard gastric or intestinal masses or stones found in ruminants such as deer. They were considered antidotes to poison.

PART 3

The Consolidation of Colonial Government (1605–1692)

Mexico's colonial period is often ignored in conventional narratives of its history, a footnote sandwiched between the two dramatic tales that mark its beginning and its end—the Spanish Conquest and the independence wars. But Mexico's colonial history is worthy of considerable attention, both because it is inherently interesting and because Mexicans developed many of the economic and social practices that shape modern lives in this period. All of this book's major themes are featured in the following documents, but one central issue that unites them all is the state's ongoing project of consolidation over the diverse peoples who constituted colonial Mexican society and the related issue of the challenges presented by these peoples, both overtly and implicitly, to consolidation.

In the late sixteenth and seventeenth centuries, the Spanish crown modified and elaborated upon the governmental institutions it had established in the first decades after the Conquest. It oversaw transformations in the Viceroyalty's labor mechanisms as *hacendados* (owners of commercial estates) and mine owners moved from the *encomienda* (tribute labor) to the use of a centralized labor distribution system, the *repartimiento,* and from this to the expansion of the free labor force. In the wake of the decimation of the indigenous population, which reached its low point of 1 million in 1620, the colonial state provided a legal framework for Spaniards' incursions into indigenous-owned land, allowing for the expansion of the large estate. It also supported the expansion of the territory's valuable northern frontier and amassed considerable wealth from the taxes collected from the region's mineral wealth, which peaked in the early seventeenth century when Zacatecas was producing one-third of Mexico's silver and one-fifth of the total world silver supply (Source 19).

Our first two sections focused on the history of the indigenous populations of Pre-Columbian Mexico and on indigenous-European relations in the first century after Contact. Throughout the colonial period, indigenous people continued to play a central role in Mexico's history. Despite their decimation in successive waves of epidemics between 1520 and 1779 and the disruption and displacement of their communities, Nahuas, Mayas, Mixtecs, Zapotecs, and indigenous people from dozens of other cultures constituted Mexico's demographic majority throughout the colonial period. As Alonso de la Mota y Escobar, Bishop of the Diocese of Guadalajara, discusses in his description of the silver mining capital of Zacatecas, Indians constituted the most important labor force in the agricultural estates and silver mines that, beginning in the 1540s, generated the Viceroyalty's astonishing wealth (Source 19). They toiled alongside the 180,000 African slaves whom the Spanish imported in the sixteenth and seventeenth centuries to augment the indigenous workforce. "The Treatment of African Slaves" outlines the state's ordinances governing their lawful treatment and some of the mechanisms it established to prevent the Afro-Mexican population from mounting a large-scale rebellion (Source 23).

Mixed-race people also populated seventeenth-century Mexico's labor force. The first generation of *mestizos* (people of Spanish and Indian parentage) and *mulatos* (people of African and Spanish parentage) in Mexico began reaching maturity fifteen years after the Spanish Conquest of 1521. These groups began to represent a significant demographic in New Spain by the late sixteenth century. Some historians have estimated that by the mid-seventeenth century one-quarter of those living in New Spain were of mixed race.* Although mestizos and mulatos occasionally held elite positions in colonial Mexican society, they more commonly occupied "middling" social positions as small merchants or artisans, or else they formed part of the laboring classes. Whatever their economic position, mixed-race people had to contend with the Viceroyalty's racial ideology, which viewed whiteness as superior (sources 27 and 31).

As well as being an expression of genuine faith, Catholicism served as a venue through which such socially marginalized people—whether Indian, African, mixed-race, or plebeian Spanish—might enhance their social positions. One religious institution in which they did this, and one typical of baroque Mexico's popular culture, was the confraternity, or lay religious brotherhood (Source 25). Indigenous traditions also shaped Mexico's cultural life in the seventeenth century. The English Dominican Thomas Gage describes how Europeans in both the Old and New Worlds enthusiastically imbibed one indigenous foodstuff: chocolate (Source 22). Other indigenous products, such as maize, cochineal (a red dyestuff), and *pulque* (liquor fermented from the maguey cactus), also developed substantial markets, beyond their traditional indigenous communities in the expanding *criollo* (American-born Spaniard) and mixed-race sectors (Source 30).

Indigenous peoples' intellectual perspectives in the mid-colonial period are most explicitly expressed in the writings of the prolific Nahua historian Domingo de San Antón Muñón Chimalpahin Quauhtlehuanitzin (Source 20). As he discusses, indigenous Mexicans might sometimes have adopted and upheld Spanish institutions, including Catholicism, even more vigorously than did Europeans, but elements of Pre-Columbian life and religious thought also endured throughout the seventeenth century and beyond (Source 24). New Spain's viceregal court, pulpits, and elite salons were also enriched by the productions of *criollo* scholars, artists, and

---

*Gonzalo Aguirre Beltrán, *La población negra de México, 1519–1810: Estudio etnohistórico,* 2nd ed. (Mexico City: Fondo de Cultura Económica, 1972), p. 219.

theologians, most prominently the nun Sor Juana Inés de la Cruz (Source 26) and Carlos Sigüenza y Góngora (Source 27), who both studied Mexico's indigenous languages and history, among other topics. Both the increased consumption of New World products and the intellectual productions of Mexican scholars mark the growth of a cultural identity in the Viceroyalty that was distinctive from that of Spain.

As it had done a century earlier in Iberia, the Catholic monarchy ruling Mexico from afar attempted to use the Church's institutions—from the inquisitorial court to the local parish priest—as mechanisms of social stability and political uniformity. The religious practices that most threatened the colonial state and church—both imports from the Old World and creations of the New—are cataloged in the Inquisition's "General Edict of the Faith" (Source 21). But as Sigüenza y Góngora's description of the Mexico City uprising of 1692 attests, nearly two centuries after the Conquest, the Spanish crown and its elite allies continued to view Mexico's indigenous population as the greatest potential challenger to the *Pax Hispanica*—the colonial peace that largely characterized Spain's maintenance of stability and order over its far-flung empire (Source 27).

19. The Silver Mining City of Zacatecas (1605)*

This account of the northern silver mining city of Zacatecas by the Bishop of the Diocese of Guadalajara, Alonso de la Mota y Escobar, is extracted from his *Descripción Geográfica de los Reinos de Nueva Galicia, Nueva Vizcaya y Nuevo León,* written around 1605 and constituting the earliest description of the northern two-thirds of New Spain. At the turn of the seventeenth century, Mota y Escobar visited all the villages of his diocese to acquaint himself with his parishioners' needs and to familiarize himself with the territory in which they lived in preparation for answering the Spanish crown's geographical questionnaire, which generated the well-known *Relaciones Geográficas* of the same era. As well as relaying the practical information requested by the royal inventory, Mota y Escobar's work conveys in its tone some traces of the celebratory descriptions of the marvelous bounty of the New World's natural wealth found in the chronicles of his contemporaries and their forebearers, including the chronicles of Amerigo Vespucci.

The Spanish discovered silver in Zacatecas and the surrounding area in 1540. By the seventeenth century, the city had become the second-most important urban center in New Spain. This excerpt conveys the centrality of silver to the colonial economy, but it also reveals other aspects of seventeenth-century life. How did the development of the Zacatecas silver mines influence the city's urban, environmental, and political life? In what ways does the source show how indigenous peoples subsidized colonial rule? While we use the term "mercantilism" (economic development for the benefit of the empire) to describe the colonial economy, what insight does this document give us about the development of local economies in New Spain? What examples do we see of cultural change as part of economic and labor activity?

---

*Alonso de la Mota y Escobar, "Descripción de Nuestra Señora de los Zacatecas (s. xvii)," in Miguel León Portilla et al., eds., *Historia documental de México,* vol. 1 (Mexico: Universidad Nacional Autónoma de México, Instituto de Investigaciones Históricas, 1965), pp. 226–231. Excerpt translated by the editors. All footnotes have been added to the original.

Description of the City of Our Lady of Zacatecas

One of the things for which a city may be celebrated is the great amount of gold or silver it produces. Zacatecas is renowned for the unlimited quantity of silver that has been extracted from it and that continues to be extracted today. . . .

At the time of its discovery, there were many forests and woodlands in this rocky land, all of which have vanished, felled when smelting was initiated, so that now except for some little wild palms, no other trees remain. Firewood is very expensive in this city because it is brought in carts from eight and ten leagues away. In the time of the heathens, the whole mountain range and its woods were a famous preserve of deer, hares, rabbits, partridges and doves, none of which had an owner in the world. The lords and *caciques* [local native leaders], whose nation and vassals were called the Zacatecos, possessed and enjoyed them, and their name has stuck to this city of Zacatecas. The wood here produces a great quantity of fruit here called *tuna,* which is fertilized and yields without any cultivation, and the wood also produces a great diversity of sweet-smelling flowers.

This treasure was discovered in the year 1540, in the following way. When Nuño de Guzmán, having finished the conquest of [Nueva] Galicia left there, his soldiers remained, spread out over the entire kingdom.* Since no more towns remained to conquer and since they had so many Indian slaves, they devoted themselves to looking for and enriching themselves from silver mines. One of these soldiers was *el bachiller* [baccalaureate] Joanes de Tolosa, a Basque, who happened to have an Aztec among his Indian slaves. The Aztec, it is said, seeing his master so anxious to discover mines and to claim silver, told him: if you so desire this substance, I will take you where you can fill your hands and satiate your lust with it. Hearing this, Joanes de Tolosa, without saying anything to his Spanish companions, left secretly and was guided by his Indian slave to this mountain range and to these minerals whereupon he started to dig out the metals and assay them. He found the hills so full of metals and of such value that there were some, although very few, with only half the silver, so that while one *quintal* [100 pounds] of earth might produce two *arrobas* [50 pounds] of silver. At the start, the smelting of each *quintal* usually produced ten, fifteen, twenty, or thirty *marcos* [marks] of silver. This caused the mines to be populated in great haste, and the first inhabitants were the soldiers who found themselves closest to the site, and at the same time many people from Mexico [City] started to come and lay claim to the silver and among them came the merchants with their merchandise. . . .

The Spaniards who first populated the place never planned to remain here, but sought only to extract the most silver they could, and so they made their houses, or better said, shacks, as journeying people in the midst of their travels might. But there

*The Spanish province of Nueva Galicia covered 180,000 kilometers of territory ranging from the Pacific Ocean to the foothills of the Sierra Madre Occidental.

was so much promise in the city that they never abandoned it and have remained here with these short, low houses and with no order to their streets. . . .

It is not known if His Majesty had given a land grant to assist in the foundation of this city, or if only the title of city, which does not include rent or property to cover its expenses. Zacatecas is subjected principally to the *Real Audiencia* [Royal Court] and is governed locally by a *corregidor* [magistrate] supplied by the *Real Consejo de Indias* [Royal Council of the Indies], who earns one thousand ducats in salary, and a municipal council that elects two *alcaldes ordinaries* [chief municipal officers] each year. There is an *aguacil mayor* [constable] and His Majesty sells the privilege of occupying this office for nineteen thousand pesos. There are three public notaries for sale, each of which sells for six thousand pesos. This city has its own municipal buildings which house the corregidor and the place where he holds his court, the jail, and the place where the *regidores* [councilmen] meet to hold council. At present, there are four of these and they are commonly sold by His Majesty for four hundred pesos each. One of the notaries serves as the clerk of the council. . . .

The houses of this city are made of adobe and mud, they all have earth floors, and few are large; some are made of stone with high roofs, but there are few of these. There are more than three hundred houses of this type. . . . There is a parish church in the middle of the city dedicated to Our Lady of the Nativity because the city was conquered from the Zacatec Indians on Her day, and the regiment takes its banner from the memory of this festival day. Two beneficiary clerics serve this church, provided, according to the *Real Patronato* [Order of Royal Patronage] by the president; there are no tithes to pay because there are no residential tithes since miners never work the soil to plant it, but only to extract metals from it.* Neither do the residents provide a salary to these curates, because these latter enjoy the privileges of the citizens, sustaining themselves with some chaplaincies that have been founded in the parish, as well as from confraternities' votive masses and frequent processions. . . .

This city also has three hundred large and small houses of the construction described above; it houses at least six hundred residents, more or less, and most of them are Spaniards. There are at times more than one hundred and sometimes two hundred people who come and go on business, bringing their merchandise. Sixty or seventy children of Spanish residents have been born here, some of whom are occupied in studying, others in being miners, and others in running agricultural estates. There are, according to what I know of this city, up to ten or twelve Portuguese and Italian foreigners in this city. I do not know if they have made arrangements with His Majesty about living in this kingdom. Of black slaves and mulattoes, women and men, there are about eight hundred. There are also some free blacks that come and go and rent themselves out to work in livestock, farming, mining, and commonly

---

*Beneficiary clerics received incomes from the fixed capital assets of a church. The *Real Patronato* (Order of Royal Patronage) was the means by which the Spanish crown, by papal concession, administered the secular church beginning in 1493.

they are bad and depraved, these free blacks, just like the other slaves, but as it is said there, "it is bad to have them, but much worse not to have them."

There are about fifteen hundred Indians of these residents in the work gangs who labor in all types of occupations in the mines, but who come and go, leaving and returning with great ease and in this way a precise number for them cannot be given, as we said earlier in the preface.

Spanish is the language that is generally spoken in this city; some Indians speak the tongues of their nations, because here there are Mexicans, Otomies, Tarascans, and those of other nations. . . .

Among the noble residents, there are few who are extremely rich and those that are, are the miners; however, among the intermediate classes of people, there are many who are rich with twenty, thirty, or forty thousand pesos and there are three or four individuals who possess one hundred thousand pesos, and all of these are merchants of public stores. But none of the stores are in Spain, as they call it here; rather they operate in Mexico, from where they bring all types of clothing from Castile, cloths, linens, silks, wine, oil, steel, spices and also clothing and silks from this land, and from China, all of which are transported to this city in carts. There are at least fifty merchandise stores whose worth ranges between two thousand and thirty thousand pesos. The merchants of the least value and wealth work in their own stores and the richest ones have servants and attendants working for them who are Spanish. . . .

There are sufficient and necessary numbers of those who perform the mechanical offices of tailor, cobbler, ironsmith, and carpenter. Of these, there are Spaniards, mulattoes, and Indians, and those that earn the most are the carpenters and masters of making engines for mining, because these are burned and damaged continuously.

Central Themes

State formation, urban life, the northern frontier, land and labor

Suggested Reading

Bakewell, Peter. *Silver Mining and Society in Colonial Mexico: Zacatecas, 1546–1700* (1971). Reprint, Cambridge: Cambridge University Press, 2002.

Benson Library, Latin American Collection. *Relaciones Geográficas* collection. See University of Texas, http://www.lib.utexas.edu/benson/rg/.

Hoberman, Louisa Schell. *Mexico's Merchant Elite, 1590–1660.* Durham, NC: Duke University Press, 1991.

Related Sources

13. Acazitli of Tlalmanalco: Nahua Conqueror on the Mesoamerican Frontier (1541)
41. Mexico in Postwar Social Turmoil (1852)

20. Chimalpahin: Indigenous Chronicler of His Time (1611–1613)*

The Nahua historian Don Domingo de San Antón Muñón Chimalpahin Quauhtlehuanitzin was born in Amecameca, Chalco, in 1579 to indigenous parents who, although nobly named, were of secondary status. At age fourteen, Chimalpahin traveled to Mexico City and began working as a steward, aide, or lay brother at the Church of San Antonio Abad in Xoloco. While there, he began writing Mexico's indigenous history and became the premier practitioner of the genre of Nahuatl annals of his day. As well as composing the *Annals* from which the following excerpts are taken, Chimalpahin also produced a lengthy history of the Indian kingdoms of the Valley of Mexico from 670 to 1612.

Chimalpahin's *Annals,* written in Nahuatl, chronicle Xoloco's history in the period from 1589 to 1615. The work also treats the activities of Nahuas affiliated with the Chapel of San Josef in Mexico City's Church of San Francisco, and it discusses public events of note in the capital and in New Spain more broadly—political appointments, natural disasters, scandals. Chimalpahin's *Annals* are in large part a record of events that he experienced himself, but his other works document his familiarity with a range of other writers, both indigenous and European, and his extensive use of oral interviews.

Little is known about Chimalpahin's contemporary readership. His work was first published in 1746, over a century after his death, but his manuscripts were sufficiently respected that by the close of the seventeenth century one of Mexico's most important luminaries, Carlos Sigüenza y Góngora, possessed a mass of them in his personal library (Source 27).

Chimalpahin's writings present a portrait of the Nahua mentality and a view of history one century after Conquest in the heart of the Spanish Empire. Students might examine them to uncover Nahua attitudes, concepts, and intellectual styles from this era. How does this Nahua historian conceive of time, place, and indigenous identity? What attitudes toward Catholicism does he convey one century after the Church's aggressive proselytization campaign began? What does this text reveal about the lives of indigenous people in the urban capital? What forms of empowerment and oppression did they experience? The following excerpts also treat the stories of three Mexican women: two indigenous vendors of chocolate and *atole* (a maize drink) and a Spanish woman. What do we learn from him about their status?

---

*Don Domingo de San Antón Muñón Chimalpahin Quauhtlehuanitzin, *Annals of His Time,* ed. and trans. James Lockhart, Susan Schroeder, and Doris Namala (Stanford, CA: Stanford University Press, 2006), pp. 195, 197, 199, 251, 253, 255, 257. Except where indicated, the footnotes included here are from the original translation, but some pertaining to translation details of Nahuatl orthography and etymology have been omitted. We have added English translations of some terms, here indicated with square brackets.

The Annals of His Time

Today, Saturday the 21st of the month of January of the year 1612, was when they went to San Josef at San Francisco to make a notification to fray Gerónimo de Zárate, chaplain at San Josef; the one who came to notify him there was señor Francisco Franco, notary of the Royal Audiencia. It was done at the order of the lords judges of the Audiencia because of a complaint against him made by María López, chocolate seller, who is from Tetzcoco but came here to Mexico Tlatilco to make her home and now belongs to Moyotlan. She complained of fray Gerónimo de Zárate because he shamed her spouse named Juan Pérez on Sunday a week after [the feast day of] San Josef; he stood him up against a stone pillar, naked and quite ill, where by the order of our father they gave him a lashing. At that time they left him almost dead, having fainted from the lashing. And [Gerónimo de Zárate] preached about him, he said in the pulpit that [Pérez] dissipated much money that had been offered to the *cofradía* [confraternity], and then he had people take him to jail and lock him up, so that he would pay it back. This happened when his wife was not present, and when she was told and found out what had happened to her spouse, she got very angry and was worried about his having been given a lashing, so that she went right away to the Royal Audiencia to make a complaint about it. And also two others went jointly to make complaint; one works as a sacristan, named Josef Gómez, and the second is a woman named María Constanza. He did the same thing to them, shamed them in public, standing them up and stripping them. Josef Gómez he publicly stood up, stripped, displayed, and gave a lashing just because he talked back with a few words. And María Constanza he publicly stood up, displayed, stripped; her breasts were exposed. The reason they went to pick her up at her home on the said Sunday was just that//* they say she didn't go to hear mass at the church of San Josef. This was not the first time, they were not the only ones to whom he did such things in the time since he entered Mexico here, for he treated all the Mexica Tenocha Moyoteca that way, because when they caused fray Gerónimo de Zárate concern or angered him about something whether little or big, he right away shamed them, stood them up in public, and did many other things here by which he mistreated everyone. In some cases it was for real sins that he would shame people and stand them up in public; he would say in the pulpit during the sermon what sins of people he had found out about. Whether something was shameful or not shameful, he would say it all in the pulpit, he would announce it in the sermon, as though he had been appointed chief justice or inquisitor. He took all the great duties of justice upon himself, as no other friar of all those who came here to be in charge of and take care of the chapel of San Josef did. And he would sell people's houses, the houses of the deceased that are in the various tlaxilacalli [territorial units]; he sought it all out and asked about it. If they told him where it was, he would right away take it from people and sell it, even if it did not belong to the church, and even if there were heirs who were truly the chil-

*In the original manuscript, Chimalpahin used diagonal lines to indicate divisions or new topics within paragraphs.

dren or grandchildren, he would ignore them and consider them as nothing. He would actually take their houses from them, remove them from them and sell them away from them. Fray Gerónimo de Zárate would take all the money they were sold for, saying, "With it I will perform masses for the deceased." But no one saw or found out that he was performing masses for the dead, nor did he give anything to the property owners. He searched out absolutely all of the testaments; he inspected them so that he found out from them what each of the deceased distributed on dying. And if he found out that a testament was in people's custody, if they didn't want to show it to him, if they didn't quickly produce it in his presence, he would lock them up in jail and also shame them for it, so that the Mexica would betray each other; whoever knew something about someone would tell and reveal it to fray Gerónimo de Zárate, so that he could seek it, could have people make it come to the surface and appear and they would reveal it to him. Whatever he saw in testaments in the way of property of the deceased, even though the deceased had passed away quite a few years ago, even though his command had already been carried out, he sought out whatever the testator had ordered in his testament and made people pay it a second time. This then is how the said father fray Gerónimo de Zárate greatly mistreated everyone; he thought nothing of the Mexica, and he thought nothing of some Spaniards, even when they implored him on someone's behalf about something. All of the many other things that he did to mistreat the Mexica cannot be said and told here, for there were a great many things that he did to people. It is not necessary to say it all, whether good or bad; let him alone give an accounting to our lord God. Let him not be talked about, forget about that. He did it of his own accord; he is responsible, for he is a friar, he is dedicated to our lord God, and in his presence he will give an accounting to him himself when he dies. Because he did such things to the Mexica and mistreated them, they thought him very evil, but although the Mexica were angry about our father because he treated them like this, they had patience with him, they kept it inside, no one dared to make it public and make complaint to the Royal Audiencia, if it hadn't been for the said María López, who was so bold as to accuse him before the lords judges of the Audiencia. She did all the things aforementioned; she entered a petition when the court was in deliberation and in her petition, she announced to the judges all the different things that he did at the chapel of San Josef to mistreat everyone. The lords heard and found out about all of it, and saw it as a very frightful thing, so that right away the judges ordered that someone go and notify fray Gerónimo de Zárate today on the said Saturday at the chapel of San Josef that his duty would no longer be at the chapel. He was to go inside the monastery, shut himself up there, and no longer take care of the Mexica. No longer was he to perform such mistreatment, shaming, and lashings as he had been inflicting on the Mexica, which appeared above. They stopped him from doing absolutely all the different things, so that he would no longer shame people, give them lashings, or stand them up in public. And they set a fine for him so that he would stay closed up inside the monastery. The commissary was not here in Mexico at that time, having gone to Guatemala, and the provincial head was not here in Mexico either; he had gone to the various altepetl all around, carrying out an inspection. But it was only for a little while, a few days, that the said Gerónimo de Zárate really stopped mistreating the Mexica in some way. He was stopped for the time being, but he did not therefore leave the chapel of San Josef, he was only prevented from holding the post of chaplain that he had been appointed to.

v* Today, Friday the 31st, the end of the month of May of the year 1613, was when María, a widow and seller of bitter atole, died. She was the spouse of the late Francisco, a tailor, and they lived here behind the church, the house of my precious revered father San Antonio Abad, [in] the tlaxilacalli of Xoloco, as it is called. The reason that the said María, seller of bitter atole, died, as was said and found out about, and the local people here in the tlaxilacalli said in this connection, was that our lord God sent down his anger, wrath, and punishment on the said woman. It was because she talked about [disparagingly] and impinged on reverence for the holy Cross, for she opposed and did not want the erection of the one that has now** been erected in the road intersection outside the house of the Spaniard Hernán Martin. This said holy Cross was the property of and was raised by our friends and younger brothers Juan Morales and Bernabé de San Gerónomio, who are married to sisters and are skirt makers, and it also belonged jointly to some other Mexica who live here in Xoloco, although not all of them belong to the said tlaxilacalli of Xoloco here. Here is what happened fifteen days ago, on a Friday: at that time the said Juan Morales and Bernabé de San Gerónimo and the others were working on what was to be the platform on which the said holy Cross was to be erected; they were putting it together. But the said María, seller of bitter atole, went to get the officers of the law. She went to make a complaint at the municipal building before the corregidor [magistrate] Don Martín Cerón; she accused the said Juan Morales and Bernabé de San Gerónimo of being the very ones who were behind working and setting things up there next to the said houses in the road intersection. And the said woman María, seller of bitter atole, claimed this road as property, which is why she went to make the complaint, saying, "It cannot be that a cross be erected there." She also said, "Very well, if they erect a cross then let them concede me just a bit of money, since the land on which they are placing the platform is my property." But it is not in truth her property, for it is the road. But is not in truth her property, for there is no doubt that it is the road.† After the said woman went to make a complaint, the corregidor sent a Spanish constable who came to arrest the said Juan Morales and Bernabé de San Gerónimo, who were working there. They did not take

---

*In the manuscript, Chimalpahin used this sign to indicate a new paragraph or the start of a new entry.

**Or recently.

†The portion beginning "Quito camo" and ending "canel ohtli" in the Nahuatl and in the English beginning "saying" and ending "is the road" is added between the lines and in the margin. Hence the repetition. Once again we have an indication that Chimalpahin was copying from something else.

them gently, for they tied the hands of both of them. It was only at the intercession of the Spaniards who live there, the vecinos,* that they untied them, and it was with hands untied that they took them to the municipal building, where they were going to keep them in custody. And the said María, seller of bitter atole, went along shouting loudly at them; all the bad and filthy language with which she went scolding at them cannot be said or told. She showed great disrespect for them, for she is a woman. But it was not this woman alone; her son-in-law made the complaint along with her. The said [Juan Morales and Bernabé de San Gerónimo] were going to be detained in the municipal building, but they were brought back outside the building, and they were not able to lock them up because of the intercession of father fray Agustín del Espíritu Santo, who is in charge of the church of San Antonio Abad here. He saw them outside the municipal building as the said Juan Morales [and Bernabé de San Gerónimo] were being taken off to be in custody, and then he said to the corregidor and the notary Juan Pérez de Ribera and the interpreter, "May you know that I am a witness that this woman María deceived you when she came saying that land on which they want to erect the holy Cross is her property. It is in the road, in the intersection that these people here whom they went to arrest are setting up and putting together the platform on which they are to raise the holy Cross. It is not on anyone's property; let it be inspected." And the said people who were going to be detained were sent back; they told them, "Don't do anything yet, let the suit take its course first." And when they had been dismissed, father fray Agustín del Espíritu Santo took the said Juan de Morales and the others to the viceroy, so that they asked the viceroy Don Diego Fernández de Córdoba, Marqués of Guadalcázar, for his permission, and he gave them permission to erect a holy Cross in the said road, which the said woman had opposed. After the orders had been issued and the viceroy had signed they finished putting together the platform, they got it ready, and they held a feast day for the blessing of the new holy Cross here at the church of San Antonio on the Sunday of the feast of the Holy Spirit, on the 26th of the month of May. The very reverend father whose name was already mentioned, fray Agustín del Espíritu Santo, blessed it. It was with great ceremony and processions that they went to raise it on the said new platform that was built. At this time the said woman seller of bitter atole was sick and very near to death. And when this said holy Cross was erected, the vicar general doctor Don Juan de Salamanca also gave them his permission, which they had requested, for the holy Cross to be raised. And it was not long after that the said María, seller of bitter atole, passed away; her son-in-law, whose name was _______, also passed away, because he helped his said mother-in-law in the complaint she had made.

v Before this that has been told, that we have just finished recounting and writing about the dispute that happened, how the said María, seller of bitter atole, had made a complaint relating to the holy Cross, here is another thing that happened first, likewise here in the tlaxilacalli of Xoloco and in [a section] called Acatlan, on the

*Although meaning only "citizen," the Spanish word *vecino* was ordinarily used for non-indigenous residents only.

other side, at the corner and close to the house of the Spaniard Diego de Senete. The said Spaniard and his spouse named Mariana Rodríguez, a Spanish woman, caused a dispute at the beginning of the said month of May, in which they likewise talked [disparagingly] about and touched on the reverence of another holy Cross, because of which they opposed the people of the said tlaxilacalli there, whose property the said holy Cross was, that their forefathers had erected there a long time ago. The said Spaniard Diego de Senete and his spouse, Mariana Rodríguez, especially this Spanish woman, opposed the holy Cross; neither of them wanted the cross to stand there close to, next to their house. And although they are residents there, it is thought that they just bought their house, although they have been there and made their home there for a long time, but the house was only a little one. Not long ago [fray Gerónimo de Zárate] sold them the house of a deceased person adjacent to their house, and it was fray Gerónimo de Zárate, who was chaplain of San Josef at San Francisco, not long ago, before he left, who gave them possession of the house, when Don Antonio Valeriano, now governor of Azcapotzalco, was fiscal, so that they amalgamated it with the house that they had had for a long time, but he did not sell them, nor did they receive possession of, the said land on which the holy Cross stands. On the other hand the said Spaniard Diego de Senete and his spouse claimed that all the land was their property, so that they ejected the said tlaxilacalli members, telling them, "Remove your cross, for the land it stands on is our property, we bought it from fray Gerónimo de Zárate." But the people of the tlaxilacalli here did not know whether our father had sold them the land along with it, and they were angered when they heard that they wanted to take their cross there away from them and were opposing them. And especially the said Spanish woman Mariana Rodríguez talked about it, opposing, scolding, and showing disrespect for the people of the tlaxilacalli; how much bad, filthy language she used with them cannot be said or told; she said that in all truth she was going to remove the cross standing there, saying that they were going to build a house there. Then the people of the tlaxilacalli above went to make a complaint, saying that the land on which the holy Cross stands is their patrimonial property. The officers of the law heard the complaint, so that they [the tlaxilacalli people] brought suit against Diego de Senete for trying to take the land deceitfully; the suit is now pending. And on the same said day when they argued and showed opposition about the holy Cross, the said Spanish woman Mariana Rodríguez began to get sick; at first she just began to have a headache, but then the next day in the morning she lay down sick in her bed. She got matlaltotonqui [a fever, possibly pleurisy], which soon became very strong, and they brought her the Sacrament from the cathedral, and she received it. On the third day the Spanish woman passed away. And it was said and found out about it, and the local people in the tlaxilacalli said that our lord God sent his anger and wrath down upon the said Spanish woman. When the suit came to an end and was finished, the officers of the law gave the land to the commoners to keep forever; the holy Cross will stand on it and no one will be able to take it away from them. And although the said

Diego de Senete tried to make a complaint, it fell to one side; his complaint was not heard. Like this, then, occurred two separate miracles here in the said tlaxilacalli Acatlan in Xoloco, close to the church of my precious father San Antonio Abad in Mexico, at the beginning of the said month of May. And I, Don Domingo de San Antón Muñón Quauhtlehuanitzin, set it down here and wrote it because both things happened right before my eyes, I really saw them.—

Central Themes

Indigenous people, state formation, urban life, popular culture, religion, gender

Suggested Reading

Chimalpahin Quauhtlehuantzin, Domingo Francisco de San Antón Muñón. *Codex Chimalpahin*, vol. 1, *Society and Politics in Mexico Tenochtitlan, Tlatelolco, Texcoco, Culhuacan, and Other Nahua Altepetl in Central Mexico.* Norman: University of Oklahoma Press, 1997.

Nesvig, Martin Austin, ed. *Local Religion in Colonial Mexico.* Albuquerque: University of New Mexico Press, 2006.

Osowski, Edward. "Passion Miracles and Indigenous Historical Memory in New Spain." *Hispanic American Historical Review* 88, no. 4 (November 2008): 607–638.

Schroeder, Susan. *Chimalpahin and the Kingdoms of Chalco.* Tucson: University of Arizona Press, 1991.

Related Sources

4. The Origin of the Nahuas and the Birth of the Fifth Sun (1596)
24. The Persistence of Indigenous Idolatry (1656)

21. The Creation of Religious Conformity (the Early Eighteenth Century)*

The Catholic kings, Ferdinand and Isabella, founded Iberia's first tribunal of the Holy Office of the Inquisition in Castile in 1478. The Spanish monarchy subsequently established eighteen other courts across its possessions in the following century, including tribunals in Lima (Peru), Cartagena (Colombia), and Mexico City, whose court followed earlier bodies headed by the regular orders and the secular church. The crown established the first audiences of the Holy Office to impose religious uniformity over its newly consolidated state, and the Inquisition's first victims were persons suspected of practicing the two religions—Judaism and Islam—perceived as the gravest threats to this consolidation.

Mexico's first *General Edict of the Faith* was published in November 1571 at the time of the founding of the Mexican tribunal. Nearly three hundred subsequent versions of the *Edict* have been located in Mexican archives. The following *Edict* dates from the reign of King Philip V (1700–1724 and 1724–1746) but varied only slightly from versions published throughout the seventeenth century. The Supreme Council of the Holy Office mandated that the *Edict* be read aloud at regular intervals in urban centers to inform and alert citizens about suspicious religious practices in order to elicit their denunciations of religious deviancy. The *Edict*'s implementation in New Spain, however, proved to be impractical. It was read only sporadically, and many listeners found it incomprehensible. Furthermore, inquisitorial records from colonial Mexico reveal that while laypeople sometimes denounced acquaintances, friends, and even family members to the court because they were disturbed by evidence of their heretical tendencies, denouncers also used the court as a means to punish their enemies and satisfy personal vendettas that had no bearing on spiritual matters.

The *Edict* provides insight into those beliefs and behaviors that the court—and the crown, by which it was ultimately controlled—found the most troubling to both spiritual purity and political stability. In this sense, documents such as this one might be understood as the instruments by which conceptions of deviancy were created. What, then, do they tell us about those behaviors and practices that most threatened the church and state? Which of the prohibited religious practices outlined here involved traditions imported from Europe and which were spiritual practices derived from the Mexican context? What sorts of Mexican-originating acts and beliefs appear to have most disturbed the court?

---

*General Edict of the Faith (16th–18th centuries). Bancroft Library, "Disposiciones varias. México, etc., 1756–1843," F 1203 D 5; "Compendio, y sumario del edicto general de la fè, y casos en el contenidos." Translated by the editors. All footnotes have been added.

Abridgement and Summary of the General Edict of the Faith, and the Cases in It Comprised

1. We the Inquisitors against heretical depravity and apostasy, by apostolic authority to all the faithful in this our district without exception, &c. We declare that the *Promotor Fiscal* [Prosecutor] of this Holy Office appeared before us and reported to us, saying: That it was well known and notorious that many people present at the publication of the General Edict of the Faith do not understand it merely through its reading, and that many others can not be present at its publication. These people are ignorant of its contents. And so that in the future, no person can claim ignorance of the Edict, he has asked that we command that in the doorways of churches be affixed a brief summary of its most substantial chapters, to ensure its most accessible and universal comprehension.

2. And we, believing the request to be just and expedient to the service of God our Lord, command that this abridgement and summary be made, so that if it is known or understood, seen, or heard that some person or persons—whether living, present, absent, or dead—has contravened in any way our Holy Faith, they should be denounced before us.

3. Especially, if it is known or heard that some person or persons has kept or keep the Law of Moses, has engaged in some ceremonies in its observance, or said that the Law is good.

4. Or if it is known or heard said that some person or persons have observed the Law of Mohamed or said that this Law is good, or engaged in some ceremonies of its observance.

5. Or if some persons follow or have followed the false sect of Martin Luther and his followers or have believed or supported some opinions of his or of other heretics.

6. Or if it is known or heard that some persons have said or affirmed that the sect of the *Alumbrados* is good or that mental prayer is of divine order, and that vocal prayer matters very little.*

7. Or if it is known or heard that some persons have injured in deed or word the Virgin our Lady or the saints in heaven, or has invoked the devil or has made a tacit or explicit pact with him, or said that witches exist, or mixed sacred things with profane ones.

8. Or that some person being a cleric of a Holy Order or a professed friar has married, or that not being priest, someone has said mass or confessed any person.

9. Or if it is known that some confessor or confessors in the act of confession or close to it, or in the confessional, or appointed places, even if not immediately after

---

**Alumbradismo* was a sect that emphasized internalized devotion, a practice that Iberian courts of the Inquisition began to prosecute in the first quarter of the sixteenth century; its prosecution had spread to Mexico by the close of the sixteenth century.

the confession, has solicited his daughters of confession, provoking them or inducing them with deeds or lewd and dishonest words.*

10. Or if someone has counselled or persuaded his penitents in the act of sacramental confession to commit the grave sins of disobedience, disloyalty, or rebellion against the King our Lord, Don Philip the Fifth, making them believe that the oath of loyalty is not obligatory.

11. Or if some person has married for the second or more times while his or her first wife or husband is still living.

12. Or if there have been astrologists or diviners, or those believing superstitions.

13. Or if for divining, or other effect, someone has consulted or asked questions of the devil in bedevilled or possessed bodies.

14. Or if, for divining, or to find stolen goods or treasures, or to predict the future concerning journeys, voyages, fleets, navies, deaths, or other things in hidden or distant places, people have used magic arts, curses, spells, omens, dreams, palm reading, rings, witchcraft, characters, or invocations of demons.

15. Or, if for divining, people have tested their luck with beans, wheat, corn, or other seeds, or with cards, dice, coins, or rings, or similar things, or mixed sacred objects with profane ones such as the evangelists, Agnus Dei, holy altarpieces, holy water, stoles, or other holy vestments.

16. Or, if they carry with them and give to others letters, memorials, recipes, or lists containing words and superstitious prayers; or circles, lines, or prohibited characters; or saints' relics, iman stones, hairs, ashes, powders, and other charms, to prevent violent and unexpected death, to provide protection from their enemies, to have good luck in all affairs, battles, and business, to effect marriage, or to attract men to women and women to the men that they desire, so that spouses and friends treat one well, and to prevent jealousy in women or in friends, to unify men, or to cause harm to them or to women, or to curse them in their persons, members, or health.

17. Or so that for these, and other effects, prayers have been used in which God our Lord is evoked, or his saints, and mixed with other invocations and indecent and disrespectful words, and that these are repeated on certain days before certain images, and at certain hours of the night, with certain numbers of candles, vessels of water, and other instruments; or that they expect things after omens and premonitions which they claim to know, or for things which they dream about when sleeping, or for which they heard spoken of in the street, or which happened to them on another day, or for the signals in the sky or the birds that fly, and other such vanities and insanities.

18. Or those who have given or give adoration to the devil, offering him sacrifices with candles, incense, copal, and other things or perfumes, and using certain unctions on their bodies invoking and adoring him with the name of the Angel of light, and anticipating answers or signs from him.

* "Daughters of confession" were female confessants.

19. Or so that for the same ends, they drink or give to others certain drinks of herbs or roots, like those that are called Peyote, the herb of Saint Mary, or by another name, with which they deceive and daze the senses, and the fantastical representations that they then see, they judge and publish afterwards to be revelations or certain notices of that which will happen.

20. Of if it is known that some people have books or any kind of writings about astrology or magical arts, superstitions, spells, omens, or witchcraft, or those of the sect of Martin Luther, or other heresies, or the Koran, or other books of the Sect of Mohamed, or Romance Bibles or any other forbidden books, prohibited by edicts, catalogues, expurgatories, and censures of the Holy Office of the Inquisition.

21. Or if any persons, failing to do what is required of them, have neglected to inform the Holy Office about any of these referred things, or has persuaded others to not inform the Holy Office about them.

22. Or if they have hidden, received, or favored any Heretic, giving them assistance and help, hiding and sheltering their persons, or their goods. . . .

Therefore, by this present Edict, we admonish, exhort, and require, that in virtue of holy obedience and under pain of major Excommunication *lata sententia trina canonica monitione pramissa,* we order that each and every one of you, if you know or have heard, seen, or heard tell that any person has done, said, had, or affirmed any of the abovementioned things, or anything else, whatever it might be, or appear to be against our Holy Catholic Faith, and those that have and teach our Holy Roman Mother Church, whether living—present or absent—or dead, come and appear before us personally or before our commissioners and qualifiers or ministers of the Holy Office (and where they may not be before curates of your parishes, who will inform us of the necessary measures) to tell them and show them, within six days following the day upon which our letter is published, or in whatever way is possible, with the warning that, once the said time has elapsed, and the abovementioned not complied with, as well as incurring the said punishments and censures, we will prosecute those who are rebellious and disobedient as well as against people who maliciously keep their mouths closed and hide these things and have evil thoughts about our Holy Catholic Faith and the censures of the Church. And so that the above said comes to the notice of all and so that nobody can claim ignorance of it, we command that it be published and affixed in this church.

Signed: *Licenciado* [Licenciate] Joseph Cienfuegos
Licenciado Don Francisco de [signature illegible]
By order of this Holy Office
don Joseph Parilla y Biezma
The penalty of Major Excommunication is absolved for no one.

Central Themes

Indigenous people, popular culture, religion, race and ethnicity

Suggested Reading

Boyer, Richard. *Lives of the Bigamists: Marriage, Family, and Community in Colonial Mexico.* Albuquerque: University of New Mexico Press, 1995.

Jaffary, Nora E. *False Mystics: Deviant Orthodoxy in Colonial Mexico.* Lincoln: University of Nebraska Press, 2004.

Lea, Henry C. *The Inquisition in the Spanish Dependencies.* New York: Macmillan, 1922. http://www.archive.org/details/theinquisition00leauoft.

Perry, Mary Elizabeth, and Anne J. Cruz. *Cultural Encounters: The Impact of the Inquisition in Spain and the New World.* Berkeley: University of California Press, 1991.

Related Sources

16. The Spiritual Conquest: The Trial of Don Carlos Chichimecatecotl of Texcoco (1539)
17. The Inquisition Seizes Don Carlos's Estate: The Oztoticpac Map (1540)
24. The Persistence of Indigenous Idolatry (1656)

22. On Chocolate (1648)*

Thomas Gage was an English Dominican who traveled through the Caribbean and New Spain between 1625 and 1637. Disillusioned by his experiences and tempted by the advantages of worldly life, Gage renounced Roman Catholicism five years after returning to England and became an Anglican clergyman. Two years later, he began writing his account of his travels, originally entitled *The English-American: His Travail by Sea and Land; or, A New Survey of the West Indies.* This text, first published in 1648, was the first eyewitness account of what it was like to live in Spanish America written by an Englishman.

In this selection, which comes from the twelfth chapter of *The English-American,* Gage describes chocolate production and details the material culture of indigenous Mexican society, both Pre- and Post-Contact. He also describes Europeans' adoption of, and attitudes toward, particular components of Pre-Columbian society for practical and pleasurable purposes. Is Gage disdainful or critical of indigenous society? He is particularly interested in the humoral qualities of chocolate. In this, he

---

*Thomas Gage, *Travels in the New World,* ed. John Eric Sidney Thompson (Norman: University of Oklahoma Press, 1958), pp. 151–159. © 1958 University of Oklahoma Press. Some of Thompson's footnotes have been omitted where they were not essential.

refers to a central medical conception that was derived from the science of ancient Greece and prevailed in early modern Europe. This theory understood the functioning of the human body according to the balance or imbalance of four essential liquids—blood, phlegm, black bile, and choler—and the properties associated with each. What is implied in his application of the European science of humors to this indigenous product?

Chapter 12. Concerning Two Daily and Common Drinks or Potions Much Used in the Indias, Called Chocolate and Atole

Chocolate being this day used not only over all the West Indias, but also in Spain, Italy, and Flanders . . . I thought fit to insert here also somewhat of it concerning my own experience for the space of twelve years. This name chocolate is an Indian name, and is compounded from *atte,* as some say, or as others, *atle,* which in the Mexican language signifieth "water," and from the sound which the water, wherein is put the chocolate, makes, as *choco choco choco,* when it is stirred in a cup by an instrument called a molinet, or *molinillo,* until it bubble and rise unto a froth. And . . . we may well call it a compounded or a confectioned drink. . . . But the chief ingredient, without which it cannot be made, is called cacao, a kind of nut or kernel bigger than a great almond which grows upon a tree called the tree of cacao, and ripens in a great husk, wherein sometimes are found more, sometimes less cacaos, sometimes twenty, sometimes thirty, nay, forty and above. . . .

From all that hath been said, the error of those is well discovered who, speaking of this drink of chocolate, say that it causeth oppilations, because cacao is astringent, as if that astriction were not corrected and modified by the intimate mixing of one part with another, by means of the grinding, as is said before. Besides it having so many ingredients which are naturally hot, it must of necessity have this effect, that is to say, to open, attenuate, not to bind. And laying aside more reasons, this truth is evidently seen in the cacao itself, which if it be not stirred, grinded, and compounded to make the chocolate, but be eaten as it is in the fruit (as many Creole and Indian women eat it), it doth notably obstruct and cause stoppings, and make them look of a broken, pale, and earthy color, as do those that eat earthenware, as pots or pieces of lime walls (which is much used among the Spanish women thinking that a pale and earthy color, though with obstructions and stoppings, well becomes them). And for this certainly in the cacao thus eaten there is no other reason but that the divers substances which it contains are not perfectly mingled by the mastication only, but require the artificial mixture which we have spoken of before.

. . . There are two sorts of cacao. The one is common, which is of a dark color inclining toward red, being round and picked at the ends; the other is broader and bigger and flatter and not so round, which they call *patlaxti* [*Theobroma bicolor,* wild cacao], and this is white and more drying, and is sold a great deal cheaper than the former. And this especially more than the other causes watchfulness and driveth away sleep, and therefore is not so useful as the ordinary, and is chiefly spent by the ordinary and meaner sort of people. As for the rest of the ingredients which make this chocolatical confection, there is notable variety. Some put into it black pepper, which is not well approved of by the physicians because it is so hot and dry, but only for one who hath a very cold liver, but commonly instead of this pepper, they put into it a long red pepper called chile which, though it be hot in the mouth, yet it is cool and moist in the operation. It is further compounded with white sugar, cinnamon, cloves, aniseed, almonds, hazel nuts . . . vanilla, *zapoyal* [ground seeds of the mamey, *Calocarpum mammosum*], orange flower water, some musk, and as much of achiote as will make it look of the color of a red brick. . . .

Now for the making or compounding of this drink, I shall set down here the method. The cacao and the other ingredients must be beaten in a mortar of stone or, as the Indians use, ground upon a broad stone which they call *metate,* and is only made for that use. But first the ingredients are all to be dried, except the achiote, with care that they may be beaten to powder, keeping them still in stirring, that they be not burned or become black, for if they be over-dried, they will be bitter and lose their virtue. The cinnamon and the long red pepper are to be first beaten with the aniseed, and then the cacao, which must be beaten by little and little, till all be powdered, and in the beating it must be turned round that it may mix the better. Every one of these ingredients must be beaten by itself, and then all be put into the vessel where the cacao is, which you must stir together with a spoon, and then take out that paste, and put it into the mortar, under which there must be a little fire, after the confection is made. . . . The manner of drinking it is divers. The one most used in Mexico is to take it hot with *atole* [a maize drink], dissolving a tablet in hot water, and then stirring and beating it in the cup where it is to be drunk with a molinet, and when it is well stirred to a scum or froth, then to fill the cup with hot *atole,* and so drink it sup by sup. Another way is that the chocolate being dissolved with cold water and stirred with the molinet, and the scum taken off and put into another vessel, the remainder be set upon the fire with as much sugar as will sweeten it, and when it is warm, then to pour it upon the scum which was taken off before, and so to drink it. . . .

The third way of taking it is the most used, and thus certainly it doth no hurt, neither know I why it may not be used as well in England as in other parts, both hot and cold. For where it is so much used, as well in the Indias as in Spain, Italy, and Flanders, which is a cold country, find that it agreeth well with them. True it is used more in the Indias than in the European parts because there the stomachs are more apt to faint than here, and a cup of chocolate well confectioned comforts and strengthens the stomach. For myself I must say I used it twelve years constantly, drinking one cup in the morning, another yet before dinner between nine or ten of the clock, another within an hour or after dinner, and another between four and five in the afternoon, and when I was purposed to sit up late to study, I would take another cup about seven or eight at night, which would keep me waking till about midnight. And if by chance

I did neglect any of these accustomed hours, I presently found my stomach fainty. And with this custom I lived twelve years in those parts healthy, without any obstructions or oppilations, not knowing what either ague or fever was. Yet will I not dare to regulate by mine own the bodies of others, nor take upon me the skill of a physician to appoint and decide at what time and by what persons this drink may be used. Only I say that I have known some that have been the worse for it, either for drinking it with too much sugar, which hath relaxed their stomachs, or for drinking it too often.

I have heard physicians of the Indians say of it, and I have seen it by experience in others, though never I could find it in myself, that those that use this chocolate much grow fat and corpulent by it. Which, indeed, may seem hard to believe, for considering that all the ingredients except the cacao do rather extenuate than make fat because they are hot and dry in the third degree. How then might this cacao with the other Indian ingredients be had in England? Even by trading in Spain for it, as we do for other commodities, or not slighting it so much as we and the Hollanders have often done upon the Indian seas. I have heard the Spaniards say that when we have taken a good prize, a ship laden with cacao, in anger and wrath we have hurled overboard this good commodity, not regarding the worth and goodness of it, but calling it in bad Spain *cagarruta de carnero* or sheep dung in good English. It is one of the necessariest commodities in the Indias, and nothing enricheth Chiapas in particular more than it, whither are brought from Mexico and other parts the rich bags of patacons only for this *cagarruta de carnero*. . . . *

Central Themes

Indigenous people, popular culture, land and labor

Suggested Reading

Crosby, Alfred. *The Columbian Exchange: The Biological and Cultural Consequences of 1492.* Westport, CT: Greenwood Press, 1972.

McNeil, Cameron L., ed. *Chocolate in Mesoamerica: A Cultural History of Cacao.* Gainesville: University Press of Florida, 2006.

Norton, Marcy. "Tasting Empire: Chocolate and the European Internalization of Mesoamerican Aesthetics." *American Historical Review* (June 2006). Available at: http://www.historycooperative.org/journals/ahr/111.3/norton.html (visited October 17, 2008).

Related Sources

5. A Treasury of Mexica Power and Gender (c. 1541–1542)
20. Chimalpahin: Indigenous Chronicler of His Time (1611–1613)
30. Mexico's Paradoxical Enlightenment (1784)

**Patacons* most commonly referred to plantains, but in this usage the word may refer to a coin worth eight *reales*.

23. The Treatment of African Slaves (the Seventeenth Century)*

Because of the low visibility of blacks and blackness in Mexico today, it is often assumed that Africans were a minor presence in colonial Mexico. In fact, they had a tremendous impact on New Spain's demography, economy, and social life. Until 1640, more African slaves were imported to Mexico than to any other part of Spanish America. The first African slave to arrive in Mexico was one Juan Cortés, who accompanied Hernán Cortés in 1519. In the first century after the Conquest, largely as a strategy for replacing the decimated indigenous population, nearly 90,000 slaves were imported to the Viceroyalty. Imports fell in the second half of the seventeenth century and continued to decline until Mexico's abolition of slavery in 1829.

The following viceregal mandate concerning African slaves provides information on a number of dimensions of their lives. Curiously, the ordinance focuses only on the activities of certain types of slave laborers and makes no mention of workers in other domains. Why do you think this ordinance does not address the activities of the slaves who worked in New Spain's lucrative silver mining industry or those who labored in textile factories or domestic service (Source 19)? Along with specifications regarding corporal and fiscal punishments for slaves and owners found to be in violation of the ordinances, this document also addresses slaves' required conversion to Christianity. Why was conversion such a preoccupation for the viceregal state? How effective was their conversion? Although the ordinances most obviously detailed the kinds of power that slave owners had over slaves, what information does this ordinance convey about the rights and freedoms conferred to—or seized by—slaves themselves?

---

*Miguel León Portilla et al., eds., *Historia documental de México*, vol. 1 (Mexico: Universidad Nacional Autónoma de México, Instituto de Investigaciones Históricas, 1965), pp. 237–240. Excerpt translated by the editors. All footnotes have been added.

Ordinances Regarding the Good Treatment That Must Be Given to Blacks for Their Preservation

First, it is charged, commanded, and ordered that all the owners of blacks take care to give good treatment to their slaves, taking into consideration that they are neighbors and Christians, giving them sufficient food and reasonable clothing, and not punishing them with cruelty nor laying hands on them without evident cause. They can not cut off their limbs nor maim them, since this is prohibited by divine and human law, under penalty of losing any slave treated this way to His Majesty and of having to pay twenty pesos to the denouncer.

Item: That all the owners of *haciendas* [agricultural estates], both sugar refineries and livestock estates, and any other properties that might have black or Indian slaves in their service, have a white man, a *mayordomo* [majordomo] or *mandador* [manager] who takes care that in the said estate there is a house or *bohío* [slave hut] that serves as a church, with an altar that has a sign of the cross and holy images, and that every morning, before the blacks or Indians go to work in the field, they go there to pray to God, commending that he care for them and save them. And on all the Sundays and festival days after eating, having had mass with the Holy Sacrament of the Eucharist on that day, everyone should gather in the said church, or house of prayer, to be taught the Christian doctrine and to be instructed in the faith. And for this, the consciences of said owners of these blacks and Indians are charged on the part of His Majesty and on my part, in his Royal name. In addition to which, the owners are levied a fine of thirty pesos for each time that the *Gobernador* [governor] visits the district they rule and finds that this order is not complied with, or that it is not a daily practice.

Item: All owners of a black or blacks are charged with His Majesty's conscience and mine in his Royal name and are commanded that when they buy black slaves, within six months after taking possession of them, they must make them learn our common tongue and give them to understand the Sacrament of Holy Baptism and baptize them and Christianize them. Because all blacks, by their inclination, are well disposed to becoming Christians and are easy to convert, and they presume the value of being Christians like us. And those who have owners who enforce this, as often happens, become very good Christians and are very devoted and virtuous and friends of reason. And if it is established that owners have been careless in this, and that the said time period has passed and they have not procured to do what is declared above, they incur as a penalty worth the value of one quarter the value of the black for the first offense, and the Gobernador must set a second period to do it in, and if the owner is remiss a second time, he loses half the value of the black; and for the third time, he loses the black entirely. . . .

Item: It is ordered and commanded that no black slave should dare to go on horseback, under pain of one hundred lashes for the first offense and two hundred for the second, and under pain of losing the horse whether it be owned by the slave or his master. And if he should be out and about without the consent of his master and captured, he should be restored to his master and two pesos should be given as reward to the captor. And the Spaniard who finds such a black slave on horseback, and does not take him and denounce him to the authorities incurs the fine of twenty pesos for the chamber, judge, and denouncer. And this is understood to apply only to blacks who are not cowboys or herdsmen of a sugar refinery, because these are given license to ride horseback because they do this in the service of their owners. But they must not be in remote places distant from the estates of their owners. But any black traveling with his owner can go on horseback.

Item: It is ordered and commanded that no black slave can carry any arm on any route, unless it be a knife without a point for cutting palms, or unless the black is a cowboy either in the pasture or traveling with livestock from one place to another who can carry a *dejarretadera* [butcher's knife] or lance. This purpose and place are the only that are permitted, under penalty, in the first instance, of one hundred lashes with a cane of the local justice; and for the second offense and those following, two hundred, and the slave will have his hand nailed to the said cane for two hours. And also the black who is a muleteer or cart driver can take with him a dagger, when he travels in this capacity, and in no other time nor place, under the said penalty, and that of losing his arms. And the Spaniard or mandador or mayordomo of his owner that has armed blacks in his charge, if he sees and does not disarm them and does not denounce them to the justice, incurs the fine of twenty pesos for the chamber, judge, and denouncer.

Item: That no slave can journey from one place to another without carrying a sealed letter of his owner or his mayordomo or mandador or *vaquero y mayoral* [overseer of a cattle ranch] which states that he travels with permission and that he journeys for so many days to such and such a place. And he who is apprehended en route in another way without such a letter, or is found on a route different from that specified in the license, should be taken and put in the stocks until such time as the justice and his owner are alerted. And the slave owner should pay the person who apprehends the slave, verifying that he is not a fugitive, three pesos, and if he is a fugitive, pays him that which the order commands. And the slave should be taken to a public jail, so that he leaves by his right according to the ordinances. . . .

Item: It is ordered and commanded that the mayordomo or mandador found on each hacienda is obliged to inspect the rooms, bohiós, and huts of the blacks in his care every night, to see if there is any black in them who does not pertain to the hacienda. And finding someone without written license, he must imprison both this black and the black who has given him shelter in his hut or bohío, and bring them captive before the authorities so that they will be punished. And much precaution should be taken in this regard and no deception committed, under penalty of twenty pesos for the chamber, judge, and denouncer. Such punishments prevent escaped blacks from traveling about. These are the principal suppliers of arms to blacks of the haciendas who conceal them to obtain the weapons.

Item: That no slave should dare to journey from one sugar refinery to another, or from one hacienda to another, after night has fallen. And if he is found doing this by the Spaniard in charge of the hacienda, he will be given by him or by his order, twenty lashes, and imprisoned. And the slave's mayordomo should be sent for and informed. And the Spaniard who does not execute this as it is declared incurs, for each instance, a fine of ten pesos for the chamber, judge, and denouncer.

Item: That no slave nor free black, nor any other person dare hide blacks who have fled their owners in their house, nor give them food to eat, nor any favor, or help in any way, under penalty that if caught, this person will be given two hundred lashes in this city and an iron shackle will be thrown on him that he will carry for the time of one year exactly. And if it is a free black, or an Indian who does this, he incurs the pain of one hundred lashes, given publicly in the streets of this city, and they must pay for the cost of lost labor accrued during the whole period of the slave's absence.

Central Themes

Land and labor, religion, race and ethnicity

Suggested Reading

Bristol, Joan Cameron. *Christians, Blasphemers, and Witches: Afro-Mexican Ritual Practice in the Seventeenth Century.* Albuquerque: University of New Mexico Press, 2007.

Martínez, María Elena. "The Black Blood of New Spain." *William and Mary Quarterly* 61, no. 3 (July 2004): 479–520.

Palmer, Colin A. *Slaves of the White God: Blacks in Mexico, 1570–1650.* Cambridge, MA: Harvard University Press, 1976.

Related Sources

25. Afro-Mexicans, Mestizos, and Catholicism (1672)
29. Maroon Slaves Negotiate with the Colonial State (1767)

24. The Persistence of Indigenous Idolatry (1656)*

The colonial state and the Church both sought the evangelization of Mexico's indigenous population. Their conversion legally justified Spain's conquest of its New World territories and ideologically facilitated the maintenance of colonial government. Missionaries also undertook natives' proselytization because of their genuine faith in Catholicism's superiority over all other religions and their fear for the perdition of the souls of the unconverted. Missionaries, beginning with the Franciscan Bernardino de Sahagún in the mid-sixteenth century, compiled histories of Mexico's native people and treatises about their spiritual practices in order to undertake their evangelical work more effectively (Source 11).

Jacinto de la Serna, a famous expurgator of native idolatry, worked within this tradition. In his writings, Sahagún had addressed the idea of native shamanism, but he did not include actual Nahuatl conjurations and incantations. Later writers, including Serna and one of his important contemporaries, Hernando Ruiz de Alcarón, from whose writings Serna drew heavily, provided more detailed information about this material. Serna was a secular priest who had served as parish priest in two partly Nahua-speaking communities in the southern Basin of Toluca. He was a graduate of the University of Mexico (an institution founded in 1551) and later served three times as its rector. Serna completed his compilation of Indian rites and ceremonies in 1656, but it was not published until 1892.

Serna conveys the outrage that missionaries felt upon detecting that despite presenting a veneer of genuine conversion to Catholicism, native people continued to practice Pre-Columbian traditions and to adhere to Pre-Conquest spirituality. What does this document reveal about how indigenous people practiced Catholicism? How did this differ from how ministers of the Church believed it should have been practiced? In what spiritual arenas and by what kind of practitioners was this faith most successfully retained? Serna obviously derided this spirituality and sought its eradication. But can we effectively examine the state of indigenous religious belief—and practice—at the time of his writing underneath his disapproving cloak of words?

---

*Jacinto de la Serna, *Tratado de las supersticiones, idolatrías, hechicerías, ritos, y otras costumbres gentílicas de las razas aborígenes de México.* See Biblioteca Virtual Miguel de Cervantes at: http://www.cervantesvirtual.com/servlet/SirveObras/01593963546705955212257/index.htm. Excerpt translated by the editors. All footnotes added to the original.

Treatise of the Superstitions, Idolatry, Witchcraft, Rites, and Other Gentile Customs of the Aboriginal Races of Mexico. Chapter One: On the State of the Idolatries Before the Congregaciones [congregations] of the Indians into Towns

1. Idolatries and Superstitions of the Indians

(2) . . . After so much light, so much preaching, and so many good works, when these people should have been full of light, they were plunged into dark obscurity. When they should have been resplendent with the works of the true Christians, instead works of true idolatry were found among them. . . . And having had faith that they were already children of the light, experience showed that they are still of darkness, for the obscurity of idolatry that they have and have kept hidden grows in them. They never left it, but rather since the start, when the faith was first preached to them, they held on to their idolatry and followed it with such cleverness that although they practiced it before the eyes of the Spaniards, even in the sight of their own priests, the Spaniards did not recognize the idolatry. And they proceeded in this with such security that although they recited the words used in sacrifices that they made to fire or to some other thing in the presence of Spaniards, these were not understood because they were sometimes mistaken, and if they were not, the Indians said them with security and with the satisfaction that they were not understood.

(3) For when some woman was in labor, so that she would be strong and spirited, they said to her *Nochpotzin, ahmo ximotequipacho, xitnochicahua ca nican mehuiltitica in nantli in tatli.* Do not be afflicted, my daughter. Be strong, for the Father and Mother are with us. They called the fire Father and Mother, and they trusted in it, that it would give her strength, and be present during her labor. And so they lived in the security of their darkness as if they lived in light. . . .

(4) And later they continued to understand their darkness for light, since they believed their superstitions and idolatries so necessary that they believed that without them nothing good would happen. And the reason that they gave for this is *Caiuh otechilhuitiaque in huehuetque, totahuan, tocolhuan.* Because our old ancient parents and grandparents did not leave us like this. And they gave such force to this tradition that passed from parents to children that they show much emotion when they see that it is being forgotten and they say: *Anh quen? cuix ilcahuiz, cuix polihuiz in otechmachtitiaque huehuetque?* What then? You have forgotten and lost what the old ancient ones have taught us? . . .

2. Invocation to a Great Number of Gods

. . . (6) It is true that those first Fathers worked admirably, zealous to teach these poor ones, to correct them of the error and deceit in which they lived. But for all this, they did not leave behind their deception and blindness, especially those who were very distant from the *cabeceras* [head towns] where the Ministers worked. Scattered in other places, the doctrine and teaching did not reach them as was necessary. Those who were dispersed under pretext of sowing, those whose towns were located in mountainous regions, and those who lived for the greater part of the year among cliffs and gorges—five in one place, four in another, and fewer in another (as today is in the highlands, lowlands, and the Huasteca)—remained in darkness and error.* And in these places, the Devil hit the hardest, because there is no one to resist him and make war against him. And he is found today in settlements of this type, in those places that are so remote that the principal teachers and zealots of idolatry have their dens and dwelling places from where they circulate and enter towns where there is doctrine and teaching (as today is done and experienced in some places), entering quietly and discreetly, waiting until they are assured of the people, circumstances, and places, to ensure they are not recognized and discovered. And little by little they spill their venom, and persuade people that they not forget the ways of their ancestors, so that in these places they would be their representatives and teachers, and they teach the formal words of their invocations and rites and ceremonies of their sacrifices, and in this, they use such circumspection and caution that no-one realizes who they want. And when they have to perform their idolatries, it is with such stealth and so hidden that they avoid discovery, verifying in this what Our Lord Christ says in Saint John, chap. 3. . . .

3. Concealment of Ceremonies and Idolatrous Rites

(9) To better conceal their deception and poison, they gild it, mixing their rites and idolatrous ceremonies with good, holy things, joining light with darkness to Christ with reverence, venerating Christ our Lord, his Holy Mother, and the saints (who some take to be Gods), together with their idols.

(10) And their concealment and dissimulation is so advanced that they perform the holy sacraments, while at the same time [they] make sacrifices to fire, sacrificing hens and animals, spilling *pulque* [maguey cactus liquor] in their presence, offering them food and drink, attributing to them any sickness that afflicts them, asking for their favor and assistance to prevent sickness from coming and giving them thanks if they obtain what they ask for. And it appears that they do this first with the Holy Sacraments, which they have in front of them, and then to the fire. And when they wish to make sacrifices and offerings to each one of these particular holy objects, they start with fire, which for greater secrecy, they have given various names in the Mexican language: *Xiuteuctli,* which means Lord of the Years and of Time; *Ixcoçauhqui,* He of the Yellow Face; *Chiucnauhyo teuctli,* Nine times Lord; *Nauhyoteuctlii,* Four times Lord. . . .

(13) They have their way of performing Confirmation, which is that a certain time after Baptism, they pierce the ears of children and perform other ceremonies, giving

*The Huastecas is the region of Mexico's eastern central coast.

them godparents as are given in the Sacrament of Confirmation. And not only that, they mix their ancient superstitions with those of the Sacrament of Marriage, so that when gifts are given to the bride, they offer them first to the fire, and after the couple is married, the mothers-in-law give away four portions of food: one to the daughter-in-law and one to the son-in-law, and they tie together the border of the clothes of the couple into one knot, according to their ancient rite. And on the fourth day of the wedding, they shake out the sleeping mats where the newlyweds have slept and with some *calabazuelas** or something similar, they cast some lots to see which of the newlyweds should go from the house of their parents to the house of the parents of the other newlywed. . . .

4. The Indians Do Not Forget Their Idolatries

(18) All of this makes it obvious that in the present, the Indians do not forget their idolatries or their idols, as was thought; for they have so much faith in them that although they believe that there is a God, they also think it is true that their idols bring them material goods. . . . For all the work that they put into harvesting and livestock raising, they always think that their profits come from the hands of their idols, or from fear of their superstitions, and the same happens with adversity which comes to them in these matters or in others. And for this reason, they take much care to placate their idols, making sacrifices of animals, food, and drink in their presence and giving them thanks for the goods that they seem to have received from them. And in these sacrifices since they can no longer spill human blood, they use the blood of chickens and animals. And there are some who, in performing all this, spill their own blood, the only blood they used in ancient times, pricking their ears, and other body parts not easily seen. . . .

(20) They also venerated the Sierra Nevada, or Volcano of Toluca, where they went regularly to make sacrifices, and to the rest of the high mountains where they had their ancient temples, which were well-made and maintained. They also made sacrifices in the principal sources of waterways, rivers and lagoons, because they also venerated water and invoked it when they sowed or reaped their crops. When they used copal or limestone, or some other substance, they called there to their gods for help and aid. And for all those things, it helped them a great deal to have put many of these idols in the foundation and base of the Cathedral and in other houses to adorn them, and they did this by chance as well as to strengthen the buildings and houses and to decorate the streets which also had them in them. The Devil used this for their greater deception and so that they would say that their gods were so strong that they put idols in the foundations and bases of the temple. And those put in the crests of houses and in the streets were put there so that they would be preserved. The places where they idolized and said their invocations [were] learned from some Indians who, as God was served, were converted and revealed the idolatry that they did with these idols. . . .

*A plant used against snakebites.

5. Idolatrous Ceremonies of the Dead and the Saints

(22) Midwives in those times used many superstitions in birth, invoking fire to help infants to be born. Doctors, male and female, are the most harmful and principal zealots of these idolatries; with the dead they use many superstitions and idolatrous ceremonies, offering food and drink to the departed, routinely providing them with supplies, which they place under the shroud for the journey to the afterlife. And they also place clean new clothing there, and the mothers of children who die put a vessel of breast milk with them so they will not lack sustenance. . . .

(25) Also when the wax and copal merchants and those who haul wood from the mountain, or rocks from the stone pit, meet together, they mix aspects of their occupations with their idolatrous ceremonies. They had people, elderly from among the ancients, who devoted themselves to conjuring rain, hail, and thunderstorms, and they reserve tribute and other personal services for these witchdoctors in order that will do this job. . . .

Central Themes

Indigenous people, popular culture, religion, race and ethnicity

Suggested Reading

Burkhart, Louise M. *The Slippery Earth: Nahua-Christian Moral Dialogue in Sixteenth-Century Mexico.* Tucson: University of Arizona Press, 1989.

Cervantes, Fernando. *The Devil in the New World: The Impact of Diabolism in New Spain.* New Haven, CT: Yale University Press, 1997.

Greenleaf, Richard E. "The Persistence of Native Values: The Inquisition and the Indians of Colonial Mexico." *The Americas* 50, no. 3 (1994): 351–376.

Tavárez, David. "The Passion According to the Wooden Drum: The Doctrinal Appropriation of a Colonial Zapotec Ritual Genre in New Spain." *The Americas* 62, no. 3 (January 2006): 413–444.

Related Sources

4. The Origin of the Nahuas and the Birth of the Fifth Sun (1596)
5. A Treasury of Mexica Power and Gender (c. 1541–1542)
15. The Tlaxcaltecas Stage a Christian Pageant, "Like Heaven on Earth" (1538)
16. The Spiritual Conquest: The Trial of Don Carlos Chichimecatecotl of Texcoco (1539)

25. Afro-Mexicans, Mestizos, and Catholicism (1672)*

Unlike Cuba and Brazil, New Spain did not import large numbers of slaves directly from Africa after 1640. Therefore, numerous brotherhoods with membership from specific regions and language groups in Africa did not exist in New Spain. By the 1700s, individuals of African descent living in New Spain had formed *cofradías* (religious brotherhoods) based around the race label *mulato* (person of African and Spanish parentage). These cofradías were either supported by religious orders and parish churches or founded with less official church regulation on *haciendas* (agricultural estates). Cofradías served primarily to honor a saint's day or a less tangible religious doctrine, such as the Holy Sacrament or the Rosary. Cofradía members maintained a decorated image of their advocation in a parish or convent church or chapel, celebrating it in yearly festivities. Members also depended on these organizations to pay for their funeral masses and burials and entrusted their brothers with the responsibility of praying for their souls. In the late seventeenth and early eighteenth centuries, the increasingly large free mulato population in towns in the Diocese of Michoacán began moving up the social pyramid. Their mobility led to conflicts between mulato, Spanish, and Indian cofradía members in such towns as Valladolid, Pinzándaro, Zitácuaro, and San Juan Peribán. Spaniards and mulatos both argued for financial or governmental control using racially explicit language and rules, believing this language would help their case.

The following are excerpts from the court records of a legal battle that members of the Cofradía of the Holy Sacrament waged in the community of San Juan Peribán in Michoacán over the issue of the legal rights and political choices of its mixed-race members. What devices do those representing the mestizo and mulato petitioners attempt to justify their rights? What do these documents suggest about relations between different races within the confraternity and within the larger community of San Juan Peribán?

---

*"Varios cofrades de Nra. Sra. de la Soledad sobre que los oficios de la cofradía se sirvan por, mulatos y no por españoles." Pinzandaro, 1712, Fondo Parroquial Sección Disciplinar, Serie Cofradías, Subserie Solicitudes, caja 1267, fojas 1–15. Casa de Morelos Archive, Morelia, Mexico. Excerpt translated by the editors and Nicole Von Germeten.

"Various confraternity members . . . dispute whether the offices of the confraternity may be served by mulatos and not by Spaniards only"

June 27, 1672

The licentiate Lucas de Uriarte Arbide, advocate of the *Real Audiencia* [Royal Court] of this kingdom, canon in the holy cathedral of this diocese of Michoacán, official *juez provisor* [chief ecclesiastical judge] and vicar general for the most illustrious and reverend *señor* [Sir] Don Francisco Sarmiento de Luna of the council of his majesty, his preacher and bishop of this diocese. In a case against Cristóbal Bernal, resident of the Valley of San Juan Peribán and current *mayordomo* [majordomo] of the confraternity of the Most Holy Sacrament, founded in the convent of Saint Francis in the name of its mulato and *mestizo* [person of Indian and Spanish parentage] brothers. Health and grace in our Lord Jesus Christ. Don Juan de Contreras, resident of said valley, declares and presents a petition before Your Illustriousness so that you will be served to do what seems most just. The petition is as follows:

Petition

Most illustrious lord, Don Juan de Contreras Figueroa, resident of the Valley of San Juan Peribán of the parish of said town, appears as head deputy elected by the brothers of the confraternity of the Most Holy Sacrament founded in the parish church of said town of San Juan Peribán in the year 1671. Since the election is contested, I am necessarily charged with verifying it, and, if necessary, stripping the voice and pledge of all the other confraternal brothers. I appear before Your Illustriousness and state that on the day of Corpus [Christi] of the current year before the *octava* [eight-day celebration] was finished, Cristóbal Bernal, resident of said Valley of Peribán, was elected [mayordomo] of the confraternity by two votes because of the affection that the Guardian Father of the convent has for him. Most votes in his favor came from mulato and mestizo brothers. One of the votes came from his own son who is not a member of the confraternity. The Spanish confraternal brothers, however, elected Don Juan de Cueva Carvajal, resident of said Valley and owner of the sugar hacienda and mill. The said confraternity was founded by Spaniards of this parish, which can be proven to Your Illustriousness so that you will be aware that Spaniards and not mulatos or mestizos founded this confraternity and you will be served to command that only Spaniards should vote for mayordomos and deputies and that neither mulatos, nor mestizos, nor any other such [individuals] can serve as mayordomos or deputies and that a new election must be held for these positions. I ask and beg that Your Illustriousness be served in accordance with which I have presented and that you command a new election be held and that no person disturb said confraternal brothers but instead that they be given their free will to select the person that appears to them the most useful to said confraternity. Signed Don Juan de Contreras Figueroa. . . .

[On June 28, 1672, in Valladollid, Lucas de Uriarte Arbide commanded that Cristóbal Bernal and the mestizo and mulatto brothers of the confraternity would have fifteen days to appear before him and present their response to the petition. *Ed.*]

Valladolid, August 1, 1672

Don Esteban de Valdez, resident of the Valley and parish of San Juan Peribán, appears with the power invested in me in this tribunal in the name of Cristóbal Bernal, resident of said Valley and current elected mayordomo of the confraternity of the Most Holy Sacrament founded in the parish church of said town and in the name [of] Juan Velásquez and Alonso de Aguilar, current deputies of said confraternity. We respectfully appear before Your Grace according to our right and that of the holy confraternity in response to a petition made by Don Juan de Contreras on June 27 of this year and in response to your command informing us of what he incorrectly presented against us. The petition says that with the affection of the Guardian Father of said convent, Cristóbal Bernal, by two votes of mulatos and mestizos, was elected mayordomo instead of Don Juan de Cueva Carvajal. The petition says that he was wrongfully elected because of this affection, and says that the brothers of the confraternity instead justly elected with their free will an honorable Spaniard, the owner of a sugar-refining hacienda who is devoted to the divine cult and who has served in the past as a deputy of said confraternity. It is known that mulatos and mestizos voted in the election and that five votes were made by leading Spanish gentlemen, and the rest were brothers of the said confraternity. Two of them had been mestizo deputies and one was a mulato. This is because since the confraternity was founded, it has had the ancient custom of voting for and electing mulatos and mestizos as deputies. For example, the mulato Pedro Ramos has been a deputy three times. . . . The captain Don Francisco Pabon, *alcalde mayor* [district governor] of the town, was mayordomo at the time; and he did not disdain having him as his deputy, because in the service of God our Lord, neither status nor color matter as long as God is served with cordial love. And most of the confraternity's membership is made up of mestizos and mulatos who help the confraternity grow, as is proven by the confraternity record books that we present. Although said confraternity was founded by Spaniards, Indians, mestizos, and mulatos have since joined and have enjoyed all the privileges of the other brothers. They vote in the elections and are elected as deputies without any contradiction or impediment. Spanish mayordomos and mestizo and mulato deputies are always elected. The Spaniards know it is an age-old custom for them to vote in elections. On one occasion, the natives elected Juan Gómez as mayordomo without any contradiction. And the natives of the town donated land to the confraternity, which was sold for 500 pesos mortgage, earning 25 pesos rent for the confraternity to spend on wax and masses. And the mulato and mestizo brothers also collect alms for the confraternity and contribute their sweat and labor to the Corpus Christi festivities when the election and the octava are held. To address the statement that this foundation was made by Spaniards and that mulatos and mestizos do not vote for Spanish majordomos and deputies: although it was founded by Spaniards, mulato and mestizo brothers were and are admitted to their meetings and can vote for mulatos and mestizos. The confraternity's record books, dating back almost to its foundation, prove this to be true, since custom makes law. And if it were the case that this confraternity of the Holy Sacrament were actually two—one for Spaniards only and the other for mulatos and mestizos—and if the latter interfered by voting in the elections of the Spaniards, this would be disputed with good reason. But since there is only one confraternity in which Spaniards, mestizos, and mulattos are mixed, and that being members of it, they become brothers, and as such, they must enjoy the graces, advantages, and prerogatives of said confraternity, which has been the custom almost since its foundation. Without question, these rights include voting and electing for a Spanish majordomo and mestizo, mulato, and Spanish deputies, especially as said mestizos and mulatos are those who most effectively secure alms both within and outside the town. In response to what was said about having a new election for majordomos and deputies: we dispute this because the election was done canonically. There is no foundation for asking this because said members willingly and voluntarily gave their votes for Cristóbal Bernal as Spanish mayordomo and Juan Velásquez and Alonso de Aguilar as mestizo deputies in the presence of the Reverend Guardian Father of the convent of San Juan Peribán who, as is customary, presided. In response to what was said about Cristóbal Bernal's son voting: this is unfounded, because he did not vote, because he is not a member. The entire allegation that Don Juan de Contreras makes in favor of Don Juan de Cueva Carvajal, his cousin and intimate friend, whom he wants to be mayordomo, is also unfounded. And the reason for his opposition to Cristóbal Bernal was his fear that he would be asked for the accounts of the confraternity dating from when he was deputy, when Bernabe de Armas was mayordomo, being then a resident of Pinzándaro and not able to be present there. In the present election, he asked many of the confraternal brothers—including us—to vote for his cousin, telling us that if we gave them, we would be admitted [to the confraternity] and not be [treated as] mestizos. When we did not want to give him our votes, because he did not suit us for the reasons given, he said that we should not, as we do now, contest the election. And for this reason, after the election was held, he snatched the books of said confraternity from the table and took them to his house without allowing the election to be ratified. And his wish to avoid appearing in this city is only done to vex us, to force us to defend ourselves and incur costs. For all of these reasons, we plead and supplicate you be served to declare the said election of the majordomo and deputies was good and legitimate, having been won by two votes and following the custom which must be observed. And we request that you reject the petition of said Don Juan de Contreras as illegitimate, that you declare that we are not obliged to respond to it, and that you command that he be required to return the books of the confraternity to said Cristóbal Bernal, who in full council was elected as majordomo. Don Juan de Contreras should be condemned according to the law for having carried off the books from the table on election day in the presence of our Reverend Father Fray Melchior del Carpio y Monroi, *definidor* [judicial council member] for this province and present guardian of this convent who presides over the council as is customary and constitutional, decreeing that the election be ratified as said books record is customary and as is commanded by the bishops. And as well we protest that we should not have to pay the costs that we have incurred in coming over thirty leagues in this time of heavy rains and also that we should be awarded damages because of the reduction of the sowing of sugar-cane on our estates, necessary for our sustenance, that appearing here has cost us. And only the service of God Our Lord and not malice moves us to act. We also request that said Don Juan de Contreras be prohibited from attending council meetings because he is a troublesome man who disturbs the meetings that must transpire in peace and order, and that the confraternity be expanded. Anyone who foments disturbances should be removed from office. The said deputies and I pledge to offer any information that might be necessary to you. We implore that in the service of God Our Lord and in Justice and we swear in the name of God Our Lord that our petition is made by Don Esteban de Valdez in our names. And we protest costs in that which is necessary.

Signed Don Esteban de Valdez, Juan Velásquez, and Alonso de Aguilar

[On August 1, 1672, Lucas de Uriarte Arbide commanded that Don Juan de Contreras return the election book of the confraternity within three days. On August 11, 1672, another member of the confraternity appeared to support the petition by Cristóbal Bernal. On August 17, 1672, Lucas de Uriarte Arbide declared that the election was valid and confirmed the elections of Cristóbal Bernal, Juan Velásquez, and Alonso de Aguilar as majordomo and deputies. *Ed.*]

Central Themes

Popular culture, religion, race and ethnicity

Suggested Reading

Bennett, Herman. *Africans in Colonial Mexico: Absolutism, Christianity, and Afro-Creole Consciousness, 1570–1640.* Bloomington: Indiana University Press, 2003.

Bristol, Joan Cameron. *Christians, Blasphemers, and Witches: Afro-Mexican Ritual Practice in the Seventeenth Century.* Albuquerque: University of New Mexico Press, 2007.

Von Germeten, Nicole. *Black Blood Brothers: Confraternities and Social Mobility for Afro-Mexicans.* Gainesville: University Press of Florida, 2006.

Related Sources

19. The Silver Mining City of Zacatecas (1605)
23. The Treatment of African Slaves (the Seventeenth Century)
29. Maroon Slaves Negotiate with the Colonial State (1767)

26. Sor Juana: Nun, Poet, and Advocate (1690)*

Sor Juana Inés de la Cruz, a prolific poet, dramatist, composer, theologian, and scholar, is now recognized as colonial Mexico's most important writer, despite her limited access to formal education because of her sex. Juana was born in either 1648 or 1651 out of wedlock to a *criolla* (American-born Spaniard) mother and a Spanish father. Her mother raised her on the family's modest estate outside Mexico City. As a child, she spent hours devouring the contents of her grandfather's small library. At age ten, Juana was sent by her mother to live with an aunt in Mexico City. There the girl's renowned intelligence brought her to the attention of the viceroy, Antonio Sebastían de Toledo, Marquis de Mancera, and his wife, Leonor Carreto. Under the vicereine's protection, Juana became a celebrated maid-in-waiting at the viceregal court in 1664.

Two options were available to noble women in colonial Mexico: marriage or the convent. Juana chose the latter, knowing that life as a nun would afford her the greatest freedom to pursue her education. She briefly joined the Discalced Carmelites in 1667 and then moved to the less rigid rule of the Jeronymite Order, entering the Santa Paula convent in Mexico City in 1669. There she amassed a considerable library, studied and wrote, taught music and drama, and, from behind the convent's *locutorio* (window grill to the outside), regularly hosted lively gatherings of courtiers, ecclesiastics, and literati.

By the late 1680s, the institutional church began to scrutinize Sor Juana's writings and activities. In 1690, Manuel Fernández de Santa Cruz, Bishop of Puebla, published a critique penned by Juana of a sermon by a Portuguese Jesuit along with a letter written under the pseudonym "Sor Philothea" in which he admonished her for devoting herself to worldly rather than spiritual studies. Sor Juana's response to this letter, a brilliant defense of her own—and all women's—right to acquire knowledge, is considered her most remarkable composition. One portion of it is excerpted here. How does she present her case in this excerpt? Why might it have so angered some of its readers? The year after her response was published, Juana came under the censure of Mexico's archbishop, Francisco Aguiar y Seijas, a man who had benefited from the civil disorder and hunger riots of 1692 that had weakened the hand of the viceroy (Source 27). Chastised by the Church and fearing an inquisitorial investigation, in 1693 Juana renounced her writings and ceased her scholarly endeavors. Her library and collections were sold for alms. She died in 1695 nursing her sister nuns during an epidemic that swept the capital.

Both a poem and a song that Sor Juana composed are included here as well. What concerns did Juana express in the poem about the sexual and social position

*Reprinted by permission of the publisher from *A Sor Juana Anthology*, trans. Alan S. Trueblood, foreword by Octavio Paz (Cambridge, MA: Harvard University Press, 1988), pp. 111, 113, 127, 129, 229–231.

of women of her day? The song is a *villancico* (carol), one of roughly fifteen that she composed to be sung in the cathedrals of Mexico City, Puebla, and Oaxaca. Juana's villancicos were aimed at popular audiences and often incorporated the concerns and language of the masses. Five of her villancicos, including the one reprinted here, feature people speaking African words; others use Nahuatl. In her villancicos, Juana also portrayed the Spanish dialects she heard—or possibly projected upon the characters in her songs. In the example here, her Spanish transforms the conventional verb constructions *dejámos* (let us leave), *vámanos* (let us go), and *vendamos* (we sell) into *dejémoso, vámoso,* and *vindamo.* Her translator, Alan Trueblood, conveyed these changes by rendering her text in a black dialect of the southern United States. What do you think of the use of this dialect? Juana drew her knowledge of Africans from her exposure to slaves on her family's *hacienda* (agricultural estate), including the *mulato* (person of African and Spanish parentage) slave who worked for her in the Santa Paula convent. What attitudes toward or impressions of black people does Juana convey in her villancico?

37 (She demonstrates the inconsistency of men's wishes in blaming women for what they themselves have caused)

Silly, you men—so very adept
at wrongly faulting womankind,
not seeing you're alone to blame
for faults you plant in woman's mind.
After you've won by urgent plea
the right to tarnish her good name,
you still expect her to behave—
you, that coaxed her into shame.
You batter her resistance down
and then, all righteousness, proclaim
that feminine frivolity,
not your persistence, is to blame.
When it comes to bravely posturing,
your witlessness must take the prize:
you're the child that makes a bogeyman,
and then recoils in fear and cries.
Presumptuous beyond belief,
you'd have the woman you pursue
be Thais* when you're courting her,
Lucretia once she falls to you.

*Thais was an Athenian courtesan who accompanied Alexander on his Asiatic conquests.

For plain default of common sense,
could any action be so queer
as oneself to cloud the mirror,
then complain that it's not clear?
Whether you're favored or disdained,
nothing can leave you satisfied.
You whimper if you're turned away,
You sneer if you've been gratified.
With you, no woman can hope to score;
whichever way, she's bound to lose;
spurning you, she's ungrateful;
succumbing, you call her lewd.
Your folly is always the same:
you apply a single rule
to the one you accuse of looseness
and the one you brand as cruel.
What happy mean could there be
for the woman who catches your eye,
if, unresponsive, she offends,
yet whose complaisance you decry?
Still, whether it's torment or anger—
and both ways you've yourselves to blame—
God bless the woman who won't have you,
no matter how loud you complain.
It's your persistent entreaties
that change her from timid to bold.
Having made her thereby naughty,
you would have her good as god.
So where does the greater guilt lie
for a passion that should not be:
with the man who pleads out of baseness
or the woman debased by his plea?
Or which is more to be blamed—
though both will have cause for chagrin;
the woman who sins for money
or the man who pays money to sin?
So why are you men all so stunned
at the thought you're all guilty alike?
Either like them for what you've made them
or make of them what you can like.
If you'd give up pursuing them,
you'd discover, without a doubt,
you've a stronger case to make

against those who seek you out.
 I well know what powerful arms
you wield in pressing for evil:
your arrogance is allied
with the world, the flesh, and the devil!

Feast of the Assumption, City of Mexico, 1679, from the Eighth Villancio, a Medley

 At the sacristan's voice
there slipped into the church
two Guinean queens
with faces of jet.
 Seeing the gaiety,
They thought they would help
and, setting baskets down,
sang the boys this song:

*[Refrain]**
Ha, ha, ha!
Monan, vuchilá!
Hé, hé, hé,
cambulé!
Gila coro,
gulungú, gulungú,
hu, hu, hu!
Menguiquilá,
ha, ha, ha!

 Fanny, this mo'nin'
we's full of glory,
don' le's sell ladyfingers
o' them almon' kisses.
We've sumpin' better:
Mary's fingers to kiss!
Ha, ha, ha! . . .
 Le's get a move on
an' skip the kitchen.
We won' sell no sweet 'taters
o' chick-peas to the gals

*Ha, ha ha! Monan vuchilá: The refrain is made up of rhythmic African words.

'cause plenty of sweet chicks
will be comin' to the fair.
Ha, ha, ha! . . .
 There never was a slave
as devout as that Handmaid
of the Lawd. She done serve Him
with her heart an' soul,
an' fo' bein' sech a good slave,
they natch'ly set her free.
Ha, ha, ha! . . .
 See her there cleavin'
the sky like a rocket,
like a pilla' of smoke
shootin' up from the incense,
sittin' down in the stars
at the right hand of the Lawd.
Ha, ha, ha! . . .

The Letter of Sor Philothea de la Cruz

. . . The venerable Dr. Arce (in virtue and cultivation a worthy professor of Scripture) in his *Studioso Bibliorum,* raises the question: *An liceat foeminus sacrorum Bibliorum studio incumbere? eaque interpretari?* (Is it legitimate for women to apply themselves to study the Holy Bible and to interpret it?)* He brings in many opinions of saints in support of the opposing view, especially that of the Apostle: *Mulieres in Ecclesiis taceant, non enim permittitur eis loqui* etc. ("Let women keep silence in the churches, for it is not permitted them to speak" [1 Cor. 14:34]). He then brings in other opinions and especially that of the same Apostle addressing Titus: *Anus similiter in habitu sancto, bene docentes* ("the aged women, in like manner, in holy attire . . . teaching well" [Titus 2:3]), with interpretations of the Church Fathers. He finally decides, in his judicious way, that to lecture publicly in the classroom and to preach in the pulpit are not legitimate activities for women, but that studying, writing, and teaching privately are not only allowable but most edifying and useful. Of course this does not apply to all women—only to those whom God has endowed with particular virtue and discernment and who have become highly accomplished and erudite, and possess the talents and other qualities needed for such holy pursuits. So true is this that the interpretation of Holy Scripture should be forbidden not only to women, considered so very inept, but to men, who merely by virtue of being men consider themselves sages, unless they are very learned and virtuous, with receptive and properly

*Juan Díaz de Arce (d. 1653) was a Mexican cleric, theologian, and university professor. The full title of his work is *Fourth Book of Expository Questions for the Fuller Understanding of the Holy Bible for the Bible Student* (1648).

trained minds. Failure to do so, in my view, has given rise precisely to all those sectarians and been the root case of all the heresies. For there are many who study in order to become ignorant, especially those of an arrogant, restless, and overbearing turn of mind, who are partial to new interpretations of the Law (where precisely they are to be rejected). Hence, until they have uttered something heretical merely in order to say what no one else has, they will not rest. Of these the Holy Spirit says: *In malevolam animam no introibit sapientia* ("For wisdom will not enter into a malicious soul" [Wisdom 1:4]). Learning does more harm to such than remaining ignorant would. A clever man once said that a person who does not know Latin is not a complete fool, but that one who does is well qualified to be one. And I add he is even better (if stupidity is a qualification) who has studied his bit of philosophy and theology and has a smattering of languages, for therewith he becomes a fool in many branches of learning and language, his mother tongue not offering room enough for a great fool.

These, I repeat, are harmed by study, for it is like placing a sword in the hands of a madman.* While a sword is a most noble instrument for self-defense, in the hands of a fool it is the death of himself and many others. Such the Divine Writ became in the possession of wicked Pelagius, perverse Arius, wicked Luther, and the other heresiarchs, such as our Dr. (he was never ours nor a doctor of anything) Cazalla.** Their learning did them harm, even though it is the best sustenance and the very life of the soul. Just as the better the nourishment a distempered and morbidly hot stomach receives, the more arid, rotten, and putrid the humors it produces, so the more these evilly inclined persons study, the worse the opinions they bring forth. Their understanding becomes obstructed by the very substance that should have nourished it; this is because they study a great deal and digest very little, in a way wholly disproportionate to the limited capacity of their understanding. On this the Apostle writes: *Dico enim per gratiam quae data est mihi, omnibus qui sunt inter vos: Non plus sapere qualm oportet sapere, sed sapere ad sobrietatem: et unicuique sicut Deus divisit mensuram fidei* ("For I say, by the grace that is given me, to all that are among you, not to be more wise than it behoveth to be wise, but to be wise unto sobriety and according as God hath divided to everyone the measure of faith" [Romans 12:3]). And truthfully the Apostle said this not to women but to men, so the *taceant* applies not only to women but to everyone not properly endowed. I will never succeed in knowing as much or more than Aristotle or Saint Augustine if I lack the aptitude of Saint Augustine or Aristotle, even though I study more than the two of them. Not only

*Sor Juana is thinking of a much-reproduced emblem of Andrea Alciato (1492–1550), the pioneer of Renaissance emblem literature: *Insani gladius* (The Sword in the Hands of a Madman).

**Pelagius (ca. 360–c. 420), British-born theologian, held that the will is free at any moment to choose between good and evil. He thus severely limited the role of God's grace and denied the efficacy of original sin. His doctrine was strongly combated by both Jerome and Augustine. The heresy of Arius (280?–336) considered the Son a subordinate being created by the Father rather than his uncreated coequal. This position was defeated at the Council of Nicaea (325). Agustín Cazalla (1510–1559), a Spanish Lutheran, onetime canon of Salamanca Cathedral, and chaplain to the King, was burned to death by the Inquisition.

that, but I will diminish and dull the workings of my weak mind by its lack of proportion to the objective.

Oh, if all of us—and myself first of all, weak woman that I am—would size up our talents before undertaking study and, even more, before writing out of a driving ambition to equal and even excel others, how little heart we would have left for it, how many errors we would spare ourselves, and how many wrong interpretations now making the rounds would not be circulating! My own errors I will put before all the rest, for if I recognized them as I ought to do, I would not write this at all. I protest that I do so only to obey you, with such misgivings as to place you more in my debt for my taking pen in hand when feeling so timid, than you would be if the works I sent you were perfect. It is just as well that everything is subject to your correction: rub it out, tear it up and reprove me, and I will be more appreciative of this than of all the vain applause others may give me: *corripiet me iustus in misericordia, et increpabit: oleum autem peccatoris non impinguet caput meum** ("The just man shall correct me in mercy and shall reprove me: but let not the oil of the sinner fatten my head" [Psalm 140:5]).

Central Themes

Popular culture, religion, gender, race and ethnicity

Suggested Reading

Merrim, Stephanie. *Early Modern Women's Writing and Sor Juana Inés de la Cruz.* Nashville, TN: Vanderbilt University Press, 1999.

______, ed. *Feminist Perspectives on Sor Juana Inés de la Cruz.* Detroit: Wayne State University Press, 1999.

Myers, Kathleen Ann. *Neither Saints nor Sinners: Writing the Lives of Women in Spanish America.* New York: Oxford University Press, 2003.

Paz, Octavio. *Sor Juana; or, The Traps of Faith,* trans. Margaret Sayers Peden. Cambridge, MA: Harvard University Press, 1988.

Sor Juana Inés de la Cruz Project. Available at: http://www.dartmouth.edu/~sorjuana/.

Related Sources

38. Female Education (1842, 1851)
46. A Positivist Interpretation of Feminism (1909)
59. Feminism, Suffrage, and Revolution (1931)
74. Jesusa Rodríguez: Iconoclast (1995)
75. Maquila Workers Organize (2006)

---

*Corripiet is evidently an erratum for corriget.

27. The 1692 Mexico City Revolt (1692)*

Carlos de Sigüenza y Góngora, like his friend Sor Juana Inés de la Cruz (Source 26), was an important Mexican luminary. Born in 1645 in Mexico City, he entered the Society of Jesus at age fifteen, took his vows two years later, but left the order in 1667 or 1669. In 1672 he became a professor of astrology and mathematics at the University of Mexico and the following year was ordained as a secular priest, serving as chaplain of the Hospital del Amor de Dios from 1682 until his death in 1700. He was also an almoner (church official responsible for distributing charity) for the Mexican archbishop Francisco Aguiar y Seijas, as well as a *corregidor general* (book examiner) for the Holy Office of the Inquisition. In addition, Sigüenza was the leading scholar of his day on Pre-Conquest indigenous history. He formed a close friendship while at the hospital with Juan de Alva Ixtlilxochitl, a prominent indigenous judge-governor who bequeathed to him a rich body of documentation about his ancestors, the indigenous nobility of Texcoco; Sigüenza would use this material, along with the writings of the Nahua chronicler Chimalpahin, in his reconstruction of the ancient history of the Mexica (Source 20).

The excerpt from Sigüenza's writing included here comes from a letter he wrote in late August 1692 to his friend, the Spanish admiral Andrés de Pez y Malzarraga, in which he described Mexico's most dramatic urban riot prior to the independence wars. Admiral Pez was then in Madrid urging the crown to finance the occupation and fortification of the Bay of Pensacola on the northwest coast of Florida, a voyage Pez undertook the following year, with Sigüenza acting as cartographer. Sigüenza probably hoped that Pez would publish his letter in the imperial capital in order to correct some false notions about the uprising that the enemies of the Mexican viceroy, the Conde de Galve, had suggested to King Charles II.

A number of circumstances provoked Mexico City's plebeian population, particularly its Indian sector, to revolt on June 8, 1692. These included pirate raids, earthquakes, flooding, a solar eclipse, and a food shortage caused by a combination of incessant rains, a crop blight, and the high price of food, along with the popular perception that the state had mishandled the food crisis. The catalyst came when a state prosecutor, Escalante y Mendoza, encountered the Indian woman described in the following passage, lying unconscious on the stairs of the viceregal palace. The woman's companions complained that she had fainted in a crush at the grain market. Escalante y Mendoza ordered that she be attended to, but did not pay her any particular attention. A short time later, an angry mob gathered in the city center, lamenting their mistreatment at the granary and brandishing a corpse they claimed was that of the Indian woman. The mob's anger escalated until it erupted in the

*Miguel León Portilla et al., eds., *Historia documental de México,* vol. 1 (Mexico: Universidad Nacional Autónoma de México, Instituto de Investigaciones Históricas, 1965), pp. 264–269. Excerpt translated by the editors. All footnotes have been added.

conflagration that Sigüenza recounts here. The viceregal state managed to reestablish its authority in fairly quick order following the riot. By the following day, the Conde de Galve had arranged the delivery of all the available corn in the region surrounding the capital to the public granary. The state also raised a merchant militia to put out the fires and hunt down all participants in the rebellion. Fifteen prisoners were ultimately executed, and nearly forty received corporal punishment for their participation in the uprising.

The excerpt from Sigüenza's letter omits his description of his most dramatic role in the riot. In the early hours of June 9, Sigüenza returned to the municipal buildings brandishing a crowbar and an ax and followed by many helpers. He cut his way through the smoldering buildings and into the archives and saved an entire collection of the city's most valuable historic records. But here Sigüenza concentrates on other aspects of the rebellion. What does his presentation reveal about his own views of the rebels, elite Mexicans, and the state? What conclusions can we draw from his description of the composition of the mob, its grievances, and its actions? These might be fruitfully compared to descriptions of later uprisings, including those presented in sources 32 and 68. In which of these three instances did the attitudes and actions of the rioters and the responses of the state and its elite allies differ most widely? How so and why?

Brawl and Mutiny in Mexico

I nearly missed what happened this past afternoon because I was at home with my books. And although I had heard some racket in the street, I thought nothing of it, for it was normal to hear such noise because we were often vexed by the constant drunkenness of the Indians. It did not even occur to me to open the glass panes on the windows of my study to see what was going on until a breathless servant came in and called loudly to me, "Sir! There is a riot!" I opened the windows in great haste, and saw a multitude of half-dressed people running to the square. Among them, some went shouting, "Death to the Viceroy and to the *corregidor* [magistrate], who have dared to take the corn and who kill us with hunger!" I set off for the square and arrived at once at the corner of Providencia, and, daring not to move, I was dumbfounded. There was an enormous crowd of people made up not only of Indians but of people of all castes. So grating were their cries and shrieks and so thick was the storm of rocks that they rained onto the palace, that these sounds exceeded the noise of the over one hundred war chests that were sounding together in the surrounding doors and windows. Of those who were not throwing stones, some waved their cloaks in their hands like flags and others flung their hats in the air while others jeered. The Indians distributed rocks to all of them with remarkable speed. It was then about six-thirty.

Bands of men came pushing their way into the square from the street where I stood (it would have been the same on others that opened into the square). Spaniards came, carrying their swords unsheathed, but seeing the same thing that had stopped me in my tracks, they too stopped. But the blacks, *mulatos* [people of African and Spanish parentage], and all who were plebeians were shouting, "Death to the Viceroy and to any who defend him!" And the Indians shouted: "Death to the Spanish and the *gachupines* [derogatory term for those whom came from Spain] who eat our corn!" And exhorting each other to be brave since no Cortés* was around to defeat them, they flooded into the square to accompany the others in throwing rocks. "Hey señoras!" said the Indians to each other in their language. "Come with joy to this war, since God wants the Spaniards to be finished in it. It does not matter if we die now without confessing! Is this not our land? So what do the Spanish want with it? . . . "

Some reinforcements of honorable people had entered through the doorway of the military barracks by the Casa de la Moneda that was next to it and from other places. These people, since they were locked in the palace, had thought they were very safe. It did not occur to them that the rioters would fight with their utmost determination if they faced no opposition. If it is true that they had loaded all their muskets the night before, as they told me, there must have been neither gunpowder nor bullets in the palace because after twenty-five or thirty musketeers had fired from the roof, not another shot was heard. Those who entered to help were ill-prepared, and of the few soldiers who were already there, two or three were very badly wounded, while another had burned his left hand when a musketoon exploded, and the remaining ones were injured from being stoned head to toe, so the auxiliaries did not do any good. They were useless, not because they came without firearms which were not available, but rather because, as they said, they did not have anyone to lead them and give them arms. And, in the end, everything there was confusion, commotion and shouting because, because neither His Excellency [the Viceroy] nor anyone in his family was at home. And few people were there except some maids and other servants. There was not even a sufficient number of soldiers (already quartered in the palace) in the Guards Corps to do their duty of presenting arms to the Captain General when he returned to the palace, such as should always be practiced among a well-disciplined infantry.

The moment the gates were shut and the people found themselves without any opposition, there arose a grating and horrific howl that struck fear in those who heard it. . . . It appeared to me that up until then, judging from their size, the number of rebels who filled the square exceeded ten thousand. . . . I returned to the square where I realized . . . that not only Indians, but people of all colors without any exception, were there. And the Indians successfully stirred up the *zaramullos* [a derogatory caste category] of the Baratillo [thieves' market] and attracted them to

---

*The reference is to Hernán Cortés, who conquered the Aztec Empire of central Mexico between 1519 and 1521.

their cause by carrying into that place the Indian woman they pretended had died. Evidence proves that Indians were there, but they were not alone. Many others who frequented *pulquerías* [taverns selling *pulque,* a liquor obtained from maguey cactus] were mixed in with them, and these (as if speaking for all of them) had encouraged the Indians days earlier [in] what they wanted to do and what they were to steal on this occasion.

In a matter as grave as that which is treated here, I would not dare to definitively state either that it was the Indians who—without the counsel of others—began the riots, or that others who were involved—among them Spaniards—persuaded them to do it. Many of those who could hear the riots affirmed and ratified the latter position, but I saw more evidence of the former. . . . [Sigüenza describes how leaseholders had left over two hundred large wooden chests holding European and local merchandise in the central square. *Ed.*] The remainder of the square was filled with stalls made of reeds and mats where Indians sold things during the day and where they slept at night. All of this commerce meant that one of the most expansive and most glorious squares in the world looks to some like a badly built village and to all like a pigpen. You are familiar with this since you have seen it many times, and you also know that it has always been understood as bad government to permit such stalls in this place (that must by its nature be open and free), because both the material they are made of and the goods in the chests is so highly flammable.

With things such as they were, since they had not succeeded in accomplishing anything by throwing stones except surrendering their arms without any benefit at all, the rebels decided to set fire to all sides of the palace. The reeds and mats from which the stalls and huts were made provided more than enough material for the task, and the Indian men and women started to rip them apart and heap them against the palace doors and set them on fire. They accomplished this in the blink of an eye. They started the fire (for I do not know what reason) next to the second large chest that was close to the palace fountains. Since it held only sugar, its flames were intense and high. Next followed the patio door, where the Treaty and Court rooms, those of the scribes of the chamber, and the stores of bullets and sealed paper were all located. After this, the jail of the court that the bailiff had locked at the start of the stir was burned, and neither he nor those who assisted him in his quarters, could impede the masses from arming themselves with carbines. . . . [Sigüenza describes the fire spreading to other governmental buildings. *Ed.*]

No sound was heard from the rebels other than "Death to the Viceroy and the Corregidor!" and with the palace already burning on all sides, the rioters moved on to the municipal buildings, where the Corregidor lived, to set it on fire as well. Since he valued his own life and that of his wife, he had fled the place, but his carriage was the first to which they set fire and pelted with rocks. While it was being consumed by flames, they brandished it around the whole square as if in triumph. Afterward, some were driven to kill the coach's mules because they were also burning, while others immediately set fire, with great mountains of burning bedrolls, reeds and planks, to the offices of the public scribes and those of the municipal council . . . [and to other buildings].

They did not need to waste even a quarter of an hour in this because of both their great numbers and the care and diligence and determination with which they worked. It is remarkable that between six in the afternoon when the riot had started, until this point—about seven-thirty—they worked their hands and mouths with equal tenacity. We have already seen how much they had already accomplished with their hands. With their voices, they were no less execrable and rude. One did not hear anything in the whole square other than "Long live the Holy Sacrament! Long live the Virgin of the Rosary! Long live the King! Long live the Santiagueños!* Long live pulque!" But to each of these acclamations (perhaps because they were watchwords used so they would know each other) they added, "Death to the Viceroy! Death to the Viceroy's Wife! Death to the Corregidor! Death to the Spaniards! Death to bad Government!" And they shouted this not so plainly as I write it here, but rather with the addition of such shamelessness, curses, and vulgarities aimed at those figures that I think have ever been pronounced before this occasion by rational men. I know very well that everyone participated in this crime, but it was Indians alone who participated in burning the houses of the city government and the palace.

I have already related how the zaramullos of the Baratillo had immediately accompanied those who passed by them with the Indian woman whom they feigned had died. Like servants or slaves who stole from their employers' houses, or those who helped such thieves or bought items from them, they began to loot goods from the square . . . they began to break through doors and roofs, that were very weak, and to load up on merchandise and coins while the Indians (who knew, because of their regular presence on the square, which of all the chests were the best stocked) set the fires.

The Indians who witnessed this saw that they should also participate in getting their hands on such considerable spoils and so, joining other Indians, mulattos, blacks, *chinos* [half-castes], mestizos, *lobos* [wolves], and vile Spaniards, gachupines and *criollos* [American-born Spaniards], that were there, they fell at once on the chests holding iron goods, to get axes and iron bars which they used to break open other chests. And those who did not have any, armed themselves with machetes and knives. . . .

At this hour, instead of an alarm, all the church bells sounded and then there appeared the reverend fathers of the Company of Jesus and of la Merced whose exhortations, accompanied with prayers of the Holy Christ and the choruses and devout pauses of the rosary might have served to calm the people. They sang litanies with soft music to the image of the Holy Mary. And the whole community came into the square. But since stones then rained on them from all around, the holy order that the priests had brought about was ruined, and they dispersed to different places, where, although they continued preaching, their efforts were fruitless because everyone whistled at them and paid them no attention.

---

*The rioters may have been referring here to the Indian confraternity of Santiago (Saint James) located in Tlatelolco.

Central Themes

Indigenous people, state formation, urban life, land and labor, race and ethnicity

Suggested Reading

Cope, R. Douglas. *The Limits of Racial Domination: Plebeian Society in Colonial Mexico, 1660–1720.* Madison: University of Wisconsin Press, 1994.

Curcio-Nagy, Linda A. *The Great Festivals of Colonial Mexico City: Performing Power and Identity.* Albuquerque: University of New Mexico Press, 2004.

Ross, Kathleen. *The Baroque Narrative of Carlos de Sigüenza y Góngora: A New World Paradise.* Cambridge: Cambridge University Press, 1993.

Related Sources

6. Markets and Temples in the City of Tenochtitlan (1519)
20. Chimalpahin: Indigenous Chronicler of His Time (1611–1613)
26. Sor Juana: Nun, Poet, and Advocate (1690)
32. Hidalgo's Uprising (1849)
60. Chronicles of Mexico City (1938)
68. Eyewitness and Newspaper Accounts of the Tlatelolco Massacre (1968)

PART 4

Late Colonial Society (1737–1816)

Eighteenth-century Mexicans experienced dramatic changes in the previous century's economy, governance, and culture. These changes exacerbated existing social tensions and instigated new ones. New Spain's population doubled over the course of the eighteenth century, reaching 6 million inhabitants. In the same period, a new dynasty transformed colonial government and provoked widespread resistance to some of its modernizing efforts. Meanwhile, an expanding economy brought greater wealth to certain sectors of the populace but a decline in the living standard of the majority. This chapter's selections document how Mexicans responded to these changes, focusing particularly on their reactions to the modernizing measures known as the Bourbon reforms. The social transformations that the Bourbon dynasty implemented and provoked were in significant measure responsible for pushing Mexicans toward participation in the drawn-out independence wars that swept the territory beginning in 1810.

While the Viceroyalty's population had increased slowly in the seventeenth century, after its Post-Conquest decline all sectors of New Spain grew rapidly in the eighteenth century. Indigenous people began a demographic recovery, and by century's end the *casta* (mixed-race) sector had expanded to as much as one-quarter of New Spain's total population. Many cities—Puebla, Guanajuato, Querétaro, and Mérida, along with the Mexican capital—experienced particularly rapid growth. This demographic explosion triggered other important changes. Urban Mexicans consumed larger amounts of locally produced manufactured goods, including textiles, as well as novel cultural products like novels and newspapers (sources 27 and 30). New Spain's overall increased population density also supported expanded local markets for foodstuffs, such as the bread and mutton whose prices are listed in the *Gazeta de México* (Source 30).

Both the agrarian and mining economies grew particularly rapidly in Mexico's Bajío region, the fertile area falling between the Viceroyalty's central valleys and its drier north. But here as elsewhere, wealth was unevenly distributed among the population. The expansion of larger estates and several years of drought, particularly in the last two decades of the eighteenth century, drove up the prices of basic commodities. These factors help explain why the first popular uprising in the era of Mexico's independence revolutions came from the Bajío region (Source 32).

Demographic changes had further ramifications in the late colonial history of the Viceroyalty. As illustrated in the period's new artistic genre, *pinturas de casta* (caste paintings) (Source 31), the growth of the casta population and the coincident social mobility of some of its members triggered greater anxiety among *criollos* (American-born Spaniards) about their position in New Spain's social hierarchy. These tensions were aggravated by such measures as the Bourbon state's strategy of strengthening its military by encouraging casta enrollment in local militias (Source 29) and its extension of privileges that had been the exclusive domain of Spaniards, such as access to the *fuero militar* (military court), to *mestizos* (people of Indian-Spanish parentage), *mulatos* (people of African and Spanish parentage), and others.

The French Bourbon dynasty that inherited control over Spanish America in 1700 and successfully defended this inheritance in the War of Spanish Succession (1700–1713) sought to overhaul the Hapsburgs' inefficiently baroque structure of government. The Bourbons applied the intellectual currents of the French Enlightenment to their colonial administration, implementing changes, for instance, in the structure and personnel of the state and the military and in the administration of taxes. The Bourbons also mandated changes in the social and cultural life of their colonies, attempting to modernize and secularize society through their support for such modern publications as the *Gazeta de México,* with its scientific treatises and discourses on more efficient agricultural practices. The Bourbons also reappropriated power from other competing groups, most especially the Catholic Church. They accomplished this by discouraging the venues of religious piety whose public ceremonies had particularly shaped Mexican Catholicism in the seventeenth century, supporting instead more personal, contemplative forms of religious worship (Source 25). In addition, they transferred power over indigenous parishes from the religious orders to the secular church. Following the practice of Portugal and France, the Bourbons even went so far as to expel the Jesuit Order from Spanish America in 1767. Administration of the order's missions in the Northwest of New Spain, which represented virtually the only presence of the Spanish state in the area at the time, was subsequently assumed by the Franciscan and Dominican Orders (Source 28).

The Bourbon dynasty did not retain absolute control in determining the nature of modernization, enlightenment, and, still less, liberty in Spanish America. As the pages of the *Gazeta de México* reveal, local concerns and traditions—particularly religious ones—remained prominent even within such Bourbon-supported projects. Mexican critiques of colonial government generally, and the Bourbon's administration in particular, became increasingly pointed at the turn of the nineteenth century. They were voiced in satire, such as in José Joaquin Fernández de Lizardi's novels (Source 34) and in political manifestos like José María Morelos's vision for a newly independent Mexican nation (Source 33). By 1821, the forces opposing continued Spanish rule had become powerful enough to secure Mexico's independence from Spain, but this was only achieved through an alliance of the territory's more radical and traditionalist elements. The alliance, then, was only temporary, and divisive conflict between liberal and conservative sectors would shape the new republic through much of the nineteenth century.

28. Indigenous Revolt in California (1737)*

Once it had secured control over south-central Mexico in the 1520s, the Spanish crown encouraged colonial governors to extend their holdings northward. This northern region became increasingly important to the crown, for as well as housing a potential port for the Manila galleons, the trading ships that sailed across the Pacific Ocean between the Philippines and New Spain, it was a frontier that delineated English and French encroachment into Spanish territory. Hernán Cortés dispatched what would be the first of many missions northwest to the Californias in 1533. This voyage was followed by a long series of unsuccessful expeditions led by explorers, mariners, pearl-fishers, and pirates. Instead, the territory was secured by the religious orders, beginning with the Jesuit Juan María de Salvatierra. In 1697, Salvatierra, accompanied by a captain, five soldiers, and a few servants, established the first mission-*presidio* (garrison) at Loreto. Within fifty years, the Jesuits had founded fifteen missions in the area. Until the crown's expulsion of the Jesuits from Spanish America in 1767, these religious communities, and the minimal military presence of their accompanying presidios, represented the only significant arm of Spain's colonial presence in the region.

The following excerpt comes from the extraordinary journal of Father Sigismundo Taraval. Taraval was born in Milan in 1700 and entered the Society of Jesus at age eighteen. He studied in Alcalá, Spain, as well as in Mexico City and was sent to serve the Jesuits in the Californias in 1730. In 1733, accompanied by three guards, he founded a new mission, Santa Rosa, on the southeast coast of the Baja Peninsula. He arrived at a time when various indigenous groups in the territory were plotting revolt against the missions' presence. Many of the conflicts originated in Indian resistance to the Jesuits' insistence that they abandon traditional social and spiritual practices, including polygamy and shamanism. The Callejue often remained loyal to the Jesuits, but several other peoples, including the Huchitíes and the Pericúes, launched repeated raids on the missions in the early 1730s, until they were forcefully subdued in 1737.

Although he produced a journal—normally considered as a private genre—we can assumed that Taraval anticipated a public readership for his writing. The Jesuits had a long-standing tradition of chronicling their missionary work in the *Jesuit Relations,* the voluminous yearly reports that Jesuit missionaries in the Americas produced. Taraval's extensive substantiation of his observations with purportedly

---

*Sigismundo Taraval, *The Indian Uprising in Lower California, 1734–1737, as Described by Father Sigismundo Taraval*, trans., with introduction and notes, by Marguerite Eyer Wilbur (Los Angeles: Quivira Society, 1931), pp. 26–37. Except where otherwise noted, any footnotes included are in the original. Footnotes containing unreferenced Latin of the citations in the text have been eliminated, as have other nonessential footnotes.

scholarly (albeit undocumented) sources further suggests that he intended for his journal to be read by the public, notwithstanding the fact that it remained unpublished until 1931. To what conclusions may we infer that Taraval wished to lead his imagined readers? Taraval's own cultural viewpoint infuses his perspective on the indigenous people he describes in these passages. What influences, sources, and attitudes obviously shaped the ways he portrayed the California Indians?

The Taraval Journal

(9) . . . When the devil began to scatter the germs of an uprising down at a point remote from the presidio, namely at Mission San Joseph, located among the Pericúe tribe on Cape San Lucas* and the seat of the first settlement in California, so potent was his fire that a spark reached on over to the other side of the farthest mission. Here it caused considerable damage and that it did not cause mischief in the intervening country was a miracle. . . .

(10) . . . What tribes inhabit this land [California] belong in the main to four totally different nations whose salient traits have been expressed as follows by one writer: "This is a fourfold people; the first division composed of women, the second of animals, the third of thieves, the fourth of men."

(11) Of these the first is the Pericúe nation, a tribe inhabiting the region lying approximately one degree below the tropic of Cancer. So effeminate are they in character that it would be difficult to find their counterpart in the entire world. And so by way of describing their manners, customs, and traits, some one has truthfully said:

> They are women in words, accents, quarrels, disputes, anger, changeableness, trust; the name alone is lacking; but you will be led astray by the very names of the men. They bear feminine names and not without uttering them. If you call for a name and Peter is mentioned, you will get Petra, if Paul, Paula, if Joseph, Josepha.

(12) Their second is the Vaicuro nation that lives between latitudes twenty-two and twenty-five degrees. Of them it may be tersely said: "They belong to the sun, the stars, the sea, the globe. They believe that a dog was their maker."

Whatever they hear from their wizards and old men about the customs, acts, and life of the dog, this they attempt to emulate. Naturally with this mode of life, their manners are akin to those of the brute. For this reason, even after the lapse of so many years, they still have no conception of eternity. If one were to judge them by

*San Joseph was thus the most southerly mission. Frequently ships bent on northern explorations or sent out to find pearls anchored off this headland. The Pericúes, or local Indians, had long been notoriously unruly and had even attempted to incite those as far north as Mission San Ignacio to rebel. They were now plotting a general uprising, and the massacre of all the fathers . . .

their actions one might question whether they were men or at least whether they realized it.

(13) The third is known as the tribe of Loreto. I am inclined to believe that this is a branch of Vaicuro and that the latter comprises three main groups, the Huchitíes, the Pericúes, and the Loretans. Although they appear to differ radically yet they have certain rites and customs in common; however, they speak totally different languages.

The tribe of Loreto is so small that, owing to the ravages of sickness, there are not so many families now as there were rancherías originally. Concerning this tribe the same writer has said: "They are petty in their faculties, and in their mind, in their souls, in their friends. If they should be measured, their defects will be even greater."

As for their beliefs I may remark that they consider the sun a most unfortunate, miserable, and unhappy creature, since it falls into the sea night after night and has to swim until dawn in order to rise again the next morning. Among this tribe the mission and pueblo of Our Lady of Loreto have been established. This is almost in the heart of conquered territory and of the crescent forming this California; as a result, it is well adapted to serve as the cornerstone for the activities of the most holy Mary of Loreto, conqueress and patroness of the Californias. Here the first landing was made; here, in her honor, was erected the first mission; here was established the royal garrison.

(14) The fourth tribe is the Cochimí, who inhabit the land extending for more than two hundred leagues beyond Mission San Xavier. No other tribes have been discovered here. These people are obsequious, humble, obedient, tractable, docile, and loyal. The farther north the Indians live, the higher seems their intelligence. For this reason toward the north lie the most successful missions, the last in my opinion being the most flourishing.* So the more to be regretted is the damage caused by the outbreak arising out of the rebellion, which will be described in due season. That this should fall victim, and not those in the center that were more or less susceptible, seems as miraculous as if fire were to ignite green wood rather than dry. Nor can I deny that the first among the northern tribes to fall made at the start considerable resistance; quite the contrary was the conduct of the Pericúes, that fell on the south. Moreover, the tribes of the north and of the south may be said to have re-enacted the historic parable of the two sons which our blessed Christ points out in his teachings, since the one who said "No," repenting later, did what his father had asked, and the one who said "Yes" failed to keep his promise.

(15) Among the Pericúe nation, three missions have been founded: San Joseph on the tip of Cape San Lucas, Santiago, and Santa Rosa. The parishioners of the latter, however, having no buildings nor neophytes, joined that of San Joseph. Two have been established among the Vaicuros: Nuestra Señora del Pilar, on the famous bay of La Paz, and that of Nuestra Señora de los Dolores (del Sur); on that of Loreto, only the latter mission. Siutated among the Cochimí are six: San Xavier, San Joseph de Comondú, Purísima Concepción, Santa Rosalía, Nuestra Señora de Guadalupe, and

*This was Mission San Ignacio, where Father Taraval had previously been stationed.

finally, Nuestro Padre de San Ygnacio. When classifying the tribes according to their basic differences they may be said to have four main languages; but to learn them with their many variations and acquire a mastery of their dialects it is actually necessary to learn six different languages, since they are as unlike as French and Spanish. The salient point of similarity among tribes of the Californias is their household possessions; otherwise they are totally and distinctly unlike. This was summarized by the said author in the following distich: "Their city is a grove, their home a cave, fruits are their food, armed weapons their furniture, wool their warmth, skin their raiment, rocks their bed. . . . "

Such are the nations, provinces, and islands of the Californias, the islands for whose conquest were opened the royal coffers of the Catholic monarchs, although they failed to found in them a single colony. These are the islands that have defied the efforts of the bravest captains who have tried their skill from the days of the invincible Hernán Cortés. These are the islands that have failed to be conquered by hundreds of expeditions, hundreds of millions of pesos, and innumerable attempts at conquest, given with valor and power, with temerity and greed in the search for pearls. And finally, these are the lands that came in for such repeated and vigorous orders on the part of their Excellencies, the viceroys, in whose interests were issued so many cédulas [decrees], and for which no pains were spared until it was finally believed they could not be conquered. . . . At the very time when it was the universal belief that all attempts must fail, their apostolic zeal led them on to this conquest, with only five men, a few alms, an old unseaworthy galliot, and a meagre stock of provisions. . . .

(17) By July of the year 1734, returning to my subject, the devil let loose, or seemingly let loose, began to practice his evil ways by scattering the seeds of rebellion at the tip of the Californias, down at Cape San Lucas, among the Pericúes, and in the first mission established among this nation, one dedicated to the noted patriarch, San Joseph.* They soon revealed the spirit that inflamed them, and although they made every effort to conceal their plots, yet before these could be put into execution they came to the attention of the venerable Father Lorenzo Carranco, the father stationed at the neighboring mission, Santiago. The holy father made constant attempts to avert this, which was accomplished at the cost of infinite labor. He then informed the venerable Father Nicolás Tamaral, the father in charge of the San Joseph mission, of all that had transpired. Thus forewarned, the blessed Father Tamaral together with his most loyal followers, if any merited this name, tried to take pre-

*The rebellion actually began at the Indian ranchería of Yeneca, belonging to Mission Santiago, where an unruly mulatto, Chicori, was captain. Among his many wives was a young woman who wished to be baptized, but Father Carranco could not receive her into the church unless she refused to live immorally with Chicori. The latter, enraged at Father Carranco's attitude toward his polygamous practices, incited his tribesmen to rebel. Miguel Venegas, *Empresas apostólicas de los padres misioneros de la compañia de Jesús de la provincia de la Nueva España obradas en la conquista de Californias* . . . , VII, 827–829.

cautions by making investigations and inquiries.* But he failed to find out anything definite, merely uncovering a series of vague rumours which invariably thrive among barbarians at new missions and so are not taken seriously. But now, perhaps because there was no loyal Indian to warn him, or possibly because the plot was kept secret from his assistants, or again the latter may have actually been the ringleaders, at all events in addition to seething, within a few days the storm broke with violence.

(18) The venerable Father Lorenzo Carranco was now clearly aware that the roads had been taken to prevent the passing of the courier with the warning. But what could he do? He gathered together without delay several Indians, men who appeared to be the most loyal, and sent them to the venerable Father Nicolás Tamaral with a letter and, in case of necessity, to conduct, guard, or defend the father.** They departed, carrying the letter, and while he took, upon receipt of it, every care and redoubled his precautions yet it was not possible to avert the calamity because of the treachery of the boys who assisted him. Possibly at first they were ignorant of what was brewing but this could not have lasted indefinitely. Invariably among barbarians, the more the missionary strives to please, exerts himself, and attempts to care for them, the more they want and the more perverse, disloyal, or ungrateful they become. A race so highly servile is made worse by presents; for the demon merely uses to wage war for his own ends the very instruments utilized by the father.

(19) Since he could not handle the situation, he returned the Indians he had sent. Thereupon the ringleaders, to protect themselves and take vengeance on the venerable Father Lorenzo Carranco, desisted from what they were about to attempt, and devoted all their wiles, tricks, and arts to persuade the natives at Santiago to inflict upon their father what they were determined to do with the one at their own mission. In the meanwhile, the natives by cunning, by promises, again by lies, and the devil with all his arts, tried to cause disorder, win converts and corrupt those at Santiago. You will soon see what happened in consequence, at my mission [Santa Rosa], the only one left in the region which the devil desired as well and made every effort to procure. So I found myself in the same, or even greater danger, because of the boldness of the Vaicuros.

---

*Father Carranco at Santiago and Father Tamaral at San Joseph were ignorant of the extent of the projected uprising. Chicori and Botón were already plotting to kill the fathers and wipe out Christianity in California, moving from south to north. By July Taraval had been warned of danger by some loyal Callejues.

**Fathers Carraco and Tamaral had no soldiers stationed at their missions. This encouraged the Indian ringleaders, who feared Spanish firearms, to revolt. Father Taraval at Santa Rosa had three guards.

Central Themes

Indigenous people, the northern frontier, religion, race and ethnicity

Suggested Reading

Konrad, Herman W. *A Jesuit Hacienda in Colonial Mexico: Santa Lucía, 1576–1767.* Stanford, CA: Stanford University Press, 1980.

Polzer, Charles. *The Jesuit Missions of Northern Mexico. The Spanish Borderlands Sourcebooks,* vol. 19. New York: Routledge, 1991.

Weber, David. *The Spanish Frontier in North America.* New Haven, CT: Yale University Press, 1992.

Related Sources

18. Father Fernández Attempts to Convert the Seris of Sonora Single-handedly (1679)
24. The Persistence of Indigenous Idolatry (1656)
37. A Woman's Life on the Northern Frontier (1877)

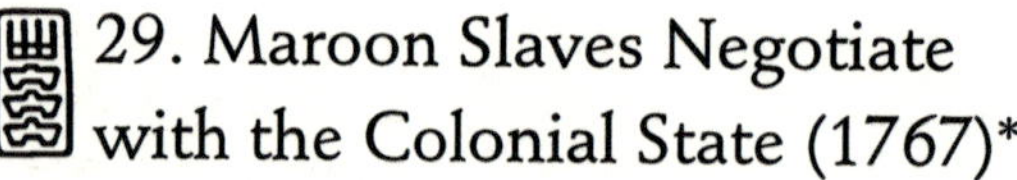

29. Maroon Slaves Negotiate with the Colonial State (1767)*

By the late eighteenth century, blacks and *mulatos* (people of African and Spanish parentage), both slave and free, constituted about 6 percent of New Spain's overall population. As had been true in the preceding century, most of them worked in mining and ranching operations in the Viceroyalty's north-central and western zones, but slaves and free blacks also lived in Veracruz, Mexico City, Oaxaca, and elsewhere (sources 19 and 23). By century's close, Afro-Mexicans were present in all but New Spain's highest social echelons. Although a relatively small percentage of the total population, in the context of the growth and increased social mobility of the *casta* (mixed-race) population, this black population threatened *criollos'* (American-born Spaniards) sense of social superiority.

Military service presented people of color with one route to social mobility. Beginning in 1760, the Bourbon dynasty that had assumed governance of Spanish America in 1700 took the unprecedented step of creating colonial armies to defend its holdings in the Americas while simultaneously expanding the size of its colonies' local militias. Since labor in these forces was not altogether attractive, the state en-

---

*Fernando Winfield Capitaine, *Los cimarrones de Mazateopan* (Xalapa, Veracruz: Gobierno del Estado de Veracruz-Llave, 1992), pp. 35–39, 45–48. Excerpt translated by the editors. All footnotes have been added. Italicized words are those italicized in the original. Spelling has been modernized and rendered consistent.

hanced the appeal of inscription by extending the privilege of the *fuero militar* (military court), previously the exclusive domain of Spaniards, to both *mestizos* (people of Indian and Spanish ancestry) and mulatos.

The Afro-Mexicans portrayed in the following documents were *cimarrones* (escaped slaves) who had formed *palenques* (escaped slave communities) in northeastern Oaxaca, near the southern tip of the present state of Veracruz. Included here is the text of the formal petition that the leader of the cimarrones, Fernando Manuel, presented before the *alcalde mayor* (district governor) of Teuitla, Oaxaca, requesting the right to lawfully found a permanent town, and the testimony of one witness who supported the town's foundation.

Later sources about the community reveal that the cimarrones did reach an agreement with the alcalde mayor. By December 1767, they had secured land titles, laid out boundary markers, and commenced construction on houses and a church. Less than a decade later, however, Teuitla's alcalde mayor wanted the town to be disbanded. He wrote the viceroy, alleging that its residents demonstrated insufficient respect for his authority and had not complied with the terms of their 1767 agreement; furthermore, he asserted, they harbored Indians, castas, and military fugitives from Veracruz, and they had usurped lands from a neighboring Indian community. The viceroy, suspicious of the alcalde's claims, refrained from disbanding the settlement.

Historians have traditionally posited that considerable animosity existed between various disempowered groups in colonial Mexico. What does evidence from the following excerpts suggest was the case here in terms of the cimarrones' relationships with other slaves, Indians, and mestizos of the laboring classes? What methods and devices did they use to advance their position?

The Maroons of Mazateopan

Before *Señor* [Sir] Alcalde Mayor of Teutila Don Andrés Fernández de Otañes, *Caballero* [Chevalier] of the Order of Calatrava.

Presented May 12 1767

I, Fernando Manuel, a black man, now a Sergeant and previously Captain of black forces called cimarrones presently found congregated in Palacios, *Breve Cocina, Mandiga,* on the banks of the *Amapa* River in this *Province of Teutila,* speak in the name of all my companions implicated in the report that I present here. To them, furthermore, I lend my voice and pledge to help them achieve their agreeable aim of transforming themselves for their own advantage. And they have given me their full consent, for all legal purposes, for this task. Before Your Mercy I appear, and state: that having deserted the sugar mills of the Villa of Córdoba, where we were slaves, because of the severity with which we were treated there, we took refuge in the highest mountains of this Province and those of Mazathiopam, forming the palenques named

Rosario, next to the woods of Anona, and San Antonio on the banks of the Quiesalapa River, and that of San Martín de Cuazathiopa, where we lived from that time on for over forty years, enduring unspeakable hardship, hunger, and discomfort. And in an attempt to end this situation once and for all, we resolved to form a stable and secure town, following the counsel of Your Mercy, to desist in traveling about as vagabonds, and to be instructed in the Christian doctrine. We seek spiritual nourishment, which we have lacked with intense pain, to repair our consciences and achieve the salvation of our souls that we desire with all our hearts. We do not doubt that we will achieve this with the protection that you offer us, and I reiterate our supplication hoping to advance our goal, which I advocate with determination, for charity and for the love of God, to avoid further spiritual and temporal difficulties and consequences because of the prosecution to which we have been exposed, despite not having ever committed harm to any living creature.

As for a fuller understanding of the stir that these palenques have caused, I suspect that that they were instigated by other blacks who fled to them long before we did, and according to what the elders tell us, they have been here since the conquest of this kingdom. But from these beginnings there now remain only the *fifty-two* people of both sexes, among them children and old people, who are described in the account that I have prepared. And although the Dragoons of the Plaza of Veracruz and the militias of the Villa of Córdoba have undertaken many missions at different times, squandering of many expenses, in attempts to catch the maroons and finish off the communities, they have been useless because the mountains are impenetrable, as is public and notorious.

In the year 1758, we were solicited by Doctor Don Apolinar de Cossío, administrator of the *Hacienda* [agricultural estate] of *Estanzuela,* to leave the mountains and our most difficult way of life. He offered to protect our freedom and, in effect, we accepted his offer and formed a fixed town in a nice, suitable, and fertile spot, which Don Fernando Carlos de Rivera de Neyra, his master, offered to us. And with this hope we journeyed near to the fields of the Hacienda, although we went with the mistrust always felt by the poor and disadvantaged that we would not get what we had been offered. At that time, we recognized as our Captain of the Mountain another black man called Macute. I was his Lieutenant, and Captain of the road, whose job was to oversee the journeys that some undertook to supply us with what we lacked, often traveling to the outskirts of Veracruz, where our comrades took what they needed and what we asked for, and brought it back to our palenques on secret routes, without doing harm to anyone. The said Captain Macute, growing more suspicious than I did of what had been offered to us, counselled us to return to the mountains and threatened to punish us if we did not. This was sufficient cause to reduce us to two groups of blacks, one in his favor and the other in mine, and we resorted to making our decision through a formal battle. And the Most Holy Virgin of Guadalupe, whom I had sworn as my advocate and patron, determined that my followers and I would triumph, and we imprisoned Capitan Macute after he had wounded himself gravely along with all those of his group who were still alive. And as a man of conscience in proof of my Christian soul, my good inclination to peace and to a settled community, we brought them to the Villa of Córdoba, so they could be delivered to their masters, as in effect was done, which is also public and notorious. Afterwards, my group and I formed the settlements where we live at present.

The hope that the two said Señores had offered us was entirely dispelled for both of them had died. Nevertheless, desiring to deserve the attainment of our goal, and in proof that we are not as bad as the general voice has wished to render us, we agreed to serve the King Our Lord in the war of 1762 with the English. And we descended determinately with this plan to the *Plaza* [Square] of Veracruz, where the Excellent Señor Viceroy the Marquis of Cruillas was arranging his defenses and we presented ourselves to His Excellency with our statement, pleading with him to concede us our liberty and a pardon from the unrest that our persecutors had wished to attribute to us. And we asked that he give us license to serve the King in the capacity of volunteers during the war as a class of Lancers of the field which His Excellency conceded us in the margin of our *Memorial* [record book], which document, to our disgrace, we have lost. But the truth of this act is found in the report that Captain Don Santiago Rodríguez Cubillo made in his naming of me as Sergeant of my companions, which he did on January 17 1765, which act I present so that once the evidence has been taken from it, it can be returned to me.

In addition to this, there is our vigilance in catching blacks who continuously flee from the sugar mills of the Villa of Córdoba, and hide in the said mountains and palenques. Only we are capable of catching them, since we have done the same things ourselves. Evidence of this truth is shown in our acts of returning slaves to Don Diego de Bringas, owner of the Mill of Toluquilla and to Don Juan Segura and Don Gaspar Mexia, which actions, so faithful and constant, since our battle with our opponents, shows that we do not desire any other thing than that we should be formally given liberty from slavery, even though, in essence, we already have it. We would like to be granted this liberty under the following circumstances and conditions:

We are obliged to solicit and turn in any escaped blacks, but in the future, the Señor Viceroy will pay us for each one according to his price, so that, our certainty of obtaining this reward, which we consider just and conforming to the laws, will spur us to the task. This will assist our masters and all the mills since in only making such a provision notorious, no-one will attempt to escape, and slaves will be reduced to working, at whatever befalls them, as is already starting to happen in the present.

As well, we pledge to be punctual in serving the King Our Lord in our capacity as Lancers any time it shall be necessary. And we shall be obedient to the royal justice of Theutila, in whose jurisdiction at the edge of the fertile land of the banks of the Amapa River and near the mountains we choose to live so that with greater ease we can catch those who attempt to hide. Your Mercy should indicate which terrain we should use and give us sufficient land, of the vast royal property that is there, so that we can maintain ourselves with its cultivation and husbandry, granting us the title of Officials of the Republic for its economic governance.

We should also be conceded the faculty and license necessary to erect a church with the name of Our Lady of Guadalupe whom we choose as our patron, in which will be celebrated the Holy Sacrament of the Mass, and other Holy acts, so that we will be indoctrinated in the Holy Fear of God, by the person whom the Most Illustrious Señor Bishop of Puebla, whose Mitre pertains to this land, serves to name. And we ask Your Mercy if you will supplicate him in our name, not doubting his Holy Pastoral zeal, about the achievement of this good end, because no less than the salvation of so many souls—who have lived in the mountains for so long, living irrationally, and burying the dead in them—depends on him.

While the foundation of these Christian intentions is verified, Your Mercy must give us an assurance in the name of the King, so that no person of any quality will disturb us, nor perturb the settlements of the Teja del Monte where we presently live, so that in this way our misgivings may cease, since although the voices that threaten some of us are insubstantial and do not harm us, they are sufficient to bring us fear, and keep us alert both day and night. With the documented assurance for which we ask, having lost the one that the Most Excellent Señor Viceroy the Marquis of Cruillas granted us, we might be somewhat calmed.

Numerous circumstances demonstrate the uselessness of the vast expense that the owners of the mills of the Villa of Córdoba have wasted on repeated occasions engaging the Dragones of Veracruz and other auxiliary forces to reduce us by force of arms, believing that this could be achieved: the inaccessibility of the mountains, the greater familiarity with which we have achieved because of our need to travel and live in them; the service that we have done for His Majesty in the past war; the benefit that the owners of the sugar mills have received from our capture and delivery of their slaves without any other compensation for this formidable task and risk with risk to our lives than that which some have voluntarily wanted to give. For this reason, we ask that his most Excellent Señor evaluate what in the future we should be given, so that there is no question about it. The termination of the instruction and teaching of the Christian doctrine risks our souls' condemnation, and in the holy fear of God Our Lord, we solicit the establishment and planning of our town by means of *reducción* [congregation]. Without a doubt, this point merits very special attention. It is equally true that this will benefit the public interest because there will no longer be any escaped black slaves to fear as there were before, and people will travel upon deserted routes without fear. And those who are slaves will not attempt to flee because they will certainly be captured and returned to their servitude. We will also happily sacrifice ourselves, whenever it is necessary and we are commanded to do so, to increase the number of Lancers of the field, a strong force, daring in its service to the king, and in the defense of these domains.

All of which substantial reasons of strong foundation demonstrate that our liberty from slavery should be conceded along with the establishment of the town and church that we have requested. And I supplicate Your Mercy will give an account of this to his Most Excellent Señor Viceroy so that such Christian desires be authorized and our difficulties ended so that we can secure the peace to which we so anxiously aspire. To this end, we release the corresponding dispatches for our security and shelter. For all of this, I supplicate and request Your Mercy. I present here the documentation of my naming as Sergeant. All that I have referred to here is true and just and I swear in the name of my companions this is not done in malice. And since I do not know how to sign, I request a witness in the presence of the Señor Alcalde Mayor.

Witnessed,
Andres de Urioste.

[This request was followed by a writ issued by Andrés Fernández de Otañes, Caballero of the Military Order of Calatrava, and Royal Commissioner of War and Alcalde Mayor of the jurisdiction, acknowledging Fernando Manuel's submission, ratified in the presence of nine companions who accompanied him and announcing that he judges it best that an investigation be undertaken to verify all aspects of the latter's proposal. There followed a list of the members of Manuel's community. After this Manuel submitted a letter dating from 1765 to which he referred in his petition, granting Manuel and his followers their freedom in exchange for their military service and naming him sergeant. Next, Andrés Fernández de Otañes issued a declaration, also dated May 12, 1767, supporting Fernando Manuel's petition and referring the matter on to the viceroy and the bishop of Puebla. This document was followed by declarations of several witnesses providing further information about the history surrounding the petition. *Ed.*]

Information

Witness #1. Prudente de Arellano, 82 years of age.

In the town of San Miguel Soyaltepeque, Jurisdiction of Teutila, on May 13 1767, I, the Alcalde Mayor, Don Andrés Fernández de Otañes, in virtue of that commanded by writ of May 12 requesting information as expressed, order the appearance before me of Prudente de Arellano, of *mestizo* [person of Spanish and Indian parentage] *calidad* [status], a blacksmith by occupation, resident of this town, who has sworn before God Our Lord and the sign of the Holy Cross according to law, and has affirmed he will tell the truth where he can in what is asked of him. And having read the petition presented by the black Sergeant Fernando Manuel of those called the cimarrones, with whom he is well acquainted, he declares that it is true that they have, in the aforementioned time, journeyed to the mountains where the palenques or settlements are located, having deserted the sugar mills of their owners because of the severity with which they were worked in slavery. This is what is heard as public and notorious, and if they had been treated well, he does not think they would have left the mills. And although at the beginning, they journeyed on the deserted routes from the Blanco River to Veracruz and Cosamaloapan and robbed travelers, regularly taking the provisions from them that they lacked so as to maintain themselves, they did not do more damage than this and retreated immediately to the mountains.

Afterwards, they did not leave there except when, from time to time, they went to furnish themselves with things that they needed in the outskirts of Veracruz where they remained hidden until their comrades, the zacateros, got them what they needed. They then returned along secret paths because they had abundant seeds for their food on the mountains because they had worked to make *milpas* [corn plots] in them, and he knows this for having heard it from the same blacks and because it is well-known in this region. And although the [owners of the] sugar mills of the Villa of Córdoba put all their efforts into dislodging them and capturing them with armed fighters, to which end the Dragones of the Plaza de Veracruz went up the mountain various times, and although militias of the country were united in this, and they spent great quantities of pesos on it, these measures were all useless because of the roughness and difficulty of the mountains, whose unpopulated gorges belonged to the Jalitatuane of this jurisdiction of Teutila.* And the declarant presumes that it is impossible to vanquish them by force of arms since experience has already shown this. And it is worth celebrating the fact that they have voluntarily desired to reduce themselves to a fixed town as they seek to do now, because in this way the spirits will be reassured that have so upset the name of these cimarron blacks who, according to what he has heard from his elders, have been here since the conquest. By means of the reducción, their spiritual solace will be achieved that instruction in the Christian doctrine alone has been deficient in achieving. And slave owners will be dispelled of the suspicion that the slaves they have in their mills will flee again since the duty that they will have, as they have previously done, to solicit and deliver them will be published as they also did with those that they caught in the battle with the opposing group of Captain Macute who did not want to establish himself in a town as desired by the followers of his lieutenant Fernando Manuel, who is now a Sergeant of the bands who live in the towns of Palacios, Breve Cocina, and Mandinga on the banks of the Amapa River of this jurisdiction that he has seen many times. And the declarant also knows that the said black Fernando Manuel descended with those of his band to the Plaza of Veracruz in the war of the year 1762 with the English and they presented themselves to the Viceroy the Marquis of Cruillas who was there arranging its defense, and that his petition amounted to the request that the Viceroy should concede them a pardon for the disorder attributed to them and grant them liberty in the name of His Majesty. He infers they achieved this according to what he has heard as public and notorious because if it was not this way they would not have served in the Lancers' Corps. And he knows that the black Fernando Manuel has the rank of Sergeant of his group, and that he has this knowledge from the land. And that the place where they wish to make their settlement is very fertile and healthy, at a distance of seven leagues from this town of Soyaltepeque and five from the *cabecera* (head town) of the *hacienda* of Estanzuela, and that it appears according to

*The Jalitatuane were a pueblo of Cuicatec Indians in the region of Teutila, Oaxaca. Peter Gerhard, *A Guide to the Historical Geography of New Spain* (1972; reprint, Norman: University of Oklahoma Press, 1993), p. 304.

what he has heard these lands pertain to the Indians who, because they are far away, do not take advantage of them because they possess sufficient lands closer to their town. And he has not heard that the said blacks have done any damage to the settlements in which they find themselves at present since the year 1758 when they were founded there, nor that there are any palenques left in the mountains. They maintain themselves on milpas of corn and peanuts that they grow and sell to the muleteers and travelers who journey along these routes for the hot lowlands. And that all that is referred to here he knows for having seen it and heard it and because it is public and notorious and it is the truth under the oath that he has sworn and having read this declaration he affirms and ratifies it. And he says he is 82 years old, more or less, and he does not sign because he can not, and he gives faith, and I, the Alcalde Mayor with the witnesses that attend me, swear for lack of a Royal and Public Scribe in over 30 leagues surrounding that I also give faith.

Andrés Fernández de Otañes.
Witness Phelipe del Azebalo
Witness Juan Manuel de las Casas.

Central Themes

State formation, land and labor, religion, race and ethnicity

Suggested Reading

Carroll, Patrick James. *Blacks in Colonial Veracruz: Race, Ethnicity, and Regional Development.* Austin: University of Texas Press, 1991.

Price, Richard. *Alabi's World.* Johns Hopkins Studies in Atlantic History and Culture. Baltimore: Johns Hopkins University Press, 1990.

Restall, Matthew, ed. *Beyond Black and Red: African-Indigenous Relations in Colonial Latin America.* Albuquerque: University of New Mexico Press, 2005.

Vinson, Ben. *Bearing Arms for His Majesty: The Free-Colored Militia in Colonial Mexico.* Stanford, CA: Stanford University Press, 2001.

Related Sources

23. The Treatment of African Slaves (the Seventeenth Century)
25. Afro-Mexicans, Mestizos, and Catholicism (1672)
30. Mexico's Paradoxical Enlightenment (1784)

30. Mexico's Paradoxical Enlightenment (1784)*

The eighteenth century saw the rise in Europe of an intellectual movement called the Enlightenment, a philosophy that sought to replace religion with science and reason as the foundation of all authority. In theory, it evoked the growth of liberty and democracy; in practice, it also involved the centralization and modernization of the state. The Bourbon dynasty, which had assumed control over Spanish America in 1700, introduced the Enlightenment into colonial government through a variety of measures in the second half of the eighteenth century. Among these was its support for the establishment of news periodicals in urban centers—among them, the *Gazeta de México.*

The *Gazeta de México,* published from 1784 to 1821, was one of New Spain's first news periodicals. The paper was created to disseminate the message of the Enlightenment to the populace and to foment the popularity of both the Spanish crown and the Mexican viceroy. Reports and communiqués from colonial bureaucrats constituted the bulk of its contents. However, the *Gazeta* also published discussions of civic and religious festivities, news of European conflicts, notices about the arrivals and departures of ships, and detailed discussions of natural phenomena. The *Gazeta*'s readership consisted of the civil and ecclesiastical bureaucracy of royal government in Mexico and the larger group of the general literate elite in the capital city and across the Viceroyalty. Most of its contents were authored by state or ecclesiastic officials.

Readers will encounter descriptions of a wide range of topics in the following *Gazeta* excerpts: natural phenomena and natural wonders, including a "monstrous" birth; religious festivals; price lists; and a treatise on the production of cochineal, a red dyestuff cultivated in Pre-Columbian Mexico that, during the colonial period, became Mexico's second-most-valuable export after silver. What attitude toward cochineal and its producers does the *Gazeta* convey? Why did its publishers decide to include notices such as this one—and the wide variety of other news items included here? What purpose might they have served? What conclusions can be drawn about the distinctive nature of the Enlightenment's development in Mexico from evidence contained in the *Gazeta*'s notices?

**Gazeta de Mexico* (Mexico City: 1784); *Gazeta de Mexico (enero a agosto de 1784)*, Colección Documenta Novae Hispaniae, vol. A-1 (Mexico: Rolston-Bain, 1983), pp. 12–13, 28, 90–92. Excerpts translated by editors. All footnotes have been added.

Gazeta de México *No. 2, Wednesday, January 28, 1784*

MEXICO CITY

[The capital city's report opens with an inventory of the number of cigars the Royal Tobacco Factory had produced in the preceding year, the amount of paper used, and a list of the number of workers employed in the factory along with the total cost of their combined salaries. The notices continue as follows:]

There has been no change in the notices regarding the following products. Bread, meat, and the rest are maintained at the following prices:

Of fine wheaten bread, well-baked and of good quality, 19 ounces for ½ *real:* and for the same price, 11 ounces of mutton, 2½ pounds of beef, 4½ ounces of lard candles and 6½ ounces of soap.

The very noble, famous, loyal and imperial city of Mexico, which if exulted with such distinguished titles, is no less complimented by those who are highly religious, pious, and devout. Upon perceiving the rate at which the epidemic illness of pleurisy from which so many have suffered and died, was spreading, it was resolved that sanctuary from such calamity should be solicited from the Very Holy María de los Remedios. And the city council, having determined that the *Novenario* [nine-day prayer cycle] would be executed on the 12th day of the current month, obtained permission from His Excellency to bring the sovereign image from her sanctuary which was done on the 15th. The next day, her image was conducted in solemn procession with the greatest magnificence, authorized by the Royal Senate, both Councils and Tribunals, from the parish church of Holy Veracruz to the Metropolitan church. She was followed by the Holy Orders according to their antiquity who sang the Hail Mary in the afternoon. The ceremonies concluded on the 24th, and the following afternoon, the image was transferred in a similar procession back to the parish church and she was restored the next morning in her sanctuary.

Beginning on the 12th, a caudate comet,* which could be seen in the evening in the sign of Pisces, and moves [through the sky] with the order for which these comets are known, nearing the Equinox and moving away from the sun, and at present not becoming more than three grades in magnitude. It is pale opaque and its location and movement suggests that it was created at the end of the year 1783 but that since it was below the sun's rays, it could not be seen until it moved away from them. This phenomenon is neither a miraculous thing, nor should be attributed with ill fate, since modern astronomers understand comets to be errant astral bodies that, like others, on certain occasions, lower their orbits and become visible from earth. This opinion is proved by the calculations of the Maqués Gisleri, who wrote in the 1720s conjecturing about the appearance of six comets in the remainder of this century in the years 1736, 1747, 1751, 1758, 1783 and 1790. The one he predicted in 1758 was seen the following March, and that of 1783 has been proven. There remains only the need for the curious to record their observations to verify the earlier

*A comet with a tail.

ones. We would observe that in a matter that is not precisely verified, the difference of one year is not notable.

Gazeta de México *No. 3, Wednesday, February 11, 1784*

CUERNAVACA

On the 10th of the current month, in the sanctuary of this village, called Tlaltenango, after many fateful symptoms, the wife of Don Josef Poblete gave birth to a monstrous but dead infant. A somewhat educated and very truthful barber provided the following description: She did not have a nose, but rather two openings in place of nostrils. Her hands stuck out of her elbows and her feet from her knees. She had small and perfectly round eyes, and a double brain (as evident in the external mass), because on top of the standard one on the head, a prominence of the size of another grew that connected the front and the back of the infant's head.

Gazeta de Mexico *No. 11, Wednesday, June 2, 1784*

OAXACA

The principal commerce of almost all the towns of the diocese of this bishopric is that of the seed called *Cochinilla,* whose second harvest is regularly undertaken in the months of April, May and June. And although this insect is very esteemed for its great utility in America as in all of Europe, until now, there has not been anyone who has given a complete account of the means by which it is produced and cultivated, and of the method that is observed to assist its growth. Without a doubt, its cultivation and trade could be further extended throughout all of New Spain, since all that is required to produce it is the Nopal cactus, the plant that it nourishes upon, if only the negligence of the territory's inhabitants had not let this very useful work be lost in many places. In former times, it was harvested in the province of Tlaxcala and in the valley of Atlixo, in Huexocinco, and in other places where it is now barely known. It seems to me that it would not be disagreeable to the public, nor of little utility to those who wanted to do the work of improving it, to provide a concise description of the little insect, and the method by which it should be cared for until the time it is harvested. . . .

Cochineal, in its perfect state, or as it is commonly called, in season, is the shape and size of a tick, with numerous wrinkles on its back that form a white shell. It has six feet, and a trunk through which it sucks the juice of the Nopal. All this pertains to the female who gives birth to innumerable little insects that are almost imperceptible at the time of their birth, which then change form and color. They are born black, and with two wings on their backs, which they lose a few days later, as is also the case with their color. They soon take on another white color, formed from a fine powder that they discharge, and that increases together with the whitening, in proportion to their increased size. The insect's magnitude, when it is born, is even smaller than that of a grain of mustard. In one month, this little hair moves for the first time, leaving it on the Nopal in the form of a white cloth; from this it is said a new seed of cochineal is formed. This mutation of hair is done up to five times in the period of its growth. And on the last time it is formed from this tunic from which is stripped another type of very small insect, that afterward grows wings in the form of a moth. And this is the male, or father who engenders the seed, since on the last time it goes out ready a few days later to start to give birth to its offspring. . . .

The method of improving cochineal is the following: In the months of October or November, Nopal that is already fairly full of cochineal is collected. The entire part that is judged ready, and in season, or in its perfect state, is collected to regenerate other new Nopales (which is called "to seed" them). Those eggs that have already been laid are then scraped from the Nopal with much care with some small straws used for this purpose. Care is taken not to drop them on the ground, so that they are not damaged or killed. They are put in baskets that are called *xicaras,* from where they are transferred to sacks made of palm, straw, or *amurga* (which they call *paztles*) that have the shape of nests, where the cochineal is stored until its birth process is completed. Indians place these nests among the leaves of the new Nopales, or as they say, between leaf and leaf. Immediately, with the natural inclination that this plant has, the offspring start to fill the leaves, or paztles, and they leave them to die naturally on them, and this cochineal that stays there dead is called the *Seed of Zactaillos,* which they say is the best.

Innumerable insects are shed from each seed, and it takes fifteen days, more or less, for them to be born, according to their nature. And in this period of time, they move other leaves to the sacks, because they do not all fit in them, and they finish all the Nopal juice, and these ones come out small and weak. They also harvest about one third of the offspring in the month of February, after the mothers have laid their eggs on the Nopal, they are harvested in the months of May or June, which they call the *second* harvest.

Central Themes

Indigenous people, urban life, popular culture, land and labor, religion, gender

Suggested Reading

Adank, Patricia Ann Drwall. "Accommodation and Innovation: The Gazeta de México, 1784–1810." PhD diss., Arizona State University, 1980.

Baskes, Jeremy. *Indians, Merchants, and Markets: A Reinterpretation of the Repartimiento and Spanish-Indian Economic Relations in Colonial Oaxaca, 1750–1821.* Stanford, CA: Stanford University Press, 2000.

Cañizares-Esguerra, Jorge. *Nature, Empire, and Nation: Explorations of the History of Science in the Iberian World.* Stanford, CA: Stanford University Press, 2006.

Related Sources

29. Maroon Slaves Negotiate with the Colonial State (1767)
34. A Satirical View of Colonial Society (1816)

31. *Casta* Paintings (1785)

Casta paintings—visual depictions of intercultural mixing—were an artistic genre native to Latin America that emerged during the eighteenth century. Little is known about who commissioned them, but it is clear that they were intended for a predominantly Spanish audience, both *criollo* (American-born) and *peninsular* (Iberian-born); most of the works have resurfaced in Spain. They typically comprised sixteen scenes that recorded the intermixing of Spanish, Indian, and African blood. The offspring of parents of different racial groups are depicted in these carefully labeled family portraits.

The artist of these two paintings, Francisco Clapera (1746–1810), produced a series of casta paintings datable to around 1785. Unlike every other known painter of such works, who were all American-born, Clapera was a Spaniard. He was born in Barcelona, but his career developed in Latin America. At age thirty, he traveled to Peru, then journeyed to Mexico three years later. There he met the Spaniard Jerónimo Antonio Gil, who would found New Spain's art college, the Royal Academy of San Carlos, in 1785. Clapera taught in the academy until at least 1791.

As well as illustrating the implications of race mixing, the pieces included here depict other features typical of the genre, including the celebration of the natural splendor of the New World and the careful recording of the material culture of daily life. In this way, casta paintings exemplify one of the central dilemmas that Spaniards in colonial Mexico confronted: racial anxiety about their inferior status vis-à-vis peninsular Spaniards, and at the same time pride in the distinctiveness that their connections to the bounteous New World conferred upon them. These tensions were exacerbated by the growth in the size of New Spain's casta population in this era and its increased social mobility.

What conclusions can be drawn about the attitudes about race mixing that these portraits promoted to their viewers? What associations might viewers of these works make with Spaniards, Indians, mestizos, blacks, and mulatos? Why did the artists always label the racial categories of each personage in these paintings? What was the purpose and effect of always depicting the phenomenon of race mixing in familial settings? What role does gender play in these images?

Francisco Clapera, "De Español, y India nace Mestiza"
(From Spaniard and Indian comes Mestiza), c. 1775
Jan and Frederick Mayer Collection, Denver Art Museum

Francisco Clapera, "De Español, y Negra, Mulato"
(From Spaniard and Black, Mulato), c. 1775
Jan and Frederick Mayer Collection, Denver Art Museum

Central Themes

Popular culture, gender, race and ethnicity

Suggested Reading

Carrera, Margali M. *Imagining Identity in New Spain: Race, Lineage, and the Colonial Body in Portraiture and Casta Paintings.* Austin: University of Texas Press, 2003.

Katzew, Ilona. *Casta Painting: Images of Race in Eighteenth-Century Mexico.* New Haven, CT: Yale University Press, 2004.

______, ed. *New World Orders: Casta Painting and Colonial Latin America* (exhibition catalog). New York: Americas Society Art Gallery, 1996.

Kellogg, Susan. "Depicting Mestizaje: Gendered Images of Ethnorace in Colonial Mexican Texts." *Journal of Women's History* 12, no. 3 (2000): 69–92.

Images

Casta Painting, 1777. Ignacio María Barreda. Real Academia Española, Madrid. Available at Vistas: Spanish American Visual Culture 1520–1820, http://www.smith.edu/vistas/vistas_web/gallery/detail/casta-ptg_det.htm.

Olson, Christa Johanna. "Casta Paintings: The Construction and Depiction of Race in Colonial Mexico." Available at: http://hemi.ps.tsoa.nyu.edu/archive/studentwork/colony/olson/Casta1.htm.

Related Sources

25. Afro-Mexicans, Mestizos, and Catholicism (1672)

32. Hidalgo's Uprising (1849)*

In 1807 Napoleon invaded Spain and installed his brother, Joseph Bonaparte, as ruler, thus presenting already disgruntled colonials in Spanish America with an opportunity to initiate challenges to colonial rule. On September 16, 1810, Miguel Hidalgo y Costilla, a liberal parish priest from Dolores in the intendancy of Guanajuato, initiated Mexico's earliest insurgency with his *Grito*—a cry for independence from the exploitation of colonial rule. Economic grievances and social discrimination prompted the masses to join Hidalgo's movement, but these concerns varied widely from those of wealthier *criollos* (American-born Spaniards), who sought

*Gilbert M. Joseph and Timothy J. Henderson, "Hidalgo and the Siege of Guanajuato," in *The Mexico Reader: History, Culture, Politics*, pp. 173–175, 177–182. © 2002 Duke University Press. All rights reserved. Used by permission of the publisher.

principally to usurp the political and financial privileges over which *peninsulares* (Iberian-born Spaniards) maintained a monopoly. Colonial peoples of diverse classes and ethnicities, however, did unite in their opposition to various reforming mechanisms that the Bourbons had introduced in the decades leading up to independence, particularly heavier and more efficiently collected taxes (sources 29, 30).

At age seventeen, Lucás Alamán, a *criollo* from a titled family, witnessed Miguel Hidalgo leading his army of the poor to sack Alamán's native city of Guanajuato. As is further illuminated in "Mexico in Postwar Social Turmoil" (Source 41), this statesman and historian would work throughout his life for a less radical road to Mexican independence. In the following excerpt, taken from Alamán's 1849 work, *Historia de Méjico,* he remembers the siege. How do the grievances and motivations of the masses, as Alamán recorded them here, compare to those seen in the earlier popular revolt of 1692 (Source 27)? What are Alamán's attitudes toward Hidalgo and his followers that he reveals in this document? How would his vision of Hidalgo's uprising have influenced the style of independence movement and government that Alamán might have supported? By the following year, Miguel Hidalgo's army was defeated, and he himself had been captured and beheaded by royalist forces. Given the evident success of Hidalgo's army in the siege of Guanajuato, what do you suppose might have led to his downfall in subsequent attacks?

The History of Mexico

In his plan of revolution, Hidalgo followed the same ideas as the backers of independence in [Viceroy] Iturrigaray's councils.* He proclaimed allegiance to King Ferdinand VII: he sought to sustain the king's rights and to defend them against the designs of those Spaniards who had negotiated their country's surrender to the French and who were then in control of Spain, men who would have destroyed religion, profaned the churches and extinguished the Catholic cult. Religion, then, played the principal role, and inasmuch as the image of Guadalupe is the cherished object of the cult of the Mexicans, the inscription put on the revolution's banner read: "Long live religion. Long live our most holy mother Guadalupe. Long live Ferdinand VII. Long live America and death to bad government." But the people who rushed to follow this banner simplified the inscription and it became the simple cry, "Long live the Virgin of Guadalupe and death to the *gachupines!*" What a monstrous pairing of religion with murder and robbery! It is a cry of death and desolation, one I heard thousands and thousands of times in the early days of my youth and after so many years it still resounds in my ears with a frightful echo!

---

*After receiving news of the Napoleonic usurpation, Viceroy José de Iturrigaray—who reigned from 1803 to 1808—allowed Mexican creoles to form a pro-creole junta (caretaker government) in the name of Ferdinand VII. This junta, along with the viceroy himself, was overthrown by conservative peninsulares on September 15, 1808.

Among a people to whom religion is disgracefully reduced to mere superficial practices; where many ministers, especially in the smaller towns, devote themselves to the most licentious lifestyle; where the dominant vice of most people is an inclination toward theft; it is not surprising that one should find, among such people, partisans for a revolution whose first steps were to free the criminals, to open the properties of the richest citizens to unlimited plunder, to incite the common people against everything that until then they had feared and respected, and to give free rein to all vice; a revolution which, moreover, later gave out military ranks freely, opening an immense field for the workers' ambitions. So it was that in all of the villages, the priest Hidalgo found so favorable a predisposition that he needed only to show himself in order to drag the masses of people along behind him. But the methods he employed to gain such popularity destroyed the foundations of the social edifice and suffocated all principles of morality and justice, and all the evils that the nation now laments flow from that poisoned fountain.

As Hidalgo, on this and later marches, passed through the fields and villages, he was joined by people who formed diverse groups or mobs. They carried sticks to which they had tied banners or multi-colored handkerchiefs displaying the image of Guadalupe, which was the standard of the enterprise and which those who adhered to the party also wore as an emblem on their hats. The cowboys and other mounted men from the haciendas, nearly all of whom were of mixed blood, formed the cavalry. They were armed with the lances that Hidalgo had made beforehand, and with swords and machetes which they customarily carried in their daily work; very few had pistols or carbines. The infantry was made up of Indians, divided by villages or bands, armed with sticks, arrows, slings and lances. Since many of them took their women and children along, they looked more like the barbarous tribes, who emigrate from place to place, than like an army on the march. The *caporals* and *mayordomos* [overseers] from the haciendas who took part became chiefs of the cavalry. The Indians took their orders from their village governors or from the captains of the hacienda work gangs. Many carried no weapons at all, and were prepared for nothing but plunder. Mounted men each earned a peso per day, while those on foot got four reales; but since no reviews were held and there was no formal enlistment, this led to great theft and mayhem, even though a treasury was established in the charge of Don Mariano Hidalgo, the priest's brother. Mariano Hidalgo did not trouble himself to provide supplies or means of subsistence for the disorderly mob. In the middle of September, when the revolution began, the corn was ripening in the fields, and in that era of wealth and prosperity for agriculture, especially in the opulent province of Guanajuato, the haciendas abounded in livestock and all sorts of foodstuffs. How unfortunate was the farm of a European which Hidalgo and his army chanced to pass by: with a tremendous cry of "Long live the Virgin of Guadalupe and death to the *gachupines!*" the Indians would scatter amid the cornfields and quickly gather in the harvest; they would open the granaries, and the grains stored there would be gone in moments; the stores, which nearly all of the haciendas had, were looted down to the bare bones. The insurgents would kill all of the oxen they needed, and if there were some Indian village nearby they would destroy even the buildings in order to cart away the roof beams and doors. The haciendas of the Americans suffered less at the start of the war, but as it progressed all came to be treated in the same way.

The city of Guanajuato is situated at the base of a deep, narrow valley which is dominated on all sides by high rugged mountains. . . . The town had perhaps seventy thousand inhabitants including those of the mining camps. Of these, the Valenciana mines, which had been for many years enjoying uninterrupted prosperity, had something like twenty thousand people. The region enjoyed great abundance: the huge sums that were distributed each week among the people as wages for their work in the mines and related haciendas sparked commercial activity; the great consumption of foodstuffs by the people and the pasturing of the many horses and mules used in the mining operations, had caused agriculture to flourish for many leagues around. In the city there were many rich homes, and many more which enjoyed a comfortable middle-class existence; commerce was almost exclusively in the hands of the Europeans, but many creole families supported themselves easily from mining related activities, and they were all respectable in the orderliness of their dress and in the decorum they observed. The people, occupied in the hard and risky labor of the mines, were lively, happy, prodigal, and brave.

So populous a city, situated amid the craggy hills which have been aptly compared to a sheet of crumpled paper, could not defend itself unless the mass of its inhabitants were united; so it was essential that its defense have the support of the common people. This was made fully clear when the intendant sounded the general alarm on September 18: a large number of people came armed with rocks, and they occupied the hills, streets, plazas, and rooftops in the early morning of the 20th, when the advance guard at Marfil believed Hidalgo was drawing near, which is why the alarm was sounded, and the intendant with his troops and armed peasants rode down the glen to meet him. The intendant, however, believed from that moment that the people were changing their minds, and he feared that the lower classes of the city would join Hidalgo when he arrived; thus, he changed his plan, deciding instead to take cover at a strong, defensible point while awaiting aid from the Viceroy. . . .

[Alamán then described how the intendant collected the city's European and much of its creole population in the public granary or *Alhóndiga,* shutting themselves in with great quantities of foodstuffs and arms and fortifying their refuge. The lower classes dispersed among the city's neighborhoods and surrounding hills. *Ed.*]

In order to win the people's hearts, the intendant, with great solemnity, published a proclamation on the morning of the 26th, abolishing the payment of tribute. This favor, which had been conceded by the regency back on the 26th of May, had not been put into effect on the pretext that a study had to be made first. Now, given the circumstances under which it was published, it was not only viewed coldly, but the lower classes of Guanajuato took it as a concession made from fear: it was met with mockery and jokes, and it ended up swaying the minds of the crowd against the government. In the moments of a revolution, the most beneficent actions done out convenience, produce a result entirely contrary to the one desired. . . .

Hidalgo . . . returned from Celaya toward Guanajuato, at every step augmenting the crowd that followed him. Riaño knew well the difficulty of his position. "The people," he told Calleja on the 26th, "voluntarily surrender themselves to the insurgents. They already did so in Dolores, San Miguel, Celaya, Salamanca, Irapuato; the same shall soon happen at Silao. The seduction spreads here, there was no security or confidence. I have fortified myself in the most suitable place in the city, and I will fight to the death, if the five hundred men I have at my side do not forsake me. I have very little gun-powder, because there is absolutely none, and the cavalry is poorly mounted and armed, with no weapons but their glass swords,* and the infantry their mended rifles, and it is not impossible that these troops might be seduced [by the rebels]. The insurgents are bearing down on me, supplies are impeded, mail is intercepted. Sr. Abarca is working actively, and Your Excellency and he together must come to my assistance, because I fear being attacked at any moment. I must not continue, because since the 17th I have not been able to rest or get undressed and it is three days since I slept for a whole hour." Such was the anguish of spirit and bodily fatigue that [Riaño] suffered in these grievous circumstances. The Europeans had grown dispirited, many of them abandoning the city and heading for Guadalajara, and the ones at the frontier of the sierra, at Santa Rosa and Villaplando did the same, as they were unprotected. . . .

[*Translator's summary:* At this point, Hidalgo sends two agents to demand that the city be surrendered and that all Spaniards be turned over to the insurgents. Intendant Don Juan Antonio de Riaño puts the proposal to a vote, and the defenders of the Alhóndiga declare that they will resist to the death. They make ready for a siege.]

The people of Guanajuato watched from the surrounding heights, some now deciding to join Hidalgo, others, no fewer in number, only watching so they would be ready when it came to pillage. The people from the mines occupied the hill next to El Cuarto; these were mostly workers from the Valenciana mine who were roused by their administrator, Dasimiro Chovell, who was believed to have reached a prior agreement with Hidalgo.

A little before twelve o'clock, in the avenue of Our Lady of Guanajuato, which is the entrance to the city from the plains of Marfil, there appeared a huge crowd of Indians with few rifles; most were carrying lances, sticks, slings, and arrows. The first of this group passed the bridge . . . and arrived in front of the adjoining trench, at the foot of Mendizábal Hall. Gilberto de Riaño—to whom his father had entrusted the command of that point, which he deemed the most hazardous—ordered them to stop in the name of the king, and since the crowd continued to advance, he gave the order to open fire, whereupon some Indians fell dead and the rest retreated hurriedly. In the avenue, a man from Guanajuato said they should go to El Cuarto Hill,

*The armaments of the regiment were bad, and the swords broke easily, which is what the intendant referred to.

and he showed them the way. The remaining groups of Hidalgo's footsoldiers, perhaps 20,000 Indians, joined by the people from the mines and the lower classes of Guanajuato, were occupying the heights and all of the houses around [the Alhóndiga de] Granaditas, in which they placed soldiers from Celaya armed with rifles; meanwhile a corps of around two thousand cavalrymen, composed of country people with lances, mixed in among the ranks of the dragoons of the Queen's regiment led by Hidalgo, climbed along the road called Yerbabuena and arrived at [the top of San Miguel Hill], and from there went down to the city. Hidalgo went to the headquarters of the Prince's cavalry regiment, where he remained throughout the action. The column continued crossing through the town in order to station itself at Belén Street, and as they passed by they sacked a store that sold sweets, and they freed all the prisoners of both sexes who were locked up in the jail—no fewer than three or four hundred persons, among them serious criminals. They made the male prisoners march on the Alhóndiga.

The intendant, noting that the largest number of the enemy rushed to the side of the trench at the mouth of Los Pozitos Street . . . thought it necessary to reinforce that point. He took twenty infantrymen from the company of the peasants to join the battalion, and with more boldness than prudence he went with them to station them where he wanted them to be, accompanied by his assistant, José María Bustamente. Upon returning, as he was climbing the stairs to the door of the Alhóndiga, he was wounded above the left eye by a rifle bullet and he immediately fell dead. The shot came from the window of one of the houses of the little plaza to the east of the Alhóndiga, and is said to have been fired by a corporal of the infantry regiment from Celaya. Thus, a glorious death ended the spotless life of the retired frigate captain Don Juan Antonio de Riaño, knight of the Order of Caltrava, intendant, *correjidor* [magistrate], and commandant of the armies of Guanajuato. . . .

The crowd on El Cuarto Hill began a barrage of stones, hurling them by hand and shooting them with slings, a barrage that was so continuous it exceeded the thickest hail storm. In order to keep the combatants supplied with stones, swarms of Indians and the people of Guanajuato unceasingly picked up the round stones that covered the bottom of the Cata River. So great was the number of stones launched in the short time that the attack lasted, that the floor of the Alhóndiga's balcony was raised about a quarter above its ordinary level. It was impossible to defend the trenches, and the troops that garrisoned them were ordered to withdraw; Captain Escalera of the guard ordered that the door of the Alhóndiga be closed. With that, the Europeans who occupied the Hacienda of Dolores were left isolated and with no recourse but to sell their lives dearly, and the cavalry on the slope of the Cata River was in the same situation or worse. Nor could the people on the roof defend themselves for long, since it was dominated by the hills El Cuarto and San Miguel, although since the latter was farther away, less damage was done from there. And despite the havoc caused by the continuous fire of the troops of the garrison, the number of assailants was so great that those who fell were very promptly replaced by others, and they were not missed. . . .

There was a store at the corner of Los Pozitos Street and Mount Los Mandamientos where they sold *ocote* [pine] chips, which the men who worked the mines by night used to illuminate the road. The crowd broke down the doors [of the store], and, loading up that fuel, they brought it to the door of the Alhóndiga and set it ablaze. Others who were experienced at subterranean labors, approached the back of the building, which was surrounded by earthen walls . . . [and they] began to drill holes to undermine the foundation. Those inside the building hurled iron flasks, of which we have spoken, through the windows down into the crowd. These would explode and bring down many people, but immediately the mob would close in tight and snuff out the flasks that had fallen under their feet, which is why there were so few wounded among the assailants, even thought a large number were killed. The discord among those under siege was such that, at the very moment when Gilberto Riaño (who was thirsty for vengeance in his father's death), Miguel Bustamente, and others were hurling flasks at the assailants, the counsellor held up a white handkerchief as a sign of peace. The people, attributing to perfidy what was nothing more than the effect of the confusion that prevailed inside the Alhóndiga, redoubled their furor and began to fight with greater cruelty. The counsellor then ordered a soldier to climb down from a window to parley; the unfortunate man fell to the ground, broken to bits. Then Martín Septiem tried to leave, confident in his priestly vocation and in the Holy Christ he carried in his hands; the image of the Savior flew into splinters as stones struck it and the priest, using the crucifix in his hand as an offensive weapon, managed to escape through the crowd, though badly wounded. The Spaniards meanwhile hearing only the voice of terror, tossed money from the windows in hopes of sparking the people's greed and thus placating the mob; others shouted their capitulation, and many, persuaded that their final hour had arrived, threw themselves at the feet of priests to receive absolution.

Berzabal, seeing the door ablaze, gathered what soldiers he could of the battalion and stationed them at the entrance: as the door was consumed by flames, he ordered his soldiers to fire at close range, and many of the assailants perished. Still, those in back of the crowd pushed forward, and the ones in front trampled over the dead sweeping everything before them with an irresistible force. The patio, stairs, and corridors of the Alhóndiga were very soon filled with Indians and common people. Berzabal, retreating with a handful of men who remained with him to a corner of the patio, defended his battalion's banners along with the standard-bearers Marmolejo and González. When these men fell dead at his side, he gathered up the banners and held them tightly with his left arm, and he held out with a sword—even though it had been destroyed by a pistol shot—against the multitude that surrounded him, until he fell pierced by many lances, still without abandoning the banners he had sworn to defend. What a worthy example for Mexican soldiers and a well-earned title of glory of the descendants of that valiant warrior!

[With Berzabal's death] all resistance ceased, and no more than a few isolated shots were heard from some who still held out, such as the Spaniard Raymayor, who did not let the Indians come near till all of his cartridges were spent. The Europeans at the Hacienda of Dolores tried to save themselves through a back door that opened upon the log bridge over the Cata River, but they found that the assailants had already taken that bridge. They then retired to the well, where—since it was a high, strong spot—they defended themselves until the last of their ammunition ran out, causing much carnage among the insurgents. . . . The few Europeans who remained alive at the end fell or were thrown into the well, and they drowned.

Central Themes

Indigenous people, state formation, land and labor, religion, race and ethnicity

Suggested Reading

Fowler, Will. "Dreams of Stability: Mexican Political Thought During the 'Forgotten Years': An Analysis of the Beliefs of the Creole Intelligentsia (1821–1853)." *Bulletin of Latin American Research* 14, no. 3 (September 1995): 287–312.

Hamill, Hugh M. *The Hidalgo Revolt: Prelude to Mexican Independence.* Gainesville: University Press of Florida, 1966.

Van Young, Eric. *The Other Rebellion: Popular Violence, Ideology, and the Mexican Struggle for Independence, 1810–1821.* Stanford, CA: Stanford University Press, 2001.

Related Sources

27. The 1692 Mexico City Revolt (1692)
33. José María Morelos's National Vision (1813)
35. Address to the New Nation (1824)
41. Mexico in Postwar Social Turmoil (1852)

33. José María Morelos's National Vision (1813)*

After the death of Miguel Hidalgo, a second major revolutionary movement developed in southern Mexico under the leadership of José María Morelos, also a priest. Morelos was a *mestizo* (person of Indian and Spanish parentage), although he was sometimes described as a *mulato* (person of African-Spanish parentage) of relatively humble origins who had at one time worked as a muleteer. He proved to have greater military skill than Hidalgo, and he also articulated a more cohesive political

*José María Morelos, "Sentimientos de la Nación o Puntos Dados por Morelos para la Constitucíon" (1813), in Miguel León Portilla et al., eds., *Historia documental de México*, vol. 2 (Mexico: Universidad Nacional Autónoma de México, Instituto de Investigaciones Históricas, 1965), pp. 110–112. Excerpt translated by the editors.

program than Hidalgo had ever advanced. Both factors allowed him to recruit supporters from all classes in the region of the Pacific lowlands. In 1813 he organized a governmental congress to convene in Chipalcingo (in present-day Guerrero State). In November 1815, the royalist forces captured Morelos, and he was defrocked and executed.

Morelos presented the following points before the Chipalcingo Congress on September 14, 1813. He had generated the ideas in dialogue with Hidalgo and other revolutionary leaders, including Ignacio López Rayón, one of Hidalgo's lieutenants. Many of Morelos's ideas served as a foundation for the development of Mexico's first comprehensive legal code. Although Morelos's ideology was obviously inspired by the ideology of the European Enlightenment, can you detect other aspects that are clearly rooted in the local context? Compare Morelos's twenty-three points to the preamble of Mexico's first Republican Constitution of 1824. What forces might explain the differences in the two documents?

Sentiments of the Nation or Points Outlined by Morelos for the Constitution

1. That America is free and independent from Spain and from all other nations, governments, or monarchies, and hereby sanctions this by giving the world the following reasons.

2. That the Catholic religion should be the only one, without tolerance for any other.

3. That all the church's ministers shall support themselves exclusively from tithes and the people should not have to make any other contributions than those of their devotions and offerings.

4. That dogma should be upheld by the hierarchy of the Church, which is composed of the Pope, the bishops, and the priests, because all plants not sown by God must be uprooted: *ominis plantais quam nom plantabir Pater meus Celestis Cradicabitur.* Mat. Cap. XV.

5. That sovereignty springs directly from the people, who wish only to invest their representatives with it. Their powers shall be divided into the Legislative, Executive, and Judicial branches. The Provinces will each elect their own representatives and these will elect all others. All those elected must be wise and honest.

6. [In all reproductions, this article is missing. *Ed.*]

7. That the representatives will be chosen for four years, after which time, the older ones will be exchanged for the newly elected.

8. The salary of the representatives will be a sufficient but not excessive sum, and at present will not surpass eight thousand pesos.

9. That public office shall be occupied only by Americans.

10. That no foreigners will be admitted to the country unless they are artisans capable of teaching others their crafts and are free of all suspicion.

11. That the fatherland will not be fully free and our own as long as the government is not reformed by fighting tyranny, establishing liberalism in its place, and expelling from our soil the Spanish enemy that has declared itself so forcibly against our nation.

12. That since good law is superior to all men, those that our congress dictates must compel constancy and patriotism, and must moderate opulence and indigence, and in these ways, improve the income of the poor, better their customs, and dispel ignorance, rapine, and robbery.

13. That the general laws apply to everyone without the exception of privileged organizations and that these shall only exist in accordance with the usefulness of their ministry.

14. That for a law to be dictated, it must be debated in Congress and decided by a plurality of votes.

15. That slavery and the distinction of castes are both abolished forever, and everyone shall be equal, and that only vice or virtue will distinguish one American from another.

16. That our ports will be open to all friendly foreign nations, but that no foreign ships, no matter how friendly, shall be based in our kingdom. There will be particular ports selected for this purpose, but in all the rest, disembarkation will be prohibited, and 10% or some other tax levied on their merchandise.

17. That everyone should maintain propriety and respect in their homes as these are sacred asylums, and penalties shall be levied against infractions.

18. That with the new legislation torture will not be permitted.

19. That the new legislation will establish as Constitutional law the celebration of December 12, in all towns, as a day dedicated to the patroness of our freedom, Most Holy Mary of Guadalupe, and all the towns are required to pay her a monthly devotion.

20. That foreign troops or those of another kingdom may not tread upon our land, unless to assist us, and in this case they shall not be part of the Supreme *Junta* [Assembly].

21. That no [religious] expeditions shall be undertaken beyond the limits of the kingdom, especially overseas. Expeditions aimed at propagating the faith to our brothers within our own lands shall be permitted.

22. That the infinite number of tributes, taxes, and assessments that must be paid shall cease, and each individual shall pay five per cent of his earnings or another equally light charge, which will not be so oppressive as the *alcabala* [sales tax] or the crown monopoly, the tribute, and others. These small contributions and the wise administration of those goods confiscated from the enemy shall suffice to cover the costs of the war and the salaries of state employees.

23. That the 16th of September shall be solemnly observed every year, as the anniversary of the day on which the voice of independence was raised and our holy liberty began. Because it was on this day that the lips of the nation parted and the people reclaimed their rights and grasped the sword to be heard, and the merits of the great hero, *señor* [sir] Don Miguel Hidalgo and his companion señor Don Ignacio Allende will be always remembered.

Chilpancingo, September 14, 1813.
José María Morelos.

Central Themes

State formation, land and labor, religion

Suggested Reading

Archer, Christon I. *The Birth of Modern Mexico, 1780–1824.* Latin American Silhouettes. Lanham, MD: Rowman & Littlefield, 2007.

Hamnett, Brian R. *Roots of Insurgency: Mexican Regions, 1750–1824.* Cambridge Latin American Studies 59. Cambridge: Cambridge University Press, 1986.

Rodriguez O., Jaime E. *The Independence of Mexico and the Creation of the New Nation.* UCLA Latin American Studies 69. Los Angeles: University of California, UCLA Latin American Center Publications, 1989.

Related Sources

32. Hidalgo's Uprising (1849)
35. Address to the New Nation (1824)
54. Land, Labor, and the Church in the Mexican Constitution (1917)

34. A Satirical View of Colonial Society (1816)*

In 1816, in the midst of the upheaval of Mexico's independence revolution, José Joaquín Fernández de Lizardi published *El Periquillo Sarniento* (*The Itching Parrot*), Spanish America's first novel. Lizardi came from a modest *criollo* (American-born Spaniard) background and began his literary career by writing satirical poems that he sold for a few cents; others were published in the *Diario de México,* a news periodical

*From José Joaquín Fernández de Lizardi, *The Itching Parrot*, trans. Kathleen Anne Porter (New York: Doubleday, 1942), pp. 152–163. Translation © 1942 by Doubleday, a division of Bantam Doubleday Dell Publishing Group, Inc. Used by permission of Doubleday, a division of Random House, Inc.

similar to the *Gazeta de México* (Source 30). When the first independence rebellions broke out in 1810, Lizardi was imprisoned on suspicion of supporting the rebels. He was released, but the state's suspicions about his sympathies were in fact justified. In 1812, Lizardi began publishing a newspaper, *El Pensador Mexicano* (The Mexican Thinker), in which he defended the freedom of the press and the right of the populace to criticize the government. Thereafter, he published many seditious pieces, including an article in which he satirized the viceroy and called upon him to revoke an edict mandating that revolutionary priests be tried by a military court (sources 32 and 33). These views ensured Lizardi's second imprisonment.

After his release, Lizardi began publishing fiction, for this genre allowed him to voice ideas impermissible in other forms. *El Periquillo Sarniento* was first published as a series, with two chapters available to subscribers each week. The series was an immediate success, and the book remained so popular during the nineteenth century that it was reprinted eleven times, although it fell out of favor with the state that came to power after the Revolution of 1910.

In this chapter from the book, we see the protagonist adopting the guise of a physician, one of a series of professions in which he dabbles and feigns expertise. The Protomedicato, the body regulating medical professionals, was in fact immensely disturbed by the existence of quack doctors in New Spain. What other elements of the following excerpt, although fictional, do you imagine accurately reflected the actual conditions of life in Lizardi's era? What do you understand to be the subversive elements of Lizardi's presentation of his society? Why do you imagine it was so popular among colonial Mexicans?

The Itching Parrot

Chapter 18. Poll Relates How He Was Employed by Doctor Physic, What He Learned from Him, How He Robbed Him, His Flight, and the Adventures That Befell Him in Tula, Where He Posed as a Doctor

I found Doctor Physic one afternoon after his siesta in his study, seated in an armchair, with a book before him and a snuffbox at his side. He was a tall man, thin of face and leg, bulky of paunch, swarthy and heavy-browed, green-eyed, sharp-nosed, big-mouthed and toothless. Besides, he was bald, and always wore a curled peruke when on the street. When I went to see him, he was wearing one of those long gowns called kimonos, covered with flowers and foliage, and a great bonnet, stiff with starch, shining from the iron. He recognized me and said, "Oh Poll, my son! From what strange horizons have you come to visit this hut?" His style did not surprise me, for I already knew he was very pedantic. I began to relate my adventures, intending to lie about whatever seemed expedient, when the Doctor interrupted me, saying he already knew all about them.

I found he wanted me for an upstairs and downstairs servant, and I foresaw my work would not be heavy; the arrangements could not be bettered, and in my situation I might have had to accept worse, but I did not know how much my wage would amount to, so I asked him, finally, how much I would earn a month. The Doctor answered, "Let me say, *claris verbis,* clearly, you will enjoy five hundred and forty-four maravedis."

"But sir," I inquired, "how much do five hundred and forty-four maravedis amount to in cash? It seems to me my work is not worth so much money."

"Yes, it is worth it, *stultisime famule,* you stupid Moor, for those hundreds amount to only two pesos."

"Well then, Doctor," I said, "I have two pesos for wages, and I consider myself content as you are, for I will get more benefit from your lessons than I did from Don Nicolás' powders and greases."

"Certainly," said Doctor Physic, "for if you apply yourself I will open Minerva's palaces to you, and that will be superabundant reward for your services, for by my doctrine alone you will preserve your health for many long years and mayhap even acquire some property and esteem."

We were agreed from that moment, and I began assiduously to flatter both him and his lady sister, Rosa, who was old, devout, and as ridiculous as my master, although I would have preferred to flatter Manuelita, their fourteen-year-old niece, who was pretty as a silver plate. But I got no chance, because the cursed old woman watched me as if the girl were made of pure gold. I stayed seven or eight months with this old man, complying with my duties perfectly; serving table, gathering the eggs, caring for the mule, running errands. The old woman and her brother thought me a saint, because I spent my leisure hours in the study, taking advantage of the liberty offered me, looking at anatomical prints, reading ancient and modern books, as much as I liked. By this reading and by observing the remedies my master prescribed for the sick poor who came to see him at his house—more or less the same remedy for every disease, for he kept in mind the proverb about doing only as much as one is paid for—I began to believe I had mastered the science of medicine. One day when he scolded me harshly and even threatened to give me a cudgeling because I forgot to give the mule her supper, I promised myself revenge and a change of luck at once.

That very night I gave the lady mule a double ration of corn and bran, and when the whole household was in its deepest sleep I saddled her with all the harness, not forgetting her blanket. I made up a bundle in which I hid fourteen books, many of them mutilated, some in Latin, some in Castilian, because, I thought, many books lend credit to doctors and lawyers, even though they may not read or understand them at all. I also bundled up my master's gown and collar, along with an old string wig, a formulary, and most important of all, his Bachelor of Medicine diploma and his certificate of examination, which documents I soon made my own by grace of a little knife and a bit of lemon, scratching and erasing enough to change the name and date. I did not forget to supply myself with money. During the time I was there, they had not paid me any wages, but I knew where the sister kept a moneybox in which she hoarded what she pared off the expenses; and as one thief robs another I emptied her bank neatly. I found, to my great satisfaction, nearly forty duros, although she had scraped them to make them slip through the narrow slot in the box. With this quite respectable viaticum I said farewell to the house at four-thirty in the morning, locking the entrance and shoving the keys back under the door.

At five or six o'clock I entered an inn, saying I had had a quarrel the night before in the one where I had been staying and wanted to change my lodging. I paid well and was attended punctually. I had coffee brought up and then put the mule in the stables with orders that she should breakfast well. I remained shut up in my room all morning without being able to decide whither I should direct my march, for I knew neither the roads nor the villages; I was at a loss where to look for a companion, for it would not be even decent for a doctor to travel without baggage or a servant. While I was pondering, one o'clock struck and my dinner was brought up. I was busy at this when a boy came to the door and begged a mouthful for God's sake. I recognized him at once; it was Andrés, Don Agustín's apprentice, a boy—I know not whether I have already said so—about fourteen years old, but well-grown as an eighteen-year-old. I called to him to come in and after a few moments conversation he remembered me. I told him that I was now a doctor and on the point of going away to some village to seek my fortune, because in Mexico there were more doctors than sick; but I was detained by my lack of a faithful servant to go with me, who must know of some village where there was no doctor. The poor boy offered himself at once, and begged me to take him as my servant. He had once gone to Tepeji del Río, where there was no doctor; it was a fair-sized village, but if we did not do well there, we would go on to Tula, a still larger village.

I dressed up my adventures for Andrés, by leading him to believe I had just been examined in medicine and would help him to pass as a barber, in case there was none in the village where we settled.

"Well sir," said Andrés, "that is all very well, but I scarcely know how to shave a dog. How can I dare try it?"

"Be quiet," I said, "don't be a coward. Fortune favors the daring and disdains the timid. You must not be faint hearted. You will become as much a barber when you have been with me a month as I became a doctor in the little while I was with my master, to whom I cannot well say how much I owe at this moment."

Andrés listened admiringly.

At three o'clock I went with him to the secondhand market, where I bought a mattress, a cowhide cover to wrap it in, a trunk; for my servant, barber to be, I bought a black waistcoat, some green breeches with the corresponding black stockings, shoes, hat, a pink jacket, a neckerchief, and a little cloak; also six razors, two lancets, a basin, a mirror, four cupping glasses, rags for towels, a pair of shears, a big clyster, and I know not what other odds and ends, the surprising thing about it being that I spent scarcely twenty-seven or -eight pesos for these supplies. All the stuff was from a secondhand market, but even so Andrés returned to the inn quite contented.

Andrés had already arranged for the journey with some drivers from Tula who had brought in a student and his baggage and were returning without a load. He had told them about our journey and they had agreed to take us for only four pesos; they were waiting downstairs for me to confirm the bargain. "Why shouldn't I agree to that, my son?" I said to Andrés. "Go and call those drivers right away." He went downstairs like a streak and came back at once with the drivers. We agreed they were to give me a mule for my baggage, a saddle animal for Andrés, and get us started before dawn. . . .

The principal gentry had visited me already and formed of me whatever opinion they like; but the common people of the village had not seen me dressed up to kill, accompanied by my shield bearer. On Sunday, when I presented myself in church dressed half-doctor and half-constable, Andrés half thrush, half-parrot, the excitement in the village was unbelievable. Since in the villages they are much given to novelties, the news that there was a doctor and a barber in town ran through all the vicinity and people came from everywhere to consult me about their infirmities. . . .

My fame grew from day to day, but what set me on the peak of the moon was the cure I made of the tax collector, though by accident and with Andrés' help. I was summoned to him one night in all haste. I went running, commending myself to God to help me out of the pinch with credit. I took Andrés, carrying his instruments, charging him in a low voice, so the servant could not hear us, to have no fear because I had none; saying that as for killing a sick man it mattered little whether he were Indian or Spaniard; that we stood a fine chance in the fight, for if the tax collector got better he would pay us well and our fame would be assured; if he died, as might be expected, considering his physicians, we would be safe in saying his hour had come and he was with God, and no one could accuse us of homicide.

Still talking, we arrived at the house, which we found a perfect Babel, with people coming and going, some of them crying, and everyone terrified. At this moment, the priest arrived with his vicar and holy oils. "This," I said to Andrés, "is a serious case. There is no middle way in it. Either we come through handsomely or we are finished. Let us see how we get out of this game." We all went into the sick-chamber together and saw the tax collector stretched out on his bed, deprived of his sense, his eyes closed, his face purple, showing every symptom of apoplexy. His wife and daughters, in a sea of tears, surrounded me and asked, "Oh, sir! What do you think? Is our papa dying?"

Affecting great serenity of spirit and a prophet's confidence, I responded, "Calm yourself, ladies, why should he die? It is only the effervescence of sanguinary humor oppressing the ventricles of his heart, stifling his cerebrum, because it presses with all the pondus of the blood upon the medular and the trachea; but all this will be stopped in an instant, for *si evaucatio fit, recedet plethora,* by evacuation we free ourselves of the plethora. . . . "

I placed my fingers on the sick man's pulse and gazed at the beams of the ceiling for a while; then I took his pulse again, doing meanwhile a thousand monkey tricks, such as arching my eyebrows, wrinkling my nose, staring at the floor, biting my lips, shaking my head, trying to stupefy those poor people by my learned pantomime. They glued their eyes upon me in profound silence, while I hoped to convince them I was a second Hippocrates at least. I began to worry in earnest about the grave state of the sick man and the difficulty of a cure, repenting that I had not told them it was serious. When I had finished taking his pulse, I looked attentively at his face, forced his mouth open with a spoon to look at his tongue, raised his eyelids, rapped his belly and feet and asked a thousand questions without coming to the point of ordering anything done, until the lady, who could not endure my delay any longer, said, "Now, sir, what do you say about my husband? Is he for this life or for death?"

"Lady," I said, "I know not what may be. Only God knows if he is for this life and the resurrection, as was *Lazarum quem resucitarit a monumento faetidum,* and according to this, he will live even though he dies. *Ego sum resurre citio et vita, qui credidit in me, etiam si mortuus fuerit, vivet. . . .* "

"Oh, Jesus!" cried one of the girls, "my little papa is dead!" She was nearest the sick man and her cry was so strange and sorrowful as she fell fainting from her chair, that we all gathered around the bed thinking he had really died.

The priest and the vicar, on hearing the uproar, rushed in, and did not know to whom to attend, the apoplectic or the hysterical, for both were deprived of their senses. The lady, now angry, said, "Leave off your Latin and see if you can or cannot cure my husband. Why did you tell me it was nothing to worry about and that he was not dying?"

"I did so, lady, in order not to alarm you," I said, "but I had not examined the sick man *methodice vel justa artis nostrae praecepta,* that is, methodically, and according to the rules of the art. But trust in God, and let us see. First put on a big pot of water to heat."

"There is more than enough of that," said the cook.

"Well then, Master Andrés," I continued, "you, as a good phlebotomist, shall give him at once, instantly, a pair of bleedings of the cava vein."

Andrés, terrified and knowing as little as I did about cava veins, tied his arms and gave him two slashes that looked like dagger wounds. The profusion of blood shocked the spectators, but when two bowls had been filled, the sick man opened his eyes and began to recognize and speak to his family standing about the bed. I had Andrés loosen the bindings and close the incisions, which were so long they cost him some work. Next, I had them anoint the man's forehead and wrists with white wine; comfort his stomach inside with egg-and-corn gruel, outside with a plaster of oil or roses, wine, coriander, and as many other meaningless things as I pleased, charging them gravely not to resupinate him.

"What is that, Father?" asked the lady; and the priest, smiling, said, "It means you must not let him lie flat."

"Well, brother, for God's sake," the matron continued to me, "let us talk a language we can all understand, like decent people."

The girl had come out of her faint and, hearing her mother said, "Yes sir; my mother talks sense. Let me tell you why I fainted just now. Because when you began to pray, like the Fathers sing for the dead when they bury them, I thought my little papa had already died and you were singing the Dead Office for him."

The priest laughed with pleasure at the girl's simplicity and the rest of us laughed with him, we were so happy to see the tax collector out of danger, taking his corn gruel and chatting serenely with everybody. I prescribed the man's regimen for the following days, offering to continue the treatment until he was entirely well. They all thanked me and when I left the lady put a gold ounce in my hand. At the time I thought it was a silver peso and cursed myself to the devil at being so badly paid. As we went home, I said as much to Andrés, who answered, "No sir, it can't be silver, because they gave me four pesos." "You must be right," I answered, and hurrying our pace we arrived home, where I saw it was an ounce of gold, yellow as pure saffron. . . .

It turned out as I had thought. As soon as the happy fate of the tax collector at my hands was known among the poor, the common people began to praise me and recommend me with open mouths, "because," they said, "if the principal gentry call him in, doubtless he is such a doctor as one doesn't find every day"; and, better still, the principal gentry were also nailed fast and generous with their praises. Only the priest could not swallow me. He commented, to the subdelegate, to the master of the mails, and others, that I might be a good doctor, but he could not believe it, because I was too pedantic and glib, and these characteristics mark a stupid man or a scoundrel, in no way to be trusted, be he doctor, theologian, lawyer, or whatever else. The subdelegate tried to defend me, saying it was natural for every man to explain himself in the terms of his calling and that should not be called pedantry. "Agreed," said the priest, "but he must always take into consideration the occasion and the persons with whom he is talking, for if I, preaching about the observance of the seventh commandment, for example, repeated, without any explanation, emphyteuses, hypotheticals, constituents, precaria, palliated usuries, pacts, retroversions, and all the rest of it, surely I would be a pedant. Moreover, if you would like to see how ignorant that doctor is, arrange for us to get together some evening and I promise you amusement listening to him gabble." "So we shall," said the subdelegate, "but how can we explain the cure he made the other night?" "I can say, without scruple," responded the priest, "that it was sheer accident." "Is that possible!" "Yes, sir. Can't you see that the sick man's bulk, his hard pulse, his darkened face, his drugged senses, his agitated breathing, all his symptoms, indicated bleeding? Why, the most ignorant old woman in my parish would have prescribed that remedy." "Well, then," said the subdelegate, "I desire to hear a conversation about medicine between you and him. Let us set it for the twenty-fifth of this month."

This conversation was repeated to me by one of the subdelegate's servants, whom I cured of indigestion free of charge, as a reward for telling me what he had heard about me in his master's house. I then devoted myself to studying my big books, so that the occasion would not catch me unprepared.

During this interval, I was called one night to the home of Don Ciriaco Redondo, the richest storekeeper in the village, who was dying of colic. "Bring your clyster," I said to Andrés, "for anything may turn up. This is another adventure and God help us out of it safely." We found the storekeeper's household as upset as the tax collector's, but here we had one advantage: the sick man could talk. I put him a thousand pedantic questions, only because it was my habit to ask them by the thousands, and from his answers I learned he was a great glutton and had just given himself a devilish stuffing. I ordered mallows cooked with soap and honey, and when this had been done I made him swallow a large dose. The miserable man and his relatives protested, saying that was not an emetic but an enema. "Take it, sir," I said, "don't you see if it's an enema as you say, it can be taken through the mouth or any other place? Now then, sir, down the dose, or die." The unfortunate man drank the nauseous brew with much reluctance and then vomited up just about half of his entrails. This exhausted him, but as the stoppage was in his intestines the pain was not alleviated.

Then I had Andrés fill the clyster and told the patient to uncover his hind end. "Never in my life," he protested, "never in my life have they done anything to me in those parts." "Well, my friend," I responded, "never in your life have you been harder pressed, nor have I in mine, for in all the years I have been a doctor I have never seen more intractable colic." After some persuasion from his relatives, the patient said, "Well, sir, let the clyster be given, if my health depends on it." *"Amen dico vobis,"* I answered, and immediately ordered everyone except the sick man's wife, for decency's sake to leave the bedchamber. Andrés filled the clyster and set about the operation; but what a dunce he was at the business! He spilled the liquid on the bed, hurt the sick man, and did nothing properly until, impatient at his stupidity, I determined to apply the remedy myself, although I had never before made the experiment. Forgetting my inexperience, I took the clyster and with the greatest decency introduced the pipe into his anus; and be it because of some talent I had that Andrés had not, or because of the sick man's apprehension working in my favor, he went on taking more and more of the decoction. I encouraged him, saying, "Hold your breath, brother, and take it as hot as you can, for your health depends upon it." The afflicted man made all the effort he could on his part—in this consists the good work of the best doctors—and in a quarter of an hour or so made a very copious evacuation, like a man who had not emptied his belly for three days. He was immediately alleviated, as he himself said; and not only that, he was perfectly cured, for once get rid of the cause and the effect ceases.

They showered me with thanks, gave me twelve pesos, and I went to my lodging with Andrés.

Central Themes

Urban life, popular culture, religion,

Suggested Reading

Lanning, John Tate. *The Royal Protomedicato: The Regulation of the Medical Professions in the Spanish Empire,* ed. John Jay TePaske. Durham, NC: Duke University Press, 1985.

Viqueira Albán, Juan Pedro. *Propriety and Permissiveness in Bourbon Mexico.* Wilmington, DE: Scholarly Resources, 1999.

Voekel, Pamela. *Alone Before God: The Religious Origins of Modernity in Mexico.* Durham, NC: Duke University Press, 2002.

Vogeley, Nancy. *Lizardi and the Birth of the Novel in Spanish America.* Gainesville: University Press of Florida, 2001.

Related Sources

30. Mexico's Paradoxical Enlightenment (1784)
50. Popular Images of Mexican Life (the Late Nineteenth and Early Twentieth Centuries)
70. Serial Satire: The Comic Book (1974)
74. Jesusa Rodríguez: Iconoclast (1995)

PART 5

The Early Republic (1824–1852)

Once having achieved independence from Spain, Mexicans confronted numerous obstacles in their efforts to establish a stable and prosperous republic for themselves. The documents in this section illuminate the foundations of these obstacles, while also delineating some of the strategies that politicians and citizens, rebels and reformers, implemented in their attempts to shape the nation's development, whether for their own personal gain or for the broader benefit of their fellow citizens.

Although it had impeded Mexico's economic and political development, Spanish rule over Mexico, and the Catholic ideology with which it was infused, had served as a powerful unifying force across the Viceroyalty of New Spain during the colonial era (sources 15, 16, 17, 18, 21, and 25). Independence undermined this ideological and administrative unity, while the military conflicts it provoked wrought havoc on Mexico's mining, agrarian, and industrial economies. Conservative circles within the new republic certainly harbored nostalgia for the relative prosperity—and cultural prestige—of the colonial era, as is clearly illustrated in the writings of Lucas Alamán (Source 41), one of the era's most important intellectuals.

Catholicism remained a significant intellectual and moral force in nineteenth-century Mexico (sources 33 and 35), retaining, for instance, its importance as a marker of common citizenship and civilization (sources 38 and 40). But the Church's power in this era continued to diminish, as had been happening since the second half of the eighteenth century. The stripping of the Church's wealth and authority would intensify in the second half of the nineteenth century, when Mexico's secular liberal ideology attained political domination (Source 42). In the first half of the century, the emergence of the liberal ideals of progress, reason, and individualism—as contrasted with conservatism's love of tradition and corporate entities—is most clearly expressed in the rationale for supporting the expansion of female education (Source 38).

What other forces emerged to fill the political and social vacuum created by the absence of Spanish colonial government and the decreasing influence of Catholicism? Beginning in the era of the independence wars themselves, Mexico came under the sway of rule by regional bosses and military leaders called *caudillos,* most notoriously embodied in the person of General Antonio López de Santa Anna (Source 36). Santa Anna, who seized the presidency eight times between 1833 and

1855, attempted to expand the power of Mexico's central government. But he was fighting against popular support for a more decentered federalism, such as that envisioned by the men who had crafted the country's first constitution, despite their faith in the growth of a nationalist sentiment and shared sense of commonality among Mexico's citizenry (Source 35).

In the early republic, local powers and the central executive often came into conflict in turmoil that impeded the country's peace and prosperity. One such conflict developed in the late 1820s in the Mexican state of Tejas-Coahuila, where the development of a local culture and economy tied to the United States caused the emergence of a political movement that sought autonomy from Santa Anna's centralist executive. The movement eventually led to the secession of Tejas from Mexico and served as a preamble to the Mexican-American War of 1846–1848. But this war, as Mexico's congressional members posit in "Mexican Views of the Mexican-American War" (Source 39), was also provoked by the expansionist ambitions of the country's northern neighbor. Such ambitions would have long-standing repercussions for both Mexico's economic development and its cultural self-formation over the course of the nineteenth and twentieth centuries.

Life on the new republic's frontiers presented particular differences from urban experiences in the country's metropolitan centers of Mexico and Guanajuato, so praised by Alamán (Source 41). Eulalia Pérez, a domestic worker in the Franciscans' San Gabriel mission at mid-century, provides a sense in her life story (Source 37) of the material and political realities of the California frontier in this era. Mexico's southeastern frontier at this time was the Yucatán Peninsula, the climatically inhospitable terrain that had formed the heart of the Post-Classic Maya states in the Pre-Columbian period (Source 8). In 1847 the Mayas of this region launched a rebellion against the Spanish inhabitants and Mexican governors of their territory that would span the next five decades (Source 39). Their central grievance turned on the changes that the country's emergent liberal economy had wrought on their landholdings and labor practices. Such grievances would resurface across the country in the later nineteenth and early twentieth centuries.

35. Address to the New Nation (1824)*

Mexico did not take a direct path from colonialism to republican nationhood. After enduring ten years of civil war, royalists and insurgents joined forces and, under the leadership of Agustín de Iturbide, declared their independence from Spain in 1821. Rather than establishing a republic, Iturbide arranged for the country's new Congress to name him emperor of Mexico, but his reign was short-lived. By 1823, internal opponents led by Antonio López de Santa Anna (Source 36) had toppled Iturbide (who is alluded to in the following source as "the unfortunate man"). Aspiring statesmen and leaders of the new nation then congregated for many months to craft Mexico's first constitution. Strongly influenced by the federalist example of the U.S. Constitution, Mexico's founding document gave limited power to the central government, reserving broad powers for those at the state level. The authors also sought to limit abuse in government by dividing the state's power between judicial, executive, and legislative branches. Unlike in the United States, however, the first Mexican Constitution did not separate the powers of church and state, and it maintained Catholicism as the country's official religion.

Rather than reproduce the articles of the Constitution itself, we include here the address to the citizens of Mexico that the president of the General Constitutional Congress, Lorenzo de Zavala, and its deputy secretaries wrote to precede it. The colonial state had imprisoned Zavala in 1814 because of his outspoken support of democratic reforms. After his release, he traveled to Madrid as a deputy to the Spanish legislature and became an active political leader in Mexico, representing Yucatán as a deputy in the First and Second Mexican Constituent Congresses of 1822 and 1824 and serving in the Mexican Senate from 1824 to 1826. In 1830 he fled from Mexico briefly because of his opposition to the increasingly powerful centralist state. After going into exile a second time, in 1835, he became the first vice president of the newly independent Republic of Texas in 1836 (sources 39 and 41).

As is evident from the following text, Zavala and his peers deeply admired the political example set by the recent history of the United States of America and also drew great inspiration from France's eighteenth-century intellectual Enlightenment. In this address, Zavala and his co-authors exhort their fellow Mexicans, using the respectful "*vosotros*" form, to join them in restoring their country to order and prosperity, particularly through a strongly federalist model of government. The address is full of idealism and optimism. What does this document identify as the sources of Mexico's recent political turmoil, and what foundation is there for the document's optimistic viewpoint? What image of Mexico and of Mexicans does Zavala construct in this document?

---

*From "Constitución Federal de los Estados Unidos Mexicanos," October 4, 1824, available at Biblioteca Miguel Cervantes, http://www.cervantesvirtual.com/FichaObra.html?Ref=13182&portal=178. Excerpt translated by the editors.

Federal Constitution of the United States of Mexico Sanctioned by the General Constitutional Congress, October 4, 1824

The General Constitutional Congress to the Inhabitants of the Federation:

Mexicans: in order to place a most beloved work—the fundamental code that might secure the fortune of the nation and serve as an indestructible base for the grand edifice of your society—in your hands that you may commit yourselves to it, the General Constitutional Congress has dutifully committed to words manifesting in a simple manner the objectives that it has considered since the first moments of its convention, the travails that impeded it, and that which is promised by your amenability and compliance with it once you begin to benefit from the joys resulting from the federal system decreed and sanctioned by the majority of your congressmen.

The Congress is not concerned here with describing either the series of events of the past fourteen years of revolution or the costly sacrifices that were necessary so that the nation would at last obtain the priceless possession of its independence. This is a subject that, in time, will redeem the history of our days. For now, it is only important that you remember that the constant blows of patriotism beat and broke the chains that had bound us to Spain. There could not have been another center of unity, nor another link joining together the diverse provinces of this great nation, than the leader who was able to acknowledge the totality of the peoples in pronouncing their independence. The impartial world will judge the events that brought a tragic end to the second revolution. However, the fact is that the state dissolved with the fall of this unfortunate man and nothing could contain the uproar from the provinces: none was superior to another, and the state, like a sinking ship, would have been submerged in the turbulence of the storm, but for the prudence and sense of the peoples in demanding the convention of the Congress which gave the nation new life. And could the Congress have ignored the voice of the people having established such eminent proof of their enlightenment? And could the congressmen have come to vote against the will of their constituents? Never have the legislators of any nation so clearly showed how public opinion directed them and guided them to follow it. Never have the representatives of a people found themselves in circumstances so favorable to knowing the desires of those whose mandate they represent. Your congressmen will return to the bosom of their families with the sweet satisfaction of having worked to conform to the spirit and needs of their constituents.

In effect, they created a government that is resolute and liberal without being dangerous. . . . They demarcated the limits of the supreme authority of the nation. And they combined these things in such a way that, with luck, their union might always promote the commonwealth and the prevention of evil. They fixed the legislative mechanism, sheltering it from all rain and ruin. They armed the executive power with sufficient authority and decorum to make it respectable domestically and worthy of all dignity abroad. They secured for the judicial power such independence that it will never cause the violation of innocence nor lend security to crime. . . .

Happily, there was both a population compliant with the voice of duty, and a model to imitate in the flourishing republic of our neighbors to the north. Happily, the Congress knew that the Mexican nation only intended to shake off its passive obedience and enter into a discussion about its interests, rights, and obligations. Happily, it has penetrated the desires and needs of its constituents and succeeded in ensuring their destiny, giving to the public spirit a steady course conforming to the opinion shaped by some eminently extraordinary circumstances which, had they not been Mexicans, would have embroiled the people in a most disastrous revolution.

The federal republic has been and must be the fruit of their discussions. Only the calculated tyranny of the Spanish mandarins was able to govern such an immense territory with one set of laws despite its enormous differences of climate and temperament and their resulting influences. What relations of correspondence and uniformity could the baked soil of Veracruz have with the frozen mountains of New Mexico? How could the same institutions govern over the inhabitants of California and Sonora or those of the Yucatán and Tamaulipas? What need do the innocent and honest people of the interior have for the many criminal laws against transgressions and intrigues that are unknown to them? The people of Tamaulipas and Coahuila might reduce their law codes to one hundred articles while the people of Mexico and Jalisco increase theirs because of the large towns that have advanced them on the route of social order. Behold the advantages of the system of federation: Each community gives itself laws that are analogous to its customs, locality and the rest of its circumstances. Each community can dedicate itself without restriction to the creation and betterment of all the branches of prosperity. It can give to its industry all the momentum possible, without suffering from the difficulties of the colonial system or of those introduced by any government who, administering from a great distance, loses sight of the interests of those it governs. It can provide for its necessities in proportion to its advances. It can put at the head of its administration subjects who, as lovers of the country, also have the knowledge sufficient to carry out this work with success. It can create the necessary tribunals for the prompt punishment of delinquents, the protection of property, and the security of inhabitants. It can conclude its own domestic affairs without stepping outside of the limits of the state's powers. In a word, its members can enter into the full enjoyment of the rights of free men.

The General Congress . . . knows that it is a very arduous undertaking to obtain through enlightenment and patriotism that which is only the work of time and experience. But in addition to the fact that the soil of America is not contaminated with the vices of old Europe, we also have the advantage of the examples of the modern peoples who have constituted themselves and enriched us with their knowledge. We have benefited from the lessons that the world has received since the happy advent of social science that cracked the cement of tyranny. And we, ourselves, have raced further ahead in fourteen years than in the previous long period of three centuries.

With such hopeful portents, what should the Mexican people not hope of their General Congress?

. . . Your representatives used simple and natural language so that today they might put in your hands the code of your fundamental laws as they have resulted from their deliberations, cemented in the healthiest principles which until today have been recognized as the basis of social happiness in civilized countries. Fortunately, they did not have to compromise with those colossuses who, at their downfall, have destabilized the revolutions of other people. If in our annals is found the name of an ambitious son of the fatherland, history will use this example to teach our grandchildren how risky one individual may be who wants to enjoy for himself all the advantages normally reserved for the entire body of society. . . .

We have employed the time usefully since the beginning of our revolution in stockpiling arms to force gothic governments to return to the darkness from which they came, and in searching for the foundations of human association in the immortal works of those sublime geniuses in which we knew we would discover the lost rights of the human race. Now the moment has arrived to apply these principles and to open the eyes of the Mexican people to flooding light. The people have proclaimed that neither force, nor worries, nor superstition will be the regulators of their government. They have declared philosophically that they have verified with Newton the secrets of nature, defined the first principles of society with Rousseau and Montesquieu, and established their foundations with these philosophical principles. They have journeyed with Columbus over the surface of the known world, with Franklin snatching lightning from the clouds and harnessing it, and with other creative geniuses who have given mankind's achievements an indestructible life and limitless reach. Finally, after putting all of mankind in communication through a thousand loops of commerce and social relations, they can not tolerate anymore anything but governments that are analogous to this order created by so many and such precious insights. The elevation of character which the American people have acquired will not permit them to fall on their knees before despotism or troubles again, as this is always disastrous to the well-being of nations.

In the midst of these advancements of civilization, however, the fatherland requires our great sacrifices as well as a religious respect for morality. Your representatives announce to you that if you would like to place this happy republic on the same level as that of our neighbors to the north, it is essential that you strive for the highest grade of civic and private virtues which distinguish this singular people. That is the only basis of true liberty and the best guarantee of your rights, and of the permanence of our constitution. Faith in promises, love of work, education of the youth, respect for peers. Here, Mexicans, are the sources from which will issue your happiness and the happiness of our descendents. Without these virtues, without the obedience required by laws and authorities, without a profound respect for our venerable religion, we will render good laws ostentatious, and in vain we will have a code full of liberal maxims, in vain we will proclaim holy liberty.

The General Congress has equal expectations for patriotism, activities of the authorities and corporations of the federation, and for those of individual states: they must pledge all their powers in order to establish and consolidate our nascent institutions. But if instead of holding tight to the orbit of their authorities, they pull away in order to overstep them, if instead of demonstrating a just observance of the Constitution and general laws, they seek to elude their observance with interpretations and deceptive descendents of the scholasticism of our education, in this case, we will then renounce our right to be free and we will easily succumb to the whims of a national or foreign tyrant who would put us in the peace of sepulchers or in the stillness of dungeons.

To you then, legislators of the states, is given the responsibility of unveiling the system of our fundamental laws, whose key consists in the exercise of the public and private virtues. The wisdom of your laws will shine in their justice and utility; and their fulfillment will be the result of a rigorous vigilance over customs. Inculcate, then, your constituents in the eternal rules of morality and public order. Teach them religion without fanaticism, love of liberty without exaltation, and the most inviolable respect of the rights of others which are fundamental to human associations. The Marats and Robespierres elevated themselves above their fellow citizens while proclaiming these principles. These monsters drenched the most enlightened nation in the world in rivers of blood and tears and immediately climbed up the stairs criminals had stained to assault the credibility of their compatriots. Washington proclaimed the same maxims but this immortal man forged the happiness of the States of the north. How do we differentiate the latter from the former two? By examining their customs and observing their steps, acknowledging that without justice, there is no liberty, and realizing that the basis of justice can not be other than equilibrium between the rights of others and our own. Here is resolved the fundamental question of social science.

Protected by such patrimony, Mexicans, what do we have to fear of our enemies? It is of no importance that our obstinate oppressors still dare to refer to us with degrading colonial language when the name Mexico is already found among those of the cultured peoples of other sovereign nations. It is of no importance that jealous and impotent Spain, presently feigns a show intended to elicit compassion from Europe and makes heard its weak voice in the cabinets of foreign monarchs. All Spain's pretensions will flame out in the consolidation of our institutions and in the forces of the sons of the fatherland who are consecrated to defend it.

You must declare to the world, then, that only the tyrannical influence of despotic governments could have sunk us in the sad degradation in which we were submerged for so many years, and that at the moment of overthrowing their domination, nothing could have prevented us from joining the great family of humanity which we hold to be sacred. Europe and the rest of America have fixed their vision on us. National honor is highly compromised in the conduct that we observe. If we divert ourselves from the constitutional path, if we do not hold dear as the most sacred of our duties to maintain order and to observe scrupulously the laws that comprise the new law code, if we do not agree to redeem this promise and instead bury it with the attacks of the villains, then, Mexicans, we will henceforth be disgraced without ever having been happy. We will bequeath to our children misery, war, and slavery, and no other recourse will remain but to choose between the sword of Cato and the sad ends of Hidalgo, Mina, and Morelos.*

Mexico, October 4, 1824.
Lorenzo de Zavala, President
Manuel de Viga y Cosío, Deputy Secretary
Epigmenio de la Piedra, Deputy Secretary

Central Themes

State formation, religion

Suggested Reading

Federal Constitution of the United Mexican States (1824), full text available in translation at: http://tarlton.law.utexas.edu/constitutions/text/AT2S1.html.

Rodriguez O., Jaime E. *The Evolution of the Mexican Political System.* Latin American Silhouettes. Wilmington, DE: SR Books, 1993.

______. *The Origins of Mexican National Politics, 1808–1847.* Latin American Silhouettes. Wilmington, DE: SR Books, 1997.

Related Sources

33. José María Morelos's National Vision (1813)
39. Mexican Views of the Mexican-American War (1850)
41. Mexico in Postwar Social Turmoil (1852)
54. Land, Labor, and the Church in the Mexican Constitution (1917)

---

*Cato was a Roman politician who opposed Julius Caesar, the would-be emperor during the last days of the Roman Republic who used his command of the army to take power in the capital. On Hidalgo and Morelos, see Sources 32 and 33. After organizing an invasion into Mexico from New Orleans, Spanish Liberal Francisco Javier Mina was captured and executed by a firing squad in 1817.

36. *Caudillo* Rule (1874)*

Upon achieving independence, Mexico was plunged into five decades of political instability under the stewardship of its new *caudillo* (local political boss) leadership. The country withstood forty-nine changes of presidency in the first thirty-three years after its break from Spain. The most notorious of Mexico's caudillos was General Antonio López de Santa Anna, who served as president on eight separate occasions. Santa Anna was born in 1794 into a Creole family and entered the Viceroyalty's royal army at age fourteen. He commenced his service in the independence wars on the royalist side, fighting against Miguel Hidalgo and José María Morelos (sources 32 and 33), but he accepted Mexico's break from Spain under the leadership of Agustín de Iturbide. When Iturbide proved too tyrannical, Santa Anna helped overthrow him in 1823. Nine years later, while still declaring himself a Liberal, Santa Anna led a revolt against the last of a string of Conservative presidents and assisted in installing a Liberal government. The following year, he led another revolt against Liberal president Gómez Farías and for the first time seized the office for himself. In 1838, Santa Anna lost a leg in a campaign against France. He later had the limb dug up and treated to full military honors. His contemporaries and later generations scorned him for his role in the secession of Texas and in the 1848 war with the United States (Source 39). When the Liberals returned to power in 1855, they drove Santa Anna into exile in Cuba.

Santa Anna was eighty, crippled, and half-blind when he wrote his autobiography, excerpted here. After being pardoned by the Mexican government, he completed his memoir in 1874 just before he returned to Mexico. A work of self-promotion, the text nevertheless conveys useful information about the nature of political life in the early republic. What does it illustrate about how caudillos maintained control and about the mechanisms they used to legitimize themselves to the public? How did Santa Anna and his contemporaries define and express their patriotism?

---

*Antonio López de Santa Anna, *The Eagle: The Autobiography of Santa Anna,* ed. Ann Fears Crawford, trans. Sam Guyler and Jaime Platón (Austin, TX: Pemberton Press, 1967), pp. 15–18, 20–24. The translators' footnotes have been omitted when they are extraneous.

The Eagle: The Autobiography of Santa Anna

Chapter Two: The Empire (1822–1823), The Republic (1824–1825)

King Ferdinand VII of Spain was so incensed by the *Plan de Iguala* and the *Treaty of Cordoba* that he ordered the official court executioner to burn them. General O'Donoju fell out of grace with his sovereign. At the same time, Iturbide succumbed to the flattery of those around him. The temptation was too great! He declared himself occupant of the Throne of Montezuma.

Although Iturbide could not foresee it, his action was highly unpopular with the people and would soon lead to his loss of power and anarchy for the country. The people strongly favored a regency with lawmaking by means of representatives. I, myself, favored such a system, and I let my opinions in support of it be known.

About this time, the Republican Party came into being for the first time. It began to attract more and more people. Many of my friends tried to coax me into joining with them, but having been reared under a monarchy, I could not favor such an extreme change and listened to their words with disapproval.*

One night the Spaniards who controlled the castle of Ulua attacked Vera Cruz and attempted to destroy the bulwarks of Santiago and Concepcion.** Their surprise attack was a failure due to the vigilance of the guards, and the Spaniards sustained heavy losses in a two-hour battle. A Spanish general, three of their officers, and one hundred forty-six soldiers of the Cataluna battalion were captured. Our imperial government considered this a glorious victory and awarded me my commission as Brigadier General.

On October 30, 1822, Emperor Augustin I (as Iturbide had declared himself) dissolved the elected Congress which had convened on February 24, declaring the Congress to be antagonistic to his imperial person. Soon thereafter he started for Jalapa, trying to draw me from my province, where I had come under denunciation of his friends.

Knowing my disapproval of his coronation as Emperor,[†] "His Majesty" stripped me of my command and ordered my transfer to Mexico City, without extending to

---

*The old revolutionary leaders Guadalupe Victoria, Guerrero, and Bravo headed the Republican party. They advocated putting aside the *Plan de Iguala* and establishing a Federal Republic. Arthur H. Noll, *From Empire to Republic,* p. 84.

**Santa Anna made overtures to the Spanish General Lemaur, commander of the Spanish troops at San Juan de Ulua. They agreed that the Spaniards might take possession of the city without meeting any resistance on the night of October 26, 1822. Santa Anna merely pretended to surrender and planned to capture the troops. The plan went awry, although the Spaniards were defeated. Hubert Howe Bancroft, *History of Mexico,* IV (San Francisco: A. L. Bancroft & Co., 1885), pp. 786–788.

†When Iturbide had promoted Santa Anna from colonel to brigadier, Santa Anna had written to him, "Hail to Your Majesty for our glory, and let this expression be so gratifying that the sweet name of Augustin I will be transmitted to our descendants, giving them an idea of the memorable actions of our worthy Liberator. They will immortalize for history how just you are, and I together with my

me the mere vestige of courtesy. Such a crushing blow offended my dignity as a soldier and further awakened me to the true nature of absolutism. I immediately resolved to fight against it at every turn and to restore to my nation its freedom.

I knew that my resolve would mean great effort and personal sacrifice, but I was determined to gain freedom at any price. I hastily made a public appearance in Vera Cruz in order to address the people. Before my troops, I proclaimed the Republic of Mexico on the second of December, 1822. I published the *Plan de Vera Cruz* and a manifesto in which I expressed my intentions, carefully stating that these were only temporary, in order for the nation itself, to be the true arbiter of its destiny.

My troops soon clashed with the imperial army under the command of General Jose A. Echavarri. Several battles were fought—some favorable to my cause, and some unfavorable. Soon the superior numbers of his forces forced my troops back into the city, where we were constantly besieged.*

On the night of January 30, 1823, the Emperor ordered an assault to be made against my forces. In three hours time, we—although but fourteen hundred in number—fought our way to complete victory. The twelve thousand besiegers were so unskillfully generaled that our withering volleys routed them into a shameful retreat, leaving the surrounding battlefield strewn with dead bodies of their soldiers.

To hide its shame, three days later the defeated army issued the ignominious *Plan de Casa Mata,* dated February 1, 1823.** This extraordinary event was destined to change the entire political complexion of the country, for two weeks later, on the nineteenth of February, discouraged by defeats and desertions, the Emperor abdicated his throne.

My victory could not possibly have been more splendid! Judge and jury that I was in these momentous times of the destiny of my country, I remained faithful to every promise in the program that I had proclaimed for the Republic. With a zeal that was almost religious in nature, I followed it to the letter! . . .

Chapter Three: The Election of Vicente Guerrero (1828), The Spanish Invasion (1829)

In the year 1828, a stormy election ensued. Manual G. Pedraza, Secretary of War, challenged the patriot of the people, General Vicente Guerrero, for the office of second constitutional President. Through skillful maneuvering and through the power

---

regiment. . . . " Quoted in Frank C. Hanighen, *Santa Anna: The Napoleon of the West* (New York: Coward-McCann, 1934), p. 23.

*Santa Anna had been joined by the old revolutionary Guadalupe Victoria. Santa Anna stormed Jalapa on December 21, 1822, suffering a devastating defeat. Santa Anna fled to join Victoria at Puente del Rey, where he suggested that they both flee to the United States. But Victoria told him: "Go and put Vera Cruz in a state of defence. You can set sail when they show you my head." Bancroft, *History of Mexico,* IV, p. 792.

**The *Plan de Casa Mata* guaranteed a republican form of government to Mexico. Also, the army agreed to reconvene the national representative Congress. Ibid., p. 795.

his office gave him, Pedraza obtained one more vote in the legislature than Guerrero. Depression and desperation followed Pedraza's election. Revolution was the natural result.

At the time of the election, I was in charge of the government of Vera Cruz. Nothing that I could do to preserve order in this grave situation was sufficient. I knew that revolution was inevitable!

In order to spare the lives of the people and to quell the whirlwind of revolution, I adhered to the pleadings of the people that Vicente Guerrero be declared constitutional President of the republic.

Pedraza's partisans declared me "outside the law," but it took me only three months to put down their attacks. The popular movement became so strong that Pedraza fled in disguise to the United States. When order was finally restored, Guerrero, the people's candidate, was declared constitutional President.

On the twenty-ninth of July, 1829, intending to reconquer Mexico, a division of the Spanish army, under the command of Brigadier General Isidro Barradas, landed at Cavo Rojo and proceeded to occupy Tampico and Fortin de la Barra without meeting any resistance. . . .

The invaders passed through the territory under my control, and I was seized with patriotic fervor. I knew that the honor of leading the defense of my country lay in my hands. Hastily I made the necessary preparations and began my campaign.

After some difficulty, I sailed from the port of Vera Cruz with a brigantine, four schooners, some small craft, two thousand three hundred foot soldiers, and as much munitions as possible. I also sent six hundred well-mounted lancers up the coast. With the true patriot's fighting spirit, I set out to brave every hazard and to seek out the invaders.*

I landed safely in La Barra de Tuxpan, sailing through the Spanish squadron cruising near Tampico under Admiral Laborde. In piraguas and canoes we crossed the Tameahua lagoon and proceeded forthwith to Tampico al Alto. Then we marched to Pueblo Viejo.

The invading general had successfully occupied the town of Villerias. Confident that he would receive reinforcements from Havana, he had left behind only a small garrison at his headquarters. This was a direct invitation for action on my part—an invitation I could not hardly fail to accept.

With a thousand soldiers under my command, I crossed the river under cover of darkness. However, the garrison stood vigilantly, and our surprise attack was frustrated. I was forced to attack the entrenchments, finally requiring them to surrender. In the midst of the formal capitulation, the commander-in-chief with his entire army

*Santa Anna was severely criticized for setting off on this reckless adventure without any orders. He left the chief seaport of the country practically unguarded against the Spanish fleet. Wilfrid Hardy Callcott, *Santa Anna: The Story of an Enigma Who Once Was Mexico* (Norman: University of Oklahoma Press, 1936), p. 72.

appeared at the city gates. Needless to say, it was an embarrassing moment for me, and I felt everyone's gaze on my face. For a few seconds, I did not know what to do.

Fortunately, luck was with me! An old general named Solomon was in command of the plaza, and despite his age, acted with unusual haste. He besieged me with foolish questions, and while he was doing so, the capitulation was drawn up. I fooled the old man by exaggerating the number of my forces, indicating that I had some twenty thousand men waiting for me at my headquarters in Pueblo Viejo. The commander-in-chief commanded old Solomon to tell him what was happening at my headquarters. The foolish old man gave him such an exaggerated picture of the situation, that the general, instead of attacking my small force, requested a parlay.

I was greatly surprised when I heard his terms. He merely desired that I abandon his headquarters and that I set a date for further negotiations. I agreed immediately, as my situation was decidedly critical. Within the hour my troops had crossed the river to safety.

I refused to meet with the invading general, as I considered his proclamations of little value. Nevertheless, I thought it my duty to point out to him the rashness of his undertaking and to advise him to retreat at once. His reply was so ridiculous that it indicated to me the full measure of his incapacity. I declined to communicate with him any further.

Hostilities resumed immediately. My first act was to cut off the enemy's lines of communication and to see that they received no further assistance. Therefore, I planned to oust them at Fortin de la Barra, which was defended by ten pieces of artillery and four companies of the Crown Battalion. I captured the pass at Dona Cecilia, which lay across the river and between the enemy headquarters, and La Barra—within a single night, my troops were securely entrenched.

Leading fifteen hundred soldiers, I commanded the general to surrender. His haughty reply infuriated me, and I attacked his forces furiously, disregarding his entrenchments and barricades. A bloody battle, lasting eleven full hours, from six in the evening to five in the morning, ensued. When their boastful leader was wounded, he surrendered unconditionally.

The commander of the enemy army had remained in his quarters throughout the entire battle. The constant pounding of our artillery and the fear of the twenty thousand men we had supposedly sent against his troops frightened him so that he sent Brigadier General Solomon to inform me of his surrender. At such surprising good fortune, I commented: "When fortune smiles on Santa Anna, she smiles fully!"

As the sun's rays spread over the banks of the Panuco River, the first Crown Division of the vanguard surrendered their arms and colors according to the rules of war—surrendering a force three times the size of my own. I permitted the officers to retain their swords. Thus, the destiny of Mexico was irrevocably assured on that memorable day!

When General Isidro Barradas was informed of the size of my forces at Pueblo Viejo, he cursed his error violently. His anguish aroused my pity. The poor man fell victim to his grief and died shortly thereafter in New Orleans.

As is the custom in Mexico, cheers and ovations greeted the conquering hero at every turn. The General Congress bestowed on me the title, *Benemerito de la patria.* I was promoted to General of Division and acquired the emblems of rank, which were pinned on me by General Manuel de Mier y Teran. This impressive ceremony took place on the very place where the invaders had surrendered. I was voted swords of honor by the various legislatures and the general public hailed me as, "Conqueror of Tampico."

I felt that the country was entering a period of peace, and I retired to my estates at Manga de Clavo for much needed rest, pleading to heaven that I would not have to answer another call to arms. But, unfortunately, I was mistaken—the uprisings continued unremittingly. General Anastasio Bustamente, Vice President of the Republic, led an uprising against President Vicente Guerrero, publishing the *Plan de Jalapa* and leading the troops of the reserve army. I stepped in immediately, demanding that Bustamente desist. But Bustamente aspired for power, and my protestations fell on deaf ears.

Knowing that his troops were inferior in number to those of Bustamente, President Guerrero retreated to the mountains at the south, hoping to hold his position with arms. The Vice President, in his own words, "without shaking off the dust of the road," placed himself in command of the Presidency. He pleaded with me to come to his aid, but I refused.

Central Themes

State formation

Suggested Reading

Fowler, Will. *Santa Anna of Mexico.* Lincoln: University of Nebraska Press, 2007.

Jones, Oakah L. *Santa Anna.* New York: Twayne Publishers, 1968.

Olivera, Ruth R., and Liliane Crete. *Life in Mexico Under Santa Anna, 1822–1855.* Norman: University of Oklahoma Press, 1991.

Related Sources

35. Address to the New Nation (1824)
39. Mexican Views of the Mexican-American War (1850)

37. A Woman's Life on the Northern Frontier (1877)*

Eulalia Pérez experienced life on Mexico's California frontier during the period in which this region was transformed from a Franciscan missionary outpost (Source 28) into a burgeoning commercial territory ceded to the United States in the 1848 war (Source 39). Pérez was born, according to some accounts as early as 1768, in Baja California's Loreto mission. As she recounted in her life story, she married Miguel Antonio Guillén, a soldier of the Loreto company, at age fifteen and gave birth twelve times during her marriage to him. The couple traveled to San Diego in 1802, and then to Mission San Gabriel outside of Los Angeles. After her husband's death in 1819, the Franciscans of San Gabriel offered Pérez work and took in her family, eventually appointing her San Gabriel's "keeper of keys," a title of great responsibility. Encouraged by the Franciscan friars, Pérez was remarried in 1832 to Juan Mariné, a retired soldier. Within the context of secularization, the mission saw the couple as a potentially friendly inheritor of mission lands. But the marriage was not a happy one; the couple eventually separated and did not succeed in maintaining their claim to land acquired from San Gabriel.

This excerpt comes from the opening of Pérez's life story, which she narrated in 1877 to Thomas Savage, an aide to the California historian Hubert Howe Bancroft. In his introduction, Savage notes that while Pérez was ancient at the time of their interview, she still possessed remarkable strength and lucidity. Her statements reveal that she was tremendously proud of the part that she and other women played in the development of California. What functions and roles did they perform in this frontier society? Her narrative also conveys an intimate sense of daily life in a frontier mission. What impression does she provide here of the social relations between the missionaries, the resident indigenous population, and the military? How does her viewpoint compare to that of Father Sigismundo Taraval (Source 28), produced a century earlier? How do her experiences compare to those of the women addressed in "The Education of Women" (Source 38)?

---

*Carlos N. Hijar, Eulalia Pérez, and Augustín Escobar, *Three Memoirs of Mexican California,* trans. Vivian C. Fisher (Berkeley, CA: Friends of the Bancroft Library, 1988), pp. 74–82.

Memoir of Eulalia Pérez

I, Eulalia Pérez, was born in the Presidio [garrison] of Loreto in Baja California.

My father's name was Diego Pérez, and he was employed in the Navy Department of said presidio; my mother's name was Antonia Rosalia Cora. Both were pure white.

I do not remember the date of my birth, but I do know that I was fifteen years old when I married Miguel Antonio Guillén, a soldier of the garrison at Loreto Presidio. During the time of my stay at Loreto I had three children—two boys, who died in infancy, one girl, Petra, who was eleven years old when we moved to San Diego, and another boy, Isidoro, who came with us to this [Alta] California.

I lived eight years in San Diego with my husband who continued his service in the garrison of the Presidio, and I attended women in childbirth.

I had relatives in the vicinity of Los Angeles, and even farther north, and asked my husband repeatedly to take me to see them. My husband did not want to come along, and the commandant of the presidio did not allow me to go, either, because there was no other woman who knew midwifery.

In San Diego everyone seemed to like me very much, and in the most important homes they treated me affectionately. Although I had my own house, they arranged for me to be with those families almost all the time, even including my own children.

In 1812 I was in San Juan Capistrano attending Mass in church when a big earthquake occurred, and the tower fell down. I dashed through the sacristy, and in the doorway people knocked me down and stepped over me. I was pregnant* and could not move. Soon afterwards I returned to San Diego and almost immediately gave birth to my daughter María Antonia who still lives here in San Gabriel.

After being in San Diego eight years, we came to the Mission of San Gabriel, where my husband had been serving in the guard. In 1814, on the first of October, my daughter María del Rosario was born, the one who is the wife of Michael White and in whose home I am now living. . . .

When I first came to San Diego the only house in the presidio was that of the commandant and the barracks where the soldiers lived.

There was no church, and Mass was said in a shelter made out of some old walls covered with branches, by the missionary** who came from the Mission of San Diego.

The first sturdy house built in San Diego belonged to a certain Sánchez, the father of Don Vicente Sánchez, alcalde [mayor] of Los Angeles and deputy of the Territorial Council. The house was very small, and everyone went to look at it as though it were a palace. That house was built about a year after I arrived in San Diego.

---

*If Doña Eulalia were 139 years old when Savage interviewed her in 1877, she would have been born in 1738 and thus 74 years old and pregnant at the time of the earthquake.

**The words *padre* and *missionero* have been used interchangeably in the dictation. They have been translated as missionary.

My last trip to San Diego would have been in the year 1818, when my daughter María del Rosario was four years old. I seem to remember that I was there when the revolutionaries came to California. I recall that they put a stranger in irons and that afterwards they took them off.

Some three years later I came back to San Gabriel. The reason for my return was that the missionary at San Gabriel, Father José Sánchez, wrote to Father Fernando at San Diego—who was his cousin or uncle—asking him to speak to the commandant of the presidio at San Diego requesting him to give my son Isidoro Guillén a guard to escort me here with all my family. The commandant agreed.

When we arrived here Father José Sánchez lodged me and my family temporarily in a small house until work could be found for me. There I was with my five daughters—my son Isidoro Guillén was taken into service as a soldier in the mission guard.

At that time Father Sánchez was between sixty and seventy years of age—a white Spaniard, heavy set, of medium stature—a very good, kind, charitable man. He, as well as his companion Father José Maria Zalvidea, treated the Indians very well, and the two were much loved by the Spanish-speaking people and by the neophytes and other Indians.

Father Zalvidea was very tall, a little heavy, white; he was a man of advanced age. I heard it said that they summoned Zalvidea to San Juan Capistrano because there was no missionary priest there. Many years later, when Father Antonio Peyri fled from San Luis Obispo—it was rumored that they were going to kill the priests—I learned that Zalvidea was very sick, and that actually he had been out of his mind ever since they took him away from San Gabriel, for he did not want to abandon the mission. I repeat that the father was afraid and the two Indians came from San Luis Rey to San Juan Capistrano; in a rawhide cart, making him as comfortable as they could, they took him to San Luis, where he died soon after from the grueling hardships he had suffered on the way.

Father Zalvidea was very much attached to his children at the mission, as he called the Indians that he himself had converted to Christianity. He traveled personally, sometimes on horseback and at other times on foot, and crossed mountains until he came to remote Indian settlements, in order to bring them into our religion.

Father Zalvidea introduced many improvements in the Mission of San Gabriel and made it progress a very great deal in every way. Not content with providing abundantly for the neophytes, he planted [fruit] trees in the mountains, far away from the mission, in order that the untamed Indians might have food when they passed by those spots.

When I came to San Gabriel the last time, there were only two women in this part of California who knew how to cook [well]. One was María Luis Cota, wife of Claudio López, superintendent of the mission; the other was María Ignacia Amador, wife of Francisco Javier Alvarado. She knew how to cook, sew, read and write and take care of the sick. She was a good healer. She did needlework and took care of the church vestments. She taught a few children to read and write in her home, but did not conduct a formal school.

On special holidays, such as the day of our patron saint, Easter, etc., the two women were called upon to prepare the feast and to make the meat dishes, sweets, etc.

The priests wanted to help me out because I was a widow burdened with a family. They looked for some way to give me work without offending the other women. Fathers Sánchez and Zalvidea conferred and decided that they would have first one woman, then the other and finally me, do the cooking, in order to determine who did it best, with the aim of putting the one who surpassed the others in charge of the Indian cooks so as to teach them how to cook. With that idea in mind, the gentlemen who were to decide on the merits of the three dinners were warned ahead of time. One of these gentlemen was Don Ignacio Tenorio, whom they called the Royal Judge, and who came to live and die in the company of Father Sánchez. He was a very old man, and when he went out, wrapped up in a muffler, he walked very slowly with the aid of a cane. His walk consisted only of going from the missionary's house to the church.

The other judges, who also were to give their opinions were Don Ignacio Mancisidor, merchant; Don Pedro Narváez, naval official; Sergeant José Antonio Pico—who later became lieutenant, brother of Governor Pio Pico; Don Domingo Romero, who was my assistant when I was housekeeper at the mission; Claudio López, superintendent at the mission; besides the missionaries. These gentlemen, whenever they were at the mission, were accustomed to eat with the missionaries.

On the days agreed upon for the three dinners, they attended. No one told me anything regarding what it was all about, until one day Father Sánchez called me and said, "Look, Eulalia, tomorrow it is your turn to prepare dinner—because María Ignacia and Luisa have already done so. We will see what kind of a dinner you prepare for us tomorrow."

The next day I went to prepare the food. I made several kinds of soup, and a variety of meat dishes and whatever else happened to pop into my head that I knew how to prepare. The Indian cook, named Tomás, watched me attentively, as the missionary had told him to do.

At dinner time, those mentioned came. When the meal was concluded, Father Sánchez asked for their opinions about it, beginning with the eldest, Don Ignacio Tenorio. This gentleman pondered awhile, saying that for many years he had not eaten the way he had eaten that day—that he doubted very highly that they ate any better at the King's table. The others also praised the dinner highly.

Then the missionary called Tomás and asked him which of the three women he had liked best—which one of them knew the most about cooking. He answered that I did.

Because of all this, employment was provided for me at the mission. At first they assigned me two Indians so that I could show them how to cook, the one named Tomás and the other called "The Gentile." I taught them so well that I had the satisfaction of seeing them turn out to be very good cooks, perhaps the best in all this part of the country.

The missionaries were very satisfied; this made them think more highly of me. I spent about a year teaching those two Indians. I did not have to do the work, only direct them because they already had learned a few of the fundamentals.

After this, the missionaries conferred among themselves and agreed to hand over the mission keys to me. This was in 1821, if I remember correctly. I recall that my daughter María del Rosario was seven years old when she became seriously ill and was attended by Father José Sánchez, who took such excellent care of her that finally we could rejoice at not having lost her. At that time, I was already the housekeeper.

The duties of the housekeeper were many. In the first place, every day she handed out the rations for the mess hut. To do this she had to count the unmarried women, bachelors, daylaborers, vaqueros [cowboys]—both those with saddles and those who rode bareback. Besides that, she had to hand out daily rations to the heads of households. In short, she was responsible for the distribution of supplies to the Indian population and to the missionaries' kitchen. She was in charge of the key to the clothing storehouse where materials were given out for dresses for the unmarried and married women and children. Then she also had to take care of cutting and making clothes for the men.

Furthermore, she was in charge of cutting and making the vaqueros' outfits, from head to foot—that is, for the vaqueros who rode in saddles. Those who rode bareback received nothing more than their cotton blanket and loin-cloth, while those who rode in saddles were dressed in the same way as the Spanish-speaking inhabitants; that is, they were given shirt, vest, jacket, trousers, hat, cowboy boots, shoes, and spurs; and a saddle, bridle, and lariat for the horse. Besides, each vaquero was given a big silk or cotton handkerchief, and a sash of Chinese silk or Canton crepe, or whatever there happened to be in the storehouse.

They put under my charge everything having to do with clothing. I cut and fitted, and my five daughters sewed up the pieces. When they could not handle everything, the father was told, and then women from the town of Los Angeles were hired, and the father paid them.

Besides this, I had to attend to the soap-house, which was very large, to the wine presses, and to the olive crushers that produced oil, which I worked in myself. Under my direction and responsibility, Domingo Romero took care of changing the liquid.

Luis the soap-maker had charge of the soap-house, but I directed everything.

I handled the distribution of leather, calf-skin, chamois, sheepskin, Morocco leather, fine scarlet cloth, nails, thread, silk, etc.—everything having to do with the making of saddles, shoes, and what was needed for the belt and shoe-making shops.

Every week, I delivered supplies for the troops and Spanish-speaking servants. These consisted of beans, corn, garbanzos, lentils, candles, soap, and lard. To carry out this distribution, they placed at my disposal an Indian servant named Lucio, who was trusted completely by the missionaries.

When it was necessary, some of my daughters did what I could not find the time to do. Generally, the one who was always by my side was my daughter María del Rosario.

After all my daughters were married—the last one was Rita, about 1832 or 1833—Father Sánchez undertook to persuade me to marry First Lieutenant Juan Mariné, a Spaniard from Catalonia, a widower with family who had served in the artillery. I did not want to get married, but the father told me that Mariné was a very good man—as, in fact, he turned out to be—besides, he had some money, although he never turned his cash-box over to me. I gave in to the father's wishes because I did not have the heart to deny him anything when he had been father and mother to me and to all my family.

I served as housekeeper of the mission for twelve or fourteen years, until about two years after the death of Father José Sánchez, which occurred in this same mission.

A short while before Father Sánchez died, he seemed robust and in good health, in spite of his advanced age. When Captain Barroso* came and excited the Indians in all the missions to rebel, telling them that they were no longer neophytes but free men, Indians arrived from San Luis, San Juan, and the rest of the missions. They pushed their way into the college, carrying their arms, because it was raining very hard. Outside the mission, guards and patrols made up of the Indians themselves were stationed. They had been taught to shout "Sentinel—on guard!" and "On guard he is!" but they said "Sentinel—open! Open he is!"

On seeing the Indians demoralized, Father Sánchez was very upset. He had to go to Los Angeles to say Mass, because he was accustomed to do so every week or fortnight, I do not remember which. He said to me, "Eulalia, I am going now. You know what the situation is; keep your eyes open and take care of what you can. Do not leave here, neither you nor your daughters." (My daughter María Antonia's husband, named Leonardo Higuera, was in charge of the Rancho de los Cerritos, which belonged to the mission, and María del Rosario's husband, Michael White, was in San Blas.)

The father left for the pueblo, and in front of the guard some Indians surged forward and cut the traces of his coach. He jumped out of the coach, and then the Indians, pushing him rudely, forced him toward his room. He was sad and filled with sorrow because of what the Indians had done and remained in his room for about a week without leaving it. He became ill and never again was his previous self. Blood flowed from his ears, and his head never stopped paining him until he died. He lived perhaps a little more than a month after the affair with the Indians, dying in the month of January, I think it was, of 1833. In that month there was a great flood. The river rose very high and for more than two weeks no one could get from one side to the other. Among our grandchildren was one that they could not bring to the mission for burial for something like two weeks, because of the flood. The same month—a few days after the father's death—Claudio López, who had been superintendent of the mission for something like thirty years, also died.

*Leonardo Díaz Barroso in 1831 was appointed deputy and commissioner of Mission San Diego.

In the Mission of San Gabriel, there was a large number of neophytes. The married ones lived on their rancherías [settlements] with their small children. There were two divisions for the unmarried ones: one for the women, called the nunnery, and another for the men. They brought girls from the ages of seven, eight, or nine years to the nunnery, and they were brought up there. They left to get married. They were under the care of a mother in the nunnery, an Indian. During the time I was at the mission this matron was named Polonia—they called her "Mother Superior." The alcade was in charge of the unmarried men's division. Every night both divisions were locked up, the keys were delivered to me, and I handed them over to the missionaries.

A blind Indian named Andresillo stood at the door of the nunnery and called out each girl's name, telling her to come in. If any girl was missing at admission time, they looked for her the following day and brought her to the nunnery. Her mother, if she had one, was brought in and punished for having detained her, and the girl was locked up for having been careless in not coming in punctually.

In the morning the girls were let out. First they went to Father Zalvidea's Mass for he spoke the Indian language; afterwards they went to the mess hut to have breakfast, which sometimes consisted of corn gruel with chocolate, and on holidays with sweets and bread. On other days, ordinarily they had boiled barley and beans and meat. After eating breakfast each girl began the task that had been assigned to her beforehand—sometimes it was at the looms, or unloading, or sewing, or whatever there was to be done.

When they worked at unloading, at eleven o'clock they had to come up to one or two of the carts that carried refreshments out to the Indians working in the fields. This refreshment was made of water with vinegar and sugar, or sometimes with lemon and sugar. I was the one who made up that refreshment and sent it out, so that the Indians would not get sick. That is what the missionaries ordered.

All work stopped at eleven, and at twelve o'clock the Indians came to the mess hut to eat barley and beans with meat and vegetables. At one o'clock they returned to their work, which ended for the day at sunset. Then all came to the mess hall to eat supper, which consisted of gruel with meat, sometimes just pure gruel. Each Indian carried his own bowl, and the mess attendant filled it up with the allotted portion. . . .

The Indians were taught the various jobs for which they showed an aptitude. Others worked in the fields, or took care of the horses, cattle, etc. Still others were carters, oxherds, etc.

At the mission, coarse cloth, serapes, and blankets were woven, and saddles, bridles, boots, shoes, and similar things were made. There was a soap-house, and a big carpenter shop as well as a small one, where those who were just beginning to learn carpentry worked; when they had mastered enough they were transferred to the big shop.

Wine and oil, bricks and adobe bricks were also made. Chocolate was manufactured from cocoa, brought in from the outside; and sweets were made. Many of these sweets, made by my own hands, were sent to Spain by Father Sánchez.

There was a teacher in every department, an instructed Indian who was Christianized. A white man headed the looms, but when the Indians were finally skilled, he withdrew.

My daughters and I made the chocolate, oil, sweets, lemonade, and other things ourselves. I made plenty of lemonade—it was even bottled and sent to Spain.

The Indians were also taught to pray. A few of the more intelligent ones were taught to read and write. Father Zalvidea taught the Indians to pray in their Indian tongue; some Indians learned music and played instruments and sang at Mass. The sextons and pages who helped with Mass were Indians of the mission.

The punishments that were meted out were the stocks and confinement. When the misdemeanor was serious, the delinquent was taken to the guard, where they tied him to a pipe or a post and gave him twenty-five or more lashes, depending on his crime. Sometimes they put them in the head-stocks; other times they passed a musket from one leg to the other and fastened it there, and also they tied their hands. That punishment, called the "Law of Bayona," was very painful.

But Father Sánchez and Zalvidea were always very considerate with the Indians. I would not want to say what others did because they did not live in the mission. . . .

Central Themes

Indigenous people, the northern frontier, religion, gender

Suggested Reading

Beebe, Rose Marie, and Robert M. Senkewicz. *Testimonios: Early California Through the Eyes of Women, 1815–1848.* Berkeley, CA: Heyday Books, 2006.

Reyes, Bárbara O. *Private Women, Public Lives: Gender and the Missions of the Californias.* Austin: University of Texas Press, 2009.

Teja, Jesús F. de la, and Ross Frank. *Choice, Persuasion, and Coercion: Social Control on Spain's North American Frontiers.* Albuquerque: University of New Mexico Press, 2005.

Related Sources

5. A Treasury of Mexica Power and Gender (c. 1541–1542)
28. Indigenous Revolt in California (1737)
38. Female Education (1842, 1851)
71. The 1985 Earthquake (1985, 1995)
75. Maquila Workers Organize (2006)

38. Female Education (1842, 1851)*

By the mid-nineteenth century an increasing number of periodicals had appeared that were directed at the female reader. Early on, editors were for the most part men, though as the century progressed and the number of opportunities for women to get an education beyond primary school increased, so did the number of female editors of and contributors to women's periodicals. Many women attended normal schools, or teacher training schools. Their training and their experiences as teachers shaped the issues they addressed as writers. Along with teachers, who most often were associated with middle-class status, women of the elite class who practiced the art of writing also contributed to such periodicals. The periodicals published poetry, an important genre among women during the nineteenth century, as well as essays on social, cultural, and political themes. Many issues also celebrated moments in history and famous figures. Such articles implicitly created an association in the public press between Mexican women and public political culture, foreshadowing the emergence of a broad movement in favor of the expansion of the rights of women.

The first selection, "The Education of Women," which appeared in *Panorama de las Señoritas Mejicanas* (1842), presents itself as correspondence between "Angélica" in Mexico and Madame Josefina Bachellery in France. The epistolary genre, including published letters, opened a space for women to speak about topics normally beyond their authorization. The letter, which was one in a series, addresses questions debated among the educated classes in Mexico at the time: women's education, domestic responsibilities, beauty, and workforce participation. The reader will also note the way the author invokes French philosophy and culture. How does this letter hint at long-standing tensions over the role of religion in women's lives? The second source, "Advice to Young Ladies," appeared in *Presente Amistoso Dedicado a las Señoritas Mexicanas* (1851).

These sources can be analyzed in the context of debates in Mexican society during the era of Liberal reform that arose shortly after their publication (Source 42). The documents can also be compared to others to show how the changing socioeconomic position of women informed conversations about their domestic responsibilities and education (sources 26, 46, 59, and 64).

---

*Josefina Bachellerry, "Educación de mugeres," *Panorama de las Señoritas Mejicanas* (Mexico: Imprenta de Vicente García Torres, 1842), pp. 177–183, available at: "Proyecto Revistas Literarias Siglo XIX," http://lyncis.dgsca.unam.mx/literaturasxix/revistas/panorama/psm27.pdf and http://www.coleccionesmexicanas.unam.mx/revistas.html; J.J.P., "Consejosalas Señoritas," *Presente Amistoso dedicado a las Señoritas Mexicanas* (1851), available at: http://lyncis.dgsca.unam.mx/literaturasxix/revistas/presente2/pa2_05.pdf. (Accessed May 12, 2008.) Excerpts translated by the editors.

"The Education of Women" (1842) by Madame Josefina Bachellery

First Letter

As you have known for some time, my dear Angélica, I have developed the project of bringing together my ideas on the education of the fair sex, and regarding an issue as serious as it is fruitful, I have thought long and hard, both for pleasure and out of obligation, with the desire to publish some new reflections.

I have taken account of the immensity of such a large undertaking, and if I have decided to confront the subject, it has been to leave my daughters and yours the results of a long career in teaching, in which so many times you have said to me that a special vocation had been given me. . . .

Until now, and you have seen it, Angélica, the education of women has not been considered for its own merit, but only from the limited and incomplete perspective of private life, and Madams Neh'er, Guizot and so many other women writers have reduced their smart exhortations and their well-informed advice to the influence of the family, to the care and vigilance of mothers; to this end, they have directed their careful and judicious observations. . . .

There exists another fairly strong objection to the best books that we have to date on the education of women, and that is that they are written for the upper classes, and not for middle class families.

Young women without a dowry and of a middling condition, that today are called upon to make their own future, like men, in seeking true instruction that leads to talent and decides their fortune, infrequently find in these studies the lessons that would stimulate and aid them. This advice, based on contemplation, in which everything occurs in orderly and measured fashion, is still not relevant to those of adventurous professions, including those of the industrialist, artist, professor, worker, or the laborer who hope for days of prosperity and well-being for their children, and who leave no other patrimony to them than those of work and patience. . . .

Without pausing to consider theories, and taking the facts as they are, it is incontrovertible that society today advances on new paths that admire the thoughtful and observant. Everything around us is freed-up, a strange and mysterious impulse pulls us to a fast and disordered movement. Everyone runs, each hurrying: great concern for well-being concerns everyone; however, it is concern for material well-being. One would expect to see the immense mixture of the people of God persecuted by the oppressive arm of the Pharaoh. . . . And would it be out of the ordinary that such perturbation would have made it indispensable to make important modifications in the education of women?

The same need, the same lack of foresight, the same mania for luxury and for equality that exhibits itself in those poor young people in silk dresses like those of the rich classes, also demands an appropriate adornment for their souls. Everywhere, the instruction of women spreads in the same way, without discernment or concern for the future. No one knows what firm hand will establish harmony in the midst of this chaos. Without a doubt, though we speak in the name of the morality of our parents, the language needed to make oneself heard is no longer the same. Before, the great art of women's education was to limit them to private life in a situation that prohibited them from moving or thinking, and everything was reduced to infinite precautions and to an excessive vigilance. Above all else, care was taken to uphold to grandparents the pure and unstained name of the family. Woman had no other function than that of wife and mother, and without intelligence, was never allowed to leave the domestic realm. Today, out of necessity or fortune, she needs to be open to rivaling men in education. I do not know if we should applaud ourselves, because I believe there is more poison than happiness in the heavy branches of the tree of science. Be that as it may, in this peaceful time of labor and industry, in which women have long participated in the dangerous and agitated life of men, a great number of them go it alone, free and mistresses of their own destiny, without there having been an educated and friendly voice to teach them knowledge and strength in the midst of that liberty; not that negative knowledge that consists of sequestering oneself away from the world, but rather one that would allow them to carry the burden that they bear.

"Advice to Young Ladies" (1851)

It is easy to give advice, but not so easy to give good advice. We dare to do so as an expression of our admiration of the fair sex, upon whom men's fortune often depends. Most frequently, mothers shape the hearts of their sons, and those sons retain for the rest of their lives the impressions of virtue and order they receive as children. If all husbands were fortunate enough to have a good wife, and all men, a good mother, homes would be happy, families blessed, older gentlemen well-taken care of, and society in an excellent state. Women, you should know your mission in the world, and make good use of it!

We will not comment on the importance of religion: its importance is such that it is impossible to imagine a perfect woman without a profound reserve of piety. If a woman were to lack religion, she would be a monster. Fortunately this, in our republic, is unknown: the female sex completely deserves the description as pious.

Compassion for the poor is another adornment of the heart that, by the grace of the Creator, sweetens life. Religion, which extricated woman from the subjection in which she lived when beneath the tyranny of gentility, obliges her to be sweet, beneficent, and charitable. Her presence is so consoling in the home of the unfortunate! Her care so attentive at the bedside of the invalid! Her tears are sweet and her favors on behalf of the unhappy are precious! . . .

In the cultivation of the moral character of a young woman with religion and virtue, one ought also to adorn her with some knowledge, which although it may not be profound, is in some way useful. She ought to flee from the two extremes, equally disagreeable, namely base ignorance and the vain ostentation of knowledge.

The former comes from not knowing anything, and the latter from misunderstanding, accompanied by an indiscreet desire to show off. . . .

When in conversation, two rules ought to be observed in order to avoid being disagreeable, and they are: amiability and modesty, which are acquired together and are mutually beneficial. A girl blessed with amiability and full of courtesy makes herself loved by all who encounter her, just as a harsh manner is not the way to attract sympathies. An air of superiority or haughtiness does not at all sit well with a woman. . . .

Music is one of the most precious adornments of the fair sex. What beauty comes from a piano when it is a woman who produces such harmonies! It is then that music exerts its power over the people who listen to it. . . .

We do not extend to young women recommendations regarding cleanliness, because it would be an offense. . . . Cleanliness and attractiveness of dress are indications of care in the most important of matters. Simplicity is an excellent pair with taste, and both with decency. . . .

The care and order of the domestic sphere depend exclusively upon the care of the woman to which it is entrusted. She is in charge of her home, the members of which obey her, even the father or husband. Rather than impose their will upon her, they should pay tribute to her. Is the house well governed? . . . Is the home disordered and abandoned? This must be because either the husband intervenes where he is not competent or because the woman is careless. . . .

To appropriately care for a family, it is, above all, necessary to establish order. Without order there is no harmony, there is no peace, and there is no happiness; all is unhappiness, unsettled, and dissonant. . . .

Domestic order rests on three principles or maxims that it is desirable for someone charged with the care of a home to keep in mind. The first is to give each member of the family an occupation that is appropriate, and ensure that they carry out this responsibility. To tolerate someone who is lazy is to give life to more laziness, because the poor example of some will infect others. The second is to make sure everything that is done, is done on time, and thus, more time will be available for everything. When things are done at the last minute, they turn out badly, and when they are done with calmness and serenity, they turn out well. . . . The third is that all things destined for the service of the individual and the family must be in their appropriate places, and that as soon as they have served their purpose, they should be returned to their places. . . .

There was a time in Mexico when, thanks to our colonizers, woman was completely happy doing nothing in her home, spending days, years, unoccupied, in tedium, when she said "I do not do anything and I do not know anything, because I am a lady." Since independence, education and customs have changed notably, and the fair sex, whose dignity and importance have been appreciated since that time, occupies herself with that which is useful and agreeable; she is dedicated to domestic labors; she is charged with the order of the home and with directing the family; she entertains with music, embroidery and the cultivation of flowers; she learns some languages; she dedicates herself to some beneficial reading, and her manners and conversation fill society with delights. . . .

Central Themes

Religion, gender

Suggested Reading

Arrom, Silvia Marina. *The Women of Mexico City, 1790–1857.* Stanford, CA: Stanford University Press, 1985.

Miller, Francesca. *Latin American Women and the Search for Social Justice.* Hanover, NH: University Press of New England, 1991.

Related Sources

26. Sor Juana: Nun, Poet, and Advocate (1690)
37. A Woman's Life on the Northern Frontier (1877)
46. A Positivist Interpretation of Feminism (1909)
59. Feminism, Suffrage, and Revolution (1931)
64. Modernization and Society (1951)

39. Mexican Views of the Mexican-American War (1850)*

The Mexican-American War (1846–1848) had tremendously important repercussions on Mexico's subsequent economic, political, and cultural life. With the war, Mexico suffered a humiliating military invasion by a foreign power twenty-five years after declaring itself an independent republic and, at the end of the conflict, ceded roughly half of its national territory—much of the present states of California, Utah, Nevada, Arizona, New Mexico, and Colorado—to the United States. In a preamble to the war, the state of Texas had seceded from Mexico in 1836 and was subsequently incorporated into the United States of America.

The following source presents a Mexican perspective on the war. When U.S. troops invaded Mexico City in 1847, members of the country's national Congress withdrew to the city of Querétaro. There a number of these delegates often gathered in the home of Guillermo Prieto, the deputy from Jalisco, to discuss the war. Their conversations were published in a series of articles between September 1848 and May 1849 under the title *Apuntes para la historia de la Guerra entre*

*Ramon Alcaraz et al., *The Other Side; or, Notes for the History of the War Between Mexico and the United States*, written in Mexico, translated from the Spanish, and edited, with notes (New York: J. Wiley, 1850), pp. 1–4, 30–32.

México y los Estados-Unidos. Because they feared potential repercussions for their criticisms of General Santa Anna's ill-considered military strategies during the war, the delegates published the book as a collective rather than taking responsibility for the authorship of individual articles (Source 36). Subsequent research revealed that the first chapter, excerpted here, was written by José María Iglesias, who would later serve as interim president of Mexico before being ousted by Porfirio Díaz in 1876 (Source 44). The congressional members were right to exercise caution about their authorship: when Santa Anna reclaimed the presidency in 1854, he ordered that all copies of the work be rooted out and burned, and he condemned its authors to exile.

Past and present critics of the war in both the United States and Mexico have viewed it as an example of American imperialism, and that view is certainly represented in the following source. But there are other sides of the story of the war as well. Are there ways in which Iglesias assigns Mexico with responsibility for the war? In Mexico one important legacy of the war was its role in shaping Mexican national identity. How does Iglesias formulate an image of the United States and of Mexico? What does he see as their relationship to one another? How are these images complicated by the fact that a majority of the Mexicans who had settled in Texas in the late 1820s and early 1830s supported its secession from Mexico and annexation to the United States, or the fact that the first vice president of the independent Republic of Texas was none other than Lorenzo de Zavala, president of the first Republican Congress of Mexico and principal author of its 1824 Constitution (Source 35)?

The Other Side; or, Notes for the History of the War Between Mexico and the United States

Chapter One: Origin of the War

To contemplate the state of degradation and ruin to which the mournful war with the United States has reduced the Republic, is painful. Nor is it pleasant to take a retrospective glance in the investigation of the causes which led to this complete overthrow. But without some explanation of the circumstances which brought on hostilities, our work would be imperfect, and would be wanting in clearness and in those acts which ought to be presented to the examination of the civilized world. . . . The Mexican Republic, to whom nature had been prodigal, and full of those elements which make a great and happy nation, had among other misfortunes of less account, the great one of being in the vicinity of a strong and energetic people. Emancipated from the parent country, yet wanting in that experience not to be acquired while the reins of her destiny were in foreign hands, and involved for many years in the whirlwind of never ending revolutions, the country offered an easy conquest to any who might desire to employ against her a respectable force. The disadvantage of her position could not be concealed from the keen sight of the United States, who watched for the favorable moment for their project. For a long time this was carried on secretly, and with caution, until in despair, tearing off the mask, they exposed the plans without disguise of their bold and overbearing policy.

To explain then in a few words the true origin of the war, it is sufficient to say that the insatiable ambition of the United States, favored by our weakness, caused it. But this assertion, however veracious and well founded, requires the confirmation which we will present, along with some former transactions, to the whole world. This evidence will leave no doubt of the correctness of our impressions.

In throwing off the yoke of the mother country, the United States of the North appeared at once as a powerful nation. This was the result of their excellent elementary principles of government established while in colonial subjection. The Republic announced at its birth, that it was called upon to represent an important part in the world of Columbus. Its rapid advancement, its progressive increase, its wonderful territory, the uninterrupted augmentation of its inhabitants, and the formidable power it had gradually acquired, were many proofs of its becoming a colossus, not only for the feeble nations of Spanish America, but even for the old populations of the ancient continent.

The United States did not hope for the assistance of time in their schemes of aggrandizement. From the days of their independence they adopted the project of extending their dominions, and since then, that line of policy has not deviated in the slightest degree. . . .

The [North Americans] desired from the beginning to extend their dominion in such manner as to become the absolute owners of almost all this continent. In two ways they could accomplish their ruling passion: in one by bringing under their laws and authority all America to the Isthmus of Panama; in another, in opening an overland passage to the Pacific Ocean, and making good harbors to facilitate its navigation. By this plan, establishing in some way an easy communication of a few days between both oceans, no nation could compete with them. England herself might show her strength before yielding the field to her fortunate rival, and the mistress of the commercial world might for a while be delayed in touching the point of greatness to which she aspires.

In the short space of some three quarters of a century events have verified the existence of these schemes and their rapid development. The North American Republic has already absorbed territories pertaining to Great Britain, France, Spain, and Mexico. It has employed every means to accomplish this—purchase as well as usurpation, skill as well as force, and nothing has restrained it when treating of territorial acquisition. Louisiana, the Floridas, Oregon, and Texas, have successively fallen into its power. It now has secured the possession of the Californias, New Mexico, and a great part of other States and Territories of the Mexican Republic. Although we may desire to close our eyes with the assurance that these pretensions have now come to an end, and that we may enjoy peace and unmoved tranquillity for a long time, still the past history has an abundance of matter to teach us as yet existing, what has existed, the same schemes of conquest in the United States. The attempt has to be made, and we will see ourselves overwhelmed anew, sooner or later, in another or in more than one disastrous war, until the flag of the stars floats over the last span of territory which it so much covets. . . .

While the United States seemed to be animated by a sincere desire not to break the peace, their acts of hostility manifested very evidently what were their true intentions. Their ships infested our coasts; their troops continued advancing upon our territory, situated at places which under no aspect could be disputed. Thus violence and insult were united: thus at the very time they usurped part of our territory, they offered to us the hand of treachery, to have soon the audacity to say that our obstinacy and arrogance were the real causes of the war.

To explain the occupation of the Mexican territory by the troops of General Taylor, the strange idea occurred to the United States that the limits of Texas extended to the Rio Bravo del Norte. This opinion was predicated upon two distinct principles: one, that the Congress of Texas had so declared it in December, in 1836; and another, that the river mentioned had been the natural line of Louisiana. To state these reasons is equivalent at once to deciding the matter; for no one could defend such palpable absurdities. The first, which this government prizing its intelligence and civilization, supported with refined malice, would have been ridiculous in the mouth of a child. Whom could it convince that the declaration of the Texas Congress bore a legal title for the acquisition of the lands which it appropriated to itself with so little hesitation? If such a principle were recognised, we ought to be very grateful to these gentlemen senators who had the kindness to be satisfied with so little. Why not declare the limits of the rebel state extended to San Luis, to the capital, to our frontier with Guatemala?

The question is so clear in itself that it would only obscure by delaying to examine it further. We pass then to the other less nonsensical than the former. In the first place to pretend that the limits of Louisiana came to the Rio Bravo, it was essential to confound this province with Texas, which never can be tolerated. In the beginning of this article we have already shown the ancient and peaceable possession of Spain over the lands of the latter. Again, this same province, and afterwards State of Texas, never had extended its territory to the Rio Bravo, being only to the Nueces, in which always had been established the boundary. Lastly, a large part of the territory situated on the other side of the Bravo, belonged, without dispute or doubt, to other states of the Republic—to New Mexico, Tamaulipas, Coahuila, and Chihuahua.

Then, after so many and such plain proceedings, is there one impartial man who would not consider the forcible occupation of our territory by the North American arms a shameful usurpation? Then further, this power desired to carry to the extreme the sneer and the jest. When the question had resolved itself into one of force which is the *ultima ratio* of nations as well as of kings, when it had spread desolation and despair in our populations, when many of our citizens had perished in the contest, the bloody hand of our treacherous neighbors was turned to present the olive of peace. The Secretary of State, Mr. Buchanan, on the 27th of July, 1846, proposed anew, the admission of an Envoy to open negotiations which might lead to the concluding of an honorable peace. The national government answered that it could not decide, and left it to Congress to express its opinion of the subject. Soon to follow up closely the same system of policy, they ordered a commissioner with the army, which invaded us from the east, to cause it to be understood that peace would be made when our opposition ceased. Whom did they hope to deceive with such false appearances? Does not the series of acts which we have mentioned speak louder than this hypocritical language? By that test then, as a question of justice, no one who examines it in good faith can deny our indisputable rights. Among the citizens themselves, of the nation which has made war on us, there have been many who defended the cause of the Mexican Republic. These impartial defenders have not been obscure men, but men of the highest distinction. Mexico has counted on the assistance, ineffectual, unfortunately, but generous and illustrious, of a Clay, an Adams, a Webster, a Gallatin; that is to say, on the noblest men, the most appreciated for their virtues, for their talents, and for their services. Their conduct deserves our thanks, and the authors of this work have a true pleasure in paying, in this place, the sincere homage of their gratitude.

Such are the events that abandoned us to a calamitous war; and, in the relation of which, we have endeavored not to distort even a line of the private data consulted, to prove, on every occasion, all and each of our assertions.

From the acts referred to, it has been demonstrated to the very senses, that the real and effective cause of this war that afflicted us was the spirit of aggrandizement of the United States of the North, availing itself of its power to conquer us. Impartial history will some day illustrate for ever the conduct observed by this Republic against all laws, divine and human, in an age that is called one of light, and which is, notwithstanding, the same as the former—one of force and violence.

Central Themes

State formation, the northern frontier

Suggested Reading

Brack, Gene M. *Mexico Views Manifest Destiny, 1821–1846: An Essay on the Origins of the Mexican War.* Albuquerque: University of New Mexico Press, 1975.

Chavez, Ernesto. *The U.S. War with Mexico: A Brief History with Documents.* Bedford Series in History and Culture. Boston: Bedford/St. Martin's, 2008.

Henderson, Timothy J. *A Glorious Defeat: Mexico and Its War with the United States.* New York: Hill and Wang, 2007.

"Invasión Yanqui: The Mexican War," available at Humanities-Interactive website: http://www.humanities-interactive.org/invasionyanqui/.

"The Mexican-American War and the Media, 1845–1848," available at Virginia Tech Department of History website: http://www.history.vt.edu/MxAmWar/INDEX.HTM.

Reséndez, Andrés. *Changing National Identities at the Frontier: Texas and New Mexico, 1800–1850.* Cambridge: Cambridge University Press, 2004.

Related Sources

35. Address to the New Nation (1824)
36. *Caudillo* Rule (1874)
41. Mexico in Postwar Social Turmoil (1852)

40. The Mayas Make Their Caste War Demands (1850)*

The year 1848 was a bad one for Mexico. The same year that the country lost half of its territory to the United States (Source 39), Maya insurgents from southern and eastern Yucatán State rebelled against the Mexican government and the local white *hacienda* (agricultural estate) owners and took control over almost three-quarters of the entire peninsula. In the ensuing "Caste War" (1847–1901), Maya leaders Jacinto Pat, Cecilio Chi, and Venancio Pec led roughly 100,000 Mayas and significant numbers of poor non-Indians in a series of spectacular and shocking victories and came within thirty miles of invading the state capital of Mérida. When large numbers of Mayas left the front lines for planting season and the indigenous leadership subsequently dissolved into factionalism with the assassinations of Pat

---

*Ernesto de la Torre Villar et al., eds., *Historia documental de Mexico*, vol. 2 (Mexico: Universidad Nacional Autonoma de México, Instituto de Investigaciones Históricas, 1964), pp. 240–243. Translated by the editors. All footnotes have been added.

and Chi, the indigenous fighters were pushed back to the eastern quarter of the peninsula. They made the town of Chan Santa Cruz in Quintana Roo the capital of an autonomous Maya state. In 1850 stone crosses positioned in front of the town's *cenote,* a natural limestone well, and dressed in native women's shirts (*huipil*) miraculously began speaking to the Mayas. Claiming to belong to the Christian God, the voices urged them to continue the fight. The followers—called the *Cruzob*—raided westward and held off the Mexican army until it managed to capture Chan Santa Cruz in 1901 and Mexico City declared Quintana Roo an official territory.

Historians still debate the motivations of the Mayas who fought, but the larger causes of the war are known. The wealthy Yucatec planter class was divided, fighting over Liberal-Conservative, centralist-federalist politics. Victorious Liberals even declared Yucatec independence in 1845, but when the Mayas almost overran their haciendas in 1847, they pleaded with the United States of America to annex the state. In the end, Liberal Yucatec governor Miguel Barbachano, whom the Mayas address in the following source, came to an agreement with Mexico: in exchange for money to outfit an army and defeat the Mayas, Yucatán would reunify with Mexico.

Many of the poor Mayas who fought had suffered from the rapid expansion of export-oriented henequen and sugar haciendas whose owners tried to ensnare their labor through debt peonage. The Yucatec Liberals had robbed many of them of subsistence farming land in 1841, when the government legally turned uncultivated public lands, or *montes,* into private real estate. Finally, the traditional Maya *batab* (governors of Maya towns) took leadership of the rebellion because successive civil governments had cut them out of their role as tax middlemen between local Maya communities and white institutions of power, especially the Church, which they had profited from since the colonial period. The Yucatec army's assassination of a prominent batab in 1847 was the final straw.

This source is a diplomatic letter from 1850 in which the Maya leaders address Governor Miguel Barbachano and the Catholic Church and lay out their demands for peace. Leaders Venancio Pec and Florentino Chan were in control of the Mayas after killing their top commander, Jacinto Pat, in Belize, but they were feeling the pressure of fighting under siege, and they badly needed supplies for their army. Note how the letter is full of colonial terminology and concepts; the fight is conceived as occurring between Indians and Spaniards, not as a civil war between different factions of nineteenth-century Mexicans. The missive is written in the colonial genre of Maya, Mixtec, and Nahua governors' petitions to higher Spanish authorities. Interestingly, the authorial voice of the letter slips between "we" and "I" in parts.

What were the specific demands of the Maya? A "caste" war means a race war. Were the rebels motivated by race? What was their opinion of the "Spaniards"? Judging from the kinds of demands the rebels made, what were the causes of the war and how had the conflict uprooted Maya society? What type of society did the Maya leadership hope to restore?

Letter Directed to Ecclesiastical Authorities and the Governor of Yucatán, January 24, 1850

1. No one should take all the armaments of my troops and if they must be confiscated, no one should dare speak of it because they are truly our own. 2. We state that they should leave us this piece of land to live on because we do not believe it is correct to live among the Spaniards, until after there is a truce and there is no war anywhere, then we will be reunited with them, but only gradually and with careful consideration. 3. On account of the order of the *señor* [lord] governor that the Indians should be resettled in their *pueblos* [towns] as soon as the troops cease pursuing them, we are obliged to assemble them so they will settle themselves in their pueblos; since they are our subordinates, they will not run from us, and with gentleness we will restore them to their pueblos. We make this known to Your Honors so that you might inform the Señor President of Mexico, in keeping with his good name. 4. When we see that no harm is done to the Indians and we have returned to our pueblos, then we will name the elders who will become *governadores* [indigenous governors], and do justice for all that presents itself. 5. Concerning the matter that there should be honored curates or fathers among us to assist in the pueblos, this we will request of you, even hoping it will happen immediately because this would please me greatly because all Christians would be welcomed with love. 6. I declare once and for all, that as long as the troops pursue the Indians with malice, they will never surrender. It should be established here, as Your Honor says, that no Spaniards should be settled among the Indians and no Indians among the Spaniards. 7. No one will prohibit the Spaniards from coming to the *pueblos de los indios* to buy or sell anything; they must be received with respect and love[;] the same was done in the past before anything happened when we lived here in peace.* 8. It is not necessary that I request montes for any pueblo in this paper signed by the lord governor, for each person knows his pueblo, and if some monte has been bought, it will be seized in order that any person whether Spaniard or Indian, even if he comes from among you, can make his milpa [corn plot] there, and in this way we will show our mutual friendship. 9. All of the king's montes in the north and east must remain restricted to the poor so that they can plant milpas there; neither can the montes in the hands of the Indians, nor those owned by the Spanish be sold. This is specified on the ancient map. 10. When the time comes for the governor to approve this paper, all of the Indians who are [in] jails in the principal towns where there are barracks should be released, and also all who have been captured. If they do not want to remain there,

---

*The *pueblo de los indios* was the legally designated indigenous community of the colonial period. Often this legal category was applied to places that had been city-states (Maya cah) in the Pre-Columbian times.

they may return to you again. It is not necessary to prohibit each person from going where they want to be so that a person does not have to be anywhere except somewhere where he is shown respect. There he must stay. And in the same way, the same thing must happen with the Spaniards. 11. The reason why I say the Indians who were recently captured should be given their freedom is because it might be the case that there are married gentlemen in some of these pueblos whose families have remained here. Also, it could happen that there is some family there and that the husband remained here so they could find each other. This I beg of you: so that each can find his missing wife or children or mother, so that they find a way to get by. It is settled. Everyone agrees that we must do for all other Christians what we do for ourselves, whether they be Spaniards or Indians. 12. A general pardon should be given as a guarantee to us that no one will be reproached for anything that has happened since the war began. We will do likewise for the Spanish. 13. If someone desires to be among you, it is fine with me, I would not say that anyone would be forced to come and live among us. The same goes for the Spaniards who are here. After the war, if they wish to go there, they should go. If here they have their way of life and do not want to leave, neither will we force them to go there. I say that no one should be prohibited from being any place, so that Indians and Spaniards will mix again in reciprocal love, and in force or in war.

Finally, I say that if the governor agrees with the things that I request, then he should write an act that should be brought for all the *indios principales* [indigenous ruling class members] to sign, for then Your Honors will speak with more success. You could then do us the favor of pleading with the commander of Valladolid that he not command an attack on any pueblo. In the meantime, we will see what the very noble and respectable lord Governor Don Miguel Barbachano resolves to do. And Your Honor, I feel compelled to inform you that you should not think that we were at fault if it so happens that a confrontation occurs; it is because the Spaniards come. The good news is that those from Valladolid do not leave to any place now, only those of Tixcacalcupul and Tihosuco, but I do not know if they still come from Valladolid when they go to Tixcucal when they travel here. Sir, may God concede to us the lord governor's protection so that all war, all reciprocal massacres, all adversity, and hatred which have dominated us as of late shall cease forever. If this is done, we will go frequently to worship Your Honor. May he grant that the pueblos will be established again and that the true God may once again be adored along with all the saints in the church. Since we have always been true believers, we are yearning to hear what Your Honor says, and wishing that you the lord governor and the entire congress will give their honorable signatures to all the things that we have asked for as long as they are good. And so, noble and respectable lord, although I might speak with Your Honor in this paper, bear in mind that I speak with the respectable lord governor and also with our lord bishop so that they can bear witness on our behalf to Your Honor, and in telling you this, we reveal to you what we must say to you. For this reason, my lord, you would be doing us a great service if you send this paper to their Honors. Either they or Your Noble Honor, will know what it is that can be done because although it is we who speak to the Spanish through this paper, everybody so desires to end this war which has hatched a thousand injuries and impoverishes both all the Indians and also all the Spaniards of the world! About that which Your Honor says about the donation for a baptism being set at three *reales* [coins worth one-eighth of a peso] and no more, and marriage at ten reales, we know this. We also know that we pay for masses. This pleases me, and all those of my race greatly and we honor all of this. And as soon as we see that there is no longer reciprocal wickedness, when we have regained our authority and freedom, then everything will be settled as it was formerly. The only thing I ask of you is that these troops cease coming as soon as the response to our paper or the great act of peace arrives. This is what I have requested in this paper. Because we only hope for this peace so that everyone can undertake that which he has to do. Right now, it is necessary to clear the milpas. One hopes only to live in liberty, in constant tranquility and in union. This I also entrust to Your Honor: that if you have a response from our Lord Bishop to the paper that I sent, that this letter be brought to me so that my heart and all these pueblos can receive the greater good it brings. Perhaps the true God will make the hour when we may rest again as desired. Dear sir, let me know if the troops will withdraw from these little pueblos, and tell me that they be only quartered in Valladolid. Give me also your opinion in response to this paper that I send you, weighing with it the response of your lord the governor with whom the true God pleads that he should send you his answer. May God Our Lord grant Your Honor health for many years to come, as is the desire of your undersigned humble servants. God and Liberty. Cruzchen, 24 January 1850.—Florentino Chan.—Venancio Pec.—Bonifacio Novelo.—Manual Antonio Gil, secretary.

Central Themes

Indigenous people, state formation, race and ethnicity

Suggested Reading

Reed, Nelson. *The Caste War of Yucatán.* Stanford, CA: Stanford University Press, 1964.

Rugeley, Terry. *Yucatán's Maya Peasantry and the Origins of the Caste War.* Austin: University of Texas Press, 1996.

Related Sources

8. The Urban Zoning of Maya Social Class in the Yucatán (1566)
39. Mexican Views of the Mexican-American War (1850)
72. The EZLN Views Mexico's Past and Future (1992)

41. Mexico in Postwar Social Turmoil (1852)*

Lucas Alamán, whose description of Miguel Hidalgo's 1810 sacking of Guanajuato is included in this reader (Source 32), is considered a founding father of Mexican conservative politics, along with Agustín Iturbide. Alamán fully supported the Plan de Iguala of 1821, a compromise plan that finally united fighting factions of Mexican Liberals and Conservatives and ended the independence war. The Plan called for the newly independent Mexico to constitutionally centralize power in a monarchy, although politicians eventually settled, with the Constitution of 1824 (Source 35), on a republic with a strong executive branch. It seems that much of Alamán's political philosophy was shaped by what he observed in Guanajuato in 1810: enraged mobs of poor people massacring Spaniards—called the derogatory name *gachupines*—and any person who appeared white. He saw clearly that Mexico could not survive as an independent nation without addressing the material concerns of its people, but the strong hand of a centralized state and shared sense of identity were required to contain class warfare and political fanaticism. A return to core values shared by all residents was required. Unlike most of Alamán's contemporaries, he did not express his patriotism through a complete and odious rejection of Spain. On the contrary, he was convinced that Spanish culture and values had civilized people and created harmony among the social classes when Mexico was part of the Spanish Empire and that nascent Mexican citizens had to choose this path if they wanted peace and prosperity in the nineteenth century.

The following excerpt is drawn from Alamán's voluminous *History of Mexico from the First Independence Movements in 1808 Until the Present Day*, published from 1849 to 1852. This work places him in the pantheon of great nineteenth-century intellectuals like Karl Marx who, with boundless authorial energy, synthesized huge sweeps of history and analyzed them sociologically. Like many of the great historians of the nineteenth century, Alamán believed that history is didactic and that readers of history should come away having learned moral and political lessons on how best to steer the direction of their own nation.

What aspects of Mexican society does Lucas Alamán criticize as causes of instability, and what aspects does he believe encourage progress? Alamán was one of the founders of Mexican conservative ideology. Yet he utilizes the concept of "progress" and seems to be calling for the removal of government intervention in the economy, ideas often attributed to Mexican Conservatives' Liberal rivals. How does his assessment of recent historical events complicate our understanding of early nineteenth-century "conservatives"?

---

*Lucas Alamán, *Historia de Mejico desde los primeros movimientos que prepararon su independencia en el ano de 1808, hasta la época presente* (Mexico: Impr. de J. M. Lara, 1852), pp. 875–883, 914–919. Excerpt translated by the editors. Alamán's footnotes, when extraneous to the meaning of the text, have been eliminated. As indicated, new explanatory footnotes have been introduced.

The History of Mexico, Chapter XII: "The State of the Nation Since Independence"

It is not my intention to give a point-by-point history of what happened in Texas, which is, for the most part, so fresh in everyone's memory. It is well-known that the settlers intended to become independent, having common cause with Zavala, who, disloyal to his fatherland, died among its enemies. In order to contain the sedition, General Santa Anna marched to that province and, after he had gained important advantages, was captured and held prisoner. This was followed by the declaration of independence, which lasted a very short time with that republic subsequently unifying with the United States and declaring that its territory extended all the way to the left bank of the Bravo River. Resisting this usurpation, the Mexican Republic engaged the United States in an unfortunate war, which terminated with a peace treaty signed in the City of Guadalupe Hidalgo (formerly the Villa of Guadalupe) on the second of February, 1848. With this, the secession was completed not only of Texas with the extended territory they tried to claim for it, but also New Mexico, Alta California in its entirety, and considerable parts of the States of Chihuahua, Coahuila, and Tamaulipas, making the total area of territory ceded 109,944 square leagues, which is equal to half of what the republic possessed at the time of Independence, as well as 1,938 square leagues as indemnity, for which was received a sum of 15 million pesos.

The consequences of the secession of such a considerable portion of the republic did not have as much importance at the time as they would later have because the boundaries of the ceded territories were so little populated that they had been more a burden than an advantage to the government of Mexico. But it quickly became apparent what might come to fruition in these extensive lands in the energetic and enterprising hands in which they had fallen when surface deposits of gold and abundant veins of mercury were discovered there just after they had left Mexico's domain. The difficulty of controlling contraband is also apparent since the borderline has moved so much closer to Mexico's population center with only the desert between them. The gravest and most immediate consequence has been the frequency and depth of the incursions of wild Indians, who previously had been halted along the line of *presidios* [garrisons] on the frontier, but who in this past year, have penetrated all the way to the outskirts of Zacatecas, devastating the rich cattle-raising *haciendas* [agricultural estates] of that state as well as that of Durango and all other places on the frontier.

It would be unfair, however, to attribute these evils to Independence. They proceed from the growth of the population of the United States, the character of this population, animated with the invading spirit of the peoples of Northern Europe from whom they descend, and from the nature of the government of that republic maintains the pretext that it does not possess sufficient power to prevent its subjects from invading the territory of neighboring nations, even those with whom it lives in absolute peace. The rapid growth of the population in these states and the fact of the borderline's movement closer to Mexico's population center has meant that the barbarians, whose vagabond life-style and occupation of hunting necessitates access to a vast expanse of country, have been compressed on one side by the population of the United States who occupy and cultivate the lands they formerly inhabited. These, in turn, have been forced to invade those lands where they find the least resistance, which happen to be those of the Mexican frontier. Their destructive forays are even beginning to reach the heart of the republic from which they had been driven away more than two centuries ago. This grave scourge has no other remedy than the extermination of the tribes who refuse to be subject to a fixed home and to procure their sustenance through farming and cattle-raising, to which they display very little disposition. The missionaries managed to settle with religion and civilization the rest of the Indians who possessed some trace—or clear evidence—of social life but they never made any progress with this race of savages.

The Spanish government would no doubt have put up a longer resistance and better defended the lost terrain, being naturally more energetic because the army on which it depended was better organized; it could have reinforced itself with European troops and it could have had a squadron with which to protect the coast . . . although this support, which the Mexicans lacked, would not have assumed more than the form of notes and protocols from the other powers of Europe. But none of these measures would have stopped the effect of continuous invasion, not from the government of the United States, nor from all the residents on the frontier, which extends for countless leagues. This is clear with respect to the ceding of Florida and in the ongoing difficulty of impeding similar aggressions respecting those territories that it has held on to in the continent notwithstanding the fact that these should be easier to defend because of their insular position. Perhaps, if the Plan de Iguala had been executed as it was conceived, it would have succeeded in protecting the national territory against dismemberment, providing that European immigrants, who have been guided by their preference for the United States, had been redirected to the Mexican provinces under the influence of the governments from whence they came, and had maintained loyalty to the new fatherland they had adopted.

One of the particular effects of independence, exacerbated by the lack of compliance with the guarantees of the Plan de Iguala must have been that of the changes that the most important sectors of the Mexican population have experienced. This population is made up of the three principal races, which we have elsewhere described in all its elements: the Spaniards, divided into two branches, European and American, the Indians, and the *castas* [mixed-race people]. Our laws have attempted to erase these distinctions, but how little the laws of man can do against those of nature and against the influence of customs and inveterate preoccupations. The latter two races have kept themselves separate and distinct, differentiated themselves through language, dress, occupations, foods, and lifestyle. The European part of the Spanish race, because of the persecution it experienced, has been overpowered by the American part. All the occupations, cause of so many grievances, cause of such ambition, and one of the principal stimuli of independence; large and small business; industry; the products of the haciendas of the *tierra caliente* [tropical lands], all this the European Spaniards lost; it was all left to the American Spaniards. And since the other two races are not fit to take part in public affairs, it is the Spanish Americans who have exclusively managed them.

There is no need to repeat here what we have already said elsewhere on the subject of the variation produced. It is easily seen that although the American Spaniards have been able to destroy their rivals, they have not filled the hole left by the ruin of these people. Disorder has crept into the debilitated civil service and, at the same time, it has lacked in individuals trained in the traditional way. Commerce and the haciendas of the tierra caliente have passed into the hands of foreigners, and the same with the business offices of the houses of even the wealthy Mexicans, which have become filled again with Spanish assistants, who then have opened the doors of the country. In the army, above all, has been noted the lack of bosses and officials of European origin, this being one of the things that produced its downfall, and this lack was also the reason why, when circumstances permitted it, they returned to employing those who remained from those who had previously been discharged.

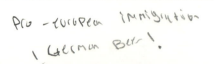

In order to fill this vacuum, to provide for the revitalization of capitals and the replacement of individuals, the Spanish caste was welcomed by those of this nation and was given residence in the country in order to increase the size of the white race by means of promoting the settlement of foreigners from all of the Catholic countries. They had been invited through the laws in the most frank manner from the start and later in diverse forms. One must distinguish this introduction of foreigners into populated regions from what had happened in the unpopulated regions, which had been specifically called "colonization." The second of these has had the sad consequences that we have seen—that of being the cause of the loss of such a large portion of territory. One greatly fears that an attempt at secession will be made under similar conditions and that one cannot stop the same circumstances and the same results. Regarding the foreigners who have come to establish themselves in populated areas, the effects have varied according to the character of the nation from which they originate: the English, accustomed to circulating large amounts of capital, launched mining operations. They intended to form rural establishments buying haciendas, but they were impeded by an imprudent law, which declared that foreigners could not acquire real estate and in commerce, storehouses were established for wholesale businesses. The sad fate of the mining operations frightened everyone else off, and except for some who still persevere today, they have a greatly decreased business, which is exercised by commissioned agents, who after they have enriched themselves, take leave of the country. They leave without a trace in order to create a place for others who would come to do the same thing without benefit to anyone in the nation. The Germans and the North Americans who are established almost exclusively in the capital and in the sea ports do the same thing. There remain only the Spanish and the French who follow different paths. The former, with the advantages that language, the similarity of customs, and the historical records and reports give them, have returned to take up all the lines of work. The people, not yet accustomed to seeing them as foreigners, have already almost forgotten the term "gachupin," distinguish them from those of all other nations, never comprehending in their spirits the category in which they must be understood. The French, among whom are included the few Italians here, quickly learning the language, familiarizing themselves with all classes of the society, are easy of character, ridiculing and criticizing all that is not French, but accommodating themselves without distaste to everything in the country. Having passionately embraced the country's interests when it was at war with the United States, France is the nation that is most sympathetic to the Mexicans and that which practicing all the professions, has caused an immense advance in all the mechanical arts, improving all their procedures, introducing good taste in building construction, furniture and clothes, and providing all the comforts and pleasures of life from architecture and machinery to confectionary and cuisine, although giving way with this advance to unchecked debauchery of which evils we will speak elsewhere. All of the restrictions that a suspicious body politic have imposed on the acquisition of real estate have been removed, and although an effort was made to place them on the retail business and the practice of the mechanical arts, this has had no effect, and all these fields remain free to competition between foreigners and nationals.

This progress in the colonization of the interior, beneficial, in one way, for the country in general, has two serious drawbacks. Foreigners encounter great advantages in maintaining their status as such, because it exempts them from mandatory military service and other burdens that are reserved only for the people of this country. They form independent colonies and there are as many of these as there are nations having commercial relations with the republic, each one recognizing as chief its minister and expecting little from Mexican laws. Rarely naturalized, they form a separate society that will never be incorporated into the nation. Counting, in addition, on the protection of their ministers, they can be too demanding and bothersome, overwhelming the government with claims that are often unjust. Meanwhile the Mexicans, disheartened by this preferential treatment, are frustrated right from the beginning, or they may place their enterprises under the name of these foreigners, who enjoy greater protection, great sums of capital, and connections with Europe and who have in their favor more knowledge in business and the arts and an aptitude for matters of style. The owners of large-scale operations are mostly English and German, and owners of retail businesses are Spanish and French while few Mexicans remain in these businesses where they are reduced to a class of employees and lawyers for those who, for the most part, encouraged this form of government. . . .

Amidst so many causes of underdevelopment, however, there has been notable progress, owing not so much to government initiatives, as to victories over the obstacles that institutions and political troubles have imposed. Even though foreign mining companies have not enjoyed the same victories, this domain has progressed extraordinarily and the treasures extracted from the Great Vein, Fresnillo, Rayas, and recently, from the mines of Nuestra Señora de la Luz in Guanajuato have been elevated to the level of prosperity equal or superior to what it had before. The amounts minted annually are now a little less than what they had been before the insurrection,* and awaiting even further improvements due to the abundance of mercury, indispensable to the amalgamation process, which comes from California and whose price has fallen to one half what it was when the mines of Mexico were provisioned only with mercury from the Almaden mines in Spain. And the California mercury is leased to private parties and the mine owners buy it from them at almost the same price as the Spanish government offered before Independence. Agriculture has returned to a more productive state than it had in that epoch and harvests are sold at higher prices than they have fetched for many years. Great industrial establishments have been formed where products are manufactured that are far superior to those that have ever been made, and progress would have been even greater if the importation of raw cotton had not been prohibited. Well-being is apparent for all those who do not depend for their living on the salaries of the government: artisans find work and in the countryside there is work for people in all agricultural operations. The bargains available on all apparel mean that even common people go about not simply clothed, but adorned in luxury. In the capital and in other major cities there are abundant outlets for entertainment, supplied in the capital by various theatres and two bull rings when before there was only one. All of this was not directly caused by independence because it could have happened without it, without incurring the other effects of independence such as the loss of territory and other adversities. Neither should it be forgotten that such advances are also the result of the general advances of the civilized world, in which Mexico for the most part has calmly and under good government participated, nor should the luck brought by mining bonanzas and abundant harvests, independent of political matters, be overlooked.

Foreign debt, with its continuous output of money without any beneficial exchange, causes the greatest harm to the economy. The loans made to businesses on customs duties, and the monies received from the salt mines and the rest of the national and church estates despite having been so ruinous for the treasury, have produced the benefit of creating numerous great, and some middling, fortunes. These, united with those that have come from mining and with those formed by people who have taken advantage of abuses and weaknesses in government, have remained rooted in the country and have driven up the prices of rural properties considerably. They have contributed to the beautification of some cities, especially Mexico and Guanajuato with the construction of sumptuous buildings, having also built some public edifices at great cost, such as the Theatre of Santa Anna in Mexico and the custom house and the warehouses in Veracruz. This accumulation of wealth, the perfection which the various arts have achieved, and the occasion these present to purveyors of high fashion, tailors, and French chefs that they have also been responsible for introducing a luxury so excessive, that gambling and social breakdown have ru-

*Mexican independence [translator].

ined some fortunes, especially those enriched by mining before they had finished developing, and they have also caused frequent commercial bankruptcy. There is no city in Europe or the United States proportionate in population, where there are so many private coaches as there are in Mexico City and the number rented in public stands is three times greater than what it was before Independence.

Society has been affected by the vicissitudes of politics and the ups and downs of private fortunes. In the first period following Independence, and especially after the fall of Iturbide, society in its entirety was politicized. Some women, addicted to insurrection, united in their social gatherings with people who had been following a certain party, while the leaders of the Scottish Rite Masons attended that of a lady who, because of her youth, beauty and talent, played the role for them of Madam Rolland of the Girondists in the French Revolution who also participated in the later ruin of the party.* The sad result of the Revolution of Tulancingo was the dissolution of the public meetings of the Masons along with the closing of their lodges, and the departure of the United States Ambassador Ponisett [*sic*] in 1829, recalled by his government, deprived the York Rite Masons of the only person who with his courteous manner and modes of French gentlemanly behavior brought a distinct lustre to their social gatherings and dances. As a result, the gatherings with connections to particular political parties ceased, leaving in their place those of little courtliness. This was most apparent in the case of the former formality of English parties whose coarseness grew sometimes to resemble the dishevelment of a Spanish dinner table. Banquets formerly marked with the solemnity of state negotiations were reduced to gatherings of a very few houses and guests; because the line of demarcation created by the excessive inequality of fortunes sharply separated families. There are not many competent to join the opulent class without risking ruin, making efforts to demonstrate wealth far above their means in order to avoid a ridiculous inferiority. Friendly society, which makes commercial life more agreeable without becoming too intimate, is almost never found. A foreigner who has not succeeded in being received into the domestic confidence of some families cannot find anything to do to pass the time other than riding a horse or wasting time in a café if he is prudent enough not to look for other distractions.

The effect of the ideas that have prevailed since the last century has been the destruction of all heraldic or administrative hierarchy. When the marks of noble distinction or those that came from civil offices were prominent—an illustrious name, a cross on the chest, a toga, a nap before lunch, a colonel's uniform, or a captain with a moderate fortune or salary—people respected those who possessed them as members of the most distinguished of classes in the state. Men toiled at great labors in order to acquire these honors, risking their lives in the countryside, or by the easier means of paying money for courtly pretenses. Now in Mexico, when all the rest have disappeared, only the army remains with a certain lustre. Some ranks within it are

*Madam Rolland's intellectual gatherings inspired the radical Girondin party in its republican and anti-monarchist stance during the French Revolution [translator].

purchased, obtained through extraordinary authorization, although these were later annulled by a decree of congress. High society was also, at least in Spanish America, much less costly. The wealthiest men, especially Spaniards of middling fortune, distinguished themselves little in their domestic comportment. With this frugal lifestyle, they gained great fortunes, with which on occasions of honor, they served the sovereign and obtained by merit the same medals that were so appreciated. Or, as a last resort, they invested in pious charities, which held their wealth in trust, and with these trusts, the memory of those who knew how [to] put their fortunes in this most noble cause.

Central Themes

State formation, the northern frontier, land and labor, gender, race and ethnicity

Suggested Reading

Hale, Charles A. *Mexican Liberalism in the Age of Mora, 1821–1853.* New Haven, CT: Yale University Press, 1968.

Martin, Luis. "Lucas Alamán: Pioneer of Mexican Historiography." *The Americas* 32 (1975): 239–256.

Related Sources

19. The Silver Mining City of Zacatecas (1605)
32. Hidalgo's Uprising (1849)
39. Mexican Views of the Mexican-American War (1850)
62. An Assesment of Mexico from the Right (1940)

PART 6

Liberalism, Conservatism, and the Porfiriato (1856–1911)

The mid-nineteenth century found the Mexican political elite working to resolve a series of issues that had emerged upon independence from Spain and persisted well after the Mexican-American War (1846–1848). Mexico lost half of its national territory in the war, and the conclusion of the conflict exposed the weaknesses of the economy and the regional factionalism that marked the country's politics. Mexican leaders debated how to encourage economic development, the nature of the relationship between church and state, and the correct balance of power between the federal and state governments.

Within this context, a generation of Mexicans emerged whose members came from middling social groups. They were mainly composed of *mestizos* (people of Spanish and Indian parentage), a group whose socioeconomic power had first emerged during the rapid economic growth of the late-eighteenth century. By the mid-nineteenth century, this middling group included individuals who had risen to social, economic, and political prominence; many first attended religious schools and then went on to public institutions of learning. For example, Benito Juárez, a Zapotec Indian from Oaxaca, attended seminary in Oaxaca City and then went on to receive a law degree. He would eventually serve as governor of the state of Oaxaca and as minister of justice and president of the Republic, strongly advancing the Liberal cause in all of these positions.

Liberals sought to usher in new relations of private property and encourage economic development, challenge the economic and political power of the Catholic Church and its moral authority over the citizenry, increase the authority of civil government, and expand political participation and conceptions of equality under the law. Liberals were not a homogeneous group: *puros* (purists) held fast to secularization, the expansion of private property, and the strengthening of the central government, while *moderados* (moderates) worked pragmatically with Conservatives. Liberal achievements included a series of laws, each named after its author. Ley Juárez (1855) eliminated ecclesiastical and military *fueros* (legal privileges) that, for example, exempted soldiers and clerics from having to stand trial in civil courts. Examining another important piece of legislation, Ley Lerdo (1856), reveals the ways in which the Liberals sought to significantly alter the Church's capacity to hold property (Source 42). This legislation also affected indigenous communities' *ejido* (community-held) land. Ley Iglesias (1857) prohibited the Church from charging high fees to administer sacraments. The Liberal Party also dominated revisions to the Constitution (1857).

Conservatives felt themselves under attack and sought to promote practices that had served them well: protection of landed estates, defense of the moral and economic authority of the Roman Catholic Church, and reliance on the military. Conservatives believed that republicanism was at the root of the country's instability and sought a strong central government, at the head of which would sit a monarch (Source 43).

Disagreement over these issues, as well as disagreements over presidential succession, led to the War of Reform (1858–1861), when the Liberal-Conservative conflict turned violent and many Mexicans took up arms. The clergy and army generally supported the cause of the Conservatives. Indigenous leaders supported both sides, depending on how their constituencies had been affected by reform legislation. Years of conflict had left the government coffers empty, and Benito Juárez, for lack of funds, suspended payment on the foreign debt. In response, France invaded Mexico. Conservatives offered to crown Archduke Ferdinand Maximilian of Austria as emperor of Mexico (Source 43). The rule of Emperor Maximilian, who arrived with Empress Carlota in Veracruz in 1864, is remembered as often for the personality of his wife as for his own efforts at Liberal-Conservative mediation; it ended with his execution for treason in June 1867. After his death, Benito Juárez returned to Mexico City and uttered words for which he is frequently cited: "People and government must respect the rights of all. Among individuals, as among nations, peace means respect for the rights of others." Despite their victory, however, Liberals remained a splintered group. Juárez had been president for almost a decade, despite the fact that the Constitution of 1857 limited presidential terms to four years and did not permit reelection. In 1871, Porfirio Díaz, an adherent of the Liberal cause who had distinguished himself in the Battle for Puebla against the French, rebelled against Juárez. Díaz eloquently expressed his reasons of rebellion in the Plan de la Noria (Source 44). Although it was a failed rebellion, in 1876, Díaz led the Rebellion of Tuxtepec (1876), which brought him to power, largely on the basis of his proclamation in support of the principle of no reelection and other principles expressed in the Plan de la Noria.

President Porfirio Díaz presided over incredible change in the areas of technology, industry, economic development, and social and cultural life. The ways in which these changes infused daily life in Mexico were both celebrated and criticized by contemporaries (sources 50 and 51). Since modernization and development did not spread evenly, Mexicans experienced this period differently depending on their social and economic position. The expansion of industrial production, especially in Mexico City, Monterrey, and the Puebla-Tlaxcala region, gave rise to new relations of work that, in turn, created tensions, which are distinctively voiced in sources 45, 48, and 49. Other voices addressed the tensions over landholding exacerbated during the Porfiriato (1876–1911) (Source 59). This period was also marked by significant changes for women, many of whom took advantage of growing educational opportunities. Women became increasingly visible in factories, and small numbers took work in government office and the professions. (Source 46).

The mid- to late nineteenth century can be seen as a period that had one foot in the past and the other in the future. Sources 42 and 44 can be evaluated in terms of Mexicans' ongoing reconciliation of the issues central to political and social life at the close of the colonial period: land use, the balance of church-state power, and federal versus state administrative jurisdiction. But these same documents can also be evaluated in terms of the way they paved the way for developments that took place during the presidency of Porfirio Díaz. Indeed, the Plan de la Noria (Source 44), written by Díaz in 1871, itself documents both of the issues that were of central concern to Mexicans at mid-century and that Díaz was unable to resolve to widespread satisfaction during his presidency.

42. The Reconfiguration of Property Rights and of Church-State Relations (1856)*

The Revolution of Ayutla (1854–1855) secured Santa Anna's final resignation from office and instituted a core group of Liberals in Mexico's federal government. They ushered in the Era of Reform, a crucial moment in Mexico's modern history. The following source, "Law of Disentailment of Church and Corporate Property"—later referred to as the Lerdo Law—was penned by Miguel Lerdo de Tejada (1812–1861) when he served as secretary of the Treasury. The law was one initiative in a broad effort to eliminate colonial structures of government and to put corporate real estate into circulation in the national economy. In this context, "corporation" does not refer to a business in the modern sense of the word, but to a legal category that derived from the colonial period and granted special rights and obligations to such entities as the Church, the military, and indigenous communities. The law stipulated that while the Church could hold property for daily functions, it could no longer hold land, for example, as an investment or in lien. The Lerdo Law also had a significant impact on indigenous community land. The law called for a radical reconfiguration of property rights and ultimately of the relationship between church and state, the impact of which was debated for decades afterward. The following are excerpts from both the law itself and the decree issued by the Ministry of Finance at the time of its enactment. Readers might consider how the law and the decree argued for the Liberal cause. How do their solutions to Mexico's ills differ from those offered by Conservatives? What in the conceptualization of this law might indicate why the Laws of Reform did not, in the final analysis, create the class of small landowners that some Liberals sought?

*"Ley de desamortización de Bienes de la Iglesia y de Corporaciones," in *Documentos para la historia del México independiente, 1823–1877,* ed. Alfonso García Macías (Mexico: Porrúa, 1988), pp. 201–216. Excerpt translated by the editors.

Law of Disentailment of Church and Corporate Property

Ministry of Finance.—His Excellency, Sir Interim President of the Republic has found it fit to send me the following decree:

Ignacio Comonfort, interim president of the Mexican republic, informs its inhabitants that: Considering that one of the greatest obstacles to the prosperity and ennoblement of the Nation is the lack of transfer or free circulation of a major portion of its real estate, a fundamental basis of public wealth, and using the faculties granted to me in the plan declared in Ayutla and reformed in Acapulco, I deem it legitimate to make the following decree:

Article 1. All rural and urban estates that are presently owned or administered by either civil or ecclesiastic corporations of the Republic, will be allotted as property to those who currently rent them, at the value corresponding to the rent that is currently paid, calculating as interest at six per cent per annum. . . .

Article 3. Corporations will be understood as comprising all religious communities of both sexes, confraternities and arch-confraternities, congregations, fraternities, parishes, *ayuntamientos* [city councils], schools, and, in general, all establishments or foundations characterized by perpetual or indefinite duration.

Article 4. Urban estates rented directly by corporations to various occupants will be allotted, capitalizing the sum of their rents, to the current occupant who pays the largest rent. With regard to corresponding rural estates, each occupant will be allotted the part that he rents.

Article 5. Urban as well as rural estates that are not rented as of the day this law is published will be allotted to the highest bidder at public auction, which will take place under the supervision of the highest political authority of the party. . . .

Article 8. Only property dedicated immediately and directly to the service and function of a corporation will be exempted from this law, even when some part immediately connected to it is rented, as is the case with convents, episcopal and municipal palaces, schools, hospitals, asylums, markets, and correctional and charitable facilities. As part of each of these properties, a house connected to them and inhabited by someone residing there for the purposes of the institution, may be included in this exception, as is the case with parochial houses and religious chaplaincies. . . .

Article 21. Those who by virtue of this law obtain rural or urban estates through auction or the process of allocation may at any time freely determine the use of or dispense of said property as with any legally acquired property. The corporations to which said property formerly belonged retain only the rights that the law grants to renters with regard to capital and revenue.

Article 25. From this day forth, no civil or ecclesiastic corporation, no matter its status, denomination or objective, will have the legal capacity to acquire property or administer real estate, with the exception of those indicated in Article 8 with respect to buildings intended for direct use or objectives of the institution.

Article 32. All the transactions for the sale of land caused by this law will be subject to taxation at the rate of five percent, which will be paid to the corresponding government office.

Article 43. Of the capital produced by the aforementioned tax, one million pesos will be set aside for the purpose of retirements, charitable assistance funds, and civil and military pensions, as well as the amortization of the coverage of civil and military employees currently in service.

Ministry of Finance to His Most Honorable Sir. On the 25th of this month of June, His Excellency the interim President of the Republic, in accordance with the unanimous agreement of his cabinet, rightfully decreed the law, copies of which accompany this letter. And although the usefulness of this law is obvious, even to those persons least informed of the true causes of the backwardness in which our country finds itself and of the methods that should be adopted to combat it, His Excellency wishes that the primary intention of this law, upon its declaration, be communicated to you, with the purpose of clarifying to you its reasoning. He doubts not that the enemies of the well-being and development of our society, constant in their tireless drive to distract the people regarding the issues that most closely affect their interests, will be prevented from distracting public opinion with regard to an issue of such vital importance for the nation.

There are two ways that the foresight of said law should be considered so that it is duly appreciated: First, as a resolution that will eliminate one of the economic errors that has most contributed to the immobility of property and that impedes the development of the arts and of industry that depend upon [the free circulation of land]. Second, as an indispensable measure to eliminate the principal obstacle that to this day exists for the establishment of a system of taxation—uniform and arranged according to the principles of science—the circulation of real estate, the natural basis of all good systems of taxation.

With regard to the first, it is without doubt sufficient to observe the immediate benefit that this resolution offers to current tenants or renters of corporate estates, as well as what the circulation of this mass of real estate that is today locked up will produce for society, and finally, the stimulation that trades and crafts will receive from the continued improvements that will be made to newly sold estates as soon as they enter into private hands. . . .

With regard to the second point, the country will benefit from resources that will accrue to the national coffers from the taxes that should be collected on the transfer of property, resources that during the difficult economic times through which the country is passing, will be put at the disposal of the government to address the most pressing needs of public administration without the state's having to recur to the ruinous methods which, unfortunately, have been utilized for many years now. Independent of this benefit, his Excellency the President proposes to form a firm base for the establishment of a system of taxation, the product of which, without inhibiting sources of public wealth, will be sufficient to fulfill the needs of the government and allow it to abolish forever all the levies which, like a tragic inheritance from the colonial era, we have retained, debilitating to a notable degree our agriculture, trades, industry, and the entire nation. . . .

Your Excellency will note that these powerful interests, which are none other than the corporations that own estates that must be sold and the current tenants and renters of those estates, are perfectly reconciled by the declarations of the law, for the former will continue to enjoy the same rents that they collect today so that they may continue to utilize them for the purposes of their institution, while the latter, transformed into owners of the estates they currently occupy as renters, will no longer have to fear that they will soon be dispossessed of the advantages that they currently enjoy, as would necessarily happen in the case that said estates were allotted to a third party. . . .

With this important measure, His Excellency the President believes that he gives to the nation an irrefutable testament of the most vehement and sincere desires that motivate him to, with firm hand, execute all the social reforms that the republic has long called for, to fully embark upon the only clear way that can lead the republic down the path to well-being and happiness, which with each passing day moves further away because of the combined acts of the mistakes that the colonial era had rooted in the Republic and the miserable and sterile revolts that after the Republic's political independence have left it in perpetual turmoil. . . .

His Excellency the President, whose heart is moved by observing the miserable condition in which the majority of the nation finds itself is also touched by the fact that such a situation cannot be improved upon in the midst of the general disorder to which the country has succumbed. By creating interests that can identify with well-understood concepts of order and progress, and successively decreeing all the appropriate means to regularize public administration in all its branches, the President firmly resolves to advance along this path, without being impeded by obstacles that may present themselves, for whatever may be the results of his work and sacrifices, his Excellency believes his good intentions will always be appreciated. . . .

To bring about these objectives, his Excellency counts upon the effective and decided cooperation of the intelligent and honorable sector of the nation, and especially upon the people at the head of public businesses. Without a doubt, your Excellency, with the erudition and patriotism which he has more than once proven he possesses, will second this measure, putting into action all the resources under his authority. . . .

God and Liberty. Mexico, June 28, 1856. Lerdo de Tejada.

Central Themes

Indiginous people, state formation, land and labor, religion

Suggested Reading

Bazant, Jan. *Alienation of Church Wealth in Mexico: Social and Economic Aspects of the Liberal Revolution, 1856–1857.* Cambridge: Cambridge University Press, 1971.

Chowning, Margaret. *Wealth and Power in Provincial Mexico: Michoacán from the Late Colony to the Revolution.* Stanford, CA: Stanford University Press, 1999.

Mallon, Florencia. *Peasant and Nation: The Making of Postcolonial Mexico and Peru.* Berkeley: University of California Press, 1995.

Vanderwood, Paul. "Betterment for Whom? The Reform Period: 1855–1875," in *The Oxford History of Mexico,* ed. Michael C. Meyer and William H. Beezley, pp. 371–396. New York: Oxford University Press, 2000.

Related Sources

52. Francisco Madero's Challenge to Porfirio Díaz (1910)
54. Land, Labor, and the Church in the Mexican Constitution (1917)
57. Petitioning the President (the 1920s)

43. Offer of the Crown to Maximilian by the Junta of Conservative Notables (1863)*

Conservatives argued that the absence of a strong centralized government was the cause of political instability, debt, and disorder in Mexico. Relying on the support of the military and the Catholic clergy, Conservatives also felt under attack by the Reform-era legislation limiting special privileges for those institutions. In 1857 Conservatives initiated a rebellion that came to be known as the War of Reform (1858–1861). While Liberals emerged victorious, the country was mired in debt; indeed, in 1861 President Benito Juárez declared the suspension of payment on all foreign debt. Later that year, Spain, France, and England sent troops to Mexico to collect moneys owed. Napoleon III, emperor of France, seeing the United States preoccupied with its own Civil War, defied the U.S. Monroe Doctrine and sought to lay claim to Mexico. A group of Conservatives sought a strong central government and supported monarchy in Mexico. Owing in part to the setbacks it suffered on such occasions as the Cinco de Mayo Battle for Puebla, France took nearly two years to seize Mexico City. In the document that follows, a group of Conservatives

*"Offer of the Crown to Maximilian," in *The Mexico Reader: History, Culture, Politics,* ed. Gilbert M. Joseph and Timothy J. Henderson (Durham, NC: Duke University Press, 2002), pp. 263–265.

formally offer the crown to Archduke Ferdinand Maximilian of Austria in 1863. What form of government does the Junta of Conservative Notables argue for, and how do they justify its appropriateness for Mexico? What about the historical context helps us understand why they took the position they did? What does this document tell us about how Conservatives saw Mexican society at this time?

Offer of the Crown to Maximilian by the Junta of Conservative Notables

1. The republican system, whether it takes the form of a federation or a centralized government, has, during the many years of its existence, been a fertile source of all the many evils that afflict our country, and neither good sense nor political reason permit us to hope that it can be remedied except by destroying the sole cause of our misfortunes at its root.

The institution of monarchy is the only one suitable to Mexico, especially in our current circumstances, because it combines order with liberty, and strength with the strictest justification. Thus, it is nearly always capable of imposing order over anarchy and demagogy, which are essentially immoral and disruptive.

2. To found the throne, it is not possible to choose a sovereign among the natives of the country (although there is no shortage of men of eminent merit), because the principal qualities that distinguish a king are those that cannot be improvised, and it is not feasible that a simple private individual should possess such qualities, much less than they can be established, without other antecedents, by a mere public vote.

3. And finally: a prince who stands out for his clearly exalted lineage, no less for his personal virtues, is the Archduke Ferdinand Maximilian of Austria. It is he who must receive the vote of the nation so that he may rule its destiny, because he is among the descendants of the royal house most distinguished for its virtues, extensive knowledge, elevated intelligence, and special gift for governance.

The Commission, accordingly, submits for the definitive resolution of the respectable Assembly, the following propositions:

1. The Mexican nation adopts for its form of government a MODERATED MONARCHY, hereditary, with a Catholic Prince.

2. The Sovereign shall take the title of Emperor of Mexico.

3. The imperial crown of Mexico is offered to His Royal Highness, Prince Ferdinand Maximilian, Archduke of Austria, for himself and his descendants.

4. In case unforeseeable circumstances prevent the Archduke Ferdinand Maximilian from taking possession of the throne that is offered him, the Mexican nation shall appeal to His Majesty Napoleon III, Emperor of the French, to indicate another Catholic prince.

Central Themes

State formation, religion

Suggested Reading

Ridley, Jaspar. *Maximilian and Juárez.* New York: Ticknor and Fields, 1992.
Servín, Elsa, John Tutino, and Leticia Reina, eds. *Cycles of Conflict, Centuries of Change: Crisis, Reform, and Revolution in Mexico.* Durham, NC: Duke University Press, 2007.

Related Sources

39. Mexican Views of the Mexican-American War (1850)
41. Mexico in Postwar Social Turmoil (1852)
56. The Catholic Church Hierarchy Protests (1917, reprinted 1926)

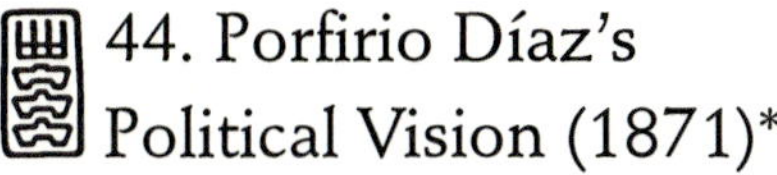

44. Porfirio Díaz's Political Vision (1871)*

As an adherent of the Liberal cause, Porfirio Díaz played a leading role in fighting back French troops as they sought, eventually successfully, to take over Mexico City, thus beginning the French Intervention (1862–1867). Díaz distinguished himself in service at the Battle for Puebla on May 5, 1862. Yet while he allied himself at this time with the Liberal cause and its chief proponent, President Benito Juárez, Díaz later led the Noria revolt in the wake of the highly contested presidential election of 1871. On this occasion, in the absence of the requisite majority vote, the decision of selecting the country's leader fell to Congress, and its members selected Benito Juárez. The Constitution (1857) did not allow for reelection, and the wartime exigencies that might have justified Juárez's extended rule no longer justified suspension of the law. Díaz denounced Juárez for returning to power again, and he criticized the corruption of Mexican institutions such as Congress and the courts. The Noria revolt failed to generate sufficient support and was quickly defeated by the federal army. Díaz then retreated to his *hacienda* (agricultural estate) in Tlacotalpan, Veracruz. In 1876, Díaz came to power with his instigation of the Revolution of Tuxtepec (1876), which reasserted many of the tenets of the Plan de la Noria. He again defended the ideal of no reelection and reiterated his earlier criticisms of the corruption of Mexican political institutions and practices. The reader might ask why such problems in the Mexican political system persisted—both before Díaz's rise to office and after.

---

*Alfonso García Macías, ed., *Documentos para la historia del México independiente, 1823–1877* (Mexico: Porrúa, 1988), pp. 321–324. Translated by Tanya Huntington and the editors.

Early interpretations of the Plan de la Noria were influenced by historians' criticisms of the Porfiriato. Some scholars have described the document as lacking a clear ideology or purpose and have seen it as an expression of the young Díaz's quest for power. More recently, some historians have begun to understand the plan as an expression of a specific political moment and a new approach to liberal politics. How is the pronouncement an affirmation of liberal ideals, and how might it represent something new?

Plan de la Noria

To the Mexican People:

Our national institutions have been placed in jeopardy by the indefinite, compulsory, and violent re-election of the Federal Executive.

In Congress, a majority regimented by deplorable, shameful methods has rendered ineffective the noble efforts of independent deputies, transforming our National Representation into a chamber of obsequious courtesans, determined to satisfy the Executive's every whim.

In the Supreme Court of Justice, the independent minority that has, on more than one occasion, saved constitutional principles from this cataclysm of perversion and immorality, has now been rendered impotent by the loss of two of its most worthy members and the admission of another who was brought in under the wing of the Executive. Since then, there have been no guarantees for legal recourse. The right honorable Judges and Magistrates of the Federal Courts have been replaced by submissive Government agents, while the principles of greatest transcendence and the interests that the people hold most dear have been left to the mercy of guard dogs.

Several States find themselves deprived of legitimate officials and subjected to unpopular, tyrannical governments, directly imposed by the Executive and sustained by federal forces. The will of the people, their sovereignty, and their laws have all been sacrificed to the blind caprice of individual power.

The Executive—a glorious personification of principles attained from the Revolution of Ayutla to the surrender of Mexico in 1867, principles that should be well tended and honored by the government in order to preserve the gratitude of the people—has been debased and vilified, compelling it to act as an instrument of hateful violence against the liberty of popular suffrage, and causing it to forget the laws and customs of Christian civilization in Mexico City, Atexcatl, Tampico, Barranca del Diablo, and La Ciudadela which, together with so many other massacres, pull us back into barbarity.

Federal income, more healthy and abundant than it has ever been before, given that people still endure the taxes levied during wartime, while neither national nor foreign debts are paid, is more than enough for all public services and should have sufficed to settle obligations incurred during the last war by covering the interests on legitimately recognized domestic and foreign debts, in addition to establishing the Nation's credit. At this time, having reduced expenses and systematized the administration of income, compliance with constitutional rule would be easy enough, freeing commerce from the obstacles and difficulties suffered as a result of the humiliating imposition of tithes, and freeing the treasury of its burdensome workforce.

But far from it: the ineptitude of some men, the favoritism shown towards others, and the corruption shared by all has crippled these bountiful sources of public prosperity: taxes are compounded, income squandered, and the Nation loses all credit while the favorites of those in power monopolize their fine spoils. For the past four years, their brazenness has tested our love for peace and our sincere dedication to institutions. Exacerbated public ills caused revolutionary movements in Tamaulipas, San Luis, Zacatecas, and other States; but most of the great Liberal party did not extend its sympathies to these restless ones, hoping to see the democratic, legal rotation of powers promised in the last elections once the Executive's constitutional period had ended, something they had not been able to achieve due to the government's policies of arbitrariness and coersion.

Because of this well-founded hope that has, unfortunately, turned out to be an illusion, all impatience was tempered, all aspirations deferred, and all thoughts turned towards forgetting past injuries and resentments; staunching the wounds of previous dissidences, and renewing the bonds of union between all Mexicans. Only the government and its agents in the Executive branch, in the chamber of Congress, and in the mercenary press, were tenaciously and capriciously opposed to the amnesty that, to their dismay, came to be decreed by a coming together of those who understood how to make the most of the intelligence and patriotic parliamentary opposition of the 5th Constitutional Congress. This law, which called upon all Mexicans to take part in the electoral struggle under the auspices of the Constitution, would have marked the beginning of an era of positive brotherhood. Any situation arising today within the boundaries of free suffrage of the people would have relied on the support of both victorious and vanquished alike.

The parties, which never share the same view of things, entered the electoral fray bursting with faith in the triumph of their ideas and interests and, defeated in fair combat, still conserve the legitimate hope that they will eventually reverse the result of their defeat, claiming the same guarantees that their adversaries enjoy; but once violence has appropriated the privileges of liberty, once bribery has replaced Republican honorability, and once counterfeiting has usurped the throne reserved for truth, the inequality of the struggle, far from creating rights of any kind, sours dispositions, and those who have been defeated by such vile treachery are compelled to reject the results as illegal and demoralizing.

The Revolution of Ayutla, the principles of Reform, and the conquest of independence and national institutions would be lost forever if the destinies of the Republic were left at the mercy of an oligarchy as inexpert as it is self-serving and anti-patriotic. Unlimited re-election is wrong, less because it results in the perpetuation of a citizen in the exercise of power than because of the preservation, through abusive practices, of ruinous collusion and the exclusion of other intelligences and interests. These are the inevitable consequences of the unlimited tenure of those employed in public administration.

And yet, the sectarians of unlimited re-election prefer their personal advantage to the Constitution, to principles, and to the Republic itself. They have turned this supreme appeal to the people into an immoral, corrupting farce, to the detriment of the very same national majesty they dare to invoke.

All the moral obligations of administration have slackened, and accomplices are sought out instead of honorable officials.

The wealth of the people has been squandered to pay off the counterfeiters of suffrage.

They have trampled the inviolability of human life, making horrifying murders a daily practice to such a degree that the macabre phrase "Ley fuga" has become proverbial.*

They have steeped the hands of their valiant supporters in the blood of the defeated, compelling them to trade in the arms of the soldier for the axe of the executioner.

They have sullied the highest principles of democracy, injured the most intimate sentiments of humanity, and besmirched the most prized and transcendental laws of morality.

They have reduced the number of independent deputies by illegally denying many districts representation of any kind, and arbitrarily swelling the ranks of re-electionists with citizens who lack any legal cause. Even so, fifty-seven representatives abstained from voting in a presidential election that the people have rejected as illegal and anti-democratic.

Impelled by these circumstances, by the instigation and demands of numerous accredited patriots from all States on both borders, in the interior, and along the shores, what am I to do?

During the Revolution of Ayutla, out of hatred for despotism, I left school to take up arms; during the war of Reform, I fought for principles; and during the struggle against foreign invasion, I upheld national independence until our government had been reestablished in the capital of the Republic.

Over the course of my political life, I have provided sufficient proof that I do not aspire to power, position, or employment of any kind. And yet I have also made serious commitments to my country for its liberty and independence, to my comrades in arms, whose collaboration has made it possible for me to surmount difficult tasks, and to myself, for I am not indifferent to public ills.

As for the call of duty, my life is a tribute to the fatherland, which I have never shirked in times of danger. My meager wealth, derived from the gratitude of my fellow citizens and improved somewhat through personal effort, as much as my scant

*The ley fuga gave authorities the legal right to shoot any person who had been detained and who attempted to flee (*fugar*, to flee). During the Porfiriato and the Revolution, the law was often invoked to justify execution, with or without any legal judgment process.

talent has made it worth, from this moment on, I devote it all to the cause of the people. Should triumph crown our efforts, I will go back to the tranquility of domestic life, preferring always the frugal, peaceful existence of the obscure laborer to the ostentations of power. If, on the contrary, our adversaries prevail, I will have done my final duty for the Republic.

We shall fight, then, for the cause of the people, and the people will be the sole heirs of victory. "Constitution of '57 and electoral freedom" will be our banner, "less government and more liberty," our agenda.

A convention of three representatives from each State, chosen by popular election, will provide a program for constitutional reconstruction and appoint a Constitutional President of the Republic, whom for no reason shall be the current wartime commander in chief. The delegates, patriots forged in honor, will bring into the arena of this convention the ideas and aspirations of their respective States, and they will know how to freely formulate and strongly uphold all truly national demands. I will only permit myself to echo those that have been pointed out to me as most pressing; but with no pretense of being in the right or in the spirit of imposing them as preconceived resolutions, making it clear from the start that I shall accept the accords of the convention without resistance or reservations of any kind.

Let the election of our President be direct and individual, and let no citizen be elected who has wielded authority for a single day the previous year, or held any position whose functions encompass the nation's territory as a whole.

Let the Congress of the Union be permitted to exercise electoral functions only in purely economic affairs, and by no means to designate top public officials.

Let the appointment of Secretaries of the executive branch and any other employee or official who enjoys salaries or fees surpassing three thousand pesos per year be subject to the approval of this Chamber.

Let the Union guarantee all Town and City Councils will have their own rights and resources, as elements that are indispensable to their freedom and independence.

Let all inhabitants of the Republic be guaranteed trial by jury of their peers that shall evaluate and determine the culpability of the accused, so that judicial officials are only conceded the faculty of applying sentences designated by pre-existing laws.

Let the hateful tithes be prohibited and the ordinance of maritime and border customs be reformed, in keeping with constitutional precepts and the manifold needs of our coasts and frontiers.

The convention shall take into account these issues and promote whatever shall lead to the reestablishment of principles, the stability of institutions, and the common good of the inhabitants of the Republic.

I shall not call upon bastardly ambitions, nor do I wish to fan the flames of deep resentment sowed by the excesses of the administration. Any national insurrection capable of returning to their reigning place the law and morality that has been violated, must be inspired by noble, patriotic sentiments of dignity and justice.

Those who love the Constitution and electoral freedom are strong and numerous enough here in the homeland of Herrera, Gómez Farías, and Ocampo to take up the struggle against the usurpers of popular suffrage.

Let all patriots, sincere constitutionalists, and men of duty lend their support to the cause of electoral freedom, and the most prized interests of the country will be saved. Let public leaders, having recognized that their powers are limited, honorably place their trust with the electorate through legal term limits, and the strict observance of the Constitution shall be a true guarantee of peace. Let no citizen impose and perpetuate himself in the exercise of power, and this revolution will be the last.

Porfirio Díaz
La Noria, November 1871

Central Themes

State formation

Suggested Reading

Garner, Paul. *Porfirio Díaz.* Harlow, UK: Pearson Education, 2001.
McNamara, Patrick J. *Sons of the Sierra; Juárez, Díaz, and the People of Ixtlán, Oaxaca, 1855–1922.* Chapel Hill: University of North Carolina Press, 2007.

Related Sources

52. Francisco Madero's Challenge to Porfirio Díaz (1910)

45. A Letter to Striking Workers (1892)*

Matías Romero Avendaño wrote the following letter to striking factory workers in 1892 while serving as minister of finance in the government of Porfirio Díaz. Romero was born in Oaxaca de Juárez in 1837 and died in New York in 1898. He studied in seminary and at the Oaxaca Institute for Arts and Sciences and later earned a law degree. With the outbreak of the War of Reform, Romero allied himself with President Benito Juárez. At age eighteen, he began working in the Ministry of Foreign Relations during the Juárez presidency. Romero eventually took up arms un-

*Ernesto de la Torre Villar, Moises Gonzalez Navarro, and Stanley Ross, eds., *Historia documental de México,* vol. 2 (Mexico: Universidad Nacional Autónoma de México, Instituto de Investigaciones Históricas, 1965), pp. 380–383. Translated by Tanya Huntington and the editors.

der the command of Porfirio Díaz and attained the rank of colonel. In 1892, when Romero wrote the letter excerpted here, he found himself again in the position of minister of foreign relations. Romero's close relationship to Díaz is also evident in the fact that at the time he was assisting Díaz with the writing of his memoirs.

In his letter, Romero outlines his vision of the relationship between the state, labor, and private industry. While President Díaz concurred with Romero on the proper relationship between labor and the state, he differed in his view of industry. Contrary to Romero, Díaz's government protected domestic industry through import tariffs. Import tariffs also served as a means of acquiring capital for the state's coffers. In his letter, how does Romero justify the protection of industry and the position of Mexico in the world economy more generally? How does he justify the protection of industry but not labor? What social actors does Romero identify, and how does he define their rights and responsibilities? How is the concept of supply and demand applied to the rights of workers? Why might this sort of argument have been considered valid during this moment of the Porfiriato?

A Letter to Striking Workers

The Executive branch of the Union is not, nor can it be, indifferent to the evils afflicting the working class of the Republic: if their wages are inadequate, if their needs are many, if it is impossible for them to save money, if they lack employment, the first one to regret this and fully concern himself with these ills is the President. . . . However, there are private ills that, while clamoring for all kinds of sympathy, fall largely beyond administrative action; such is the case of those that afflict the class you so honorably represent.

The Government has the law as its norm and justice as its aspiration. Given the institutions that govern us, it is unfeasible to restrict freedom of hiring or to intervene directly in the improvement of basic working conditions. No legal document authorizes this, nor do any economic interests oblige the Government to dictate salaries, or prices, or working hours. Our institutions, founded on the high principles of human freedom and regard for property, ban the Government from meddling directly in labor-management relations and will not allow any action whatsoever other than enforcing each party's legitimate and recognized rights under penalty of incurring serious liabilities. The Government can only contribute to improving labor conditions by indirect means such as keeping the peace, the promotion of industry and the investment of both national and foreign capital in native elements of the country's wealth, and thus ensure national credit. The Government believes it has done everything in its power and proposes to do all that is licit in order to achieve these results.

In your demands, you invoke your right to work. This right necessarily brings with it the obligation to procure said work, and our institutions do not consign any such obligation either to the Government or to private citizens. Without overstepping its bounds and incurring liabilities, the Government cannot, thus, take on the obligation of supplying workers with jobs much less oblige anyone else to supply them. And if this cannot be done by ministering the law, how might it possibly be accomplished if considerations of justice and public welfare are considered? Labor is subject, by unavoidable natural phenomena, to the law of supply and demand. This demand, be it high or low, falls beyond administrative action; the Government cannot regulate it without detriment. It would be equally unjust and inconvenient to impose the duty of hiring workers upon management as it would be to subject consumers with the obligation of purchasing merchandise lying stagnant in a warehouse. Soon enough each of these measures would pervert prices, limit production, and bring about widespread ruin.

The consumer is just as worthy of consideration as the producer. There is no reason to favor the latter to the detriment of the former. And given that the State must impose sacrifices upon individuals in order to attain the common good, it must not exaggerate or swell these to benefit certain social classes. Moreover, given the impossibility of protecting everyone at once, its duty is to procure that benefits will befall the majority, rather than the minority; upon the mass of consumers, rather than isolated groups of producers. There can be no doubt that the excess labor and insufficiency of our workers' wages, with all their disastrous consequences, are largely due to the shortage of merchandise of all kinds, caused mainly by the high customs tariffs that have prevailed in this country.

Far be it from this account to suggest that the President, exercising the faculties awarded him by Congress, should set about modifying customs tariffs with a view to damaging, or worse yet, ruining the industries that have developed in the shadow of high protective taxes; for although he believes it would have been more in the country's general interests for capital and workers employed in protected industries to have been dedicated to the development of other industries, for which our soil and conditions hold exceptional advantages, he comprehends that any sudden change in economic policy would lead to serious disruption and could result in the immediate bankruptcy of the capital invested in the manufacturing industry, as well as the unemployment, albeit temporary, of the hands it employs.

No individual would presume to rely upon his provider because he does not produce as much as he consumes; in as much as he's produced enough to pay for what he acquires, he is free and independent. Nations are the same way; the richest and most powerful ones are those that maintain the broadest trade relations with foreign countries; the ones that, to be concise, buy more abroad. Trade relations are exchange relations; in order to trade extensively, it is necessary to produce on a large scale. Foreign trade is a barometer of domestic production given that each unit of value introduced from abroad presupposes one of equivalent or greater value created in the importing country. It is not easy for a nation to produce all that it needs for its consumption without buying anything from the outside, while selling all that is left over to foreigners.

Therefore, in certain regions, given their natural or social conditions, agricultural production or the manufacturing of certain items is very cheap whereas these same articles are very costly to produce in other regions that do not possess these conditions.

By nature, Mexico possesses special advantages for the production of certain fruits. And if capital and energies nationwide are channeled into producing them, the economic situation will become much more favorable to what we have now. The mining industry, for example, has no tariff protection. Importation of gold and silver in the Republic is entirely duty-free, and yet this industry has developed and sustained itself, taking on extraordinary importance despite the fact that the price of silver has gone down considerably in foreign markets over the past few years.

It is beyond our scope here and inappropriate in an official communication of this nature to deal with other considerations regarding this issue that involves economic matters of such great import in order to demonstrate, for example, that if part of the capital and labor invested in manufacturing industries had been applied to the production of certain agricultural crops, such as coffee, conditions would be quite different for workers, capitalists, and the Nation as a whole.

Central Themes

State formation, land and labor

Suggested Reading

Hart, John Mason. *Anarchism and the Working Class, 1860–1931.* Austin: University of Texas Press, 1976.

Lear, John. *Workers, Neighbors, and Citizens: The Revolution in Mexico City.* Lincoln: University of Nebraska Press, 2001.

Porter, Susie S. *Working Women in Mexico City: Material Conditions and Public Discourses, 1879–1931.* Tucson: University of Arizona Press, 2003.

Wiener, Richard. *Race, Nation, and Market: Economic Culture in Porfirian Mexico.* Tucson: University of Arizona Press, 2004.

Related Sources

47. Precursors to Revolution (1904, 1906)
48. The Cananea Strike: Workers' Demands (1906)

46. A Positivist Interpretation of Feminism (1909)*

By the turn of the century, growing numbers of women attended postsecondary school, especially normal school (teacher education); entered professions, becoming lawyers, doctors, and journalists; read and wrote for the feminine press; and participated in public culture in new ways. And while some women had always worked outside of the home, a growing number of them were ever more present in the life of Mexican cities. Such shifts in woman's position in society challenged the status quo and positivist conceptions of order. Positivism, a philosophy that emerged in France at the beginning of the nineteenth century, posited that scientific methods and knowledge offer the only rational means of understanding not only the natural world but the social world as well. Horacio Barreda was one of many members of the Mexican elite who interpreted the changes in women's roles through the lens of positivism. Barreda published a series of essays titled "Study of Feminism" in *Revista Positiva* in 1909. Beginning in 1901, *Revista Positiva* served for fourteen years as a space for discussion of positivist ideas, including the dissemination of the thought of Auguste Comte. Barreda's essays on feminism provide insight into the ideological currents of positivism as they related not only to the position of women in society but also to a host of concepts including progress, history, economic development, and order. What can we learn about the positivist worldview from Barreda's approach to the topic of feminism? Why might Barreda have used Pre-Columbian history to make his argument? What social or ethnic hierarchies does Barreda affirm by situating his analysis of women in Aztec history?

---

*Lourdes Alvarado, ed., *El siglo XIX ante el feminismo: Una interpretación positivista* (Mexico: Universidad Nacional Autónoma Metropolitana, 1991), pp. 123–128, 130–134, 140. Excerpt translated by the editors.

Of Feminism in Mexico . . .

. . . Is not the true role of woman to provide man with all the attention and sweetness of the home, receiving from him in exchange all the means of survival that he acquires by means of work?

—Madame de Vaux

The Mexican woman is the true priestess of the home; the home is her temple, and it is her pedestal; there is her tabernacle of the immaculate pages of her history. . . . The home of the great Mexican lady does not have a boudoir, it has a sanctuary; to enter, one ought bow one's head and kneel.

—(*La mujer mexicana*). Concepción Gimeno de Flaquer

. . . In summary, we will appreciatively evaluate the influence of the Aztec antecedents, of Latin civilization—transmitted by means of Spanish domination—as well as the external influence of modern societies that might shape our social environment, whether by means of alternative educational [models] or because of their geographical location, as, for example, with the United States of America. . . .

As for conjugal relations, it can be said that they were satisfactory, given the level of development of the Mexica civilization. To have some idea of how this worked, it is sufficient to examine the character of matrimony in Aztec society.

Although it is true that polygamy was allowed, it is important to note that this form of human matrimony was in fact severely regulated and its practice quite restricted, given the fact that the obligation to justify that one had the pecuniary resources to support a given number of women reduced the polygamous unions to a sort of privilege of the well-off classes, and this sort of practice could not spread among the popular classes. . . . The principle that man was required to provide for women's subsistence was thus recognized by means of this severe economic requirement imposed upon polygamy; and, this rule had the intention of assuring the domesticity of the female sex. . . .

The organization of filial, fraternal, and conjugal relations, as they existed among the Mexica of old, exerted an influence on private life, affirming the idea of domestic subordination on the basis of age and sex, which provided for the order and stability of the family. . . .

The ceremonies associated with birth, marriage, and death, as well as the nature of education the priestly class provided to young men and women, due to custom and religious sanction, tended to strengthen the ideas, feelings, and prejudices that, in private and public life, maintained a division in the roles of the sexes. . . .

If the newborn was female, then there was placed [next to her] a broom, a *malacatl* [weaving tool] and a *petatl* [woven mat] that would serve as a seat when she did her work within the house. These work implements indicated to woman that her destiny was domestic activity, and that her place was at the heart of the home. . . .

If we add to this series of private and public influences, the naturally submissive nature that characterizes the Aztec race, we see that the absence of a subversive and turbulent spirit was characteristic in these people, as the historian Ramírez confirms in making the fair assertion that during the entire duration of the Mexica civilization, the people never rebelled against their masters. . . .

During the colonial period, the Latin influence, obeying the double force of the history of feudal and Christian morality, perfected the institution of the Mexica family . . . and it was by these means that it came to consolidate the constitution of conjugal relations, with the consecration of marriage based on monogamy, at the same time that along with the legal institutions of *mayorazgos* [entailed estates] and with mutual obligations that Catholic morality imposes upon fathers and sons, it improved filial and fraternal relations, affirmed subordination based on age, and destroyed the absolute authority of the head of household. . . .

While it may be true that from a certain perspective one could lament the seclusion in which Mexican women lived during the viceregal era, whether in monasteries or within the heart of the home, it would be worth finding out, before making categorical pronouncements against such a state of affairs, what would have been the advantages for the domestic sphere and the morality of both of the sexes, if the Hispanic-American woman had participated with all her will in this negative emancipation that since the end of the fifteenth century shook the very foundations of society in Europe, corrupting customs, altering moral sentiments, and seriously undermining the foundations of the family. This great revolutionary movement, which had been indispensable for the societies of the old continent to pass from one order of being that was already spent to another in harmony with the new needs called for by progress, meanwhile, was extremely harmful to the moral and social order, and therefore, essentially corrosive of family relations. The psychic nature of woman, her great domestic mission, and her social destiny would have gained nothing, to be sure, by getting caught up in this avalanche of negations accumulated by such a social tempest. The superior physical organization of Mexican women allowed for the preservation among us of the sacred depository of human morality, while the moment of regeneration of positive morality arrived, thus saving it from revolutionary chaos, just as Eneas saved the tutelary gods from the burning city; however, in order to do this, it is necessary to protect our women from the contagion and corrosive force of negativism; and her seclusion in the heart of the home, the vigilance of ladies in waiting and tutors, the circumspect living and family life, just as we are taught by Spanish customs, was preferable to seeing women dragged down by social dissolution.

Whatever the case may be, the Mexican woman, happily protected from Protestant ferment by her Catholic education, and alien to any habit of anarchic independence, was able to preserve the characteristics of a superior spiritual nature, to which the Mexica civilization, as well as the Latin civilization, transmitted by Spanish domination, contributed so much.

As a necessary consequence of the separation of Church and State, the most important social event to occur since Independence, the ideas of teleology and inappropriate opinions with regard to superstitions, have been restricted to all those individual acts related with private life and with issues of personal conscience, without the possibility of invoking them with regard to questions of public life or in relations of a social order. . . .

However, the effect of public life on that of private life has produced in our country a kind of woman perfectly prepared to receive a broad and complete positivist education, which will improve her intellectual and moral character as a purely human quality and that shows her the degree to which scientific knowledge of the social order and a positive appreciation of her duties as wife and mother can satisfy her intelligence and fill her heart. This essential group of women, which is the average type of Mexican woman, observed with instinctive distrust and even with aversion by the aristocratic classes, who are less emancipated, is the one that is important to consider here, because it is the one that finds itself most in harmony with the character of our social evolution.

The Mexican woman, due to her education, to the customs and tendencies cultivated by Spanish domination, has to this day continued to obey the influence of Latin civilization without the civilizations of Anglo origin having been able to significantly alter these customs and predilections. . . .

The Mexican woman cannot compete in physical strength or muscular development with either the Anglo-Saxon or German woman. Her constitution is weaker, her shape more delicate, her stature generally lesser; however, her nervous system is more excitable, and larger, and so too, then, her sensitivity, which turns out to be more delicate, and even exaggerated on many occasions. . . . Her notable prudence often gives her a truly heroic constancy to withstand, with admirable selflessness, pain and all types of suffering. . . .

The individualism that North American customs foment, the brutal competition that their industrial activities confirm, and the intellectual promiscuousness that contributes to the development of their mental and religious anarchy, results in the fact that among the proletarian class there exists no family life; male egotism has led to the expectation that not only the woman, but the child as well are obliged to contribute to family subsistence, searching for their daily bread in factories and workshops. . . .

Therefore, the sense in which we ought to encourage feminism in Mexico will consist in the affirmation of the domestic situation of woman, for which she finds herself admirably prepared, and in order to achieve it, seeking a complete positivist education to inculcate in each [man and woman] a clear notion of the respective mission of the sexes.

Central Themes

Indiginous people, urban life, land and labor, religion, gender

Suggested Reading

Arrom, Silvia. *The Women of Mexico City, 1790–1857.* Stanford, CA: Stanford University Press, 1985.

Ramos Escandón, Carmen. "The Social Construction of Wife and Mother: Women in Porfirian Mexico, 1880–1917." In *Kinship, Gender, Power: A Comparative and Interdisciplinary History,* ed. Mary Jo Maynes et al., pp. 275–286. London: Routledge, 1996.

Vaughan, Mary Kay. *The State, Education, and Social Class in Mexico, 1880–1920.* DeKalb: Northern Illinois University Press, 1982.

Related Sources

5. A Treasury of Mexica Power and Gender (c. 1541–1542)
38. Female Education (1842, 1851)
59. Feminism, Suffrage, and Revolution (1931)
64. Modernization and Society (1951)

47. Precursors to Revolution (1904, 1906)*

At the turn of the century, while the Porfirian elite celebrated "order and progress," other Mexicans spoke loudly and clearly of the uneven distribution of the benefits and costs of this so-called progress. Through labor organizing, political mobilization, and an opposition press, a liberal movement emerged, prominent among which were the three Flores Magón brothers—Ricardo, Jesús, and Enrique. The Flores Magón brothers arrived in Mexico City from Oaxaca at the turn of the century and, along with Antonio Horcasitas, founded the newspaper *Regeneracíon.* The title of the newspaper came from the concept of biological regeneration—the capacity of an organism to reconstruct and repair itself. In this spirit, the editors sought to describe the path toward the regeneration of Mexico. The newspaper went through a process of evolution, which is partly reflected in the newspaper's slogan. Originally it read "Independent Legal Periodical"; four months later, it was changed to "Independent Periodical of Combat." The Flores Magón brothers suffered repeated imprisonment

---

"Valle Nacional," in *Regeneración, 1900–1918* (Mexico: Ediciones ERA, 1977), pp. 170–172; "Ricardo Flores Magón, programa del Partido Liberal," in *Historia documental de México,* vol. 2, ed. Miguel León Portilla et al. (Mexico: Universidad Nacional Autónoma de México, Instituto de Investigaciones Históricas, 1965), pp. 407–411. Translated by the editors and Tanya Huntington.

for their work on the newspaper and for their involvement in other activities. In 1904, Ricardo Flores Magón was forced to leave Mexico and moved to the United States, where he continued to suffer persecution for his political activities. The newspaper came to serve as a voice for the Mexican Liberal Party (Partido Liberal Mexicano, PLM, established in 1906) organizing committee. Secret police hired by President Díaz and aided by the U.S. government destroyed the printing press and suspended the committee's right to publish the paper. By 1910 the newspaper was published in Los Angeles, California, and the slogan had become "Revolutionary Periodical." With the outbreak of armed insurrection in Mexico, the PLM split: one group returned to Mexico City to support Francisco Madero; the other group remained in Los Angeles and continued to promote anarchist ideals. In what way was the Liberal Party program a continuation of Liberal ideals in Mexico? How might we understand the long-held demands that were so central to the Liberal cause as revolutionary in 1910? How might the position of Mexico in the world economy have contributed to the conditions described in these documents?

"Valle Nacional," Regeneración, *1904*

In all the time of Mexico's memory, slavery today will be linked with the name of the demon that makes its existence possible. His name is Porfirio Díaz. And the most beastly of his works is in Valle Nacional.*

Fellow Mexican citizens: take note that there are only two methods by which to carry off the innocents to this purgatory. One is by means of a political boss, who operates directly; the other, by means of an *enganchador* [labor boss]. This latter operates with the willing cooperation of a political boss. This latter, as unfortunately you well know, is named by the State governor. Responsible to no-one, except the governor, who pays him an annual tribute, and never asks for account of his work.

And there you have the despicable political boss from Pachuca, for example!

He grabs whomever he wants in the streets. He takes him to jail. He accuses him of some imaginary crime, but the victims never appear. When the devil fills the jail, he sends them off to Valle Nacional. Naturally, after he is paid he has the pleasure of giving a part of this blood-money to his distinguished patron, his excellency Don Pedro A. Rodríguez, governor of the State of Hidalgo.

Fellow citizens: you might know of a friend who was not sent directly to Valle Nacional by a political boss. This is how it is, you see, for the majority work for an enganchador. Why? Because to traffic in human beings is illegal. Those most responsible hide behind enganchadores, the latter of whom carry out their business under the aegis of the former. This way they laugh at the idea of being prosecuted.

How does the enganchador spin his web? He advertises that he seeks workers. They will receive high wages, three pesos a day, good food, lodging in good housing,

*Valle Nacional, Oaxaca, a center for commercial agriculture production, especially tobacco.

without having to pay rent. The poor worker, who receives perhaps fifty cents a day, falls in the trap. He signs the contract. He receives an advance of five pesos, which he is encouraged to spend. A few days later, corralled with others, gullible like himself, he arrives in Valle Nacional. There, he and his companions of misfortune are sold to the tobacco plantations owners.

And how, fellow citizens, do government representatives rationalize their participation in the business of slavery? "What"—they proclaim indignantly—"did not said individual receive an advance of five pesos? This is a debt that he rightly must repay. . . . " These venal hypocrites throw up their hands at the constitutional rights of the worker. Indeed, when, under Porfirio Díaz, has the majority enjoyed their constitutional rights?

And what about the plantation owners? They cynically protest that theirs is not a system of slavery. By no means. It is a purely contractual agreement. Yes Sir, the worker signed the contract. And for this reason, he is obliged to the circumstances in which he finds himself. . . . What the upright plantation owners do not say is that instead of the three pesos a day promised by the enganchador, the salary stipulated in the contract, which the illiterate worker signed with the mark of an X, was only later filled in by either the enganchador or the plantation owner. Wages are customarily set at fifty cents a day.

And now imagine, fellow citizens, what happens next:

The trapped worker is rarely paid in cash. He receives credit in the company store, which belongs to the plantation owner. The prices charged there, for clothing and other necessities, are up to ten times higher that in towns outside of Valle Nacional. But that is not all. The slave is required to repay the price of his own purchases. It is *impossible* to work enough to pay off his debt.

The slave dies, generally within a year!

Why, you might ask, horrified with admiration, perhaps, does a healthy man die after eight to ten months in Valle Nacional? Because the wretched creature is required to work from sun up, throughout the long, cruel, humid hours of the day underneath the burning sun, and when the sun goes down because it sinks beneath the continuous and merciless beatings meted out by the overseer, who forces him to withstand such conditions to the limits of his strength; because the poor nourishment and the filthy living conditions turn him into easy prey for malaria or other tropical diseases. . . .

And because of the terrifying knowledge that he will never be able to regain his freedom!

But you could say: "Díaz himself does not directly benefit from this terrible business!" Fine. We will give him the benefit of the doubt. However, what of the governors of Veracruz, Oaxaca, Hidalgo—his underlings—who do benefit from it? Who named these governors? Porfirio Díaz. They in turn designate their associates. If Díaz wanted, he could get rid of slavery tomorrow. And not only in Valle Nacional, but in the henequen plantations of Yucatán; in the wood and fruit industries of Tabasco, Oaxaca, Morelos, and almost half the states of Mexico.

Why doesn't he do it? Because he needs these human hyenas. Pale imitations of he himself, he needs them to uphold his authoritarian power. But the day of liberation is near. Prepare yourselves for it, my fellow citizens!

—Enrique Flores Magón, *Regeneración,* 1904

Mexican Liberal Party Program

1. Reduction of presidential terms to four years.

2. Termination of the re-election of Presidents and State Governors. These officials will not be eligible for re-election until two terms after they have served.

3. Disqualification of the Vice President from performing legislative duties, or any other office of popular election; authorization of the same to hold offices conferred by the Executive branch.

4. Ban on obligatory military service and foundation of a National Guard. Those who offer their services to the regular Army will do so of their own free will. Military ordinance will be revised to eliminate any part of it that could be construed as oppressive and humiliating to the dignity of man; and, the wages of those who serve in the National Militia will be improved.

5. Reform and regularize Articles 6 and 7 of the Constitution, eliminating restrictions imposed upon freedom of speech by *res privada* or public peace, declaring punishable in this regard only the absence of truthfulness entailing libel, blackmail, and moral violations of the law.

6. Abolition of the death penalty, with the exception of traitors to the Fatherland.

7. Expand the accountability of public officials, imposing severe prison terms upon delinquents.

8. Restitution of the territory of Quintana Roo to Yucatán.

9. Elimination of military courts in peacetime.

10. Increase the number of primary schools to the degree that all places of learning that are cloistered, because they pertain to the Clergy, may be replaced advantageously.

11. Obligation to provide wholly non-religious instruction in all schools of the Republic, whether they are government-run or private, holding accountable all directors who fail to readjust themselves to this precept.

12. Declare education obligatory up until the age of fourteen, it being the duty of the Government to convey protection by any means possible to poor children whose destitution could cause them to lose the benefits of instruction.

13. Pay elementary schoolteachers a living wage.

14. Require the teaching of rudimentary arts and crafts and military instruction, preferably with a focus on civic instruction, at present so sorely neglected in all schools of the Republic.

15. Dictate that foreigners, by the act of purchasing real estate, lose their primary nationality and become Mexican citizens.

16. Prohibit Chinese immigration.

17. Churches are to be considered as places of business and, as such, obligated to keep accounts and pay corresponding taxes.

18. Nationalization, in keeping with the Law, of all real estate held by members of the Clergy by means of front men.

19. Expand punishment as specified under the Laws of Reform against those who violate said Law.

20. Abolition of schools controlled by the Clergy.

21. Establish a maximum eight-hour workday, with a minimum wage of the following proportions: $1.00 for the general populace, where the average salary is lower than that specified here, and more than one peso for those regions in which living expenses are higher, where this salary would be insufficient to keep the worker out of poverty.

22. Regulation of domestic service and of those who work in private homes.

23. Adopt measures so that bosses who pay by the hour do not evade the enforcement of maximum hours or minimum wage.

24. Completely prohibit the employment of all children under age fourteen.

25. Require the owners of mines, factories, workshops, etc. to maintain the best hygienic conditions possible on their premises, keeping all hazardous areas in a state that will not endanger workers' lives.

26. Require bosses or rural landowners to provide workers with hygienic lodgings when the nature of their work demands that they receive shelter from said bosses or landowners.

27. Require bosses to pay indemnities for work-related accidents.

28. Nullify all current debts owed by field workers to their masters.

29. Adopt measures preventing landowner abuse of sharecroppers.

30. Require those who lease homes and properties to indemnify those renting their lands for any necessary improvements they have made.

31. Prohibit bosses, under severe penalty of law, to pay workers in any way other than cash money; prohibit and punish those who impose fines on workers, or dock their wages, or delay the payment of their earnings for more than one week, or deny those being terminated from work the immediate payment of what they have earned; ban of company stores.

32. Prevent all businesses or negotiations from hiring as employees and workers more than a minority percentage of foreigners. Prohibiting, without exception, Mexicans from being paid less than foreigners among workers of the same class, or that Mexicans be paid differently from foreigners by the same establishment.

33. Declare Sunday an obligatory day of rest.

34. Landowners are obliged to render productive all that they possess; any extension of land left fallow by the owner will be recovered by the State and used in keeping with the following Articles:

35. Mexicans who reside abroad will, upon request, be repatriated by the Government, which will pay their travel expenses and provide them with land for cultivation.

36. The State will give land to anyone who so requests, under no other condition than having them use it for agricultural production, not sale. The maximum extension of land the State can award a person will be established.

37. So that this benefit cannot be used solely to the advantage of the few who have the wherewithal to cultivate land, but also by the poor who lack the tools to do so, the State will create or support an Agricultural Bank that will extend low-interest loans to poor farmers, redeemable in installments.

38. Abolition of head and poll taxes,* leaving in Government hands the analysis of the best way to lower the Stamp tax until its full abolition becomes feasible.

39. Ban all assessments on capital lower than $100.00, exempting from this privilege churches and other businesses that are considered hazardous and which should have no right to the guarantees extended to useful businesses.

40. Stockpiles, luxury items, and vices are to be taxed, while assessments will be lightened on articles of basic need. The rich will not be allowed to adjust their retainers with the government in order to pay fewer taxes than those imposed by law.

41. Legal protection proceedings are to be made more practical by simplifying the necessary procedures.

42. Restitution of the Free Zone.

43. Establish civil equality for all children fathered by the same man, eliminating differences established under current Law between legitimacy and illegitimacy.

44. Establish, whenever possible, penal rehabilitation colonies instead of the jails and penitentiaries where delinquents suffer sentences today.

45. Elimination of political bosses.

46. Reorganization of municipalities that have been suppressed; fortification of municipal power.

47. Measures to suppress or restrict stockpiling, pauperism, and shortages of basic goods.

48. Protection of the indigenous race.

49. Establish bonds of union with other Latin American countries.

50. Upon the triumph of the Liberal Party, the goods of those officials enriched under the current Dictatorship will be confiscated, and implementation of the Chapter of Lands will be applied to all that is produced thereby—especially restitution to the Yaquis, Mayas, and other tribes, communities, or other individuals from lands that were taken away from them—and towards paying down the National Debt.

51. The first National Congress to meet following the downfall of the Dictatorship will annul all reforms made to our Constitution by the Government of Porfirio Díaz; our Magna Carta will be reformed as soon as possible in order to put this Program into effect; laws will be created as needed to attain the same objective; articles of the Constitution will be regularized as well as those of other laws that so require; and all issues will be studied that are considered to be of interest to the Fatherland, whether or not they are proclaimed in the present Program; and the items that constitute it here will be reinforced, especially in the areas of Labor and Land.

**Impuesto sobre capital moral y de capitación.*

Central Themes

Indigenous people, state formation, land and labor, religion

Suggested Reading

Hodges, Donald C. *Mexican Anarchism After the Revolution.* Austin: University of Texas Press, 1995.

MacLachlan, Colin M. *Anarchism and the Mexican Revolution.* Berkeley: University of California Press, 1991.

Traven, B. *The Rebellion of the Hanged.* New York: Knopf, 1952.

Related Sources

44. Porfirio Díaz's Political Vision (1871)
45. A Letter to Striking Workers (1892)
47. Precursors to Revolution (1904, 1906)
48. The Cananea Strike: Workers' Demands (1906)
52. Francisco Madero's Challenge to Porfirio Díaz (1910)
54. Land, Labor, and the Church in the Mexican Constitution (1917)
63. We the Undersigned (1941, 1945)

48. The Cananea Strike: Workers' Demands (1906)*

On June 1, 1906, workers at the Consolidated Copper Company mine in Cananea, Sonora, went on strike. The event is considered a precursor to the Mexican Revolution, in part because of the efforts of the Mexican Liberal Party (Partido Liberal Mexicano, PLM) to unite the miners and assist them in formulating their demands and presenting them to their employer. In January 1906, the miners formed the Liberal Brotherhood Union Club (Club Unión Liberal Humanidad), which was affiliated with the PLM. When negotiations with employers broke down, the workers went out on strike. Mine owner William C. Greene turned to President Porfirio Díaz for support, and when the latter did not act quickly enough, Greene sought the assistance of the U.S. ambassador. Still dissatisfied, Greene called private security forces from across the border into Mexico to put down the strike. In the years following, organized workers took up the strike as a symbol of their cause. Throughout the years, working Mexicans have celebrated the organizational force

*Ernesto de la Torre Villar, Moises Gonzalez Navarro, and Stanley Ross, eds., *Historia documental de México* (Mexico: Universidad Nacional Autónoma de México, Instituto de Investigaciones Históricas, 1965), vol. 2, pp. 406–407. Translated by Tanya Huntington and the editors.

of the miners and the demands they made, decrying what they have considered evidence of the Mexican state's preferential treatment of foreigners. What was revolutionary about the demands of the Cananea workers? How do those demands compare with those made by workers years later (sources 71 and 75)?

The Cananea Strike: Workers' Demands

Memorandum:

1. Working people declare a strike.

2. The workers will labor only under the following conditions:

i. The firing of Luis the overseer (Level 19).

ii. Minimum wage for a worker will be five pesos for an eight-hour workday.

iii. The Cananea Consolidated Copper Co., throughout its entire work force, will employ 75% Mexicans and 25% foreigners, for the former have the same aptitude as the latter.

iv. Honorable men are placed in the care of the cages, in order to avoid any sort of conflict.

v. All Mexicans employed to work by this company will have the right to promotions as long as they are qualified.

Mexican workers: A government elected by the people so that it guides them and satisfies their needs in as much as possible: Mexico does not have this.

Furthermore: A government that is made up of ambitious men who tire the patience of the people with their criminally self-interested activities, elected by the worst of them in order to help them get rich: Mexico does not need this.

The people elect their representatives to govern them, and not to ridicule and humiliate them; that is a Republic.

People, rise up and go forward. Learn what it seems that you have forgotten. Gather together and discuss your rights. Demand the respect that is owed you.

Each Mexican who is mistreated by foreigners is worth the same or more than them, if he unites with his brothers and demands his rights.

It would be an unheard of exaggeration to say that a Mexican is not equal to a Yankee, a Negro, or a Chinaman, in the very land of Mexicans. That this might otherwise be the case is because of the worthless government that gives advantages to adventurers and in so doing devalues the true owners of this unfortunate land.

Mexicans, awake, unite. The Fatherland and our dignity demand it.

Central Themes

The northern frontier, land and labor,

Suggested Reading

French, William E. *A Peaceful Working People: Manners, Morals, and Class Formation in Northern Mexico.* Albuquerque: University of New Mexico Press, 1991.

Heyman, Josiah M. *Life and Labor on the Border: Working People of Northeastern Sonora, Mexico, 1886–1986.* Tucson: University of Arizona Press, 1991.

Lear, John. *Workers, Neighbors, and Citizens: The Revolution in Mexico City.* Lincoln: University of Nebraska Press, 2001.

Related Sources

45. A Letter to Striking Workers (1892)
54. Land, Labor, and the Church in the Mexican Constitution (1917)
63. We the Undersigned (1941, 1945)
71. The 1985 Earthquake (1985, 1995)
75. Maquila Workers Organize (2006)

49. Land and Society (1909)*

Andrés Molina Enríquez (1868–1940) worked within a long tradition of nineteenth-century Liberals who sought new relations of landholding and the breakup of the *hacienda* (large landed estate) as a means of encouraging economic development. As with earlier generations, Molina Enríquez associated new property relations with new social relations and political cultures. Molina Enríquez wrote as a journalist and published in the most respected newspapers of his day. The following excerpt comes from his book *Los grandes problemas nacionales* (*The Nation's Great Problems,* 1909), the work for which he is best known. In this analysis of Mexican history, Molina Enríquez focuses on what he considers to be key historical moments: the period after 1821 (for which he coined the term "the era of national disintegration") and the Reform Era. He explores the ramifications of these two historical moments with regard to the status of indigenous peoples and the emergence of the *mestizo* (person of Indian and Spanish heritage) as a political, economic, and social actor. He also discusses in great detail the "integral period," a period that was char-

*Molina Enríquez, Andrés, *Los grandes problemas nacionales* (Mexico: Imprenta de A. Carranza e Hijos, 1909), pp. 57, 58, 69–71, 319–321, 328. Excerpts translated by Tanya Huntington and the editors. Italics are from the original.

acterized by stability and unity imposed by the personality and authority of President Díaz and was the focus of his criticism. Molina Enríquez earned a law degree from the Toluca Institute of Science and Literature, but he always considered himself more sociologist than lawyer. In formulating his arguments for land reform, Molina Enríquez drew on theory and law, but especially on sociology and history.

The following excerpt from *The Nation's Great Problems* allows us to acknowledge the role that intellectuals played in the Revolution—in this case with regard to land reform. In addition to *The Nation's Great Problems*, Molina Enríquez also authored the Plan de Texcoco, in which he critiqued Francisco Madero's limited implementation of the Plan de San Luís Potosí (Source 52). Andrés Molina Enríquez was a strong proponent of land reform and a central contributor to the formulation of Article 27 of the Constitution of 1917 (Source 54). However, he did not support the Cárdenas administration's focus on the *ejido* (communally held land tenure system) as the most important component of agrarian reform.

In the following selection from *The Nation's Great Problems,* what categories shape Molina Enríquez's analysis? What does Molina Enríquez identify as the active forces in Mexican society? How does his argument build on earlier ways of thinking about different ethnic groups? Does he introduce new ideas about those groups? How might we use his observations about different social groups and the press to evaluate newspapers as a source for historical knowledge? Finally, what sorts of social and political change does Molina Enríquez associate with economic development?

The Nation's Great Problems

As a result of the redistribution of Indian lands, the Indians lost these lands. It could not have happened any other way. Community presented clear advantages to indigenous people. While communal lands were generally barren and of poor quality, they offered the indigenous people themselves a way to live out all stages of their evolution, from that of being savage hordes to that of being a people incorporated into general civilization. These lands rendered many uses that indigenous people could enjoy without undue exertion, without capital, and most importantly, without any appreciable deterioration of these lands. Among the advantages we can point to are those that come from mountainous lands, such as lumber that can be taken and sold as firewood, beams, kindling, or charcoal, or used to light and heat homes, or to fuel ovens in order to make tiles, bricks, and pottery. In the plains, there are pastures that can be used to feed animals—not only large animals, but small ones, like turkeys, chickens, etc. In areas of water, they can hunt ducks and other birds, or catch fish and other animals used for food, and many other benefits such as clay, *tequesquite,** lime, etc., which Nature does the work of producing and

*A gray, mineral salt commonly used in the preparation of tortillas.

adorning, leaving the indigenous people to exert what small effort corresponds to their degree of evolution to consume or market them. Moreover, Community offered indigenous people the advantage of land ownership, and of not losing that possession to the detriment of their meager fortunes. . . . Independent Mexico has not been able to find a more efficient means of aiding the indigenous race than that of Community. . . .

Now then, since vacant land was divided among the have-nots and previous ownership respected, suddenly these have-nots, who had not been capable of owning anything, were transformed into landowners, causing them to skip the intermediate state of occupation, and giving them advantages they did not understand and were not able to exploit, while at the same time imposing upon them obligations that were necessarily burdensome, such as titles, tax payment, successive notary processes, determination of succession, etc. It is understandable that in this case, deprived of the communal advantages with which they had lived and given the imperative need to survive, and also given the encumbrances associated with owning property, most indigenous people did not use their parcels, but sold them. And thus they were sold under conditions of great supply, reduced demand, and the pressing need for finalization. Then, the mestizos rushed in to buy. Indigenous people's land parcels that had been valued at five, ten, fifty pesos were sold for two, five, twenty, etc. Some states tried to block these ruinous dispossessions and imposed severe penalties upon the buyers; but this was useless and highly prejudicial because the lands were wasted, having been sold nonetheless with no other prerequisite than title transfers. And so on and so forth, to the present day. Oftentimes, and of this we can personally bear witness based on observations made over the course of nine years in various small communities, mestizos have administered the redistribution of indigenous towns. They have bought up nearly all the lands, they have issued the corresponding titles, and they have, of course, gathered up these titles, paying taxes on behalf of grantees. Many of the Indians who were allocated land were not owners for so much as one day, and if an investigation were to be carried out regarding sales prices, it would find that one parcel had cost the buyer a few pieces of bread, another, a few *cuartillos** of corn, or, in most cases, a few jars of *pulque* [liquor fermented from the maguey cactus] or a few cuartillos of white lightning. Once the indigenous people were divested of their land parcels, they no longer had any place to live. There was no longer any firewood, cr beams, or kindling, or charcoal to sell; no sticks of pine to light their homes, no chili peppers to put in their tortillas; no driftwood with which to fire the clay pieces of their pottery industry; nothing to feed their animals; no hunting, no fishing, no plants to eat, and nothing for them to eat themselves. They lacked, in other words, for everything; they would no longer be peaceful men, and instead became mercenary soldiers, ready to follow any agitator who came along. . . .

---

*A common unit of measurement in New Spain, roughly equivalent to a quart.

Treatment given by Mr. General Díaz to the mestizos.—On the one hand, the mestizos, triumphant and predominant after having rung in the *integral period,* showed their thirst for material gain more than ever. Greedy for wealth and hungry for pleasure, they felt they had been hoodwinked by the Reform, which had not succeeded in satisfying them. Mr. General Díaz, who recognized in them his own kind—his race, his nationality, and his future—took it upon himself to satisfy them. To that end, he put them all on the National Payroll. In the classification we so opportunely made of the racial elements that composed the national population when the Ayutla Plan was proclaimed, we stated that mestizos were divided into four groups, to wit: *ranchers, employees, professionals,* and *revolutionaries.* Among this last group, which included Díaz's oldest, most devout and most loyal partisans, or better yet, his friends, he has distributed and continues to distribute positions of power and of trust—even making one of his friends President of the Republic—as well as those duties that have maintained and continue to maintain the concentration of power, the ones that have been necessary and continue to be necessary for his authority to operate smoothly. He has appointed and continues to appoint them Ministers, Governors, Chiefs of the Militarized Zone, Army Commanders, etc. From the groups of *professionals* and *employees,* he has drawn and continues to draw all the remaining officials of his administration. From the group of *ranchers* he drew, has drawn, and likewise continues to draw the Officers and Commanders of the Army. And as someone who profoundly knows all mestizos, he has allowed and continues to allow them to take advantage of their positions, traffic with influence, and enrich themselves, satisfying all of their ambitions and sating all of their appetites. He has known and still knows that many of them have negotiated and continue to negotiate, have profited and continue to profit, have led and continue to lead, lives of disorder, if not vice, but none of this has caught or continues to catch his eye. . . .

Treatment given by Mr. General Díaz to the "criollo gentlemen" and the "criollo clergy."—Meanwhile, the *criollos* [American-born Spaniards] in their two groups, *the criollo gentlemen* and the *criollo clergy,* demanded their share too. The *criollo gentlemen,* as we have already stated, were divided between *conservative criollos* and *moderate criollos;* and the *criollo clergy,* between superior church officials and *reactionaries*—all those who avidly supported the clergy in order to protect their interests. The *conservative criollos* asked for nothing, nor have they ever asked for anything, other than respect for their vast holdings; Mr. General Díaz has conceded this to them. These *criollos* have abstained from taking an active role in politics, remaining content to wield with relative vigor the influence of their enormous fortunes in close proximity to powerful officials. Whenever these fortunes are at stake, as a whole or in pieces, whenever taxes are at stake, whenever rural security is at stake, one sees them appear. And one might almost say that in fiscal and administrative affairs, nothing can be done without their acquiescence; they have kept agriculture in the state of ruin and misery in which it remains. The *moderate criollos* have, in fact, asked for and obtained their piece of the public pie, but they have done so in, shall we say, a palatial manner that is peculiar to them. Mr. General Díaz has received them warmly and given them positions of honor, ones that shine and are symbolic, but very rarely has he given them any active office. . . . In today's daily press here in the capital of the Republic, they are represented by *El Tiempo*. This newspaper—expensive, grand, and rebellious even in the eyes of the church, enemy to the Americans because of religious differences, enemy to the *new criollos* and *mestizos* for having usurped the goods of the church, and friend to Europe out of blood affinity—represents, in effect, the *criollo gentlemen* very well. Back when the division between the two groups of *criollo gentlemen* was more marked, *El Tiempo* represented the *conservatives* and *El Nacional* the *moderates.* Among the *criollo clergy,* this group of dignitaries has stopped meddling with politics in order to dedicate themselves to their noble ministry, and yet, Mr. General Díaz has procured and succeeded in gaining their good will and sympathy, softening the rigor of the laws of Reform, honoring their top dignitaries, etc. etc. . . . The vehicle of *reactionary criollos* in the daily press of the capital of the Republic is currently *El País.*

Treatment given by Mr. General Díaz to the "new criollos" or "liberal criollos."—The *new criollos* or *liberal criollos,* having made their services worthwhile during the Intervention, have been more difficult to please. Although they were already well favored, they asked for more and have obtained much more than they had asked for, thanks to their condition as intermediaries between the *criollo gentlemen,* on the one hand, and the mestizos and indigenous peoples, on the other. . . .

They will never be as strong as the *mestizos* are and lack their political orientation. Today, in the daily press of the capital of the Republic, the *new criollos* are represented by *El Imparcial,* a newspaper that confuses the prosperity of the *new criollos* with that of the nation. . . .

Treatment given by Mr. General Díaz to indigenous people.—Among the indigenous element, the ranks of the *displaced* have felt nothing but depredation and, in his view, have merited nothing more than repression and punishment. Mr. General Díaz knew he had to give them appropriate treatment with his accustomed energy. Moreover, he has always favored the incorporation of these indigenous people into the general mix of population without attending to the evolutionary state in which they are found, as shown by the warm reception given to the Kikapoos—under, of course, the compulsory condition that in all circumstances, they live in peace. With regard to Indians from the other two ranks, that is to say, the *incorporated* and *subjected indigenous peoples,* within the four groups of social action they have formed—that is to say, the group of *lesser clergy,* that of *soldiers,* that of *communal property owners,* and that of *laborers*—one might rightly say that they were already far from any real or pretended passivity that might have characterized them during the colonial era. They were also already making their requests, and in a certain sense, somewhat demandingly. Mr. General Díaz attended to them at the time, continued to attend to them, and attends to them still. As for the *Indians in the lesser clergy,* he has kept them happy by easing the Laws of Reform, most especially in terms of what is known as public worship, allowing them, from time to time, to freely manifest their semi-idolatrized Christianity during their festivals, processions, etc. As for the *revolu-*

tionary Indians, for the most part they have been employed as soldiers, being paid salaries in a timely fashion that are superior to those of laborers; and he has given the rest salaried labor, through great public works, that comes very close to a soldier's wages. As for the *communal property–owning Indians,* he has kept them quiet, delaying the redistribution of their towns and helping them to defend said towns, while hearing their complaints and manifestations against the hacienda owners, against the Governors, etc. As for the *Indian laborers,* that is to say, the peons of the fields, who have been least favored in a direct fashion, he has somewhat ameliorated their condition by simply maintaining the peace that allows them to grow their crops and thus earn a steady income. The indigenous people have no representation whatsoever in the press. . . .

Unity and solidity of Mr. General Díaz's character—. . . .

Aside from the aforementioned groups, there are no longer any capitalist groups, or great individual property owners, so that all capital and all major property is held among those groups that are preferentially privileged, joined together by a narrow solidarity of origin. And these are so few, that on the whole they scarcely account for fifteen per cent of the total population. As a result, major national interests are concentrated in the hands of a privileged minority who, by virtue of their position, [suck] all the wealth from our country with growing greed, impoverishing national existence with corresponding rapidity. We do not find it necessary to prove the previous statement, given that it belongs to the realm of public and notorious facts. One can count on one's fingers in each city, in each market plaza, the names of the major businessmen, and in each of the major businesses, those same names appear; names that, by the way, the oppressed classes know all too well. On a daily basis, companies, trusts, etc., are made and unmade, always under the same names. . . . We are the first to wish that national wealth might be better distributed in peacetime, because we understand that this could very well, under certain circumstances, foster rage among these lesser groups when the day of judgment and retribution comes. . . .

The unification of customs.—Judging by what the newspapers they publish say, criollo groups in our country believe that the customs of a people are something they sustain because they want to: they suppose that by merely wishing it, these customs can be changed. Where our country is concerned, they fume against the customs of indigenous people and mestizos, in an attempt to compel both former and latter to follow and observe European customs. The pretension would be truly laughable, if it were not put into practice and did not give rise to numerous highly censurable measures.

In our country, the way in which criollos make their actions against mestizos and against the indigenous felt most is with regards to customs. According to the *criollos,* all national customs are an inconvenience. Several times, *El Imparcial* has preached against national cuisine, for example, declaring it complicated, unsubstantial, and even hazardous, counseling that it be traded for this or that; they have also declared an all-out war against pulque. We have already demonstrated in *Problema de la población* that national cuisine is a derivation of our general and undeniable need to nourish ourselves with corn. The use of chili peppers obeys the same need: the use of pulque, likewise. In as much as a great deal of our population will necessarily always live off of corn, it will also need a national cuisine that consists of chili and pulque. As far as garments are concerned, there is something more to be said. There can be no doubt that the less human life needs in order to sustain and perfect itself by artificial means, the more perfect it will be. Now then, if the lion's share of the units of our population can live and attain well-being with light garments, tailored this way or that, it's only natural to try and perfect these garments, rather than impose Russian counterparts. The garments from Northern Europe that are imposed upon our soldiers, for example, are truly absurd, just as *charro* [horseman] outfits are logical for our rural police. The same can be said with regard to living arrangements. If thanks to the mildness of our climate, it is not necessary to accumulate rooms, depriving them of the air, light, and sun of our cheerful patios, it is absurd to build homes this way just so that they might resemble those of other countries. We do not need heating, or the introduction of chimneys and furnaces; it would be ridiculous if it were not so disastrous. Even in terms of the nomenclature of our cities, if our way of being has us accustomed to the picturesque habit of designating streets with names joined to traditions that are more or less interesting based on our previous existence, it is truly worthy of censure that these names be erased and the traditions to which they refer be made to disappear, only to substitute them with numbers or empty names for the benefit of foreign consumption. It would be only natural for the foreigners visiting Mexico to be the ones who procure to understand our customs. . . .

Although what has already been said in general terms might be enough for what we propose to do, we believe it is convenient to call the attention of our readers to the countless tasks *criollos* carry out to incline us towards adopting, if not European customs, which we cannot understand due to the few examples of them before us, at least American customs, most particularly in two areas: that of business among men, and that of feminism among women. . . .

The brusqueness with which, with few exceptions, of course, Americans residing in Mexico make known the energy of their character; the dissimulation, deceit, and falsehood that they consider to be high-spiritedness; the spirit of speculation with which they generally disguise a true lack of probity; and the lack of scruples that they call a practical spirit, will teach us nothing good and plenty that is bad, just as they have, in effect, been teaching us. . . .

Our customs of the seclusion and passivity of women, more in harmony with her nature, will mean, in and of itself, that she forms better families in Mexico than does the liberated American woman in the United States. In time, perhaps, our superiority over the United States will depend upon this, because the better the individuals that make up the total family perform their own function, the stronger the family as a whole. And the Fatherland and society, as we have already demonstrated, are derived from the family. Meanwhile, this absurd American feminism has produced such a profound disturbance in the Mexican family that one does not need great observational skills to see that something more than the well-being of women has developed in the shadow of that feminism, to wit, their prostitution. . . .

Consequences of the fixed notion of patriotism.—When the convergence of the ideal and the fundamental correction of our existing property system has been fully realized, current differences regarding what one ought to understand the Fatherland to be will disappear. There will no longer be anyone who believes the Fatherland is defined by the high esteem of Mexican values abroad, nor anyone who believes that it is patriotic to do in Mexico what the Cuban criollos have done in their country; nor anyone who believes that it is patriotic to invite a new foreign intervention, whether it be European or American; nor anyone who believes that it is patriotic to deny our customs and despise our statesmen, insult priests, and murder foreigners. The notion of patriotism will be firmly determined and limited to the following simple terms: ALL OF US, LIKE SIBLINGS IN A FAMILY, ARE FREE TO EXERCISE OUR FACULTIES OF ACTION. BUT UNITED BY THE FRATERNITY OF COMMON IDEALS, WE ARE COMPELLED BY VIRTUE OF THAT SAME FRATERNITY TO EQUITABLY DISTRIBUTE, ON THE ONE HAND, THE ENJOYMENT OF THE COMMON HERITAGE THAT NOURISHES US, AND TO TOLERATE, ON THE OTHER, ANY MUTUAL DIFFERENCES DERIVED FROM SAID ENJOYMENT.

Central Themes

Indigenous people, state formation, urban life, land and labor, religion, gender

Suggested Reading

Kourí, Emilio, *A Pueblo Divided: Business, Property, and Community in Papantla, Mexico.* Stanford, CA: Stanford University Press, 2004.

Shadle, Stanley F. *Andrés Molina Enríquez: Mexican Land Reformer of the Revoltuionary Era.* Tucson: University of Arizona Press, 1994.

Tutino, John. *From Insurrection to Revolution in Mexico: Social Bases of Agrarian Violence, 1750–1940.* Princeton, NJ: Princeton University Press, 1986.

Van Young, Eric. *Hacienda and Market in Eighteenth-Century Mexico: The Rural Economy of the Guadalajara Region, 1675–1820.* Lanham, MD: Rowman & Littlefield, 2006.

Related Sources

42. The Reconfiguration of Property Rights and of Church-State Relations (1856)
46. A Positivist Interpretation of Feminism (1909)
54. Land, Labor, and the Church in the Mexican Constitution (1917)
59. Feminism, Suffrage, and Revolution (1931)
62. An Assessment of Mexico from the Right (1940)
67. Rubén Jaramillo and the Struggle for *Campesino* Rights in Postrevolutionary Morelos (1967)

50. Popular Images of Mexican Life (the Late Nineteenth and Early Twentieth Centuries)

The work of José Guadalupe Posada (1852–1913) has served as inspiration to myriad artists, both inside and outside of Mexico. At an early age, Posada discovered his talent for copying artwork, whether religious cards or small printed pictures. He studied at the Municipal Academy of Drawing, apprenticed himself to a lithographer in 1879, and then worked for a small newspaper. In 1884, Posada set up a shop in Mexico City, El Porvenir, where he illustrated books, pamphlets, and the penny press. Posada was an expert printmaker and worked in engraving, etching, and woodcut techniques. Much of his work appeared on broadsheets—one-page stories about newsworthy events such as natural disasters, crime, political intrigue, and folktales. The illustrations were accompanied by text, often presented in poetic form or as a *corrido* (Mexican folk ballad) (Source 51). Broadsheets could be purchased on the streets from market vendors and at fairs and plazas at a low cost.

Posada is perhaps best known in the United States and in Mexico for his use of the *calavera* (playful skeleton), which often carried the message that everything in life—from power to suffering—ends in the same way: in death. The images below treat a range of themes. What perspectives do the images and text provide regarding modernization and urban life? What perspective is given on relations with the United States? Do these portrayals differ from other sources in this reader?

Gran Calavera Eléctrica

—QUE SE LES VA A REGALAR—

CALAVERA MUY FACHOSA DE PURA ELECTRICIDAD.

El primero de Noviembre,
Como diablos correrán

Los eléctricos vagones
Qua á Dolores llegarán.

¡Qué hechiceras van á estar
Ese día de calaveras;
Han de ser todas eléctricas
Con sorbete y con pialeras.

A esta reunión eléctrica
Están convidados varios;
Aquellos muertos fachosos
Y de los más endiablados.
"Chucho el Roto ha de asistir"
Cón todos sus compañeros
Que eléctricos han de estar
Gastando muchos dineros
Los *lagartos* de Plateros,
También están convidados
Para asistir á la bola
Donde estarán muy jalados.

Como diablos correrán,
Los eléctricos vagones
Que en menos de un santiamén
Los jalarán á Dolores

La electricidad estará,
De lo más fuerte, Señores;
Habrá muertos y esqueletos,
En sus caballos rabones

Las pípilas de Santa Ana,
Juntas con las del Carrizo
Han de ir también á almorzar
Cucarachas y mestizos.

Van á adornar el Panteón.
Para hacer la gran jamaica,
Donde efectuarán el baile,
El almuerzo y merendata.

Los instrumentos que toquen,
Serán de puros huesitos;
Con harta electricidad
Tocarán allí solitos.

Y entonces las calaveras
Bailarán sus jarabitos,
Con esqueletos eléctricos
Estando muy borrachitos

Los músicos han de estar
Eléctricos también todos,
Pues tocarán muchas piezas
Y danzas de los demonios

A la luz de muchos focos
De nuestra electricidad,
Saldrán de las sepulturas
Los muertos allí á danzar,

Las Mercedarias también
Eléctricas estarán,
Y armando la grande bola
Bailarán allí el cancán.

Mariana; la trompa de hule,
Pípila de la Agüitita,
Estará también eléctrica
Con la tuerta Mariquita.

Cuando el almuerzo ya esté,
Sentados á la redonda,
Comerán mole de perro
Y tripas de rata hedionda.

Allí estará Juan el manco
Con toditita su recua,
Que eléctricos estarán
Bailando hasta de cabeza.

Harta guasa y harta copa:
¡Viva la electricidad!
¡Que brinden las calaveras
Con júbilo sin igual!

En la jamaica han de de estar,
Todas vestidas de chinas,
Con sus botines de raso
Y rebozo de bolita.

Todo el pulque de Mazapa,
Lo tienen ya contratado,
Junto con el de Cuautenco;
Los dos muy bien recurados.

Habrá mucha barbacoa,
Pues Don Diego el carnicero
Ha comprado perros gordos
Para en el horno cocerlos.

Gertrudis la Pingajosa
Que es la muertera mayor,
Se vestirá de catrina
Para hacerles el amor.

El bolón es general,
Pues los vivos y los muertos
Como á las dos de la tarde.
Han de estar ya muy eléctricos.

También en esa gran fiesta,
Los electricos gendarmes
De ver aquel gran rebumbio,
Les darán hasta calambres.

A las cuatro de la tarde,
Ya no se podrá aguantar,
Tanto eléctrico borracho
Que en el Panteón estará.

En esa hora los gendarmes
Que parecen zopilotes,
Cargarán vivos y muertos,
Cual si fueran tejocotes.

Los eléctricos vagones
¡Cuantas gentes llevarán
Para hacerlas calaveras
Con pura electricidad!

En fin, que lleguen los Muertos.
La fiesta está cerca ya;
A pasearse y á gozar:
¡Que viva la electricidad
Que vivan las calaveras!
Qqe descansan en Dolores,
Los trenes también eléctricos
Que los llevan á montones:
Un padre nuestro por ellos
Y un Requien á los vagones.
Un responso por las ánimas
Y los borrachos gritones.

José Guadalupe Posada, "Grand Electric Skeleton"

Pictorial Collections, Center for Southwest Research, University Libraries, University of New Mexico

EL MOSQUITO AMERICANO

El Mosquito Americano
Ahora acaba de llegar;
Dicen se vino á pasear
A este suelo mexicano.

Dizque el domingo embarcó
Allá en Laredo de Texas,
Y que al Saltillo llegó
Picándoles las orejas,
En la Estación á unas viejas
Que bien las hizo marchar,
Hasta las hizo sudar
Este animal inhumano;
Luego empiezan á gritar:
El Mosquito americano.

A Guanajuato marchó,
Esto es cosa de reir;
Él al centro no llegó,
Pero si estuvo en Marfil.
Ya no podrán sufrir
Tan malcriado y altanero,
Pues le picó en el trasero
A un militar veterano.
Porque es mucho, muy grosero
El Mosquito americano.

Tomó el rumbo de Irapuato
Y por Pénjamo pasó;
De allí luego regresó
Por el pueblo de Uriangato,
La hacienda de Villachato
La dejó muy derrotada;
Toda la gente asustada
La encontró el vale Mariano,
Nana Emeteria gritaba:
El Mosquito americano.

Por la puerta de San Juan
Piedra Gorda y la Sandía,
Una viejecita decía:
¡Jesús, qué fiero animal!
Dígame usted Don Pascual
¿No le ha llegado el Mosquito?
Dicen que es muy chiquitito,
Y también muy inhumano;
¿Qué dice tata Pachito
El Mosquito americano?

José Guadalupe Posada, "The American Mosquito"
Pictorial Collections, Center for Southwest Research, University Libraries, University of New Mexico

MEXICO, MAYO DE 1892 NUM. 1

GACETA CALLEJERA

Esta hoja volante se publicará cuando los acontecimientos de sensación lo requieran.

El Motín de los Estudiantes.—Lluvia de piedras.—Los sucesos de la noche.—El café de la Concordia.—El Universo.—Heridos.

La *reelección* y la *no reelección*, han venido á sacar á la sociedad mexicana del estado de marasmo en que se hallaba, despertando en todas las clases sociales, cuando menos, una curiosidad palpitante por conocer los movimientos de los dos bandos que se levantan ,y esperando el resultado de una cuestión que tiene que ser de muchas trascendencias, sea el que sea el resultado que ponga fin á este tan discutido asunto.

De todo punto imparciales en la cuestión, nos limitaremos á dar á conocer al público los acontecimientos que ocurran, puramente como relatores de los hechos, sin que tomemos partido en ninguno de los dos bandos que ahora luchan.

Los estudiantes de las escuelas Nacionales superiores, son los que, como en otras ocasiones, forman el alma de los dos campos *reeleccionista* y *anti-reeleccionista*. Los segundos organizaron para el domingo 15, una manifestación pública, que tuvo verificativo con su correspondiente programa.

Este programa fué ejecutado puntualmente, reuniéndose en el Jardín de S. Fernando, gran número de estudiantes y obreros que á las nueve de la mañana salieron de aquel punto siguiendo el camino señalado. En el trayecto, la comitiva aumentó de un modo colosal, formando una larguísima procesión que algunos calculan en cerca de cuatro mil almas. En la calle del Empedradillo dos jóvenes estudiantes pronunciaron discursos, subidos en un carro que conducía pulque. Frente al zócalo, un artesano se dirigió al pueblo, siendo de notar el buen juicio de su alocución y comprendiéndose desde luego que obedecía á convicciones muy bien razonadas, sin degenerar en apasionamientos necios ni en insultos que no deben figurar en tales casos. Se nos ha dicho que este Sr. es el redactor en jefe del periódico "El Fandango." En la calle de la Monterilla otro joven estudiante tomó la palabra. En la de Balvanera otro individuo que dijeron ser impresor, subió á un carro repartidor de carne y desde allí habló. En la Merced, un estudiante de la Escuela Normal pronunció otro discurso. En una casa de la calle de Jesús Mara, un anciano desde el balcón dirigió al pueblo una arenga y en la Academia un ciego tomó igualmente la palabra.

De regreso la procesión para San Fernando, por la Alameda un joven se subió á un coche para pronunciar una poesía. Por algún desorden cometido, un policía trató de llevarse á un joven; pero fue acometido por la multitud, y tuvo que huir refugiándose en una casa de la calle de la Mariscala. Continuó luego la comitiva hasta San Fernando donde por última vez tomaron la palabra dos jóvenes, disolviéndose luego la reunión

El día 16 el bando reeleccionista hizo su manifestación, figurando algunos gremios obreros, entre ellos los trabajadores de la fábrica de tejidos de San Antonio. Cuatro músicas acompañaban á los manifestantes, figurando en la procesión un carro alegórico.

Frente al Zócalo, algunos estudiantes del bando contrario atacaban la reelección, y sin que sepamos explicarnos el significado de ello, vimos volar algunas piezas de pan.

Al medio día, al salir los estudiantes de la Escuela Preparatoria, prorrumpieron en *vivas* y *mueras*, y en la misma calle de San Ildefonso se hallaban algunos soldados de la Gendarmería montada que trataron de disolver las masas, y fueron apedreados, siendo en este lance los faroles del alumbrado los que pagaron las injurias.

A las siete de la noche se habían citado los anti-reeleccionistas para reunirse en la calle de Sta. Inés. Antes de esa hora comenzó una bolita de estudiantes en la calle de San Ildefonso á poner en mala situación las cosas, y reunidos en el punto indicado, desfilaron para las calles de Plateros lanzando gritos desaforados y arrojando piedras á los faroles y á las casas. En el café de la Concordia hicieron pedazos los cristales y otro tanto pasó con el almacen "El Universo" de la calle de la Profesa, no conformándose allí con destrozar los cristales del aparador, sino que extrajeron de éste cuanto había. Siguieron rumbo á la Alameda y allí rompieron multitud de faroles y en el callejón de López apedrearon á las hijas de la alegría que en él habitan.

La policía y la Gendarmería montada hicieron esfuerzos inauditos por reprimir el desorden; pero era absolutamente imposible contener aquellas masas frenéticas. Por el rumbo de Santa Ana, el escándalo llegó también á un grado extremo.

Se nos ha dicho que muchas desgracias personales han ocurrido siendo considerable el número de heridos tanto de los bolistas como de gendarmes municipales y de la montada, lo que puede muy bien ser, pues algunas de las piedras lanzadas han de haber causado perjuicios personales.

Imp. Santa Teresa núm. 1.—Mexico.

José Guadalupe Posada, "The Mutiny of Students" (street newspaper)

Pictorial Collections, Center for Southwest Research, University Libraries, University of New Mexico

José Guadalupe Posada, "Cemetery of Ancient Epitaphs"

Pictorial Collections, Center for Southwest Research, University Libraries, University of New Mexico

VISITA Y DESPEDIMENTO AL SEÑOR DE IXTAPALAPA.

QUE SE VENERA EN DICHO PUEBLO.

VERDADERO RETRATO DEL SANTO ENTIERRO DEL SEÑOR DE IXTAPALAPA.—TIENE CONCEDIDA INDULGENCIA PLENARIA Á TODOS LOS FIELES QUE VISITEN SU SANTUARIO.

Jesucristo aplaca tu ira,
Tu justicia y tu rigor,
Y por tu preciosa sangre,
¡Misericordia, Señor!

Desde tu solio inmenso
Señor, vuelve hacia nos;
Contritos imploramos
Tu gracia y tu perdón.

VISITA AL SEÑOR DE IXTAPALAPA.

A tu presencia Señor,
venimos los de tu pueblo
á implorar con gran fervor
que por tu piadoso celo
perdones á un pecador.

Ante tu imagen sagrada
vengo á postrarme de hinojos,
y en tu celestial mirada
se fijan mis pobres ojos
quedando mi alma admirada.

¡Dios mio! ten piedad de mí,
soy de este pueblo nativo,
porque en su centro nací,
y si en él tranquilo vivo
sólo, Señor, es por tí.

Niños, niñas y varones
de más ó menos edad,
consagran sus corazones
á tu divina bondad
en sus santas oraciones.

¡Oh Señor de Ixtapalapa!
míranos con compasión,
y cúbrenos con tu capa
en esta grande aflicción
que sobre nos se descarga.

El agua nos va faltando
en nuestra vasta corriente,
pues los ríos se están secando
y en los pozos y en la fuente,
Señor lo estamos notando.

Con gran fervor te pedimos
que el agua nunca nos falte
los que en tu pueblo vivimos;
que tu bondad no se exalte
por lo mucho que exigimos.

De Ixtacalco é Ixtlahuaca,
de Tejupilco y Texcoco,
de Mixcoac y Tlalnepantla,
han venido poco á poco
á adorar tu imagen santa.

Lleno tu sagrado templo
á cada instante se vé,
pues todos dan un ejemplo
con su fervorosa fe
y cristiano sentimiento.

José Guadalupe Posada, "Visit and Farewell to the Señor de Ixtapalapa Who Is Venerated in Said Village"

Pictorial Collections, Center for Southwest Research, University Libraries, University of New Mexico

Central Themes

Indigenous people, urban life, land and labor, religion

Suggested Reading

Beezley, William. *Judas at the Jockey Club and Other Episodes of Porfirian Mexico.* Lincoln: University of Nebraska Press, 2004.

______. *Mexican National Identity: Memory, Innuendo, and Popular Culture.* Tucson: University of Arizona Press, 2008.

Miliotes, Diane Hellen. *José Guadalupe Posada and the Mexican Broadside.* Technical notes by Rachel Freeman. Chicago: Art Institute of Chicago; New Haven, CT: distributed by Yale University Press, 2006.

Related Sources

51. *Corridos* from the Porfiriato (the Early 1900s)
60. Chronicles of Mexico City (1938)
70. Serial Satire: The Comic Book (1974)

51. *Corridos* from the Porfiriato (the Early 1900s)*

Public discussions occur in many spaces, many of them already presented in this collection—from public speeches, cartoons, and news reporting that appears in newspapers to books, petitions, and official documents such as legislation. The following documents are written transcriptions of *corridos.* Derived in part from the eighteenth-century Spanish romance, the corrido, often in poetic form, is a narrative song or ballad put to music, usually the simple accompaniment of a single guitar. A corrido typically begins with a greeting from the singer to his or her audience and an opening or prologue to the story that will be told. After telling a story, the corrido often closes with a moral. Corridos have been written about a wide variety of themes, including historic events, tales of famous people, sensationalistic reports of natural disasters and crime, and love stories. More recently, the *narco-corrido,* which does not always adhere to the historic form of the genre described here, is a tale of the contemporary drug trade. The heyday of the corrido was the period from Mexican independence through the Revolution, a time when much of the country was illiterate and the corrido served as a principal form of entertainment, communication, and preservation of memory.

---

*Higinio Vazquez Santa Ana, *Canciones, cantares y corridos mexicanos* (Mexico: Segundo Tomo, León Sánchez, 1925–1931), pp. 244–245, 247–249. Excerpts translated by the editors.

Corridos were transmitted orally as well as on broadsheets sold on the streets and in markets. As an art form, the corrido was eclipsed in part by the spread of mass communication media such as television and radio. Nevertheless, they continue to be sung throughout Mexico and beyond its borders. While one of the more widely known corridos, "La Cucaracha," relates events associated with Pancho Villa and pokes fun at the revolutionary general Venustiano Carranza, the following corridos tell of events associated with modernization and politics. What sort of perspective on history do we learn from the corrido? Do the perspectives offered here differ from other conversations regarding the changes associated with modernization?

"The Corrido of the Rural Police"

How handsome the *rurales*
of the big-rimmed hats,
with red *sarape* [blanket]
and leather garb.

It is worth seeing the *rurales,*
of any splendid squadron,
and how well they present themselves
in any formation.

They are the honor of the Nation,
for their thorough discipline
because the *rural* always walks,
taking care of the rural byways.
And that is why the children say
how handsome the *rurales!*

With sword at waist
and Remington by his side,
he defies any danger
while mounted on a fine steed.

Accompanied by his woman
he goes far and wide.
And like a strong oak,
they cannot dominate him.
He is the valiant soldier
of the big-rimmed hat.

Always happy and cheerful,
and never of bad humor,
the *rural* speaks of love
with all the young girls.

With the vagabonds, gamblers,
and lovers of tobacco
wherever they may be,
they belong to the god Baccus,
for they are so good humored [and]
dressed with red sarape.

When the rural troops
are in any town
with their sonorous bugles
they fill all with admiration.

In the local gathering places,
they can be seen throwing back a drink.
The women go crazy,
and even forget to tend the fires,
upon seeing their fine steeds
and leather garb.

"The Corrido of the Electric Trains"

Oh, how beautiful, how blessed
it is to ride the electric train
and sit there so happy,
so free!

Oh! How beautiful, how swift
one travels so dauntless
on this classy train
without fears or anxiety.

The bell so sonorous,
is heard with jubilation,
and it always arrives so swiftly
anywhere it goes.

It is a magnificent invention
that can be seen today in Mexico,
[and] that so surprises
everyone in the Capital.

It seems diabolic,
but it is only scientific,
and the shining, admirable
result of progress.

And the city is full of delight.
Enthusiasm is widespread.
Because the new era
and the height of enlightenment have been commemorated.

The close of the century arrived,
fastened with a golden brooch,
sure that with [the] next one
there will be many more good things to come.

Now, all so content,
together we sing frenetically.
Long live the electric train!
Long live enlightenment!

The great battalion thirteen,
and so, so many people—
all were festooned
and all the songs were played.

The fifteenth of January
of the year nineteen hundred
the new event took place
during the afternoon.

There were speeches and toasts
and a sumptuous banquet,
pleasure reigning everywhere
and order of the most enduring.

—It's as if something from the Devil
—Well, now you see Don Simón,

that the train goes on its own
has no compare.

Among the townspeople
and even those from the highest ranks
talk of the train is heard,
with fright and with surprise.

—What foreign devils!
says a nasally old lady,
Such inventions of the wicked
to earn their daily bread!

—For there is no doubt,
says another of ninety,
it's the devil himself,
believe me you, Doña Petrona.

—They say they are electric,
but this is just a pretense
to conceal
there is something of Satan about.

—God save us, Casildita,
from riding in one of those cars,
surely they would take one
straight to Hell.

—I don't even want to see them.
The priests can excommunicate us,
Aunt Bruna,
I am off to confession.

—Well, of course, it is the devil
who pulls those train cars along, by damn!
These days, Doña Charo,
everything is electric.

—Didja' see the electric light,
the telegraph, an' phonograph,
and a thousand other things,
that frighten almost everyone.

—Any old thing, *comadre* [dear lady],
of these things in which the devil may abound,
they say they are electric,
just so as not to scare us.

—But that is not the case, no, no, no,
and they try to fool us,
so that soon we are turned over
to Mister Don Satan.

—And there have already been two deaths
out by Chapultepec;
the trains ground them up
before they even knew it.

—Am I wrong? Well, just tell me,
if this isn't something from hell.
Oh, caramba! In my time,
would this sort of thing [have] been done!

And in this sort of way
the old ladies talk today,
frightened by the occurrence
of the modern streetcars. . . .

There is no risk of being run over
because they can be stopped,
on the spot,
more quickly than mules.

Cordial greetings to our current president,
who with intelligence knows how
to unite peace with progress.

Central Themes

State formation, urban life, popular culture, gender

Suggested Reading

Herrera-Sobek, María. *The Mexican Corrido: A Feminist Analysis.* Bloomington: Indiana University Press, 1990.

Simmons, Merle. *The Mexican Corrido as a Source of an Interpretive Study of Modern Mexico, 1870–1950.* Bloomington: Indiana University Press, 1957.

Vanderwood, Paul J. *Disorder and Progress: Bandits, Politics, and Mexican Development, 1910–1917.* Albuquerque: University of New Mexico Press, 1992.

Related Sources

50. Popular Images of Mexican Life (the Late Nineteenth and Early Twentieth Centuries)
55. Revolutionary *Corridos* (1917, 1919)
60. Chronicles of Mexico City (1938)

PART 7

The Mexican Revolution (1910–1940)

By 1910, Mexico had experienced unprecedented growth. President Porfirio Díaz had removed restraints on trade, passed legislation that facilitated the sale and development of land, and encouraged foreign investment. Foreign capital from Spain, France, Britain, and the United States had complemented Mexican capital in advancing industrial development, and a growing working class had adapted to new relations at work. The expansion of commercial agriculture wrought significant change in labor conditions and land distribution. The strong central government that oversaw this growth remained in power through the cultivation of patronage at the regional level and, over time, increasingly through corrupt electoral politics, control of the press, and repression of dissent. The documents in this section give the reader an idea of the cacophony of voices and the range of interests that responded to these conditions in the making of the Mexican Revolution. Each document can be evaluated from the point of view of the sector of the population it represents. And by comparing the various documents, we can gain insight into the interests that were sometimes united in the Revolution, as well as the causes of conflict between different groups. These groups included the followers of Francisco I. Madero (Source 52); Emiliano Zapata's supporters, who adhered to the priorities voiced in the Plan de Ayala (Source 53); and the Constitutionalists, the dominant voices in shaping the Constitution of 1917 (Source 54). What do these documents reveal about how these groups might have either forged alliances or fallen into conflict based on their conceptions of what was at stake?

Traditionally, scholars have written of the Mexican Revolution as a struggle over land, a struggle among elites, or a convergence of regional conflicts that resulted from the modernization projects of the Porfiriato (1876–1911). As evidenced in Article 123 of the 1917 Constitution, however, it was also a workers' revolution (Source 54). How the 1917 Constitution addressed the concerns of labor might be evaluated against workers' grievances from the period preceding the Revolution (sources 45, 47, and 48). The Constitution would quickly become a central point of reference, not only in Mexican law, but for popular political culture more generally. While the Constitution addressed some long-standing concerns, it failed to resolve others, and it significantly altered the relationship between the church and state, which sparked that conflict anew (sources 56 and 63).

The documents collected in this section give an idea of the evolution of the Revolution from the idealizations of early declarations of objectives and expectations (sources 52 and 53) to the solidification of new relations of rule with the institutionalization of new laws (Source 58). And just as multiple interests challenged one another during the violent period of the Revolution, so too did Mexicans continue to struggle for what they understood the Revolution to mean in the postrevolutionary 1930s. Many women continued to argue that the slogan "effective suffrage, no reelection" meant that under Mexican law, they too had the right to vote. Women activists also worked for a range of causes, from improving women's education and employment opportunities to bettering conditions for mothers (Source 59). The "Petitioning the President" sources also allow us to formulate some idea of how average people from around the country interpreted the ideals espoused by the revolutionary government (Source 57). In addition, the letters suggest the unique relationship that Lázaro Cárdenas, as president of Mexico, developed with its citizens.

The presidency of Lázaro Cárdenas (1934–1940) is considered by many the period when the system that would serve as the basis of Mexican politics for decades to follow was created. Cárdenas came into office as the Great Depression reverberated throughout Mexico. His policies worked on the premise that the way to reinvigorate the economy was for the government to take a more active role in directing economic development. His administration supported large infrastructure projects such as the construction of highways and dams. During his presidency, the Mexican government distributed millions of acres of land to peasants. Furthermore, Cárdenas created four central trade unions that were closely allied to the state and intertwined with the political party system. The government also nationalized several industries, including railroads and oil (Source 61).

How might we trace the evolution of material conditions and ideas from the previous period into this era of revolution? What continuities and changes appeared in the ideas held by both the state and the public about religion? How, during this period, did the expansion of women's participation in the professions and in the Revolution alter the ways people spoke about them? What might the changes in material culture, described here by Salvador Novo, have meant for residents of urban Mexico (Source 60)?

52. Francisco Madero's Challenge to Porfirio Díaz (1910)*

As president of the Partido Nacional Antireeleccionista, Francisco I. Madero wrote his Plan de San Luís Potosí in San Antonio, Texas, in 1910. Madero had fled from Mexico to Texas when, at the time of the 1910 elections, President Porfirio Díaz had had him jailed. Rather than name the manifesto after the place where it was proclaimed, a U.S. city, Madero named it after the Mexican city from which he had fled the country. Copies of the plan soon arrived in Mexico City, and on November 18, 1910, government forces discovered an anti-Díaz conspiracy organized by Aquiles Serdán in Puebla. The police assassinated Serdán and several of his co-conspirators. Nevertheless, the Plan de San Luís Potosí inspired people from a wide range of circumstances throughout the country to take up arms against the Díaz government. Which different groups of people might have found inspiration in which aspects of the proclamation? While other proclamations raised similar concerns regarding the abuse of power and access to resources, how does this document construe those issues? The terms and expectations set out in the proclamation would shape politics for decades to come. In reflecting on later periods in Mexican history, the reader might return to this document to see how ideas laid out here continued to have relevance.

Plan de San Luís Potosí

People, in their constant efforts that the ideals of liberty and justice triumph, are forced, at certain historical moments, to make their greatest sacrifices.

Our beloved country has reached one of those moments. A force of tyranny, to which we Mexicans were not accustomed to suffer since we won our independence, oppresses us to such a degree that it has become intolerable. In exchange for that tyranny we are offered peace, but for the Mexican nation it is a shameful peace because its basis is not law, but force; because its object is not the glory and prosperity of the country, but to enrich a small group who, abusing the power of their position, have converted government offices into fountains of exclusive personal benefit, unscrupulously exploiting lucrative concessions and contracts.

The Legislative and Judicial powers are completely subordinated to the Executive Office; the division of powers, the sovereignty of the states, the liberty of the common councils, and the rights of citizens exist only on paper in our Magna Carta;

*From U.S. Congress, Senate Subcommittee on Foreign Relations, *Revolutions in Mexico,* 62nd Cong., 2nd sess. (Washington, DC: U.S. Government Printing Office, 1913), pp. 724–730, passim. Translated by the editors.

in fact, it might almost be said that what reigns in Mexico is martial law; the justice system, instead of imparting protection to the weak, merely serves to legalize the plundering committed by the strong; the judges instead of being the representatives of Justice, are the agents of the Executive, whose interests they faithfully serve; the chambers of congress have no other will than that of the dictator; the governors of the States are designated by him and they in turn designate and similarly impose the municipal authorities.

As a result, the entire administrative, judicial, and legislative machinery obey a single will, the caprice of General Porfirio Díaz, who during his long administration has shown that the principal motive that guides him is to maintain himself in power and at any cost.

As a result of such a system of government, profound discontent has been felt throughout the Republic for many years; however General Díaz, with great cunning and perseverance, has succeeded in annihilating all independent elements, so that it was not possible to organize any sort of movement to take from him the power of which he made such bad use. The evil constantly became worse, and the vehemence of General Díaz to impose a successor upon the Nation in the person of Mr. Ramon Corral* carried that evil to its limit and caused many Mexicans, although lacking recognized political standing, since it had been impossible to acquire it during the 36 years of dictatorship, to throw ourselves into the struggle to recover the sovereignty of the people and our rights on purely democratic grounds.

The National Anti-reelection Party (Partido Nacional Antireeleccionista), among other parties dedicated to the same ends, was organized, proclaiming the principles of effective suffrage and no reelection, as the only thing that would save the Republic from the immanent danger with which it is threatened by the extension of a dictatorship, every day more onerous, more despotic, and more immoral.

The Mexican people succeeded in supporting this party, and, responding to the call that it made, sent representatives to a Convention in which the National Democratic Party (Partido Nacional Democrático) was also represented, which also represented the will of the people. Said Convention designated candidates for the presidency and vice-presidency of the Republic, with said nominations falling to Mister Francisco Vázquez Gómez and myself, as vice-president and president, respectively.

While in a completely disadvantageous situation, due to the fact that our adversaries could depend upon full official forces, to which they recurred unscrupulously, we believed that our duty, to serve the people, required that we accept such an honorable designation.

In Mexico, as a democratic Republic, public power can have no other origin, nor basis than the will of the people, and the latter cannot be subordinated to methods fraudulently carried out.

---

*Ramón Corral Verdugo (1854–1912), vice president of Mexico from 1904 to 1911.

For this reason the Mexican people have protested against the illegality of the last election and, desiring to use successively all the recourses offered by the laws of the Republic, in due form asked for the nullification of the election by the Chamber of Deputies, notwithstanding they recognized no legal origin in said body and knew beforehand that, as its members were not the representatives of the people, they would carry out the will of General Díaz, to whom exclusively they owe their investiture.

In such a state of affairs the people, who are the only sovereign, also protested energetically against the election in imposing manifestations in different parts of the Republic; and if the latter were not general throughout the national territory, it was due to the terrible pressure exercised by the government, which always quenches in blood any democratic manifestation, as happened in Puebla, Vera Cruz, Tlaxcala, and other places.

But this violent and illegal system can no longer continue.

I fully realize that if the people have designated me as their candidate for the presidency it is not because they have had an opportunity to discover in me the qualities of a statesman or of a ruler, but the virility of the patriot determined to sacrifice himself, if need be, to obtain liberty and to help the people free themselves from the odious tyranny that oppresses them.

From the moment I threw myself into the democratic struggle I knew very well that General Díaz would not bow to the will of the nation; and, the noble Mexican people, in following me to the polls, also knew perfectly the outrage that awaited them; but in spite of this, when necessary, the people offered up a significant contingent of martyrs for the cause of liberty, and with wonderful stoicism went to the polls where they suffered all sort of abuse.

But such conduct was indispensable to demonstrate to the whole world that the Mexican people are fit for democracy, that they are thirsty for liberty, and that their present rulers do not measure up to their aspirations.

Furthermore, the attitude of the people before and during the election, as well as afterwards, shows clearly that they energetically reject the government of General Díaz and that, if those electoral rights had been respected, I would have been elected for President of the Republic.

Therefore, in accordance with the national will, I declare the recent election illegal, and therefore the Republic without rulers, and I assume the presidency of the Republic on a provisional basis, until the people designate their rulers pursuant to the law. In order to attain this end, it is necessary to throw from power the audacious usurpers whose only claim to legality is reflected in a scandalous and immoral fraud.

With all the honor required of the situation, I declare that it would be a weakness on my part and treason to the people, who have placed their confidence in me, not to put myself at the front of my fellow citizens, who anxiously call me from all parts of the country, to compel General Díaz by force of arms, to respect the national will.

The current government, though it originates in violence and fraud, from the moment it was tolerated by the people, might be considered by foreign nations as having certain legal standing until the 30th of next month, at which time its powers expire; however, as it is necessary that the incoming government, which was spawned by the recent fraud, not be recognized or take power, or that at the least it encounter the majority of the Nation protesting, with arms in hand against this usurpation, I have designated Sunday the 20th of November so that beginning at six in the afternoon on, in all populations throughout the Republic, [the people] raise up in arms in accordance with the following.

Plan

1. The elections held in June and July of the current year for president, vice-president, Supreme Court justices, and delegates and senators are declared null and void.

2. The current government of Porfirio Díaz is no longer recognized, nor any of the authorities whose power ought to come from popular election, for not only were they not elected by the people, they have lost the little claim to legal authority they might have had and, by means of the power placed at their disposition by the people and for the defense of their interests, perpetrating and sanctioning the most scandalous electoral fraud recorded in the history of Mexico.

3. In as much as possible, and in order to avoid the difficulties inherent in any revolutionary movement, it is declared that all laws and regulations promulgated by the current administration will remain in effect, reserving the right, in due time and in accordance with the constitution, to reform those laws that are found in flagrant violation of the principles proclaimed in this manifesto. All legislation, judicial decisions and decrees that sanction the management of funds and accounts of all Porfirian administration representatives; for as soon as the Revolution succeeds, investigative commissions will be formed in order to judge the obligations that federal, state, and municipal government might have incurred.

In all instances the agreements made by the Porfirian government with foreign governments and businesses before the 20th of the month will be honored.

In violation of the Law of Vacant Lands, and by agreement of the Ministry of Development, or by the error of national courts, numerous small land-holders, the majority of them indigenous peoples, have been dispossessed of their lands. In all fairness, those lands that were taken away by such arbitrary measures should be returned to their former owners, and it is declared that such arrangements and resolutions are subject to revision, and it is required of those who acquired lands by such immoral means, or their heirs, return those lands to their original owners, and pay indemnization for losses suffered. Only in instances where lands have passed on to a third person before the proclamation of this manifesto, will the former owners receive indemnization from those who benefited from the divestiture.

4. In addition to the Constitution and existing laws, the [principle] of no reelection of the president and vice-president of the republic, state governors and municipal presidents is the Supreme Law of the Republic, while related constitutional reforms are enacted.

5. I assume the position of Provisional President of the United States of Mexico with the authority necessary to engage in war against the illegitimate Government of General Díaz.

As soon as the national capital and more than half of the states of the Federation are in the hands of the People (*el Pueblo*), the provisional president will within a month call for special general elections and will turn over power to the President that is elected, as soon as the results of the election are known.

6. The provisional President, before turning over power, will notify Congress of the use made of the powers conferred by this manifesto.

7. On the 20th of November, beginning at six in the afternoon, all citizens of the Republic will take up arms in order to depose the authorities that now govern. The towns that are far from lines of communication will do so beginning at sundown.

8. When the authorities offer armed resistance, they will be made by force of arms to respect the will of the people, but in such cases the laws of war will be vigorously observed, calling special attention to the restrictions related to not using explosives or shooting prisoners. Attention should be called, as well, to all Mexicans, to respect foreigners in their person and interests. . . .

Fellow citizens: If I call upon you to take up arms and bring down the Government of General Díaz, it is not only due to the violations committed during the recent elections, but in order to save the Fatherland from the dark future that awaits it under the continued dictatorship and the nefarious scientific (*científico*) oligarchy, that without scruples and with great speed is taking up and wasting national resources, and that if we allow to remain in power, in a very short time will have completed its work: it will have committed a public offense and devalued the [Mexican] people; it will have sucked all the wealth from the country and left it in utter misery; they will have stained the Fatherland with bankruptcy, which weak, impoverished, and hamstrung, will find itself inert to defend its borders, its honor, and its institutions.

With regard to myself, I have a clear conscience and no one can accuse me of promoting the revolution for personal gain, for it comes from the will of the people, which did everything possible to come to a peaceful agreement I was even willing to denounce my candidacy if General Díaz had permitted the Nation to choose even if it were the vice president of the Republic; however, dominated by incomprehensible pride and willingness to succumb to revolution before ceding an inch, before returning to the people an atom of their rights, before complying with the promises he made to the Nation in the Noria and Tuxtepec [manifestos], even if it were during the last years of his life.

He himself justified the present revolution when he said: "Let it be that no citizen imposes himself and perpetuates the exercise of power and that this will be the last revolution."

If interests of the Fatherland had weighed upon General Díaz more than his own sordid interests and those of his advisors, making some concessions to the people, this revolution would have been avoided; but now that he has not done it. . . . So much the better! Change will be more rapid and more radical, for the Mexican people, in place of lamenting like a coward, will accept as a brave challenge, and now that General Díaz intends to rely on brute force to impose upon them this offensive yoke, the people will recur to the same force in order to shake off this yoke, to throw this evil man from power and re-conquer their liberty.

San Luís Potosí, October 5, 1910.
Francisco I. Madero

Central Themes

State formation, land and labor

Suggested Reading

La France, David G. *The Mexican Revolution in Puebla, 1908–1913: The Maderista Movement and the Failure of Liberal Reform.* Wilmington, DE: SR Books, 1989.

Ross, Stanley R. *Francisco I. Madero: Apostle of Mexican Democracy.* New York: Columbia University Press, 1955.

Young, Elliot. *Catarino Garza's Revolution on the Texas-Mexico Border.* Durham, NC: Duke University Press, 2004.

Related Sources

44. Porfirio Díaz's Political Vision (1871)
47. Precursors to Revolution (1904, 1906)
53. Revolution in Morelos (1911)
54. Land, Labor, and the Church in the Mexican Constitution (1917)

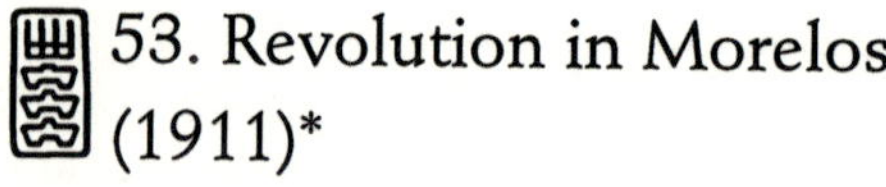

53. Revolution in Morelos (1911)*

When Francisco I. Madero declared the Plan de San Luís Potosí, diverse groups whose grievances dated back decades, if not longer, took up arms in support of Madero and the Revolution. The peasants of the southern state of Morelos, who recognized Emiliano Zapata as their leader, formed one such group. Upon taking the presidency, Madero called upon the Zapatistas to disarm themselves before he would consider attending to their demands. The armed peasants lost patience with

*Emiliano Zapata et al., "Plan de Ayala," in *Documentos interesantes de la revolutión de ideales;* and *Manifiexto del General Emiliano Zapata* (Puebla, Mexico: Imprenta Commercial, 1913), pp. 19–28. Translated by the editors.

him and in November 1911 convened in a small town in southern Puebla to draw up and proclaim the Plan de Ayala, which was signed by more than sixty Zapatista generals, captains, corporals, and lieutenants. A careful reading gives insight into the culture from which this document, central to the agrarian movement in the region, emerged. The Plan de Ayala reveals the ways the people of Morelos, over time, engaged with national political leaders. The Plan de Ayala did not call for the outright elimination of *haciendas* (agricultural estates) but sought some form of coexistence with them; in so doing, it was not as radical as the manifestos of other agrarian movements, such as those issued in 1915 by rivals to Venustiano Carranza that called for land to be given to any village that could demonstrate it had insufficient land for its needs. By examining Madero's manifesto along with the Plan de Ayala, readers may be able to discern why the Zapatistas might have initially supported Madero as well as the source of the tensions that would emerge. What precisely does the manifesto call for? How does the manifesto justify those claims? How does historical consciousness play a role in the formulation of those claims?

Plan de Ayala, November 25, 1911

Plan for Liberation of the sons of the State of Morelos, affiliated with the Insurgent Army, which defends the fulfillment of the Plan of San Luis, and with the additional reforms it has believed necessary to include for the betterment of the Mexican Fatherland.

We the undersigned, constituted in a Revolutionary Junta to sustain and carry out the promises made to the country by the Revolution of November 20, 1910, solemnly declare before the civilized world which sits in judgment of us, and before the Nation to which we belong and which we love, propositions which we have formulated to end the tyranny which oppresses us and to redeem the Fatherland from the tyranny which oppresses us, and which are outlined in the following plan:

1. Taking into consideration that the Mexican people, led by the caudillo Don Francisco I. Madero, went to battle and shed their blood to retake liberties and vindicate their rights which had been trampled upon, and not so that one man take power for himself, thus violating the sacred principles which he swore to defend under the slogan "Effective Suffrage and No Reelection," thus denigrating the faith, the cause, the justice, and the liberties of the people; taking into consideration that the man to whom we refer is Don Francisco I. Madero, the same who initiated the aforementioned revolution, who imposed his will and influence as a norm of governance on the Provisional Government of the ex-President of the Republic, the Esteemed (*licenciado)* Francisco L. de Barra, causing with this deed, and in a deceitful and ridiculous manner, repeated bloodshed and multiple misfortunes for the Fatherland, having no intentions other than satisfying his personal ambitions, his boundless

instincts as a tyrant, and his profound disrespect for the fulfillment of the preexisting laws emanating from the immortal Constitution of '57, written with the blood of revolutionaries of Ayutla.

Taking into account: that the so-called Chief of the Liberating Revolution of Mexico, Don Francisco I. Madero, through lack of integrity and utter weakness, did not bring about a satisfactory end to the revolution which he gloriously initiated with the help of God and the people, since he left standing most of the governing powers and corrupt oppressive forces of the dictatorial government of Porfirio Díaz, which are not nor can in any way be representative of National Sovereignty, and which, for being bitter adversaries of ourselves and of the principles which even now we defend, are causing the country's ills and opening new wounds in the heart of the Fatherland, to give it its own blood to drink; taking also into account that the aforementioned Sr. Francisco I. Madero, present President of the Republic, seeks to avoid fulfillment of the promises which he made to the Nation in the Plan of San Luís Potosí, having postponed to the Ciudad Juárez agreements the aforementioned promises, and by nullifying, pursuing, jailing, or killing revolutionary forces who helped him occupy the high post of President of the Republic, which he did by means of false promises to, and numerous deceptions of, the Nation.

Taking into consideration that the oft-cited Francisco I. Madero has tried with the brute force of bayonets to silence and to drown in blood the people who ask, solicit, or demand from him the fulfillment of the promises of the revolution, calling them bandits and rebels, condemning them to a war of extermination without conceding or granting a single one of the guarantees which reason, justice, and the law prescribe; taking equally into consideration that the President of the Republic Francisco I. Madero has made of Effective Suffrage a bloody mockery of the people by imposing, against the will of the same people, licenciado José M. Pino Suárez in the Vice-Presidency of the Republic, or governors of the States, designating men such as the so-called General Ambrosio Figueroa, scourge and tyrant of the people of Morelos, or scandalously consorting with the Científico party, feudal landlords, and oppressive *caciques* [local leaders], enemies of the Revolution he proclaimed, so as to forge new chains and follow the pattern of a new dictatorship more shameful and more terrible than that of Porfirio Díaz, for it has been patently clear that he has undermined the sovereignty of the States, trampling on the laws without any respect for lives or interests, as has happened in the State of Morelos, and other states, leading us into the most horrendous anarchy recorded in contemporary history.

Given these considerations we declare the aforementioned Francisco I. Madero inept at fulfilling the promises of the Revolution of which he was the author, because he has betrayed the principles by means of which he deceived the people and was able to rise to power: incapable of governing and because he has no respect for the law and justice of the people, and a traitor to the Fatherland, because with blood and fire he humiliates the Mexicans who want liberties, only to please the *científicos* [technocrats], landlords, and bosses who enslave us, and from today on we continue the revolution begun by him, until we achieve the overthrow of the dictatorial powers which exist.

2. Sr. Francisco I. Madero is no longer recognized as Chief of the Revolution and as President of the Republic, for the reasons already expressed, in order to overthrow this official.

3. The illustrious General Pascual Orozco, the second of the Don Francisco I. Madero, is recognized as Chief of the Liberating Revolution, and in case he does not accept this difficult post, recognition as Chief of the Revolution will go to General Don Emiliano Zapata.

4. The Revolutionary Junta of the State of Morelos manifests to the Nation under formal oath: that it adopts as its own the plan of San Luís Potosí, with the additions expressed below, for the benefit of the oppressed *pueblos* [towns], and it will make itself the defender of the principles it defends until victory or death.

5. The Revolutionary Junta of the State of Morelos will not allow agreements or compromises until it achieves the overthrow of the dictatorial forces of Porfirio Díaz and Francisco I. Madero, for the Nation is tired of false men and traitors who make promises as liberators, and who upon arriving in power forget them and become tyrants.

6. As an additional part of the plan, we give notice: the pueblos or citizens who have legal title to real estate will take possession of the lands, forests, and water, which, in the shadows of corrupted justice, landlords, científicos, or bosses have usurped, maintaining at any cost with arms in hand the mentioned possession; and the usurpers who believe they hold rights to [those properties] will be heard before the special tribunals which will be established upon the triumph of the revolution.

7. In virtue of the fact that the immense majority of Mexican pueblos and citizens are owners of no more than the land they walk on, suffering the horrors of poverty without being able to improve their social condition in any way or to dedicate themselves to Industry or Agriculture, because lands, timber, and water are monopolized in a few hands, for this cause there will be expropriated the third part of those monopolies from the powerful proprietors, with prior indemnization, in order that the pueblos and citizens of Mexico may obtain *ejidos* [communally held land], colonies, and foundations for pueblos, or fields for sowing or laboring, and the Mexicans' lack of prosperity and wellbeing may improve in all and for all.

8. The landlords, científicos, or caciques who directly or indirectly oppose the present Plan, shall have their property nationalized, and the two third parts which otherwise would belong to them will go for indemnizations of war, and pensions for widows and orphans of the victims who succumb in the struggle for the present Plan.

9. In order to carry out the procedures regarding the aforementioned properties, the laws of disentailment and nationalization will be applied as appropriate: as norm and example, shall be those laws put into effect by the immortal Juárez regarding ecclesiastical properties, which punished the despots and conservatives who have always sought to impose upon us the ignominious yoke of oppression and backwardness.

10. The insurgent military chiefs of the Republic who rose up in arms at the call of Don Francisco I. Madero to defend the Plan of San Luís Potosí, and who oppose with armed force the present Plan, will be judged traitors to the cause which they defended and to the Fatherland, since at present many of them, to humor the tyrants, for a fistful of coins, or for bribes or connivance, shed the blood of their brothers who claim the fulfillment of the promises which Don Francisco I. Madero made to the Nation.

11. The expenses of war will be taken in conformity with Article II of the Plan of San Luís Potosí, and all procedures employed in the Revolution we undertake will be in conformity with the same instructions which said plan determines.

12. Once the revolution we carry out is realized, a Junta of the principal revolutionary chiefs from the different States will name or designate an interim President of the Republic, who will convoke elections for the organization of federal powers.

13. The principal revolutionary chiefs of each State, in council, will designate the governor of the State to which they belong, and this appointed official will convoke elections for the necessary organization of public powers, with the purpose of avoiding compulsory appointments which bring about the misfortune of the people, like the well-known appointment of Ambrosio Figueroa in the State of Morelos and others who drive us to the brink of bloody conflicts, fomented at the will of Madero the dictator and the circle of científicos and landlords who have influenced him.

14. If President Madero and other dictatorial forces of the present and former regime want to avoid the immense misfortunes which afflict the Fatherland, and if they possess true sentiments of love for it, let them immediately renounce the posts they occupy, and by doing so they will in some way staunch the grave wounds which they have opened in the bosom of the Fatherland, since, if they do not do so, on their heads will fall the blood and the anathema of our brothers.

15. Mexicans: consider that the cunning and bad faith of one man is shedding blood in a scandalous manner, because he is incapable of governing; consider that his system of government is choking the Fatherland and trampling our institutions with the brute force of bayonets; and thus, as we raised up our weapons to elevate him to power, we again raise them up against him for failing to keep his promises to the Mexican people, and for having betrayed the Revolution initiated by him. We are not personalists, we are partisans of principles and not of men!

Mexican People, support this plan with weapons in hand and you will bring about the prosperity and well-being of the Fatherland.

Ayala, November 25, 1911
Liberty, Justice, and Law.

[This] is a true copy taken from the original. Camp in the Mountains of Puebla, December 11, 1911.

Signed, General in Chief Emiliano Zapata. [followed by more than sixty signatures]

Central Themes

Indigenous people, state formation, land and labor

Suggested Reading

Brunk, Samuel. *Revolution and Betrayal in Mexico.* Albuquerque: University of New Mexico Press, 1995.

Hart, Paul. *Bitter Harvest: The Social Transformation of Morelos, Mexico, and the Origins of the Zapatista Revolution, 1840–1910.* Albuquerque: University of New Mexico Press, 2005.

Womack, John. *Zapata and the Mexican Revolution.* New York: Vintage Books, 1968.

Related Sources

42. The Reconfiguration of Property Rights and of Church-State Relations (1856)
49. Land and Society (1909)
52. Francisco Madero's Challenge to Porfirio Díaz (1910)
54. Land, Labor, and the Church in the Mexican Constitution (1917)
55. Revolutionary *Corridos* (1917, 1919)
67. Rubén Jaramillo and the Struggle for *Campesino* Rights in Postrevolutionary Morelos (1967)

54. Land, Labor, and the Church in the Mexican Constitution (1917)*

By mid-1915, Venustiano Carranza and his forces had defeated Pancho Villa in the north and the Zapatistas in Morelos. While in 1915 Carranza had allied himself with some sectors of organized labor, late the following year he put down a general strike in Mexico City. By September 1916, Carranza had called into session a Constitutional Convention, meeting in Querétaro, where delegates drew up the Constitution of Mexico that is still in use today. While Carranza sought to use the Constitution of 1857 as the foundation for the new constitution, representatives to the convention pushed for more progressive social reforms than those favored by Carranza. Furthermore, the mobilized population—including *campesinos* (rural workers), workers, and other groups—had pushed for change. For example, a series of military decrees had responded to workers' demands and thus laid the foundation for the recognition of new relationships between workers, employers, and the state. The Mexican Constitution was the first constitution to include social rights,

*Bibliotéca Virtual Miguel de Cervantes, "La bibliotéca de las culturas hispánicas," available at: http://www.cervantesvirtual.com/servlet/SirveObras/08146396711992773087857/index.htm (accessed March 30, 2009). Excerpts translated by the editors.

two years prior to the German Constitution (1919), which emerged during the Weimar Republic. Constitution Day, honored as a national holiday on February 5, commemorates both the Constitution of 1857 and that of 1917. The reader will see evidence that issues raised during the Era of Reform are reiterated here, as well as new conceptions of the rights and responsibilities of citizens, the state, private interests, and foreign powers that emerged during the Revolution. The reader will see in other documents in this volume when and how Mexicans have secured their rights by invoking concepts laid out in the Constitution of 1917.

Article 27

Ownership of the lands and waters within the boundaries of the national territory is vested originally in the Nation, which has had, and maintains, the right to transmit title thereof to private persons, thereby constituting private property.

Private property shall not be expropriated except for reasons of public use and subject to payment of indemnity.

The Nation shall at all times have the right to impose on private property such limitations as public interest may demand, as well as the right to regulate the utilization of natural resources which are susceptible to appropriation in order to conserve them and to ensure a more equitable distribution of public wealth. In light of this objective, necessary measures shall be taken to divide up large landed estates; to develop the operation of small landed holdings; to create new agricultural centers with the lands and waters they need; to encourage agriculture in general; and, to protect natural resources and property from damage to the detriment of society. Centers of population which at present neither have lands nor water, or do not possess them in sufficient quantities for the needs of their inhabitants, shall be entitled to grants thereof, which shall be taken from adjacent properties, while respecting at all times the rights of small land holdings in operation.

In the Nation is vested direct ownership of all natural resources of the continental shelf and the submarine shelf of the islands; of all minerals or substances that in veins, ledges, masses or ore pockets, form deposits of a nature distinct from the components of the earth itself, such as the minerals from which industrial metals and metalloids are extracted; deposits of precious stones, rock-salt and the deposits of salt formed by sea water. . . .

. . . [Ownership] by the Nation is inalienable and imprescriptible, and the exploitation, use, or appropriation of the resources concerned, by private persons or by companies organized according to Mexican laws, may not be undertaken except through concessions granted by the Federal Executive, in accordance with rules and conditions established by law. . . . The Federal Government has the power to establish national reserves and to abolish them. . . . In the case of petroleum, and solid, liquid, or gaseous hydrocarbons, no concessions or contracts will be granted, nor may those that have been granted continue, and the Nation shall carry out the exploitation of these products, in accordance with the provisions indicated in the respective regulatory law.

It is exclusively a function of the Nation in general to conduct, transform, distribute, and supply electric power to be used for public service. No concessions for this purpose will be granted to private persons and the Nation will make use of the property and natural resources required for these ends. . . .

Legal capacity to acquire ownership of lands and waters of the Nation shall be governed by the following provisions:

(i) Only Mexicans, by birth or naturalization, and Mexican companies have the right to acquire ownership of lands, waters, and their appurtenances, or to obtain concessions for the exploitation of mines or of waters. The State may grant the same right to foreigners, provided they agree before the Ministry of Foreign Relations to consider themselves as nationals in respect to such property, and bind themselves not to invoke the protection of their governments in matters relating thereto. . . . Under no circumstances may foreigners acquire direct ownership of lands or waters within a zone of one hundred kilometers along the borders [of national territory] and of fifty kilometers along the shores of the country. . . .

(ii) Religious institutions known as churches, regardless of creed, may in no case acquire, hold, or administer real estate or hold mortgages thereon; such property held at present either directly or through an intermediary shall revert to the Nation. . . . Places of public worship are the property of the Nation, as represented by the Federal Government, which shall determine which of them may continue to be devoted to their present purposes. Bishoprics, rectories, seminaries, asylums, and schools belonging to religious orders, convents, or any other buildings built or intended for the administration, propagation, or teaching of a religious creed shall at once become the property of the Nation by inherent right, to be used exclusively for the public services of the Federal or State Governments, within their respective jurisdictions. All places of public worship hereafter erected shall be the property of the Nation. . . .

(v) Banks duly authorized to operate in accordance with the laws on credit institutions may hold mortgages on urban and rural property in conformity with the provisions of such laws but may not own or administer more real property than is actually necessary for their direct purpose. . . .

(vii) The centers of population which, by law or in fact, possess a communal status shall have legal capacity to enjoy common possession of the lands, forests, and waters belonging to them or which have been or may be restored to them. . . .

(viii) The following are declared null and void:

(a) All transfers of the lands, waters, and forests of villages, *rancherías* [settlements], groups, or communities made by local officials, state governors, or other local authorities in violation of the provisions of the Law of June 25, 1856, and other related laws and rulings. . . .

(x) Centers of population which do not have *ejidos* [communally held lands] or which are unable to have them restored to them due to lack of titles, impossibility of identification, or because they had been legally transferred, shall be granted sufficient lands and waters to establish them, in accordance with the needs of the population; but in no case shall they fail to be granted the area needed, and for this purpose the land needed shall be expropriated, at the expense of the Federal Government, to be taken from lands adjoining the villages in question. . . .

(xiv) Landowners affected by decisions granting or restoring communal lands and waters to villages, or who may be affected by future decisions, shall have no ordinary legal right or recourse and cannot institute injunction proceedings.

Article 123

The Congress of the Union, without contravening the following basic principles, shall formulate labor laws which shall apply to:

(A) Workers, day laborers, domestic workers, artisans, and in a general way, to all labor contracts:

(i) The maximum duration of work for one day shall be eight hours.

(ii) The maximum duration of night work shall be seven hours. The following are prohibited: unhealthful or dangerous work, industrial night work, and all work after ten o'clock at night by minors under sixteen years of age.

(iii) Workers between twelve and sixteen years old shall have a maximum workday of six hours. The work of children under twelve cannot be the object of a contract.

(iv) For every six days of work, a worker must have at least one day of rest.

(v) During the three months prior to childbirth, women shall not perform physical labor that requires excessive physical effort. In the month following childbirth, they shall necessarily enjoy the benefit of rest and shall receive their full wages and retain their employment and the rights acquired under their labor contract. During the nursing period, they shall have two special rest periods each day, of a half hour each, for nursing their infants.

(vi) The minimum wage that each worker must enjoy will be sufficient, taking into account the conditions of each region, to satisfy the basic necessities of a worker's life, his education, and his honest pleasures, considering him as the head of the family. In all businesses, whether agrarian, commercial, industrial, or mineral, workers have the right of participating in the profits, which will be regulated according to paragraph 9.

(vii) Equal wages shall be paid for equal work, regardless of sex or nationality.

(viii) The minimum wage shall be exempt from levies, compensation, or deductions.

(ix) The rate of minimum wage and the distribution of profits referred to in paragraph 6 will be fixed by Special Commissions that will be formed in each municipality, and subordinate to the Board of Conciliation and Arbitration that will be established in each state. In the absence of these Commissions, the minimum salary will be fixed by the respective Board of Conciliation and Arbitration.

(x) Wages must necessarily be paid in money of legal tender and cannot be paid in goods, promissory notes, or any other token intended as a substitute for money.

(xi) Whenever, due to extraordinary circumstances, the regular working hours of a day must be increased, one hundred percent shall be added to the amount for normal hours of work as remuneration for the overtime. Overtime work may never exceed three hours per day nor should it happen for three consecutive days. Men under sixteen years of age and women of any age may not be admitted to this kind of labor.

(xii) In any agricultural, industrial, or mining enterprise or in any other kind of work, employers shall be obliged to furnish workmen comfortable and hygienic living quarters for which they may collect rent that shall not exceed one half percent monthly of the assessed valuation of the property. They also must establish schools, hospitals, and any other services necessary to the community. If the enterprise is situated within a town and employs more than one hundred workers, it shall be responsible for the first of the above obligations.

(xiii) In addition, in these same work centers, when the population exceeds two hundred inhabitants, a tract of land of not less than five thousand square meters must be reserved for the establishment of public markets, the erection of buildings destined for municipal services, and recreation centers. Establishments for the sale of intoxicating liquors and houses for games of chance are prohibited in all work centers.

(xiv) Employers shall be responsible for labor accidents and for occupational diseases of workers, contracted because of or in the performance of their work or occupation; therefore, employers shall pay the corresponding indemnification whether death or only temporary or permanent incapacity to work has resulted, in accordance with what the law prescribes. This responsibility shall exist even if the employer contracts for the work through an intermediary.

(xv) An employer shall be required to observe, in the installation of his establishments, the legal regulations on hygiene and health, and to adopt adequate measures for the prevention of accidents in the use of machines, instruments, and materials of labor, as well as to organize the same in such a way as to ensure the greatest possible guarantee for the health and safety of workers as is compatible with the nature of the work, under the penalties established by law in this respect.

(xvi) Both employers and workers shall have the right to organize for the defense of their respective interests, by forming unions, professional associations, etc.

(xvii) The laws shall recognize strikes and lockouts as rights of workmen and employers.

(xviii) Strikes shall be legal when they have as their purpose the attaining of an equilibrium among the various factors of production, by harmonizing the rights of labor with those of capital. In public services, it shall be obligatory for workers to give notice ten days in advance to the Board of Conciliation and Arbitration as to the date agreed upon for the suspension of work. Strikes shall be considered illegal only when the majority of strikers engage in acts of violence against persons or property, or in the event of war, when the workers belong to establishments or services of the Government. . . .

(xx) Differences or disputes between capital and labor shall be subject to the decisions of a Board of Conciliation and Arbitration, consisting of an equal number of workers and employers, with one from the Government. . . .

(xxvii) The following conditions shall be considered null and void and not binding on the contracting parties, even if expressed in the contract:

(a) Those that stipulate a day's work that is inhumane because it is obviously excessive, considering the nature of the work. . . .

(c) Those stipulating a period of more than one week before payment of a day's wages;

(d) Those indicating as the place of payment of wages a place of recreation, an inn, café, tavern, bar, or store, except for the payment of employees of such establishments;

(e) Those that include the direct or indirect obligation of acquiring consumer goods in specified stores or places;

(f) Those that permit the retention of wages as a fine;

(g) Those that constitute a waiver by the worker of indemnification to which he is entitled due to labor accidents or occupational diseases, damages occasioned by the non-fulfillment of the contract, or by being discharged;

(h) All other stipulations that imply waiver of any right designed to favor the worker in the laws of protection and assistance for workers. . . .

Article 130

The federal powers shall exercise the supervision required by law in matters relating to religious worship and outward ecclesiastical forms. Other authorities shall act as auxiliaries of the Federation.

Congress cannot enact laws establishing or prohibiting any religion.

Marriage is a civil contract. This and other acts of a civil nature concerning persons are within the exclusive competence of civil officials and authorities, in the manner prescribed by law, and shall have the force and validity defined by said law.

A simple promise to tell the truth and to fulfill obligations that are contracted is binding on the one who so promises, and in the event of failure to fulfill them, this person shall be subject to the penalties that the law prescribes for this purpose.

The law does not recognize religious groups called churches as legal entities.

Ministers of denominations shall be considered as persons who practice a profession and shall be directly subject to the laws enacted on such matters.

Only the legislatures of the States shall have the power to determine the maximum number of ministers of denominations necessary for local needs.

To practice the ministry of any denomination in the United States of Mexico, it is necessary to be a Mexican by birth.

Ministers of denominations may never, in a public or private meeting constituting an assembly, or in acts of worship or religious propaganda, criticize the fundamental laws of the country or the authorities of the government, specifically or generally. They shall not have an active or passive vote nor the right to form associations for religious purposes.

Permission to dedicate new places of worship open to the public must be obtained from the Secretariat of Government, with previous consent of the government of the State. There must be in every church building a representative who is responsible to the authorities for compliance with the laws on religious worship in such building, and for the objects pertaining to the worship. . . .

No privilege shall be granted or confirmed, nor shall any other step be taken which has for its purpose the validation in official courses of study, of courses pursued in establishments devoted to the professional training of ministers of religion. . . .

Periodical publications of a religious character, whether they be such because of their program, title, or merely because of their general tendencies, may not comment on national political matters nor provide public information on acts of the authorities of the country nor on matters relating directly to the functioning of public institutions.

The formation of any kind of political group, the name of which contains any word or indication whatever that it is related to any religious denomination, is strictly prohibited. Meetings of a political character may not be held in places of worship. . . .

The acquisition by private parties of personal or real property owned by the clergy or by religious organizations shall be governed by Article 27 of this Constitution.

Trials for violation of the above provisions shall never be heard before a jury. . . .

Central Themes

Indigenous people, state formation, land and labor, religion, gender

Suggested Reading

Bortz, Jeffrey. *Revolution Within the Revolution: Cotton Textile Workers and the Mexican Labor Regime, 1910–1923.* Stanford, CA: Stanford University Press, 2008.

Hart, John Mason. *Revolutionary Mexico: The Coming and Process of the Mexican Revolution.* Berkeley: University of California Press, 1987.

Middlebrook, Kevin. *The Paradox of Revolution.* Baltimore: Johns Hopkins University Press, 1995.

Niemeyer, E. V., Jr. *Revolution at Querétaro: The Mexican Constitutional Convention of 1916–1917.* Austin: University of Texas Press, 1974.

Related Sources

47. Precursors to Revolution (1904, 1906)
49. Land and Society (1909)
52. Francisco Madero's Challenge to Porfirio Díaz (1910)
53. Revolution in Morelos (1911)
55. Revolutionary *Corridos* (1917, 1919)
58. Plutarco Elías Calles: The Legal Challenges of the Postrevolutionary State (1928)
61. The Responsibility of Government and Private Enterprise to the Mexican People (1937–1938)

55. Revolutionary *Corridos* (1917, 1919)*

The earlier discussion regarding *corridos* (ballads) serves as context for consideration of revolutionary corridos (Source 51). The corridos included in this selection record two very different historic events from the era of the Mexican Revolution: the Constitutional Convention of 1916–1917 and the murder of Emiliano Zapata. How might our perspective on these events change by reading these corridos? What sort of tone does each corrido set, and how might that tone contribute to a certain perspective on national events?

Fragment of "The Corrido of the Constitutional Congress of Querétaro" (1917)

Now Venustiano Carranza
has got his convention delegates
to straighten up the laws
that he will give to the people.

Come on, sweetie, let's go!
Put on your purple sandals,
let's go to Iturbide theater, an'
you'll see the delegates.

---

*Higinio Vazquez Santa Ana, *Canciones, cantares, y corridos mexicanos,* segundo tomo (Mexico: Imprenta M. Leon Sánchez, 1931), pp. 237–240, 247–248. Translated by the editors.

Let them talk, insult each other, and shout,
Down and up they'll go,
and he who brings the most *pinole* [sugar candy]
will be the one to swallow the most spit.

And even if they all get upset
and speak of Constitution,
those that are here are not everyone,
nor are all the important ones here.

I say to the congressmen:
Do not fight so continuously
And instead of becoming a Congressional representative
end up with something done.

Come on, woman, and I'll buy for you
your little *guichol rebozo* [shawl].
You will hear the delegates
air their dirty laundry.

There is a little of everything in the Congress,
as they say in Saltillo, a little chile, pork, and sweets,
and also *picadillo* [minced meat].

Everyone has some gift,
as the priest says.
Some the gift of gab,
others that of stubbornness.

Amaya, who is president,
shouts at them: Sons of *huarache!**
I fought for the North
before any of you no-good people!

And the lawyer Cañete
tells him: Listen, president,
I am going to donate my laws
So that you might know how to treat the people. . . .

**Huarache* is a sandal. Here the word is less important for what it means than to allow the corrido to play on the phrase "sons of bitches."

And here the singing ends,
These verses so common.
Long live Venustiano;
Long live the delegates!

"The Death of Emiliano Zapata" (1919)

Listen, dear sirs, to the corrido relating
a sad event;
For in Chinameca, thinking he was safe,
Zapata, the great insurgent was killed.

April of nineteen hundred
nineteen, will remain
in the memory
of the *campesino* [rural worker]
like a stain on history.

Bells of Villa Ayala,
Why do you ring so sorrowfully?
—It is that Zapata has died
and Zapata was a brave man.

The good Emiliano who loved the poor
Wanted to give them freedom;
for this the Indians of all villages,
with him went to fight.

From Cuautla to Amecameca,
Matamoros and el Ajusco,
The recruits of
Don Porfirio they had the pleasure to encounter.

Trinitaria [wild pansies] of the fields
on the plains of Morelos,
if you ask for Zapata,
they will say that he already ascended to the heavens.

Zapata said to Don Pancho Madero,
when Madero was already governing:
—If you don't give lands, you will see the Indians
once again take up the battle.

He stood up to Mister Madero,
To Huerta and Carranza,
For they did not want to carry out
His manifesto, the Plan de Ayala.

Run, run, little rabbit,
Go tell your brothers:
Mister Zapata, the bane of the tyrants,
has already died.

Riding with elegance on his cinnamon-colored mare,
he was a *charro* [horseman] to admire;
And in bringing down a bull,
And pulling down the bull by the tail was the strength
of a top horseman.

Play a tune from the lowlands
on the *charanga* [brass band].
A bull is rolling in the sand,
Because Zapata is one of the good ones.

A frog in a small puddle
Sings in his serenade:
—Where was there a better charro
than my General Zapata?

With lots of enthusiasm the people applaud
And even the little girls agreed
That Zapata the chief and his generals
Do good wherever they go.

With a *jaripeo* [rodeo] they celebrated
His victory in the scuffle
and among his fellow southerners,
that he is a charro, no one denies.

En route to Huehuetoca
thus a bird inquired
—Traveler, what did they do
with the famous leader?

He was born among the poor, lived among the poor,
and it was for them he fought.
—I don't want riches, I don't want honors—,
he said to all.

In the siege of Jojutla
One of the elders said:
—Bring General García,
so that he [will] accompany me to the front.

In the shade of a guava tree
Two crickets sang:
—Mister Zapata, terror of the *gachupines* [derogatory word for European-born Spaniards],
has already died!

When the scuffle has ended
pardon the prisoners,
heal the wounded,
and to the poor, give them money.

Little star that at night
hangs from far off peaks,
where is our leader Zapata
who was the punishment of the rich?

—When I have died—he says to a subaltern—
you will tell the boys:
with weapon in hand you will defend your *ejidos* [communally held land]
like a man should.

He says to his loyal assistant
when they went about in the hills:
while I am alive, the Indians
will be the owners of their land.

Sweet-smelling little poppy
from the hills of Guerrero,
you will never again see
the famous fighter.

With great sorrow he says to his old lady:
—I feel beaten down,
so everyone should rest, I am the wanderer
Like a bird without a nest.

Generals come and go,
They say to calm us;
and not able to do good by him,
they made a plan to deceive him.

Sing, sing little sparrow,
in your melodious song tell:
General Zapata fell
By the hands of traitors.

Don Pablo González orders Guajardo
to act as if he surrendered,
and upon his arrival at camp
shoot Zapata with their guns.

Guajardo says to Zapata:
I and my troops surrender;
in Chinameca I await you,
and we will have a drink.

Turbulent little stream,
What did that carnation tell you?
—He says that Zapata has not died,
and he will return.

Central Themes

Indigenous people, state formation, popular culture, land and labor

Suggested Reading

Brunk, Samuel. *The Posthumous Career of Emiliano Zapata: Myth, Memory, and Mexico's Twentieth Century.* Austin: University of Texas Press, 2008.

Hart, John Mason. *The Coming and Process of the Mexican Revolution.* Berkeley: University of California Press, 1997.

Knight, Alan. *The Mexican Revolution.* vols. 1 and 2. Lincoln: University of Nebraska Press, 1986.

Simmons, Merle E. *The Mexican Corrido as a Source for Interpretive Study of Mexico, 1870–1950.* Bloomington: Indiana University Press, 1957.

Related Sources

51. *Corridos* from the Porfiriato (the Early 1900s)
53. Revolution in Morelos (1911)
54. Land, Labor, and the Church in the Mexican Constitution (1917)
58. Plutarco Elías Calles: The Legal Challenges of the Postrevolutionary State (1928)
67. Rubén Jaramillo and the Struggle for *Campesino* Rights in Postrevolutionary Morelos (1967)

56. The Catholic Church Hierarchy Protests (1917, reprinted 1926)*

Tensions between the Mexican government and the Catholic Church date back to at least the Era of Reform. The Catholic hierarchy opposed aspects of the Constitution of 1917 from the start. And whereas President Álvaro Obregón had not focused on the anticlerical articles of the Constitution, President Plutarco Elías Calles sought to enforce them. In February 1926, as conflict between the Catholic Church, the Catholic faithful, and the federal government intensified, the Catholic Church once again made its protest public by republishing its criticisms in a leading Mexico City newspaper, *El Universal*. In the protest, Archbishop José Mora y del Río lays out several arguments, many of which date from mid-nineteenth-century church-state conflicts in Mexico (sources 42 and 43). On July 31, 1926, the archbishop declared a strike that would last for three full years. During this time, many priests refused to celebrate central rites such as baptism and last rites. Others did so secretly. Such divisions underlay the Cristero Rebellion (1926–1928), which would leave many dead and the country greatly divided. How is the written protest an expression of tensions that dated back to the Era of Reform, or even earlier—to concerns that José María Morelos had expressed in the Era of Independence (Source 33)? How does the protest use the concepts of nation and citizen?

---

*Ernesto de la Torre Villar et al., eds., *Historia documental de Mexico*, vol. 2 (Mexico: Universidad Nacional Autonoma de México, Instituto de Investigaciones Históricas, 1964), p. 630. Translated by the editors.

The 1917 Constitution wounds the sacrosanct rights of the Catholic Church, of Mexican society, and of Christian individuals; it proclaims [principles] contrary to the truths taught by Jesus Christ, which are the treasure of the Church, the greatest patrimony of humanity, and it violently uproots the few rights conceded by the Constitution of 1857. . . .

Not presuming to implicate ourselves in political questions, we seek rather to defend, in a manner possible for us, the religious freedom of Christian people in the face of this abrupt attack inflicted on religion; we confine ourselves to forceful but decorous protest against this aggression. . . .

1st In accordance with the doctrines of the Roman Pontiffs . . . and motivated also by patriotism, we are far from approving armed rebellion against the established authorities, while not believing that passive submission to any government implies intellectual and voluntary approval of antireligious and unjust laws that emanate from it. Neither do we intend that Catholics, our faithful supporters, should therefore be deprived of the rights granted them as citizens to work legally and peacefully to counter national laws, when these offend their conscience and their rights. . . .

Our only motive is to comply with the obligation that defense of the rights of the Church and of religious freedom requires of us. . . . As heads of the Catholic Church in our fatherland, we protest against the tendency of the Constitutional Assembly, destroyer of religion, culture, and traditions. . . .

For all the aforementioned reasons, we protest against all such aggressions that diminish religious freedom and the rights of the Church and we declare that we do not recognize any act or pronouncement, even those issued from a lawful ecclesiastic within our diocese, if it is contrary to these declarations and protests. . . .

Central Themes

State formation, religion

Suggested Reading

Butler, Matthew. *Popular Piety and Political Identity in Mexico's Cristero Rebellion: Michoacán, 1927–1929.* New York: Oxford University Press, 2007.

Connaughton, Brian F. *Clerical Ideology in a Revolutionary Age: The Guadalajara Church and the Idea of the Mexican Nation, 1788–1853*, trans. Mark Alan Healy. Calgary: University of Calgary Press, 2003.

Curly, Robert. "Anticlericalism and Public Space in Revolutionary Jalisco," in *The Americas* 65, no. 4 (2009): 511–533.

Meyer, Jean. *The Cristero Rebellion: The Mexican People Between Church and State, 1926–1929,* trans. Richard Southern. Cambridge: Cambridge University Press, 1976.

Related Sources

30. Mexico's Paradoxical Enlightenment (1784)
42. The Reconfiguration of Property Rights and of Church-State Relations (1856)
43. Offer of the Crown to Maximilian by the Junta of Conservative Nobles (1863)
54. Land, Labor, and the Church in the Mexican Constitution (1917)

57. Petitioning the President (the 1920s)*

In Mexico, the practice of petitioning dates back to the colonial period. The following documents are petitions and letters directed to the president of the Republic, sent at different times and from different locations throughout the country. Each letter suggests the range of means by which Mexicans interacted with the federal government and illustrates the sorts of issues that emerged at the regional level in the aftermath of the Revolution. We might ask questions about the genre of letters to the president as well as regarding the specific content of these letters. What insight do these letters provide into what people hoped to gain from writing to the federal government during this period? With regard to content, how might we think of the Revolution as providing an opening for such petitions? How do racial tensions manifest themselves in these letters, and how might we explain the nature of such tensions in Mexico at this time? What do the letters reveal about unintended consequences of the Revolution?

Telegram (1922)

Telegram. Hermosillo, Sonora, June 27, 1922.

President of the Republic.—

Since the 12th of this month, by order of the Governor, nationals who are members of the society I represent, and many others who do not pertain to any organization, all businessmen, farmers, and peaceful workers have been detained in the jail of this city and in other places. This has been done without their being notified of the reason for their detention and without their being allowed to defend themselves. All possible means have been exhausted, with no success in getting the Governor to concede to those detained any of the guarantees usually granted to the most hardened criminals. I respectfully beg that you order the Most Honorable Governor to allow the incarcerated compatriots to defend themselves, so that if they are culpable, they be justifiably punished. Those of this society and those who are neutral that have been detained number one hundred and thirty-six, and businesses and families are abandoned and suffering to the point of breaking, without reason. And, according to news circulating around here they are trying to expel the detained without trial. I implore you Mister President in the name of humanity and justice for my compatriots. Interim President Chee Kung Fong. Juan Lin Fu.

---

*María del Carmen Nava Nava, *Los abajo firmantes: Cartas a los presidentes,* Colección Retrato Hablado (Mexico: Secretaría de Educación Pública, Unidad de Publicaciones Educativas, 1994), pp. 66–67, 112, 164. Translated by the editors.

Telegram (1924)

Mexican Telegraphic Company
March 1 1924
To His Excellency President Obregón, México

The Chinese residents of Sonora complain of the losses and privations they will suffer if the new law is enforced that obliges them to settle only within certain zones. My government would receive it as evidence of good friendship if your Excellency used all his influence to obtain the nullification of such a severe law.

Sun Yat Sen
President of the Republic of China

Letter (1922)

Honorable Sir Álvaro Obregón, Constitutionalist President of the United States of Mexico:

We the undersigned, *vecinos* [residents] of the age of majority of Mixquiahuala de Juárez, Actopam, Hidalgo, respectfully declare:

That by virtue of the innumerable difficulties which, for reasons of politics have put our lives and those of our families in danger, disturbing the public peace, creating a conflict which people have unjustifiably wanted to characterize as agrarian, though it is not, for in no part of the Republic would the agrarian question have been better resolved than in Mixquiahuala de Juárez; however, passions that have been stirred up have caused this conflict, in which the National Agrarian Commission is involved, for the facts of the case have been presented to them on various occasions, as you will see below; however, said Commission, despite efforts we have made to be heard, has remained deaf to our protests; and, there has not been any resolution to the decisions and good deeds that you, Mister President, have carried out to resolve the conflict, and for this reason we once again recur to you to demand justice.

General Facts

1.—*Years from 1622 to 1922.*—Beginning in the year 1622, the *pueblo* [town] of Mixquiahuala de Juárez began to file complaints regarding the Ulapa *Hacienda* [agricultural estate] regarding land issues, the result of which were various declarations, all of which found in favor of the pueblo. However, bad governments, which have come one after another since that date until the year 1915, did not take into account that we were protected by reason, and that justice was ours, and disregarding the decisions of the tribunals, never resolved the case.

2.—This being the case, and in accordance with the Plan de Ayala of 1915, and as the respective Acts verify, the lands that the *pueblo* [town] demanded were restituted, enacting, finally, a provisional distribution of lands in which all the petitions for parcels that were presented were attended to.

3.—With the Constitutional Government already established, in accordance with the decree of January 6, 1915, the Governor of the State was petitioned and from him we received recognition of the provisional possession of lands, with the Governor of the State naming an Executive Committee for the *Ejidos* [communally held lands] of Mixquiahuala, which continued to distribute parcels.

4.—In the year 1919, the Federal Government sent as delegate of the National Agrarian Commission, Engineer Don Ignacio L. Figueroa, who made it known that he was not going to give us lands, but rather, that he came as a mediator between the owners of Ulapa Hacienda and the vecinos of this pueblo, in order that the lands would be bought by those who had a right to receive parcels as long as the size of said parcels did not exceed fifty hectares. And indeed, such parcels were established. (All of the previous can be verified in the presidential resolution agreed upon in the distribution of ejidos of Mixquiahuala de Juárez.)

5.—On January 29, 1922, as warranted by clauses I and II of Article 40 of the Law of Ejidos of December 25, 1920, the pueblo of Mixquiahuala was called together to carry out election of the Administrative Committee of Ejidos of the pueblo. The election was carried out in accordance with the terms set forth by law and in accordance with democratic practices. Later, the Local Agrarian Commission of the State of Hidalgo, and the governor of the same [state] recognized those elections.

6.—While having already taken definitive possession of those lands since the year 1920, as a result of the agreement made by the government of Adolfo de la Huerta to grant ejidos to our pueblo, the situation began to change, and modifications were imposed upon the distribution of lands, lands which had already been granted to us and of which we had already taken possession; and, lacking legal standing that would have determined the means by which it should be carried out, and having elected the Administrative Committee, and having been signed by those people of standing of the pueblo, and of the most intellectual and moral distinction to correct the previous divisions, . . . we began to work the land, advancing along a path of order and equity, when professional politicians interfered with the intention of resolving an agrarian conflict which did not exist.

7.—The aforementioned Committee functioned until the month of July of last year, without having mediated a single protest during this time, when tempers were incited by political passions, which is substantiated by the fact of the election of deputies, and then an agitator by the name of Manuel Hera, partisan of the *agrarista** representative Matías Rodríguez, who had initiated his electoral candidacy in the Tula Electoral District, to which our pueblo pertains, and who turned to the

*Adjective to describe someone who allied himself with the agrarian politics of the Mexican federal government.

National Agrarian Commission with foolish complaints, and we do not know what sort of influence he exercises or what he must have done, but the fact of the matter is that last year on August 3 the State of Hidalgo Attorney for Ejidos, [called] for a new election. . . .

8. The situation has become untenable, our lives are at risk, public peace has been disrupted, and in the name of the highest right, the right to life—that no one can take away—we turn to you, Mister President, so that you impose your authority and with all your effort resolve the conflict which people have wanted to say is agrarian by nature, and is not. For this reason we the undersigned have invoked our right to make, to you, Mister President, the following requests:

First.—That an Attorney for Pueblos be designated so that, in accordance with circular number 22, issued October, 1922, he call together all heads of family to elect an Administrative Committee.

Second.—That the president of the Republic send a person of the utmost trustworthiness to oversee this election.

Third.—That the election be carried out according to the following stipulations: I. That a census of all the families of this pueblo be made, a census that will be overseen by the Presidency. . . .

These, Mister President, are our requests, which fall within the law, and, so, we hope you will attend to our entreaty. . . . Justice is what we ask for . . . Mixquiahuala de Juárez, March 22, 1923. Signatures follow.

Letter (1927)

It is with pleasure that we, all the members of the "Women's Union," send along a photograph that was taken the day of the inauguration of our workshop for the production of work clothing [made] with the canvas and denim that, with such good will, you provided us with, so that we might better ourselves economically; and, as a result of which, as of today has opened to new horizons. We once again repeat our thanks and with pleasure offer our constant support in the social and economic improvement of women.

Effective suffrage. No re-election.

El Puerto de Concepción Tep, Aguascalientes, the 10th of February, 1927.

Signing for the Women's Board of Directors, General Secretary, Miss Refugio García and Secretary of the Intr. [Interior] Miss Jesus Muñóz.

Juan Navarrte, Representative of the Community and Chief of Civil Defense of Zinzinmacato, Morelia Municipality and District.

Central Themes

Indigenous people, state formation, land and labor, gender

Suggested Reading

Olcott, Jocelyn. *Revolutionary Women in Postrevolutionary Mexico.* Durham, NC: Duke University Press, 2005.

Peña Delgado, Grace. "At Exclusion's Southern Gate: Changing Categories of Race and Class Among Chinese Fronterizos, 1882–1904." In *Continental Crossroads: Remapping U.S.-Mexico Borderlands History,* ed. Samuel Truett and Elliot Young. Durham, NC: Duke University Press, 2004.

Warman, Arturo. *We Come to Object: The Peasants of Morelos and the National State,* trans. Stephen K. Ault. Baltimore: Johns Hopkins University Press, 1980.

Related Sources

47. Precursors to Revolution (1904, 1906)
49. Land and Society (1909)
53. Revolution in Morelos (1911)
54. Land, Labor, and the Church in the Mexican Constitution (1917)
63. We the Undersigned (1941, 1945)
67. Rubén Jaramillo and the Struggle for *Campesino* Rights in Postrevolutionary Morelos (1967)

58. Plutarco Elías Calles: The Legal Challenges of the Postrevolutionary State (1928)*

With a new constitution and a growing set of government offices, the Mexican government expanded to accomplish the work of putting into effect the goals of the Revolution. The government, as a series of institutions, was tenuously held together by a group of politicians who had emerged from the military phase of revolution. The fragility of this coalition was revealed when President Álvaro Obregón was shot by a Catholic zealot in 1928, and the question of presidential succession fell into question. Plutarco Elías Calles, the incumbent president, made a speech before Congress on September 1, 1928, urging his fellow revolutionaries to consider how to proceed. The speech lays out some of the challenges that Mexicans faced at the moment. What are those challenges, and how might we understand them as integral to the transition away from earlier forms of governance in Mexico? In what ways was Calles limited by other political movements of the era—for example, Maderismo, as expressed in the Plan de San Luís Potosí or the military (Source 52)? How might we consider this speech an early step toward the creation of the National Revolutionary Party (Partido National Revolucionario, PNR), a precursor to the Party of the Institutionalized Revolution (Partido Revolucionario Institutional, PRI) in 1946?

---

*Gilbert M. Joseph and Timothy J. Henderson, *The Mexico Reader: History, Culture, Politics* (Durham, NC: Duke University Press, 2002), pp. 421–426.

Mexico Must Become a Nation of Institutions and Laws

The death of the president-elect is an irreparable loss which has left the country in an extremely difficult situation. There is no shortage of capable men: indeed, we are fortunate to have many capable individuals. But there is no person of indisputable prestige, who has a base of public support and such personal and political strength that his name alone merits general confidence.

The general's death brings a most grave and vital problem to public attention, for the issue is not merely political, but one of our very survival.

We must recognize that General Obregón's death exacerbates existing political and administrative problems. These arise in large measure from our political and social struggle: that is, they arise from the definitive triumph of the guiding principles of the Revolution, social principles like those expressed in articles 27 and 123 [of the Constitution], which must never be taken away from the people. At the start of the previous administration, we embarked on what may be called the political or governmental phase of the Mexican Revolution, searching with ever increasing urgency for ways to satisfy political and social concerns and to find means of governing appropriate to this new phase.

All of these considerations define the magnitude of the problem. Yet the very circumstances that Mexico now confronts—namely, that for perhaps the first time in our history there are no *caudillos* [regional or military leaders]—give us the opportunity to direct the country's politics toward a true institutional life. We shall move, once and for all, from being a "country ruled by one man" to a "nation of institutions and laws."

The unique solemnity of this moment deserves the most disinterested and patriotic reflection. It obliges me to delve not only into the circumstances of this moment, but also to review the characteristics of our political life up until now. It is our duty to fully understand and appreciate the facts which can ensure the country's immediate and future peace, promote its prestige and development, and safeguard the revolutionary conquests that hundreds of thousands of Mexicans have sealed with their blood.

I consider it absolutely essential that I digress from my brief analysis to make a firm and irrevocable declaration, which I pledge upon my honor before the National Congress, before the country, and before all civilized peoples. But first, I must say that perhaps never before have circumstances placed a chief executive in a more propitious situation for returning the country to one-man rule. I have received many suggestions, offers, and even some pressures—all of them cloaked in considerations of patriotism and the national welfare—trying to get me to remain in office. For reasons of morality and personal political creed, and because it is absolutely essential that we change from a "government of caudillos" to a "regime of institutions," I have decided to declare solemnly and with such clarity that my words cannot lend themselves to suspicions or interpretations, that not only will I not seek the prolongation of my mandate by accepting an extension or designation as provisional president, but I will never again on any occasion aspire to the presidency of my country. At the risk of making this declaration needlessly emphatic, I will add that this is not merely an aspiration or desire on my own part, but a positive and immutable fact: never again will an incumbent president of the Mexican Republic return to occupy the presidency. Of course, I have absolutely no intention of abandoning my duties as citizen, nor do I intend to retire from the life of struggle and responsibility that is the lot of every soldier and of all men born of the Revolution. . . .

Historical judgment, like all a posteriori judgments, is often and necessarily harsh and unjust, for it overlooks the pressing circumstances that determine attitudes and deeds. I do not intend to review the history of Mexico merely to cast blame on the men who became caudillos owing to the frustrations of our national life. Those frustrations—the inert condition of the rural masses, who have now been awakened by the Revolution; the sad, nearly atavistic passivity of citizens of the middle and lower classes, who fortunately have also been awakened—inspired those caudillos to identify themselves . . . with the fatherland itself. They styled themselves "necessary and singular" men.

I need remind no one of how the caudillos obstructed—perhaps not always deliberately, but always in a logical and natural way—the formation of strong alternative means by which the country might have confronted its internal and external crises. Nor need I remind you how the caudillos obstructed or delayed the peaceful evolution of Mexico into an institutional country, one in which men are what they should be: mere accidents, of no real importance beside the perpetual and august serenity of institutional laws. . . .

I would never suggest such a path if I feared, even remotely, that it could cause us to take a single step backward from the conquests and fundamental principles of the Revolution. . . . [I suggest this path] out of the conviction that effective freedom of suffrage must be extended even to groups representing the reaction, including the clerical reaction. This should not alarm true revolutionaries, for we have faith that the new ideas have affected the conscience of nearly all Mexicans, and that the interests created by the Revolution are now much stronger than those represented by the reaction, even if it were to be victorious. The districts where the political or clerical reaction wins the vote will, for many years at least, be outnumbered by those where the progressive social revolutionaries triumph.

Not only will the presence of conservative groups not endanger the new ideas or the legitimate revolutionary institutions; their presence will also prevent revolutionary groups from weakening and destroying themselves through internal squabbling, which is what happens when one finds oneself without an ideological enemy. . . .

We revolutionaries are now sufficiently strong—having achieved a solid basis in law, in the public consciousness and in the interests of the vast majority of people—that we need not fear the reaction. We invite that reaction to take up the struggle in the field of ideas, for in the field of armed combat—which is the easier of the two forms of struggle—we have triumphed completely, as those groups representing liberal ideas of social progress have always done. . . .

I would not be behaving honorably if I did not point out the many dangers that could result from dissension within the revolutionary family. If such dissension should occur, it would be nothing new in the history of Mexico, which has at times abounded in shady, backroom political dealings that brought to power ambitious, unprincipled men who weakened and delayed the final triumph of progress and liberalism in Mexico, surrendering themselves, whether consciously or not, to our eternal enemies.

I have spoken of our political adversaries with special tolerance and respect, even going so far as to declare the urgency of accepting the representatives of every shade of the reaction into the Chamber of Congress if they win in perfectly honorable democratic struggles. Having said this, I should be permitted to insist that, if one day ambition, intrigue, or arrogance should fracture the revolutionary group that for so many years was united in the struggle for a noble cause—that of the betterment of the great majority of the country—then the conservatives will once again seize the opportunity to insinuate themselves. If this happens, it is almost certain that the reaction will not need to secure a direct military or political triumph. History and human nature permit us to foresee that there will be no shortage of disaffected revolutionaries who, upon failing to find sufficient support from the disunited revolutionary factions, would call insistently at the doors of our old enemies. This would not only endanger the conquests of the Revolution, but it would surely provoke a new armed social conflict that would be more terrible even than those the country has already suffered; and when the revolutionary movement triumphed, as it must triumph, after years of cruel struggle, Mexico would be bled dry and would lack the strength to resume the march forward from the point where it was interrupted by our ambitions and dishonor.

Finally, in my triple capacity as revolutionary, division general, and chief of the armed forces, I will address myself to the army. . . . We have an opportunity that is perhaps unique in our history. In the period that follows the interim presidency, all men who aspire to the presidency of the country, be they military men or civilians, will contend on the fields of honorable democracy. As I have so frankly pointed out, there will be many dangers for Mexico—dangers that imperil the revolution and the fatherland itself. Anyone who, during those anxious moments, abandons the line of duty and [tries] to seize power by any means other than those outlined in the Constitution, will be guilty of the most unforgivable criminal and unpatriotic conduct.

All members of the national army must be conscious of their decisive role in those moments. They must embrace the true and noble calling of their military career: to give honor and fidelity to the legitimate institutions. Thus inspired by the duties imposed upon them by their mission, they must reject and condemn all whispers and perverse insinuations from ambitious politicians who would seek to sway them. They must choose between doing their duty, and thereby winning the gratitude of the Republic and the respect of the outside world, and betraying the Revolution and the fatherland at one of the most solemn moments in its history. The latter course of conduct could never be condoned by society or history.

Central Themes

State formation

Suggested Reading

Buchenau, Jürgen. *Plutarco Elías Calles and the Mexican Revolution.* Lanham, MD: Rowman & Littlefield, 2007.

Knight, Alan, and Will Pansters. *Caciquismo in Twentieth-Century Mexico.* London: Institute for the Americas, 2005.

Related Sources

52. Francisco Madero's Challenge to Porfirio Díaz (1910)
53. Revolution in Morelos (1911)
54. Land, Labor, and the Church in the Mexican Constitution (1917)
67. Rubén Jaramillo and the Struggle for *Campesino* Rights in Postrevolutionary Morelos (1967)
69. Theft and Fraud (1970)

59. Feminism, Suffrage, and Revolution (1931)*

Margarita Robles de Mendoza, a tireless defender of the rights of women, was particularly active during the 1920s and 1930s. In this era, women increased their political and professional participation in Mexican life and rallied to pressure the federal government to fulfill promises made to them during the Revolution. Robles de Mendoza founded several organizations that worked both within and outside of Mexico to advance the status of women. She organized and served as head of the Union of American Women (Unión de Mujeres Americanas), and she led the Women's Section of the ruling political party, the Partido National Revolucionario (PNR). She was also Mexico's representative to the Interamerican Women's Commission (CIM). Robles de Mendoza challenged accepted ideas regarding Mexican women, such as the assumption that they were inherently religious and conservative, and that such tendencies had led them to oppose the Revolution. In word and deed, Robles de Mendoza called for acceptance of women as full citizens who had the right to exercise the vote and to participate in all aspects of Mexico's social, economic, and political life. When, in his December 1935 address to the nation, President Lázaro Cárdenas made statements in support of women's suffrage, women who had been ac-

*Margarita Robles de Mendoza, *La evolucion de la mujer en Mexico* (Mexico: Imp. Galas, 1931), pp. 97–104. Translated by the editors.

tive in a variety of organizations responded by building on the work of women like Robles de Mendoza and stepped up their efforts to secure the vote (Source 61).

The following article was published in 1931 as a collection of articles that had appeared over the previous several years in other venues, often the main Mexico City newspapers. It conveys the basis for Robles de Mendoza's claims for increased rights for women as well as of the sorts of arguments against which she had to contend. How does Mendoza address issues raised earlier in the century with regard to women and education, work, and public activity (sources 38 and 46)? Can you discern the sorts of justifications for restrictions on women's rights against which Mendoza argues? What gender norms does she not challenge? What accepted truths about the definitions of democracy, motherhood, and feminism does Robles de Mendoza challenge?

Feminism and Suffrage

New names for new things. Whether because of the newness of the term, or a lack of familiarity with its meaning, feminism is frequently spoken of mistakenly and with confusion.

The word is of recent introduction to the language; however it is surely not because it is new that there is confusion. Rather, this is due to a lack of care and clarity when the subject is breached.

There are male writers who define feminism as "the brutal struggle between man and woman." They surely forget that we live in an era of "passivism" and "good will," and that nothing noble comes from violence. There are, to be sure, women who, while they have worked for years for the social advancement of their sisters, say emphatically: "I am not a feminist," and there are some who are even ashamed of associating themselves with those who proclaim themselves feminists.

Feminism is the name given to the modern movement that seeks to defend the individual, economic, social, and political rights of women; however, this does not mean that all feminist women are necessarily and systematically rabid suffragists. They might be interested in the economic or social aspects of the movement, and not at all interested in interfering in political issues. In the same way, the world of politics is of no interest to an infinite number of talented and very useful men.

The vote is not all there is to feminism. The movement seeks the vote only as a means to achieve economic or social goals; however this is never an obsessively exclusive goal. Suffrage is a concession that feminists seek because they believe it is neither reasonable nor democratic that women are denied the vote when so many of them are morally, intellectually, and even physically superior to many men who enjoy this privilege. Those women who wish to do so will exercise this right. It is not the case that all men exercise it [the right to vote], for if they did we would not see cases of Nations and States where only two per cent of the citizenry votes.

Feminism seeks respect for women's selfhood, that she be treated as a human being and as a prescient adult; it does not seek to abuse, but to share, participate, and cooperate.

From the time we are little girls, we learn, along with our first letters, "that one place cannot be occupied by two bodies at the same time." How, then, could we seek to displace from their positions those [men] who, due to ancient custom and preeminent qualifications, successfully carry out those responsibilities?

A place for women in the social realm. We ask only that in the realm of human society we are given the opportunity to put into play our abilities. Time and the exercise of those abilities will surely demonstrate if they are small or large.

In the first half of the nineteenth century, Comte was of the opinion that women had to be raised up and educated fully, but he wanted to see women excluded from material responsibilities and kept from participation in public matters. He was not aware that the industrial age was upon him, dragging women along with it, and that this would force him to clip the wings of his fantasy without, in so doing, losing the affective power that he attributed to women, nor her capacity to maintain her active and intellectual energies in continual subordination to sentiment. Now that positivism has failed as a philosophical system because of our bitter experiences in an age of crushing materialism, we march on the path toward spiritualism, with ever greater reason. We must seek broader horizons. Those who presume to see everything through a prism of that which is physical and palpable to the senses are out of touch with the times.

Feminism does not tear women from the home. We are abundantly aware that we are different from men; it is precisely because of this that we hope that there might be those who, in all life's activities, in thinking and feeling like we women do, can interpret and understand these "differences." For this reason, we are delighted to hear musical compositions written by women and we admire paintings and sculptures made by female hands. For this reason, we feverishly applaud the female public speaker; the female poet and dramaturge enthralls us because in works by women there are traces of the collective female soul, because in them we feel the vibrations of our spirit. It is for this reason as well that we ask that not only male criteria be taken into consideration in the making of laws, but that our criteria be taken into account as well, because women better understand women. It is for this reason as well that we want women to participate in juries and in the meting out of justice. Society is made up of two elements. Why should it be only one of them that produces, labors, and receives the satisfaction of its efforts?

Feminism does not propose to yank women from the home; rather, it seeks to provide a home for the woman who does not have one, and to accustom her to be the creative force within this sanctuary. By home, naturally, we understand, not the usual domicile, with its more or less adequate material comforts, but rather the space within which, as in a sanctuary, the most pure affections are enclosed, where the unification of elevated aspirations and the enthusiasm for cooperation among members of the family reign.

Better women will make better mothers. Undoubtedly the different stages through which women have acted in the world have not left her satisfied. From the time of the patriarchate until now, she has sometimes been master of her destiny by means of force or sexual attraction, but most often she has been a slave, subjected to egotistical impositions. What she seeks now is neither throne nor chain, but rather a moral equality that gives her soul the opportunity of completing the state of being one who is loved.

We have looked to the *soldadera* [female soldier] as a prototype of Mexican feminism, precisely because she is the one who most has shared in the life of her man. In a state of sublime primitivism, she has faithfully followed in his footsteps, and by his side she has sung his victory songs, and cried with grief at his defeat. He has taken her with him everywhere. Wife, friend, comrade, partner, all this she has been for her man, and this is exactly what feminism wants all women to be, whatever their level of culture or social position may be. Equal rights for men and women make their responsibilities equivalent, and equalize participation in matters pertaining to their life in common as well.

This is not to shun the sacrosanct obligation of deeming women the principal protagonist in the realm of human creation; however it does allow that nature does not choose all women to perpetuate the species, nor does compliance with this biological function carry with it the necessary preparation to conscientiously fulfill their obligations. . . .

Faced with a child who suddenly contracts diphtheria, the woman who knows first aid is more useful than the one who becomes hysterical and only knows how to cry, even when the former might have had to leave the house for a few hours to go to school, a clinic, or hospital to learn first aid while the other stayed at home sitting sweetly by the fireplace doing crochet.

A mother who at evening time sits with her child to help him with his history or algebra lessons, who takes an interest in his life at school, and who then comments to her husband about her favorite book, or who enjoys with him the pleasures of classical music, after having applied her knowledge of physics or chemistry to the care of her house or in the preparation of food, demonstrates a more perfect behavior than the one who, shielding herself behind "feminine ignorance," is startled by difficult words from science, or the one who uses a false modesty with regard to issues of transcendental importance, or the one who willy-nilly mixes ingredients that are prejudicial to the health of those who sit at her table.

The admission of women to universities is relatively recent, and we have already seen that their contributions to the advancement of the common good have not been inconsequential.

There is no need for alarm, for maternal love is a primal instinct and as such it cannot easily be destroyed or made dormant. There may be women who do not possess it, just as there are women born blind or without a sense of smell; but these women form the minority, and in any case, would be the same whether or not they gained economic, social, or political rights. There have always been the *marimacho* [butch] type—women who are discontent with their sex and seek compensations that lead them to behave ridiculously; and there have also been men who wanted to be women and who carry themselves with mannerisms; but these small anomalies of nature are the "fungus" on the tree of life.

Love continues to be the supreme ideal of all societies. There is no normal woman who voluntarily prefers the hazards of the struggle to earn her daily bread over the tranquility of the home. Those who throw themselves outside of the home do so impelled by economic necessity or moral imperative, and with regard to these women, it is preferable that they go out armed and not deprived of the possibility of success.

Feminists do not accept arbitrary limits in their lives. As human beings, they believe they have the same right as men to follow the path that pleases them and, of course, they are ready to suffer the consequences of their actions. They seek equality before the law and the treatment by society that corresponds to them as adults.

It is incongruous that children and the insane are not considered responsible for their actions, and in contrast all the force of the law is applied to women as it is to men. Women are considered equal when they are at fault. However, when it comes to the concession of rights, be they economic, social, or political, they are not conceded these rights "because they do not know how to make good use of them."

The most hardened man softens to the point of tears upon viewing the lioness who defends her cubs from the attacks of other wild beasts and, contrarily, condemns the woman who, leaving behind her dressing room and the vanity of finery, spends eight hours in front of a machine, and with each turn of the transmission or with her decline in status, delivers a blow to the wolf of misery that bares its teeth at the door of her house.

For such heroines, feminism holds warm embraces and words of encouragement; it is for them that feminism asks for equal wages when the results of those efforts are equal to those of men.

Far from the factory, the office, or the laboratory, far from the halls of justice, when, beyond the hustle and bustle of the daily struggle, they come together, now and forever, yesterday and tomorrow, with more or less refinement and nuance, he will be the man and she the woman.

Central Themes

Urban life, land and labor, gender

Suggested Reading

Mitchell, Stephanie, and Patience A. Schell. *The Women's Revolution in Mexico, 1910–1953.* Lanham, MD: Rowman & Littlefield, 2007.

Olcott, Jocelyn, Mary Kay Vaughan, and Gabriela Cano, eds. *Sex in Revolution: Gender, Politics, and Power in Modern Mexico.* Durham, NC: Duke University Press, 2006.

Porter, Susie S. *Working Women in Mexico City: Public Discourses and Material Conditions, 1879–1931.* Tucson: University of Arizona Press, 2003.

Related Sources

26. Sor Juana: Nun, Poet, and Advocate (1690)
38. Female Education (1842, 1851)
46. A Positivist Interpretation of Feminism (1909)
54. Land, Labor, and the Church in the Mexican Constitution (1917)
60. Chronicles of Mexico City (1938)
64. Modernization and Society (1951)

60. Chronicles of Mexico City (1938)*

Salvador Novo López (1904–1974) was one of Mexico's most celebrated and prolific writers. Novo worked in a wide range of media: theater, poetry, prose, translation, television, and historical essay. He is identified with *los contemporáneos,* a group of writers who emerged during the postrevolutionary period. He was a central contributor to the group, including as cofounder (along with Xavier Villarrutia) of the literary magazines *Ulises* (1927) and *Contemporáneos* (1928). Novo is known for his satiric verses and recognized as a skilled essayist. His poetry mocked modernism and what Novo saw as the propensity in Mexico at the time to open itself wholeheartedly to outside influences. In this sense, his work is considered nationalistic by some. Much of Novo's work is profoundly informed by history. In contrast to many of the documents included in this section on the Mexican Revolution, Novo's work focuses not on the countryside but on urban Mexico. Indeed, he is considered by many the official chronicler of Mexico City, and the first selection displays his love for that city, expressed in attention to the details of daily life and its transformation. The National Literature Prize was awarded to Novo in 1967.

The two essays included here draw on Novo's observations of the city and echo documents that he might have seen in his work as a Mexico City archivist. In bringing to life the color, smells, people, and practices of urban life, Novo also comments on modernization during his time. What changes does he note, and what do those changes mean, according to Novo, for Mexico City residents? How does Novo write about labor and consumption, two important issues in 1930s urban Mexico? How might we read Novo's essays as a critique of postrevolutionary Mexico? What comments does Novo make on class, ethnicity, and national culture?

---

*Salvador Novo, *Toda la prosa* (Mexico: Empresas Editoriales, S.A., 1964), pp. 79–83, 100–103. Translated by Tanya Huntington and the editors.

In Defense of What's Been Used

Not allowing ourselves to fully enjoy any person, place, or thing is one of the most deplorable signs of our time. Once we've acquired something, a new and improved model comes along to tempt our fickle ambition, inciting us to abandon the undiminished pleasures of a love affair, a car, a necktie, or a house, and exchange them for another one that boasts the ability to turn into a bed with an arthritic click of its back seat; or one that's been streamlined, or endowed with air conditioning, or silk-lined rails. The assembly line tears us brusquely away from an affection that had only just begun to flower within the lukewarm confines of our person; it takes the toy from our hands and leaves us with the enigma of a newer, colder one whose lights we don't quite understand how to turn on, whose *clutch** doesn't obey our former motor coordination—and once again, we adapt, so that a few months later, the phenomenon can repeat itself.

In this sense, the era of private property was far happier than ours. People had their pianos, their furniture, their wives, and their horses—and they lasted for as long as minor upkeep could maintain them. From the start, our ancestors took special pride in true "quality" (a word that modern advertising has stripped of all meaning), choosing objects of daily, moderate usage that filled their peaceful lives. They didn't have to risk a design change in some clothing-related fashion trend that had slowly, organically evolved, suddenly leaving the little woman (or the bed shared with said little woman) *passé*. It was enough for china, *buggy*, household, beings, and belongings to be good, solid, and presentably decent.

And then along came the invention of machines, no less. Any book or leader, whichever is closest at hand, will be more than happy to explain all of the Industrial Revolution's terrible implications for the members of a productive class that, under feudalism, had secured the privilege of having their own private little workshops in which things—nice and well-made things—were made by hand. They also managed to develop a worthy love for their trade and were known as "masters." They hadn't yet been felled (not until the machines appeared, that is) by the iron fist of a new master, a collective, alien workshop that hunger, not vocation, compelled them to join. But in order to explain this chaos, both books and leaders—preoccupied with saving humanity—part from the principle of compassion towards the exploited masses who, having grown more vehement and having turned a blind eye to the reality of their sentimental natures, believe they can fully dispense with all that, and translate the happiness of men into having men eat rational, scientific, and wholesome diets. Then they don revolutionary garments, both practical and uniform, inhabit *standard* housing, and satisfy their instincts in monotonous ways.

Neither books nor leaders, no matter how enlightened they may seem, take into account any desire of our time beyond that of inverting the schematics of the distri-

*English words in italics appear as such in the original.

bution of wealth. What irritates them about machines isn't the fact that they exist, but rather that they remain in the hands of those who own them; that only a few can gaze upon their gold-filled trunks, wrung from the sweating brows of thousands of comrades who toil alongside machines; that their *closets* are stuffed with suits of artificial wool woven by workers who dress in denim; that their obesity idles on eight cylinders assembled by athletic salaried employees who arrive at the factory in jalopies. But upon taking a closer look, we find that what irritates them isn't really the most irritating thing about machines.

Halfway from structure to superstructure, somewhere in between naked hunger and spiritual elevation, machines have come to build an inexorable bridge out of their awe-inspiring products. The result is that we all have to cross it. Nobody's free any longer to remain on this bank or that, or to reach the other side by swimming and thus breach the distance between their desire to hear music and the pleasure of playing it on a piano—something that fashion and the hybrid need to tune in London, Shanghai, and Australia have replaced with a twelve-bulb Philco.

While biology sends us off to work, in the purest sense of employing our energies solely by transforming them into individual pleasure, something useful in and of itself, economic-social *usefulness*—that absurdity of materialist logic—is the monstrous industrial spawn of a civilizing doctrine that aspires to forget the fact that in this universe, identifying A with A is an abstraction that has been debunked every step of the way by the facts, by phenomena and by objects; that the non-biological, non-vocational labor that individuals are forced to perform in our mechanized society is to each and every one of them just as displeasing and repulsive as the unnecessary and fictitious collective happiness and pleasure that books and leaders struggle to guarantee through the conquest of a twenty-hour work week, higher wages, vacations, union congresses—not to mention the obligation to consume suits, automobiles, radios, films, and collective congresses.

What's irritating about machines isn't the way the factories they form part of are managed. Under the pitiless hand of a capitalist corporation, or cooperative, or cog in the revolutionary gear of a Gosplan* that predetermines their performance (and shoots *as Trotskyites* all those who, biologically destined to efficiently perform as gardeners, are put to work at a seeding machine that they "sabotage" by breaking it); the lamentable- thing is that they intend to make us all equal in utilitarian happiness through their products. They make objects that are more and more perfect, and less linked to us, more and more "in our stead." Because aside from increasingly limiting our activity—disabling an organism that is made to adapt itself to the cold, wind, and sun, and doing so directly and gloriously; and providing it, in exchange, for a modest price, with ultraviolet rays in the bedroom, technical massages and wool socks—these new and improved objects have taken their toll on the spirit, engendering within a truly senseless psychosis of possession and persecution of the superfluous-individual,

*"Gosplan" refers to the Soviet Union State Planning Committee.

which passes for the useful-collective. And no matter what the final result of the class struggle turns out to be, those who possess machines as well as those who operate them today; those who manage them as well as those who set them in motion tomorrow; all will be to blame for machines having destroyed the sense of that which is enduring in man.

Which, incidentally, has come to pose the secondary, but no less primordial conundrum of second-hand items. Divorcées, automobiles, suits, and shoes all remain in such good shape when we've abandoned them for a newer model, that it makes no sense to destroy them simply because we no longer have any use for them. There have always been those who settled for *second best*, but this considerable portion of humanity, one that finds highly convincing reasons to hang a *sarape* from Saltillo instead of a Persian tapestry in its living room, has never before had greater opportunities for satisfaction. Opportunities born from those wasted by the rich or the naïve, troubled victims of a psychosis of inauguration, who dispense with the nut the moment it's been shelled.

Collectors and antiquarians elude this broad group of second-hand buyers of things, because what they seek are books, paintings, works of art: that is to say, things that are of no use whatsoever. And yet they are joined, without being any the wiser, by a fact inherent to all second-hand objects, whether they are as useful as an illuminated manuscript or a Goya, as serviceable as a 1934 Chevrolet or a pair of Florsheims acquired at the Lagunilla flea market: the human warmth of the previous owner, manifest in the fingerprints its pages boast, or the comfortable sinkage of old cushions, in the molding of the footwear or suit to the peculiarities of a poor person's anatomy, on which anything sits well. Without knowing it, without realizing it, antiquarians and buyers of second-hand objects have come together in the search for a human imprint that is absent from new, mechanical products, but already present, lukewarm, familiar, and satisfactory in used ones. When the artisan created his objects by hand, he was working, therefore, in the best biological and vocational sense of his aptitude; he expressed himself by doing so and communicated to his creation a desire for immortality that made it lasting, pleasing, beautiful, and immediately and indispensably useful to that kindred spirit who, upon acquiring it, understood and treasured it, proud to permanently possess it and incapable of trading it in for a newer model. Quite the opposite takes place now that objects are made not by men, but by machines. Set upon seeing who will finish first, machines and man compete to win with uniformly accelerated drive, the former, through their production of superfluous novelties; the latter, in his capacity to consume them as soon as they appear on the market.

The trouble is that highway accidents, shootings, and several other resources of which modern technology has availed itself to absorb the surplus of spouses and cars, find their efficiency thwarted by correlating progress in the construction of roads, the adoption of four-wheel brakes, and emergency surgery. Imminent Justice conspires against the destructive zeal of these "premièrers," and has shown itself to be a faithful ally of all those who love what's used. These are the ones—sensible, conservative—who turn up their noses at the ephemeral flower, awaiting instead its seasoned fruit. They know all too well that a second-hand car can now venture out onto any highway, that it can attain any speed the pedal can impress upon it; that the *spray* can be tightened in order to avoid wasting so much fuel, and that one more dent in its already much-hammered fenders hardly matters. Very similar considerations—and tactics—can be applied to any other half-used object.

In conclusion, the portion of humanity that laughs last continues to laugh best; the one that bears on its shoulders a suit that originally belonged to someone else, and in its brain, a second-hand doctrine. The one that inhabits a home whose vanquished humidity already conferred its rheumatism on the over-anxious individual who inaugurated it, wherein is heard a 1933 radio—just as good, but much cheaper, than the 1938 model the neighbor is paying for in distressing installments—because at the end of the day, he and his neighbor are going to be listening to exactly the same drivel.

This sensible portion of humanity that enjoys used items, who are looked down upon so unjustifiably by the other half that peels their fruit for them, is not necessarily composed of beings who can't afford the latest, but rather by individuals who exercise their will, measure their coexistence, await their chance, and take advantage of others' experience. Its ranks tend to be filled by very distinguished persons. King Edward VIII, for example. . . .

The Markets

"When I travel—says André Gide—, I am attracted to four things above all: the public garden, the market, the cemetery, and the Palace of Justice." I am reminded of these words, which begin the *Souvenirs de la Cour D'Assises,* now that the coming of a new Palace of Justice has quickly dispersed the extremely peculiar "Colonial Paradise" that was the El Volador [market], which had suddenly aged, at the same time that it is made classic by the most recent psychological description of the market that we find in *Pero Galín* by Genaro Estrada.

Perpetual flea market, El Volador offered us the most delicious of provincial Mexican traditions in the possibility of haggling over and of discovering in it anything from orange leaves to broad-rimmed hats. Its peculiar location meant that long before the exodus, the products that had previously been exclusive to El Volador spontaneously appeared in other various, more accessible locations which nevertheless were no less constantly crowded—and this they call progress. This is how the Volador-style of life came about at the La Lagunilla and Mixcoalco markets, at the same time that all the rest, from Martínez de la Torre to the Mercado Juárez, from the San Cosme to the "2nd of April" and that of San Juan, allowed in their midst, or their co-midsts, products that until that moment had not appeared in the usual commercial trade. And alongside the vegetables—greens—, and the fresh and bright egg stands, one finds cream from Toluca, and butter wrapped in leaves, fruit (oh, and now they are Californian, like the movies!), in boxes from which emerge the sweet, old-fashioned little apples, San Juan pears, *capulines,** *tejocotes,*** and fresh jícama, Córdoba mangoes, Tabasco bananas, avocados, *cuaresmeño*† chiles, pomegranates, quinces, and black and small zapotes: along with this, and much more, along with the fish, the chickens in perpetual dive, the dough and tortillas, the herbalists and the little boys who carry baskets or "the nets that they used in the olden days to go to the beach," [along with all this,] the Siro-Lebanese community, which has a great sense of color, began to put up stalls to sell cloth and ready-made clothing.

And given that cloth does not rot, their invasion was unstoppable. What in the olden days was a normal market gave way—precisely—to the sweetest new styles; and green grocers, little egg shops, etc., retreated to open up and install themselves in other, less confusing locations. The Department of Sanitation, zealous in its mission, forgot, in its electropure arrangements, the poetic consideration of folklore, and eliminated and sterilized the tortilla and meat vendors, saving contemptible individual stomachs at the expense of the traditional collective and, we might even say, national beauties.

The vogue of tin cans, herald of tinplate-civilization, helped the work of the cooks enormously—albeit with so many artistic disadvantages! Now one buys tomato sauce, *pickles,* and "Tabasco" in stores called *Piggly Wiggly* and they even deliver to your home whatever you order by telephone. Manual labor is in a truly Western decline.

Why don't we take the example of the maid. And let us not worry about her duties within the house, for the execution of which, in place of a broom made of straw with which they used to clean out the corners so well, they now use brushes for waxing and even electric *vacuum cleaners,* to say nothing of the electric irons which are the cause of those delicious anafres lights, and the collection of irons to test with a finger, moistened with spit, of the maid, made an indescribable "Chhhh"; nor of the coffee "Fortaleza" or "Teka," which has also banished the practice of toasting at home and the music of the coffee grinder, or the chocolate that is no longer ground on the *metate* [grinding stone]. Let us, instead of examining her personal life, see to what degree the transformation of markets has affected her, in as much as we are able.

We know, from the solemn testimony of History, how the Indians, in their propensity for trinkets, facilitated the flight of Aztec gold in exchange for Castillian glass beads. Habits have not changed much, and although the best gold that remains is that of our customs, even this is fleeing, like in olden days, in exchange for glass beads, which today are called *chaquiras* [glass beads].

---

*Small wild cherries native to Mexico.

**Mexican Hawthorn berries.

†A large variety of jalapeño with dark skin marked by long dark-brown streaks.

It used to be that maids made their own clothing—of wide and folded petticoats, with some sort of ruffle, a blouse fastened with embroidered ties and lace, made from brilliant pink cloth that sits so well on the earthen-brown skin of their arms. They wore necklaces made of cut paper and real gold earrings made by very skilled hands. On their chest they had, in distinctive fashion, a button with a picture of the one who, sooner or later, would steal them away. And all this covered with a heavy and graceful *rebozo* [traditional Mexican shawl] upon which rested, like two interjections, their black medieval braids.

None of this is left to us any longer. In the market there are dresses that hang like ghosts, and the maids fit very well in them. There are those made of percale for daily use, but they do not have long and wide petticoats but rather slips irregularly cut, with absurd lace and incongruous ruffles. For days off, there are dresses of blue silk, embroidered with white beads, orange with black appliqué, or those completely and inexorably red. These suggest La Malinche, who gets out her beads and buys herself a dress. She also buys meat-colored stockings (meat of what color?) and a purse. In the purse she carries a photo-mirror of he who, sooner or later, will steal her away. All she has to do now is cut her hair, and she ought to do so.

Ancient markets, the authentic ones, are now only seen in the villages of Mexico. In our city, the markets have become specialized and the ladies find their greatest pleasure in acquiring cloth at La Lagunilla to make their clothing, flowers in San Juan, provisions and fruit for their pantry at La Merced. This latter market has the totally brutal appearance of a railroad boxcar. Wholesale transactions are done there. La Lagunilla has, by contrast, the affable appearance of a bazaar that on Sundays extends and grows into the neighboring streets for the sale of all sorts of old objects: lamps, chairs, books.

San Juan market is also a specialized market. When the old Flower market was thrown out of the *Zócalo* [main plaza], a separation of the sale of flowers for the living and flowers for the dead was achieved. The [vendors] situated themselves along the front of the Alameda, near these horrible agencies that all day long show seven wakes in search of a dead person. The others appeared in San Juan market. They are there—red, yellow, blue, fresh—attempting to counter with their aroma the strong smells emitted by the oyster shops, mixed up with phonographs and radios, the last cry of the innocence and sweetness of life, and in defense against the boxed flowers that appear in elegant homes where they "say it with flowers" by telegraph.

Central Themes

Urban life, popular culture

Suggested Reading

Corona, Ignacio, and Beth E. Jorgensen, eds. *The Contemporary Mexican Chronicle: Theoretical Perspectives on the Liminal Genre.* Albany: State University of New York Press, 2002.

Monsiváis, Carlos. *Mexican Postcards,* trans. and with an introduction by John Kraniauskas. London: Verso, 1997.

Novo, Salvador. *The War of the Fatties and Other Stories from Aztec History,* trans. Michael Alderson. Austin: University of Texas Press, 1994.

Related Sources

6. Markets and Temples in the City of Tenochtitlan (1519)
22. On Chocolate (1648)
34. A Satirical View of Colonial Society (1816)
50. Popular Images of Mexican Life (the Late Nineteenth and Early Twentieth Centuries)
51. *Corridos* from the Porfiriato (the Early 1900s)
70. Serial Satire: The Comic Book (1974)

61. The Responsibility of Government and Private Enterprise to the Mexican People (1937–1938)*

Mexican economic sovereignty has often been tied up in tensions between Mexican workers and foreign-owned companies. Such was the case with the Cananea labor strike of 1906 (Source 48) and later in the century with the workers in the *maquilas* (multinational-owned factories) along the U.S.-Mexico border (Source 75). Such tensions reached a high point under the presidency of Lázaro Cárdenas (1934–1940), whose economic policies gave the state an increasing role in guiding economic development. By the 1920s, Mexico had become the world's second-largest oil producer. In 1937 a labor dispute between Mexican oil workers and foreign-owned oil companies intensified. The conflict played out in several arenas, one of which was the courts. The Mexican Council of Conciliation and Arbitration and then the Mexican Supreme Court both ruled in favor of the Mexican workers. The oil companies refused to recognize the legitimacy of the courts or the demands

**Mexico's Oil* (Mexico City: Government of Mexico, Mexico City, 1940), pp. 93–94; *El petróleo de México* (Mexico: Gobiernode Mexico, 1963), anexo 41; "Cárdenas Speaks," in *Readings in Latin American Civilization: 1492 to the Present,* ed. Benjamin Keen (Boston: Houghton Mifflin, 1955), pp. 362–364.

of Mexican workers. The Mexican government compiled a study, more than nine hundred pages long, in which it laid out its case, based in extensive study of the role of foreign investors in the oil industry and the legal aspects of the case. Excerpts of the study and selected photographs appear here. The reader might consider how the text and photographs complement each other. And how do these sources confirm popularly held ideas about foreigners in Mexico during the Mexican Revolution?

The conflict also played out in the political realm and on the streets. On March 18, 1938, Cárdenas made a radio address, which appears here as well, to the Mexican people to announce the nationalization of the oil companies. Cárdenas also called for citizens to help the government pay for the expropriations. By the thousands, ordinary citizens and organizations of all kinds contributed money and personal belongings, and people paraded in the streets in support and celebration. Still today, the day is celebrated as a national holiday. Following the expropriation, Cárdenas founded Petróleos Mexicanos (PEMEX), which would play a central role in the Mexican economy for decades to come and which served as a model to other countries that sought greater control over the natural resources of their own country. In the address that follows, how does Cárdenas justify expropriation? How does he speak of the rights of private industry, of the nation, and of its people?

The Real Purposes of the Companies

With a few exceptions, the objective of the oil companies in establishing themselves in Mexico has been the extraction of the petroleum wealth of our soil, the existence of which had been evident for centuries because of the abundant seepages in various parts of the country, particularly in the region of the Gulf Coast. Their organization and the original nature of their plants were for the most part designed for the transport and shipment of the products abroad.

In some cases, the original objectives were different. In this connection we refer primarily to the Pierce Company, which was established in Mexico at the end of the last century for the purpose of supplying the domestic market with illuminating oil (kerosene), at that time in great demand. In general, the activities of this company have remained unchanged, as most of its refined products are destined for local consumption. Doheny began operating in Mexico upon the suggestion of the President of the Central Railways, many kilometers of whose lines traversed the Pánuco region, extremely rich in seepages. The immediate aim was to find oil to supply the railway system with the economical fuel to substitute the coal which it was then obliged to import in large quantities.

But if the original intention of Doheny was not to export, if it was later, when the development of his oil interests began to boom. The concession which he obtained for the construction of a pipeline to the Central Plateau, after making alluring promises to the Mexican Government of the great benefits that would be conferred on the center of the country by a supply of petroleum for its economic development, was exploited, together with the privileges it included, to import free of duty the materials and equipment he required for development operations. Instead of constructing the promised pipeline (which he never did) he built others to Tampico, with their respective loading terminal, for the purpose of exporting on a large scale the oil wealth he was discovering.

A superficial inspection of the kind of plant and equipment of the oil companies and of the orientation of their activities proves conclusively that everything has tended towards the purpose of depriving Mexico of the innumerable benefits derived from petroleum exploitation and to send them abroad to the advantages of other countries. A comparison of the volume of products left within the country with the volume of exports is the most eloquent confirmation of this condition. For example, while in 1918, 63,828,326 barrels were produced, 51,767,219 barrels, or 81 per cent, were exported. In 1922, our production was 182,278,457 barrels, of which 180,866,282 barrels, or 99 percent, were exported.

The pipeline systems, storage plants, pumping stations, terminals, loading wharves, etc., in Tampico, Puerto Lobos, Tuxpam, Nanchital, and Minatitlán have for the most part been designed, constructed, and equipped preferably or exclusively for exportation.

A typical case is the so-called Puerto Lobos (there never existed, nor was there ever subsequently constructed, a port, properly speaking, at this place); exclusively for purposes of exploitation, pipelines were laid from the rich oil fields of the Golden Lane to Puerto Lobos, the name given to the large portion of open coast southeast of a long strip of land which separates Tamiahua Lagoon from the Gulf of Mexico, and which extends from a few kilometers to the northeast of the City and Port of Tuxpam to the mouth of the Pánuco River. In the said Puerto Lobos, storage and pumping plants, loading wharves with submarine pipelines, and three small topping plants were constructed. Through this point and during the period of the most intensive exploitation of the Golden Lane (1918 to 1925), seven companies exported 194,265,000 barrels of crude oil, fuel oil, and distillates, with a value of approximately 430,430,000 pesos. Of all this enormous exported wealth, the country received nothing but the relative benefit of taxes collected. And neither Puerto Lobos nor the nearby port of Tuxpam underwent any beneficial transformation which might have converted them into real ports.

The fact is that Mexico has been considered by the majority of the oil companies as a colony from which to extract raw materials and to which manufactured goods may be sold.

It has been necessary for Mexico to take various measures in order to obtain, even though gradually and against the most bitter opposition of the companies, some effective benefit from this petroleum wealth, which is national and, by reason of traditional legal principles, belongs to the Nation.

It has been very difficult for Mexico to derive any benefit from the exploitation of its oil resources carried on principally by foreign enterprises, as they not only refused for a long time to accept the legal principles of national sovereignty over the petroleum of the subsoil and our systems of taxation, but have systematically sold at excessively high prices the products which they leave in the country.

The various measures adopted by the government have been, although slowly, producing fruitful results, and indirectly these measures have been aided by the increasing competition which the companies are meeting in foreign oil markets. It is to be hoped that eventually the whole, or at least the major part, of these valuable products will be consumed in this country.

At present, 61 per cent of our total production is exported, in place of the 99 per cent which, as we mentioned above, was exported in 1922. Our consumption has increased from 11 to 12 million barrels, in 1928 and 1929, to a little over 18 million barrels in 1936.

As may be seen, in spite of the progress made in national consumption and, therefore, in the benefit of our general progress, more oil is still being exported than is allocated to domestic requirements.

For Mexico, the exploitation of its oil resources has been for a long time the source of almost continuous difficulties and internal disturbances, and even of serious international conflicts. All this has been caused by the rebellious attitude of the oil companies in their dealings with the authorities emanating from the Revolution, and in opposition to the principles and provisions enacted by them in pursuit of a just recovery of national wealth. In general, the activities and policies of the majority of the companies have not been marked by a friendship for and cooperation with our country which has granted them such generous hospitality.

Their relations with the authorities have not been those of frank and decided cooperation; on the contrary, their general standard of behavior has been a systematic opposition not only to the laws and dispositions issued but even to the technical regulations on the observance of which the operators have been more benefitted than the Nation. Their activities, whether in the acquisition of concessions and exploitation rights or in the purchase of lands and contracting of leases, have not, in many cases, been notable for the scrupulousness of the methods employed.

That is why the present Administration has placed among the policies of its Six-Year Plan, as the expression of an urgent national necessity, the goal of "making effective the nationalization of the subsoil; of modifying the present system of concessions; of denying concessions contrary to the national interest; of guaranteeing the national oil supply; of preventing monopolization of oil lands; and of intervening to establish an equilibrium between the economic forces of the petroleum industry, stimulating the development of national industries and creating an organism of support and regulation."

Images of Oil Workers

Drinking Fountains

El petróleo de México (Mexico, DF: Secretaría del Patrimonio Nacional, 1963).

English Colony, Tacoteno, Minititlán, Veracruz

El petróleo de México (Mexico, DF: Secretaría del Patrimonio Nacional, 1963).

Recreation Centers for Foreign Management
El petróleo de México (Mexico, DF: Secretaría del Patrimonio Nacional, 1963).

Workers' Camp, Poza Rica, Veracruz
El petróleo de México (Mexico, DF: Secretaría del Patrimonio Nacional, 1963).

Restrooms, South Side

El petróleo de México (Mexico, DF: Secretaría del Patrimonio Nacional, 1963).

Cárdenas Speaks

The history of this labor dispute, which culminates in this act of economic emancipation, is the following:

In connection with the strike called in 1934 by the various worker' unions in the employ of the Compañia Mexicana de Petróleo "El Águila," the Federal Executive agreed to intervene as an arbitrator to secure a conciliatory agreement between both parties.

In June, 1934, the resultant Award was handed down and, in October of the same year, this was followed by an explanatory decision establishing adequate procedure for revising those resolutions which had not already been agreed to.

At the end of 1934 and early in 1936, the Chief of the Labor Department, delegated by me for that purpose, handed down several decisions with respect to wage levels, contractual cases, and uniformity of wages, on the basis of the Constitutional principle of equal pay for equal work.

The same Department, for the purpose of eliminating certain anomalous conditions, called the representatives of the various trade-union groups into a conference at which an agreement was reached on numerous pending cases, others being reserved for subsequent investigation and analysis by commissions composed of labor and employer representatives.

The Union of Oil Workers then issued a call for a special assembly in which they laid down the terms of a collective contract which was rejected by the oil companies on its presentation.

Out of consideration for the wishes of the companies and in order to avert a strike, the Chief of the Labor Department was instructed to secure the acquiescence of both parties to the holding of a worker-employer convention to be entrusted with the task of establishing, by mutual agreement, the terms of the collective contract. The agreement to hold the convention was signed November 27, 1936, and in the meetings the companies presented their counter-proposals. Because of the slow progress being made, it was then decided to divide the clauses of the contract into economic, social, and administrative categories, so that an immediate examination of the first-named group might be undertaken.

The difficulties preventing an agreement between the workers and the companies were clearly revealed by the discussions; their respective points of view were found to be very far apart, the companies maintaining that the workers' demands were exaggerated and the workers, for their part, pointing to the companies' intransigence in refusing to understand their social necessities. As a result of the breakdown of the negotiations, the strike began in May, 1937. In response to my appeals, the companies then offered an increase in wages and a betterment of certain other conditions, and the Union of Oil Workers decided to resume work on June 9th, at the same time bringing an economic action against the companies before the Board of Conciliation and Arbitration.

As a result of these events, the Board of Conciliation and Arbitration took jurisdiction in the case and, in accordance with the provisions of the law, a commission of experts, composed of persons of high moral standing and adequate preparation, was designated by the President of the Board.

The commission's report found that the companies could afford to meet the disbursements recommended in it, namely, an annual increase of 26,332,756 pesos, as against the offer made by the seventeen oil companies at the time of the strike in May, 1937. The experts specifically stated that the conditions recommended in the report would be totally satisfied with the expenditure of the sum stipulated, but the companies argued that the amount recommended was excessive and might signify an even greater expenditure, which they estimated at a total of 41,000,000 pesos.

In view of these developments, the Executive then suggested the possibility of an agreement between the representatives of the Union of Oil Workers and the companies, duly authorized to deal with the dispute, but this solution proved impossible because of the refusal of the companies.

Notwithstanding the failure of this effort, the Public Power, still desirous of securing an extra-judicial agreement between the parties at issue, instructed the Labor Authorities to inform the companies of its willingness to intervene with the purpose of persuading the Labor Unions to accept the interpretations necessary to clarify certain obscure points of the Award which might later lend themselves to misunderstandings, and to assure the companies that in no case would the disbursements ordered by the Award be allowed to exceed the above-mentioned sum of 26,332,756 pesos; but in spite of this direct intervention of the Executive, it was impossible to obtain the results sought.

In each and every one of the various attempts of the Executive to arrive at a final solution of the conflict within conciliatory limits, and which include the periods prior to and following the *amparo* action [legal injunction] which has produced the present situation, the intransigence of the companies was clearly demonstrated.

Their attitude was therefore premeditated and their position deliberately taken, so that the Government, in defense of its own dignity, had to resort to application of the Expropriation Act, as there were no means less drastic or decision less severe that might bring about a solution of the problem.

For additional justification of the measure herein announced, let us trace briefly the history of the oil companies' growth in Mexico and of the resources with which they have developed their activities.

It has been repeated ad nauseam that the oil industry has brought additional capital for the development and progress of the country. This assertion is exaggeration. For many years, throughout the major period of their existence, the oil companies have enjoyed great privileges for development and expansion, including customs and tax exemptions and innumerable prerogatives; it is these factors of special privilege, together with the prodigious productivity of the oil deposits granted them by the Nation often against public will and law, that represent almost the total amount of this so-called capital.

Potential wealth of the Nation; miserably underpaid native labor; tax exemptions; economic privileges; governmental tolerance—these are the factors of the boom of the Mexican oil industry.

Let us now examine the social contributions of the companies. In how many of the villages bordering on the oil fields is there a hospital, or school or social center, or a sanitary water supply, or an athletic field, or even an electric plant fed by the millions of cubic meters of natural gas allowed to go to waste?

What center of oil production, on the other hand, does not have its company police force for the protection of private, selfish, and often illegal interests? These organizations, whether authorized by the Government or not, are charged with innumerable outrages, abuses, and murders, always on behalf of the companies that employ them.

Who is not aware of the irritating discrimination governing constructing of the company camps? Comfort for the foreign personnel; misery, drabness, and insalubrity for the Mexicans. Refrigeration and protection against tropical insects for the former; indifference and neglect, medical service and supplies always grudgingly provided, for the latter; lower wages and harder, more exhausting labor for our people.

The tolerance which the companies have abused was born, it is true, in the shadow of the ignorance, betrayals, and weakness of the country's rulers; but the mechanism was set in motion by investors lacking in the necessary moral resources to give something in exchange for the wealth they have been exploiting.

Another inevitable consequence of the presence of oil companies, strongly characterized by their anti-social tendencies, and even more harmful than all those already mentioned, has been their persistent and improper intervention to international affairs.

The oil companies' support to strong rebel factions against the constituted government in the Huasteca region of Veracruz and in the Isthmus of Tehuantepec during the years 1917 to 1920 is no longer a matter for discussions by anyone. Nor is anyone ignorant of the fact that in later periods and even at the present time, the oil companies have almost openly encouraged the ambitions of elements discontented with the country's government, every time their interests were affected either by taxation or by the modification of their privileges or the withdrawal of customary tolerance. They have had money, arms, and munitions for rebellion, money for the anti-patriotic press which defends them, money with which to enrich their unconditional defenders. But for the progress of the country, for establishing an economic equilibrium with their workers through a just compensation of labor, for maintaining hygienic conditions in the districts where they themselves operate, or for conserving the vast riches of the natural petroleum gases from destruction, they have neither money, nor financial possibilities, nor the desire to subtract the necessary funds from the volume of their profits.

Nor is there money with which to meet a responsibility imposed upon them by judicial verdict, for they rely on their pride and their economic power to shield them from the dignity and sovereignty of a Nation which has generously placed in their hands its vast natural resources and now finds itself unable to obtain the satisfaction of the most elementary obligations by ordinary legal means.

As a logical consequence of this brief analysis, it was therefore necessary to adopt a definite and legal measure to end this permanent state of affairs in which the country sees its industrial progress held back by those who hold in their hands the power to erect obstacles as well as the motive power of all activity and who, instead of using it to high and worthy purposes, abuse their economic strength to the point of jeopardizing the very life of a nation endeavoring to bring about the elevation of its people through its own laws, its own resources, and the free management of its own destinies.

With the only solution to this problem thus placed before it, I ask the entire Nation for moral and material support sufficient to carry out so justified, important, and indispensable a decision.

The Government has already taken suitable steps to maintain the constructive activities now going forward throughout the Republic, and for that purpose it asks the people only for its full confidence and backing in whatever dispositions the Government may be obliged to adopt.

Nevertheless, we shall, if necessary, sacrifice all the constructive projects on which the Nation has embarked during the term of this Administration in order to cope with the financial obligations imposed upon us by the application of the Expropriation Act to such vast interests; and although the subsoil of the country will give us considerable economic resources with which to meet the obligation of indemnization which we have contracted, we must be prepared for the possibility of our individual economy also suffering the indispensable readjustments, even to the point, should the Bank of Mexico deem it necessary, of modifying the present exchange rate of our currency, so that the whole country may be able to count on sufficient currency and resources with which to consolidate this act of profound and essential economic liberation of Mexico.

It is necessary that all groups of the population be imbued with a full optimism and that each citizen, whether in agricultural, industrial, commercial, transportation, or other pursuits, develop a greater activity from this moment on, in order to create new resources which will reveal that the spirit of our people is capable of saving the nation's economy by the efforts of its own citizens.

And, finally, as the fear may arise among the interests now in bitter conflict in the field of international affairs that a deviation of raw materials fundamentally necessary to the struggle in which the most powerful nations are engaged might result from the consummation of this act of national sovereignty and dignity, we wish to state that our petroleum operations will not depart a single inch from the moral solidarity maintained by Mexico with the democratic nations, whom we wish to assure that the expropriation now decreed has as its only purpose the elimination of obstacles erected by groups who do not understand the evolutionary needs of all peoples and who would themselves have no compunction in selling Mexican oil to the highest bidder, without taking into account the consequences of such action to the popular masses and the nations in conflict.

Central Themes

State formation, land and labor

Suggested Reading

Hayes, Joy Elizabeth. *Radio Nation: Communication, Popular Culture, and Nationalism in Mexico, 1920–1950.* Tucson: University of Arizona Press, 2000.

Jayne, Catherine E. *Oil, War, and Anglo-American Relations: American and British Reactions to Mexico's Expropriation of Foreign Oil Properties, 1937–1941.* Westport, CT: Greenwood Press, 2001.

Schuler, Friedrich E. *Mexico Between Hitler and Roosevelt: Mexican Foreign Relations in the Age of Lázaro Cárdenas, 1934–1940.* Albuquerque: University of New Mexico Press, 1998.

Related Sources

39. Mexican Views of the Mexican-American War (1850)
41. Mexico in Postwar Social Turmoil (1852)
48. The Cananea Strike: Workers' Demands (1906)
50. Popular Images of Mexican Life (the Late Nineteenth and Early Twentieth Centuries)
54. Land, Labor, and the Church in the Mexican Constitution (1917)
63. We the Undersigned (1941, 1945)

PART 8

The Institutionalization of the Revolution (1940–1965)

The year 1940 marked the end of the presidency of Lázaro Cárdenas, and scholars often view this date as also marking a turn in the direction of politics in Mexico. As the journalist Jorge Denegri observed, this was the year when the Revolution got down off its horse and into a Cadillac, signaling a shift in politics, in consumer habits, and in emphasis from rural to urban life. With regard to politics, President Manuel Ávila Camacho significantly slowed the redistribution of land, minimized his support for organized labor, and virtually abandoned the Cárdenas educational program, though he continued to support education. For many Mexicans, the shift in politics provided greater openings for protesting aspects of revolutionary policy that they found odious. The National Action Party (Partido de Acción Nacional, PAN), established in 1939, voiced many of those concerns, as did individuals who, continuing the practice of writing directly to government representatives, protested against Cárdenas's so-called socialist education (sources 62 and 63).

The 1940s also marked a period of unprecedented growth in Mexico. The economy grew at the rate of 6.5 percent between 1940 and 1970. Following the global economic crisis of the 1930s, Mexican leaders saw that countries that emphasized the export of raw materials were disadvantaged vis-à-vis industrialized economies. The outbreak of World War II led to domestic product shortages and gave the government added impetus to follow a policy of import substitution industrialization (ISI), a model of development implemented throughout Latin America at this time. The model of development upon which Mexico embarked, which emphasized the expansion of commercial agriculture and of industrial production, wrought profound changes on the country. Whereas in 1930 Mexico was a predominantly agricultural country, with agriculture the primary mode of production and two-thirds of the population living in the countryside, by 1970 industry accounted for more than one-third of total production and two-thirds of the population lived in urban areas. The expansion of commercial agriculture transpired in such a way that small landholders could not compete with large agricultural interests, and many were forced off their land. Commercial agriculture did not create sufficient jobs, and many Mexicans left for the cities. The economist José E. Iturriaga provides a panorama of this change, as well as the social change associated with it, for some

Mexicans—in the realms, for example, of marriage and family life (sources 60 and 64). Iturriaga also discusses the underside of modernization in Mexico: unequal distribution of income and of access to resources.

Mexicans responded in different ways to the unequal access to material and political resources that characterized this period of economic growth. Rubén Jaramillo's experience illustrates the limitations on citizens' participation in political activism in this era. Previously, Jaramillo had found ways to participate in the political system, but those possibilities became increasingly restricted, and in 1962 he and his family were tragically murdered (Source 67). His story can be evaluated within the context of the struggle for land in Morelos, Mexico, a struggle that had begun in the previous century (sources 53 and 54). During the 1950s, railroad workers also attempted to change their working and living conditions. When Demetrio Vallejo and his fellow workers found that existing channels for political expression did not serve them well, they went on strike. Vallejo was jailed at Lecumberri prison, but his incarceration did not stop him from publicizing injustices throughout the 1960s (Source 70).

Other Mexicans responded to the restriction of economic and political opportunity by turning to the already well-established practice of migrating to the United States (Source 63). There they might find work and live side by side with others who had migrated decades earlier or who had lived in the U.S. Southwest since the time when it was the Northwest of Mexico. As the labor disputes in Delano, California, grape fields showed, U.S. citizens of Mexican heritage and Mexicans resident in the United States did not always work side by side without tensions. Nevertheless, as Luis Valdez writes, an integral aspect of those labor struggles was the telling of Mexican history in ways that empowered *la raza* (the Mexican people, or literally, the race) and the labor movement (Source 66).

Throughout the period, the telling and reinterpretation of Mexican history has had profound cultural and political ramifications. One might read Valdez's interpretation of Mexican history within the context of both racism in the United States and the meanings of race and culture that prevailed in Mexico during the previous decade of the 1950s. The Mexican government had continued to uphold education as an important achievement of the Revolution, while at the same time government financial support declined. The government continued to build primary and secondary schools; however, secondary school attendance remained low. Working conditions for teachers—especially their salaries—declined, and participation in the teachers' union became increasingly politicized. At the same time, education served as an important means of touting the achievement of the Revolution. Indeed, as textbooks from the 1950s show, the education system contributed to certain conceptions of the Mexican Revolution and of Mexican history dating back to the Pre-Conquest period (Source 65).

62. An Assessment of Mexico from the Right (1940)*

Manuel Gómez Morín wrote the following document on the occasion of the Second Convention of the National Action Party (PAN). Morín worked as a lawyer for most of his life and took important positions in both the private and public sector, including work for the Bank of Mexico, for the federal government, and as rector of the National Autonomous University of Mexico (UNAM). Along with Luis Calderón Vega, he was a founding member of the National Action Party in 1939. Morín served as the first president of the party, from 1939 to 1949. Morín's political thought, which played a central role in shaping the ideology of the PAN, was deeply influenced by his religious faith and belief in Catholic theology; his identification with, and celebration of, Spanish culture; and his critique of the ruling political party, the PRN (and as of 1946, the PRI). The speech reprinted here was made in 1940, at the close of the presidency of Lázaro Cárdenas, and it can be understood as a denunciation of the policies and practices by which the Cárdenas presidency distinguished itself, as well as a more general denunciation of the path taken by the Mexican Revolution. The PAN has played an important role in the Mexican electoral process, party politics, and in formulating a critique of the ruling party, the PRI. In the year 2000, the election of the first PAN president, Vicente Fox, would make a significant contribution to eroding the political monopoly of the PRI, a monopoly it had exercised for over seventy years.

Morín uses events from Mexican history to make his case and to persuade his audience. To which moments does he refer, and how does he use those examples? While Morín criticizes the Cárdenas presidency for its support of Republican Spain ("the Spanish issue"), what aspects of Mexico's relationship with Spain does he celebrate? There are many ways to use spirituality and religious doctrine to inform political thought. In what ways does Morín do so? How does Morín's use of history differ from how history is used in other documents in this collection?

---

*Acción Nacional (Mexico) and Manuel Gómez Morín, *Diez años de Mexico: Informes del Jefe de Accion Nacional* (Mexico: Editorial Jus, 1950), pp. 43–69. Translated by the editors.

Address for the Second Convention of National Action, Given on April 20, 1940

Our Assembly meets in a period of confusion and bitterness in the entire world. These are crucial times during which all affairs of Politics and Economy, of the social structure and the Law, of conceptions of the State and international relations, are invaded by the dark shadows that a regressive movement has been creating for many years.

The Current Crisis

The war extends and constantly deepens its related ills, and is also imbued with threats of all kinds for the future. However, more than war, and even more than violence itself, the situation of the world today is fearfully shadowed by the abandonment of moral and legal norms that made human coexistence possible, by the constant recourse to lies and to confusion, and by the loss of spiritual means of understanding and ordering personal and collective life.

Consideration of current ills overwhelms. And, among them, that which seems to be the central cause and origin of all the rest: the incapacity of intelligence to illuminate social events, to adequately regulate them. Its primary task, on the contrary, is to increasingly obscure and make incomprehensible the labyrinth of its action, its purposes, and its motives. Disconnected from the reality that it has not tried to understand, and with which it has no other contact than constant struggle, [it is] the source of new confusion; estranged from that which is the source and goal of all true social works—the affirmation of a moral duty—intelligence labors in a vacuum, it comes back on itself and is bound to succumb because it has forgotten *the Truth, the Way, and the Life.*

Those who, in contrast, invoke the prodigious reach of intellectual work in the fields of science forget that intelligence is nowhere more humble than there, and is therefore progressively more tied to its source. Above all, they also forget that in sharp contrast with the fruits of intellectual work applied to the understanding of the physical world, in that which treats human phenomenon, understanding of this vital relationship between intelligence and its source, its essence and its purpose, intellectual work has achieved only sinister simulacrum, ever-growing ruptures in the heart of the human community, and ephemeral pyrotechnics of clarity that do not light the way, and serve only to make more evident the dense darkness in which we men are submerged. . . .

The International Situation

For many long years we have sacrificed the international position that should belong to Mexico, to follow artificially adopted paths and directions that come to us from outside.

Such is the case with the behavior of Mexico in the Society of Nations, demagogic behavior, frequently grotesque, seriously diminishing the prestige that might be ours were we to act with modesty and dignity. Such was the attitude of the Government with regard to the whole misfortunate Spanish issue, in which, unjustifiably and needlessly, not only did it ally itself with the lowest international interests, but due to inane inexperience or maladroitness of its own fault, was converted into a mere agent of those interests, and perhaps has been compromised in who knows what unmentionable dealings.

Such is the case with regard to the politics of the continent. Reason and tradition mark for us a clear path. We have long forgotten, for many years now, the maritime routes that were ours. And to forget, in such cases, is to lose. For having thus forgotten, one hundred years ago, we also quickly lost the land routes, over mountains and deserts, that the spent sandals of missionaries and determined conquistadors and settlers had traveled. . . .

National Problems

The same occurs with regard to domestic issues. In the use of the natural resources of the Country, as in the construction of public works; in the structuring of new forms of the Economy, as in the provision of public services; in the planning and management of social problems, as in the most minimal issues of Administration; in the organization of education, as in the incidences of political life, instead of severe action, informed by knowledge of the truth, directed toward the Common Good, a lack of forethought and vain whim have been preferred. Proclamations have been made in favor of immediate selfish political interest; and, in essence, by following the objectives and tactics of the "mafia." Lies serve as the banner of the regime, unscrupulous propaganda as a recourse to power, and as a norm for conduct, deceitfulness.

Nothing has been done, not even to build upon what little has been achieved since 1917, to define the terms of a firm politics based on the natural resources of Mexico, let alone to bring about this development for national benefit. On the contrary, either the true problem is forgotten and supplanted with others that are simply incidental and serve only to redirect the Government's attention, national efforts, and even Mexico's particular position in the international sphere—as in the case of petroleum—or they waste their energies in minor conflicts or in abandonment, as in the case of mining, or they close the doors to all private initiative under the pretence of supplanting it with official action that is either never realized or is realized only for twisted ends and with lamentable effect. . . .

Agrarian Questions

Thirty years ago, it seemed that a new light shone on the panorama of the Mexican countryside. In some ways, paths toward salvation were rediscovered that since 1810 had been forgotten, and that during the second half of the previous century, since the Reform, had appeared definitively blocked. The existence of a serious agrarian problem in Mexico was recognized and an initial solution was found, a beginning, perhaps incomplete, but simple and useful for struggle. During many years, the necessity of this struggle took precedent over all other aspects of the question. There was violence, destruction, and annihilation, the price for the treason committed from Independence to the Reform; and afterwards there was the forgetting of reality through routine and self-interest. Once having defeated the military, political, and economic resistance that opposed itself to the solution of the problem, Mexico waited in vain for resolution. Because at first there was a generous and humane movement to give Mexico the incomparable treasure of a rural population of individuals placed, justifiably, on their own land, land that they loved and worked in peace, and that was productive because of aptly-applied efforts, and which, day-by-day, expanded by means of conquest of the immense zones that still await the caress of the plough and the blessing of the sower of seed. But what came forth from Mexico, like one of its most pure desires, was quickly transformed by pettiness into a mere source of speculation and political power. And after thirty years, the problem remains intact, aggravated. And all the sacrifices made to this point have been a useless waste, because new and greater efforts would be needed to once again properly channel the issue and arrive at a truly satisfactory solution. The current Government, which for so many reasons began with its hands full of possibilities, has had magnificent opportunities to resolve this problem. It has not wanted to do so. Here as well, it has, instead, preferred the contemptible applause of the "mafia," the transitory deception of the *campesino* [rural worker], the use of political force derived from the substance of the same problem, the feigning of a struggle over a serious productive solution of benefit to the Republic; however, this would have required capabilities, honesty, persistence, and the greatest fruits of such labors would have appeared only many years later, still in time to be praised by history, but too late to take political advantage and for the satisfaction solely of vanity.

The State's ignorance of resources available to organize the functioning of agrarian credit compromises credit and the very basis of the national monetary system; the State destroys the few formal and established systems of production within the Republic and crudely imitates institutions not only foreign and incomprehensible, but already condemned by experience and reason; the regime increasingly winds itself up in the lies of an organization that it calls campesina and autonomous, but which is nothing but a bureaucracy subordinate to politics; it is important to take heed of the grains Mexico no longer produces, even though the Republic is at peace. . . .

Pretense

It is not without reason that it is said that part of our misfortune is due to the colonial structure of our economy. To be more precise, one would have to say, "the colonial structure that is being imposed on our economy." For since the last third of the past century, the motor of the Country's economic forces (not always effective or well-directed) [has] tended to overcome colonial forms. And it would have been possible to achieve this. And it would have even been possible to achieve the necessary and productive discernment between those aspects of the colonial economy that were mistaken or sickly or impossible, and those that, given the specific situation of Mexico, should not only be preserved, but encouraged because they strengthen our personality and our possibilities and coincide with the true needs of our emerging nationality, contributing substantially to it, now that our dependent economic and political ties with Spain are broken. . . .

And why bother speaking about what is happening with regard to education? Nothing is more painful for us, and for Mexico, and nothing more important for them, the international left-wing, obscurantist, and charlatan "mafia," than the destruction of the School in Mexico, and the violent imposition of a system that is irrational, antiscientific, obscurantist, and corrupting of intelligence and customs. . . .

For this reason, National Action presents to the Nation today—as it did last September when it presented an essential interpretation of the individual, society, State, authority, Fatherland—a program that simultaneously shows how the principles of doctrine are the living source of concrete and immediate solutions, and also the necessary path to reorder essential aspects of the life of Mexico.

Elections

We have never thought, nor would it be wise to think, that the resolution of the serious national problems that we face [depends] upon an election. The highest aspirations of collective life, the best accomplishments of the State, and the fulfillment of national objectives are not goals that can be achieved by means of the minimal effort of the vote. . . .

From this emerges the need and the origin of our Organization: to define a doctrine, to define a fundamental programmatic position, to promote the integral adoption of a new style of life, to give a new tone to both individual conduct and collective action, to recuperate for the entire Nation a sense of origin, a trajectory, and a destiny, that it appears to have lost. From this, as well, comes our oft-repeated affirmation: before and after the vote, above all election, above and beyond connections with Power, true political action in its only generous human form becomes an integral and interwoven aspect of all other obligations of individual life and the invincible web of collective life. . . .

1910–1940

What can we expect from the election?

The usual system of false Mexican democracy has been that it is the Government who elects. This is how it was during the long Porfirian era. This is how it continued to be in 1934, when the current Government emerged from an election in which the people did not participate at all because the results were already known to have been decreed by those who at the time were the owners of the Country. . . .

What is happening in Mexico today is extraordinarily similar, in more than one respect, to what happened in 1910. But it is more important, more profound, and more extensive.

Now, as then, the Nation and the Government are separate, they are antagonistic; the regime is obsolete, imprisoned in the chains of conventionalism that it itself has created, reduced to the band of followers who benefit and prosper off it. . . .

A Call to Action

Therefore, in 1910, the Constitution had made a date with destiny for the people of Mexico. However, vanity, a lack of understanding of reality, and the desire for power, led the regime to miss that date, and the people themselves, disorganized, lacking the structure that would make possible social movements, and without serious upheavals, also missed that date. Action became explosion. And the consequences are known.

This date appears once again, for a new generation. . . .

Central Themes

State formation, land and labor, religion, race and ethnicity

Suggested Reading

Mabry, Donald J. *Mexico's Acción Nacional: A Catholic Alternative to Revolution.* Syracuse, NY: Syracuse University Press, 1973.

Mizrahi, Yemile. *From Martyrdom to Power: The Partido Acción Nacional in Mexico.* Notre Dame, IN: University of Notre Dame Press, 2003.

Newcomer, Daniel. *Reconciling Modernity: Urban State Formation in 1940s León, Mexico.* Lincoln: University of Nebraska Press, 2004.

Sherman, John. *The Mexican Right: The End of Revolutionary Reform, 1929–1940.* Westport, CT: Praeger, 1997.

Related Sources

41. Mexico in Postwar Social Turmoil (1852)
43. Offer of the Crown to Maximilian by the Junta of Conservative Nobles (1863)
56. The Catholic Church Hierarchy Protests (1917, reprinted 1926)
58. Plutarco Elías Calles: The Legal Challenges of the Postrevolutionary State (1928)
63. We the Undersigned (1941, 1945)

63. We the Undersigned (1941, 1945)*

The following two letters, written by Mexican citizens to government representatives during the 1940s, demonstrate the persistence of certain issues in postrevolutionary Mexico. The first letter concerns the question of education. President Lázaro Cárdenas had continued the expansion of the educational system carried out during the 1920s, and during the 1930s education professionals had infused the content of curriculum with new meaning. While for some this meant that the content of education came more into line with the ideals of the Revolution that emphasized social responsibility, others considered the Cárdenas-era curriculum "socialist" and merely a continuation of revolutionary attacks on religious faith. For this latter group, the election of Manuel Ávila Camacho (1940–1946) signaled a possible opening in which to voice their concerns. In the first letter, how does the author speak of patriotism? The second letter voices the concerns of Mexican workers in the United States. During the late 1940s, many Mexicans migrated to the United States to work under the auspices of the *bracero* (guest worker) program, a program sponsored by both the U.S. and Mexican governments. With this program, the United States got the workers it sought, and the Mexican government benefited from work opportunities for some of the country's unemployed. How do these Mexican workers in the United States conceive of their rights? As in the analysis of all letters, it is important to pay attention not only to the body of the letter but to the closing as well. What slogans did people use to close their letters, and what might those slogans tell us about political language at the time?

---

*María del Carmen Nava Nava, *Los abajo firmantes: Cartas a los presidentes,* Colección Retrato Hablado (Mexico: Secretaría de Educación Pública, Unidad de Publicaciones Educativas, 1994), pp. 53, 135. Excerpt translated by the editors.

Letter (1941)

February 13, 1941
H. Chamber of Deputies of the Union
Mexico, DF.

The undersigned, in representation of the San Pedro C. Sinarquist group [Ciudad Hidalgo, Michoacán], address ourselves to you, most honorable representatives, asking that Article Three of the Constitution currently in effect be revoked, that the Socialist School and co-education be terminated, and that freedom of instruction be reestablished, so that many private schools might function and parents not find themselves forced to send their children to official schools or leave them without any education at all. We also beg of you that the communists be eliminated from the Ministry of Education so that they do not obstruct our patriotic work.

Effective Suffrage, No Reelection.

Leader of the Sinarquist group
Román Bucio
Mexico, DF.

Letter (1945)

November 18, 1945
Yakima, Washington, U.S.A.

To the Most Honorable President of the United States of Mexico,
Dear Mister President,

In the name of nearly one thousand Mexican workers, we inform you that since the last few days of October, upon completion of the agricultural jobs for which we were contracted, and without taking into consideration our cooperation with this country, we have been detained in this concentration camp, suffering the rigors of winter.

This unjustified detention causes us and our families significant economic hardship, as we have not earned wages since the date indicated. By emphatically protesting this arbitrary treatment we beg that by legal means you enter into negotiations with this government for the payment of back wages, to which we have a right, and that we are immediately returned to Mexico, according to the relevant clause in our collective contract.

Most respectfully,
Aquileo Bravo
Signatures follow.

Central Themes

The northern frontier, land and labor, religion

Suggested Reading

Bantjes, Adrian A. *As If Jesus Walked the Earth: Cardenismo, Sonora, and the Mexican Revolution.* Oxford: Scholarly Resources, 1998.

Gonzalez, Gilbert G. *A Century of Chicano History: Empire, Nations, and Migration.* New York: Routledge, 2003.

Gutiérrez, David G. *The Columbia History of Latinos in the United States Since 1960.* New York: Columbia University Press, 2004.

Meyer, Jean. *The Cristero Rebellion: The Mexican People Between Church and State, 1926–1929.* Cambridge: Cambridge University Press, 1976.

Schell, Patience A. *Church and State in Revolutionary Mexico City.* Tucson: University of Arizona Press, 2003.

Related Sources

54. Land, Labor, and the Church in the Mexican Constitution (1917)
65. Official History (1951)
66. Chicano Consciousness (1966)

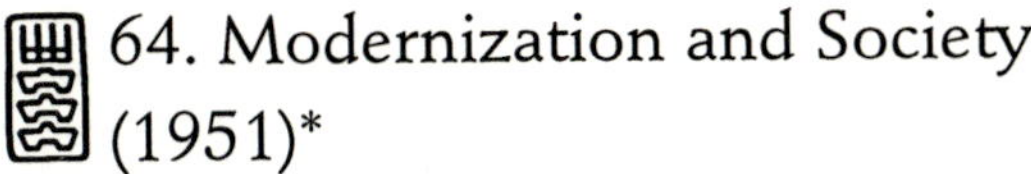

64. Modernization and Society (1951)*

The following are excerpts from a study of the Mexican economy and society, financed by the National Finance Company, SA, that was meant to "harmonize Mexican economic development." In the work's prologue, its author, José E. Iturriaga, explains that culture is essential to economic development, for it plays a central role in Mexicans' capacity as consumers. Iturriaga also directs his attention to the significant cultural impact of modernization on Mexican society and family life. The bulk of the study is devoted to an analysis of three social classes, which he defines as "popular," "middle," and "upper." To conduct his analysis, Iturriaga drew on a range of theories and claimed "an eclectic set of criteria by which classes are distinguished by economic level, levels of culture, and habits of conduct—all of these criss-crossing in different equations." In your estimation, does Iturriaga argue that there is a causal relationship between cultural and economic phenomenon, and if so, how?

---

*José E. Iturriaga, *La estructura social y cultural de México* (Mexico: Fondo de Cultura Económica, 1951), pp. 3–5, 13–17, 26, 29. Excerpts translated by the editors.

While a middle class emerged in Mexico at least as early as the late nineteenth century, according to the study, between 1895 and 1940, the Mexican middle class grew from 8 to 16 percent of the population and was concentrated in urban areas. During the 1950s, social scientists and politicians paid increasing attention to the middle class. Iturriaga associates the middle class with urbanization, citing Leo Muffelman: "The city is born—underlines Muffelman—and with it, the middle class." This growth is the result, claims Iturriaga, of agrarian reform, industrialization, and urbanization. How does Iturriaga explain urbanization in Mexico, especially when he contextualizes it within Latin America more generally? How does Iturriaga explain changes in the family and the social roles of women?

The Social and Cultural Structure of Mexico: Part 1: The Social Structure

1. The Countryside and the City

The fundamental characteristic of the social organization of Mexico today is that of an agrarian society, although it is far different from that which existed immediately prior to the revolutionary era. That is to say, the symptoms that plague a feudal system have been disappearing, without this meaning that Mexico has stopped basing its social life upon agricultural activities. To be more clear: with independence, the country suffered deep alterations, evolving from the *latifundio* [large landed estate] to smaller plots of land or to *ejidos* [communally held land] or to small land holdings; the basic social structure of Mexico continues to be rural, which is evident in the fact that in 1940, 64.91% of the population lived in rural towns and the remaining 35.09% lived in cities. . . .

Between 1910 and 1940, the social structure of Mexico began an uninterrupted process of transformation, an indicator of the progressive growth of our urban population and a proportionate decline of our rural population, a process which it would be useful to describe schematically in as much as it would serve as the basis for better understanding the evolution of social classes, [to] the analysis of which the following chapter is dedicated. . . .

During the most bloody phase of the Revolution, from 1910 to 1920, the rural population diminished and that of the cities grew, due to the desire on the part of *campesinos* [rural workers] for security and a means of making a living that could be found in urban centers; this, independent of the fact that numerous campesinos emigrated to the United States, a country that during the First World War needed workers in its industry and agriculture. The violence of the armed struggle during the decade of 1910–1920 is made evident with this illustrative fact: in 1910 the country had 70,830 towns and in 1921 there were only 62,879, which means that this phase of our Revolution depopulated or destroyed 7,951 localities, of which the great majority were rural. If we detail the depopulation of these nearly eight thousand localities by region, we corroborate a well-known fact: that the Revolution was more bloody in the North and center of the country than in the South. . . .

In other Latin American countries, the phenomenon of the hypertrophy of urban populations due to causes unrelated to industrialization is the same, even when there was no long-term armed revolution like ours, which leads a part of the population to concentrate in cities. This is to say, Latin American urban centers—excepting, among others, Monterrey, Mexico, and São Paulo, Brazil—are subject to a dizzying rhythm of growth without necessarily experiencing corresponding industrial growth, such as occurred in more representatively industrial countries: the United States, England, France, Germany, etcetera. . . .

During the decade of the thirties, with peace secured in the countryside and agrarian reform enacted during the *sexenio* [six-year presidential term] of President Cárdenas, the most natural thing would have been for the rural population to have increased in proportion to the urban population; however, it did not occur that way. Quite the opposite: the rural population continued to decline (relative to the urban), in virtue of the fact that the country's industrialization began to take shape in those years, so that in 1940 the rural population of Mexico was, as we have already said, 64.91% and the urban population 35.09%. . . .

2. The Family

The Cause of Weakening Family Ties

When the Revolution broke out in 1910, the first cause of the weakening of family ties occurred: the massive displacement of the campesino population uprooted many heads of family from their homes and places of origin, who moved to cities within Mexico or who emigrated abroad in search of stability or better opportunities; and this does not take into account those who joined the popular army or different factions and who died in battle. . . .

The growth of cities is the other direct cause of the weakening of the family. In effect, the rural population that is able to set up home in large urban centers is then submitted to a depressing influence on their habits and customs due to the influence of the city, which exerts a liberating force on the many restrictions imposed upon individual conduct in small communities. That is to say, the city breaks the feeling of neighborliness that characterizes small towns, so that the rigid social censure that is so characteristic of small towns ceases to function. And because of this, divorce and other forms of breakdown of the family appear with more frequency in urban centers than in the countryside. This is the case to such an extent that, despite the fact that in 1940 the rural population was twice the size of the urban population, in the latter, there were four times as many divorces registered than in the former. Put another way, in 1940 the practice of divorce was eight times more likely in urban areas than in rural populations. . . .

Another factor that contributes to the weakening of family ties as they existed in the past is the incorporation of women into the economically active population. In effect, of the personnel who [occupied] all Mexican industry in 1940, 14.44% were women; commerce and banking employed 17.50% women; public administration employed 22.04% women; in the liberal professions, women were 9.39%; in unidentified occupations [a census category] 12.52%; and in paid domestic labor 85%. Put another way, in that year, there were 532,544 women working in waged labor outside of the home. The consequences of this fact are obvious and have been studied exhaustively in recent years: women who worked before marriage often have an attitude of economic self-sufficiency which women of the past did not possess, so much so that this attitude taints the marriage with less stability, for it is known that a significant degree of family stability originates in the absolute economic dependence of the wife upon the husband.

While it may be true that in general the standard of living of the population has improved, the poverty that continues to exist among a considerable sector of families acts as yet another factor that contributes to the disintegration of the home. If this is true, and it is, it might seem contradictory to say that on the one hand, families in the past were more cohesive, and on the other hand, that poverty was greater in the past. However, the apparent contradiction is explained by the following reasons, among others: because poverty did not exert its force as an active agent in the disintegration of the home due to a rigid religious censorship in the past; because of the absence of a law regulating family relations [the 1917 Law of Family Relations] that legalized divorce; and in general because of the lack of a climate of liberation for women, which increasingly imposes itself upon modern societies. . . .

Poverty within rural households results in a phenomenon that is worth brief consideration: the movement of women dedicated to paid domestic service to cities—153,000 in 1940—[who] do not always return to their homes of origin because when they make advances and ascend in social category, they take jobs and expand the female labor force in factories. And when the environment of the city degrades their habits and moral customs, they end up expanding the ranks of prostitutes. Data that is useful to mention in this regard shows that servants tend to make up a considerable percentage of single mothers, which is to say the extreme form of household disintegration, because the father neither acknowledges paternity nor accepts or fulfills the corresponding paternal responsibilities.

The aforementioned causes for the disintegration of family ties as they have been known in Mexico would be sufficient. However, apart from strictly economic and sociological local factors that encourage such modifications in family structure, there are other reasons worth mention: imitation of our neighbor, the United States, a country where the disintegration of the family has reached one of the highest levels in the world. There is no need to adopt a moralistic tone to affirm that, along with the aforementioned causes, we must add one more: the crisis in traditional ethical values that denies responsibility for paternity on the part of the head of the family. . . .

One of the great themes in modern sociology is that of the lack of cohesion of the family, and it seems that—within the context of the social morality associated with the Industrial Revolution—there is no obvious solution to this problem. A simplistic solution might be found in confining women to strictly domestic labors, eliminating large urban centers, and returning to the moral climate that predates the Industrial Revolution. Such measures, however, are obviously impracticable. . . .

3. Social Classes

As in all modern societies, within Mexican society there are three classes: the popular classes, the middle, and the upper, a division that derives from occupation, economic status, and the degree of access to culture among each class.

We have arrived at the following results: in 1940, 83.08% of the population was of the popular classes, 15.87% of the middle classes and 1.05% of the upper classes. . . . This evolution of our social classes during the last 45 years . . . is the result of the combination of three decisive factors: (a) the new regime of rural property introduced by the Revolution; (b) urban growth; and (c) the gradual industrialization of the country.

Central Themes

Urban life, land and labor, gender

Suggested Reading

Cross, John C. *Informal Politics: Street Vendors and the State in Mexico City.* Stanford, CA: Stanford University Press, 1998.

Moreno, Julio. *Yankee Don't Go Home! Mexican Nationalism, American Business Culture, and the Shaping of Modern Mexico, 1920–1950.* Chapel Hill: University of North Carolina Press, 2003.

Mraz, John. *Nacho López, Mexican Photographer.* Minneapolis: University of Minnesota Press, 2003.

Niblo, Stephen. *Mexico in the 1940s: Modernity, Politics, and Corruption.* Wilmington, DE: Scholarly Resources, 1999.

Related Sources

46. A Positivist Interpretation of Feminism (1909)
54. Land, Labor, and the Church in the Mexican Constitution (1917)
59. Feminism, Suffrage, and Revolution (1931)
60. Chronicles of Mexico City (1938)
62. An Assessment of Mexico from the Right (1940)

65. Official History (1951)*

The extent and content of education was an important and much contested achievement of the Mexican Revolution. The Ministry of Education helped to expand the number of schools—especially in urban areas but perhaps more significantly in rural Mexico. A corps of teachers were trained for this work, and with official texts in hand, they served as central figures in the interpretation of knowledge and message. The ministry also worked to make significant changes to the content of education in Mexico, playing an integral role in disseminating new conceptions of Mexican history and government messages about the role of government and nation in the lives of Mexicans.

The following selection is from the official, state-approved third-grade textbook. It begins with a preamble directed to schoolchildren, followed by selected lessons in early Mexican history. How does the text define history, and in what other ways might we understand history? One question we ask of history is why things happened the way they did. To what does this textbook attribute causation, and how might that fit within the political moment of 1950s Mexico? What lessons might we learn from this text about 1950s conceptions of ethnicity, culture, and the state? When comparing this document to related sources (see the end of the selection), how might the conceptions of ethnic groups communicated in this textbook have shaped conflicts over the land during the 1920s and 1940s in which indigenous people were involved?

To the Children

In this book, modest, yet written from the heart, are the origins of the Mexican Fatherland.

Here you will excitedly contemplate the profound, mysterious, and heroic life of the indigenous peoples, and that of the productive transplanted Spaniard, so full of energy, who enriched the life of Mexico with new knowledge and important material and spiritual goods.

You will accompany the Mexican Nation at its birth, which has instilled in you the most fervid hopes.

We already know that, even though you are still young, you love Mexico very much for the simple reason that it is your Country, because you were born on its

---

*Hector Campillo Cuautli, *La nación Mexicana: Sus orígenes*, Texto oficial y ejercicios de historia para los alumnus de tercer año de la escuela primaria, Aprobado por la Secretaría de Educación Pública, (Mexico: Cuadros Vivos, 1951), preface and pp. 124–125, 190–193, 226–227, 232–233. Excerpts translated by the editors.

blessed soil, and because you live in it alongside your parents who gave you life and who work tirelessly for your care and education.

But beyond loving it a lot, you ought [to] love it well, which is only possible by learning about it. It is for this reason that you study its territory in Geography and its life in History.

This little book that we have made for you, illustrated with beautiful images, is the first part of the History of Mexico. Next year, you will study the remaining history, and in the same way that you now learn how the Mexican people came into being, you will then learn how our nationality developed, and this study will be of the utmost importance for your understanding of your patriotic duties.

There is no other subject that you ought [to] study with more love than National History. There are people who believe that History is not important, because without studying it, all good citizens know that it is their obligation to work for the betterment of their Country by behaving as well as they can; however, such people forget that each people is great in its own way, and for this reason, no country has become great by simply imitating others that are already great.

In order to be a great and dignified people, one must be loyal to oneself, one's ancestors, and their most noble acts.

It is for this reason that you ought to study the History of Mexico with the utmost affection, dedicating to it all your intelligence and great respect for the truth.

Do not think that History is a story. At times it seems as if it were, because it is enjoyable and agreeable and tells of interesting things; but it is not [a story]. A story is made up and History is the truth. It does not matter that sometimes there are truths that are not pleasing. When this happens, the worst that we can do is get mad or discouraged, or try to deny or hide these truths, while at the same time exaggerating those that please us, or try to invent agreeable lies. If we corrupt History, we are lost, because we can never improve that which is wrong.

What would happen to a person who did not want to take into account his mistakes or faults? They would never be corrected, he would never improve, never progress. On the contrary, each day would be worse, because past mistakes would pile up on new ones, and new ills would compound upon past ills.

The same wrongs, and even worse, can come from hiding or falsifying the truths of history that we do not like. What we have to do is work so that we do not again repeat either mistakes or shortcomings, and so that the good and beautiful pages of our History rise above those that cause us pain. And never, never devalue our people, not even in their most disagreeable moments, but rather think that it is precisely in the most difficult moments that the Country most needs the love of its children. It is only fair that glorious moments and illustrious figures inspire satisfaction and noble pride and that we feel pain for the unfortunate; but love must be inextinguishable.

The greatest lesson of History can be summed up in three great loves: love of Country, love of Humanity, and love of the Truth.

"Social Differences"
La Nación Mexicana: Sus orígenes, p. 125

LX. Social Differences

The Aztec tradition says that the social differences that existed in their society date from the era of Izcóatl and Moctezuma I.

According to this tradition, the people suggested to Izcóatl that if he liberated them from the oppression of Azcapotzalco, they would happily work for the king, the priests, and the warriors, and this was how the latter became the privileged classes which lived without working.

What is certain is that social classes already existed well before these two kings; they already existed amongst the Aztecs upon their arrival to the Valley, and that social classes existed as well, to a very significant degree, among the Toltecs, the Quiché Mayas, the Tarascans and the Mixtec-Zaptoec. Among all of these peoples, there were priests and warriors, the powerful and the unproductive, and a mass of workers that was rarely subjugated.

What we ought to understand about the aforementioned tradition is that with the imperial wars, the number and arrogance of the warriors and priests increased and the condition of the people was made harder, which meant that social differences became increasingly blatant and onerous.

Activities

Observe:

1. Do all the people represented in this picture appear to be of the same social class? 2. Which are the ones of a higher social standing? 3. Who is the young one who is on his knees? 4. What is the appearance of the seated man?

"The Conquistador: Hernán Cortés, standing on the bridge of his ship, contemplating beautiful Mexico, which he will bring to light and the renown of the world."
La Nación Mexicana: Sus orígenes, p. 191

XCIII. The Conquistador

HERNÁN CORTES was born in a region of Spain called Extremadura.

To please the wishes of his parents, who wanted him to become a *licenciado* [title of higher education], he studied at the University of Salamanca for a time; however, he wanted to be a soldier and he went to Seville with the intention of signing up for the army. An accident kept him from embarking with the army to Italy, and so he went to America and took part in the conquest of Cuba under the command of Diego de Velázquez.

He lived on this island uneventfully, when he was assigned to organize an expedition for the conquest of Mexico. At this point begins the truly historic life of Hernán Cortés.

He was able to understand it as such, and for this reason displayed incredible energy in the preparations for this great enterprise.

He quickly brought together 10 ships and 500 soldiers, and left with them from Santiago de Cuba on the 1st of February, 1519.

Following the route of Hernández de Córdoba and Grijalva, he arrived in Tabasco, however, now the Indians did not welcome him peacefully, and he had to fight with them in some very intense battles.

"Moctezuma II, Emperor of Mexico"
La Nación Mexicana: Sus orígenes, p. 193

XCIV. Moctezuma II, Emperor of Mexico

When the first Spaniards arrived on Mexican soil, the Emperor Moctezuma II Xocoyótzin who ruled the Great Tenochtitlán, sent them splendid gifts, accompanied with entreaties that they let him die in his throne.

This was a big mistake, because it was giving up. This is how Cortés understood it, who, in order to scare him more, made his horses jockey around and shot off his guns in front of the ambassadors of Tenochtitlán.

He achieved what he wanted, for the envoys drew what they had seen and explained the drawings to the Emperor, which filled him with fear when he remembered the prophesy of Quetzalcóatl.

Moctezuma II called for Netzahualpilli, the king of Texcoco, and called the most wise of the Aztecs and Zapotecs to consult with them as to whether those men were those foretold by the Toltec god upon his expulsion from Tula. They all agreed that it was, and for this reason Moctezuma experienced doubts that were so great, that he was unable to hide them even in the face of his own enemies.

Activities

Observation:

The Emperor Moctezuma II appears seated in the throne. How does he appear?

What can you see in the faces of the two Indians with him?

What are they showing him?

What is the relationship between these things and the moral despondency of the king? (Remember the prophesy from the time of the Toltecs.)

"Political Consequences"
La Nación Mexicana: Sus orígenes, p. 227

CXI. Political Consequences

CORTÉS ORGANIZED the country under a single government with the same laws, giving it the name of New Spain. He was the first governor.

As Mexico was the most important of the Spanish conquests it was governed by viceroys, that is to say, by rulers of high standing, almost equal to that of the Spanish kings; in this way the inhabitants of all the regions that now constitute our Republic—Indians of different races, *mestizos* [people of Spanish and Indian parentage], or *criollos* [American-born Spaniards]—all became accustomed to feeling Mexican and to love one another as compatriots.

This is how, in the course of an extended coexistence, Mexican nationality was formed [and later] consecrated by Father Hidalgo in his time with the glorious independence movement.

This was surely the most important consequence of the conquest, because it was for this reason that a union of dispersed and different tribes of Indians came to be Mexican, whose process of integration advanced rapidly, thanks to the patriotic feelings of all its children, without distinction of race or color.

Activities

1. Describe this scene and state the significance. 2. Correlation. Study the evolution of the mestizo race and the current role that it plays in the demographic life of the country. 3. Discuss the importance of the ethnic integration of the Mexican in the mestizo type.

"Ethnic Consequences"
La Nación Mexicana: Sus orígenes, p. 232

CXIV. Ethnic Consequences

THE SPANIARD as an individual is sometimes a proud man, and prone to violent short-temperedness; however, the populating of the lands that he conquered and colonized is a living testimony to the fact that his soul contains a profound feeling for humanity; he never considered any people so inferior as to be loathe to mix with them, nor did he accept the odious idea that there are inferior races that are destined to perish or en masse to serve forever others who consider themselves superior.

The consequence of this way of being was that, beginning with Cortés himself and his captains, the conquistadors and colonizers fully mixed with the Indians, which brought into being a new human type, the mestizo type, that currently constitutes the most important element of the Mexican population.

This work of national biological integration should proceed as if it conforms to a natural law, and a moment will come when the people of Mexico will unify materially in a new type, just as it is unified spiritually by the love for its Country.

Questions

1. As an individual, how does the Spaniard sometimes behave?
2. What does the existence of the Spanish colonies prove about the genetic condition of the Spaniard?
3. What were the consequences of this?
4. What will happen with the population of Mexico?

Central Themes

Indigenous people, state formation, popular culture, race and ethnicity

Suggested Reading

Joseph, Gilbert M., Anne Rubenstein, and Eric Zolov, eds. *Fragments of a Golden Age: The Politics of Culture in Mexico Since 1940.* Durham, NC: Duke University Press, 2001.

Vaughan, Mary Kay. *Cultural Politics in Revolution: Teachers, Peasants, and Schools in Mexico, 1930–1940.* Tucson: University of Arizona Press, 1997.

______. *History Textbooks in Mexico in the 1920s.* Buffalo: State University of New York, Council on International Studies, 1974.

Related Sources

4. The Origin of the Nahuas and the Birth of the Fifth Sun (1596)
10. Hernán Cortés and Moteucçoma Meet, According to a Spanish Conqueror (1568)
11. Moteucçoma and Hernán Cortés Meet, According to a Nahua Codex (c. 1555)
12. The Nahua Interpreter Malintzin Translates for Hérnan Cortés and Moteucçoma (1580)
63. We the Undersigned (1941, 1945)

66. Chicano Consciousness (1966)*

The Treaty of Guadalupe Hidalgo, which ended the Mexican-American War in 1848, created the first generation of Mexican Americans in the United States in its decree that the 100,000 Mexicans living in territory ceded to the United States were henceforth American citizens (Source 39). For the remainder of the nineteenth century, Mexicans continued to cross the fairly porous border between the two countries, and immigration into the U.S. Southwest increased in the next century, particularly in the era of the Mexican Revolution. Nearly 500,000 Mexican Americans were then forcibly repatriated to Mexico during the Great Depression. When the United States experienced labor shortages during World War II, the country sought Mexican immigrants, using the *bracero* (guest worker) program to once again encourage agrarian workers to cross the border. Chicanos have formed a core element of the agrarian workforce in the U.S. Southwest ever since. They have also played a central role in the U.S. agrarian labor movement since the 1930s, and their period of greatest activism was during the mid-1960s.

---

*Luis Valdez, "The Tale of La Raza," in *The Chicanos: Mexican American Voices,* eds. Ed Ludwig and James Santibañez (Baltimore: Penguin Books, 1971), pp. 95–100.

In his essay "The Tale of La Raza," Luis Valdez reflects on this history and on the story of a famous strike that migrant Mexican grape pickers staged in Delano, California, in 1965–1966. The labor leader César Chávez and the union he helped to found, the National Farm Workers Association (NFWA), coordinated the event, which began with a 250-mile march from Delano to Sacramento and included Chávez's nationally publicized twenty-five-day hunger strike, as well as call for a national grape boycott. Luis Valdez, whose parents were farmworkers, founded El Teatro Campesino, a theater group that performed in the fields and on the backs of flatbed trucks for workers on strike. Valdez is also the author of the Plan de Delano. A prolific writer and director, Valdez is considered one of the fathers of Mexican American theater. In this essay, he assigns history a central role in forming the Chicano character. To what historical episodes or personages does he refer? What interpretations does he give to them? What is it about the United States in the 1960s that can help us understand Valdez's uses of Mexican history?

The Tale of the Raza

The revolt in Delano is more than a labor struggle. Mexican grape pickers did not march 300 miles to Sacramento, carrying the standard of the *Virgin de Guadalupe,* merely to dramatize economic grievances. Beyond unionization, beyond politics, there is the desire of a New World race to reconcile the conflicts of its 500-year-old history. *La Raza* is trying to find its place in the sun it once worshiped as a Supreme Being.

La Raza, the race, is the Mexican people. Sentimental and cynical, fierce and docile, faithful and treacherous, individualistic and herd-following, in love with life and obsessed with death, the personality of the *raza* encompasses all the complexity of our history. The conquest of Mexico was no conquest at all. It shattered our ancient Indian universe, but more of it was left above ground than beans and tortillas. Below the foundations of our Spanish culture, we still sense the ruins of an entirely different civilization.

Most of us know we are not European simply by looking in a mirror—the shape of the eyes, the curve of the nose, the color of skin, the texture of hair; these things belong to another time, another people. Together with a million little stubborn mannerisms, beliefs, myths, superstitions, words, thoughts—things not so easily detected—they fill our Spanish life with Indian contradictions. It is not enough to say we suffer an identity crisis, because that crisis has been our way of life for the last five centuries.

That we Mexicans speak of ourselves as a "race" is the biggest contradiction of them all. The *conquistadores,* of course, mated with their Indian women with customary abandon, creating a nation of bewildered half-breeds in countless shapes, colors, and sizes. Unlike our fathers and mothers, unlike each other, we *mestizos* [people of Spanish and Indian parentage] solved the problem with poetic license and called ourselves *la raza.* A Mexican's first loyalty—when one of us is threatened by strangers from the outside—is to that race. Either we recognize our total unity on the basis of *raza,* or the ghosts of a 100,000 feuding Indian tribes, bloods, and mores will come back to haunt us.

A little more than 60 years ago the Revolution of 1910 unleashed such a terrible social upheaval that it took 10 years of insane slaughter to calm the ghosts of the past. The Revolution took Mexico from the hands of New World Spaniards (who in turn were selling it to American and British interests) and gave it, for the first time and at the price of a million murders, to the Mexicans.

Any Mexican deeply loves his *mestizo patria,* even those who, like myself, were born in the United States. At best, our cultural schizophrenia has led us to action through the all-encompassing poetry of religion, which is a fancy way of saying blind faith. The Virgin of Guadalupe, the supreme poetic expression of our Mexican desire to be one people, has inspired Mexicans more than once to social revolution. At worst, our two-sidedness has led us to inaction. The last divine Aztec emperor was murdered in the jungles of Guatemala, and his descendants were put to work in the fields. We are still there, in dry, plain American Delano.

It was the triple magnetism of *raza, patria,* and the Virgin of Guadalupe which organized Mexican American farmworkers in Delano—that and César Chávez. Chávez was not a traditional bombastic Mexican revolutionary; nor was he a *gavacho,* a gringo, a white social worker type. Both types had tried to organize the *raza* and failed. Here was César, burning with a patient fire, poor like us, dark like us, talking quietly, moving people to talk about their problems, attacking the little problems first, and suggesting, always suggesting—never more than that—solutions that seemed attainable. We didn't know it until we met him, but he was the leader we had been waiting for.

Although he sometimes reminds one of Benito Juárez, César is our first real Mexican-American leader. Used to hybrid forms, the *raza* includes all Mexicans, even hyphenated Mexican-Americans; but divergent histories are slowly making the *raza* in the United States different from the *raza* in Mexico. We who were born here missed out on the chief legacy of the Revolution: the chance to forge a nation true to all the forces that have molded us, to be one people. Now we must seek our own destiny, and Delano is only the beginning of our active search. For the last hundred years our revolutionary progress has not only been frustrated, it has been totally suppressed. This is a society largely hostile to our cultural values. There is no poetry about the United States. No depth, no faith, no allowance for human contrariness. No soul, no mariachi, no chili sauce, no pulque, no mysticism, no *chingaderas* [screw-ups]. . . .

The pilgrimage to Sacramento was no mere publicity trick. The *raza* has a tradition of migrations, starting from the legend of the founding of Mexico. Nezahualcoyotl, a great Indian leader, advised his primitive *Chichimecas,* forerunners of the Aztecs, to begin a march to the south. In that march, he prophesied, the children would age and the old would die, but their grandchildren would come to a great lake. In that lake they would find an eagle devouring a serpent, and on that spot, they would begin to build a great nation. The nation was Aztec Mexico, and the eagle and the serpent are the symbols of the *patria.* They are emblazoned on the Mexican flag, which the marchers took to Sacramento with pride. . . .

Huelga means strike. With the poetic instinct of the *raza,* the Delano grape strikers have made it mean a dozen other things. It is a declaration, a challenge, a greeting, a feeling, a movement. We cried *Huelga!* to the scabs, *Huelga!* to the labor contractors, to the growers, to Governor Brown. With the Schenley and DiGiorgio boycotts, it was *Huelga!* to the whole country. It is the most significant word in our entire Mexican-American history. If the *raza* of Mexico believes in *La Patria,* we believe in *La Huelga.* . . .

The Virgin of Guadalupe was the first hint to farmworkers that the pilgrimage implied social revolution. During the Mexican Revolution, the peasant armies of Emiliano Zapata carried her standard, not only because they sought her divine protection, but because she symbolized the Mexico of the poor and humble. It was a simple Mexican Indian, Juan Diego, who first saw her in a vision at Guadalupe. Beautifully dark and Indian in feature, she was the New World version of the Mother of Christ. Even though some of her worshippers in Mexico still identify her with Tonatzin, an Aztec goddess, she is a Catholic saint of Indian creation—a Mexican. The people's response was immediate and reverent. They joined the march by the thousands, falling in line behind her standard. To the Catholic hypocrites against the pilgrimage and strike the Virgin said *Huelga!*

The struggle for better wages and better working conditions in Delano is but the first, realistic articulation of our need for unity. To emerge from the mire of our past in the United States, to leave behind the divisive, deadening influence of poverty, we must have bargaining power. We must have unions. To the farmworkers who joined the pilgrimage, this cultural pride was revolutionary. There were old symbols—Zapata lapel buttons—and new symbols standing for new social protest and revolt; the red thunderbird flags of the NFWA, picket signs, armbands. . . .

The NFWA is a radical union because it started, and continues to grow, as a community organization. Its store, cafeteria, clinic, garage, newspaper, and weekly meeting have established a sense of community the Delano farmworkers will not relinquish. After years of isolation in the barrios of Great Valley slum towns like Delano, after years of living in labor camps and ranches at the mercy and caprice of growers and contractors, the Mexican-American farmworker is developing his own ideas about living in the United States. He wants to be equal with all the working men of the nation, and he does not mean by the standard middle-class route. We are repelled by the human disintegration of peoples and cultures as they fall apart in this Great Gringo Melting Pot, and determined that this will not happen to us. But there will always be a *raza* in this country. There are millions more where we came from, across the thousand miles of common border between Mexico and the United States. For millions of farmworkers, from the Mexicans and Filipinos of the West to the Afro-Americans of the South, the United States has come to a social, political, and cultural impasse. Listen to these people, and you will hear the first murmurings of revolution.

Central Themes

The northern frontier, land and labor, religion, race and ethnicity

Suggested Reading

Acuña, Rodolfo F. *Occupied America: A History of Chicanos.* New York: Pearson Longman, 2007.

Meier, Matt S., and Feliciano Rivera. *Mexican Americans/American Mexicans: From Conquistadors to Chicanos.* New York: Hill and Wang, 1993.

Mexican Migration Project (oral histories of Mexican migrants). Available at: http://mmp.opr.princeton.edu/expressions/stories-en.aspx.

Vargas, Zaragosa. *Labor Rights Are Civil Rights: Mexican American Workers in Twentieth-Century America.* Princeton, NJ: Princeton University Press, 2005.

Related Sources

53. Revolution in Morelos (1911)
65. Official History (1951)
67. Rubén Jaramillo and the Struggle for *Campesino* Rights in Postrevolutionary Morelos (1967)
71. The 1985 Earthquake (1985, 1995)
75. Maquila Workers Organize (2006)

67. Rubén Jaramillo and the Struggle for *Campesino* Rights in Postrevolutionary Morelos (1967)*

Rubén Jaramillo was born in Tlaquiltenango, Morelos (1900). At the age of fifteen, he joined Zapata's army (Source 53). By the close of the 1920s, he had become an important agrarian leader who supported the presidency of Lázaro Cárdenas. In 1938, Jaramillo inaugurated a sugar-processing cooperative in Zacatepec, Morelos, and was elected to the mill's first Council of Administration and Oversight. Under President Manuel Avila Camacho (1940–1946), state support for cooperative endeavors, workers' rights, and land reform dwindled. Jaramillo was often forced to go underground in order to avoid death threats meant to end his continued work on behalf of *campesinos* (rural workers). Nevertheless, Jaramillo was able to parlay the power he accrued as a popular campesino representative. In 1958, President Adolfo López Mateos named him as a special delegate of the main campesino organization, the National Peasant Confederation. During the 1960s, Jaramillo supported land

*Rubén Jaramillo, *Autobiografía* (Mexico City: Editorial Nuestro Tiempo, 1967), pp. 13–15, 19–20, 23–25, 39, 74–75, 104–105. Excerpts translated by Tanya Huntington and the editors.

invasions and the formation of a production collective. On May 23, 1962, judicial police and soldiers kidnapped Jaramillo, his pregnant wife, and their three sons and shot them near the Pre-Columbian ruins of Xochicalco. No one was ever brought to trial for the crime.

Jaramillo's *Autobiography* was written in the third person; Jaramillo claimed that his religious convictions prohibited him from speaking in a way that celebrated himself. The reader might ask what aspects of Mexican political culture would have reinforced Jaramillo's desire to deemphasize the self while at the same time telling his story. What does Jaramillo's story tell us about how Mexican politics worked and how they changed over time? The journalist Froylán Manjarrez brought the autobiography to light by having it published in the 1960s, and we might well ask how Jaramillo's portrayal of Mexican history and bureaucracy might have dovetailed with the sort of critiques being made by Mexican youth at that time.

Autobiography (1967)

1. Origins and Revolution

His father was called Atanasio Jaramillo, the great-grandson of General Julián Jaramillo Corral, friend and collaborator of Don Benito Juárez, who was known as the Most Meritorious of the Americas. Don Atanasio passed away in the year 1903, widowing Mrs. Romana Ménez Nava de Jaramillo and leaving her with the following children: Beatriz, Antonio, Francisco, Rubén, Porfirio, and Reyes Jaramillo.

The Jaramillos came from the Zacualpan mines in the State of Mexico. Don Atanasio Jaramillo was a mining expert, and Doña Romana was a campesina. They both had numerous relatives in Cuernavaca, Yautepec, Tlaquiltenango, and Jojutla way back before these towns came to form part of the State of Morelos, because they originally belonged to the State of Mexico. Around the year 1902, approximately 38 years after the foundation of what is today the State of Morelos, the Jaramillos moved to the Morelos area for work in the construction of canals, [and this is] where they had their children. After several years of sporadic work, Don Atanasio was felled by a serious bout of lung disease and they returned to their native land, where he passed away soon after. A year later, Mrs. Jaramillo returned to the State of Morelos with her children, all of them minors, and declared as her residence the township of Tlaquiltenango, where it is known that Francisco, Rubén, Porfirio, and Reyes Jaramillo were born. . . .

Mrs. Romana Ménez Nava, Jaramillo's widow, suffered, together with her children, the most harsh devastation of the Revolution of 1910. When rights were suspended in 1912 and 1913, she went to live in the mountains of the township of Tlaquiltenango, feeding not only her children, but providing food for the revolutionaries as well.

But around the months of May or June in 1914, she was bit by a scorpion and passed away near a place called Los Elotes, in the township of Tlaquiltenango. . . .

The year 1914 went by, and in late 1915 Jesús Zorrillo, who was around age 18, and one of his friends convinced Jaramillo of the revolutionary ideals of "Land and Liberty." Their comrade Rubén Jaramillo agreed to take up arms by joining the revolutionary group under the command of J. Zorrillo, and that is how Rubén M. Jaramillo began his career at arms. . . .

Despite his young age, he knew how to treat these people, and in this manner, in the Jaramillista camp, there were always rations while others lacked them because citizens from elsewhere supplied him with all the necessities. And one always saw Jaramillo surrounded by local people, and he, with the simple, affable character that never failed him, attended to them all. These people's appreciation and recognition of Jaramillo was so great, that even today he relies on their esteem and is spoken very well of, to such a degree that the powerful forces that have persecuted him since the year 1943 because he continues to uphold his revolutionary ideals in favor of the people, have never been able to stop him, no matter how hard his very influential federal and civil enemies have tried. . . .

Then [during the 1920s] he went to work for the oil companies at El Ebano. There he realized that this industry belonged to foreigners, and that the revolutionaries who were active in these areas received large sums of money from the companies in return for not causing them any damage, and for this reason, he no longer was inclined to join them and kept on working.

At the Aguabuena sugar plantation there was a man from the town of Amacuzac named Luis Jaime who was a great employee of the plantation, and he kept Jaramillo well informed regarding revolutionary affairs. And one fine day, this friend said to him: "Things aren't going well. They say that Don Venustiano Carranza, because of the presidential elections, is distancing himself from his main leaders, including General Álvaro Obregón, who also wants to be President of the Republic; and everyone knows he [Obregón] already controls most of the army generals and it is possible that a putsch will take place. Moreover, they say he's already made commitments to landowners and also to the revolutionaries, to whom he promised to fulfill the Ayala Plan by handing over the land to the people, so that the Zapatista ideals will be fulfilled by General Obregón. . . ."

When Jaramillo heard this he immediately communicated it to his friends, and everyone was happy, except for Jaramillo, who, as always, was suspicious, and said: "Although the news is reason to celebrate, it also gives reason to be cautious, for the agreements that Obregón has made with landowners could result in the disillusionment of the great and just aspirations of the Revolution; it could well be that although we all have land, we continue to work as cheap labor for the owners. We will see what these agreements consist of."

2. Institutions, Closed Doors

The beautiful plains that in distant times, back when Tlaquiltenango was in the State of Mexico, were known as the Jegüital Plains, were in the old days of the monopolistic land-owners a veritable hideout for wild animals, and a nesting ground for flocks of ducks, and the roads turned to mire.

In view [of] such living conditions among the farmers in Tlaquiltenango, Rubén M. Jaramillo commented on this terrible, disastrous, and sad situation. But happily, one fine day he went over to the shack of a man by the name of Nicéforo Gómez for a pound of sugar, and in the paper they wrapped the sugar in, which was a piece of newspaper, there was a small article that read:

"The Agricultural Credit Bank, with offices in Mexico City, opens its doors to all farmers with provisional possession of their lands, so that they may obtain credit from the Bank in order to cultivate these lands. Credit will only be given to those who organize and form agricultural credit associations that number 11 associates or more, wherever possible, but only if the number of associates is odd, not even. For more information, ask the manager of said Bank for a full set of instructions, or send a commission to the Bank to receive more detailed instructions. . . . "

And so, Rubén Jaramillo, who at this time could barely read—his wife, Misses Epifania R. de Jaramillo, first taught him his letters, and the professor Tomás Molina taught him a bit more—with the aforementioned article, headed to the home of Antonio Aguas and presented him with the question of obtaining credit from the Agricultural Credit Bank. Indeed, Mister Antonio Aguas invited Delfino García and many others from the group who had originally taken the initiative to take possession of land, and all were in agreement. Three days after the conversation between Jaramillo and Aguas, there was a gathering of no fewer than fifty campesinos at the home of Lucas Villalba.

"Comrades, we've called this small meeting to make you see the sad conditions we live in, and which we find it just to bring to an end. All those present here have received a plot of land so that, by sowing it and harvesting its crops, we can live in ease. But unfortunately, none of us feels happy with his land, because we don't have the necessary resources to work it and make it as productive as it should be. It's truly a shame to see our fields so fertile, yet not rendering sufficient fruits to support ourselves and our families. And what little they do render is snatched away from us at ridiculous, starvation prices, by local and foreign hoarders, making them richer and us poorer. You see how cheap our rice is, to the point that, in truth, its cultivation is not cost-effective, and with such stingy prices, it isn't possible for our economic life to improve; the lands will be impoverished and us along with them, and we will never remedy our condition as hungry people. And there's no reason why, being the owners of such good lands, we should be so miserably poor. I ask you whether what I'm saying is true or not." And everyone said it was true. . . .

Next, he said: "I'm asking you if you'd be willing to organize and form an agricultural credit association, to obtain from the Bank of the same name the monetary credit we need to cultivate our *ejidos* [communally held land]." They all responded that they agreed to organize, and one of those present asked: "What are the requirements?" Jaramillo said: "I'm getting to that. Comrade Antonio Aguas has a newspaper clipping indicating the prerequisites." The newspaper was read before everyone present and, once the reading was finished, Jaramillo asked: "Are you aware of the prerequisites?" Everyone said: "We are." "And how do you find them?" They responded: "Perfectly fine." "So then, shall we get to work?" "Yes," they all answered in unison. . . .

Jaramillo was invited by General Cárdenas to a luncheon at the natural springs in Tehuixtla with Mr. Elpidio Perdomo, who was State Governor, in attendance. This was around December 1938, that is to say, ten months after becoming an advisor. It was during this meal that General Cárdenas indicated that the future President of the Republic would be General Don Manuel Ávila Camacho. Jaramillo said to General Cárdenas: "And won't he betray us? You know how Don Maximino is." To which General Cárdenas replied: "Don Manuel is a good man, and not all the fingers on his hands are alike. I want the farmers to support General Ávila Camacho through you." Jaramillo told him, "I don't sympathize with the Ávila Camachos because their track record in the State of Puebla is dubious with regards to our revolutionary ideology, the means by which our people might break free of all hindrances, and if this man returns us to the past, we won't be in agreement. . . ."

[The following relates to Jaramillo's response to a plot to assassinate him.] Thus it was that at four in the afternoon on that same day the townspeople arrived. There, Jaramillo, taking the prisoner by the arm, presented himself to the group and told them: "I bring with me this young man so that you may know him." And he asked him: "Why did you come to these parts?" The young man answered: "To assassinate you, boss." "In exchange for what?" "For 45,000 pesos, and a position in the government or on the plantation." "What weapon were you given to accomplish this?" Answer: "A regulation .45 caliber pistol." Jaramillo said: "Could this be it?" The young man said: "That's the one!" Rubén M. Jaramillo told everyone present, "What would you do to this man if you were in my shoes?" Some said they should kill him, after hanging him first; this was the judgment of most of the townspeople, but Jaramillo said: "That's what I should do, but such an attitude would cast me in the same criminal role as the ones who hired this young man who, because he didn't know the instincts of these people, let himself be overwhelmed by the offers they made, not thinking that these same people later on would have him killed, just as they have done with others who, like this young man, have fallen for the flattery of these hypocrites. Thus they have vilified many good people from our simple, humble town. But in this case, I do not intend to do harm to the one who intended to do me wrong, and I want to repay this boy's wrong with right, [this boy] whom I consider less guilty than those who hired him, those who one day, not long from now, God will place in our hands, and then they will answer for all the evil deeds they have availed themselves of to intimidate citizens who speak in the name of justice for the people and the law. . . ."

Jaramillo told Felipe Morán: "Here, take him with you, just as I indicated before." The youth somewhat nervously asked that he be allowed to sing a song of gratitude, which made tears fall from the eyes of the men and women present. Once the song was over, sobbing with emotion, he gave Jaramillo a strong embrace and, wiping his eyes, took his leave. . . .

10. Policy Against the Revolutionary Struggle

Everyone returned to work energetically. This was on September 13, [1945,] in Mexico City. Jaramillo continued working at the "April 2nd" market, and was an *henriquista* [a supporter of General Henríquez Guzmán] at the time, but in the end, General Henríquez Guzmán withdrew from the race, so that in the end he didn't register the party [with the government] or declare himself a candidate for President of the Republic nationwide. . . .

In that same month, the head of the Markets Office, who was nicknamed "La Mona,"* called all the market administrators together, and once they were gathered, he said to them: "I've called you here to tell you it is the will of the President of the Republic, General Manuel Ávila Camacho, to be substituted in power by Mr. Miguel Alemán Valdés, the current Secretary of the Interior. As a result, by the following month of November, a meeting will take place in the México Arena Theater in order to launch his candidacy, and therefore it is necessary that all of you administrators bring tenants from the market stands with you that day. This won't be in vain, given that starting now, each of you can tell me how many people you can bring."

Next he took from his desk many packets of one thousand peso bills. "Let me know the number of people you'll bring." Then the administrator of La Merced market said, "I'll bring six thousand with me." "Here you are: $6,000.00." Then he said to the administrator of La Lagunilla: "You, how many will you bring?" And he said, "Six thousand." And he said: "Here you are: $6,000.00." Then the administrator of Villa de Guadalupe said, "Five thousand for me." And he said, "Here you are: $5,000.00," and thus they were all chained together.

Only Rubén M. Jaramillo was able to say, when he was asked in turn: "I, Mr. Aguirre, am a democrat who loves justice, independence, and liberty for my people, and I cannot do what my colleagues have done. My conscience, my freedom, and my reputation as a Mexican cannot be bought. I serve the government for the salary it pays me and to do the job commended to me, but not to deliver tenants into anyone's hands. If they, in keeping with the freedom they enjoy under our laws, wish to surrender themselves, it will be up to their free and spontaneous will to do so, but it won't be because I have seduced them. . . . "

---

* *Translator's note:* This nickname is feminine and means "pretty one."

Central Themes

Indigenous people, land and labor

Suggested Reading

Boyer, Christopher. *Becoming Campesino: Politics, Identity, and Agrarian Struggle in Postrevolutionary Michoacán, 1920–1935.* Stanford, CA: Stanford University Press, 2003.

Hart, Paul. *Bitter Harvest: The Social Transformation of Morelos, Mexico, and the Origins of the Zapatista Revolution, 1840–1910.* Albuquerque: University of New Mexico Press, 2005.

Padilla, Tanalís. *Rural Resistance in the Land of Zapata: The Jaramillista Movement and the Myth of the Pax Priísta, 1940–1962.* Durham, NC: Duke University Press, 2008.

Related Sources

53. Revolution in Morelos (1911)
54. Land, Labor, and the Church in the Mexican Constitution (1917)
57. Petitioning the President (the 1920s)

PART 9

Neoliberalism and Its Discontents (1968–2006)

If the period from 1940 to 1968 saw the institutionalization of the Mexican Revolution by the political party that claimed to embody its objectives, the era from 1968 to the present has seen the dismantling of much of this institutionalization. The documents in this final section address the events that led to the end of the Partido Revolucionario Institucional (PRI)'s eight-decade monopoly of the Mexican state. They focus on the three events that played the biggest role in securing the PRI's downfall. These selections also illustrate how, in recent decades, Mexicans have addressed the unfulfilled goals of the Revolution of 1910 through their writing, organizing, and armed rebellion, evoking in all of these the challenges posed by generations of earlier rebels and critics.

The first major event leading to the collapse of the PRI's monopoly on power was the Tlatelolco Massacre of October 2, 1968 (Source 68). On this dreadful date, the Mexican army brutally repressed widespread student protest against the presidency of Gustavo Díaz Ordaz. In the wake of the killing, Mexicans reeled in disbelief that their government had both exercised such excessive force against its own citizenry and disavowed its involvement in the violence. Two decades later, a second disaster further dislodged the population's faith in the legitimacy of the PRI. On September 19, 1985, an estimated ten thousand Mexicans died in a major earthquake that devastated the Mexican capital and surrounding area (Source 71). Mexicans grew incensed at the slowness and inadequacy of the state's emergency responses to the crisis. In the absence of government leadership, citizens turned to each other in attempting to rebuild broken lives in the chaos of the aftermath.

The third major force that pushed the PRI from power at the turn of the twenty-first century was an insurgent movement that had first declared war on what it called an illegitimate Mexican state on January 1, 1994. By the late 1990s, popular support for the Ejército Zapatista de Liberación Nacional (EZLN) was growing, both domestically and internationally, through its eloquent written communications and media ingenuity, its success in negotiating the San Andrés peace agreements of 1996, and its articulation of the Mexican populace's grievances against the federal government (Source 72).

Critiques of the PRI and its antecedents that had surfaced in Mexico in more muted tones in earlier periods (sources 56, 57, 62, and 67) became more frequent and more pointed in the last four decades of the twentieth century. Many of them centered on the state's mishandling of these three episodes (sources 68 and 71), but some also tackled issues such as governmental corruption of the social benefits that Mexico offered its citizens, including public housing (Source 69). Some critiques appeared in conventional epistolary form (sources 69 and 73), but others followed the well-worn tradition of Mexican satire in such genres as the comic book (Source 70) and the cabaret script (Source 74). In all its forms, criticism of the government grew in confidence and popularity, and by the late 1990s it was a ubiquitous narrative of daytime television and the stuff of street performance—children, for instance, begged at traffic lights wearing convict uniforms and plastic masks representing ex-President Carlos Salinas de Gortari.

Vicente Fox of the Partido de Acción Nacional (PAN) was elected president of Mexico in the historic elections of July 2000. His party's ideology originated in the Catholic Cristero Rebellion of 1928 and was formalized in 1939 and 1940 (Source 63). While some observers expressed cautious optimism that the PAN's assumption of power heralded the advent of democracy in Mexico, many others, including the dramatist Jesusa Rodríguez (Source 74), charged that PAN rule merely signified the perpetuation of PRI-style politics coupled with a conservative social agenda. One of Fox's prominent campaign promises had been to investigate the Mexican "dirty wars" that transpired particularly under the presidencies of Presidents Díaz Ordaz (1964–1970), Luís Echeverría Álvarez (1970–1976), and José López Portillo (1976–1982). Skepticism about Fox's intention to promote real change heightened when members of the research team who helped prepare the special prosecutor's "Historical Report to Mexican Society," released in November 2006, immediately denounced the report for its inaccuracies, which included the elimination of entire chapters of the earlier drafts (Source 76).

One set of PRI initiatives that Fox and his successor, President Felipe Calderón Hinjosa, adopted and magnified were based in the economic policies known in Mexico as neoliberalism. This economic model called for deregulation of the state-controlled economy, which had been a central tenet of Mexican revolutionaries' responses to the liberal economy of the Porfiriato (1876–1911) (sources 49 and 61). Neoliberal policy in Mexico has eliminated protective tariffs and state monopolies, courted foreign capital, and privatized previously public-controlled sectors, including health care and education. President Carlos Salinas de Gortari (1988–1994) provoked heated responses to his government's promotion of neoliberalism with his modification in 1992 of the protections extended to small landholders in the 1917 Constitution (sources 54 and 73). The PRI had laid a cornerstone of its neoliberal program as early as 1965 with the creation of the Border Industrialization Program by which it enticed multinational firms to establish factories on Mexico's northern frontier in exchange for tax benefits and a pool of inexpensive labor. The PRI also viewed the program as a solution to the rising unemployment in Mexico caused by the end of the *bracero (*guest worker) program (Source 66). Ten years later, the border zone was dotted with over four hundred *maquilas* (multinational-owned factories), and by the late 1990s over three thousand operated in this region where employers were unhampered by state regulation of environmental, health, or safety issues (Source 75).

Mexicans entered the twenty-first century under new political leadership while questioning whether it would lead them in new directions. As illustrated in the ideas of the activist Luis Valdez (Source 66), the insurgent Subcommandante Marcos (Source 72), the playwright Jesusa Rodríguez (Source 74), and the labor activist Jaime Cota (Source 75), Mexicans also continued to look to the past as a way of understanding their present. It is perhaps no coincidence that the latter two of these disparate figures make reference to the writings of the outspoken nun of the seventeenth century, Sor Juana Inés de la Cruz (Source 26). Rodríguez, Cota, and many others use history to interpret the contradictions of Mexican society, to praise its accomplishments, and to inspire those who seek to change it. For Mexicans live in a society where knowledge of the past matters, where subway station names, pop song lyrics, and even rearview mirror decorations frequently refer to historic figures and events. Since at least the time of the Aztecs' first emperor, Itzcoatl, burner of books, Mexicans have taken seriously the power that historical events—and their recording—can exert on those living in the present.

68. Eyewitness and Newspaper Accounts of the Tlatelolco Massacre (1968)*

In 1968 the Mexican state violently repressed a student movement that challenged the authoritarianism of the Partido Revolucionario Institucional (PRI). In the months leading up to the 1968 summer Olympic Games, students from several Mexico City postsecondary institutions began protesting state spending on preparations for the Games, which they believed would benefit only a small segment of Mexican society. Their grievances quickly escalated. Imprisonment and *granadero* (paramilitary riot police) brutality against demonstrators provoked further protests. The National Strike Committee (CNH) orchestrated a public campaign in which students disputed the state's intolerance of political dissent, demanded the release of political prisoners, and contested the PRI's impunity in a five-decade-long history of single-party rule. In August the CNH organized a protest of half a million people in Mexico City's *Zócalo* (main plaza); it was the largest antigovernment demonstration in Mexican history. The state responded with tanks and armored cars. One student was killed, and further protests followed.

On October 2, 1968, students staged a demonstration in the Plaza de las Tres Culturas in the District of Tlatelolco. Against a backdrop of Aztec ruins, a sixteenth-century Franciscan mission, and recently built low-income housing projects, five thousand students and supporters gathered to hear speeches and register dissent. The army and police units arrived, but the demonstrators refused to disband. Helicopters circled overhead, and the army and paramilitary units opened fire on the students. The Mexican state and the families of those killed on the Plaza that day continue to disagree about which group initiated the bloodshed that followed and about the number and identities of those killed. Shortly after the massacre, official government statistics admitted only eight deaths, although the state later acknowledged that as many as forty-three people had died. Human rights organizations placed the number at four hundred or higher. The state's refusal to ever satisfactorily address its participation in this violence had significant repercussions on subsequent history. One of the Tlatelolco Massacre's most important consequences was that public awareness of the state's use of violence against its own citizens initiated a crisis of confidence in the PRI that led to the unraveling of the party's hegemonic control of the country.

Included here are two of the hundreds of eyewitness descriptions of the massacre collected by the journalist Elena Poniatowska, along with several newspaper articles

---

*Elena Poniatowska, *Massacre in Mexico,* trans. Helen R. Lane, pp. 219–221, 258–259. Copyright ©1975 by The Viking Press; original copyright © 1971 by Ediciones Era SA de CV. Used by permission of Viking Penguin, a division of Penguin Group (USA) Inc.; newspaper sources are listed with each excerpt. Excerpts translated by the editors.

and editorials about the events. Scholars have often asserted that a media blackout left the horror of the Tlatelolco Massacre of 1968 unreported. Throughout the era of the PRI monopoly on state power, Mexico's news media were heavily state-controlled. Until 1990, for instance, the federal government used its newsprint monopoly to influence newspapers' editorial content and reporting. However, as documented in the following news stories from several Mexico City dailies published in the first days following the Tlatelolco Massacre, a total media blackout did not occur.

Compare the first eyewitness accounts to those provided in the news publications. In what ways do the different reports of events coincide or differ? How might we explain those similarities and differences? What details from the accounts included here suggest why this event so profoundly shocked the Mexican populace? Where and how do the news pieces and editorials cautiously critique the state? What lies at the root of the outrage some of the articles express toward the students? Elements of individual articles also present the potential for interesting analysis. Why might *El Sol* have decided to reproduce UPI reporter Mike Hughes's complete report in its pages? What changes from his earlier address (Source 62) are reflected in Lázaro Cárdenas's address to the Mexican populace reproduced here, and what has remained the same? Some commentators, including the writer Octavio Paz, have compared the 1968 massacre to earlier Mexico City uprisings, including that of 1692 (Source 27). Is there any foundation to this comparison?

María Alicia Martínez Medrano, Nursery-School Director

There was nothing we could do but keep running. They were firing at us from all directions. We ran six or eight feet, keeping under cover, and then ten or twelve feet out in the open. Rifle fire sounds very much like a jet taking off. There was nothing to do but keep running. We heard the display windows of the shops on the ground floor of the Chihuahua building shatter, and we suddenly decided we ought to make a run for the stairway. As I stood down there, babbling all sorts of nonsense, I also suddenly remembered all my many friends and comrades at the meeting and got terrible cramps in my stomach. I remembered names, faces. As I reached this stairway that the people from the CNH who were going to speak had been going up and down all during the afternoon, I met Margarita and Meche, who said to me in the most despairing tone of voice, "María Alicia, our children are up there on the fourth floor!"

For the first time I had the feeling I might be able to do something useful amid all this confusion and suffering, despite my sense of utter helplessness, and I said to them, "I'll go up there with you."

The youngster who had saved my life—by leaping on me and throwing me to the floor there on the speakers' stand when they first started shooting at us—went upstairs with us: he was my armor, my cape, my shield. I have no idea who he was. I have a photographic memory, but I can't remember his face at all. . . . The three of us started up the stairs, and on the first landing we met another youngster. I had seen him on the speakers' stand there on the fourth floor of the Chihuahua building, too, talking with various Movement people as though he knew them very well. I remember him particularly because he'd apparently been wounded in the right wrist and had a white handkerchief wrapped around his hand.

"Don't leave, *señora,* it'll all be over soon," he said to me.

I was about to go downstairs again, because I'd spied some girl friends of mine down on the esplanade. But the boy took me by the arm and very solicitously helped me up the stairs. I was touched by this courageous behavior on the part of yet another student here, and went upstairs with him.

Then Mercedes shouted, "*Señor,* my children are there upstairs!"

Margarita shouted that her children were up there, too, and I stopped there on the stairs and looked at the youngster escorting me, thinking that the courage of those kids is really incredible sometimes. Many hours later, I discovered that my escort was one of the assassins guarding the stairway so that none of the CNH people would escape. He took us back downstairs then, and I remember that we were caught up in a whole crowd of people and shoved to the corner of the Chihuahua building, and that meanwhile there was a steady hail of bullets from the buildings.

A girl came by shouting, "You murderers, you murderers!" I took her in my arms and tried to calm her down, but she kept screaming louder and louder, until finally the youngster behind me grabbed hold of her and started shaking her. I noticed then that her ear had been shot off and her head was bleeding. The people in the crowd kept piling one on top of another, seeking shelter from the rain of bullets; we were all right on each other's necks, and I felt as though I were caught in the middle of a riot or squeezed in a sardine can.

I stood there staring at the tips of the coffee-colored shoes of some woman. Several rounds of machine-gun bullets suddenly raked the spot where we were standing, and I saw one bullet land just a few inches from that woman's shoe. All she said was, "Oh, my goodness!" and another voice answered, "Make a run for it. If you stay here you'll be even worse off; you're sure to get hurt here." We all started running again and just then I spied a red Datsun with a young girl at the wheel. She'd been shot, and I saw her collapse on top of the steering wheel; the horn kept blowing and blowing. . . . The youngsters kept saying, "Don't look, don't look." We ran on toward one of the buildings behind Chihuahua.

Gilberto Guevara Niebla of the CNH

The government's only proof of its contention that there were "sharpshooters" involved is the fact that General Hernández Toledo was wounded during the "activities" that day. Nonetheless there are a number of significant details that demolish this argument. In the first place, General Toledo was wounded in the back, and if we take into account the fact that he was passing just in front of the Foreign Relations building, proceeding in the direction of the Plaza de las Tres Culturas, when he was struck by the bullet, we may conclude that the shot came from his own troops, either from one of his own men in the rear guard, or from the helicopters that were participating in the slaughter at that point, hovering overhead and firing down at the crowd helplessly trapped in the Plaza. In the second place, this reconstruction of events is further substantiated by the fact that the bullet which hit the General was of the same caliber as an AR-18 rifle cartridge, this rifle being a brand-new weapon which has heretofore been used almost exclusively by the United States Marine Corps in Vietnam. Moreover, even though the precise circumstances which led to General Toledo's receiving this bullet wound have yet to be determined, the fact that the shots apparently came from some nearby building, plus the fact that it has not yet been determined what person or persons were doing the shooting, leads one to suspect that the bullets were fired by one or several special sharpshooters, who were undoubtedly very well trained and able to hit their precise targets from the very first and provide perfect cover for the rear guard. All the apartments of the buildings around the Plaza were carefully searched by the Army troops and the police, and no weapons of the type mentioned were found anywhere. All this is further corroborated by the fact that the agents of the Olimpia Battalion are known to have also fired on the troops approaching the Plaza or already inside it at that particular moment.

Ángel Martinez Agis, Reporter, Excelsior, *Thursday, October 3, 1968*

"Chihuahua" Building: 6 o'clock

Bengala lights, perhaps a signal
Police arrived, pistols in their hands
Shots. All at apartment 210

Third floor "Chihuahua" building. A few more than 10,000 people in the Plaza "Three cultures." Three students have taken the microphone. One for introductions, another from the Politécnico and one more from the University.*

On the central balcony of the building are the journalists, some photographers and cameramen, reporters and foreign correspondents.

The speakers attacked politicians, some journalists, and they even went so far as to propose a boycott against a city newspaper.

*The "Politécnico" was the National Politechnical Institute, whose students, along with those from the National Autonomous University of Mexico (UNAM), were the most active in the movement.

Workers were received amid applause. It was said that they were railroad workers. They displayed a banner that said "Railroad Workers Support the Movement and Do Not Recognize the Romero Flores–GDO Talks."

Some of them even announced the beginning of progressive strikes.

Four green Bengala lights fell on the pools of water in the square. It was 6:10.

Several hundred Judicial Police agents, from the national Attorney General's Office, from the Federal Security Office arrived and shouted at the journalists, "Get down from there!" They carried pistols in their hands.

Those same agents told the students:

"Stop there. No one move. . . . "

The Shooting Begins

The journalists barely got down before rapid shooting began. Shots in the air. Rapid bursts of machine gun fire. Everyone running. Elevators blocked; the agents covered access to the two stairways.

Below, in the plaza, people milled around. They fell, they tumbled down the stone stairway in front of Santiago Tlatelolco Church.

On bullhorns could be heard: "Don't go! Don't go! . . . "

At the same time, the army arrived by the side of the Foreign Relations building. More shots.

Here on the third floor some forty students from the National Strike Committee were arrested. Darkness. There was no light in the building. Sócrates is among those detained. Handcuffed.

Crouching down, up against the wall, moved on by the shouting of the agents themselves, two journalists descend to the second floor. Some fifteen or twenty minutes, while the shooting continues without stop.

Agents and journalists, together, up against apartment 210. The lock gave way. There is no one. Its inhabitants have fled.

In the hallway of the apartment there are two telephones, and everyone wants to use them.

The chief of the DFS speaks on the phone. "Are there snipers?"

By telephone, the same chief of the DFS informs:

"If we even so much as move, they will shoot at us here. There are snipers. We need you to send a convoy of civilian ambulances to see if they will let them through and take out the wounded. They should come with sirens blaring to show that they are ambulances. . . . "

Care of the Wounded

Tourniquets are applied to some of the wounded agents to keep them from bleeding. The lights have returned.

An Army Captain uses the telephone. He calls the Ministry of Defense. He informs them of what is happening.

"We are responding with all that we have. . . . "

Machine guns, pistols—45s, 38s, and 9 millimeters could be seen.

Shots from below towards above. Small explosions, even. More machine gun blasts.

Almost two hours later the agents and the journalists descend. First the detainees. They are lined up against the wall with their hands in the air.

The chief of the DFS receives information from a military official. He mentions the dead, two soldiers among them; and, General José Hernández Toledo was wounded by two bullets when he was leading the troops. He is in serious condition.

The agents, dressed in civilian clothing, gather on the first floor, next to the elevators and they leave. It was 8:30.

The Plaza of the Three Cultures, the church, and Vocational School Number Seven can be seen. There are soldiers crouched and hidden, seated in jeeps, machine guns at their sides. More military ambulances. Cars recognizably from the Army in Nonoalco, next to the Foreign Relations building.

The agents, with white gloves on the left hand, the journalists with handkerchiefs tied around theirs, exit with their arms raised, until they reach Nonoalco.

All the streets are closed off by traffic police, up to Santa María la Redonda. Motorcycles, patrols. Later a group of grenadiers.

The army combed the buildings, the streets. . . .

"Bloody Tlatelolco," **Excelsior**, *Editorial Page, Thursday, October 3, 1968*

Desolation has returned to invade the Mexican capital, the heart of the Republic. The presence of the military called in to disperse a gathering in the Plaza of Three Cultures, left behind an atrocious wake of death and blood. And in the conscience of sensible citizens, [there is now] an endless desperation, a severe, unsettling anguish.

Because the facts of last night do not clarify anything, they do not provide answers. On the contrary, they have created new offenses. Intransigence and force serve only to widen the breach of resentment, to distance the possibility of reconciliation.

Although it is true that the behavior of the students—and that of a good number of teachers—at times surpassed the limits of sensibility and turned insolent and unconsciously challenging, overestimating their own strength. But it is no less true that the response to such extremes was neither prudent nor appropriate.

The overflowing of arrogance—which meant that the President of the Republic, on the same day that he was to give his State of the Nation, was forced to appear in the Zócalo to enter into dialogue with the nonconformists—was behavior fitting puerile and arrogant adolescents.

The spilled blood dramatically and vehemently demands a reconsideration of how next to proceed. For it is not by killing ourselves that we ought to build a Mexico that we love and hope to share in peace—even given our bitter disagreements.

However, the Government is made up of adults, people who know how pride tends to blind, how self-importance leads to resentment. These adults know that youthful ardor and passion lead to futile and dangerous insolence. Yet, such maturity ought to come into play in the future—and we will expect it to—in all its greatness.

"Insidious News from UPI: On This Date We Cancel the News Agency's Service," El Sol *Morning Edition, Thursday, October 3, 1968*

Like an irrefutable demonstration of the flightiness and malevolence with which some foreign correspondents are informing the world of the events that occurred in this country, we make known to the Mexican public the message that Mr. Mike Hudges [*sic*], of UPI, sent last night to their New York offices for retransmission to all subscribers within its reaches, asserting facts that we have been able to confirm are absolutely false.

THE JOURNALISTIC ASSOCIATION GARCÍA VALSECA, which serves innumerable readers with seriousness and truth, cannot let this insidious information stand. In demonstration of protest, as of this date, [the association] cancels the UPI service, and hopes that said news agency gives satisfaction to the Mexican people.

The cable in question says:

> Mike Hughes
>
> Mexico, October 2 (UPI)—A spokesperson for the International Olympics Committee commented that a danger exists that the Olympics that are scheduled to begin here on the 12th will be cancelled, due to the student disturbances, during the most recent of which, occurring this evening, the Army shot on demonstrators.
>
> Sources in the Committee observed that there is no rule that mandates that the Olympic Games should be cancelled in a climate of instability, but they added that in the original Games, those of Ancient Greece, such a rule did exist.
>
> Furthermore, the source indicated that an atmosphere of considerable violence could lead to a decision to cancel the Games in any case. Sources suggested that while they did not wish to meddle in the internal politics of Mexico, the Olympic Games Organizing Committee was obligated to guarantee the security of the athletes and visiting dignitaries. They added that when people are killed in the streets, the organizers could clearly not offer any guarantees.

The executive committee of the International Olympic Committee, made up of nine members, which is in session here, would certainly discuss the recent events and it would be quite possible that they recommend cancellation of the Games in Mexico to the full committee, which will gather here on the seventh of this month, five days before the scheduled beginning of the opening ceremonies.

The President of the International Olympic Committee, the American Avery Brundage, could not be contacted for comment.

Observers indicated that the Organizing Committee had to take into consideration the declaration made by student leaders last Monday, in which they stated that they hoped the Olympics would take place in peace, "but not this kind of peace."

With approximately half of the 8 to 11 thousand athletes already registered in the Olympic Village housing, in addition to the presence of several hundred foreign journalists, officials would of course be reluctant to cancel the Games; however, they might feel obliged to do so.

The athletes have discussed the situation in the international center at the Olympic Village, however, they will not make any formal declarations with regard to the situation because they do not have full knowledge of what has occurred.

Thus far they have not been restricted from going about the city, though it is thought that they might be restricted to the Village, unless they leave in groups, in order to avoid any mishaps.

José A. Perez Stuart, "Opinion," El Universal, *Saturday, October 5, 1968*

No citizen, Mexican, Flemish, Brazilian, Argentinian, Italian, etcetera, would dare argue that their government is perfect. In this world, there is no perfect government.

However it is preferable to have a government—with all its faults—that every day betters itself democratically, economically, socially, culturally, and morally, than to be under a communist dictatorship.

The Marxist-Leninist mafia that seeks to carry our Fatherland away into chaos, disorder, and anarchy, and whose objective is the implementation of a totalitarian regime, has at last been found out, and since the events of Tlatelolco, repudiated.

It is lamentable to see how young people have been used by agitators for satanic purposes. Agitators use those young people who do not stand strong before life and who have not freed themselves from the tumult of emotions that consumes them and that turns them into an unprincipled mass of no value, who seek only material gain like simple "useful idiots."

Many innocent people, or those who lack judgment, have not wanted to see that inside the "student" movement is a handful of individuals who treat the people and

PRECAUCION

—¡Es González, el que vive en Tlatelolco!

"Precaution—It's González, the one who lives in Tlatelolco!"
(editorial cartoon on Tlatelolco)
El Universal, Saturday, October 5, 1968.

their followers like a simple jumping off point—as we stated previously—for the purposes of implanting a government of foreign ideology, and once this was done, there would not be any freedom of expression, freedom to gather in groups, nor—the bandied about idea—university autonomy.

And it is not that we are "witch hunters" or anything like it, rather that we stand with our feet firmly on the ground and we see things as they are.

And we will not change our opinion about this only because they replaced banners of "Che" Guevara, the guerilla, with those of Zapata: this attitude should be considered merely one more Marxist tactic.

Students: we have an [illegible word] event of the utmost importance—and although we do not [illegible text], we ought to place above all else the name of our Fatherland: Mexico.

Mexicans: have faith in the youth that until today has been [illegible text] and that communist lies of [illegible word] and against one sole name will seize the arms of Faith, Truth, and Justice and will give their lives in defense of the Fatherland.

Youth will respond, because it knows that the places of the [illegible word] are for cowards. People who are lovers of freedom, justice, and love are advancing: against all, for God, and for Country.

"General Lázaro Cárdenas Condemns the Agitators: He Calls on the Sense of Responsibilities in Defense of National Unity," El Heraldo de México, *Sunday, October 6, 1968*

Last night former President Lázaro Cárdenas denounced antinational and foreign elements that seek to bring about the disintegration of the country by means of arms and terror, and called on the State and the students to resolve their conflict with mutual respect and a spirit of reason.

Cárdenas said that all Mexicans must be aware that "enemy forces" are taking advantage of the internal conflicts to distort and change them and that "it is indispensable to call for mediation and a sense of responsibility in defense of national integrity."

The declarations of the ex-President were written, signed, and sent to journalists.

In them, he affirmed that "the venues of understanding are not closed" and he considers that efforts must be made to find an "urgent" solution to our present conflicts.

"Without the youth losing their rights, all Mexicans are obliged by their patriotism, to exclude violent methods and prepare themselves to accept the wisdom of justice and liberty," he added. . . .

Central Themes

State formation, urban life, popular culture

Suggested Reading

Hodges, Donald Clark, and Daniel Ross Gandy. *Mexico Under Siege: Popular Resistance to Presidential Despotism.* London: Zed Books, 2002.

Mabry, Donald J. *The Mexican University and the State-Student Conflicts, 1910–1971.* College Station: Texas A&M University Press, 1982.

National Security Archives. *The Dead of Tlatelolco: Using the Archives to Exhume the Past.* Electronic Briefing Book 201. Available at: http://www.gwu.edu/~nsarchiv/NSAEBB/NSAEBB201/index.htm.

Orme, William A. *A Culture of Collusion: An Inside Look at the Mexican Press.* Coral Gables, FL: North-South Center Press, University of Miami, 1997.

Zolov, Eric. *Refried Elvis: The Rise of the Mexican Counterculture.* Berkeley: University of California Press, 1999.

Related Sources

27. The 1692 Mexico City Revolt (1692)
71. The 1985 Earthquake (1985, 1995)
76. Lies Within the Truth Commission (2006)

69. Theft and Fraud (1970)*

Many workers, though certainly not all, came out of the Mexican Revolution stronger in their organizational force, and with more federal government support, than they had when they entered it. Scholars generally agree that the government engaged in practices of economic and political support for some organizations while neglecting and intimidating others. Out of these practices emerged a system of political bosses who formally represented urban workers and *campesinos* (rural workers), for example, but who in fact reported more to the interests of the government. Such *charrismo* (corrupt politics) characterized the railroad industry, which erupted in protest in 1959. The late 1950s were characterized by economic crisis: the devaluation of the Mexican peso and stagnation of real wages. Mexicans from a range of locations in the workforce organized to demand better working conditions. Railroad workers emerged as among the most prominent, for both the impact of their movement and the dynamism of their leaders, who included Demetrio Vallejo.

In rejection of charrismo, railroad workers elected Vallejo to represent them as the head of the Railroad Workers Union. The railroad played an important role in the Mexican economy, both as a means of moving material goods and people and as an important sector of organized workers. And so, when railroad workers went on strike, they paralyzed the country. In response, President Adolfo López Mateos suppressed the strike and had Vallejo incarcerated in Lecumberri prison. Vallejo was imprisoned for over eleven years, but this did not stop him from engaging in politics, as is evident in the following letter, which was written from Lecumberri in 1970. The letter demonstrates Vallejo's engagement with issues beyond those strictly defined by the workplace and continues to critique the structure of Mexican politics and its close association with the distribution of domestic resources. How can Vallejo's words help us understand how Mexican politics worked? How can we use Mexican history to help explain how the Mexican state took the form that it did?

*Demetrio Vallejo, *Cartas y artículos desde la carcel (1960–1970)* (Mexico: Editorial Posada, 1975), pp. 42–47. Excerpts translated by Tanya Huntington and the editors.

Theft and Fraud in Housing Construction

For many years now, there's been a lot of talk about the housing problem in our country and nothing has been done to solve it in terms of planning. Units like Tlatelolco and Villa Olímpica have been constructed as a means to political, lucrative, and propagandistic ends. Tlatelolco was built during the now extinct administration of President López Mateos at a cost of nearly 2 billion pesos. A waste of money, but at least his goal was to rent these apartments at economical rates. And so it was, until the new regime of Díaz Ordaz decided to sell to the tenants, but only after increasing the gains more than threefold to match the real value of the apartments. For example, a great many families had been paying 250 in rent every month; now they were compelled to vacate the premises unless they bought their apartments for 94,000 pesos by paying 800 a month.

This process demonstrates that the government has followed the example of bankers, and is now profiting from the construction and sale of housing, given that it sells real estate for more than double its actual value. However, everything was built with the people's money, which means that the tenants (as representatives of the people) must pay usurious interests upon making their purchase despite the fact that the money invested in construction belongs to them. In this case, as in all public works carried out by the State, the beneficiaries are contractors, middlemen (including the *charro** union leaders), and top or mid-level government officials. These are the ones who are taking away the lion's share of all construction projects, especially housing construction.

Taking money from the bureaucrats themselves, the Institute of Social Services and Safety for State Workers (ISSTE) makes loans to its members for residential construction, but besides charging interest on the sum being loaned, these members don't have the option of turning to trusted contractors, but are obligated to use the services of whomever has been designated by the Director of the Institute. One might suppose that this gentleman would jealously guard the workers' funds, or that he would want these buildings to incorporate high quality materials, thus adjusting their real value to the amount being invested. But this isn't the case. The constructions are shoddy, and they are built and completed whenever the contractors desire. Housing with a real value of 100,000 pesos costs 200,000, not counting the monetary interest from the loan. How much does the Director of the Institute get for awarding a contractor or construction company an exclusive contract? It's anyone's guess! But this is the sole reason why the director compels the person requesting the loan to accept the contractor he's designated. And if the borrower refuses? He simply isn't given the loan.

Anarchy in housing construction is rampant. This disorder is deliberately provoked by government officials in order to stimulate theft. Eight years have passed since construction was completed at the Tlatelolco complex, and hundreds of apartments are still vacant or unsold despite intense government propaganda—similar to that of

**Translator's note:* The term *charro* refers to traditional cowboy dress in Mexico and suggests something gaudy, garish, or vulgar; it also connotes corrupt politics.

any good entrepreneur—on television, in newspapers, and in magazines. The expense has undoubtedly had repercussions on the pricing of this real estate.

It's the same story with the Villa Olímpica complex. It's a ghost town. Nowadays no one will risk occupying the apartments, and those who've already done so have repented, because they are very small, too narrow, and badly constructed with shoddy material; the doors are defective, the sewage services are in poor condition, and the ceilings and roof terraces have no drainage. All occupants concur that by the time they're finished paying, they are going to have to purchase or build new apartments for themselves. The prices fluctuate between 200 and 260 thousand pesos to buy, and over 2,000 pesos each month to rent.

There's a lot of talk about building affordable housing and yet, only luxury apartments are being built, even if they don't sell or aren't rented, because the "profit" is in the construction. And that's all public officials care about, as is the case of the "Morelos Residential Community" created for State workers who are building the National Bank of Mexico and the Mexican Mortgage Association, profiteered by Agustín Legorreta and Antonio Esperón Azueta, respectively. This unit or community will have 910 residences and will cost 167 million pesos. Of these 910 residences, 310 will be sold at 80,000 pesos. And for the 600 that remain, prices will fluctuate between 140,000 and 165,000 each. Doing some quick math, the 310 residences will bring in 24,800,000 pesos and the 600 that remain 91,500,000 pesos, at an average price—in the latter case—of 152,500 pesos each. Both groups total 116,300,000 pesos. Therein lies the conundrum. Because if the financiers are going to invest 167 million pesos and will only get 116,300,000 pesos upon selling all of the residences, that means the "poor things" will lose no less than 50,700,000 pesos. Is this because the same bankers who say farmers aren't worthy candidates for credit are now becoming more humane in the construction and sale of housing? The ruthless logic of gross profit rules this out as a charitable act. What's really going on is that public officials, like bankers, are propaganda experts who always alter the sum total of their investments in order to impress the people for political gain. Hiding, thus, the fraud they've committed due to the shoddy quality of the materials used in housing construction, because of which the tenant-buyer will pay inflated rent and more than double the actual value in interest. Every day, this kind of housing can be found for sale in the newspapers. Which only goes to show that supply has surpassed demand.

The new Federal Labor Law establishes that businesses with 100 or more workers are obliged to build rooms for them, charging them in rent 6 percent annually of the residential property value. If workers were to compel the authorities to enact this legal precept, one might say that approximately 50 percent of the housing problem would be solved by this means on a short-term basis. The rest of the problem could be solved if an honest, revolutionary government expropriated lands by virtue of public usage to build high quality, economical housing, compelling banks to provide sufficient credit at reduced interest rates and, in the event that they were to oppose this initiative, by nationalizing them.

Management at the Construction Laboratory of the National Housing Institute announced last year that it has achieved an effective, major reduction in housing construction costs. It specified that it has six different models of homes, the cheapest being 25,000 pesos, to be built on 50 square meters; while the most expensive are to be built on 86 square meters at a price of 40,000 pesos. All six models consist of 3 bedrooms, a bathroom, a kitchen, and a dining room. Also in the affordable housing program, there are 7 different models of homes that cost from 18,000 to 20,000 pesos each. These can be acquired by persons with a monthly family income of 750 to 1,250 pesos, which is 80 percent of the national population.

If by presidential decree, the National Housing Institute has achieved a major, effective reduction in the cost of housing construction, why doesn't the government apply this same method and technique? It must be because neither the officials, nor the charro leaders, nor the bankers could rob enough. The Mexican Labor Congress (CTM) Residential Unit constructed in the Atzacoalco colony provides a typical example of how these charro leaders steal.* Workers accused Mr. Raúl Rivas, Section 19 of the Mexico City Federation of Workers, of asking them to pay 3,000 pesos in order to occupy each home. Since this housing unit will consist of 2,500 residences, this theft would add up to 7,500,000 pesos. Did this actually take place? No one can say. The charro leaders of the CTM gave indications that the accusation would be looked into, but nothing more has happened—given the tempting nature of the sum.

Dishonesty and the lack of a government-planned housing policy create disorder. As the refrain says, a turbulent river is a fisherman's gain, although the only fishermen here are high-ranking officials, bankers, and charro union leaders.

But the landlords have also taken advantage of this anarchy to make a killing, setting exorbitantly high rents and increasing them each time an apartment contract is renewed, or using inhumane, dirty methods in connivance with the authorities to evict tenants. This was the case of building no. 20 on Republic of Cuba Street, whose inhabitants went to President Díaz Ordaz to request his intervention so that justice might be done, since they were to be thrown out on the street despite the fact that they've lived in these apartments for over thirty years and have always paid their rent on time.

Therefore, the State must plan to build affordable housing and exert the necessary legal pressure to contain the voracity and maneuvering of these landlords. Rent ceilings that correspond to the sum total of the investment must be fixed. And raising the rent each year, as these landlords have been doing arbitrarily, must be prohibited.

July 4, 1970.

Central Themes

State formation, land and labor

Suggested Reading

Van Hoy, Teresa Miriam. *A Social History of Mexico's Railroad.* Lanham, MD: Rowman & Littlefield, 2008.

---

* *Translator's note:* Mexico City is divided into neighborhoods known as *colonias* or colonies.

Related Sources

63. We the Undersigned (1941, 1945)
67. Rubén Jaramillo and the Struggle for *Campesino* Rights in Postrevolutionary Morelos (1967)
70. Serial Satire: The Comic Book (1974)

70. Serial Satire: The Comic Book (1974)*

An immensely popular tradition in Mexico, comics date back at least to the José Guadalupe Posada era of the late nineteenth and early twentieth centuries and have only grown in popularity since the 1940s (Source 50). Unlike in the United States, where comic books featuring superheroes are targeted primarily to young males, Mexican *historietas* (comic books) feature middle- and working-class protagonists, deal with the stories of their daily lives, and appeal to a much broader audience. Their popularity cuts across lines of region, age, gender, and class. As late as 1990, eight of the top ten periodicals in Mexico were comic books. One of the other reasons for their appeal has been that while more conventional print media—newspapers and magazines—were subject to the PRI's invasive censorship, historietas sometimes managed to present and reflect more critical political views (Source 68).

Eduardo del Río, born in 1934, known by his pen name Rius, is one of the most popular cartoonists in Mexico. Rius wrote *Los Supermachos* (The Super-Machos) and *Los Agachados* (The Cowering Ones) during the 1960s and 1970s. His work was frequently critical of the Mexican government, and his activism followed a similar vein. He expressed interest in a range of issues and sought, through comics and simple text, to reach a broad audience. *Los Supermachos* portrays life in a little town in central Mexico called San Garabato Cuc. It contains such sharp social commentary that the state pressured its publisher, Editorial Meridiano, to censor it. Rius departed and published his second serial, *Los Agachados,* elsewhere. President Gustavo Díaz Ordaz ordered Editorial Meridiano to confiscate all available early editions of *Los Supermachos,* so very few from the earlier period exist. The following excerpt comes from a volume published in 1974 in the series' tenth year of publication. Some critics believe the series lost its satirical edge with Rius's departure. Do you think this is true? What sorts of social commentaries are contained in this excerpt? Why do you think Rius originally entitled the series *Los Supermachos*? Look also at the quotations from readers' letters reproduced here. What do they indicate about the views and concerns of fans of the series?

**Los Supermachos* 452 (September 5, 1974): 1–4, 6, 13.

LOS SUPERMACHOS DE SAN GARABATO CUC. PRESENTA. ¿CÓMO LLENAR LA PANZA.

COMEMOS MAL Y NOS ALIMENTAMOS PEOR, PORQUE AQUELLO CON LO QUE LLENAMOS LA PANZA SUELE SER POCO NUTRITIVO Y DE MUY DIFÍCIL DIGESTIÓN.

EL PROBLEMA SE HA ACENTUADO EN LOS ÚLTIMOS TIEMPOS COMO RESULTADO DEL ENCARECIMIENTO DE LA VIDA.

NO HAY PRESUPUESTO QUE ALCANCE, PUES DE UN DÍA PARA OTRO LOS PRECIOS SUBEN, SUBEN Y SUBEN.

MIENTRAS EL GOBIERNO NO CONTROLE LOS PRECIOS DE LOS ARTÍCULOS DE PRIMERA NECESIDAD, LA INFLACIÓN CONTINUARÁ HASTA UN PUNTO EN QUE LO ÚNICO QUE NO PODREMOS INFLAR SERÁ LA PANZA.

1

"How to Fill Your Gut," from **The Supermachos**, *September 5, 1974 (Tenth Year), Weekly Magazine*

The Supermachos of San Garabato Cuc Present
"How to Fill Your Gut"

Traditionally, the Mexican has been a mal-nourished person.
"Nutrition-less, food-less, milk-less, gut-less, and color-less."

We eat poorly and are fed worse, because what we tend to fill our guts with is usually lacking in nutrition and difficult to digest.

"So difficult that even the solitary protest."

The problem has gotten worse lately as a result of the increasing cost of living.

"But the communists are to blame."

There is no salary that suffices, 'cause from one day to the next prices go up, up, up.

"And panties go down, down, down."

While the Government does not control prices of basic goods, inflation will continue to the point at which the only thing that we will not be able to inflate is the gut.

"Allow me to contradict that opinion."

¿Y USTÉ TAMBIEN VIENE A COMPRAR?
VENGO A HACERME LA ILUSIÓN DE QUE COMPRO. AQUÍ NO ADMITEN "TRAVELERS CHEC'S."
FONDA
LA CHINA
¿18 PESOS EL KILO DE PAPAS?... ¡SAN GARABATO NOS PROTEJA! ¿HASTA DONDE VAMOS A LLEGAR?
PERO MARCHANTITA, SON PAPAS PROTEINIZADAS...
¿Y ESO QUE ES?
QUE TIENEN SU BUENA DOTACIÓN DE CARNE...
¡UF, QUÉ ASCO! ¿DE MANERA QUE PARA COLMO ESTÁN AGUSANADAS?...
ASÍ SON MÁS NUTRITIVAS, EMERENCIANITA ...NO SEA FIJADA.
ADEMÁS... ¿YO QUÉ CULPA TENGO DE QUE TODO ÉSTE TAN CARO?... A MÍ TAMBIEN ME LAS SUBEN DE PRECIO...
MENTIRA, PUS QUÉ: SI SUPIERA QUE ME IBAN A HACER CASO LO DENUNCIABA A LAS AUTORIDADES...

"Are you here to shop?"

"I am here just to pretend that I am shopping. They don't accept travelers' checks here."

"18 pesos a kilo for potatoes? Saint Garabato protect us! When will this ever end?"

"But my dear little shopper, the potatoes have been filled with protein. . . . "

"And that means what?"

"That they have a good portion of meat. . . . "

"Eew, disgusting! So on top of everything they are full of worms?"

"That way they are more nutritional my dear shopper . . . don't get caught up in details."

"Besides . . . what fault is it of mine that everything is so expensive? They are raising prices on me as well. . . . "

"Well, that is a lie: if I thought they'd pay any attention to me at all I would denounce you to the authorities."

POR MÍ QUÉJESE CON QUIEN QUIERA, MARCHANTA... YO TAMBIÉN TENGO QUE VIVIR.
¡VOY A QUEJARME A LA OEA!..
EN LA OEA NO SE VALE... AHÍ SÓLO ADMITEN CHISMES CONTRA CUBA...
TOTAL, QUE NO HAY NI A QUIEN QUEJARSE...
AL CONTRARIO, SOBRA CON QUIEN QUEJARSE... LO MALO ES QUE NADIE LE HACE A UNO CASO..
DEBÍAN DE INVENTAR UNA OFICINA DE QUEJAS PA' QUE PUDIERA UNO QUEJARSE.
YA LA HUBO, NOMÁS QUE LE LLEGARON TANTAS QUEJAS, QUE YA NO TUVIERON DONDE ALMACENARLAS... Y MEJOR LA CERRARON.
¿Y RESOLVÍAN LAS QUEJAS?
PERO SI ESA OFICINA NO ERA PARA RESOLVER LAS QUEJAS. ERA OFICINA DE QUEJAS NADA MÁS. SI USTED TENÍA UNA QUEJA QUE ENTREGAR, AHÍ SE LA RECIBÍAN Y LA ARCHIVABAN.
UJULE, PUS QUÉ POCA.
PUES SÍ, FUE EN TIEMPOS DE DON ADOLFO LÓPEZ MATEOS. BUENO, QUÉ PUES: ¿SE DECIDE POR LAS PAPAS O SEGUIMOS NUESTRA VISITA DE INSPECCIÓN?...

"It is all the same to me, complain to whomever you like shopper . . . I also have to make a living."

"I am going to complain to the OAS [Organization of American States]."

"It is not worth complaining to the OAS, they only pay attention to rumors about Cuba."

"So then there is no one to complain to. . . . "

"On the contrary, there are more than enough to complain to . . . the problem is that no one will pay you any attention. . . . "

"They ought to create an office to hear complaints so that one could complain."

"There already was one, only they received so many complaints that they had to file them away . . . and decided that it was just better to close down."

"And did they resolve the complaints?"

"But this office was not for resolving complaints. It was an office for complaints, and nothing more. If you had a complaint to turn in, they would receive it and file it away."

"Wow, well, that's not much."

"Well, of course, it was in the time of Don Adolfo López Mateos. So then: shall we take the potatoes or should we continue our inspection visit?"

LA DESNUTRICIÓN SOCIAL PROVIENE DE LA IGNORANCIA, LA SUBCULTURA, LA POBREZA Y LA EXPLOTACIÓN, Y EGENDRA MAYOR IGNORANCIA, EXPLOTACIÓN Y POBREZA.

NO HAY QUE CONFUNDIR LA DESNUTRICIÓN AGUDA QUE SIGUE A LAS GRANDES CATÁSTROFES, LA CUAL SUELE SER PASAJERA.

TAMPOCO HAY QUE CONFUNDIR LA DESNUTRICIÓN SOCIAL CON LA ESPECÍFICA Y REGIONAL QUE AFECTA EN FORMA EVENTUAL A UNA DETERMINADA ZONA, NI CON LA DESNUTRICIÓN INDIVIDUAL Y OCASIONAL.

1º FAMILIA DESNUTRIDA: SOCIAL.

4

2º DESIERTO CON HUESOS HUMANOS: REGIONAL O DE ZONA.

3.º BORRACHITO: INDIVIDUAL Y OCASIONAL.

Mexico has for many years suffered from social malnutrition, an insufficient level of nutrition that affects the entire community and has lasted throughout history.

"I was malnourished."

"Not I."

Societal malnutrition comes from ignorance, underdeveloped culture, poverty, and exploitation, and it fosters greater ignorance, exploitation, and ignorance.

"Can you teach me to read?"

"I will teach you to write, because I don't know how to read."

Acute malnutrition should not be confused with malnutrition that appears in the wake of big catastrophes, the latter of which tends to be passing.

"Why did you pay with two tickets?"

"Because my malnutrition is also a passenger."

Neither should malnutrition be confused with that which affects specific regions, nor with individual and occasional malnutrition.

1st Malnourished family: Societal
2nd Desert with human bones: regional or [in] specific zones
3rd A drunk: individual and occasional . . .

"LA MORTALIDAD PRENATAL EN MÉXICO ES ALTA (44 X 1000) Y LA INFANTIL HA AUMENTADO DE 60.9 EN 1965 A 68.5 EN 1970," ESCRIBE EL DR. MARTÍNEZ.
MURIÓ, SIN HABER AMADO.
DIRÁS SIN HABER COMIDO.
LA MALA NUTRICIÓN NO SÓLO AFECTA EL DESARROLLO FÍSICO Y MENTAL DEL INDIVIDUO, SINO TAMBIÉN EL DESARROLLO DE LA SOCIEDAD A LA QUE PERTENECE.
¡DESNUTRIDO!
LAS SOCIEDADES QUE PADECEN DESNUTRICIÓN SOCIAL NO PUEDEN DESARROLLARSE SALUDABLEMENTE. SON SOCIEDADES CONFORMISTAS QUE ARRASTRAN SUS INCAPACIDADES Y SUS INEPCIAS SIN DARSE CUENTA DE ELLAS.
¡ERES UN IMBÉCIL!
GRACIAS. ES LA PRIMERA VEZ QUE ALGUIEN ME DICE ALGO BONITO.
DESDE LOS TIEMPOS MÁS REMOTOS, EL MEXICANO POBRE SE HA ALIMENTADO MUY MAL. CUANDO LLEGARON LOS ESPAÑOLES, HABÍA 1,000 POBRES POR CADA SEÑOR PUDIENTE.
¿SOLAMENTE LOS RICOS IBAN AL EXCUSADO?
TELMA TIXOU
6

"Maternal mortality is high in Mexico (44 [out of] 1,000) and infant mortality has increased from 60.9 in 1965 to 68.5 in 1970," writes Dr. Martínez.

"She died without having loved."

"Without having eaten, you might say."

Poor nutrition not only affects the physical and mental development of the individual, but the development of the society to which the individual belongs as well.

"@#OØ"

"Malnourished!"

Societies that suffer social malnutrition cannot healthily develop. They are societies made up of people who accept their fate and drag along their disabled and inept population, without taking them into account.

"You are an imbecile!"

"Thanks. That is the first time anyone has said anything nice to me."

Since ancient times, the poor Mexican has been poorly fed. When the Spanish arrived there were 1,000 poor for each wealthy landlord.

Thelma Tixou

"Only the rich went to the bathroom? . . . "

Letters to *Los Supermachos*

Many of the letters that we receive are so interesting that we cannot resist the temptation to print them here, even if only in excerpts. A scarcity of paper means that we can only do it once in a while, as we do here at the close of this edition.

" . . . Along Reforma [Paseo de], at Mariano Escobedo, you will find the Diana the Hunter Fountain, the idea exists of moving this most beautiful statue to Venustiano Carranza Park, out there to the East of the City, which we consider to be an inconceivable and serious mistake. . . .

. . . Diana the Hunter, created by the sculptor Olaguíbel, and placed in the center of one of the few beautiful fountains we have here in Mexico, which forms a central part of the Paseo de la Reforma, and is an integral part of the character of our city . . .

. . . just as in Madrid the Cybele Fountain, and in Rome that of Neptune, Mexico has one for Diana. . . .

. . . Who would admire her in such a far off park, abandoned, and only accessible to sports enthusiasts with membership to that same park?

. . . The fountain could be moved, piece by piece, to the glorieta at Reforma and Niza [Streets], where there is currently a palm tree that [is] on the verge of dying. This way all of Mexico could continue to admire this precious and beautiful work of art that gives so much character to our city and its principal boulevards. . . . "

Arqu. Carlos del Razo,
Sierra Nevada 766,
México, D.F.

" . . . On page 24 of issue number 442, titled 'The Screw-up and the Shameless Little Sons of Screw-ups' [*El desmadre y sus hijos de los desmadritos*], you give an example from Oaxaca and the case of majordomos [*mayordomías]*. . . .

. . . It is worth mentioning that you are mistaken in saying that they [mayordomías] force an Indian to take on the costs associated with a religious celebration. Perhaps this may have been the case in the previous century when people respected religion, but a mayordomía is a lucrative public post that the PRI hands out: it is nothing but deal-making.

. . . These sorts of celebrations occur in the Tehuantepec Isthmus, and the mayordomo is the one who gains the most, because everyone celebrates him and gives him presents. . . . "

Ray de la Rosa
Puebla, Pue.

. . . Sunday, June 9, at 10 at night, at the entrance to the cockfighting ring located on Virrey de Mendoza Street, in this city of Zamora, Mich., there was an altercation between the military and the police. . . .

. . . The police were searching people entering the ring in order to keep anyone from entering armed with guns, when several civilians arrived, who were later found to be plainclothes military personnel. One policeman attempted to search the leader of the group, however this individual not only did not allow himself to be searched, he also smacked [the policeman] around several times, which led a representative of the judicial police to intervene and disarm the aggressor and take him out into the street, where the detained man identified himself as colonel Héctor Magallanes Solís, of the Eighth Infantry Regiment. . . .

. . . In the midst of all this, a military squadron under the command of a sub-lieutenant arrived, with bayonets flying and guns ready, and detained the judicial police, and then took the judicial policeman back to the barracks with them. . . .

. . . Such incidents are common in this city, where the military do, or not, as they wish. . . .

. . . Hopefully General Cuenca Díaz, Secretary of Defense will put a stop to such disorder that degrades the Army. . . . "

A Reader (whose name we do not reveal)
Zamora, Mich.

" . . . Friday, March 21, I left San Diego headed for Tijuana and Mexico City. I boarded a bus and at customs in Tijuana I, and all the passengers aboard the bus, began our crossing. . . .

. . . The customs agents began to ask for money in exchange for not searching our bags, and if we did not give it to them, they threatened, they would stop us at every single toll booth and take all of our luggage from the bus and thoroughly search every single piece. . . .

. . . One woman who had a small television set had to hand over $150.00 in order to keep it, and then at the next stop at customs they took it from her because they said it was against the law to bring such items into the country. . . .

. . . At each customs stop, the guards shouted cynically from the door: 'Everyone out to pay a tip.' . . .

. . . Some middle-class American tourists were also on the bus, and they were astonished that such things could occur in a country that they had thought of as civilized. . . .

. . . How is it possible that the authorities allow such armed assaults on the part of their subordinates? . . . Why are they then surprised when there are kidnappings and assaults and Lucío Cabañas* up in the hills[?] . . . "

Abel Cadima Saavedra,
465 17th St.
San Diego, Calif.

*Lucío Cabañas was a student leader of the armed group Party for the Poor (*Partido de los Pobres*), which engaged in guerrilla activities from their base in the mountains of Guerrero during the 1970s.

. . . Have you noticed, Calzonzin my friend, that all the trucks that tow away improperly parked cars, causing them severe damage, have Tlaxcala license plates? . . .

. . . This smells to me like a rotten little business taken on by our Tlaxcala neighbors, for when one goes down to the impound lot to recover their car, or what is left of it, they charge you a fortune in order, according to them, to pay for the tow truck. . . .

. . . Who in fact owns these tow trucks, all equally old and *dilapidated* and all from the State of Tlaxcala? . . .

Hermenegildo Quiroz,
Plaza del Carmen 2,
México, D.F.

Central Themes

State formation, popular culture

Suggested Reading

Campbell, Bruce. *"Viva la Historieta!": Mexican Comics, NAFTA, and the Politics of Globalization.* Jackson: University Press of Mississippi, 2009.

Hinds, Harold E., and Charles M. Tatum. *Not Just for Children: The Mexican Comic Book in the Late 1960s and 1970s.* Contributions to the Study of Popular Culture 30. Westport, CT: Greenwood Press, 1992.

Rubenstein, Anne. *Bad Language, Naked Ladies, and Other Threats to the Nation: A Political History of Comic Books in Mexico.* Durham, NC: Duke University Press, 1998.

Related Sources

34. A Satirical View of Colonial Society (1816)
60. Chronicles of Mexico City (1938)
69. Theft and Fraud (1970)
74. Jesusa Rodríguez: Iconoclast (1995)

71. The 1985 Earthquake (1985, 1995)*

An estimated ten thousand people died in the massive earthquake that devastated Mexico City on September 19 and 20, 1985. Despite the history of seismic activity in this area, the Partido Revolucionario Institucional (PRI) government was ill prepared to handle the disaster, particularly where it struck newly constructed high-rises in the city center. Among the dead were hundreds of seamstresses who worked in sweatshops in cheaply constructed buildings. In the wake of the disaster, survivors in this industry organized themselves into the 19th of September Union. Included here is the testimony of one sweatshop worker in a series on experiences of the earthquake that journalist Elena Poniatowska first published in the Mexico City daily *La Jornada*. What indications does her account contain about why this natural disaster provoked widespread political protest? What did the tragedy reveal to both textile workers and *Jornada* readers about the paternalistic guise favored by both the state and the financial elites?

For several years, the 19th of September Union managed to function independently of organizations like the heavily co-opted Confederación de Trabajadores de México (CTM), although it eventually succumbed to the structural limitations that constrained organized labor under PRI rule. Also included here are excerpts from an interview with Evangelina Corona, the first secretary-general of the 19th of September Union. It was conducted in her home in Nezahualcóyotl, a working-class municipality northeast of the Federal District, and published in a book commemorating the tenth anniversary of the earthquake and the union's creation. According to Corona, what forces eventually hindered the effectiveness of the union? How did the reality that she and her coworkers experienced differ from the ideals set out in the 1917 Constitution (Source 54)? What circumstances may have had a different impact on the apparent success of the organizations of Maquila workers fifteen years later (Source 75)?

---

*Elena Poniatowska, *Nothing, Nobody: The Voices of the Mexico City Earthquake,* trans. Aurora Camacho de Schmidt and Arthur Schmidt (Philadelphia: Temple University Press, 1988), pp. 142–145. Used by permission of Temple Uniersity Press. Gonzalo Martré and Angélica Marval, *Costureras: Debajo de los escombres* (Mexico: Grupo Editorial Planeta, 1995), pp. 63–64, 80–88. Excerpts translated by the editors.

"Eight Hundred Factories and Sweatshops Totally Destroyed: The Earthquake Revealed the Exploitation of Women Textile Workers"

Eleven stories were reduced to three at San Antonio Abad 150, a building that is today the symbol of the tragedy of the seamstresses.

Clandestine sweatshops existed on a great many streets: at José María Izazaga 65, in just one eight-story building, fifty sweatshops; on Fray Servando, on Xocongo, on Mesones (Sportex), on Pino Suárez; almost all second-class—if not fifth-class—buildings, loaded with machinery and heavy rolls of fabric. No wonder the floors came down. San Antonio Abad 164 was also reduced to dust. At Manuel José Othón 186, close to the corner of San Antonio Abad, the textile workshops continued to function in spite of the stench of cadavers, the rubble, and the fear.

The seamstresses at Dimension Weld, Amal, and Dedal were the first to realize that their bosses weren't going to help them. What's worse, they saw how the machinery was carried out before anybody worried about the six hundred entombed *compañeras* [coworkers]. If anyone was beaten and done violence in this year of 1985, if anyone has suffered, it is precisely these women. The earthquake showed that of all those exploited in the Federal District, none are more so than the workers of the clothing industry. Domestic service may constitute the leading employer of poor women in our country, but second place goes to sewing. Seated on the sidewalk of Lorenzo Boturini Street is Juana de la Rosa Osorno, fifty-five, who works for Dimension Weld de México, S.A., employed by Elías Serur:

Now with this disaster, she says, putting her hands under her green and white checkered apron, we're here in the street waiting for people's charity to be able to eat. The boss is not a bad person; he's just fickle. He offers one thing, then another; he changes his mind; we can never come to an agreement. He first yelled at us, "The machinery is yours with my compliments. I've lost it all, my life is buried here."

His life is not buried there; if any lives are buried, it's those of the compañeras. The boss came running when he heard that the building had fallen down. He drove from his house in Las Lomas. But we were here. And the dead were here, bleeding among concrete and steel mesh. Elías did not suffer a scratch. So why should he say that his life had been buried here? Maybe he meant his safe. Maybe he means that his safe is his life. That's what happens to the rich, right?

I myself didn't die because my shift starts at 7:30. I've been working for fifteen years. I have two children. My daughter is twenty-seven; the boy is sixteen, and he's in high school. I'm a widow, and here in the San Antonio Abad encampment they asked me to be in charge of the kitchen. I used to start at 7:30 and end at 5:30. Occasionally, I worked until eight and sometimes even Saturdays and Sundays. . . .

In Dimensión Weld [according to another worker], there wasn't even a first-aid kit, and if we had to be excused to go to the bathroom, and we took a little longer, he would come and knock on the door of the stall:

"What's the matter?"

"I'm taking care of my physiological needs."

"Well come now, you've been there for ten minutes or you've been there for a quarter of an hour; go back to work or I'll have to dock the time from your paycheck."

I do overlay. I was working on sport shirts. I'm a highly qualified seamstress. I was making 11,300 pesos a week more or less before taxes. I had no social security nor loans of any sort. When I had to buy my eyeglasses, it took about four months of pleading before Elías told the cashier to lend me the money. In reality, the only thing that I have to thank the boss Elías for is that when my father died recently, he gave me a leave of absence of a week, but without pay. In fifteen years of work, that week without pay is what I am grateful for.

We have seen no government aid, period—only from churches, from private persons who come open their trunk and bring out big pots of rice, tortillas, and beans, and they tell us to come and have some lunch. Young people have come; I don't know from what organization. But the boys have been here; they bring oil for me to cook with. . . .

In Dimensión Weld, there were 130 of us. Here on this avenue there are many factories. The one with the most casualties was Dedal, where a whole big bunch of women died, because their shift started at seven. They took out three bodies last night, all made mincemeat.

At Manuel Gutiérrez Nájera and San Antonio I don't know how many of them are still missing. The relatives are there, waiting in tents. Just imagine what a barbaric thing that is. We've left behind our lungs, our hearts, all our efforts, down there under that concrete. Shouldn't the boss compensate us in some way? We live in tenements, we rent small rooms, we pay rent while they, the owners, live in mansions, have cars, they travel, but we are the ones who take pains to work, to produce, to live. Of course, they started the business, but we moved it forward on our backs. That's my thinking.

I left my eyes behind in Dimensíon Weld. Now I can only see with my glasses on. I used to eat by the lockers, I brought my food in a dinner pail. Then they put some tables by the entrance. There are many of us and all of us are poor. We can't afford to eat at a diner, so we'd bring our beans or whatever God had given us for that day.

Evangelina Corona Interview

INTERVIEWER: Doubts emerge after ten years: why didn't the Union "19th of September" not grow as was expected?

EC: . . . One of the principal reasons that the union stopped growing was that the people who played a central role in the movement, from the beginning, charged too high a price. What does this mean? It means that the people who guided us got into disagreements. They fought in front of all of the women workers, with the result that women took sides with one or another person, group, or movement. This led to divisions, and of course, as we all know, a house divided cannot grow. I also believe that the primary reason that it did not grow was bad information, misinformation. Much was said about the union. That it shut down businesses, that it was red, aggressive. That is to say, all the characterizations we heard at the local board. And the businessmen, fearful and afraid, said: "I prefer to shut down my business, fire the women workers, before the '19th of September' comes in," all because of the negative slant of the publicity among businessmen where this sort of thing was happening. One of the principal protagonists was in fact Robert's [a major clothing store] and its owner. He was the one who made the complaint against the Federal Ministry for having officially registered the union. He asked that the registration be annulled on the grounds that an illegitimate board had requested it. Sometimes, when we were renegotiating contracts with local boards, he presented documents alleging that the union was not legal, that it had been filed by a secretary lacking legal competence. This is another reason the union did not grow.

We believe a third reason, apart from the defamation, is the struggle that the union developed. The struggle for restoration of working women's labor rights. And what was this? It was that not a single union had really demanded that the employers in the textile industry comply with the law. It was always . . . "I give you money, you say you fix things, and don't fix anything." And with us, many employers found they could not do things this way, because our commitment was with the workers, not with the bosses. This was not really strangling businesses, but saying to them: "You are earning such and such amount, and it is fair that you share your earnings with the workers." How is that? Well, with a fairer wage, more deserving, one is able to live on it and survive. This is what we asked. Our intention was not to strangle business. We, as a union, and above all when I represented the union, were of the opinion that the strangle business was to kill the source of employment for the more or less significant number of seamstresses that there were at that time. That it is better to share a bit of the work. To make progress, that was our idea. But many employers were used to "I am the only one who profits here," they kept all the profit. For us there were not even dividends. Many times there was not even Social Security. And many others did not even pay overtime. At least not in the way the law stipulates. They would in some way subsume it in the production quota demanded of us. This is what, as a union, we could no longer support and they said: "The union is what closes down businesses and finishes off employers." So it was this sort of defamation on the part of employers towards the ones who entered into dialogue with them with regard to reparations for those who had been injured, it was a serious problem. Many lawyers representing employers, well, they said that this had never occurred. They had never given severance pay, and no one had ever fought such a hard fight. When they paid severance to those of us who had lost our jobs, we earned twelve days compensation regardless of the number of years we had worked; we were able to get twenty days for a year more, and the services stipulated in the law; it was already September, just about time for Christmas bonuses and vacation for many people. We were able to secure vacation time at that moment. All this meant that the union gained in stature with the workers, but on the other hand, it grew as a threat to employers. This is one of the reasons why the union could no longer expand. But the principal reason it could no longer grow was due to the divisions that emerged among the different groups that advised the union. . . .

INTERVIEWER: At that time, 1991, were working conditions in the workshops and factories in general, and not only those belonging to the union, the same as before the earthquake, or did the workers make gains?

EC: In general there were changes. Perhaps it would be better to say advances, but in regard to the consciousness of workers; with regard to working conditions you couldn't say that there was much improvement. Since '85 many business owners established small workshops all over the place and thus avoided any compliance whatsoever with the law. This leads us to suspect that the working women, rather than improve their conditions, were going to end up worse off. Of course, the other issue is that at this time, the majority of working women were in the midst of the critical economic straits in which the country found itself because they could no longer find jobs and there was a lot more repression than before. This was the situation when Salinas came into power. A situation wherein companies are unaccustomed to sharing with workers is very strong. And then came all the changes to the law, and the creation of more taxes. This led many businesses to close, jobs decline, and to some degree the adoption of the attitude: "Either you work longer hours, or produce more for less money." That, I believe, is how women's earning capacity has gotten worse instead of better. . . .

INTERVIEWER: How might we characterize the current situation with regard to protective contracts? The CTM [Confederación de Trabajadores de México] and the CROM [Confederación Regional Obrera Mexicana] continue to provide protective contracts to employers?

EC: It is as simple as this, they protect the employer more than the worker. The situation has not changed a bit. . . .

INTERVIEWER: What did Evangelina Corona do for the seamstress union during the three years she was a representative to Congress?

EC: The truth is that she did not do anything. Absolutely nothing. She did not have a chance to do so. When we wanted, for example, the thing about Social Security, the thing about the Retirement Savings System, the senators representing the official party could not have cared less about such a discussion. They never accepted such a possibility, never understood that this represented an aggression against workers. We argued too, about the work day; however, when I objected to a production project, we argued that it was not possible because it implied squeezing even more from working women. The same with flexible work schedules. "I, the boss, need you to stay and work until two at night, and you have to do it." For working women, this is just one more form of oppression. We could not do anything. Not because we did not want to, but because we found ourselves in the Chamber of Deputies with a majority and the CTM, a Congress full of supposed workers' representatives, who did not give a hoot about workers. What they wanted was to be in good standing with their president, their patron. So really we could not do anything. . . .

Central Themes

State formation, urban life, land and labor, gender

Suggested Reading

Brickner, Rachel K. "Mexican Union Women and the Social Construction of Women's Labor Rights." *Latin American Perspectives* 33, no. 6 (2006): 55–74.

Cook, Maria Lorena. *Organizing Dissent: Unions, the State, and the Democratic Teachers' Movement in Mexico.* University Park: Pennsylvania State University Press, 1996.

Porter, Susie S. *Working Women in Mexico City: Material Conditions and Public Discourses, 1879–1931.* Tucson: University of Arizona Press, 2003.

Preston, Julia, and Sam Dillon. *Opening Mexico: The Making of a Democracy.* New York: Farrar, Straus and Giroux, 2004.

Rodriquez, Victoria E. *Women's Participation in Mexican Political Life.* Boulder, CO: Westview, 1998.

Tirado, Silvia. "Weaving Dreams, Constructing Realities: The Nineteenth of September National Union of Garment Workers in Mexico." In *Dignity and Daily Bread,* ed. Sheila Rowbotham and Swasti Mitter. New York: Routledge, 1994.

Related Sources

48. The Cananea Strike: Workers' Demands (1906)
54. Land, Labor, and the Church in the Mexican Constitution (1917)
68. Eyewitness and Newspaper Accounts of the Tlatelolco Massacre (1968)
75. Maquila Workers Organize (2006)

72. The EZLN Views Mexico's Past and Future (1992)*

The Ejército Zapatista de Liberación Nacional (EZLN) burst into international consciousness on January 1, 1994, when it occupied several cities in Chiapas, among them San Cristóbal de las Casas and Ocosingo. Launching the public face of its movement on the day the North American Free Trade Agreement (NAFTA) went into effect, the EZLN declared that neoliberalism in general and NAFTA in particular exacerbated the historic exploitation of the state's land, labor, and resources. For several days, these masked fighters—later known as the "Zapatistas"—occupied San Cristóbal's municipal palace and issued the first in a series of "Declarations" from the Lacondón Jungle. The Zapatistas disputed the legitimacy of Carlos Salinas de Gortari's presidency, charged the Partido de Revolucionario Institucional (PRI) with unconstitutionality, and appointed themselves defenders of Mexico's impoverished majority. The EZLN came to some rapprochement with the federal government at the time of the 1996 San Andrés peace accords, but today the group contends that the federal government never honored its commitments to these agreements. Indisputably, the widely popular—and well-publicized—Zapatistas played an instrumental role in cementing the downfall of the PRI in the 2000 federal elections.

The Zapatistas are at the forefront of a new wave of revolutionary political movements that have made effective use of the Internet and other media to captivate broad audiences and effectively engage civil society in their political struggles. The following excerpt comes from an essay that the eloquent EZLN spokesperson Subcommandante Marcos wrote in 1992 and released publicly on January 27, 1994. Like many of his writings, "Chiapas: The Southeast in Two Winds: A Storm and a Prophecy"—published in *La Jornada*, a liberal Mexican news daily, and on the Internet—was received by an enormous audience. Why do you think Marcos adopts the tone toward his audience that he adopts in this piece? What is the presumed relationship of the reader to the history discussed? In his essay, Marcos presents a particular view of Mexican history. What is it?

---

*Subcomandante Marcos, *Chiapas: El sureste en dos vientos, una tormenta y una profecia* (1992), originally from www.ezln.org/documentos/1994/199208xx.en.htm (accessed September 26, 2007); see also Irish Mexico Group, EZLN Communiques, at: http://flag.blackened.net/revolt/mexico/ezln/marcos_se_2_wind.html.

"Chiapas: The Southeast in Two Winds: A Storm and a Prophecy"

The First Wind: The One from Above

Chapter One

This chapter tells how the supreme government was affected by the poverty of the Indigenous peoples of Chiapas and endowed the area with hotels, prisons, barracks, and a military airport. It also tells how the beast feeds on the blood of the people, as well as other miserable and unfortunate happenings.

Suppose that you live in the North, Center, or West of this country. Suppose that you heed the old SECOTUR [Department of Tourism] slogan, "Get to know Mexico first." Suppose that you decide to visit the Southeast of your country and that in the Southeast you choose to visit the state of Chiapas. Suppose that you drive there. . . . Suppose that you take the Transístmica Highway. Suppose that you pay no attention to the Army barracks located at Matías Romero and that you continue on to Ventosa. Suppose that you don't notice the Department of Government's immigration checkpoint near there (the checkpoint makes you think that you are leaving one country and entering another). Suppose that you decide to take a left and head towards Chiapas. Several kilometers further on you will leave the state of Oaxaca and you will see a big sign that reads, "WELCOME TO CHIAPAS." Have you found it? Good, suppose you have. You have entered by one of the three existing roads into Chiapas: The road into the northern part of the state, the road along the Pacific coast, and the road you entered by are the three ways to get to this Southeastern corner of the country by land. But the state's natural wealth doesn't leave only by way of these three roads. Chiapas loses blood through many veins: Through oil and gas ducts, electric lines, railways, through bank accounts, trucks, vans, boats and planes, through clandestine paths, gaps, and forest trails. This land continues to pay tribute to the imperialists: petroleum, electricity, cattle, money, coffee, bananas, honey, corn, cacao, tobacco, sugar, soy, melon, sorghum, mamey, mango, tamarind, avocado, and Chiapaneco blood flows as a result of the thousand teeth sunk into the throat of the Mexican Southeast. These raw materials, thousands of millions of tons of them, flow to Mexican ports and railroads, air and truck transportation centers. From there they are sent to different parts of the world: The United States, Canada, Holland, Germany, Italy, Japan, but with the same fate—to feed imperialism. The fee that capitalism imposes on the Southeastern part of this country oozes, as it has since from the beginning, blood and mud.

A handful of businesses, one of which is the Mexican State, take all the wealth out of Chiapas and in exchange leave behind their mortal and pestilent mark: in 1989 these businesses took 1,222,669,000,000 pesos from Chiapas and only left behind 616,340,000,000 pesos worth of credit and public works. More than 600,000,000,000 pesos went to the belly of the beast.

In Chiapas, Pemex [the national oil company] has 86 teeth clenched in the townships of Estación Juárez, Reforma, Ostuacán, Pichucalco, and Ocosingo. Every day they suck out 92,000 barrels of petroleum and 517,000,000,000 cubic feet of gas. They take away the petroleum and gas, and in exchange leave behind the mark of capitalism: ecological destruction, agricultural plunder, hyperinflation, alcoholism, prostitution, and poverty. The beast is still not satisfied and has extended its tentacles to the Lacandona jungle: eight petroleum deposits are under exploration. The paths are made with machetes by the same campesinos who are left without land by the insatiable beast. The trees fall and dynamite explodes on land where *campesinos* [rural workers] are not allowed to cut down trees to cultivate. Every tree that is cut down costs them a fine that is 10 times the minimum wage, and a jail sentence. The poor cannot cut down trees, but the petroleum beast can, a beast that every day falls more and more into foreign hands. The campesinos cut them down to survive, the beast to plunder. . . .

The tribute that capitalism demands from Chiapas has no historical parallel. Fifty-five percent of national hydroelectric energy comes from this state, along with 20% of Mexico's total electricity. However, only a third of the homes in Chiapas have electricity. Where do the 12,907 kilowatts produced annually by hydroelectric plants in Chiapas go? . . .

What does the beast leave behind in exchange for all it takes away? . . .

Education? The worst in the country. At the elementary school level, 72 out of every 100 children don't finish the first grade. More than half of the schools only offer up to a third grade education and half of the schools only have one teacher for all the courses offered. There are statistics, although they are kept secret of course, that show that many Indigenous children are forced to drop out of school due to their families' need to incorporate them into the system of exploitation. In any Indigenous community it is common to see children carrying corn and wood, cooking, or washing clothes during school hours. Of the 16,058 classrooms in 1989, only 96 were in Indigenous zones. . . .

The health conditions of the people of Chiapas are a clear example of the capitalist imprint: One-and-a-half million people have no medical services at their disposal. There are 0.2 clinics for every 1,000 inhabitants, one-fifth of the national average. There are 0.3 hospital beds for every 1,000 Chiapanecos, one-third the amount in the rest of Mexico. There is one operating room per 100,000 inhabitants, one-half of the amount in the rest of Mexico. There are 0.5 doctors and 0.4 nurses per 1,000 people, one-half of the national average. . . .

Welcome! You have arrived in the poorest state in the country: Chiapas.

Suppose that you drive on to Ocosocoatla and from there down to Tuxtla Gutierrez, the state capital. You don't stay long. Tuxtla Gutierrez is only a large warehouse which stores products from other parts of the state. . . . You go on to Chiapas de Corzo without noticing the Nestlé factory that is there, and you begin to climb up into the mountains. What do you see? One thing is certain, you have entered another world, an Indigenous world. . . .

Three hundred thousand Tzotziles, 120,000 Choles, 90,000 Zoques, and 70,000 Tojolabales inhabit this Indigenous world. The supreme government recognizes that "only" half of these 1,000,000 Indigenous people are illiterate.

Continue along the mountain road and you arrive in the region known as the Chiapaneco highlands. Here, more than 500 years ago, Indigenous people were the majority, masters and owners of land and water. Now they are only the majority in population and in poverty. Drive on until you reach San Cristóbal de las Casas, which 100 years ago was the state capital (disagreements among the bourgeoisie robbed it of the dubious honor of being the capital of the poorest state in Mexico). No, don't linger. If Tuxtla Gutierrez is a large warehouse, San Cristóbal is a large market. From many different routes the Tzotziles, Tzeltales, Choles, Tojolabales, and Zoques bring the Indigenous tribute to capitalism. Each brings something different: wood, coffee, cloth, handicrafts, fruits, vegetables, corn. Everyone brings something: sickness, ignorance, jeers, and death. . . . Welcome to San Cristóbal de las Casas, a "Colonial City" according to the history books, although the majority of the population is Indigenous. Welcome to Pronasol's huge market. Here you can buy or sell anything except Indigenous dignity. Here everything is expensive except death. But don't stay too long, continue along the road, the proud result of the tourist infrastructure. In 1988 there were 6,270 hotel rooms, 139 restaurants, and 42 travel agencies in this state. This year, 1,058,098 tourists visited Chiapas and left 250,000,000,000 pesos in the hands of restaurant and hotel owners.

Have you calculated the numbers? Yes, you're right: there are seven hotel rooms for every 1,000 tourists while there are only 0.3 hospital beds per 1,000 Chiapaneco citizens. Leave the calculations behind and drive on, noticing the three police officials in berets jogging along the shoulder of the road. Drive by the Public Security station and continue on, passing hotels, restaurants, large stores and heading towards the exit to Comitán. Leaving San Cristóbal behind you will see the famous San Cristóbal caves surrounded by leafy forest. Do you see the sign? No, you are not mistaken, this natural park is administered by . . . the Army! Without leaving your uncertainty behind, drive on. . . . Do you see them? Modern buildings, nice homes, paved roads. . . . Is it a university? Workers' housing? No, look at the sign next to the cannons closely and read: "General Army Barracks of the 31st Military Zone." With the olive-green image still in your eyes, drive on to the intersection and decide not to go to Comitán so that you will avoid the pain of seeing that, a few meters ahead, on the hill that is called the Foreigner, North American military personnel are operating, and teaching their Mexican counterparts to operate radar. Decide that it is better to go to Ocosingo since ecology and all that nonsense is very fashionable. Look at the trees, breathe deeply. . . . Do you feel better? Yes? Then be sure to keep looking to your left, because if you don't you will see, seven kilometers ahead, another magnificent construction with the noble symbol of SOLIDARIDAD on the facade. Don't look. I tell you, look the other way. You don't notice that this new building is . . . a jail (evil tongues say that this is a benefit of Pronasol; now campesinos won't have to go all the way to Cerro Hueco, the prison in the state capital). . . . Pass by Cuxulja and instead of following the detour to Altamirano drive on till you reach Ocosingo: "The Door to the Lacandona Jungle. . . . "

Good, we have arrived at the intersection. Now to Ocosingo . . . Palenque? . . . Other places? Different places? In what country? Mexico? You will see the same. The colors will change, the languages, the countryside, the names, but the people, the exploitation, the poverty and death are the same. Just look closely in any state in the Republic. Well, good luck. . . . And if you need a tourist guide please be sure to let me know. I'm at your service. Oh! One more thing. It will not always be this way. Another Mexico? No, the same . . . I am talking about something else, about other winds beginning to blow, as if another wind is picking up. . . .

The Second Wind: The Wind from Below

Chapter Five

This chapter tells how the dignity of the Indigenous people tried to make itself heard, but its voice only lasted a little while. It also tells how voices that spoke before are speaking again today and that the Indians are walking forward once again but this time with firm footsteps. They are walking together with other dispossessed peoples to take what belongs to them. The music of death that now plays only for those who have nothing will now play for everyone. It also tells of other frightful things which have happened and, they say, must happen. . . .

In the municipal seat of Ocosingo, 4,000 Indigenous campesinos from the organization ANCIEZ [Emiliano Zapata National Independent Alliance] march from different points of the city. Three marches converge in front of the Municipal building. The municipal president doesn't know what it's all about and flees. On the floor of his office is a calendar indicating the date: April 10, 1992. Outside Indigenous campesinos from Ocosingo, Oxchuc, Huixtaán, Chilón, Yajalon, Sabanilla, Salto de Agua, Palenque, Altamirano, Margaritas, San Cristóbal, San Andre's and Cancuc dance in front of a giant image of Zapata painted by one of them, recite poetry, sing, and speak. Only they are listening. The landowners, businessmen, and judicial officials are closed up in their homes and shops, the federal garrison appears deserted. The campesinos shout that Zapata lives and the struggle continues. One of them reads a letter addressed to Carlos Salinas de Gortari [president of Mexico, 1988–1994] in which they accuse him of having brought all of the Agrarian Reform gains made under Zapata to an end, of selling the country with the North American Free Trade Agreement and of bringing Mexico back to the times of Porfirio Díaz. They declare forcefully that they will not recognize Salinas' reforms to Article 27 of the Political Constitution. At two o'clock in the afternoon the demonstration disperses, in apparent order, but the causes persist. With the same outward appearances everything returns to calm. . . .

The viceroy dreams that his land is agitated by a terrible wind that rouses everything, he dreams that all he has stolen is taken from him, that his house is destroyed, and that his reign is brought down. He dreams and he doesn't sleep. The viceroy goes to the feudal lords and they tell him that they have been having the same dream. The viceroy cannot rest. So he goes to his doctor and together they decide that it is some sort of Indian witchcraft and that they will only be freed from this dream with blood. The viceroy orders killings and kidnappings and he builds more jails and Army barracks. But the dream continues and keeps him tossing and turning and unable to sleep.

Everyone is dreaming in this country. Now it is time to wake up. . . .

The storm is here. From the clash of these two winds the storm will be born, its time has arrived. Now the wind from above rules, but the wind from below is coming. . . .

The prophecy is here. When the storm calms, when rain and fire again leave the country in peace, the world will no longer be the world but something better.

The Lacandona Jungle, August 1992

Central Themes

Indigenous people, state formation, land and labor, race and ethnicity

Suggested Reading

Gilbreth, Chris, and Gerardo Otero. "Democratization in Mexico: The Zapatista Uprising and Civil Society." *Latin American Perspectives* 28, no. 4 (July 2001): 7–29.

Hayden, Tom, ed. *The Zapatista Reader.* New York: Thunder's Mouth Press/Nation Books, 2002.

Womack, John, Jr. *Rebellion in Chiapas: An Historical Reader.* New York: New Press, 1999.

Related Sources

47. Precursors to Revolution (1904, 1906)
49. Land and Society (1909)
67. Rubén Jaramillo and the Struggle for *Campesino* Rights in Postrevolutionary Morelos (1967)
73. Popular Responses to Neoliberalism (the Late 1990s)

73. Popular Responses to Neoliberalism (the Late 1990s)*

One of the most concrete manifestations of Mexico's adoption of neoliberal economics in the 1990s was President Carlos Salinas de Gortari's alteration of state policy on communal landholding, as articulated in Article 27 of the Constitution (Source 55). In theory, this article limited the size of large-scale estates, banned foreigners from holding property, and restored *ejido* (communally held) land to those populations that had possessed it before the presidency of Porfirio Díaz. The ejidal system established that the federal government technically owned this land, but that peasants had the right to farm and profit from it in perpetuity. The largest distribution of this land occurred during the presidency of Lázaro Cárdenas (1934–1940). In its development, the ejidal system had many shortcomings, including the poverty of the land the state sometimes distributed and peasants' lack of access to capital to develop it. Salinas's reform to this system removed the ban on private ownership of ejidal land. Supporters of the measure argued that the change would help end rural poverty and improve low agrarian productivity while providing financial opportunities to small landholders. Critics saw it merely as a means whereby the law ceased to protect poor farmers from forced sale to large landholders and corporations. Disputes between proponents of the two positions sparked across the Mexican countryside, including in Chiapas in the wake of Salinas's reforms (Source 72).

Conflicts over foreign incursions into national territory also arose in municipal centers. One of the most heated occurred in the scenic colonial town of Tepoztlán, Morelos, a gathering place for both domestic and international progressive organizations. In 1995 citizens of Tepoztlán organized themselves into a movement that successfully contested the plans of the multinational conglomerate Kladt Sobrino (KS) to develop an eighteen-hole golf course, a country club, and a subdivision of eight hundred luxury homes in the historic town. The following is an open letter created by the movement organizing resistance to the development. By comparing this text with earlier sources (sources 7, 20, 27, and 53), readers might study how this group consciously or unconsciously drew from the historic concept of the rights of the indigenous *pueblo* (people or town) as a means of legitimizing their grievances against the state and foreign interests. How does this text compare to petitions from earlier eras (sources 29, 57, 63)?

---

*Carta al C. Presidente de la República at Committee for Tepozteco Unity (CUT) website: http://www.tepoz10.0rg/documentos/index.htm. Translated by the editors.

Open Letter of Protest

To the Citizen President of the Republic
To the Citizen Secretary of the Interior
To the National Institute of Ecology
To the Political Parties
To the Non-Governmental Organizations
AND ABOVE ALL, TO EL PUEBLO OF MEXICO:

El Pueblo of Tepoztlán, despite recent national events, continues to believe that NO ONE SHOULD BE ABOVE THE LAW. With respect to the profoundly ILLEGAL intent of the company KS and the government of the state of Morelos to build a large subdivision and golf club in Tepoztlán, we declare that:

1. The people of Tepoztlán are morally and legally in the right with regard to the legitimate ownership of their communal lands, given that there is a 1929 decree clearly establishing this. The "purchase" alleged by KS is evidently illegal, its sole foundation being the corruption of the officials who legitimized it and continue to support it today.

2. All of the lands where they intend to build the aforementioned subdivision are located within the TEPOZTECO NATIONAL PARK, within the WILD FLORA AND FAUNA PROTECTION ZONE, along the CHICHINAUTZIN-AJUSCO BIOLOGICAL CORRIDOR; therefore they belong to the NATIONAL SYSTEM OF PROTECTED AREAS and cannot for any reason be devastated in order to build a residential subdivision. This is clearly established by the General Law of Ecological Equilibrium and Environmental Protection currently in effect.

3. Water needed for the subsistence of the Tepoztecan population as well as that of other towns in the state of Morelos depends heavily on the replenishment of groundwater in the region where their golf course is supposed to be built. Moreover, the company's claim that it will irrigate over one million square meters of land with pure aquifer water—while at the same time supplying hundreds of swimming pools and luxury homes—when the wells in the region are suffering severe reductions in capacity, is a crime against the local population.

4. Municipal zoning regulations expressly prohibit the construction of residential subdivisions and golf clubs in that area.

5. The National Institute of Ecology (INE), in accordance with law, chose not to approve environmental impact studies presented on two separate occasions, because it believed that the company had omitted studies of fundamental importance, such as the impact on the local climate, water, soil, population, flora, fauna, landscape, etc. The INE responded thus to the company KS: "As long as Constructora Tzemantzin [Kladt Sobrino, KS] can not demonstrate the environmental feasibility of this project, and until this General Department issues a Resolution of Environmental Impact as per the terms specified under Environmental Legislation, NO WORKS OR ACTIVITIES WHATSOEVER OF THE TEPOZTECO GOLF CLUB SHALL BE CARRIED OUT; OTHERWISE, THE COMPANY WILL BE SUBJECT TO ANY SANCTIONS IT HAS INCURRED."

6. State Governor Jorge Carrillo Olea, seconded by his Secretary of "Environmental Development," the nefarious ex-environmentalist of Swiss origin Ursula Oswald, has decided to join the company's campaign, promoting in diverse media the construction of the subdivision: threatening any regents who oppose the project with imprisonment, firing government employees who have taken positions against the golf course, inventing civil, criminal or agrarian lawsuits against local residents opposed to the project, pressuring ejido, communal, and municipal authorities, local residents, etc. The local press is filled with indications, threats, and accusations formulated by the Governor and Mrs. Oswald against the Tepoztecan people. Carrillo Olea's **Great Alliance** consists of businessmen and government officials allied against the rights of the people of the state of Morelos.

7. Above and beyond all this, the resolution of the Tepoztecan people stands: NO TO THE RESIDENTIAL SUBDIVISION AND GOLF CLUB ON TEPOZTECAN LANDS! KM and government officials know that the population will not allow this construction to take place, yet they insist on using threats, provocations, and intimidation. During a Popular Assembly against the Golf Club attended by over 3,000 people outside the Municipal Presidency of Tepoztlán, the company bussed in hundreds of thugs from Cuernavaca to confront the population; but their provocation failed. The company has attempted to confront the town by deceitfully offering jobs and by handing out money left and right. In the state's most impoverished and needy communities, they publicized an alleged hiring campaign, deceiving and manipulating people, and trying to use this against the Tepoztecan population with the argument that there would be work for everyone. The history of this company in the state of Morelos shows us that the offer of progress and jobs for everyone is nothing but a con game, an attempt to turn the population against itself. These worthy people no longer let themselves be fooled. They are tired of all this mockery and injustice, both from the businessmen and from corrupt government officials. We declare state governor General Jorge Carrillo Olea and the KS company responsible for any harm, imprisonment or direct or indirect repression suffered by any member of the Tepoztecan community. How long will they continue to violate the Mexican Political Constitution in order to favor the groups and mafias of economic and political power in the State of Morelos and nationwide? Does General Carrillo Olea intend to continue employing the methods of his colleague, Rubén Figueroa, in order to eliminate all those who oppose his policies?

POPULAR ASSEMBLY OF THE TEPOZTECAN PEOPLE

Central Themes

State formation, land and labor

Suggested Reading

Stolle-McAllister, John. *Mexican Social Movements and the Transition to Democracy.* Jefferson, NC: McFarland & Co., 2005.

Waters, Jody. "Text, Context, and Communicative Practice Within an Alternative Discourse of Development: The 'No Al Club De Golf' Movement of Tepoztlan, Morelos." PhD diss., University of Texas at Austin, May 2002. Available at: http://www.lib.utexas.edu/etd/d/2002/watersj022/watersj022.pdf#page=4.

Related Sources

53. Revolution in Morelos (1911)
54. Land, Labor, and the Church in the Mexican Constitution (1917)
62. An Assessment of Mexico from the Right (1940)
72. The EZLN Views Mexico's Past and Future (1992)

74. Jesusa Rodríguez: Iconoclast (1995)*

Director, actor, playwright, performance artist, and social activist, Jesusa Rodríguez delighted audiences in her Mexico City cabaret and in international venues for decades with her hilarious satires of Mexico's past and present. The following excerpts come from a play that she wrote in 1995 for Channel 40 television in Mexico City. In it, she juxtaposes various episodes from Mexico's ancient and recent history, including the life of Sor Juana Inés de la Cruz (Source 26), the censorship of Mexico's Holy Office on the Inquisition (Source 21), the neoliberal era of Carlos Salinas de Gortari (Source 73), the rise to power of the Partido de Acción Nacional (PAN, here referred to as "the NAP") (Source 62), the Zapatistas (Source 72), and the powerful influence that U.S. political and economic life exerts on Mexico. To what extent does Rodríguez distort these episodes from Mexican history in her humorous presentation of them? Why does she juxtapose the past with the present in this piece? How do her satires compare with Mexican satires from other periods (sources 34 and 70)?

---

*Jesusa Rodríguez, "Sor Juana in Prison: A Virtual Pageant Play," trans. Diana Taylor, with Marlène Ramírez-Cancio, in *Holy Terrors: Latin American Women Perform,* ed. Diana Taylor and Roselyn Costantino (Durham, NC: Duke University Press, 2003), pp. 211, 213–214, 221-223, 225.

Sor Juana in Prison: A Virtual Pageant Play

Characters:
SOR JUANA INÉS DE LA CRUZ
LISY/LYSY
ATTORNEY
PROSECUTOR

The spectacle that you are about to see is the result of years of experimentation with high tech. It is the Blessed Year of Our Lord 2000, and thanks to Him the National re-Action Party has come to power in Mexico and finally restored decency and good manners to the social and political life of our country.

Any resemblance to real life is purely virtual.

The scene takes place in Sor Juana's jail cell in the Almoloya penitentiary. Stage left is the nun's desk, filled with books, ancient geometrical instruments, a pen, an inkwell, and a small Macintosh computer, the first kind to be introduced into the market. Downstage center is a single cot, and above it, a video screen. To the right, a black grand piano.

Sor Juana laughs as she reads a letter to the press from former president of Mexico Salinas de Gotari in November 1995. The text of that letter and a photograph of the ex-President dressed as Sister [Sor] Philothea is projected on the screen.

JUANA: Ha, ha, ha, this guy was really something! What a man! With one little letter written from his virtual exile he activated a whole group of politicians and intellectuals. "It was all a huge conspiracy," he said. Ha, ha, ha. What a guy, smart-ass, and with that he got off the hook. He never got accused of anything, he was never forced to testify about the murders and the collapse of the country, he never returned a penny of what he stole, come on, he didn't even get kicked out of the Party. No doubt about it: either this guy was a genius, or his peers were total assholes.

Oh well. The important thing is that the epistolary genre is alive and well again in Mexico. This can be my chance to get out of here. I have to send a message to the media, though it's probably like throwing a letter in a bottle out to sea—or better, launching a bit into cyberspace. Naturally, only letters sent from abroad matter around here. I've got it! I'll answer the ex-President's letter! It never occurred to anyone to respond back then, and a five-year-old news item might interest the press.

I will title it: "Sister Sor Juana Gets Sore."

To my most illustrious Ex-president, Ex-man, Ex-Cell-Intense, Carlos Salinas Kissinher, Bare-on of Bumsfeld, Chain-me, and lineage of the Fucksy, folksy Bush:

It is no will of mine, but my indignation, that has held up my reply these many years. It can hardly be a surprise that at the outset my bundling digital pen encountered two obstacles. The first, and for me the most obdurate, I find myself imprisoned in the Almoloya jail, where I was brought, deceived by men who said they believed in the NAP (later I found out it meant the right-wing "National Action Party" that you supported to gain power). Perversely, they scrambled the seventeenth and the twenty-first centuries through virtual technology—imposing a reign of terror and persecution in Mexico, refrying ancient laws to the detriment of people like me, who refuse to have their brains fried and prefer to think freely. . . .

The second impossibility is that they have placed in my cell, as if it were the convent of St. Jerome, a false, two-dimensional library, courtesy of The Official Press, hologram furniture, and an obviously obsolete Internet system. I would have preferred the Quadra 605 and not this Apple BCE. To top it all off, they want me to write their speeches for them, write splendid praises to their fundamentalism, and build triumphant arches to President Fucks and Bush, which, needless to say, is not in my nature.

Actually I know a lot of those guys get off jack-free. Take Cheney: although he did good things, that all seemed bad, he didn't do any bad things that seemed worse. But me, they have in chains, to beat and humiliate me just for being a woman and inclined to COGITATION. I write desperately because today the attorney—believe it or not, NAP has put a nun in charge of the tribunal—today she will pass sentence on my case and I have reasons to fear she won't give me a chance to defend myself.

In short, I know that you (to resort to the language of NAP) don't give a fuck, but whereas thou hast more influence than any among the NAPPERS, I appeal to thy merciful Internet beseeching thy intercession on my behalf from the bottom of your hard drive. From this Convent of Our Father Saint Ignatius of Almoloya, your least fortunate, Juana Inés de la Cruz. . . .

PROSECUTOR: . . . I want you to know that your virtual performance art piece on the Birth of Christ does not qualify, and it is prohibited on the grounds that it offends intimacy, genitality, and human reproduction according to the regulations for spectacles mandated by the municipality.

JUANA: But Mother! This performance is being presented in the Capital!

PROSECUTOR: But you have Susan Sarandon in the cast, and she's a hippie radical, plus Trudy Guiliani says it's a piece of shit. . . . According to chapter 9 on the law of public spectacles, Article 140, it is absolutely forbidden to display a naked human body in any establishment, as well as any sexual acts that go against morality and good manners, as well as any other act that goes *contra natura.*

JUANA: But, Mother, what is really contra natura in my view is the current attack on Iraq and our civil liberties.

PROSECUTOR: We have resolved that issue. Don't you read the newspapers? But don't change the topic. We have concluded that your show is destabilizing. Why do the subalterns have to speak? Don't you understand that it provokes subversion? People are the ones who provoke violence. Why would they go out in their cars if they know they're going to get stolen? Provocation. Anyway, you're an emissary from the past. Can you tell me why you mention events from 1995 in your performance?

JUANA: I'm only trying to give some historical fundamentals.

PROSECUTOR: I see. Fundamentals, is it? And they say that we're the fundamentalists.

(The President comes on the screen with whatever news made the headlines that day. "Economic recovery is not only wishful thinking. It's bushwhacked idiocy.")

JUANA: By the way, Mother, who is that guy? No one remembers him anymore.

PROSECUTOR: He was a functionary of the past regime, but he died at the hands of his wife. And because we're behind in cataloguing, his name hasn't been entered into the database yet.

JUANA: And what happened to Subcommandante Marcos?

PROSECUTOR: His cause became meaningless. Now that we've exterminated all the Indians in the country, the Zapatista movement has become obsolete—good riddance! . . .

JUANA: All right, Mother. I want to know exactly what I stand accused of.

PROSECUTOR: You stage the birth of the Messiah live, and that goes against the intimacy of human persons according to Article 39 of the regulations. Moreover, in that scene, you include a total frontal nudity with the objective of attracting morbid attention, and increasing your revenues.

JUANA: But, Mother, that is not correct. I never staged frontal nudity.

PROSECUTOR: What are you talking about? Let's look at that nativity scene.

(Image of the Manger with the classic Virgin and Child pose.) There! You see! The baby is stark naked! . . .

PROSECUTOR: And you, enemy of Mexico, give it up. You're going to rot in Almoloya. Here is the sentence passed by the Holy Tribunal:

EDICT: In exercise of the power vested in us, we, the NAPPING Inquisitors against depraved heresy and apostasy declare:

Hitherto, the virtual performance art piece proposed by the nun, Sor Juana Inés de la Cruz, is banned *In Totum.* Or better still, the work of the aforementioned nun is banned in *Totototum Piarum Aurium.* And it will be banned by the Holy Orifice in any language, even for those who do not know how to read, even in books-on-tape. It cannot be translated, nor printed, nor pirated on pain of *Excomunio Ipsofacto Incurrenda.* And aforementioned nun will remain in custody for the rest of her days to write the hagiographies of the saints: Saint Jesse Helms, Saint Strom Thurmond, and Saint Clarence Thomas. . . .

Ours by the grace of God.
Mexico, ever true
National reAction Party.

JUANA: (*Desperate*) Gods! This was the democratic change we were waiting for? We've moved from the dinosaurs to the fundamentalist troglodytes. Poor Mexico, so close to God, so far from the United Way. The beginning of the NAP for the elite, and the end of the nap for the workers. The worst torture is to lose hope. I will write my epitaph.

"I, Juana Inés de la Cruz, ratify my version of events and sign it with my blood. I wish I could let all of it out in benefit of the truth. I beg my beloved sisters to take pity on this country and not vote either for the dinosaurs or the troglodytes. I, the worst of all: Juana Inés de la Cruz."

Central Themes

State formation, urban life, popular culture, religion, gender

Suggested Reading

Franco, Jean. "A Touch of Evil: Jesusa Rodríguez's Subversive Church." *Drama Review* 36, no. 2 (Summer 1991): 48–61.

Gladhart, Amalia. "Monitoring Sor Juana: Satire, Technology, and Appropriation in Jesusa Rodríguez's 'Sor Juana En Almoloya.'" *Revista Hispánica Moderna* 52, no. 2 (1999): 213–226.

"Jesusa Rodríguez," available at Hemispheric Institute website: http://hemisphericinstitute.org/cuaderno/holyterrorsweb/jesusa/index.html.

Taylor, Diana. "'High Aztec' or Performing Anthro Pop: Jesusa Rodríguez and Liliana Felipe in 'Cielo de Abajo.'" *Drama Review* 37, no. 3 (Autumn 1993): 142–152.

Related Sources

21. The Creation of Religious Conformity (the Early Eighteenth Century)
26. Sor Juana: Nun, Poet, and Advocate (1690)
34. A Satirical View of Colonial Society (1816)
62. An Assessment of Mexico from the Right (1940)
70. Serial Satire: The Comic Book (1974)
73. Popular Responses to Neoliberalism (the Late 1990s)

75. Maquila Workers Organize (2006)*

Mexico's northern frontier underwent considerable transformation beginning in the 1970s with the initiation of the Border Industrialization Program, which sought to boost the country's economy and lower unemployment rates by securing foreign investment in the manufacturing sector. Mexico would provide tax benefits and inexpensive labor to companies that wished to establish manufacturing ventures inside its borders. The new assembly plants—*maquilas*—overwhelmingly employed women who traveled to the border region from across the country to seek employment. As well as confronting exploitative working conditions in the maquila industry, these women and their families were exposed to the environmental hazards created in the deregulated atmosphere of the border region. Maquila workers have sometimes managed to successfully confront many of these issues.

The following are excerpts from the script of *Maquilapolis: City of Factories*, a documentary film that records the experiences of women working in Tijuana's maquila industry. *Maquilapolis* was produced and directed by Vicky Funari and Sergio de la Torre in collaboration with the women who formed three organizations fighting for improved labor and environmental conditions: Grupo Factor X, Chilpancingo Collective for Environmental Justice, and the Promotoras por los Derechos de las Mujeres. Against the odds, these women managed to powerfully and effectively organize themselves. How were they able to do this? How did their experiences compare to those of the women who formed the 19th of September Union in the wake of the 1985 earthquake (Source 71)? How might the collaborative nature of the production of *Maquilapolis* have contributed to the resulting film?

**Maquilapolis: City of Factories* (unpublished script, used by permission).

Maquilapolis: City of Factories

. . . MAQUILA WORKERS: In 1994, with NAFTA, the North American Free Trade Agreement, Tijuana became even more fertile soil for sowing factories. By the end of the 1990s there were nearly 4,000 factories on the border, and we maquila workers numbered more than a million.

VARIOUS WORKERS:
I assemble filters.
I assemble electrical components.
I assemble oxygen masks.
I place rings in the machine.
I tape electronic pieces.
I assemble urinary bags.
I assemble furniture.
I package telephones.
I inspect lenses.
I package pantyhose.
I assemble power cords.
Television parts.
Toys.
Oxygen sensors.
Intravenous tubes.
Batteries.

MARÍA LOURDES LUJÁN AGUIRRE: My name is María Lourdes Luján Aguirre. I am 29 years old. . . . I've turned on the camera and I'll tell you a little about my life. I live in a neighborhood called Chilpancingo. This is a shot of where I live. There's my son playing basketball with his Dad. There's the river, where people cross. The bus is about to ford the river. The goats use the bridge too. I've always lived in this neighborhood, Chilpancingo, and the river has always been here. When I was a kid it was clean. When I got a little older and started working in the factories, I saw that the water was changing colors. Now sometimes it's black, green, red or foamy. The water used to be crystalline and I used to bathe here. What I loved was that families used to come to camp and swim. I look at the sad reality now, how the river has been destroyed. I wish my kids could have enjoyed this river as I did.

OLGA RENDÓN: The "Industrial City" is up on the mesa, and we're down below. All their chemicals end up in our neighborhood. People here have gotten sores on their legs and feet like she has, and we think they're from the water. For three days the water has had this color and smell.

María Lourdes Luján Aguirre: When it's like this, my nose blocks up and I struggle to breathe. I get sick over and over, my arms get . . . sometimes I'm OK, but I always have spots.

Olga Rendón: My daughter has spots too, but hers are brown and always itchy. My son too, he gets hives all over his body. And my niece too.

María Lourdes Luján Aguirre: I don't want my children to live with this problem. That's what motivates me to find a solution. . . .

Carmen Durán: I met Lourdes at Grupo Factor X, where we took workshops in women's rights and labor rights. As a *promotora* [women's rights advocate], you promote the law. What little you know, you pass on. I can't stay quiet anymore. I have to defend whatever right is being violated. You sow the seeds of what you have learned. You are a student, and gradually you become a teacher. . . .

Lupita Castañeda: Within globalization, a woman factory worker is like a commodity. And if that commodity is not productive, if she's not attractive for globalization because she starts to defend her rights, then they look for that commodity elsewhere. . . .

Carmen Durán: Remember David and . . . Samson? Wait . . . and Goliath! . . . Goliath, sorry, I went a little far afield. David beat him even though Goliath was so big. See, you're David and [you're] fighting Goliath, which is Sanyo, a huge, world-famous company. They can have all the money in the world but they won't be able to take away your dignity. Your dignity can defeat anybody.

María Lourdes Luján Aguirre: I started as a promotora because of a sign inviting 10 women to participate in a health survey for the San Diego Environmental Health Coalition. When I started to do the surveys I noticed problems: kids born without fingernails. Skin allergies like this one on my face. I learned about cases of hydrocephalus where they have to put a shunt in the brain. I saw cases of anencephaly when babies are born without a brain and die at birth. The birth defects here are because of the pollution, especially the waste left by Metales y Derivados. It is an abandoned factory with 6,000 tons of lead slag, left exposed to the elements. Metales y Derivados was a lead recycling plant. These are cast-off car batteries brought to Mexico to retrieve the lead they contain.

Magdalena Cerda (Environmental Health Coalition): In 1994, ROFEPA, the Office of Environmental Protection, shut down Metales y Derivados. The factory was abandoned and left contaminated with toxics like sulfuric acid, cadmium, plastic and lead.

MARÍA LOURDES LUJÁN AGUIRRE: They say they covered everything with tarps, but you can see that the tarps are torn up. The barrels where they dumped the slag are filled with holes, eaten away. A few years ago, they dug a hole 30 feet deep and they found lead. Wind and rain bring lead down through our streets.

Workers pass by and get lead on their shoes. They bring it into their workplaces and homes. When the government shut the factory, the owner fled. He went to the U.S., to San Diego. He owns the parent company there and reports a million dollars of profit each year.

MAGDALENA CERDA: This person, Jose Kahn, has an arrest warrant in Mexico but they can't arrest him because he's in San Diego.

MARÍA LOURDES LUJÁN AGUIRRE: We wanted them to extradite him so he would clean up the factory, but to clean Metales y Derivados will cost millions of dollars. We've learned that it's up to the Mexican government to clean it, and they say that they don't have the money to do it.

MAGDALENA CERDA: When we talk of globalization we see that these companies can go anywhere in the world. But along with their capital comes their impact on the environment and on people's health. . . .

LUPITA CASTAÑEDA: I was working in a pantyhose factory. The factory had a union, but the workers didn't even know it existed. A problem arose, and we realized it was a union in name only because we went to see the union representative and there wasn't one.

JAIME COTA and CARMEN DURÁN: In the maquiladora industry most unions are "ghost unions." You can't see them, you don't know they exist. These unions don't live off dues paid by the workers. They live off money that the employer pays them. So the union protects the employer. . . .

VIANEY MIJANGOS: Mexico's Federal Labor Law is pretty good for workers. But the authorities won't uphold the law. Since the 70s, the International Monetary Fund and the World Bank have made a series of loans to the Mexican government. But these loans come with conditions. The Mexican government signed a letter of intention promising the IMF that Mexican workers' salaries would not go up. So these institutions force Mexico to break its own laws.

JAIME COTA: There's a poem by a lady named Sor Juana Inés de la Cruz. Whose sin is worse: the one who sins for pay, or the one who pays to sin? Who is more to blame for violating our labor law: the government which is corrupted by the multinationals, or the multinationals which pay Mexico to break the law? . . .

MARÍA LOURDES LUJÁN AGUIRRE: We formed the collective [Chilpancingo Collective for Environmental Justice] after the San Diego Environmental Health Coalition came here. It's a U.S.-Mexico collaboration. . . . We were a small group. It was hard at the beginning. Now we are growing. We had our meetings in people's homes . . . and now we've found an office of our own. . . .

MAGDALENA CERDA: We took many strong actions and they never responded. Then we started getting international media coverage, and they started to worry. At the start of this year, 2004, our government and the U.S. Environmental Protection Agency told us there was U.S.$85,000 to begin the clean-up of Metales y Derivados.

MARÍA LOURDES LUJÁN AGUIRRE: They see that we are strong, so they are complying with all of our demands. It's like they're afraid of us. How is it possible that high-ranking officials, faced with our little committee of 5 women—that we're making such trouble for them?

YESENIA PALOMARES: We're just housewives, or busybodies, you might say. Imagine, 5 women making a government official tremble! . . .

MARÍA LOURDES LUJÁN AGUIRRE: On June 24, the Secretary of the Environment is coming here and supposedly on that day we'll sign the accord. The accord will establish the clean-up process from start to finish.

GOVERNMENT OFFICIAL: The government welcomes you to the signing of the collaboration agreement for the clean-up of the Metales y Derivados site. Joining us for this important event: Governor Eugenio Elorduy. From the U.S. Environmental Protection Agency: Jerry Clifford. Representing the Chilpancingo Collective: Lourdes Luján and Marta Cervantes.

MARÍA LOURDES LUJÁN AGUIRRE: Thank you for hearing us after 10 years of struggle. Signing this accord between government and community will be an example in the fight for a safe environment. We will make history with this bi-national clean-up. We want to affirm that Tijuana is nobody's trashcan. . . .

CARMEN DURÁN: How do you see globalization in Tijuana in recent years?

AXAYACATL: Maquiladoras turn Tijuana into a city of cheap labor. They exploit these unskilled workers. They're like "haciendas," plantations from a century ago. If we follow Tijuana's example and become a nation of plantations, we'll never get out of this. . . .

Central Themes

The northern frontier, land and labor, gender

Suggested Reading

Cravey, Altha J. *Women and Work in Mexico's Maquiladoras.* Lanham, MD: Rowman & Littlefield, 1998.

Iglesias Prieto, Norma. *Beautiful Flowers of the Maquiladora: Life Histories of Women Workers in Tijuana.* Translations from the Latin America Series. Austin: University of Texas Press, Institute of Latin American Studies, 1997.

Maquilapolis website: http://www.maquilapolis.com/project_eng.html.

Salzinger, Leslie. *Genders in Production: Making Workers in Mexico's Global Factories.* Berkeley: University of California Press, 2003.

Related Sources

45. A Letter to Striking Workers (1892)
48. The Cananea Strike: Workers' Demands (1906)
54. Land, Labor, and the Church in the Mexican Constitution (1917)
63. We the Undersigned (1941, 1945)
71. The 1985 Earthquake (1985, 1995)

76. Lies Within the Truth Commission (2006)*

In the 2000 presidential election, one of Vicente Fox's central campaign promises was the establishment of a truth commission that would investigate state involvement in Mexico's "dirty wars." In 2002, Fox established the Office of the Special Prosecutor for Social and Political Movements of the Past (Fiscalía Especial para Movimientos Sociales y Políticos del Pasado, FEMOSPP), but many Mexicans criticized the Office's ineffectiveness and disparaged the shortcomings of the final report it published in November 2006. The eight-hundred-page *Historical Report to Mexican Society* acknowledged the government's responsibility in police and army executions of over seven hundred people without trial since World War II. But the prosecutor who headed FEMOSPP, Ignacio Carillo Prieto, did not succeed in indicting the officials, including former President Luís Echeverría, whom the report held responsible for the violence.

---

*"Open Letter to the Fox Administration," May 30, 2006, National Security Archive, http://www.gwu.edu/~nsarchiv/NSAEBB/NSAEBB180/letter_limonetaltofox.pdf.

Three authors of the *Historical Report,* Alberto López Limón, José Luis Moreno Borbolla, and Agustín Evangelista Muñoz, wrote the letter reprinted here in May 2006 when the Fox government hesitated to publish the report and appeared to be preparing to terminate further investigations by FEMOSPP. As well as conveying concern over the integrity of the Prosecutor's Office and its work, the letter reveals their prevailing concern with history. What does this letter suggest are some of the important uses of history? The Mexican public also features importantly in the letter, as both addressee and lever of moral authority. How does the idea of Mexico's citizenry evoked here compare to its evocation in earlier contexts (sources 35 and 62)?

Open Letter to the Fox Administration

Mexico, Federal District, May 30, 2006
To Public Opinion:
To the Candidates for President of the Republic:

In the recent interview with BBC of London, President Vicente Fox stated that the Office of the Special Prosecutor for Social and Political Movements of the Past (FEMOSPP) will conclude the work assigned to it, with a Report to the Nation, on April 15; in a similar vein, newspaper headlines make reference to the termination of the Commission, the closure of which is justified by the stepping down of Ignacio Carrillo Prieto and the meager administrative results of said Commission.

The signators below express our concern about this for the following reasons:

Because there is no special body dedicated to attending to denunciations presented by family members of victims of crimes against humanity from '68, '71, the "dirty war," and subsequently, all continuity is lost in the work carried out by the Special Commission. Declarations made by representatives of the National Office of the Attorney General (PGR) do not clear up the doubts that emerge in this regard: How will the investigations already in progress and those that may be made in the future move forward? Will they begin again from zero? Will the work of the individuals associated with this institution be thrown out? If with the FEMOSPP as the "only avenue" of investigation, the results were meager, how will this issue, which is intimately tied to justice, truth, and the fight against impunity, be addressed? It is for these reasons that we demand that the presidential candidates address this topic as part of the national agenda, as an important aspect of the defense of Human Rights.

We are concerned about the final destination of the documental and testimonial archive gathered by the General Office of Analysis, Information, and Document Research, throughout its work, the results of which are contained in the "Report to the Nation." These include thousands of copies of documents from the National General

Archive (AGN), as well as from the newspaper libraries and the testimonies of relatives of the victims of the "dirty war" and former militants in political organizations. The PGR has not made any announcements with regard to this issue. The fruits of the labor of classification and organization of said documentation cannot be placed in a forgotten archive of the Office of the Attorney General because they are public documents, which should be accessible to all those interested in consulting them. Not one of them is included in the investigations conducted by the Public Prosecutor's Office, and they are not therefore subject to legal censure. The work of gathering and classifying documents, we insist, should not be squirreled away by any government employee. Furthermore, the original documents that the administration took from the National General Archive should be returned, for they are national property and should be available for free and open consultation by the public.

We demand that the Report to the Nation, which was submitted to the Special Commission on December 15, 2005, and which the public prosecutor's office turned over to President Vicente Fox, be published and widely distributed. The Report has a clear and unequivocal audience: Mexican society. It also proposes a mechanism for continuing work on the historical reconstruction of this period of our national life.

The signatures below appear in alphabetical order:

[Followed by 268 signatures]

Central Themes

State formation

Suggested Reading

Aguayo Quezada, Sergio, and Javier Treviño Rangel. "Neither Truth nor Justice: Mexico's De Facto Amnesty." *Latin American Perspectives* 33 (2006): 56–68.

Rubio-Freidberg, Luis, and Susan Kaufman Purcell. *Mexico Under Fox.* Publication of the Americas Society and CIDAC. Boulder, CO: Lynne Rienner, 2004.

Related Sources

67. Rubén Jaramillo and the Struggle for *Campesino* Rights in Postrevolutionary Morelos (1967)

68. Eyewitness and Newspaper Accounts of the Tlatelolo Massacre (1968)

Glossary

alcabala. Sales tax
alcalde mayor. District governor
alcalde ordinario. Chief municipal officer
alhóndiga. Public granary
altepetl. Sovereign ethnic state of the Nahuas; after the Conquest, the Spaniards called it the *pueblo*
auto de fe. The Inquisition's ceremony of public condemnation
ayuntamiento. City council
bracero. Guest worker. Refers to the Mexican workers with whom the United States contracted during World War II, primarily to perform agrarian labor
cabeccera. Head town
cacique. Local native leader (colonial period); political boss (postindependence)
campesino. Rural worker
casta. Literally "caste"; usually signifying mixed-race people but sometimes designating plebeians of any racial category
caudillo. Local political boss
charro. Horseman
científicos. Writers, technocrats, and politicians who advocated economic liberalism
cofradía. Confraternity; religious brotherhood
compañero. Comrade
congregación. Concentration, or "congregation," of scattered populations into towns
corregidor. Magistrate; governor of a district
corrido. Ballad
criollo. American-born Spaniard
ejido. Communally held land
encomienda. Grant of indigenous tribute and labor
fueros. Courts; legal jurisdictions
gachupín. Derogatory word for a European-born Spaniard
gobernador. Governor
hacienda. Agricultural estate for commercial production
hacendado. Owner of a commercial estate
junta. Assembly
latifundio. Large landed estates
macehuales. Indian commoners
mayordomo. Majordomo; steward
mestizaje. Race mixing

mestizo. Person of Indian and Spanish parentage
milpa. Corn plot
mulato. Person of African and Spanish parentage
peninsular. Spaniard born on the Iberian Peninsula
plaza. Square
presidio. Garrison
principales. Noblemen
Promotor Fiscal. Prosecutor
Provisor. Chief ecclesiastical judge
pueblo. A town; a people; a community
pulque. Liquor fermented from the maguey cactus
ranchería. Settlement
real. A coin worth one-eighth of a peso
Real Audiencia. Literally the "Royal Court"; refers to the Spanish crown's principal judicial body in New Spain, which also occasionally acted in a legislative capacity
reducción. Congregation; the concentration of scattered populations into towns
regidor. Municipal councilman
señor. Lord; sir; mister
sexenio. Six-year presidential term
Zócalo. Main plaza

Index